Management Control Systems
TEXT AND CASES

The Willard J. Graham Series in Accounting

Consulting Editor
ROBERT N. ANTHONY
Harvard University

Management Control Systems

TEXT AND CASES

ROBERT N. ANTHONY
Ross Graham Walker Professor of Management Control

JOHN DEARDEN
Herman C. Krannert Professor of
Business Administration

both of the
Graduate School of Business Administration
Harvard University

Third Edition   1976

RICHARD D. IRWIN, INC.   Homewood, Illinois   60430

Irwin-Dorsey Limited   Georgetown, Ontario   L7G 4B3

Third Edition

4 5 6 7 8 9 0 Q 5 4 3 2 1 0 9 8

Case material of the Harvard Graduate School of
Business Administration is made possible by the
cooperation of business firms who may wish to remain
anonymous by having names, quantities, and other
identifying details disguised while basic relationships
are maintained. Cases are prepared as the basis for
class discussion rather than to illustrate either effective
or ineffective handling of administrative situations.

ISBN 0-256-01816-2
Library of Congress Catalog Card No. 75–43163
Printed in the United States of America

PREFACE

This third edition of our book follows closely the format of the second edition. All of the text, however, has been rewritten. In particular, the first four chapters are almost entirely new. Also, we have added new chapters on multinational organizations (Chapter 13) and service organizations (Chapter 14). New cases have been added in other chapters and several cases included in the second edition have been deleted.

The book continues to focus on the subject of management control. It does not deal extensively with topics such as cost accounting and budgeting procedures, which are discussed in separate accounting courses. Instead, its focus is on newer topics, not usually discussed in such courses—topics such as the control of discretionary costs, profit centers and the programming process.

The book is designed for a one-semester course for students who have had a course in management accounting and who wish to study management control in greater depth. (Most of the material in the book is currently being used in a second-year course in the management control field at the Harvard Business School.) Few of the cases require a detailed knowledge of accounting or finance and many of them have been used successfully in management education courses in which many of the participants have had no formal accounting courses.

Most of the cases have been used at the Harvard Business School. Many have also been used at other institutions. All have been selected for their interest and value as a basis for class discussion. They are not necessarily intended to illustrate either correct or incorrect handling of management problems. As in all cases of this type, there are no right answers. The educational value of the cases comes from the practice the student receives in analyzing management control problems and in discussing and defending his or her analysis before the class.

Acknowledgments

The course from which the material in this book was drawn was originally developed at the Harvard Business School by the late Ross G. Walker. We wish to acknowledge his pioneering work in the development of both the concepts underlying the course and the methods of teaching these concepts. Recognition is also offered to the following members of the Harvard Business School faculty who have contributed much to the development of this book: Francis J. Aguilar, Robert H. Caplan, Charles J. Christenson, Russell H. Hassler, Regina E. Herzlinger, Robert A. Howell, Gerard G. Johnson, F. Warren McFarlan, Richard F. Vancil, and John R. Yeager. In addition, we wish to acknowledge the assistance provided us by Robert H. Deming, James S. Hekimian, John Mauriel, Chei-Min Paik, and Jack L. Treynor. Jane Barrett and Ann Carter supervised the preparation of various stages of the manuscript, and their assistance is gratefully acknowledged.

Authors of cases in this third edition, other than those written by or under the direction of the authors of the book are as follows:

Case 1–1, Wallace Box, by Richard Vancil, Harvard University. Case 2–2, Clark Chemical Company, by Russell Hassler, Harvard University. Case 3–1, Empire Glass Company, by David Hawkins, Harvard University. Case 3–2, Thurber Division, by T. J. Burns, Ohio State University. Case 4–1, Pierce Irwin Corporation, by Gerald Wentworth, Stanford University, copyright © by the Board of Trustees of Leland Stanford University. Case 5–3, Mercury Stores, Inc., by William H. Newman and Charles E. Summer, *The Process of Management: Concepts, Behavior and Practice* (Englewood Cliffs, N. J.: Prentice-Hall, Inc., 1961). Case 5–5, Seneca Steel Corporation, by Jeanne Deschamps under the direction of Jay Lorsch, Harvard University. Case 6–1, Bultman Automobiles, Inc., by David Hawkins and Andrew McCosh, Harvard University. Case 6–3, Thunderbolt Manufacturing Company, by R. H. Ambromeit under the direction of R. H. Caplan, Harvard University. Case 7–1, Birch Paper Company, by Neil Harlan, Harvard University. Case 8–2, Diversified Products Corporation, by William Rotch, University of Virginia, copyright © by the University of Virginia. Case 8–3, Long Manufacturing Company, by Neil Harlan, Harvard University. Case 8–7, Schoppert Company, by Dwight Ladd, copyright © by IMEDE, Management Development Institute, Lausanne, Switzerland. Case 8–8, General Electric Company (B), by Richard Vancil, Harvard University, Case 9–1, Hastings Electronics Company, by Charles D. Orth, Harvard University. Case 10–2, Northwest Aggregates Corporation, by Leo Guthard and H. Edward Wrapp, Harvard University. Case 11–3, Wellington Company, by Richard Vancil, Harvard University. Case 11–4, Cotter Company, by Richard Vancil, Harvard University. Case 12–1 and 12–2, Mainline Manufacturing Company (A) and (B), by Gerard G. Johnson under the direction of John Yeager, Harvard University. Case 12–3, Perkins Engine, by John Ratichek under the direction of Warren McFarlan, Harvard University. Case 12–4, Binswanger & Steele, Inc., by K. B. Westheimer under the direction of J. Sterling Livingston, Harvard University. Case 15–1, Disease Control Program, by Charles J. Christenson, Harvard University. Case

15–2, Metropolitan Museum, by Richard Kopelman under the direction of Fred Foulkes, Harvard University. Case 15–3, Hyatt Hill Health Center, by Marc Shulman under the direction of Regina Herzlinger, Harvard University. Case 16–1, Northeast Research Laboratories (B) by Professor Richard T. Johnson, Stanford University. Case 16–2, Construction Associates, Incorporated, by William Holstein, Harvard University.

Except where otherwise noted, all cases in this book are copyrighted by the President and Fellows of Harvard College, and we appreciate their permission to reproduce them here. We owe an even greater debt to the many businessmen who cooperated with us in the preparation of these cases, and to the administration of the Harvard Business School for supporting our efforts in case collection and the development of this course.

April 1976   ROBERT N. ANTHONY
                                                   JOHN DEARDEN

CONTENTS

PART I

An Overview

Chapter One

THE NATURE OF
MANAGEMENT CONTROL

In this chapter we describe the nature of control in general and of management control in particular. In order to do this, we distinguish between management control and other planning and controlling processes that are found in organizations, and we also distinguish between the management control function and other functions of management. The chapter concludes with an overview of the management control structure and the steps in the management control process.

THE NATURE OF CONTROL

When the brake pedal is pressed, an automobile slows down or stops. When the accelerator is pressed, the automobile goes faster. When the steering wheel is rotated, the automobile turns. With these devices, the driver *controls* the speed and direction of the vehicle. Without them, the automobile would not do what the driver wanted it to do; that is, it would be out of control. A business company, or indeed any organization, must also be controlled; that is, there must be devices that insure that it goes where its leaders want it to go. The control of an organization is, however, much more complicated than the control of an automobile. We shall lead up to a discussion of control in organizations by describing the control process in simpler situations.

Control in Simple Situations

A control system is a system whose purpose is to maintain a desired state or condition. Any control system has at least these four elements:

1. A measuring device which detects what is happening in the parameter being controlled, that is, a detector.

3

2. A device for assessing the significance of what is happening, usually by comparing information on what *is actually happening* with some standard or expectation of what *should be happening,* that is, a selector.
3. A device for altering behavior if the need for doing so is indicated, that is, an effector.
4. A means for communicating information among these devices.[1]

These elements are shown diagrammatically in Exhibit 1–1. We shall illustrate them in three situations: the thermostat, the regulation of body temperature, and human behavior.

Exhibit 1–1

ESSENTIALS OF A CONTROL SYSTEM

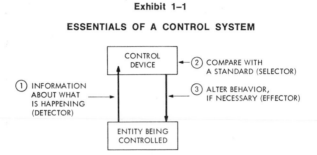

Thermostat.   The thermostat that is hooked to a furnace is a control system that has the elements listed above: (1) the thermostat contains a thermometer (detector) which measures the current temperature in the room; (2) the thermostat compares this measurement with a preset standard, the desired temperature (selector); (3) if the current temperature is significantly below the preset standard, the thermostat causes the furnace to turn on and to send heat to the room, and when the temperature reaches the preset standard, the thermostat causes the furnace to shut off (effector); and (4) electrical circuits convey information from the thermometer to the comparison part of the thermostat and convey instructions from the thermostat to the furnace.

Body Temperature.   Most mammals are born with a built-in standard of desirable body temperature. In humans, it is 98.6 F. The control of body temperature is achieved as follows: (1) sensory nerves scattered throughout the body (detectors) measure the current temperature and transmit information about it to the hypothalamus center in the brain; (2) the hypothalamus compares information on current body temperature with the standard of 98.6 (selector); (3) if this comparison indicates that the current temperature is significantly above the standard, the hypothalamus activates devices to reduce it (panting, sweating, opening of skin pores); and if the

---

[1] For a more complete discussion, see Norbert Wiener, *Cybernetics* (New York: John Wiley, 1948). Cybernetics is defined as "control and communication in man and machine."

current temperature is significantly below the standard, the hypothalamus activates devices to increase it (closing of skin pores, shivering) (effector); and (4) nerves convey information to and from the hypothalamus.[2]

Note that the control system for body temperature has the same elements as those for the control of room temperature, but that there are at least two important differences that make an understanding of the body temperature system more difficult than an understanding of the thermostat. First, the system is more complicated: sensors are scattered all through the body, the hypothalamus acts on both plus and minus deviations from normal, and the actions that it takes involve a variety of muscles and organs. Second, although we know *what* the hypothalamus does, we do not really understand exactly *how* this is done.

Human Behavior. Consider an automobile driver on a highway where the speed limit is 55 mph. The driver has a control system that acts as follows: (1) the eye observes the speed as stated on the speedometer and communicates this speed to the brain (or perhaps the sense of speed is communicated by a general perception of movement): (2) the brain compares the current speed with the limit of 55 mph; (3) if this comparison indicates that the speed is too fast, the brain directs the foot to ease up on the accelerator, and (4) nerves convey these messages to and from the brain.

Although this control system has the same essential elements as the other two, it has an additional complication: we cannot state with confidence what, if any, action the brain will direct if actual speed exceeds 55 mph. Some people obey the speed limit and therefore will ease up on the accelerator; others act only when the actual speed considerably exceeds 55 mph, and still others obey the speed limit at certain times, but not at other times. In these circumstances, although a control system exists, we cannot predict what will happen when the brain receives information about the automobile's speed.

Control in Organizations

The control system in an organization has the same essential elements as those described above. An organization has a desired state, which is specified in its goals. Information about the actual state of the organization is compared with the desired state, and if there is a significant difference, action is taken. The control process in an organization is more complicated than the corresponding process in the simple situations in several respects, however.

First, unlike the thermostat or body temperature, the standard that is used as a basis for assessing the significance of what is happening is not preset. Rather, it is the result of a conscious management process, called planning. In the planning process, management decides what the organization should

---

[2] S. A. Richards, *Temperature Regulation* (London: Wykeham Publications Ltd., 1973).

be doing, and the control process compares actual accomplishments against these plans. Thus, in an organization there is a close connection between the planning process and the control process, so close that for many purposes they should be viewed as a single process.

Second, like human behavior, but unlike the thermostat and body temperature regulation, the system does not operate automatically. Some of the detectors (that is, the instruments for detecting what is happening in the organization), can be mechanical, but important information is often detected through the manager's own eyes, ears, and other senses. There can be automatic ways of comparing reports of what is happening against some standard, but usually a determination of whether or not the difference between actual and standard is significant must be made by human beings, and the action taken to alter behavior also involves human beings; that is, in order to effect change, one manager must interact with another manager. Operations researchers use the term "black box" to describe an operation the exact nature of which cannot be observed and which therefore cannot be expressed in mathematical symbols. The control system in an organization is a black box; a thermostat is not.

A third difference, which follows from the second, is that the connection between the observed need for action and the behavior required to obtain the desired action is by no means as clearcut as it is in the case of the simple control systems. In the selector stage, the manager may decide "costs are too high," but there is no easy or automatic step, or series of steps, that is guaranteed to bring costs down to what they should be.

Fourth, control in an organization requires coordination. An organization consists of many parts, and the control system must insure that the work of these parts is in harmony with one another. This need did not exist at all in the case of the thermostat, and it existed only to a limited extent in the case of the various organs that influence body temperature.

Finally, control in an organization does not come about solely, or even primarily, as a result of actions taken by an external regulating device like the thermostat. Much control is *self* control; that is, managers act the way they do, not primarily because they are given specific orders by their superiors, but rather because their own judgment tells them the appropriate actions they should take. The persons who obey the 55 mph speed limit do so, not because the sign commands them to do so, but rather because they have consciously decided that it is in their best interests to obey the law.

Thus, control in an organization involves a variety of functions, some of which are not present in the simple situations that often come to mind when the word "control" is used. These include: (1) *planning* what the organization should do, (2) *coordinating* the activities of the several parts of the organization, (3) *communicating* information, (4) *evaluating* information and deciding what, if any, action should be taken, (5) *influencing* people to change their behavior, and (6) *processing information* that is used in the other functions.

PLANNING AND CONTROL PROCESSES

We have discussed the control process in organizations in general terms. Actually, there are many types of control functions in an organization, and they differ in important ways. Also, there are several types of planning, some of which are closely related to control, and others not closely related. We shall classify these planning and control activities into three categories: (1) strategic planning, (2) management control, and (3) operational control.

These three planning and control activities are part of the information system of a company. The field of information systems includes all activities having to do with the *systematic* flow of information within an organization It thus excludes only nonsystematic information, such as letters or memoranda on subjects that are not encompassed within the regular information structure. Exhibit 1–2 is a schematic representation of all information systems. In this section we describe the three planning and control processes listed in this diagram. (The other elements in the diagram are discussed in Chapter 3.)

Exhibit 1–2

OVERALL CLASSIFICATION SCHEME

Our purpose is to establish the boundaries of the subject area of interest to us, that is, management control systems, and the description of the other topics in Exhibit 1–2 is therefore intended to clarify these boundaries. They do not purport to be complete descriptions of the other areas.

Obviously, we do not mean to imply that the three planning and control processes can be separated by sharply defined boundaries; one shades into another. Strategic planning sets the guidelines for management control, and management control sets the guidelines for operational control. The complete management function involves an integration of all these processes, and the processes are complementary. The processes are sufficiently distinct, however, so that those who design and use planning and control systems will make expensive errors if they fail to take into account both the common characteristics of a process and the differences between processes. We describe these similarities and differences and point out some of the errors made when they are not recognized.

Management Control

Management control is the process by which managers assure that resources are obtained and used effectively and efficiently in the accomplishment of the organization's goals. We shall explain this definition by discussing the key words and phrases in it.

Process. A management control system consists of a process and a structure. The process is the set of actions that take place, and the structure is the organizational arrangements and information constructs that facilitate this process. By analogy, in the body temperature control system, the way the system regulates temperature is the process, and the neurons, muscles, hypothalamus and other organs are the structure. The word "system" is often used with two overlapping meanings: in one sense, the organization itself is a system; an another sense, management control is a system. The context usually makes clear which sense is intended.

Managers. Management control is a process for the use of managers, and it involves the interaction of one manager with another. Line managers are the focal points in management control. They are the persons whose judgments are incorporated in the approved plans, and they are the persons who must influence others and whose performance is measured. Staff people collect, summarize, and present information that is useful in the process, and they make calculations that translate management judgments into the format of the system. Such a staff may be large in numbers; indeed, the control department is often the largest staff department in a company. However, the significant decisions are made by the line managers, not by the staff.

Since managers are human beings, psychological considerations are dominant in management control. Activities such as communicating, persuading, exhorting, inspiring, and criticizing are an important part of the process.

Management control is the control that managers exercise over other managers. Foremen, who are managers, exercise control over production workers, and sales managers exercise control over individual salesmen, but the principles involved in such control are in important respects different from management control.

Goals. The goals[3] of an organization are set in the strategic planning process; in the management control process these goals are generally taken as given (occasionally, information obtained during the management control process may lead to a change in goals). The management control process is intended to facilitate the achievement of these goals. The broad strategies and policies that have been decided on in the strategic planning process are also taken as givens in the management control process.

Efficiency and Effectiveness. By *effectiveness,* we mean how well an organization unit does its job—that is (to quote the dictionary), the extent to which it produces the intended or expected results. *Efficiency* is used in its engineering sense—that is, the amount of output per unit of input. An efficient machine is one which produces a given quantity of outputs with a minimum consumption of inputs, or one which produces the largest possible outputs from a given quantity of inputs.

Effectiveness is always related to the organization's goals. Efficiency, per se, is not related to goals. An efficient responsibility center is one which does whatever it does with the lowest consumption of resources; but if what it does (i.e., its output) is an inadequate contribution to the accomplishment of the organization's goals, it is ineffective.

For example, if a department that is responsible for processing incoming sales orders does so at a low cost per order processed, it is efficient. If however, the department is sloppy in answering customer queries about the status of orders, and thus antagonizes customers to the point where they take their business elsewhere, the department is ineffective; the loss of a customer is not consistent with the company's goals.

Resources. In doing its work, an organization unit uses resources. These include both tangible resources, such as material and equipment, and also human resources. Managers are responsible for both the acquisition of these resources and for seeing to it that they are used efficiently and effectively.

Assurance. The definition states that managers *assure* that resources are obtained and used effectively and efficiently, not that managers personally *do* the work of obtaining and using resources. Managers, when they are acting as managers, do not themselves do the work. Their function is to see to it that the work gets done by others.

System characteristics. Following is a list of the principal characteristics of a management control system:

1. A management control system focuses on *programs* and *responsibility cen-*

---

[3] In this book we use the word *goals* for the broad, overall aims of the organization and *objectives* for the more specific statements of planned accomplishments in a given time period. Some people use these two words interchangeably, and others reverse the meanings given above. The words *target* and *aim* are also used as synonyms for either word. Confusion can result if these differences in intended meaning are not understood.

ters. A program is a product, product line, research and development project, or similar activity that the organization undertakes in order to achieve its goals. A responsibility center is an organization unit headed by a responsible manager.

2. The information in a management control system is of two general types: (1) *planned data,* that is, programs, budgets, and standards; and (2) *actual data,* that is, information on what is actually happening, both inside the organization and in the external environment.

3. Ordinarily, a management control system is a *total* system in the sense that it embraces all aspects of a company's operation. It needs to be a total system because an important management function is to assure that all parts of the operation are in balance with one another; and in order to coordinate these activities, management needs information about each of them.

4. The management control system is usually *built around a financial structure;* that is, resources and revenues are expressed in monetary units. Money is the only common denominator which can be used to combine and compare the heterogeneous elements of resources (e.g., hours of labor, type of labor, quantity and quality of material, amount and kind of products produced). Although the financial structure is usually the central focus, nonmonetary measures such as minutes per operation, number of employees, and reject and spoilage rates are also important parts of the system.

5. The management control process tends to be *rhythmic;* it follows a definite pattern and timetable, month after month and year after year. In budget preparation, which is an important activity in the management control process, certain steps are taken in a predescribed sequence and at certain dates each year: dissemination of guidelines, preparation of original estimates, transmission of these estimates up through the several echelons in the organization, review of these estimates, final approval by top management, and dissemination back through the organization. The procedure to be followed at each step in this process, the dates when the steps are to be completed, and even the forms to be used can be, and often are, set forth in a policies and procedures manual.

6. A management control system is, or should be, a coordinated, integrated system; that is, although data collected for one purpose may differ from those collected for another purpose, these data should be reconcilable with one another. In particular, it is essential that data on actual performance be structured in the same way—that is, have the same definitions and the same account content—as data on planned performance. If this is not done, valid comparisons of actual and planned performance cannot be made. In a sense, the management control system is a *single* system, but for some purposes it is useful to think of it as a set of interlocking subsystems, one for programming, another for budgeting, another for accounting, and another for reporting and analysis.

Strategic Planning

Strategic planning is the process of deciding on the goals of the organization, on changes in these goals, on the resources used to attain these goals, and on the policies that are to govern the acquisition, use, and disposition of these resources.

The word *strategy* is used here in its usual sense of deciding on how to combine and employ resources. Thus, strategic planning is a process having to do with the formulation of <u>long-range, strategic, policy-type plans</u> that change the character or direction of the organization. In an industrial company, this includes planning that affects the goals of the company; policies of all types (including policies as to management control and other processes); the acquisition and disposition of major facilities, divisions, or subsidiaries; the markets to be served and distribution channels for serving them; the organization structure (as distinguished from individual personnel actions); research and development of new product lines (as distinguished from modifications in existing products and product changes within existing product lines); sources of new permanent capital, dividend policy, and so on. Strategic planning decisions affect the physical, financial, and organizational framework within which operations are carried on.

Distinctions between Management Control and Strategic Planning. Briefly, here are some ways in which the strategic planning process differs from the management control process.

A strategic plan usually relates to some part of the organization, rather than to the totality; the concept of a master planner who constantly keeps all parts of the organization at some coordinated optimum is a nice concept, but an unrealistic one. Life is too complicated for any human, or computer, to do this.

Strategic planning is essentially *irregular*. Problems, opportunities, and bright ideas do not arise according to some set timetable; rather, they are dealt with whenever they happen to be perceived. The appropriate analytical techniques depend on the nature of the problem being analyzed, and no overall approach (such as a mathematical model) has been developed that is of much help in analyzing all types of strategic problems. Indeed, an overemphasis on a systematic approach is quite likely to stifle the essential element of creativity. In strategic planning, management works now on one problem, now on another, according to the needs and opportunities of the moment.

The estimates used in strategic planning are intended to show the *expected* results of the plan. They are neutral and impersonal. By contrast, the management control process and the data used in it are intended to influence managers to take actions that will lead to *desired* results. Thus, in connection with management control it is appropriate to discuss how tight an operating budget should be. Should the goals be set so high that only an outstanding manager can achieve them, or should they be set so that they are attainable by the average manager? At what level does frustration inhibit a manager's best efforts? Does an easily attainable budget lead to complacency? And so on. In strategic planning, the question to be asked about the figures is simply: Is this the most reasonable estimate that can be made?

Strategic planning relies heavily on external information—that is, on data collected from outside the company, such as market analyses, estimates of costs and other factors involved in building a plant in a new locality, technological developments, and so on. When data from the normal information system are used, they usually must be recast to fit the needs of the specified problem being analyzed. For example, current operating costs that are collected for measuring performance and for making pricing and other operating decisions usually must be restructured before they are useful in deciding whether to close down the plant. Another characteristic of the relevant information is that much of it is imprecise. The strategic planner estimates what will probably happen, often over a rather long time period. These estimates are likely to have a high degree of uncertainty, and they must be treated accordingly.

In the management control process, the communication of objectives, policies, guidelines, decisions, and results throughout the organization is extremely important. In the strategic planning process, communication is much simpler and involves relatively few persons; indeed, the need for secrecy often requires that steps be taken to inhibit communication. (Wide communication of the decisions that result from strategic planning is obviously important; this is part of the management control process.)

Strategic planning is essentially applied economics, whereas management control involves both economics and social psychology.

Both management control and strategic planning involve top management, but middle managers (i.e., operating management) typically have a much more important role in management control than in strategic planning. Middle managers usually are not major participants in the strategic planning process and sometimes are not even aware that a plan is being considered. Many operating executives are by temperament not very good at strategic planning. Also, the pressures of current activities usually do not allow them to devote the necessary time to such work. Currently, there is a tendency in companies to set up separate staffs to gather the facts and make the analyses that provide the background material for strategic decisions.

These and other differences between management control and strategic planning are summarized in Exhibit 1–3.

Strategic planning and management control activities tend to conflict with one another in some respects. The time that management spends in thinking about the future is taken from time that it could otherwise use in controlling current operations, so in this indirect way strategic planning can hurt current performance. And, of course, the reverse is also true. More directly, many actions that are taken for long-run, strategic reasons make current profits smaller than they otherwise would be. Research and some types of advertising expenditures are obvious examples. The problem of striking the right balance between strategic and operating considerations is one of the central problems in the whole management process.

Exhibit 1–3

SOME DISTINCTIONS BETWEEN STRATEGIC PLANNING
AND MANAGEMENT CONTROL

Characteristic	Strategic Planning	Management Control
Focus of plans	On one aspect at a time	On whole organization
Complexities	Many variables	Less complex
Degree of structure	Unstructured and irregular; each problem different	Rhythmic; prescribed procedures
Nature of information	Tailor-made for the problem; more external and predictive; less accurate	Integrated; more internal and historical; more accurate
Communication of information	Relatively simple	Relatively difficult
Purpose of estimates	Show expected results	Lead to desired results
Persons primarily involved	Staff and top management	Line and top management
Number of persons involved	Small	Large
Mental activity	Creative; analytical	Administrative; persuasive
Source discipline	Economics	Social psychology
Planning and control	Planning dominant, but some control	Emphasis on both planning and control
Time horizon	Tends to be long	Tends to be short
End result	Policies and precedents	Action within policies and precedents
Appraisal of the job done	Extremely difficult	Much less difficult

Operational Control

Operational control is the process of assuring that specific tasks are carried out effectively and efficiently.

As the definition suggests, the focus of operational control is on individual tasks or transactions: scheduling and controlling individual jobs through a shop, as contrasted with measuring the performance of the shop as a whole; procuring specific items for inventory, as contrasted with the management of inventory as a whole; specific personnel actions, as contrasted with personnel management; and so on.

The definition does not suggest another characteristic that applies to most activities that are subject to operational control, namely, that these activities are capable of being programmed. In order to explain what these activities are, we need first to develop the concept of outputs and inputs.

Outputs and Inputs. Outputs are the goods, services, or other effects created by an organization. Inputs are the resources the organization consumes. Every organization has, or at least is intended to have, outputs, even though they may not be readily measurable or even clearly definable;

that is, every organization does something, and that something is its output. In a business, outputs are goods and services. In a school, the output is education; in a hospital, patient care; in a law office, advice and counsel; in a government, public service or defense posture. Similarly, the inputs may range from easily valued items, such as purchased parts, to such intangible items as executive thought.

Moreover, every unit within an organization has outputs. In the case of factories, the outputs are goods. In all other units—personnel, transportation, sales, engineering, administration, and so on—outputs are services. Since these services are often not priced, the amounts are difficult to measure. Nevertheless, the outputs exist.

One of the important management tasks in an organization is to seek the *optimum* relationship between outputs and inputs. In many situations, it is rarely, if ever, possible to determine the optimum relationship between outputs and inputs objectively; instead, the choice of a relationship is a matter of subjective judgment. This is true because there is no scientific or objective way of determining how output will be affected by changes in inputs. How much should a company spend for advertising? Are additional fire trucks, or schoolteachers, or policemen worth their cost? Informed people will disagree on the answers to questions of this type.

The term *discretionary costs* is descriptive of the type of inputs for which an objective decision cannot be made as to the optimum quantity to be employed. An important management control function is to make judgments as to the "right" amount of discretionary costs in a given set of circumstances. These are, by definition, subjective judgments, and such judgments fall within the management control process.

In other situations, there is at least the possibility that an optimum relationship between outputs and inputs can be found. It is unrealistic to imply that this relationship can ever be determined in an absolute sense, inasmuch as new and better ways of doing things are constantly being developed; therefore, a more realistic meaning of "optimum" is this: The optimum is that combination of resources, out of all *known* combinations, that will produce the desired output at the lowest cost. If the optimum input-output relationship for a given activity can be predetermined, then the inputs that should be employed in a given set of circumstances can be described and reduced to rules; that is, they can be programmed.

Distinctions between Management Control and Operational Control. As an example of an activity to which operational control is applicable, consider the inventory area. If the demand for an item, the cost of storing it, its production cost and production time, and the loss involved in not filling an order are known, then the optimum inventory level and the optimum production or procurement schedule can be calculated. Even if these factors cannot be known with certainty (as, of course, is the case with all future events), sound estimates nevertheless can be made, inventory levels and production or procurement schedules based on these estimates can be calculated, and reasonable men will agree with the results of these calculations. An inventory control system using rules derived from such calculations is an example of operational control.

By contrast, consider the legal department of a company. No device can measure the quality, or even the quantity, of the legal service that constitutes the output of this department. No formula can show the amount of service the department should render or the optimum amount of costs that should be incurred. Impressions as to the "right" amount of service, the "right" amount of cost, and the "right" relationship between the service actually rendered and the cost actually incurred are strictly subjective. They are judgments made by management. If persons disagree on these judgments, there is no objective way of resolving the disagreement. Yet the legal department, as a part of the whole organization, must be controlled; the chief counsel must operate within the framework of policies prescribed by top management. The type of control necessary in this situation is management control.

Examples of activities that are susceptible to operational control are automated plants, such as cement plants, oil refineries, and power generating stations; the direct production operations of most manufacturing plants; production scheduling; inventory control; the order-taking type of selling activity; and order processing, premium billing, payroll accounting, check handling, and similar paperwork activities.

Examples of activities for which management control is necessary are the total operation of most manufacturing plants, which includes such judgment inputs as indirect labor, employees' benefit and welfare programs, safety activities, training, and supervision; most advertising, sales promotion, pricing, selling (as distinguished from order-taking), and similar marketing activities; most aspects of finance; most aspects of research, development, and design; the work of staff units of all types; and, of course, the activities of top management.

The type of control appropriate for the whole of any unit that carries on both programmed and nonprogrammed types of activities is management control. Thus, the control of one division of a company is management control. The control of the whole accounting department is management control, even though operational control is appropriate for certain aspects of the work such as posting and check writing.

Some people believe that the distinction between the two classes of activities described above is merely one of degree rather than of kind; they say that all we are doing is distinguishing between situations in which control is easy and those in which control is difficult. We think the distinction is more fundamental, and hope this will be apparent from the following brief list of characteristics that distinguish management control from operational control.

whereas data in a management control system are often retrospective and are summaries of many separate events. Computer specialists who do not make such a distinction dream about a system that will display to the management the current status of every individual activity in the organization. Although this *could* be done, it *should not* be done; management does not want such detail. Management does not need to know the time at which lot No. 1007 was transferred from station 27 to station 28; rather, it needs to know only that the process is, or is not, proceeding as planned, and if not, where the trouble lies.

Similarly, operational control uses exact data, whereas, management control needs only approximations. Material is ordered and scheduled in specific quantities and employees are paid the exact amount due them, but data on management control reports need contain only two or three significant digits and are therefore rounded to thousands of dollars, to millions of dollars, or even (in the U.S. government) to billions of dollars.

An operational control system requires a mathematical model of the operation. Although it may not always be expressed explicitly in mathematical notation, a decision rule states that given certain values for parameters $a, b, \ldots n$, action X is to be taken. Models are not so important in management control. In a sense, a budget and a PERT network are models associated with the management control process, but they are not the essence of the process.

The formal management control *system* is only a part of the management control *process,* actually a relatively unimportant part. The system can help motivate the manager to make decisions that are in the best interests of the organization, and the system can provide information that aids the manager in making these decisions; but many other stimuli are involved in motivating the manager, and good information does not automatically produce good decisions. The success or failure of the management control process depends on the personal characteristics of the manager—his judgment, his knowledge, his ability to influence others.

In operational control, the system itself is relatively more important. Except in fully automated operations, it is an exaggeration to say that the system *is* the process, but it is not much of an exaggeration. An operational control system ordinarily states what action should be taken; it makes the decisions. As with any operation, management vigilance is required to detect an unforeseen foul-up in the operation or a change in the conditions on which the technique is predicated, and to initiate the necessary corrective action. And management will be seeking ways to improve the technique. In general, however, the degree of management involvement in operational control is small, whereas in management control it is large.

As new techniques are developed, there is a tendency for more and more activities to become susceptible to operational control. In the factory, the production schedule that was formerly set according to the foreman's intuition is now derived by linear programming. And although not very long ago it was believed that operational control was appropriate only for factory operations, we now see models and formulas being used for certain marketing decisions, such as planning salesmen's calls and planning direct-mail advertising. This shift probably will continue; it is a large part of what people have in mind when they say, "management is becoming increasingly scientific."

The differences between management control and operational control are summarized in Exhibit 1–4.

Exhibit 1–4

SOME DISTICTIONS BETWEEN MANAGEMENT CONTROL AND OPERATIONAL CONTROL

Characteristic	Management Control	Operational Control
Focus of activity	Whole operation	Single task or transaction
Judgment	Relatively much; subjective decisions	Relatively little; reliance on rules
Nature of structure	Psychological	Rational
Nature of information	Integrated; financial data throughout; approximations acceptable; future and historical	Tailor-made to the operation; often non-financial; precise; often in real time
Persons primarily involved	Management	Supervisors (or none)
Mental activity	Administrative; persuasive	Follow directions (or none)
Source discipline	Social psychology	Economics; physical sciences
Time horizon	Weeks, months, years	Day-to-day
Type of costs	Discretionary	Engineered

OTHER MANAGEMENT PROCESSES

Authors classify the functions of management in various ways. An old classification, which is still widely used, is that of Fayol: planning, organizing, commanding, coordinating, and controlling.[4] It is obvious that the description of management control in the preceding section encompasses several of these functions, for it includes, at least, planning, coordinating, and controlling. The danger exists that the preceding description can create the impression that management control is the *whole* of management. This obviously is not the case; management control is only a part of management.

We have already identified another important management function, strategic planning. An even more important function is the one which Fayol called

---

[4] Henri Fayol, *Industrial and General Administration*, trans. J. A. Coubrough (Geneva: International Management Institute, 1929). Originally published in 1916.

organizing and which others call staffing, or the personnel function. Managers must make judgments on hiring, promotion, and reassignment; they must decide where a person best fits in the organization, what the person's responsibilities should be, and the relationships of persons to one another; and managers must create an environment that encourages employees to work effectively. Judgments about people are probably much more important to the success of an organization than its control system. Good people can overcome the defects in a management control system, but even the best management control system will not lead to satisfactory results without good people to operate it.

Managers also have an expertise in the particular function they are involved in. The production manager knows about production; the marketing manager knows about marketing. Our discussion of management control does not touch on this functional expertise.

Finally, managers do not spend all their time in the management function itself. The sales manager may close a deal with an important customer. The production manager may "get his hands dirty" with some problem in the plant. The financial vice president personally negotiates credit arrangements.

For these reasons, the discussion of management control in this book is by no means a discussion of the whole process of management, nor is it a description of all that managers do.

OVERVIEW OF MANAGEMENT CONTROL SYSTEMS

Much of the management control process involves informal communication and interactions. Informal communication occurs by means of memoranda, meetings, conversations, and even by such signals as facial expressions. Although these informal activities are of great importance, they are not amenable to a systematic description. In addition to these informal activities, most companies also have a *formal* management control system. It consists of some or all of the following phases:

1. Programming.
2. Budgeting.
3. Operating and accounting.
4. Reporting and analysis.

As indicated in Exhibit 1–5, each of these activities leads to the next. They recur in a regular cycle, and together they constitute a "closed loop." These four phases are described briefly below, and are discussed in depth in later chapters.

Programming. Programming is the process of deciding on the programs that the company will undertake and the approximate amount of resources that are to be allocated to each program. Programs are the principal activities that the organization has decided to undertake in order to implement

Exhibit 1–5

PHASES OF MANAGEMENT CONTROL

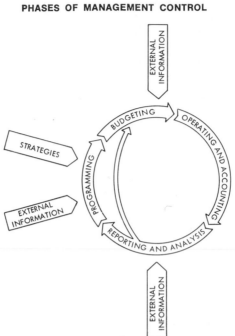

the strategies that it has decided upon. In a profit-oriented company, each principal product or product line is a program. If several product lines are manufactured in the same plant, the plant itself and additions or modifications to it may be identified as a program. There are also various research and development programs, some aimed at improving existing products or processes, others searching for marketable new products.

Budgeting. A budget is a plan expressed in quantitative, usually monetary, terms that covers a specified period of time, usually one year. In the budgeting process each program is translated into terms that correspond to the sphere of responsibility of each manager who is charged with executing the program or some part of it. Thus, although the plans are originally made in terms of individual programs, in the budgeting process the plans are translated into terms of responsibility centers. The process of developing a budget is essentially one of negotiation between the manager of a responsibility center and his superior. The end product of these negotiations is an approved statement of the revenues that are expected during the budget year, and the resources that are to be used in achieving the company's goals for each responsibility center and for the company as a whole.

In addition to the monetary statement of plans, the plan for the year also includes a statement of objectives that are to be accomplished during the year. These objectives are usually expressed in nonmonetary terms.

Operating and Accounting.   During the period of actual operations, records are kept of resources actually consumed (i.e., costs) and of revenues actually earned. These records are structured so that cost and revenue data are classified both by programs and by responsibility centers. Data classified according to programs are used as a basis for future programming, and data classified by responsibility centers are used to measure the performance of responsibility center managers. For the latter purpose, data on actual results are reported in such a way that they can be readily compared with the plan as set forth in the budget.

Reporting and Analysis.   The management control system serves as a communication device. The information that is communicated consists of both accounting and nonaccounting data, and of both data generated within the organization and data about what is happening in the environment outside the organization. This information keeps managers informed as to what is going on and helps to insure that the work done by the separate responsibility centers is coordinated.

Reports are also used as a basis for control. Essentially, such reports are derived from an analysis that compares actual performance with planned performance and attempts to explain the difference. Based on these formal reports, and also on information received through informal communication channels, managers decide what, if any, action should be taken. They may, for example, decide to change the plan as set forth in the budget, and this leads to a new planning process. It is for this reason that the phases shown in Exhibit 1–5 are depicted as a closed loop with one phase leading to the next.

Case 1–1

Wallace Box Company

In May, 1961, Milton Purcell, a Boston management consultant, paid a visit to Fall River, Massachusetts, to meet William Barrett, president of the Wallace Box Company. Mr. Barrett had asked Mr. Purcell to help him, he said, "to take a look at where my company is right now, and help me make any necessary plans."

As Mr. Barrett explained the situation to Mr. Purcell, "The company is making satisfactory profits, and I expect it to continue to do so.[1] But although I am not concerned about current profitability, I do want to be sure that nothing has been overlooked in making the business as efficient as is feasible." He went on to suggest that Mr. Purcell might start his review by looking at the company's accounting and control system, simply because this particular aspect had not been studied by an outsider for some time; he reiterated that he was not dissatisfied with the present setup. Major elements in the system were a complete budget, a standard cost system for all elements of manufacturing costs, and a regular reporting procedure that produced monthly financial statements by the middle of each succeeding month. Mr. Purcell agreed to follow the approach suggested by Mr. Barrett. His investigations revealed the information that follows.

COMPANY HISTORY

The company had had its beginnings in 1850, when George Wallace, a Scottish papermaker, settled in Fall River and started a small paper mill. In 1897, control passed to a local converter who had previously taken the bulk of the mill's output. From that time on, the company operated as an integrated manufacturer of folding boxes.

Mr. Barrett had acquired a majority interest in the company in 1921, after several years of unprofitable operations had taken it to the verge

---

[1] Five-year financial statements are reproduced in Exhibits 1 and 2.

Exhibit 1

BALANCE SHEETS, DECEMBER 31, 1956–60

(000)

	1960	1959	1958	1957	1956
ASSETS					
Cash	$ 216	$ 407	$ 641	$ 392	$ 684
State and municipal bonds	475	604	467	618	577
Accounts receivable (net)	581	609	610	383	337
Inventories	1,183	1,033	822	863	764
Total Current Assets	$2,455	$2,653	$2,540	$2,256	$2,362
Cash value of life insurance	419	418	408	322	310
Securities and cash held for plant and equipment replacement	985	985	485	485	485
Plant and equipment (net)	1,914	1,529	1,576	1,575	1,176
	$5,773	$5,585	$5,009	$4,638	$4,333
LIABILITIES					
Accounts payable	$ 312	$ 355	$ 442	$ 326	$ 312
Accrued liabilities	56	89	31	88	85
Income taxes	316	419	331	359	423
Total Current Liabilities	$ 684	$ 863	$ 804	$ 773	$ 820
Replacement reserve, plant and equipment	985	985	485	485	485
Capital stock:					
Common	900	900	900	900	900
6% preferred	600	600	600	600	600
Earned surplus	2,604	2,237	2,220	1,880	1,528
	$5,773	$5,585	$5,009	$4,638	$4,333

Exhibit 2

CONDENSED INCOME STATEMENTS, 1956–60

(000)

	1960	1959	1958	1957	1956
Sales	$7,478	$7,344	$6,086	$6,170	$5,374
Manufacturing expenses	5,228	4,795	4,302	4,464	3,780
Gross profit	$2,250	$2,549	$1,784	$1,706	$1,594
Selling, administrative, and general expenses	906	954	649	586	496
Profit-sharing and retirement plan contributions	171	179	155	151	132
Income before taxes	$1,173	$1,416	$ 980	$ 969	$ 966
Income taxes	608	740	511	509	515
Net income	$ 565	$ 676	$ 469	$ 460	$ 451
Dividends paid	198	162	126	108	108
Balance to surplus	$ 367	$ 514	$ 343	$ 352	$ 343
Note: Depreciation	$ 201	$ 177	$ 174	$ 153	$ 138

of bankruptcy. Under Mr. Barrett's management, annual losses were reduced, and the company showed a profit in 1925. It had not lost money in any year since that time, although it had not covered its preferred dividend in 1932. Mr. Barrett and his family owned or controlled 75 percent of the company's stock; the remainder was held by executives or retired executives who had obtained it under an incentive compensation plan that Mr. Barrett had instituted soon after he had taken over the company.

In describing those early years to Mr. Purcell, Mr. Barrett said, "I'll never forget the hard times we went through. The company was in urgent need of refinancing, and there just seemed to be no money available for a small, unprofitable company. I made up my mind there and then that if I succeeded in putting Wallace back on the road to recovery (which I did), I would take all possible steps to build up its financial strength to a level that would almost guarantee that we would never again be short of funds at a crucial moment. You see as a small company we've never had the flexibility that larger companies have, but we find ourselves needing money just the same way that they do. They can always fall back on their banking relationships, or on their big financiers. But in a crisis, we don't have access to those sources of funds. We have to look after ourselves. Call it New England conservatism, if you like. I regard it as prudent business management."

Wallace manufactured paperboard cartons for a wide variety of uses, primarily as packages for consumer products. The box factory used paperboard made in the firm's adjoining mill. Mill production was geared to the needs of the box factory, according to the production manager. "In general, we produce paperboard only for immediate use in production. We keep very little paperboard in inventory." The plant complex also included a 60,000-square-foot warehouse (built at a cost of $300,000 in 1960), where finished orders were stored pending delivery. The warehouse was currently about 60 percent full; it had been built large enough to provide for the company's needs until 1966. The company had approximately 425 employees in 1961.

MARKETING SITUATION

The company's marketing area included the New England states (primarily Massachusetts and Connecticut), New York, New Jersey, and eastern Pennsylvania. There were seven sales engineers who were compensated on the basis of a nominal salary plus commission. Three of them operated from the Fall River plant; the other four were based in a sales office in New York City.

Mr. Barrett told Mr. Purcell "One of our major assets is our excellent reputation for product quality and customer service. We control our product quality to a far greater degree than do many of our competitors, because we control practically all the elements that go into our final product. In addition to the normal operations of making our own paperboard and doing the various printing, cutting and creasing, folding, and gluing operations, we even make our own dies and grind and mix our own inks."

Mr. Barrett emphasized that the industry was characterized by strong competition. Wallace met this by fulfilling special design requests, by actively catering to all customer requirements, and by strict adherence to promised delivery dates. Whereas all cartons were manufactured to order, some finished goods were kept in storage at customers' requests. The rate charged for such storage was .75 percent per month, covering interest and storage costs; Mr. Barrett thought that this was adequate. In May, 1961, finished orders priced at approximately $250,000 were overdue for delivery; i.e., customers had postponed acceptance of these orders beyond scheduled delivery dates. Mr. Barrett was not disturbed about this, however, as he had reassured himself that the bulk of these orders were from good customers whose financial integrity was unquestioned. "Anyway, this isn't too big a part of our finished goods inventory, and we have confirmed orders for all of it—overdue or not."

Mr. Purcell inquired whether Mr. Barrett could give him the reasons for his statement that the industry was highly competitive. "This," Mr. Barrett said, "is basically the fault of the potential overcapacity that exists in most plants. The production process requires that paperboard mills run a continuous three-shift operation, but the typical industry box plant usually operates only one and one-half shifts per day. Because of this overcapacity, competition for high-volume orders is particularly vicious, and price-cutting is common, especially among the larger producers. On the other hand, we have avoided the temptation of going after the high-volume, low-margin business of some of the large national companies for whom we manufacture specialty cartons. If you get big enough, you find that you have to do high-volume work to keep your plant busy, and that often goes at break-even prices, unlike specialty work. We've managed to keep our size down to the point where we do a large volume of specialty business—we're good at it—and we don't have to bother with high-volume work."

Mr. Barrett told Mr. Purcell that pricing was a crucial element in marketing. Prices were prepared by the company's estimators for each bid or order, on the basis of sales specifications and the appropriate standard cost elements according to tables the company had developed for this purpose. Total costs, as calculated, were then increased by certain percentages for selling and administrative expenses, profit, sales commissions, and cash discounts. These percentages were determined annually when the company's budget was drawn up. A record of the percentages used from 1956 to 1961 is shown in Exhibit 3, and a representative price estimate is reproduced in Exhibit 4. Mr. Barrett remarked, however, that the price calculated in the estimate was often adjusted, for quotation purposes, to meet competitive conditions, to reimburse the company for additional costs not included in the estimate, or to pick up some of the savings, if any, known to be realized

Exhibit 3

ADD-ON PERCENTAGES USED IN PRICE ESTIMATING

	1961	1960	1959	1958	1957	1956
Administrative and selling expenses* (percent of manufacturing cost, excluding material)	45%	47%	46%	39%	46%	42%
Profit (percent of total delivered cost)	20	20	20	20	20	20
Commission and discount† (3% and 1%, respectively, of the total of delivered cost plus profit)	4	4	4	4	4	4

* Including factory overhead, amounting generally to one-half of the percentage added on.
† A provision against expenses incurred as percentages of sales.

by the customer through the special design or service provided by the company.

Mr. Purcell was interested to hear from Mr. Barrett that it was customary for estimators in the trade to meet regularly under the auspices of a trade association to price sample boxes according to their own formulas. The price of the paperboard would be given, for the purpose of these comparsions; Wallace normally priced paperboard, in its own estimates, at 10 percent over mill cost, which, Mr. Barrett was sure, was less than nonintegrated manufacturers would normally have to pay. It seemed that Wallace's prices were usually in the lowest tenth in these comparisons, a fact that gave Mr. Barrett not inconsiderable pleasure. In practice, he said, most producers probably varied from their formulas in quoting to customers. But, he pointed out, whereas most of his competitors were shaving prices below formula, Wallace's quoted prices were higher than the calculated estimate about 65 percent of the time, identical about 20 percent of the time, and lower 15 percent of the time. "It all depends on the competition, and on your assessment of the whole situation."

ACCOUNTING AND BUDGETING

The paperboard mill, headed by its own superintendent, was treated as a single cost center. The box factory, also under a superintendent, had 10 principal cost centers, each consisting of a press or a group of similar presses and associated equipment, and each headed by a foreman. Minor operations such as ink manufacture, quality control, and the storage warehouse also were treated as separate cost centers. The paperboard mill was operated 24 hours a day, and the presses were operated 16 hours a day, either 5 or 6 days a week, depending on demand. Considerable variation was possible in the output per hour, and for this reason the foremen were paid partly on an incentive plan, which was based largely on the comparison of their actual

Exhibit 4

PRICE ESTIMATE

ITEM: 1 million boxes 6⅛ × 2¾ × 1½, printed 2 colors and varnish, on .024 caliber white patent coated, news backed.

PREPARATORY COST	Production Per Hour	Rate	/MM Unit	/MM Material Cost	/MM Mfg. Cost	M Unit	M Material Cost	M Mfg. Cost	M Unit	M Material Cost	M Mfg. Cost
Original Plates	F. or E.										
Electros 9¾ x 9¼ (91)		18.94	28	530 32							
Wood				15 99							
Rule				34 09							
Composing											
Die Making	③	4.85	41.8		202 73						
Make Ready – ptg.	2X	12.80	30.0		384 00						
Make Ready – C. & C.	11.55	11.25	15.8		177 75						
44¼ Total Preparatory Cost				580 40	764 48						
QUANTITY COST											
Board 65,005 (3¾)	171.00 +25			5557 93							
Board (32.5025)				25 00							
Ink		.37	300	111 00							
Ink 30"		.75	300								
		.45	231	328 95							
Cases Corrugated	700	.30	1429	428 70							
Cellulose Material											
Board, Storage & Handling		1.87			60 78						
Cutting Stock											
Printing		} 22.766									
Cut and Crease					813 09						
Stripping	.933-4	.178+120			391 60						
Cellulose											
Auto Gluing		[.562]	466 +11.24		477 24						
Hand Gluing											
Wrapping or Packing		6.503			92 93						
Inspection											
Total Quantity Cost				6451 58	1835 64						
Total Preparatory Cost				580 40	764 48						
Total Cost to Make				7031 98	2600 12						
Selling & Commercial		45+8	(% $)		1178 05						
Material Forward					7031 98						
77" Shipping 56+		7.25+2	60,287		220 54						
Freight and Cartage		.40			241 15						
Total Cost					11271 84						
Profit		20%			2254 37						
Total Selling Price					13526 21						
Finished Stock St'g											
Commission & Dis.		4%			541 05						
Total Selling Price					14067 26						
Selling Price per M – Calculated					14 07						
Selling Price per M – Quoted					15 30						
Form 40											

hourly output with predetermined standards for different types of paperboard or cartons.

The annual budget was drawn up under the direction of James Lewis, the treasurer. The budget was synthesized from estimates of sales prepared by the sales staff and from corresponding activity rates and cost expectations

developed by manufacturing personnel. The manufacturing people participated in discussion of the relevant portions of the budget. Mr. Lewis used
his experience with past budgets to combine the separate elements into a
meaningful whole. The budget was stated in terms of a specified dollar
amount per month for each major expense item in each manufacturing cost
center. Separate schedules listed budget allowances for selling, administrative, and general expenses. This scheme made possible the annual determination of the selling and commercial expense percentage to be used in price estimates. (See Exhibit 3.) While no formal capital rationing system was
used, all capital expenditures were reviewed both before and after being
incurred, on an annual basis for an overall review and on an individual
basis as specific projects were undertaken. The annual budget also facilitated
the development of standard costs for use in price estimating and inventory
valuation. For the inventory purpose, all costs were included through factory overhead; i.e., costs such as selling and other administrative were
excluded from inventory and charged off as incurred.

REPORTS—INTERNAL

Mr. Barrett received a variety of internal and trade association reports
on a regular basis. The internally generated reports were as follows.

1. Balance sheet.
2. Profit and loss statement, monthly (Exhibit 5).
3. Cost center spending report, monthly (Exhibit 6).
4. Selling, general, and administrative expense statement, monthly.
5. Overdue accounts receivable, monthly (usually aggregated between
   $60,000 and $100,000).
6. Overdue shipments, monthly.
7. Inventory breakdown, monthly. Typical percentages were: finished goods,
   50 percent; work in process, 35 percent; and raw materials, 15 percent.
8. Raw material shrinkage report, monthly.
9. Cash and securities listing, monthly.
10. Sales, weekly.
11. Sales recapitulation, monthly. This analyzed sales against budgets, and
    included profit and expense estimates.
12. Salesmen's report, monthly.
13. Carton shop production, monthly. This included operating hours statistics
    and efficiency percentages.
14. Foremen's bonus report, monthly.
15. Outstanding orders, weekly.
16. Progress schedule, weekly.
17. Machine production report, daily.
18. Quality control report, monthly.
19. Other special reports, prepared as the need arose.

Exhibit 5

PROFIT AND LOSS STATEMENTS*
(Abbreviated)

	November 1960	December 1960	12 Months 1960
Board Mill			
Net sales of board	$ 12,427	$ 12,842	$ 144,797
Transfers to carton factory	167,885	140,973	1,969,599
Total sales and transfers	$180,312	$153,815	$2,114,396
Cost of sales and transfers	162,830	139,401	1,895,581
Standard profit or (loss)	$ 17,482	$ 14,414	$ 218,815
Burden variance†	1,417	5,552	18,609
Over or (under) earned burden†	(2,600)	(6,539)	18,343
Inventory adjustment	—	(2,370)	(2,370)
Profit or (loss) board mill	$ 16,299	$ 11,057	$ 253,397
Carton Factory			
Net sales of cartons	$628,259	$626,463	$7,068,025
Cost of sales:			
Materials	273,144	275,196	3,038,625
Scrap and cuttings sales	(1,657)	(1,978)	(24,427)
Manufacturing	142,265	141,712	1,693,488
Remakes	5,427	350	23,207
Miscellaneous charges	24,907	8,983	20,301
Selling and commercial	31,457	31,283	374,326
Shipping and storage	19,366	17,782	207,603
Leased machines	2,607	(309)	24,126
Salesmen's commissions	18,192	19,216	197,684
Total cost of sales	$515,708	$492,235	$5,554,933
Standard profit, cartons	$112,551	$134,228	$1,513,092
Burden variance†	32,856	41,501	320,712
Over or (under) earned burden†	(52,793)	(52,853)	(575,221)
Inventory adjustment	(323)	17,215	535
Profit, carton factory	$ 92,291	$140,091	$1,259,118
Miscellaneous income and costs	$ 675	$ (4,393)	$ (49,156)
Total profit from carton and board sales	108,590	151,148	1,512,515
Gain for period	$109,265	$146,755	$1,463,359
Less: Bonus and profit sharing	15,771	16,501	324,956
Net gain for period	$ 93,494	$130,254	$1,138,403
Less: Reserve for income taxes	48,332	66,058	590,175
Net income after taxes	$ 45,162	$ 64,196	$ 548,228

* These statements are those produced internally for management use (see text). Differences between the 12-month statement and the figures in Exhibit 2 are accounted for by year-end and audit adjustments not determined when the above were compiled.

† Explained in more detail in the structure of and notes to Exhibit 6.

Mr. Barrett said he usually reviewed the first four reports carefully, although he sometimes put off for several months the cost center spending review. These reports were distributed to executive and operating personnel, as

Exhibit 6

SPENDING REPORT
COST CENTER #014
(Five Two-Color Miehle Printing Presses)

	1960 Standards (5 Weeks)	1960 Standards (4 Weeks)	November 1960 (5 Weeks) Actual	November 1960 (5 Weeks) Variance	December 1960 (4 Weeks) Actual	December 1960 (4 Weeks) Variance	Year 1960 (52 Weeks) Standards	Year 1960 (52 Weeks) Actual	Year 1960 (52 Weeks) Variance: Gain or (Loss)
Fixed charges	$ 4,190	$ 3,352	$ 4,190		$ 3,352		$ 43,576	$ 43,576	
General press, fixed overhead	2,701	2,426	2,701		2,426		30,212	30,212	
General press, variable overhead	10,909	8,749	9,399	$1,510	8,721	$ 28	113,628	103,541	$10,087
Press supplies	274	219	135	139	373	(154)	2,849	3,279	(430)
Repairs	1,009	808	1,754	(745)	1,472	(664)	10,500	16,560	(6,060)
Power	900	720	666	234	484	236	9,360	6,369	2,991
Labor, pressmen	10,032	8,025	7,502	2,530	5,315	2,710	104,328	73,957	30,371
Labor, press helpers	3,688	2,950	2,984	704	2,074	877	38,352	28,978	9,374
Liability insurance and payroll taxes	1,029	823	825	204	580	243	10,700	8,107	2,593
Total Cost	$34,732	$28,072	$30,156	$4,576	$24,797	$3,276	$363,505	$314,579	$48,926
Standard credit			(28,463)		(19,266)			(267,585)	
Burden variance			4,577		3,274			48,927	
Over or (under) earned burden			(6,270)		(8,805)			(95,921)	
Gain or (loss)			(1,693)		(5,531)			(46,994)	
Number hours makeready			668		389			6,390	
Number hours machine time			1,441		1,047			13,783	
Number hours total	2,600	2,080	2,109		1,436		27,040	20,173	
Production units per hour			2,984		3,036			3,049	
Fixed cost per hour	$ 2.65	$ 2.78	$ 3.27		$ 4.02			$ 3.66	
Variable cost per hour	10.71	10.72	11.03		13.25			11.93	
Total cost per hour	13.36	13.50	14.30		17.27			15.59	

NOTES:
1. Standard credit = Actual hours worked × Standard hourly costs.
2. Over or (under) earned burden = Standard credit − Standard costs.
3. Gain or (loss) = Actual costs − Standard credit = Over or (under) earned burden + Burden variance.

appropriate, for information and action when necessary, such as the production manager's review, with the departmental foreman, of cost center spending statements. Most of the other internally generated reports were prepared primarily for other executives and were sent to Mr. Barrett for his information.

REPORTS—EXTERNAL

Mr. Barrett paid close attention to several reports he received regularly from the Folding Paper Box Association of America, the industry trade association. These were as follows:

1. Quarterly Economic Report.   This 16-page report was prepared by a consulting economist. The first half dealt with current economic trends, and the second half went into specifics in analyzing the probable effects of these trends on different segments of the paperboard carton industry.
2. Industry Statistics.   This was a monthly report, by month and cumulative, in dollars and tons, quoting sales, new orders, and other related statistics. Figures were quoted by company code number. Because of his many years of experience in the industry, Mr. Barrett thought that he could identify some of the companies from the characteristics of the data they reported. Sample sheets are summarized in Exhibit 7. Wallace's code number in the exhibit is 617.
3. Industry Operating Results.   This annual booklet summarized percentage operating results and ratios, by types and sizes of company. An excerpt from the 1960 report is shown in Exhibit 8. The report was usually issued in the early part of the summer.

Each following Tuesday, Mr. Barrett also received several weekly reports from the National Paperboard Association. He studied these reports carefully in order to keep currently informed on important industry data. These reports covered nearly 90 percent of the paperboard manufacturing industry, and quoted data by company name. They included:

4. Paperboard Production and Operating Summary.   This stated paperboard production tonnage by type, activity percentage (relative to a 144-hour week), and percentage of industry production, all on a previous-week and cumulative basis.
5. Orders Received, Manufactured and Unfilled.   This covered paperboard tonnage, by type, on a previous-week and cumulative basis.
6. Paperboard Stock Report.   The information was stated in tons, by type, at the end of the week.

ORGANIZATION

An abbreviated organization chart for the company is shown in Exhibit 9.

Exhibit 7

INDUSTRY STATISTICS, JANUARY 1–APRIL 30, 1961*

(Issued May 9, 1961)

Folding Paper Boxes
Shipments and Orders Entered

	Dollars							Tonnage						
	Per Cent of Industry				Total Shipments This Year To-Date	Percent This Year Over or Under Last Year	Total Orders Entered This Year To-Date	Per Cent of Industry				Total Shipments This Year To-Date	Percent This Year Over or Under Last Year	Total Orders Entered This Year To-Date
Company Code	Entire Year 1958	Entire Year 1959	Entire Year 1960	Year To-Date 1961				Entire Year 1958	Entire Year 1959	Entire Year 1960	Year To-Date 1961			
213	.26	.26	.31	.29	863,574	0.3	952,382	.30	.32	.42	.41	3,008.1	13.9	3,337.0
215	.28	.30	.32	.28	835,513	−14.1	1,150,489	.16	.18	.17	.14	1,047.9	−18.2	1,575.0
224	.26	.30	.39	.35	1,017,501	− 2.0	972,453	.12	.13	.16	.14	1,001.3	−13.5	1,339.5
225	.14	.18	.18	.21	624,651	4.1	642,276	.09	.10	.10	.12	843.7	− 2.6	1,064.1
226	.30	.32	.29	.29	859,072	−16.2	842,015	.29	.34	.31	.33	2,368.0	−18.1	2,238.2
227	.03	.03	.04	.04	113,246	0.4	107,767	.06	.06	.07	.08	547.8	1.7	528.3
248	.12	.12	.12	.17	494,562	12.6	426,458	.09	.08	.09	.12	863.0	9.4	1,082.1
259	.31	.32	.36	.37	1,089,287	− 3.6	976,258	.19	.18	.20	.18	1,311.3	− 8.4	1,424.6
318	.11	.13	.14	.14	409,557	6.3	505,507	.09	.10	.11	.10	736.4	− 9.5	961.5
351	.83	.79	.76	.73	2,134,350	− 0.8	2,073,000	.80	.76	.70	.65	4,707.5	− 4.2	4,468.1
352	1.85	1.86	1.87	1.68	4,969,802	13.4	5,342,981	1.79	1.74	1.82	1.68	12,214.8	12.7	13,742.4
423	.61	.68	.61	.61	1,798,319	− 2.9	2,196,793	.59	.66	.59	.62	4,551.6	5.3	5,167.1
451	2.64	2.61	2.37	2.21	6,504,923	−15.7	6,940,605	2.70	2.73	2.34	2.17	15,776.4	−21.7	20,660.4
519	.61	.59	.58	.58	1,717,143	− 5.9	1,799,074	.58	.58	.57	.56	4,094.1	− 8.7	4,515.0
521	.37	.41	.38	.42	1,222,353	−14.3	1,095,846							
540	.10	.10	.10	.11	314,435	9.4	275,550	.11	.11	.11	.12	845.8	6.9	861.1
553	1.49	1.20	1.14	1.12	3,288,523	−13.0	4,525,314	1.47	1.18	1.10	1.13	8,259.5	− 8.8	10,936.1
554	.72	.63	.60	.40	1,185,394	−29.8	901,286	.85	.77	.74	.55	3,972.6	−21.7	3,127.5
616	.20	.22	.23	.23	664,342	−23.2	506,889	.18	.19	.21	.21	1,528.1	−24.0	1,068.6
617	.64	.75	.77	.85	2,502,532	− 7.2	2,455,316	.49	.55	.58	.67	4,907.4	1.7	4,764.3
618	.17	.17	.16	.19	545,417	− 8.1	511,141	.16	.15	.15	.17	1,242.9	− 6.7	1,284.7
643	.31	.31	.30	.30	872,382	− 9.3	861,063	.25	.27	.26	.26	1,886.5	− 6.2	1,838.0

Eastern Area

Code														
647	.16	.17	.18	.20	575,843	9.8	.12	.13	.15	.15	514,102	1,109.7	3.8	1,026.6
652	1.70	1.67	1.63	1.72	5,063,439	6.9	2.11	2.08	1.96	1.98	4,797,477	14,373.2	3.5	13,316.2
660	.37	.41	.36	.38	1,115,315	—1.1	.32	.34	.31	.33	438,412	2,415.0	—7.3	824.9
714	.05	.06	.06	.06	166,697	—13.8	.05	.05	.06	.07	181,909	533.5	—12.8	584.1
720	.12	.12	.09	.08	236,850	—32.0	.08	.07	.06	.05	292,959	353.6	—34.7	553.5
721	.35	.28	.31	.30	872,417	—7.7	.27	.22	.27	.21	800,290	1,561.8	—31.8	1,636.6
723	.06	.06	.06	.07	220,259	21.4	.03	.03	.03	.03	139,406	24.7	24.0	172.4
726	.49	.42	.37	.36	1,066,132	—14.2	.55	.48	.40	.39	1,106,131	2,833.1	—13.7	3,186.7
733	.60	.55	.61	.62	1,813,079	—7.8	.68	.64	.66	.69	1,703,650	5,034.1	6.2	4,824.6
742	.09	.09	.08	.08	236,499	—3.9	.09	.09	.08	.08	199,949	566.2	—11.1	457.8
751	.20	.21	.22	.24	693,850	—4.2	.20	.20	.22	.22	797,763	1,621.6	9.7	2,002.3
752	.14	.15	.16	.16	457,815	—5.5	.15	.18	.18	.18	510,369	1,323.0	3.6	1,513.3
753	.21	.22	.21	.23	669,736	—3.5	.24	.27	.29	.31	580,067	2,267.9	7.3	2,135.4
834	.26	.29	.35	.37	1,079,598	—8.9	.17	.18	.21	.21	1,023,624	1,541.0	—14.5	1,558.0
836	.21	.18	.21	.20	574,114	—16.5	.16	.13	.16	.16	558,642	1,129.8	—14.2	1,289.9
917	.09	.09	.09	.10	292,897	—4.1	.06	.06	.06	.07	291,796	476.3	—3.5	596.8
Eastern Area Total	17.45	17.25	17.01	16.74	49,161,418		16.75	16.45	16.01	15.66	49,997,009	113,994.3		122,623.0
Southern Area Total	3.74	3.83	4.06	4.05	11,947,931		4.09	4.15	4.27	4.26	12,620,050	31,145.0		33,585.5
North Central Area Total	23.94	24.21	24.43	24.49	72,127,835		24.22	24.54	25.10	25.31	75,533,636	184,354.3		204,601.2
Pacific Area Total	2.94	3.05	2.99	3.01	8,905,238		3.04	3.24	3.12	3.09	10,081,433	22,500.9		25,792.9
Reporting Companies Total	48.07	48.34	48.49	48.29	142,142,422		48.10	48.38	48.50	48.32	148,232,128	351,994.5		386,602.6
Balance of Industry	51.93	51.66	51.51	51.71	152,209,249		51.90	51.62	51.50	51.68		376,467.8		
(Millions) Total Industry	909	944	940	294			2.314	2.367	2.313	0.728				

Exhibit 8

COMPARATIVE INDUSTRY OPERATING RESULTS, 1960*

STATEMENT OF OPERATION FOR THE YEAR 1960

	Median	Integrated Box Manufacturers with Sales Volume over $4 Million† Range of Middle 50%			Wallace Box Company
Net sales	100.00%	100.00%		—	100.00%
Total materials used	56.16	50.42%	to	62.34%	43.48
Manufacturing wages and salaries	21.63	18.29	to	23.90	21.61
All other manufacturing expense	10.15	7.17	to	11.76	6.69
Total cost of goods sold	86.49%	82.24%	to	92.08%	71.78
Gross profit on sales	13.51%	7.93%	to	17.77%	28.22
Total administrative expense	4.61	3.44	to	6.17	7.57
Total selling expense	7.38	6.04	to	8.93	8.17
Total administrative and selling expense	11.99	9.29	to	14.78	15.74
Net profit from operations	1.52%	(2.05%)	to	6.01%	12.48
Total income credits	.26	.17	to	.50	1.98
Total	1.78	(1.96)	to	6.55	14.46
Total income charges	.48	.20	to	2.17	2.58
Net profit before federal and state income taxes	1.30%	(3.76%)	to	6.55%	11.88
Net profit after federal and state income taxes	.80%	(3.76%)	to	3.14%	4.81

BREAKDOWN OF MATERIALS USED

As a Percentage of Net Sales

	Median				Wallace Box Company
Paperboard	46.58%	41.47%	to	54.15%	34.86
Ink	2.28	2.09	to	2.83	1.68
Corrugated containers	2.66	2.11	to	3.18	2.78
Other materials	5.27	2.38	to	6.60	4.16
Total	56.79%‡	49.37%	to	61.08%	43.48

Exhibit 8—Continued

OTHER FINANCIAL RATIOS§

	Integrated Box Manufacturers with Sales Volume over $4 Million†	
	Median	Range of Middle 50%
Current ratio	4.0	2.57 to 5.43
Number of weeks' sales in:		
Finished goods inventory	6.0	4.56 to 7.17
Total inventory	8.7	8.31 to 9.06
Sales per dollar of:		
Net worth	$ 2.57	$ 2.52 to $ 2.75
Working capital	4.89	4.76 to 5.01
Inventory as a per cent of:		
Sales	16.79%	15.98% to 17.42%
Working capital	82.99	69.45 to 96.53
Net worth	41.17	36.16 to 46.18
Current assets to net worth	75.20	72.35 to 78.05
Fixed assets to net worth	41.02	34.11 to 47.93
Total assets to net worth	131.26	113.32 to 149.19
Return on investment, basis of:		
Net worth	(3.10%)	(8.68%) to 2.49%
Total assets	(1.82%)	(7.96%) to 4.53%

† The published data broke down integrated manufacturers into two groups—sales below and above $4 million.

‡ Varies from the median reported for total materials in the Operating Statement because not all the companies submitting figures were able to break down their material costs into the categories listed above.

§ Wallace's figures were not inserted by Mr. Lewis, because he said the company's financial situation was sufficiently different from the average company's to make these comparisons of dubious value.

Exhibit 9

PARTIAL ORGANIZATION CHART

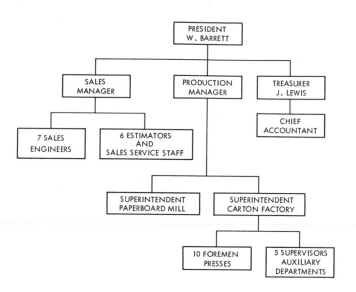

QUESTION

You are asked to appraise the planning and control system of this company. What are the *important* points you think should be made to Mr. Barrett? Include suggestions for any changes that you think should be considered.

Chapter Two

BEHAVIOR IN
ORGANIZATIONS

In this chapter we describe certain characteristics of organizations and of the behavior of people who work in organizations. These are characteristics that influence the design and use of management control systems. We also describe in some detail the function of the controller, the staff person who is responsible for these systems.

ORGANIZATION STRUCTURE

Although organizations come in all sizes and shapes, for the purpose of analyzing the appropriate management control structure, we can refer generally to three main types: (1) a functional organization, in which each manager is responsible for a specified function, such as production; (2) a divisional organization, in which each divisional manager is responsible for all, or almost all, of the functions that are involved in a product line or group of product lines, and (3) a matrix organization, in which there are two organizational structures, one arranged by functions and the other by projects. Abbreviated organization charts for each type are shown in Exhibit 2–1.

Functional Organizations

In a functional organization, each manager is responsible for one of the several functions that collectively are involved in generating profits or doing whatever the goals of the organization may be.

Functional organizations have the potential of great efficiency. For a great many activities, efficiency increases as the size of the activity increases, up to some point where there are no further "economies of scale" to be realized. The reason that efficiency increases is that large-scale operations permit

Exhibit 2–1

TYPES OF ORGANIZATION

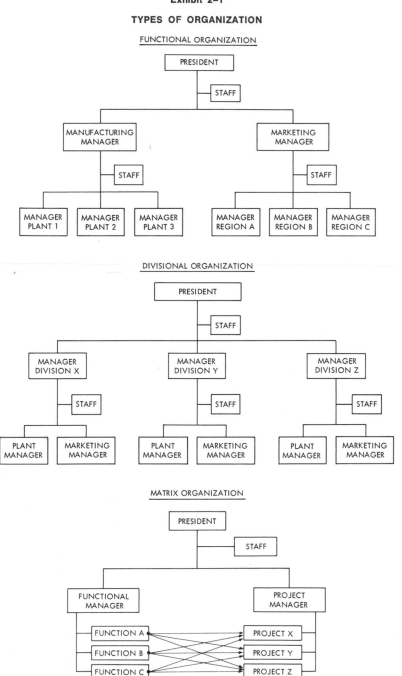

the utilization of increasingly specialized inputs. A general purpose machine tool operated by a skilled machinist may be able to produce 100 parts per hour, whereas a specially designed piece of equipment may produce 1,000 parts per hour and require only a part time operator. Specialization of human resources can also yield economies of scale; the learning curve of a production worker is perhaps the most common example.

Further, the quality of manufacturing supervision and technical services, such as engineering and quality control, is likely to be better when those activities are centralized under one manufacturing manager. Scattering those resources across product divisions would both lower the quality of the personnel that might be used and reduce the efficient utilization of their services. Similar arguments might be made about the efficiency of the marketing organization as a large functional activity.

A disadvantage of a functional organization is that responsibility for earning profits cannot be assigned unambiguously to individual managers. If one manager is responsible for manufacturing a product and another manager is responsible for marketing that product, then the profits on that product result from the joint efforts of each. It may be quite difficult, or impossible, to identify how much of the total profit is attributable to each manager. Further, in a functional organization, top management must plan and coordinate the activities of the functional units and resolve disputes between their managers. These factors make control more difficult in a functional organization.

Effective decision making in a functionally organized business is hampered by the fact that no subordinate has the same broad perspective of the business that the president or general manager has. Many decisions, and almost all of the important ones, will affect more than one function in the business. Delegating the authority for such decisions to one functional manager may result in a different decision (because of his functional bias) than if the decision were made by another functional manager or by the general manager.

Divisional Organizations

For control purposes, a division in a divisional organization can be treated almost as if it were an independent entity. The division manager can develop a strategy for his particular business, finding a competitive niche for it that may be different from the strategy being pursued by other division managers with different product lines. Tactically, a product division can also be more responsive to current customer needs. The division manager has the authority to change the production schedule in response to the request of an important customer; in a functional organization, such a request must go "through channels," which may be ponderous and time-consuming. Moreover, divisions may be an excellent training ground for young managers, fostering entrepreneurship and increasing the number of centers of initiative in a corporation.

Since division managers are responsible for both the manufacturing and the marketing activities for the products in the division, they control the main elements that affect the division's profitability, and they therefore can be held accountable for their division's results. They cannot be held quite as accountable as if the division manager were the chief executive of an independent company because the division is a part of the larger organization and decisions made by higher management and interactions with other divisions do impinge on the division manager's responsibility; nevertheless, the division manager can be held accountable for profits to a greater degree than the manager of a unit in a functional organization. The management control process is therefore inherently more straight-forward in a divisional organization than in a functional organization.

Of course, responsibility centers within a division are functional units, and the control problem is the same for these units as for a whole company that is functionally organized except that it is on a smaller scale.

Matrix Organizations

In a matrix organization, there is one basic organization structure in which responsibility centers are arranged by functions, and alongside this structure—or superimposed on it—there is another structure in which the focus of responsibility is by projects. As used in this context, a project is any task or group of tasks involved in reaching a specified end objective. Preparing an advertising campaign, developing a new project, or building a new plant are examples of such objectives. Each project is set up for a specific purpose. The project manager uses personnel, material, and/or services from the various functional units in accomplishing that objective, and when the objective is achieved the project is terminated.

A shipyard is an example of a matrix organization. The basic organization structure is by functional shops—plumbing shop, electrical shop, machine shop, and so on. Each ship overhaul is a project. The project manager calls on the functional shops for the resources required for the job. If these resources are personnel, they work under the supervision of the project manager while assigned to the project. If the shop furnishes material or services, the responsibility for the cost, quality, and timely delivery of these items is partly that of the shop manager and partly that of the project manager.

Consulting firms, research/development organizations, construction companies, manufacturers of aircraft and other complicated equipment, and many other companies have a matrix organization. In most companies, teams are created for various special purposes, and these teams are equivalent to projects.

The management control problems in a matrix organization are obviously more difficult than those in the other two types. Planning must mesh the requirements of the projects with the resources that are available in the functional units. Coordination involves scheduling the activities of the several units so that projects are completed on time but personnel are not idle. Control is difficult because profitability is the joint responsibility of several managers.

Implications for Systems Design

If ease of control were the only criterion, companies would be organized into divisions whenever it was feasible to do so because in a divisional organization each divisional manager is held responsible for the profitability of the division's product line and presumably plans, coordinates, and controls the elements that affect its profitability. Control is not the only criterion, however. A functional organization may be more efficient because the larger functional units give the economies of scale. A divisional organization requires a somewhat broader type of manager than the specialist who manages a function. A matrix organization permits personnel with similar skills to have a home base in a functional unit whose manager is responsible for developing these skills. These matters are discussed in more depth in Chapter 6 with respect to divisional and functional organizations, and in Chapter 16 for matrix organizations.[1]

Because of the apparently clearcut nature of the assignment of profit responsibility in a divisional organization, designers of a management control system sometimes recommend such an organization without giving appropriate weight to the other considerations involved in organization design. In the final analysis, the systems designer must fit the system to the organization, not the other way around. In other words, although the control implications of various organization structures should be discussed with top management, once management has decided that a given structure is best, all things considered, then the system designer must take that structure as a given and design the best system he can for it. Enthusiasts for some control technique may overlook this essential point.

This point is also important in other contexts. For example, many advertising agencies follow the practice of shifting account supervisors from one account to another at fairly frequent intervals, so as to bring a fresh point of view to the various advertising programs. This practice increases the difficulty of measuring the performance of an account supervisor because the fruits of an advertising campaign may require a long time to ripen. Nevertheless, the systems designer should not insist that the rotation policy should be abandoned simply because to do so would make performance measurement easier.

------

[1] For an excellent discussion of the complex factors that must be considered in making a basic change in organization structure, see Alfred D. Chandler, Jr., *Strategy and Structure* (Cambridge, Mass.: MIT Press, 1962).

MANAGEMENT BEHAVIOR

In Chapter 1 we described several types of control systems and pointed out that control of body temperature was more complicated and more difficult to understand than the electromechanical control of room temperature with a thermostat, and that control that involved the human brain, such as in driving an automobile, was even more complicated and difficult to understand. Control in an organization is more complicated and difficult to understand than any of these. Why is this?

A portion of the explanation is that an organization consists of many parts, and the coordination of the activities of these parts is complicated. This is by no means the whole explanation, however, for the electrical distribution network of large sections of the country requires that millions of consuming and generating units be tied together in a single system, yet breakdowns in this system are rare. Nor does the fact that the organization is affected by unanticipated external forces explain the difficulties, for the human body adjusts its temperature to external conditions that change more rapidly and vary more as a percentage of the norm than those affecting the typical organization.

The most important difference between an organization and the examples of simpler control systems given in Chapter 1, is that in an organization, control occurs through the interactions of human beings. Human behavior is complicated and not well understood, and the optimum control techniques in an organization are correspondingly complicated and not well understood.

Basic Concepts

As is the case with any system, an organization is "in control" when it is behaving in accordance with predetermined standards. In an organization these standards are called *goals*. They are determined by top management, and top management wants all operating managers to work so as to achieve these goals.[2] If an organization were like a heating system, this would be easy: top management would issue orders and operating managers would execute them, just as the furnace is turned on when the thermostat directs it to do so.

Managers are not like furnaces, however. For one thing, managers differ greatly as to their ability to carry out their responsibilities. The ability of a given manager depends partly on innate traits, and partly on his education, his experience, and his suitability for the job to which he is assigned. These characteristics obviously have a great deal to do with how well a manager performs. The systems designer must accept the fact that these differences

---

[2] For simplicity, we shall refer to top management and operating managers as if there were only two management levels in an organization. Although most organizations have several levels, similar considerations apply with respect to each of them.

do exist, and that they are one of the reasons why it is impossible to predict exactly the response of individual managers to stimuli provided by the system.

Operating managers differ from furnaces in two other principal ways. First, they may, or they may not, understand what top management wants them to do: this is the problem of *perception*. Second, they may, or they may not, react in the way that top management wants them to react; this is the problem of *motivation*. We shall discuss each of these problems.

Perception

In order to work toward the goals of the organization, operating managers must know what these goals are and what actions they are supposed to take in order to achieve them. Through various channels, the operating managers receive information as to what they are supposed to do. In part this information is conveyed by budgets and other formal documents, and in part it is conveyed by conversations and other informal meanings. This information often is not a clear and unambiguous message as to what top management wants done. An organization is complicated, and the actions that should be taken by one part of it to accomplish the overall goals cannot be set forth with absolute clarity, even under the best of circumstances. Furthermore, the messages received through the various information channels may conflict with one another, or managers may interpret them in different ways. For example, the budget mechanism may convey the impression that managers are supposed to make current profits as high as they can, whereas from other sources they learn that it is desirable to reduce current profits in order to increase future profits. In short, the operating manager's perception of what he is supposed to do is vastly less clearcut than the message that the furnace receives from the thermostat.

Much can be done to reduce the amount of ambiguous and conflicting information that the manager receives. This topic is discussed in more detail in Chapter 3.

The Informal Organization. An important cause of conflicting and erroneous perceptions of desired actions is the existence of an informal organization alongside the formal organization. The lines on an organization chart depict the formal organization, that is, the formal authority and responsibility relationships of the several managers. The organization chart may show, for example, that the production manager of Division A reports only to the general manager of Division A. In actuality, however, the production manager of Division A communicates with various other people in the organization: other managers in Division A, managers in other divisions, and managers and staff people at headquarters. In extreme situations, the production manager may pay very little attention to the messages he receives from his division manager. Moreover, the goals of the informal organization may not be consistent with the goals of the formal organization. The relationships not depicted on the organization chart constitute the informal organization. By definition, they are not included within the formal management control system. They are nevertheless important in understanding the realities of the management control process.

A manager's perceptions involve his understanding not only of *what* he is supposed to do, but also of *how strongly* top management wants a certain course of action. In various ways, top management signals the degree of importance that should be attached to the control process—by the amount of time that it devotes to the process, by the speed and vigor of its reaction to reports which it receives, and in general by its attitude toward control. An organization in which top management disregards control is, to all intents and purposes, leaderless.

Functional Fixation.   Erroneous perceptions may arise for strange reasons. Among them is the phenomenon called *functional fixation,* which means that people tend to interpret certain terms according to the definition that they have become accustomed to through prior experience with these terms, even though a different definition is intended in the control system currently being used. In the usual case, the system designer assumes, erroneously, that "everyone knows" that a term means what the designer thinks it means, and therefore he does not take the trouble to define it. In the extreme case, managers may, because of their background, assume that a term has a different meaning from that intended even though a different definition is explicitly given; they may not read or comprehend the definition. For example, in a certain company, the term "labor cost" may be intended to mean the sum of salary cost and fringe benefits, but a manager may, because of a fixation developed in school or in another company, interpret labor costs as including salary only. There is an unfortunate tendency for system designers to assume that everyone else defines terms in the same way they do.

Motivation

Managers react to information, as they perceive it, in different ways. Their reactions depend on their motivation. Motivation occurs within the individual; it is inner directed. External stimuli can influence a person's motivation, but the motivation itself reflects the person's reaction to these stimuli. As a basis for understanding motivation we describe briefly the relationship between individuals and the organization of which they are a part.

Personal Goals.   Each person in an organization is called a *participant.* A person becomes a participant—that is, he joins an organization—because he believes that by doing so he can achieve his *personal* goals. His decision to contribute to the productive work of the organization once he has become a member of it is also based on his perception that this will help achieve his personal goals.

An individual's personal goals can be expressed as *needs.* Some of these needs are *material* and can be satisfied by the money that he earns on the job;

that is, he needs enough money to provide for himself and for his family. Other needs are *psychological.* People need to have their abilities and achievements recognized; they need social acceptance as members of a group; they need to feel a sense of personal worth; they need to feel secure; they need the freedom to exercise discretion; they may need a feeling of power and achievement.

The relative importance of these needs varies with different persons, and their relative importance to one person varies at different times. For some people, earning a great deal of money is a dominant need; for others, monetary considerations are must less important. Only a relatively few people attach much importance to the need to exercise discretion or the need for achievement, but these few persons tend to be the leaders of the organization.[3] The relative importance that persons attach to their own needs is heavily influenced by the attitude of their colleagues and of their superiors.

Incentives. Individuals are influenced both by positive incentives and negative incentives. A *positive incentive,* also called a reward or a reinforcement, is the satisfaction of a need, or the expectation that a need will be satisfied. A *negative incentive,* also called a punishment, is the deprivation of satisfaction of a need, or the fear of such deprivation. Most of the research studies on human incentives use students as subjects, and those few studies conducted in a business environment tend to focus on salespersons, production workers, clerical employees, and other nonmanagers. There are obvious difficulties in conducting controlled experiments with managers as subjects. Despite the paucity of research evidence, there seems to be support for the following generalizations:

> Individuals are more strongly motivated by positive incentives than by negative incentives.
>
> Monetary compensation is an important incentive, but beyond the subsistence level the amount of compensation is not necessarily as important as nonmonetary rewards. Nevertheless, the amount of a person's earnings is often important indirectly as an indication of how his achievement and ability are regarded. (A person earning $50,000 a year may be disgruntled if a colleague whom he perceives to have only equal ability earns $51,000 a year.)
>
> The effectiveness of incentives diminishes rapidly as time elapses between an action and the reward or punishment administered for it. This is why it is important that reports on performance be made available and acted on quickly. Management control cannot wait for the annual financial statements that appear three months or so after the year has ended.

---

[3] McClelland argues that there is a relationship between the strength of the achievement motivation of the leaders of an organization and the success of that organization and that a similar relationship helps explain why certain countries have a rapid economic growth at certain times while others do not. See David McClelland, *The Achieving Society* (1971); and David C. McClelland and David G. Winter, *Motivating Economic Achievement* (New York: The Free Press, 1969).

Needs may be unconscious, or they may be expressed as aspirations or objectives. Motivation is weakest when the person perceives an objective as being either unattainable or too easily attainable. Motivation is strong when the objective can be attained with some effort and when the individual regards its attainment as important in relation to his needs.

The incentive provided by a budget or other statement of objective is strongest when the manager participates actively in the process of arriving at the budgeted amounts.

A person who perceives his work as being worthwhile or important is more highly motivated than one who does not.

A person needs to know, on some fairly regular basis, whether the results of his efforts are regarded by his superior as being satisfactory.

Objectives are likely to provide strong incentives only if the manager perceives these objectives to be fair.

Objectives are likely to provide strong incentives only if managers feel committed to attaining them. The commitment is strongest when it is a matter of public record, that is, when the manager has explicitly agreed to the objective.

Managers tend to accept reports of performance more willingly and to use them more constructively when the reports are presented to them in a manner that they regard as objective; that is, without personal bias.

Persons are receptive to learning better ways of doing things only when they personally recognize the inadequacies of their present behavior.

Beyond a certain point, pressure for improved performance accomplishes nothing. This optimum point is far below the maximum amount of pressure that conceivably could be exerted.

Individuals differ in their needs and in their reactions to incentives of various types. An important function of the manager at each level is to adapt his application of the management control system to the personalities and attitudes of the individuals whom he supervises. Thus an impersonal system can never be a substitute for interpersonal actions; rather, the system is a framework that should be adapted by the manager to fit individual situations.

Compensation.   In many companies managers are compensated in part by a salary and in part by a bonus that is based on performance. This bonus can be a powerful incentive. The bonus and the method of arriving at it can take any of several forms, and the direction and strength of motivation is greatly affected by the particular forms that are selected.

The basis for the bonus can be entirely objective, entirely subjective, or anywhere in between. An objective bonus is one that is based strictly on a formula, such as the calculated profitability of a division. The measure of profitability can be for the individual division, for the company as a whole, or for the combination of the two. The time span for the bonus calculation can be a single year, or a period of two, three, or four years.

A bonus system which is primarily objective, which focuses on a division's profitability, and which has a short time span is appropriate when the division manager has a considerable degree of autonomy, when cooperation with other divisions is relatively unimportant, and when the division manager is unlikely to take short-run actions that hurt long-run profitability. By contrast, a bonus system which is based primarily on top management's subjective appraisal, which focuses on the profitability of the company as a whole, and which may cover a period of several years, is appropriate when top management exerts a direct influence on decisions that affect the divisions, when divisions must cooperate with one another, when the short-run profitability of a division cannot be measured with reasonable accuracy, and when a long-run view is encouraged. Many permutations of these sets of characteristics are obviously possible and lead to a wide variety of bonus plans.

Alternatives also exist for the form of bonus payment. It may be paid in cash or in stock options, and in either case the payment may be made immediately, or it may be deferred for a number of years. These payment options also affect the motivation that the bonus provides.

Clearly, the power of the bonus and the existence of such a variety of alternatives suggest that it is worthwhile to devote much study and thought to devising a bonus plan which will provide the optimum motivation.[4]

Goal Congruence. Since an organization does not have a mind of its own, the organization itself literally cannot have goals. The "organizational goals" that we have referred to are actually the goals of top management. Top management wants these organizational goals to be attained, but other participants have their own personal goals that *they* want to achieve. These personal goals are the satisfaction of their needs. In other words, participants act in their own self-interest.[5]

The difference between organizational goals and personal goals suggest a central purpose of a management control system: The system should be designed so that actions that it leads people to take in accordance with their perceived self-interest, are actions that are also in the best interests of the organization. In the language of social psychology, the management control system should encourage *goal congruence;* that is, it should be structured so that the goals of participants, so far as is feasible, are consistent with the goals of the organization as a whole. If this situation exists, a decision that a manager regards as being good from his own viewpoint will also be a good decision for the organization as a whole. As McGregor states:

---

[4] This section was based on Malcolm S. Salter, "Tailor Incentive Compensation to Strategy," *Harvard Business Review,* March–April 1973, p. 94. See also: American Management Association, *Financial Motivation for Executives* (New York: American Management Association, 1970).

[5] It follows that in a literal sense all persons are "selfish." This does not imply a cynical view of human nature, however. For most people, self-esteem is a need, and self-esteem requires that a person help other people, often at some sacrifice of his own pleasure or profit.

The essential task of management is to arrange organizational conditions and methods of operations so that people can achieve their own goals best by directing their own efforts towards organizational objectives.[6]

Perfect congruence between individual goals and organizational goals does not exist. One obvious reason is that individual participants want as much salary as they can get, whereas from the viewpoint of the organization, there is an upper limit to salaries, beyond which profits will be adversely affected. As a minimum, however, the system should not encourage the individual to act *against* the best interests of the company. For example, if the management control system signals that the emphasis should be only on reducing costs, and if a manager responds by reducing costs at the expense of adequate quality or if he responds by reducing costs in his own responsibility center by measures that cause a more than offsetting increase in costs in some other responsibility center, he has been motivated, but in the wrong direction. It is therefore important to ask two separate questions about any practice used in a management control system:

1. What action does it motivate people to take in their own perceived self-interest, and
2. Is this action in the best interests of the company?

Cooperation and Conflict

The lines connecting the boxes on an organization chart imply that the way in which organizational goals are attained is that the top manager makes a decision, he communicates that decision down through the organizational hierarchy, and operating managers at lower levels of the organization proceed to implement it. It should now be apparent that this is *not* the way in which an organization actually functions.

What actually happens is that each operating manager reacts to the instructions of top management in accordance with how those instructions are perceived and how they affect his personal needs. Since usually more than one manager is involved in carrying out a given plan, the interactions between managers also affect what actually happens. For example, although the manager of the maintenance department is supposed to see to it that the maintenance needs of the production departments are satisfied, the needs of that production manager's department may be slighted if there is friction between the maintenance manager and production manager. More importantly, many actions that a manager may want to take to achieve his own goals have an adverse effect on other managers and on overall profitability. Managers argue about which of them is to get the use of limited production capacity or other scarce resources, or about potential customers that several managers want to solicit. For these and many other reasons, conflict exists within organizations.

---

[6] David McGregor, *The Human Side of Enterprise* (New York: McGraw-Hill, 1960).

At the same time, the work of the organization will not get done unless its participants work together with a certain amount of harmony. Thus, there is also cooperation in organizations. Participants realize that unless there is a reasonable amount of cooperation, the organization will dissolve, and the participants will then be unable to satisfy *any* of the needs which motivated them to join the organization in the first place.

An organization attempts to maintain an appropriate balance between the forces that create conflict and those that create cooperation. Some conflict is not only inevitable; it is also desirable. Conflict results in part from the competition among participants for promotion or other forms of need satisfaction; and such competition is, within limits, healthy. A certain amount of cooperation is also obviously essential, but if undue emphasis is placed on engendering cooperative attitudes, the most able participants will be denied the opportunity of demonstrating their full potentialities.

Organizational Climate. As noted above, perceptions about an organization's goals and about decisions that a manager should take to achieve these goals come not only from the formal control system but also through the informal organization. Both the formal and informal structure combine to create what is called the organizational climate. As defined by Andrews:

> The term 'climate' is used to designate the quality of the internal environment which conditions in turn the quality of cooperation, the development of individuals, the extent of members' dedication or commitment to organizational purpose, and the efficiency with which that purpose becomes translated into results. Climate is the atmosphere in which individuals help, judge, reward, constrain and find out about each other. It influences morale—the attitude of the individual toward his work and his environment.[7]

Organizational climate has important influences on motivation. Since to a certain extent an organization is "the lengthened shadow of an individual," the attitude of the chief executive officer toward control is an important ingredient of the climate. The nature of the management control process in a given organization is much affected by the "style" of the top management in that organization. Some chief executive officers rely heavily on reports and other formal documents; others prefer conversations and informal contacts. The formal system must be consistent with top management's preferences. It follows that if a new top management, with a different style, takes over, the system should change correspondingly.

By its very nature, "climate" cannot be described concretely. Some alternative characteristics are as follows:

Focus on results versus focus on following the rules.

Individual accomplishment versus being a member of the team.

---

[7] Kenneth R. Andrews, *The Concept of Corporate Strategy* (Homewood, Ill.: Dow-Jones-Irwin, Inc., 1971), page 232.

Exhibit 2–2

TYPES OF CONTROL IN ORGANIZATIONS

Controls Administered by	Direction for Controls Deriving from	Behavioral and Performance Measures	Signal for Corrective Action	Reinforcements or Rewards for Compliance	Sanctions or Punishments for Non-compliance
Organization	Organizational plans, strategies, responses to competitive demands	Budgets, standard costs, sales targets	Variance	Management commendation Monetary incentives, promotions	Request for explanation Dismissal
Informal group	Mutual commitments, group ideals	Group norms	Deviance	Peer-approval, membership, leadership	Kidding, Ostracism, hostility
Individual	Individual goals, aspirations	Self-expectations, intermediate targets	Perceived impending failure, missed targets	Satisfaction of "being in control" Elation	Sense of disappointment Feeling of failure

Source: Gene W. Dalton and Paul R. Lawrence, eds., *Motivation and Control in Organizations* (Homewood, Ill.: Richard D. Irwin, Inc., 1971).

Initiative and risk taking versus "not rocking the boat."

Individual gains versus enhancement of organizational objectives.

Tough mindedness in dealing with people versus avoidance of unpleasant actions.

The purpose of the management control system is to insure compliance with policies versus the purpose is to obtain results.

The management control system is an aid to managers versus the system should be circumvented or disregarded.

The relative importance of participatory management versus authoritarian management.[8]

Types of Control

One way of summarizing the foregoing comments on motivation is indicated in Exhibit 2–2, taken from Dalton. Dalton points out that three types of control are always present. There is, first, the formal control mechanism that is administered through regular organization channels, and which is the most clearly visible type of control simply because it is manifested in budgets, reports of performance, and other documents. Second, there are the controls associated with the informal organization. Third, there are the controls associated with the manager as an individual. In the ideal world, all these controls would be working in the same direction, but in the real world this ideal is never fully achieved.

Variations in Controls

The general nature of control that is appropriate in a given situation varies according to the nature both of the work involved and of the individual manager. Three dimensions of the work are important:

1. The amount of management discretion,
2. The amount of interdependence, and
3. The time span of performance.

Management Discretion. The work done by an organization unit can be located along a scale with routinized production or clerical operations at one end, and creative, unspecifiable activities, such as research at the other. For activities at or near the routine end, specific performance standards can be established, and rewards (for example in the form of bonuses) can be related to how actual performance compares to these standards. For activities at the other end of the scale, specific standards are not feasible; indeed, an attempt to impose them is likely to have dysfunctional consequences.

Interdependence. Organization units can also be located along a scale according to their degree of independence from, or interdependence with,

---

[8] This list is adapted from an unpublished paper by Professor Robert H. Caplan.

other units. To the extent that the work of the whole organization requires that individual units cooperate closely with one another, controls that focus on the performance of an individual unit can be dysfunctional.

Time Span.   Finally, organization units can be arrayed according to the time span between the initiation of action and results. A selling organization whose job is to visit customers and take orders is at one extreme (with a short time span), and an organization responsible for all the efforts involved in introducing a new product is at the other extreme (with a long time span). When the time span is short, performance measurement can be, and should be, frequent, and actual performance can be compared with short-run standards. When the time span is long, any measurement of interim performance should be regarded as being highly tentative.

Personal Differences.   In addition to these differences in the nature of the work, the control system should also take account of differences in the motivation and other personality characteristics of individual managers to the extent that this is feasible. Generally, these differences affect the way one manager deals with another in using the system, rather than differences in the way the formal system is constructed.

FUNCTION OF THE CONTROLLER

We shall use the word "controller" as the name for the person who is responsible for the design and operation of an organization's information systems. This use is only for convenience in exposition, for in practice there are all sorts of variations in nomenclature. The person who has the title of controller may in fact be responsible for all information systems, or he may be responsible for only some of them. In some organizations, a person with the title of information systems manager may be largely responsible for the function, and the controller may be responsible only for accounting systems. In other organizations, a person with the title of financial vice president has overall responsibility for information systems; the controller, who then has responsibility for some part of this area, reports to the financial vice president.[9]

Despite the variations in practice, it is useful conceptually to think of a function that has to do with information systems, and of a person who is responsible for that function. As a practical matter, most companies have not yet grouped all information-related activities into a single organization unit because of the difficulties involved in doing so.

---

[9] Incidentally, the spelling "comptroller" is also used. This spelling originated with an error made some two hundred years ago in translating from French to English, but the erroneous spelling has become embedded in dozens of federal and state statutes and in the bylaws of many companies, and it is therefore difficult to eradicate. "Comptroller" is *pronounced* exactly the same as "controller."

Controller Responsibilities

Stated most broadly, the controller is, or should be, responsible for the design and operation of all systems for processing recurring, quantitative information that relates to resources. Resources are personnel, materials, services, and money.

The degree of responsibility for these systems varies. For budgets and financial reports of performance, the controller typically has the primary responsibility for the development and operation of the system (always keeping in mind that, as pointed out in Chapter 1, line managers make the decisions that are incorporated in the system). For systems specific to a certain function, such as the personnel records of the industrial relations department, or the materials control and production scheduling systems in a factory, the functional specialist has primary responsibility, and the controller's responsibility is to insure that these systems dovetail into the overall information system in a coherent, unambiguous, and efficient manner. The controller may also be responsible for the management of cash, for obtaining loans, for insurance protection, and for similar activities, although strictly speaking there are part of the financial function, rather than the controller function.

More specifically, the controller may be responsible for any or all of the following activities:

1. Design, install, and operate an accounting system that provides information for operating purposes, for management, and for external parties.

2. Prepare financial statements, financial reports to government agencies, and other reports for external parties.

3. Prepare tax returns.

4. Design, install and operate programming and budgeting systems. Coordinate the programming and budgeting processes.

5. Prepare and analyze reports on performance.

6. Participate in the design and operation of other systems that are used in operations (e.g., production control, inventory control.)

7. Participate in the design and operation of systems for obtaining and disseminating information from sources external to the organization.

8. Assist managers by analyzing and interpreting reports and by analyzing program and budget proposals. Specifically, assist them in expressing plans in appropriate financial terms, by providing analytical assistance to determine the financial impact of alternatives, by analyzing plans submitted, by determining financial resource requirements, and by consolidating the plans of various segments into an overall corporate plan.

9. Using appropriate internal audit and control procedures, assure the validity of information, establish adequate safeguards against theft and defalcation, and perform operational audits.

10. Develop controller personnel and participate in the education of management personnel in matters relating to the controller function.

11. Manage the personnel and equipment involved in processing information.[10]

The contrast between the wording of Items 1 and 4, on the one hand, and Items 6 and 7, on the other hand, should be noted. The controller is directly responsible for accounting, programming, and budgeting systems, which collectively may be called *financial* systems because most of the information in these systems is stated in monetary terms. The controller "participates" in the design of other systems, such as production control systems. The principal responsibility for these other systems is with the organization that the system is designed to serve; for example, the production organization is principally responsible for the design and operation of the production control system. The controller's responsibility with respect to such systems is to insure, insofar as feasible, that systems throughout the organization are efficient and compatible with one another, that is, that one system provides information for another, that unnecessary duplication is eliminated, and that common terminology is used in all systems.

Relation to Line Organization

The controller function is a staff function, not a line function. Although the controller is usually responsible for the design and operation of the *system* by means of which control information is collected and reported, the *use* of this information in actual control is the responsibility of line management. The controller is something more than an accountant and something less than a chief executive. In addition to his responsibility for collecting figures, the controller may also be responsible for analyzing figures, for pointing out their significance to management, and for making recommendations as to what should be done. Moreover, he may police the adherence to limitations on spending laid down by the chief executive. He controls the integrity of the accounting system and is responsible for safeguarding assets from theft and fraud. In recent years the controllership function has become increasingly important in companies generally.

The controller does *not,* however (unless de facto he *is* the chief executive), make or enforce management decisions. The responsibility for control runs from the president down through the line organization, not through the controller, who is a staff officer.

The controller does make some decisions. In general, these are decisions that implement policies decided on by line management. It is not easy to draw a sharp line between the type of decisions that the controller makes and the type that is appropriately made by line management. For example, a member of the controller organization often decides on the propriety of the expenses listed on a travel voucher; line managers usually prefer not to get involved in discussions of whether the traveler spent too much on meals,

---

[10] This statement adapted from Donald J. Trawicki, *Survey of Financial Management* (New York: Touche Ross & Co., 1971), p. 11.

or whether he should have traveled by tourist class rather than first class. But who should decide whether the trip itself should be made in the first instance? In some companies, the travel requests are approved by the controller; in other companies, they are approved by line management.

Although not directly relating to the controller function, the following comment by George F. Kennan, who created and headed the policy planning staff of the Department of State illustrates the frustrations that a staff man can experience:

Saturday, November 19, 1949

Pondering today the frustrations of the past week, it occurred to me that it is time I recognized that my Planning Staff, started nearly three years ago, has simply been a failure, like all previous attempts to bring order and foresight into the designing of foreign policy by special institutional arrangements within the department. Aside from personal shortcomings, the reason for this seems to lie largely in the impossibility of having the planning function performed outside of the line of command. The formulation of policy is the guts of the work of the department, and none of it can successfully be placed outside the hierarchy which governs operations. No one can regiment this institution in the field of ideas except the Secretary. He can take as much independent advice as he likes from outside the institution; he can take it orally from "special assistants" or "counselors" or other official advisors. But when it comes to any formalized staff effort, anything that has to be put down in writing and is designed to serve as a major guide for action, the operating units—the geographic and functional units—will not take interference from any unit outside the line of command. They insist on an effective voice in policy determination; if one of them cannot make its voice alone valid, it insists on the right to water down any recommendation going to the Secretary to a point where it may be (perhaps not) meaningless but at least not counter to its own views. If an unwelcome recommendation does find the Secretary's approval, they will perhaps give it a perfunctory recognition, but they will pursue basically their own policies anyway, secure in the knowledge that no one can really survey their entire volume of work, that the issues which agitate the present will soon be outdated, and that the people who are trying to force their hand will soon be gone. This is only human, and much more justifiable than it sounds. It is my belief, in the light of this discouraging experience, that the only way the thing will work is if a Secretary of State will thresh out a basic theoretical background of his policy and then really set up some sort of an educational unit through whose efforts this system can be patiently and persistently pounded into the heads of the entire apparatus, high and low.

The heart of the difficulty lies in the fact that my concept of the manner in which our diplomatic effort should be conducted is not shared by any of the other senior officials of the department; and that the Secretary is actually dependent on these officials, for better or for worse, for the execution of any foreign policy at all.[11]

---

[11] George F. Kennan, *Memoirs, 1925–1950* (Atlantic Monthly Press, 1967), pp. 267–68.

In order to avoid these frustrations there must be a close personal association between the controller and top management.

Organization of the Controller Function

Simon and his colleagues point out that accounting information is used to answer three different kinds of questions:

Score-card questions:	"Am I doing well or badly?"
Attention-directing questions:	"What problems should I look into?"
Problem-solving questions:	"Of the several ways of doing the job, which is the best?"

This leads them to the conclusion that there is generally much to be gained from separating, to a considerable degree within the controller's department, the personnel and units responsible for each of three major kinds of functions:

1. Bookkeeping, and preparation and distribution of periodic accounting reports.

2. Assistance to the operating departments in current analyses of accounting information for score-card and attention-directing purposes.

3. Participation in the use of accounting information for problem solving on a special-studies basis.[12]

In addition to these three types of organization units, the controller organization normally would contain separate units for:

4. The operation of data processing equipment (unless this is included in the accounting unit).
5. Assistance in the preparation and revision of programs.
6. Assistance in the preparation and revision of budgets.
7. Internal auditing.

The Divisional Controller

Many companies are organized into divisions, each headed by a manager who has considerable autonomy, and each with a controller. The divisional controller inevitably has a divided loyalty. On the one hand, he owes some allegiance to the corporate controller, who is presumably responsible for the overall operation of the control system. On the other hand, he owes allegiance to the division manager, since he is responsible for furnishing staff assistance to his manager. The relative strength of these two ties varies among companies. Many believe that the division controller's *primary* allegiance should be to the division manager. The Simon *et al.* study, which

---

[12] Simon, Guetzkow, Kozmetsky, and Tyndall, *Centralization vs. Decentralization in Organizing the Controller's Department* (New York: Controllership Foundation, Inc., 1954).

although not recent is one of the few published studies of the controller function, puts it as follows:

> There are two general types of arrangements of the lines of formal authority in the companies studied. In some, the factory controller or chief accounting executive is completely under the formal authority of the company controller. In other companies he is "functionally" responsible to the company controller, "administratively" to the factory manager.
>
> It was observed that when the accounting department lacks acceptance and active support from the top levels of the manufacturing department, it may be unsatisfactory to divide authority over the factory accountant between the company controller and the factory manager. But in organizations where top executives of the operating department regard the controller's services as important management tools, a system of divided authority appears to work as well as a plan in which the factory controller or district office manager reports solely to the company controller.
>
> Of greater importance than the lines of formal authority is the question of how much leeway should be given the accounting man, at a decentralized location, to run his own shop. Whether authority was centralized or decentralized, it was found that the greatest service was provided to factory management when the factory accountant felt that he had authority to provide reports to the factory management as requested, within the minimum standards of accounting policy and procedure laid down by the company controller's department.
>
> Whatever the formal arrangements, it seemed that appointments and removals of factory accountants are almost always a matter of negotiation and agreement between the controller's department and the factory manager. Admitting this joint responsibility, there is probably some advantage in placing the formal power of appointment in the controller's department.[13]

The corporate controller is normally responsible for specifying the "ground rules" within which the divisional control system must operate, and he often participates in the selection of division controllers and in decisions regarding their compensation, but if the corporate controller goes much beyond this—if, for example, he expects the division controller to keep him informed of what is going on in the division, rather than having such information channeled through the division manager—he runs the risk that the division controller will be regarded as a "spy from the front office," rather than as a valuable staff aid to division management. If this attitude develops, the division controller may become ineffective. The relationship described above is usually characterized as a "dotted line" relationship; that is, the strong, solid line of responsibility on an organization chart runs between the controller and his division manager, whereas a weaker, dotted line runs between the division controller and the corporate controller.

In some companies division controllers do report directly to the top finan-

---

[13] Simon et al. *Centralization vs. Decentralization,* pp. 8 and 9.

cial officer of the corporation. Perhaps the best known of these is the International Telephone and Telegraph Corporation. Mr. H. C. Knortz, senior vice president and comptroller of that company, describes the practice as follows:

ITT maintains a "solid line" relationship in its finance operations from my office down through the lowest element of the financial organization in the fields. This represents the customary controls over hiring, firing, bonus and merit increases. Obviously, a number of these steps are carried out in consultation with the senior operating executive at the local installation.

Although at the Headquarters level we have a segregation between the Treasurer's office and the Comptroller's office, this segregation disappears when one enters the division. There the senior financial executive reports to the ITT Comptroller and very often has reporting to him in his capacity as Director of Finance both a Treasurer and a Comptroller. Obviously, the Treasurer's Department provides strong "functional" guidance in respect to such items as cash handling, capitalization, and borrowing.

The direct line of command proceeds not only to a Division comptroller or Director of Finance, but actually extends down into third tier subsidiaries or plant location. Thus, although our German subsidiary is one of the largest companies in Germany, its financial head actually reports to the representative of the common shareholder (the ITT Comptroller in New York).

We presently administer approximately 200 subsidiaries at the Headquarters reporting level although many of these, in their turn, consolidate numerous subsidiaries. Since our program has been in operation for about 6 years, there would have been many opportunities to enter into internecine warfare, had that been a particular potential of this system. As a matter of fact, only 5 controversies have developed. In 2 of these cases the operating executives were removed; in 2 the comptrollers were removed; in the 5th case both parties were given new assignments. This is an unusually good record and was achieved largely because of the support given to this program by all of the Headquarters executives.

It should be noted that we do not tolerate private reporting from the individual comptrollers. All reports that they file with New York must also be filed with their local managers. Of course, the adequacy of the reporting is subjected to constant monitoring between directors of financial controls who act as group comptrollers and by a very powerful internal audit group.

We are entirely satisfied with the techniques used in this control of our financial function and we have been complimented by noting that those of our executives who left for other organizations often chose to install this approach to the financial monitoring. I would recommend the technique for general use in industry wherever multiple plants or divisions are concerned. There is, of course, little need for this application in a more centralized activity.[14]

The fact that in some companies the relationship between divisional and corporate controllers is "dotted line" whereas in other companies it is "solid line" reflects a difference in top management philosophy about the appro-

---

[14] Personal communication, 1971.

priate amount of delegation of responsibility. Even in companies in which the division controller's primary loyalty is to the division manager, it is expected that the division controller will not condone or participate in the transmission of misleading information or the concealment of unfavorable information; his overall ethical responsibilities should not countenance such practices.

The specific responsibilities of a divisional controller are indicated in the following list of criteria that one company uses in evaluating their performance:

1. *Accounting and Financial Reporting.* Timeliness and accuracy of regular reports submitted to division management and corporate controller's office. Does he meet schedules and deadlines and are his reports accurate and reliable?

2. *Knowledge of Division Operations.* Comprehensive but detailed understanding of division operations. Does he and can he explain accounting reports, reflecting an in-depth comprehension of trends and reasons for specific results? Does his overall understanding of operations and current conditions result in his anticipating and predicting the effect of operational decisions and directions?

3. *Performance Against Objectives.* Has he accomplished the objectives agreed to for the period under review? List objectives, dates of completion and quality of results achieved.

4. *Compliance With Policy.* Attitude and cooperation in complying with Corporate policies. Does he understand necessity of and reasons for policies? Does he seek compliance by other managers and fulfill his responsibilities in assuring overall compliance by his division?

5. *Management Contribution.* Influence and effect on the division management group. Is he respected and viewed by the division president and other key executives as an important and essential factor in the overall management of the business? Is his counsel sought and does he have a significantly positive impact on management decisions and operations?

6. *Accounting Knowledge.* Is he professionally trained as an accountant or does he have sufficient other training and experience to be considered reasonably expert in most accounting areas. If not sufficiently competent in certain areas, does he seek appropriate assistance? Is he expanding his accounting knowledge and developing himself as an accountant?

7. *Integrity and Professionalism.* As the chief financial and control executive of his division, does he recognize and accept his responsibility to the corporation and to the standards of integrity implicit in his role? Does he exercise a degree of independence and professionalism in reporting and advising line management and the corporate controller of conditions and circumstances which might otherwise be ignored or not reported?

8. *Cooperativeness.* Attitude and performance in responding to corporate requirements and requests. Does he respond positively to requests for

regular and special information by the corporation? Will he assist other divisions and corporate staff in improving over-all accounting and control programs and procedures?

9. *Organization and Staff.* What is the quality and performance of his subordinates and staff? Is he developing a professional competence in his organization and has he developed subordinates for promotion within the company?

10. *Initiative and Drive.* Has he initiated constructive changes and improvements in his own operations? In other divisional functions over which he has a direct or indirect control responsibility? Does he take an aggressive and positive position with regard to improving the overall operational control and procedures of the division?

SUGGESTED ADDITIONAL READINGS

BARNARD, CHESTER I. *The Functions of the Executive.* Cambridge, Mass.: Harvard University Press, 1938.

BRUNS, WILLIAM J., JR. and DON T. DECOSTER. *Accounting and Its Behavioral Implications.* New York: McGraw-Hill, Inc., 1969.

CHANDLER, ALFRED D., JR. *Strategy and Structure.* Cambridge, Mass.: MIT Press, 1962.

CYERT, RICHARD M., and JAMES G. MARCH. *A Behavioral Theory of the Firm.* Englewood Cliffs, N.J.: Prentice-Hall, Inc., 1963.

DALTON, GENE W., and PAUL R. LAWRENCE, eds. *Motivation and Control in Organizations.* Homewood, Ill.: Richard D. Irwin, Inc., 1971.

HOFSTEDE, G. H. *The Game of Budget Control.* Assen, Netherlands: Van Gorcum & Company, 1967.

KATZ, DANIEL, and ROBERT L. KAHN. *The Social Psychology of Organizations.* New York: John Wiley & Sons, Inc., 1966.

LAWRENCE PAUL R. and JAY W. LORSCH, *Organization and Environment,* Homewood, Ill.: Richard D. Irwin, Inc., 1969.

LORSCH, JAY W. and PAUL R. LAWRENCE. *Studies in Organization Design.* Homewood, Ill.: Richard D. Irwin, Inc., 1970.

MARCH, JAMES G., and HERBERT A. SIMON. *Organizations.* New York: John Wiley & Sons, Inc., 1958.

MINTZBERG, H. *The Nature of Managerial Work.* New York: Harper & Row, 1973.

SIMON, HERBERT A. *Administrative Behavior,* 2d ed. New York: The Macmillan Company, 1957.

SKINNER, B. F. *Beyond Freedom and Dignity.* New York: Appleton, Century-Crofts, 1971.

TANNENBAUM, ARNOLD. *Control in Organizations.* New York: McGraw-Hill, Inc., 1968.

VROOM, V. H. *Work and Motivation.* New York: John Wiley & Sons, Inc., 1964.

Case 2-1

Rendell Company

Fred Bevins, controller of the Rendell Company, was concerned about the organizational status of his divisional controllers. In 1975 and for many years previously, the divisional controllers reported to the general managers of their divisions. Although Mr. Bevins knew this to be the general practice in many other divisionally organized companies, he was not entirely satisfied with it. His interest in making a change was stimulated by a description of organizational responsibilities given him by the controller of the Martex Corporation.

The Rendell Company had seven operating divisions; the smallest had $10 million in annual sales, and the largest over $100 million. Each division was responsible for both the manufacturing and the marketing of a distinct product line. Some parts and components were transferred between divisions, but the volume of such interdivisional business was not large.

The company had been in business and profitable for over fifty years. In the late 1960s although it continued to make profits, its rate of growth slowed considerably. James Hodgkin, later the president, was hired in 1970 by the directors because of their concern about this situation. His first position was controller. He became executive vice-president in 1973 and president in 1974. Mr. Bevins joined the company as assistant controller in 1971, when he was thirty-three years old. He became controller in 1973.

In 1970, the corporate control organization was primarily responsible for (1) financial accounting, (2) internal auditing, and (3) analysis of capital budgeting requests. A budgetary control system was in existence, but the reports prepared under this system were submitted to the top management group directly by the operating divisions, with little analysis by the corporate control of organization.

Mr. Hodgkin, as controller, thought it essential that the corporate control organization play a more active role in the process of establishing budgets and analyzing performance. He personally took an active role in reviewing budgets and studying divisional performance reports, and hired several young analysts to assist him. Mr. Bevins continued to move in the same direction after his promotion to controller. By 1975, the corporate organization was beginning to be well enough staffed so that it could, and did, give careful attention to the information submitted by the divisions.

Divisional controllers reported directly to the divisional general managers, but the corporate controller always was consulted prior to the appointment of a new division controller, and he also was consulted in connection with salary increases for divisional controllers. The corporate controller specified the accounting system to which the divisions were expected to conform, and the general procedures they were to follow in connection with budgeting and reporting performance. It was clearly understood, however, that budgets and performance reports coming from a division were the responsibility of that division's general manager, with the divisional controller acting as his staff assistant in the preparation of these documents. For example, the divisional general manager personally discussed his budget with top management prior to its approval, and although the divisional controller usually was present at these meetings to give information on technical points, his role was strictly that of a staff man.

Most of the divisional controllers had worked for Rendell for 10 years or more. Usually, they worked up through various positions in the controller organization, either at headquarters, in their division, or both. Two of the divisional controllers were in their early thirties, however, and had only a few years' experience in the headquarters controller organization before being made, first, divisional assistant controller and then divisional controller.

Mr. Bevins foresaw increasing difficulties with this relationship as the corporation introduced more modern control techniques. For one thing, he thought the existing relationship between himself and the divisional controllers was not so close that he could urge the development and use of new techniques as rapidly as he wished. More important, he thought that he was not getting adequate information about what was actually happening in the divisions. The divisional controllers' primary loyalty was to his division manager, and it was unreasonable to expect that he would give Mr. Bevins frank, unbiased reports. For example, Mr. Bevins was quite sure that some fat was hidden in the divisional expense budgets, and that the divisional controllers had a pretty good idea as to where it was. In short, he thought he would get a much better idea of what was going on in the divisions if reports on divisional activities came directly from controllers working for him rather than for the divisional manager.

Mr. Bevins was therefore especially interested in the controller organization at the Martex Company as he learned about it from E. F. Ingraham, the Martex controller, when he visited that company.

Until his visit to Martex, Mr. Bevins had not discussed the organization problem with anyone. Shortly thereafter, he gave William Harrigan, his assistant controller, a memorandum describing his visit (see the appendix) and asked for Mr. Harrigan's reaction. Mr. Harrigan had been with Rendell for 25 years, and had been a divisional controller before going to headquarters in 1972. Mr. Bevins respected his knowledge of the company and his opinion on organizational matters. Mr. Harrigan was accustomed to speaking frankly with Mr. Bevins. The gist of his comments follows.

I don't think the Martex plan would work with us; in fact, I am not even sure it works at Martex in the way suggested by the job descriptions and organization charts.

Before coming to headquarters, I had five years' experience as a divisional controller. When I took that job, I was told by the corporate controller and by my general manager that my function was to help the general manager every way I could. This is the way I operated. My people got together a lot of the information that was helpful in preparing the divisional budget, but the final product represented the thinking and decisions of my general manager, and he was the person who sold it to top management. I always went with him to the budget meetings, and he often asked me to explain some of the figures. When the monthly reports were prepared, I usually went over them, looking for danger signals, and then took them in to the general manager. He might agree with me, or he might spot other things that needed looking into. In either case, he usually was the one to put the heat on the operating organization, not me.

We did have some problems. The worst, and this happened several times a year, was when someone from the corporate controller's office would telephone and ask questions such as, "Do you think your division could get along all right if we cut $X out of the advertising budget?" Or, "Do you really believe that the cost savings estimate on this equipment request is realistic?" Usually, I was in complete agreement with the data in question and defended them as best I could. Once in a while, however, I might privately disagree with the "official" figures, but I tried not to say so.

Questions of this sort really should be asked of the general manager, not of me. I realize that the head office people probably didn't think the question was important enough to warrant bothering the general manager, and in many cases they were right. The line is a fine one.

This business of the division controller's being an "unbiased source of information" sounds fine when you word it that way, but another way to say it is that he is a front office spy, and that doesn't sound so good. It would indeed make our life easier if we could count on the divisional controllers to give us the real lowdown on what is going on. But if this is to be their position, then we can't expect that the general manager will continue to treat his controller as a trusted assistant. Either the general manager will find somebody else to take over this work unofficially, or it won't get done.

I think we are better off the way we are. Sure, the budgets will have some fat in them, and not all the bad situations will be highlighted in the operating reports, and this makes our job more difficult. But I'd rather have this than the alternative. If we used the Martex method (or, rather, what they claim is their method), we can be sure that the divisional controller will no longer be a member of the management team. They'll isolate him as much as they can, and the control function in the division will suffer.

QUESTIONS

1. What is the organizational philosophy of Martex with respect to the controller function? What do you think of it? Should Rendell adopt this philosophy?

2. To whom should the divisional controllers report in the Rendell Company? Why?

3. What should be the relationship between the corporate controller and the divisional controllers? What steps would you take to establish this relationship on a sound footing?

4. Would you recommend any major changes in the basic responsibilities of either the corporate controller or the divisional controller?

Appendix

Notes on Martex Controller Organization

Mr. Ingraham, the corporate controller, reports directly to the president and has reporting to him all division controllers and other accounting, data processing, and analysis groups. The Martex Company's organization charts and descriptions of responsibility are included herein (Exhibits 1, 2, 3, and 4), and indicate the structure and function of the organization.

The controller's organization is charged with the responsibility of establishing cost and profit standards in the corporation and of taking appropriate action to see that these standards are attained. It reviews all research projects, and assigns names and numbers to them in order to coordinate research activities in the various divisions and their central research. The organization also handles all matters involving cost and profit estimates.

The present size of divisional controllers' staffs ranges from three to twenty-two. Division controllers are not involved in preparing division profit and loss statements; these are prepared by a separate group for all divisions and the corporation.

LINE-STAFF RELATIONSHIPS

A division manager has no staff of his own, not even a personal assistant. He receives staff assistance from two sources.

First, he has some people assigned to him from the general staff—typically, a controller, an engineer, and a purchasing agent.

All division management and all the corporate staff are located in the corporate headquarters building. However, the "assigned staff" are located physically with their staff colleagues; for example, a divisional controller and his assistants are located in the controller's section of the building, not near his divisional manager's office.

Second, the division can call on the central staff to the extent that the manager wishes. The divisions are charged for these services on the basis of service rendered. The central staff units are listed in the General Staff Services box of Exhibit 2.

DIVISION MANAGER-CONTROLLER RELATIONSHIP

The success of the Martex controller organization and its relations with divisional managers appears to be largely the result of managers' and controllers' having grown up with the arrangement and accepting it long before they arrived at their managerial positions.

Some additional factors that appear to contribute to their successful relationship are the following:

1. A uniform and centralized accounting system.
2. Predetermined financial objectives for each division.
   a. Growth in dollar sales.
   b. A specified rate of profit as a percent of sales.
3. Profit sharing by managers and controllers.

ACCOUNTING SYSTEM

The controller's division has complete control of the accounting system. It determines how and what accounts will be kept. The controller's division has developed an accounting system that is the same for all divisions. Mr. Ingraham pointed out that no division had a system perfectly tailored to its needs, but he believes that the disadvantages to the divisions were more than offset by having a system uniform over all divisions and understood by all concerned. Mr. Ingraham indicated it was likely that if Martex divisions were free to establish their own accounting systems, every division would have a different one within two years, and interpretation by corporate management would be difficult, if possible at all.

The accounting system appears to provide a common basis for all divisional financial reports and analyses, and it aids in maintaining the bond of confidence between division managers and controllers.

DIVISION OBJECTIVES

The corporation has established two financial objectives for each division. These are (*a*) growth in dollar sales, (*b*) a specified rate of profit as a percent of sales.

These objectives are determined in advance by recommendations of the controller's division with the advice and counsel of divisional managers. The objectives are long-range in nature; the target profit rate has been changed only three times since 1950.

The particular percentage of sales selected as the target profit rate is based on several factors, among which are (1) the patentability of products, (2) a desired rate of return on investment, (3) the industry's margin of profit, and (4) the industry's rate of return on investment. These factors and others determine the profit rate finally selected.

Within limits, attainment of these financial objectives represents the primary task required of division general managers by corporate management.

PROFIT SHARING

Divisional managers receive about 75 percent of their total compensation from profit sharing and stock options. Divisional controllers receive about 25 percent of their compensation from profit sharing—half from a share in divisional profits, and the other half from corporate profits.

DIVISION MANAGERS' VIEW OF THE SYSTEM

Mr. Ingraham indicated that divisional managers like to have divisional controllers report to the corporate controller because (1) it gives them an unbiased partner armed with relevant information, (2) the controller is in a better position to do the analysis needed for decision-making, and (3) when cost reports are issued there is little or no argument about them among affected parties.

Exhibit 1

POSITION DESCRIPTIONS FROM THE MARTEX MANAGEMENT GUIDEBOOK

Controller

The trend of modern business management is to change the basic concept of the controller's position from that of an administrative function concerned largely with accounting detail to that of an important position in management as it relates to the control of costs and the profitable operation of the business as a whole.

The more our business becomes diversified with operations scattered throughout the U.S.A., the greater is the need for an officer to whom the president delegates

Exhibit 1—Continued

authority with respect to those factors affecting costs and profits in the same manner as he may delegate authority to others in strong staff positions.

In our vertical type of organization there is great need for an appointed officer whose responsibility it is to establish budgetary standards of operations and objective per cent of profit on sales targets for each of the operating divisions and domestic subsidiaries. He shall also establish budgetary standards of operation for staff functions in line with divisional and over-all company profit objectives. When the standard of operations or profit target is not attained, the controller has the right and the responsibility within his delegated authority to question the failure and recommend changes to accomplish the desired result.

The controller shall work with the various divisions of the company through divisional controllers assigned to each major operating division and staff function. It is not intended that the controller take the initiative away from the division managers, since the responsibility for efficient operations and profits are assumed by the managers. However, the controller and his staff should have the right and the responsibility to expect certain operating results from the division head, and when a difference of opinion occurs as to the reasonableness of the demand for results, the matter should then be referred by either party to the president.

Along with the foregoing, the following responsibilities are an essential part of the position and apply to the corporation and its subsidiaries:

1. The installation and supervision of all accounting records.
2. The preparation, supervision, and interpretation of all divisional and product profit and loss statements, operating statements, and cost reports, including reports of costs of production, research, distribution, and administration.
3. The supervision of taking and costing of all physical inventories.
4. The preparation and interpretation of all operating statistics and reports, including interpretation of charts and graphs, for use by Management Committees and the board of directors.
5. The preparation, as budget director, in conjunction with staff officers and heads of divisions and subsidiaries, of an annual budget covering all operations for submission to the president prior to the beginning of the fiscal year.
6. The initiation, preparation, and issuance of standard practice regulations and the coordination of systems, including clerical and office methods relating to all operating accounting procedures.
7. Membership of the controller or his designated representative in all division and subsidiary Management Committees.

He shall be responsible for the selection, training, development, and promotion of qualified personnel for his organization and their compensation within established company policy. He shall submit to the president an organization plan for accomplishing desired objectives.

The controller may delegate to members of his organization certain of his responsibilities, but in so doing he does not relinquish his over-all responsibility or accountability for results.

Treasurer and Assistant Treasurers

Subject to the rules and regulations of the Finance Committee, the treasurer is the chief financial officer and generally his functions include control of corporate funds and attending to the financial affairs of the corporation and its domestic and foreign subsidiaries wherever located. More specifically the duties and responsibilities are as follows:

Banking: He shall have custody of and be responsible for all money and securities and shall deposit in the name of the corporation in such depositories as are approved by the president all funds coming into his possession for the company account.

Exhibit 1—Continued

Credits and Collections: He shall have supervision over all cashiers, cash receipts, and collection records and accounts receivable ledgers. He shall initiate and approve all credit policies and procedures.

Disbursements: He shall authorize disbursements of any kind by signature on checks. This includes direct supervision over accounts payable and payroll departments and indirect supervision over all receiving departments for the purpose of checking on the accuracy of invoices presented for payment. He shall maintain adequate records of authorized appropriations and also determine that all financial transactions covered by minutes of Management and Executive Committees and the board of directors are properly executed and recorded.

General Financial Reports: He shall prepare and supervise all general accounting records. He shall prepare and interpret all general financial statements, including the preparation of the quarterly and annual reports for mailing to stockholders. This also includes the preparation and approval of the regulations on standard practices required to assure compliance with orders or regulations issued by duly constituted governmental agencies and stock exchanges.

He shall supervise the continuous audit (including internal controls) of all accounts and records and shall supervise the audit and procedures of Certified Public Accountants.

Taxes: He shall supervise the preparation and filing of all tax returns and shall have supervision of all matters relating to taxes and shall refer to the general counsel all such matters requiring interpretation of tax laws and regulations.

Insurance Property Records: He shall supervise the purchase and placing of insurance of any kind including the insurance required in connection with employee benefits. He shall be responsible for recommending adequate coverage for all ascertainable risks and shall maintain such records as to avoid any possibility that various hazards are not being properly insured. He shall maintain adequate property records and valuations for insurance and other purposes and, if necessary, employ appraisal experts to assist in determining such valuations and records.

Loans: He shall approve all loans and advances made to employees within limits prescribed by the Executive Committee.

Investments: As funds are available beyond normal requirements, he shall recommend suitable investments to the Finance Committee. He shall have custody of securities so acquired and shall use the safekeeping facilities of the banks for that purpose. As securities are added or removed from such vaults or facilities, he shall be accompanied by an authorized officer of the Corporation.

Office Management: He will be responsible for the coordination of all office management functions throughout the company and its domestic subsidiaries.

Financial Planning: He shall initiate and prepare current and long-range cash forecasts, particularly as such forecasts are needed for financing programs to meet anticipated cash requirements for future growth and expansion. He shall arrange to meet sinking fund requirements for all outstanding debenture bonds and preferred stock and shall anticipate such requirements whenever possible.

He shall have such other powers and shall perform such other duties as may be assigned to him by the board of directors and the president.

The treasurer shall be responsible for the selection, training, development, and promotion of qualified personnel for his organization and their compensation within established company policy. It is expected that since he will have to delegate many of the duties and responsibilities enumerated above, he shall confer with and submit to the president an organization plan and chart.

The treasurer may delegate to members of his organization certain of his responsibilities together with appropriate authority for fulfillment; however, in so doing he does not relinquish his over-all responsibility or accountability for results.

The treasurer is a member of the Finance, Retirement, and Inventory Review Committees.

Exhibit 2

MARTEX CORPORATION

Organization Chart, Division A, January 1, 1975

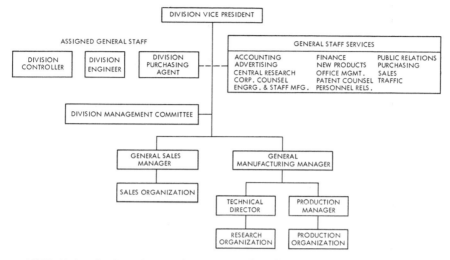

NOTE: Various levels on the chart do not necessarily indicate relative importance of positions.

Exhibit 3

MARTEX CORPORATION

Organization Chart of Controller's Division, January 1, 1975

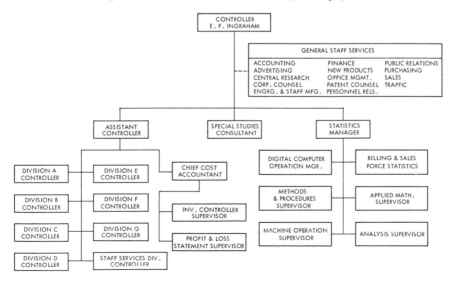

Exhibit 4

MARTEX CORPORATION

Organization Chart of Treasurer's Division, August 1, 1975

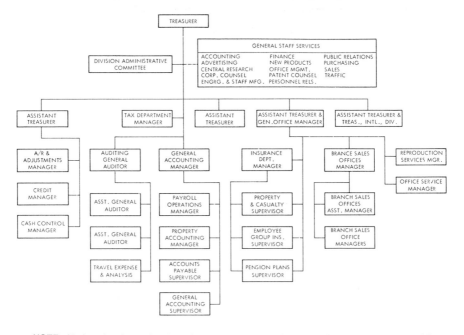

NOTE: Various levels on the chart do not necessarily indicate relative importance of positions.

Case 2-2

Clark Chemical Company

The Clark Chemical Company had just completed a management reorganization. Under the plan adopted, the organization structure had been changed from a functional one—with vice presidents of sales, manufacturing, legal, and industrial relations, all reporting to the president—to a divisional setup. Four operating divisional vice presidents, each with responsibility for a group of products, now reported to an executive vice president. Each vice president had "profit and loss responsibility" for his division and corresponding authority, subject only to such restrictions as maximum limits on capital expenditures, legal and patent matters, and general company policy matters. A chart of the new organization is shown in Exhibit 1.

The Clark Chemical Company was currently celebrating its fiftieth anniversary; during the fifty years of its life the volume of the company's sales had grown from a few thousand dollars to over thirty-seven million dollars. This growth had come through developing and specializing a series of chemical products for industrial users.

THE ACCOUNTING AND FINANCIAL FUNCTION

At about the same time that the organizational changes were being made, the company employed Sidney Green to head up its accounting and finance function. Mr. Green came to the company from a firm of similar size in which he had acted as assistant controller and assistant treasurer. He was known by his associates as a man who had some firm ideas as to what a good controller organization should do in a decentralized operation and was aggressive in advancing those ideas. As one of his first steps he worked out the organization of his own unit, as shown in Exhibit 2. He was able to staff each section with an able young man having somewhat similar ideas as to the appropriate role of the controller in business management.

The next step the new controller took was to ask each of his section heads to submit a program for carrying out the responsibilities of his section. At a series of staff meetings these programs were presented and discussed. These meetings provided an opportunity for each section to gain an understanding of the whole job to be done; they also facilitated the elimination of unnecessary duplication and the covering of areas where gaps occurred.

THE PROBLEM

The financial planning and analysis section of the controller's office submitted as its program the report shown in Exhibit 3. This program was approved by Mr. Green, the controller. John Kay, the head of the financial planning and analysis section immediately began to work out detailed plans to carry out his program. As noted in Part V of Exhibit 3, he undertook to develop both a written and oral report to the executive vice president covering the results of monthly operations for each division in the company. Mr. Kay had selected a number of men in his section and assigned to each of them the responsibility for getting familiar with operations of a particular division. After monthly operating statements had been prepared, the individual responsible for each division set out to prepare an analysis of the division for which he had responsibility. To do this he frequently called on members of the operating divisions for explanations, forecasts, and various other kinds of information.

After this plan had been in operation for several months, Mr. Green attended a management meeting of the executive officers and operating vice presidents. When the meeting was opened to general discussion, the following discussion took place.

SAM JOHNSTON. (v.p. of division A). Mr. President, I have a bone to pick with Sidney (controller) here, and I might as well get my gripe out on the table. I object to the way Sidney's man Kay goes about getting explanations of monthly operating results. Not that he's obnoxious or anything, I just don't approve of the whole idea. First, we have to tell him what he needs to know and this takes time. Then he goes back to his office and writes up what we have told him. Secondly, and more important, is the management philosophy involved. I believe each operating division should make its own report and explanations of what happened last month. The controller's office should furnish us the statements and we should do the analysis and explaining. Not only is this easier, but it's part of our job. We should have to explain to the executive vice president, and we need to know anyway to run our division well. Well, that's quite a speech, but it's how I feel.

SIDNEY GREEN. Am I clear in thinking you don't object to Kay's or his men's behavior, just the principle involved?

SAM JOHNSTON. That's right. They are a nuisance but pleasant about it.

SIDNEY GREEN. Don't you think in time Kay's men would learn your operation and then they could help you? After all, we've only been doing this a few months.

SAM JOHNSTON. We will take all the help we can, if it doesn't cost anything, but on this point, we are helping you to do what we have to do anyway.

SIDNEY GREEN.   You mean you think it is not the duty of the controller to report on, and analyze the results of operations of the divisions? That's fundamental to good control.

SAM JOHNSTON.   Absolutely, it's not the controller's job to analyze operations and report to the boss. That's my job. Now, I agree that you have a responsibility to the boss. It seems to me that your job should be to be sure we are using the right figures. Further, I can accept the idea of your reviewing our explanations and analysis, and reporting whether you agree with us. Your function, though, would be a review one. Now that we are in this discussion, I'd sure like to get a decision from the president on this point.

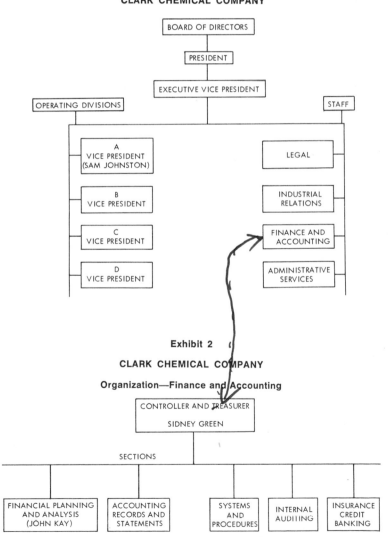

Exhibit 1

CLARK CHEMICAL COMPANY

Exhibit 2

CLARK CHEMICAL COMPANY

Organization—Finance and Accounting

Exhibit 3

CLARK CHEMICAL COMPANY

Financial Planning and Analysis Program

I. Work with top management and divisions in developing projections of business operations and setting goals.
   a) Annual plan or budget
   b) Five-year forecast
   c) Cash requirements
   d) Capital expenditure program
II. Interpret management plans in financial terms. Make or assist in economic studies of proposed facility and equipment investments, research programs, markets, industries, and possible company acquisitions to provide guidance to top management and divisions.
   a) Estimate of research project cost, elapsed time, anticipated results.
   b) Estimate of plant and facility startup cost, volume requirements, payoff period, return on investment.
   c) Estimate of market development cost, elapsed time.
   d) Examine capital structure of companies desirable for acquisition and evaluate profitability. Recommend financial terms for purchase.
   e) Other studies as needed.
III. Appraise current investments and operations, indicating where financial improvements might be made.
   a) Receivable balances and terms.
   b) Inventory levels and evaluation of content related to sales outlook.
   c) Product line P & L's and investment.
   d) Cash balances and working capital levels. Make short term projections.
IV. Work with operating personnel in developing operating goals and setting expense controls. Explore methods of maximizing operating margin and minimizing investment under various conditions.
   a) Operating margin and return on investment goals.
   b) Departmental expense budgets.
   c) Relationship of expenses to volume—fixed and variable.
V. Report on current performance related to yardsticks (annual budget, departmental expenses, capital expenditure program, etc.).
   a) In personal meetings, written reports, and division heads' meetings, report on overall and divisional results related to annual budget. Monthly basis.
   b) Capital expenditure program—appraise progress during current year both as to stage of completion and actual cost of projects. Quarterly basis for first six months and monthly thereafter.
   c) Develop and maintain charts to more effectively portray trends.
VI. Assist in developing long-range plans for the overall company.
   a) Assist in determining direction of company.
   b) Assist operating divisions in developing divisional plans.
   c) Participate in review of progress.
VII. Analyze cost data to develop overhead rates for use in pricing intercom-

pany transactions and other uses. Provide assistance for developing inter-departmental service charges.

    a) Research department cost rates.

    b) Factory overhead rates.

    c) Others.

VIII. Maintain competitive company and customer financial data.

    a) Appraise interim and annual financial reports and alert management to significant facts or trends.

    b) Become acquainted with operating and financial arrangements of other companies for practical application in Clark Chemical Company.

    c) Maintain scrapbook of competitive company and customer articles found in current periodicals.

IX. Maintain economic statistics not kept elsewhere in the company.

Indicated below is the manner in which the financial planning and analysis section would carry out the attached program. The numerals below correspond directly with those on the outline of the program.

I. This section would, in conjunction with top management, determine the necessary information to be requested from the various divisions and departments to develop the several plans and programs. The section would coordinate the flow of information and physically put the data in finished form ready for evaluation. The section, where possible, would make constructive suggestions or recommendations concerning the data developed and the problems encountered—recommendations both to division managers and to top management.

II. The section would become involved in these special studies most likely as a result of a request from division managers or top management and would participate at the time of developing the figures and thus be in a position to see that all financial aspects have been considered.

III. Projects in this area would be started at the initiation of this section, top management, or the divisions with the objective that recommendations for constructive action would result. Work on product line studies would be done in conjunction with divisional personnel.

IV. Work in this area would usually take place during budget preparation periods or when sudden changes in plans appear imminent. Initiation during times other than budget periods would probably come from top management or operating personnel. However, this section might recommend to management changes in the course of action from time to time.

V. This category covers reporting to top management and divisional personnel and would be done at the initiative of the section.

VI. In the long-range planning area the section should be a participant contributing ideas and making necessary studies as well as commenting on progress.

VII. Most of the functions in this area would be performed at the request of the operating divisions or staff departments.

VIII. Functions in this area would be accomplished both at the request of top management and divisions and at the initiation of this section.

IX. The accumulation of economic statistics would be done on a routine basis and would be restricted to those statistics not maintained elsewhere in the company.

Case 2–3

Tanner Corporation

As a consequence of an unfortunate incident that had occurred recently in the Process Systems Division of Tanner Corporation, John Bentwood, Chairman of the Audit Committee of the Board of Directors, was considering whether he should support a proposed change in the Committee's relationship with divisional management. This change was designed to increase the Committee's ability to find out what was going on in the company.

Tanner Corporation was a large, diversified company organized into 31 operating divisions. The company was well established, had operated profitably for many years, and had expanded steadily, both through internal growth and through acquisitions. In 1975 its sales revenue was approximately $900 million. Its Board of Directors had 12 members; nine were outside directors, plus Seth Remick, the president (who was also chairman); the executive vice president; and the financial vice president, Spencer Brody.

The Audit Committee

The audit committee of the Board was created in 1972. At that time, there was a general movement to set up such committees in publicly held corporations. Its impetus came in part from recommendations made by the New York Stock Exchange, the Securities and Exchange Commission, the American Institute of Certified Public Accountants, and the major public accounting firms. The recent tendency for the Securities and Exchange Commission and the courts to increase the responsibilities of boards of directors for overseeing corporate affairs, and the fines and other penalties levied on board members that were found not to exercise the appropriate amount of diligence were also important stimuli. A Conference Board survey showed that about 45 percent of 504 manufacturing companies had audit committees in 1973, compared with less than 20 percent in 1967.[1] In the formal

---

[1] *Corporate Directorship Practices: Membership and Committees of the Board* (New York: Conference Board Report No. 588, 1973), p. 62.

Board minutes that established the audit committee, its purpose and functions were given as follows:

The Audit Committee will be comprised of not less than three nor more than five nonmanagement Directors. Its purpose is to assist the full Board of Directors in fulfilling the Board's fiduciary responsibilities with respect to the Corporation's accounting, internal control, and reporting practices.

The Audit Committee's activities on behalf of the Board shall include, but not be limited to, the following:

1. Recommend the selection, each year, of the independent auditors for the Company.
2. Review with financial management and the independent auditors the proposed auditing program for the ensuing year and suggest changes in emphasis or scope as necessary. This will encompass both the independent and internal audit programs.
3. Review with financial management and the independent auditors, both together and separately, the results of the audits, including the audited financial statements, with particular attention to:
   a. the conformance of the statements to generally accepted accounting principles.
   b. the full disclosure of all material matters affecting the Company's operations and financial condition, and their fair presentation.
   c. the scope and effectiveness of the audit activity.
4. Review with the independent auditors their recommendations for improvements in internal control, and assure that appropriate action is taken in response to these recommendations.
5. Report at least annually to the full Board on the above matters.

These functions were believed to be fairly typical of those of audit committees in general.

In 1975, the Committee consisted of four members:

John Bentwood, Chairman, partner in a managing consulting firm, and a certified public accountant with long experience in accounting and control systems.

Francis Dube, a lawyer whose firm had no connection with the company.

Guay Hamel, executive vice president of a large manufacturing company.

George Spring, senior vice president of Tanner Corporation's principal commercial bank.

Hamel had been elected to the Board in 1973 and became a member of the audit committee in 1974. The other three members had been directors for many years and were original members of the audit committee.

Prior to the establishment of the audit committee, there had been no formal channel of communication between the Board and members of management other than the president; that is, the agenda for Board meetings was set by Remick, and although issues were presented to the Board by various members of management, each issue was accompanied by Remick's recommendations. In some cases the Board voted against his recommendations, and in other cases, proposals were sent back for further study. In Bentwood's opinion, these differences were simply differences of judgment among men of good will; that is, they did not indicate friction between the Board and management.

Although the only formal channel between the Board and management was through the president, board members had many informal contacts with members of management, and Remick encouraged such contacts. Bentwood said:

Of course, at every Board meeting we meet management people, not only the inside Board members, but also those who are presenting proposals to us, and we get to know these people in the luncheons and other activities that are associated with Board meetings. Also, we make a trip at least once a year during which we visit several divisions, observe what is going on as carefully as we can, and form impressions about the many management people that we meet.

As can be seen from the minute quoted above, the formation of the audit committee created two new formal channels of communication. First, the Committee was authorized to meet privately with the independent public accountants. Such meetings were held annually, and the engagement partner of the public accounting firm was asked specifically whether he had any relevant comments beyond those which were contained in the usual "management letter," that is, the letter setting forth the public accountant's observations on the adequacies of the company's control system and recommendations for improving it. In no case did the partner bring up topics other than those contained in the management letter, but he did indicate certain topics that he thought should be emphasized. For example, the 1974 letter suggested that internal audit activity devoted to computer-based systems should be stepped up, and the partner stressed the importance of this. The partner also made complimentary remarks about the cooperation his firm received from the financial management organization and the competence of that organization.

The second new formal channel of communication was between the audit committee and the financial vice president. The committee met two or three times a year with Brody, who was usually accompanied by members of his staff. There was no thought of excluding the president, and Remick usually did attend part of each meeting. Remick was not present most of the time, however, stating that the matters to be discussed did not involve him.

Process Systems Division

In 1971 Tanner Corporation acquired a small company whose management had developed new technology for automating production processes in a variety of chemical companies. The Process Systems division was an outgrowth of this acquisition. The division developed a general approach to process automation for a given industry, with heavy emphasis on special purpose computers, and it then adapted this general approach to the needs of specific companies on a contract basis. It built many of the components required for the new system, adapted other components, and purchased still other components. Usually, the contract with the Process Systems division required that it install the system and make it ready to operate. Most contracts were for at least $100,000, and some were much larger.

In the first year, customers were hard to find, but after a few successful installations, sales volume increased. It doubled in 1973 over 1972 and more than doubled again in 1974. Because of development costs and the relatively expensive professional organization that the division assembled, overhead costs were high. In 1974, for the first time, the division reported a profit, but it was a relatively small percentage of sales. Sales volume continued to increase in 1975, and in that year a sizeable profit was expected. Actual reported performance for the first six months of 1975 exceeded these expectations.

In July 1975, however, Brody, the financial vice president, received a letter from an accountant in the Process Systems division who recently had been discharged on grounds of incompetence. The ex-employee alleged that division management was furnishing false reports to the corporation. The letter contained so many specifics that Brody decided to have the matter looked into, and he sent a member of the internal audit staff to investigate. Within a week, the internal auditor reported that it was indeed likely that a serious problem existed, but that intensive work was required to measure its magnitude.

Brody immediately called in the public accountants to make a special audit of the division. He also reported the existence of the problem to the audit committee, and they in turn reported it to the board of directors. Throughout the investigation that followed, the Board was kept fully informed.

By September, the investigation had uncovered the facts summarized below. The division had been audited by the internal auditors in September 1974, in accordance with the regular audit program in which some divisions were assigned to outside auditors and others to internal auditors. That audit included an attempt to validate the inventory, but the cost accounting system was found to be so unreliable that it was not feasible to make a good check against the physical inventory. At that time, the internal auditors called attention to the system defects, acknowledged that these were probably caused by the fact that the system had not kept up with the rapid growth of the division, and recommended improvements.

Sometime in 1974, control over the work-in-process inventory records had been lost. A job cost record was established for each component of each contract, but not all the material, parts and other costs of the component were recorded on these records. When the components were billed to the customer, the job cost record was used as the basis for calculating cost of goods sold, but since costs on this record were incomplete, cost of goods sold was understated and gross margin was correspondingly overstated. The total effect of correcting this error was to wipe out the division's reported profits for 1974 and to change the results for 1975 from an expected profit of $1 million to a loss of $1 million, on sales volume of $10 million.

A careful examination of the economics of the division led to the conclusion that selling prices for contracts already written were too low, and that the advantages of the new system to the customer were not sufficiently great to permit prices to be increased to a point where a satisfactory return on investment could be earned.

The division was therefore discontinued. This was done by completing the backlog of contract work. During the phase-out period it was possible to reduce fixed costs so substantially that the eventual net loss on the whole operation was relatively insignificant.

Audit Committee Reactions

Members of the audit committee discussed the implications of this incident at length, both in formal meetings and informally. Dube and Spring were of the opinion that although there was clearly a breakdown in the control system, it was primarily attributable to the rapid growth in the division's activities. They pointed out that the failure to charge all costs to the job cost cards seemed to have started either shortly before or shortly after the 1974 audit, and in any event was not prevalent enough at the time of that audit to be a matter that the auditors reasonably could be expected to detect. They also pointed out that as soon as corporate management learned of the problem, it took prompt action and kept the audit committee and the board fully advised.

Hamel, the new member of the Board, felt differently. Here is a systems breakdown that corporate management didn't know about until an ex-employee spelled it out for them, he said. Furthermore, by hindsight, we can see that the inventory reported by the division was growing at a rate that was out of line. (Others replied that it was easy to see this by hindsight, but that at the time, the inventory growth was regarded as a commendable attempt to stockpile components and parts to fill the huge backlog of orders.) Admittedly, the final outcome in this case had practically no effect on profits, Hamel said, but there may be other more serious problems somewhere in the corporation that we have no inkling of. The Board is responsible.

Hamel thereupon suggested to his colleagues that it might be a good idea to add the following sentence to the stated functions of the audit committee: "In carrying out its responsibilities, the audit committee may meet privately with the independent auditors, with internal auditors and with other employees, and can undertake such additional analysis as it deems necessary." His thought was that the audit committee would meet annually and privately with the manager of internal audit (who reported to the financial vice president), and that it would publicly encourage communication of relevant information from any corporate employee to the audit committee.

Spring was strongly opposed to this proposal, on three grounds. First, he said, the internal audit manager would not report anything to the audit committee that he had not already discussed with the financial vice president; if he did, he should be fired for disloyalty. Second, the very idea conveyed an implication of distrust of management that was distasteful to him. Third, he envisioned the possibility that the audit committee would be deluged with crank letters that it was unequipped to handle. Dube tended to agree with Spring.

As of the end of 1975 Hamel's suggestion had been discussed only within the committee. Bentwood felt that if a formal proposal along the lines suggested by Hamel were made, it probably would be accepted by Remick and Brody; to oppose such a proposal could be regarded as tantamount to an admission that there was something to hide. He also felt that they would feel hurt by such a proposal, and that it might lead to tension between management and the board. Based on years of contact, Bentwood had a high regard for both the ability and the integrity of Remick and Brody. He was, however, mindful of the new responsibilities that boards of directors were asked to assume, and the possibility of SEC or stockholder suits if at any time the board did not act with diligence.

Case 2–4

Magnell Company

The Magnell Company marketed equipment and supplies primarily for use on petroleum wells. On December 20 of a recent year, the company mailed out its usual Christmas bonus checks to each of its more than 400 employees. This bonus averaged a week's salary for each employee and totaled something in excess of $80,000.

Mr. John Magnell, chairman of the board, who was also the majority stockholder, raised a question about this bonus at the next board meeting, held the following January. He had never liked the idea of paying a Christmas bonus. It was not that he had any basic objection to paying a bonus to his employees, but he felt that so long as it was an outright gift with no implications of reward for superior performance, it not only was not appreciated by the employees who received it, but had no corresponding benefits to the company. In fact, he said that he would no longer authorize the payment of employees' bonuses until the management presented to him a plan which would embody the following essential elements:

1. It would reward performance which resulted in improving the company's profit position and therefore would provide an incentive to employees to achieve this goal.
2. It would not be paid to everyone. Rather, the plan would extend only to those employees whose positions were such that they could affect substantially the company's profit position. Among this group of employees the plan would have to provide that in order to receive a bonus one must earn it. This meant that some would receive a bonus and some would not.
3. The formula for figuring the bonus must provide for an amount large enough to furnish an incentive for superior performance.
4. The amount to be disbursed should be roughly the same as in previous years; but because of the rearrangement in distribution, the amounts received by individuals who qualified would be substantially increased.

The chairman reviewed with the president the financial statements for 1968. Among the points he made were:

1. Of more than 40 retail outlets, over 20 per cent had sales amounting to less than their break-even point.
2. Assets of the company totaled something more than $14,000,000, of which about $5,000,000 was invested in inventory, $8,000,000 in receivables, and $1,000,000 in fixed assets, including over $300,000 in autos and trucks.
3. The company's sales for the year just passed had declined somewhat from the previous year's total volume of almost $50,000,000. But, at the same time, operating expenses had continued to rise steadily.
4. With net profit (before taxes) of only $1,300,000 in 1968, return on investment was less than 10 per cent. In 1967, return on investment was close to 12 percent.

Initial Steps

The next day, at a regular staff meeting of the company's principal officers the president led a discussion and they talked over the assignment which lay before them. There was some sentiment in the group for seeking the services of an outside management consultant on the problem, but the consensus was that at least a first effort should be made with the talent at hand, thus saving the consultant's fee and perhaps discovering a formula better adapted to this company's needs than an "outsider" would devise.

At the end of this meeting the president appointed a committee to draft a bonus plan. It consisted of the controller, who was to serve as chairman; the general sales manager; and the director of purchases. The first problem they tackled was identification of the areas of operation where improvement would have a direct bearing on the return investment percentage to which the chairman had obviously attached considerable significance. The committee decided that there were three such areas:

1. Sales and/or gross profit ratios.
2. Purchasing.
3. Management of the company's assets and employees.

Consideration of Salesmen and Purchasing Office

After identifying these categories, the next step to be considered was how to identify an individual employee's contribution to, or responsibility for, improved performance in these areas. The sales manager foresaw great difficulties in identifying improved sales volume with an individual salesman, principally because of the nature of the supply industry. He made three points:

1. Many of the company's best customers placed their orders with the company because of financial ties through credit.
2. Personal friendships existed between the top officers of some companies which were good customers and the top officers of Magnell Company.
3. Many of the major customers apportioned their business among suppliers of an area.

All of these conditions made it relatively unimportant which salesman called upon and serviced the account. The volume of business from these customers would remain virtually unchanged, without regard to the salesmen's efforts.

The sales manager recognized a further problem. In the supply industry, it is customary for a field salesman to call upon and service the tool pusher or drilling superintendent at a field location; but when orders are placed, they are placed at a remote city which happens to be the headquarters location of the customer involved. The city salesman is sure to feel that his receipt of this order is a reward for the service he has rendered the Purchasing Department of the customer; whereas the field salesman is equally sure that except for his superb service and efforts with the field staff of the customer, the order would never have been placed. The sales manager believed that to have the various salesmen in competition with each other to receive credit for orders would result in detriment rather than gain to the company's overall sales effort.

The director of purchases also foresaw problems in attempting to recognize and reward individual buyers. Without developing all of his reasons, they can be summarized by stating that the discounts obtained on an order are related to factors over which the buyer has so little control as not to be a valid basis for a bonus award.

Consideration of Assets and Employees

The controller viewed as somewhat easier the task of identifying and measuring performance within the area of management of the company's assets and its employees. He pointed out that most of the company's assets consisted of inventory and receivables and that good management of either one of these assets involved maximum turnover and minimum loss, both of which were easy to identify through accounting records.

Expense control also was a direct result of good management of employees; and since the greatest items of company expense, other than payroll, were the operation of the company's fleet of automobiles and trucks, long-distance telephone expense, and entertainment and travel expense, improvement in any of these areas would be easy to measure from accounting records. By the same token, the gross income at any given field store in relation to the expenses incurred furnished a "natural" for measuring improvement. It would be easy to identify exactly the investment at any field store. He believed that the managers of the stores, in the final analysis, held the key to improved management of assets and people necessary for a better return on investment. He also believed that store managers had been largely sales-oriented and had never really given much consideration to the idea that they had capital entrusted to their custody upon which a satisfactory rate of return had to be earned.

Most of the managers of the stores had a high school education or less; and since the accounting work was all performed in the headquarters office, the managers of these stores understood very little of the relationship between their performance and the return on investment of their stores. It was the controller's view that a concentrated management training program for store managers, supplemented by a bonus plan, would make them conscious of the necessity of increasing profits through better management and would furnish them the incentive to put better practices into effect.

The controller recognized that there were obstacles which had to be overcome, such as identifying sales allocated to a store because of delivery into its territory even though the store really could lay no claim for credit. The biggest single item involved was oil country tubular goods (pipe), principally because pipe historically had been in short supply and had been distributed to customers on an allocated basis, rather than in response to any special sales effort.

Preparation and Discussion of Plan

When the committee reported back to the president, it was the consensus that the controller should be assigned to devise a bonus plan along the lines outlined above.

Shortly thereafter, the controller submitted to the president the bonus plan shown in the Appendix.

The president looked over the plan quickly and observed that it was drawn to include only store managers and district managers. He said, "You can bet your bottom dollar that the salesmen on the road aren't going to be happy when they hear about a bonus plan for store managers. What does the general sales manager have to say about the proposed plan?"

The general sales manager made it clear that he did not think well of it, because:

1. The plan was discriminatory against salesmen.
2. The plan tended to overemphasize the importance of the management function at store locations, whereas the really important key to improved performance lay in increased sales volume.
3. Any bonus paid purely on application of a formula based upon accounting records would result in some inequities. Some payments would be made to those who did not deserve them, and some who were deserving would not receive a bonus.

In spite of the misgivings of the general sales manager, the draft of the plan was submitted to the chairman.

One final obstacle had to be overcome before the matter could be considered concluded; namely, how to announce to the personnel that their Christmas bonus would be discontinued and that in its place a limited bonus plan, open only to managers, would be substituted. A gratuitous circumstance contributed very substantially to the solution of this potentially serious problem. A wage survey conducted by the Office of Personnel had disclosed that the Magnell Company had not kept pace with the industry in its basic salaries and that an adjustment was needed to correct this condition.

Therefore, it was agreed that if the chairman decided to implement the bonus plan, the announcement of the discontinuance of the Christmas bonus would coincide with the announcement of the over-all wage increase, which was slightly in excess of the Christmas bonus. It, therefore, would be possible to announce that in lieu of the Christmas bonus an amount in excess of this was now being added to their regular compensation.

Appendix

A Bonus Plan for Store Managers and District Managers

February 25, 1969

I. *General Statement of Plan*

This bonus plan is designed to provide store and district managers with an opportunity to earn additional compensation for improved performance as reflected by an increased return on the company's investment at the stores under their management.

II. *Prerequisites of the Plan*

In order for the plan to work fairly, both to the company and to the managers involved, it is necessary that the manager at each location:

A. Be given sufficient authority over the management of his assets, personnel, and the sales program within his assigned territory to give him substantial control over his performance.

B. Be charged with accountability and responsibility for the performance of his store or stores.

C. Be furnished with adequate yardsticks to measure his performance, and that the information used to measure performance be based upon highly accurate reports of achievement.

III. *Definition of Terms*

The following definitions are to be applied to the terms wherever they are used:

A. *Investment*—Investment at each location will include the annual average of the following:

    1. Month-end inventory, at cost, maintained at the store, excluding

      a) Casing, tubing, and drill pipe

      b) Used machinery which the Machinery Department determines should be charged against the General Office inventory account.

      c) Central stocks placed at a given location at the direction of the Purchasing Department.

    2. Investment in automobiles and trucks assigned to the location, at depreciated cost.

    3. Investment in furniture and fixtures (including shelving, air conditioners, typewriters, counters, desks, chairs, file cases, adding machines, etc.), at depreciated cost.

    4. Amounts invested in receivables growing out of bonusable sales credited to the location.

    5. The funds maintained in agents' bank account at each location.

    NOTE: Company-owned real estate, such as store buildings, lots, etc., are not classified as an "investment." Rental will be charged for the use of these facilities and will be included in the monthly store expenses.

B. *Bonusable Sales*—Bonusable sales are those for which a manager will receive credit in computing his bonus. They will include the following:

    1. Allocated direct sales of machinery, supplies, and aluminum, plastic, and line pipe, except those sales which result exclusively from the activities of General Office or Sales Office personnel.

    2. Stock shipments out of a store's inventory, except casing, tubing, and drill pipe.

    3. Allocated sales accomplished through emergency order buy-outs.

    Casing, tubing, and drill pipe are omitted from bonusable sales because in today's market no appreciable effort or expense on the part of store personnel are required to sell these items. All available pipe of this type could be easily disposed of through the General Office by allocation to a few customers. On the other hand, such pipe allocated to a store, either by way of direct sales, or to its inventory, constitutes a lead item which, properly used, can be a device for generating sales of supplies and equipment which are classified as bonusable sales.

If and when conditions change, so that the sale of casing, tubing, and drill pipe becomes competitive and the market changes from a seller's to a buyer's market, these items may be included in bonusable sales.

Stock shipments are identified as bonusable sales rather than allocated stock sales on the theory that a store which maintains an inventory and has the cost of such inventory included in its investment, is the store whose management has foreseen the requirements for the material and has stocked its inventory to meet such requirements, even though it may be sold by another store in another location.

C. *Bonusable Gross Profit*—Bonusable gross profit is the balance remaining after deducting cost of sales from bonusable sales.

D. *Bonusable Net Profit*—The bonusable net profit is the profit left after subtracting expenses from bonusable gross profit.

E. *Expenses*—Expenses are those operating costs in addition to cost of sales which will be deducted from bonusable gross profit determining bonusable net profit. Such expenses shall include:

1. Regular monthly direct store expense.
2. The pro rata share of total District Office expense.

   The pro rata share of total district expense of the District Office, divided by the number of stores in the district.

3. Cost of routine General Office services which apply to bonusable sales.

   Every sale involves certain direct expenses over and above those incurred at a store or district arising out of the fact that certain routine services necessary to consummate the sale are performed at the General Office. If these services were not rendered on a centralized basis in the General Office where they can be handled more economically by the use of skilled specialists and modern machines and equipment, they would have to be performed individually at each store point.

   Examples of the routine services referred to are as follows:

   a) Processing of orders, including pricing, costing, invoicing, recording, collection, and maintenance of customers' accounts.

   b) Purchasing of materials for inventory and direct shipments.

   c) Maintaining and servicing accounts payable.

   d) Credit investigations and issuing lines of credit.

4. Actual cost of special General Office services. This includes:

   a) Making quotations at managers' request.

   b) Repossession or special collection efforts involving employment of a collection agency or prosecution of a claim in the courts.

c) Sales assistance. Special assistance from the General Office staff is available upon request to complete a sale. Most often this applies to the sale of a rig or other heavy machinery. For example, when a store determines that a customer within its territory is in the market for the purchase of a rig or other heavy machinery items, such sales can ofttimes be expedited by calling upon the Machinery Sales Division to furnish a machinery specialist to appraise machinery or to work out the details of sale and terms of payment. The services of such specialists are available to a store, but their services require incurring expenses of travel, entertainment, communications, and the time of personnel. The expenses incurred will be charged directly against the store on an actual cost basis, whether the sale for which the services were requested is consummated or not. Money is wasted each year within the company by requesting such services when the opportunity for consummating the sale is extremely remote. A store or district manager must share in the responsibility for incurring such expenses and share in the risk that is involved in incurring needless expense.

5. Operating losses incurred as a result of the following will be charged directly against the responsible store as an expense when determination is made by the bonus committee that the loss resulted from negligence, bad judgment, or failure to adhere to prescribed company policy or procedure by store personnel:

    a) Inventory shortages

    b) Loss of or cost of repairs to damaged property

    c) Loss on sale of assets

    d) Bad debt losses

F. *Return on Investment*—Return on investment at any given location may be computed in terms of percentage by dividing the total of all investment items (A above) into the bonusable net profit (D above).

G. *Bonus Committee*—The bonus committee is a committee of three company executives appointed by the general manager to review facts and circumstances of any questions arising out of administration of the bonus plan which are not specifically covered in this statement of the plan and to render decisions which will resolve such questions.

IV. *Earning a Bonus*

The purpose of this bonus plan is to create an incentive for managers to improve the return on the company's investment at the stores under the management of the respective store managers and district managers. It would be highly desirable to outline at this point a specific formula which would permit a manager to know in advance the exact amount of bonus that he would be able to earn if he achieved certain specific improvements in his operation. Unfortunately, it has not been possible to reconstruct information on past performance at the various store locations which would permit a completely accurate measure of past performance in those areas of management which are held to be subject to improvement. In order to establish such a measure with the degree of accuracy which is believed to be necessary, it is going to be essential that additional information be recorded over a period of at least one year. Until this period has elapsed and the necessary information can be compiled, it is not believed that a completely acceptable basis for judging improvement can be determined.

In lieu of a precise formula for computing a bonus based on improvement, the entire matter of awarding a bonus to district and store managers for the year 1969 is going to be left in the hands of a bonus committee appointed by the general manager. At the end of the current year, this committee will review the achievements of each store and will make an independent determination of whether a bonus shall be awarded to the store manager and responsible district manager. This committee admittedly will not be able to arrive at a conclusion as to the achievement at each store on a basis of mathematical certainty. It will, however, take into account all known factors of measurement and will make its determinations of bonus awards based on their best judgment of improved return on investment in 1969 over the 1968 performance.

While it is not possible to provide a formula at this time which will permit a computation in advance of what bonuses will be awarded, it is possible to state at this time the general basis upon which bonus award determinations will be made. This general basis will be as follows:

A. *Bonus will be based on improved return on investment in 1969 over 1968.*

For all stores combined, the average return realized from bonusable sales during the year 1968 was 10.5 percent. However, since the whole basis of this bonus plan is to provide an incentive for every manager to improve his performance, bonus awards will be made to managers for improvement over their 1968 performance, whether this performance was above or below the 10.5 percent average.

B. *A reward for holding your own.*

There will undoubtedly be cases in which a store achieves a return on investment in 1969 which is the same that it was in 1968. In such cases, recognition will be given for holding your own by the awarding of a bonus. It is probable, however, that the bonus awarded under these circumstances will not be as generous as that which is made to those managers whose stores have shown an increased return on investment. It is also probable that the award made to a manager whose store earned a satisfactory or better return on investment in 1968 and held his own in 1969 will be more generous than that to the manager whose return in 1968 was less than satisfactory and who held his own in 1969.

C. *A premium for achieving a satisfactory return.*

It is probable that the manager of a store which earned less than a satisfactory return on investment in 1968 but was able to improve his return on investment in 1969 to a point which reached or exceeded the company-wide average will receive special consideration in the form of a premium bonus over and above that which would have been earned solely on the basis of improvement from the previous year's performance.

D. *Some will earn no bonus.*

It probably is inevitable that there will be those stores whose 1969 performance measured in terms of return on investment will not be as good as their 1968 performance. At those stores where the 1968 performance was less than satisfactory and the 1969 performance got worse, it is highly probable that no bonuses will be paid to the managers of such stores.

In those cases where even though the 1969 performance was not as good as 1968, but the return on investment in 1969 is still considered satisfactory, there will be a bonus awarded to the store manager involved, although the amounts will be less than those awarded to managers who held their own or showed improvement.

V. *Computing Bonuses for District Managers*

A district manager's bonus will be determined by the return on total investment in the district from all bonusable net profit earned by the stores in his district. In general, the same considerations will be given in determining the bonus awards to be made to district managers as have been outlined above, except that the performance of all stores in the district will be taken into account in measuring the district manager's achievements.

VI. *What Will be the Amounts of Bonus Awards?*

It is not possible at this time to state with any degree of certainty the exact amount of bonus awards. This is because, first, the amount which will be available for distribution as bonuses will be directly related to the profit which is earned by the company for the year 1969 and, second, it is going to be necessary to have at least one year's experience in determining the profits which will be generated by improved performances which justifies bonus awards. Until such experience has been acquired, it is going to be necessary to call upon managers to rely upon the fairness of the bonus committee. About the only guide that can be given at this time as to the amount of the bonus awards which is in the minds of the bonus committee is that it is believed that a minimum bonus of $600 should be awarded in those cases where a bonus is believed to have been earned and that for superior performance it is hoped that bonuses may reach a high that will approximate 10 percent of the manager's annual salary.

(Sections VIII, IX, and X of the plan are omitted.)

(Section VIII described monthly reports on performance to be submitted by store managers and district managers.)

(Section IX described modifications to be made to the basic plan under exceptional circumstances. Managers with less than six months' service in a store and managers of new stores that had been opened for less than a year were ineligible for the bonus. The bonus committee could revise the base return on investment ratio if the geographical area allocated to the store changed. The bonus committee could award a bonus to a manager who was transferred from a store in which he demonstrated "good qualities of management" to a new store.)

(Section X authorized the bonus committee to amend the plan and to hear appeals from managers who believed they were unfairly treated.)

Chapter Three

INFORMATION

In this chapter we first describe recent developments in the field of information theory and show that although the techniques proposed by the theorists have few practical applications in business organizations, the theories do provide insights that are valuable in understanding the nature and use of information in these organizations. We then discuss some of the characteristics of the information that is used in the management control process.

INFORMATION THEORY

Information is a fact, datum, observation, perception or any other thing that adds to knowledge. The number 1,000 taken by itself is not information; it doesn't add to anyone's knowledge. The statement that 1,000 students are enrolled in a certain school *is* information.

Information is obtained either by direct observation or by communication. Most of a manager's information is obtained by communication. Even in the simplest responsibility center, the manager could not observe with his own senses everything that is going on, nor would he want to devote his time to doing so, even if it were possible. Instead, the manager relies on information that is communicated to him in various ways, ranging from informal conversations to formal reports.

Information is to be distinguished from reality (or "the state of nature" in the language of information theory). Suppose that a petroleum company is considering the purchase of drilling rights on a certain piece of property. There is in reality a certain quantity of crude oil on that property. No one knows what that quantity is, however. The petroleum company does have some information that helps it to estimate the amount of oil that probably exists—information derived from knowledge of geological formations, drilling on nearby properties, seismic explorations, and so on. This information is useful in helping the company decide whether to buy the drilling rights, but it is not, and cannot be, a perfect description of reality, which is the actual amount of crude oil that exists on the property.

Value of Information

Suppose the oil company can buy drilling rights to the property for $10 million, and it is convinced that the $10 million investment would be worthwhile if the property contained at least 10 million barrels of crude oil. It is uncertain as to how much oil the property does contain. It can reduce this uncertainty by obtaining additional information, for example by conducting additional seismic shots or by asking the opinion of a petroleum geologist. In order to obtain this information, it must incur additional costs. Information theory describes a technique for deciding how much the company can afford to pay for this additional information. Since the technique is usually described in the context of problems involving sampling, the amount that the company can afford to pay is called the *expected value of sample information.*

More generally, the approach can be used to describe the nature of an optimum information system in a company. In an optimum system, the difference between the expected value of sample information furnished by the system and the cost of obtaining this information is at a maximum.

There are several catches to the use of information theory in the real world, however. Catch 22 is that the expected value of information depends on the decision maker's judgment. If the petroleum company, on the basis of information now available, is already pretty well convinced that the property does contain at least 10 million barrels of crude oil, additional information is much less valuable to it than would be the case if it were more uncertain about the true state of nature, that is, the quantity of crude oil. Information theory provides a technique for probing the decision maker's own judgment as to how valuable additional information would be, but the technique requires the identification of the decision maker's *subjective probabilities* (i.e. his current belief as to the likelihood that various quantities of crude oil exist on the property) and his utiles (i.e. how strongly he feels about the necessity for making the right decision). In order to identify these amounts, a lengthy dialogue between the decision maker and the analyst is required, and its outcome is tentative at best. Thus, although the approach has the appearance of being objective, the values used in the technique actually are highly subjective.

Furthermore, the theory requires that there be a clear specification of the problem under consideration and of the nature and cost of the additional information that might be purchased as an aid in making the decision. Most business problems are not that clear cut. In the usual case, the problem is not sharply defined and there are several alternative solutions. Moreover, information in an information system is used for several purposes, and it is usually not feasible to associate a specific piece of information with a specific problem and hence compare its value with its cost.

Finally, many decision makers draw on the information that flows through an information system. The problem of quantifying the judgments of each of them as to the expected value of additional information can be insuperable.

Thus, the practical application of information theory is limited to problems like the oil well drilling rights situation described above; that is, problems in which the decision is both important enough to warrant the expenditure of much management time in quantifying the value of additional information and also specific enough so that the nature of additional information that might be obtained, the extent to which it will reduce the decision maker's uncertainty, and its cost can all be stated.[1]

For our purposes, this aspect of information theory provides only some useful general notions (which could perhaps be derived equally well by common sense): The purpose of information is to reduce a decision maker's uncertainty about the "state of nature," that is, about what is the actual situation in the real world; and the value of additional information should exceed its cost.

Noise

Suppose that the chief executive officer reads in a report that the actual profit of one of the divisions in the company in the preceding month was 10 percent below the budgeted profit. This message could convey to him the signal that the performance of this division was unsatisfactory; the division was not contributing as much to the company's profit goal as the budget indicated that it should. This signal might be correct, but, on the other hand, for any of a number of reasons that are discussed in later chapters, it might not be correct; the performance of the division might in fact be perfectly satisfactory. An information system that conveys ambiguous messages of this sort is said to be *noisy*.

Information theory provides approaches to measuring the amount of noise in an information system. These techniques have turned out to be valuable in studying ways to improve electrical systems, such as the telephone system, but they have no practical application to management systems, beyond suggesting the common sense ideas that noise is present in all such systems, that it never can be eliminated, but that measures to improve the clarity of the messages in the system are worthwhile.

Relevance

A person receives through his senses vast quantities of information, more than he possibly needs or can use, but his brain acts to *filter* most of it, and he is consciously aware of, and acts on, only a tiny fraction. For example,

---

[1] For a thorough explanation of the technique and how to apply it to such problems, see Howard Raiffa, *Decision Analysis: Introductory Lectures on Choices under Uncertainty* (Reading, Mass.: Addison-Wesley, 1968).

the ears of an automobile driver pick up innumerable sounds which are disregarded, but if the sound of an engine knock appears, the brain brings this message to his consciousness for appropriate action. Similarly, a business information system is constructed with the objective of filtering out unneeded information and conveying only relevant information to the decision maker.

The difference between "territory" and "map" provides a useful analogy. There is a territory called California, which is a reality; however, the reality is so complex and has so many dimensions that there is no conceivable way of describing it completely. There are also maps of California. The task of the map maker is to extract from reality the information that is relevant to the person using the map. For example, if an automobile driver asks what is the fastest way from San Francisco to Los Angeles, he can obtain an answer, "Take Interstate 5," without any map at all. If he wants more detailed information about alternative routes, interesting sights along the route, and so on, a map can be designed to provide this information. If he wants to know the location of a certain street in Los Angeles, a map of California will not suffice; he will need a map of Los Angeles. Map makers do not know the information that various users want to obtain from the map, but they include only information that they believe will be relevant, they do not include so much information that the map will be difficult to understand, and they prepare different maps for different purposes.

Likewise, designers of management information systems cannot know exactly what information about the organization will be relevant. They nevertheless attempt to extract from reality that information that they believe to be relevant, to filter out irrelevant information, and to communicate various types of information to users of the system according to their perception of the needs of each user. The idea of relevance has great practical importance, particularly since the advent of the computer. It is easy to design a system that spews forth mountains of information; it is much more difficult to decide what small fraction of that information is likely to be useful.

Precision

There are two types of quantitative information: counts and measurements. Counts can be precise; if one counts twelve persons in a room, the number is exact, in the sense that there are not twelve and a fraction. A measurement is never precise. Measurements are always approximations. With modern radar, the distance from a point on the earth to a point on the moon can be measured within an accuracy of a few feet, but there is that margin of error of a few feet. All measurements are estimates that are accurate only within a range.

Most messages in a management information system are measurements, rather than counts. All accounting information (with the trivial exception of the amount of cash in a small business) is derived from measurement.

Inventory quantities may be obtained by counts, but the monetary amount of inventory is a measurement. Measurements of such items as the expenses of an accounting period are likely to be fairly rough approximations.

It is illogical to criticize a management information system, or any measurement system, on the grounds that it is not precise. The question is whether it is good enough for the intended purpose. For example, the practice of allocating overhead costs to products is sometimes criticized on the grounds that there is no precise way of determining how much of the overhead cost is attributable to each product. This is an unwarranted criticism. There are ways of measuring the share of total overhead cost that is associated with each product, and although these measurements are only approximations, they are sufficiently good approximations so that, for certain purposes (such as measuring the cost that the buyer should pay under a cost-type contract) the decision maker is better to have them than not to have them.

Many accounting measurements are also not precise because they are *surrogates*. A surrogate is a substitute measure of some phenomenon that is used because it is not feasible to measure the phenomenon directly. Profit, as defined according to certain prescribed rules, is often used as an overall measure of a division's performance. Profit is a surrogate for the real performance of the division. It is never a precise measure of that performance, but it may nevertheless be good enough to be useful to the manager.

Not only is precise measurement impossible, it is also undesirable. The more precise the measuring instrument, the more it costs. There is no point in spending money to increase the precision of measurement beyond the degree of approximation that is needed in order to make sound decisions. Referring back to the oil well problem described earlier, the decision maker would like to know that there is, or is not, at least 10 million barrels of crude on the property. He does not need to know what the exact quantity is, and estimates of how much there is are useful only in helping evaluate how much room for error there is between the estimate and the decision criterion of 10 million barrels.

In a management information system, there is usually a tradeoff between precision and *timeliness*. An estimate of sales revenue for a month that is made available on the first day of the following month is usually more useful to the manager than an estimate that reaches him two weeks later, even though the latter is more accurate because it has been double checked, reports from outlying offices have been included, and so on.

TYPES OF INFORMATION

Information can be either systematic or nonsystematic. Our discussion is generally limited to information that flows through a formal system, but it is important to keep in mind the fact that a great deal of information reaches the manager from sources outside the formal system. Newspaper and other news media, conversations, and even a manager's perception of a colleague's facial expressions are important sources of information. Many managers give more attention to such sources than to the formal reports.

Information can be external or internal. Much information that is relevant to the manager flows into the organization from the outside environment. This information can be systematic—regular reports from trade associations, government agencies, and so forth—or it can be unsystematic. Information from and about the environment that surrounds the organization is important, but we do not discuss it extensively in this book because of its wide variety. Our description is primarily concerned with information that is generated inside the organization.

Accounting Information

Information can be accounting or nonaccounting. Although both types of information are important, we tend to give more attention to accounting (i.e. financial) information. The reason is that the management control system is built around an accounting core. The outputs of a responsibility center are the goods and services that it provides to other responsibility centers or to customers; accounting provides a way of aggregating these often heterogeneous products into a single amount, revenue. The inputs of a responsibility center are the hours of labor services, pounds of materials, and units of various services that it uses; accounting provides a way of aggregating these heterogenoeus inputs into a single amount, expense. Profit, which is the difference between revenue and expense, is an overall measure of the performance of the responsibility center, encompassing within it the results of actions that create revenue and the expenses associated with those actions.

Not only does accounting provide a way of aggregating physically unlike elements, an accounting system is also a disciplined way of doing this. The fundamental rule that debits must always equal credits, and the safeguards built into the system of recording and summarizing transactions provide assurance that there is appropriate support for the validity of the numbers that flow through the system and that part of a given transaction has not slipped through a crack and disappeared. Errors, and even fraud, can sometimes occur, but these are relatively uncommon, and users, in most circumstances, can trust accounting numbers more than they can trust numbers that come from a system that is not governed by the debit-and-credit mechanism.

Obviously, accounting information is not perfect. The reported profitability of a responsibility center is never a complete or accurate measure of its performance. Furthermore, in many responsibility centers it is not feasible to measure output in monetary terms and therefore it is not feasible to measure profitability. Also, in certain responsibility centers, accounting measurements are relatively unimportant. In certain staff units, for example, the control of the unit's expenses is a trivial matter; the quality of the work that it does is the most important criterion of performance, even though quality cannot be measured in accounting terms.

Another inadequacy of accounting information is that considerable time elapses between the occurrence of an event and the issuance of an accounting report on that event. If an automated machine starts to turn out parts that exceed prescribed tolerance limits, someone needs to get information on that event immediately; they cannot wait for an accounting report on spoilage costs.

Because of these inadequacies, accounting information is supplemented by various types of nonaccounting information: reports of labor efficiency and personnel turnover as well as labor costs; reports of material usage and spoilage, as well as material costs, and so on. This information is important, and in some cases it is more important than the accounting information. For example, a report of orders booked, which strictly speaking is not an accounting number, is usually a more important indicator of the performance of a marketing organization than the accounting number called revenue. Nevertheless, bookings do not tell the whole story; profitability depends on how much of the revenues generated by these bookings ultimately flows down to the bottom line.

When we refer in this book to a *financial control system,* we mean that part of the management control system that collects, reports, and uses accounting numbers. In emphasizing the financial control system, we do not intend to minimize the importance of other information. Our reason for focusing on accounting information is that it provides a coherent framework for the management control system in the organization as a whole. Most nonaccounting information can be related to appropriate parts of this framework. Thus, information about increased spoilage from a machine is originally presented in nonaccounting terms, but the effect of this situation ultimately shows up in an accounting report of the increased costs in the responsibility center and a corresponding decrease in the profitability of the company.

Operating Information

By far the largest quantity of information that flows through a business is *operating* information, that is, information that is generated in the course of day-to-day operations. There is great variety in this information, but in general terms it can be classified into a relatively few main streams, some of the most important of which are:

A *production* stream, consisting of records showing the detail on orders received from customers, instructions for producing the products to meet these orders, and records of work in process and finished goods inventories. The nature of the production stream varies widely in different industries, but it tends to be similar for companies within a given industry. In some industries, such as banks and insurance companies, the majority of employees process "paper" in essentially the same way that employees in a factory process material.

A *purchasing and materials* stream, consisting of records having to do with materials and services ordered, with their receipt, with keeping track of materials while they are in inventory, and with their issue to the production departments.

A *payroll* stream, consisting of records which show how much each employee has earned, the nature of the work that employees did, and how much they have been paid. Because payroll records must conform to requirements set forth in social security regulations, there is a great deal of similarity in the payroll records of most companies.

A *plant and equipment* stream, consisting of records showing the cost, location, and condition of each significant noncurrent asset, together with the related depreciation data.

A *sales and accounts receivable* stream, consisting of detailed data on each order booked, each sales transaction, the credit to accounts receivable that is generated by the transaction, amounts that customers pay, and amounts that customers currently owe.

A *finance* stream, consisting of records of cash movements and cash balances, investments, borrowings and payments made to lenders, and dividends and other transactions with shareholders.

A *cost* stream, consisting of records of costs incurred in manufacturing goods or rendering services.

A *responsibility accounting* stream, consisting of the revenues, expenses and investment of responsibility centers.

With the exception of the responsibility accounting stream, these streams of information are required for purposes other than management control. Much information used in the management control process is derived by summarizing data that was originally generated for other purposes. The additional cost of using these data for management control purposes is relatively small. Indeed, there is such a tremendous difference in the cost of summarizing information that exists in these operating streams and the cost of collecting data *de novo,* that systems designers often specify that management control information be obtained from operating information, even though the available data are not quite what is desired.

MANAGEMENT CONTROL INFORMATION

In the management control process, information is used for planning, for coordinating, and for control. Although we shall discuss the specifics of this information in later chapters, it is appropriate here to make some general comments, particularly on the nature of information that is used for the control process per se.

Information Reports versus Control Reports

As we pointed out in Chapter 1, the management control process in an organization differs from a mechanical or electrical control device, such as a thermostat, in several important respects. One of these is that the information requirements of the thermostat can be completely specified, whereas the information requirements of management control cannot be specified. In order to do its job, the thermostat need only measure the temperature of the room, but in order to do their job, managers must be aware of all important matters that bear on the organization's work in trying to achieve its goals.

To the extent that the manager's needs for information can be predicted, reports can be designed that will meet these needs. One such report is the *control report,* which essentially reports actual performance compared with planned performance. However, in planning and coordinating the work of the organization, management needs information beyond that contained in control reports. Management therefore also receives *information reports,* that is, reports intended to tell management what is going on, but not specifically designed to facilitate the control process. These reports may or may not lead to action. Each reader studies them to detect whether or not something has happened that is worth looking into. If nothing of significance is noted, which is often the case, the report is put aside without action. If something does strike the reader's attention, an inquiry or action is initiated. The information on these reports comes both from the accounting system and also from a wide variety of other sources. Included are reports of orders received, the status of accounts receivable, the status of inventories, general news summaries, stock market prices, actions of competitors, and government regulations.

The important point is that a management control system cannot be viewed as consisting entirely of a set of reports, each designed to show information that is relevant in the control process. It also consists of a wide variety of reports which may, but also may not, contain relevant information.

Control Information

Exhibit 3–1 is a diagram of the essentials of the management control process that provides a basis for making comments about the type of information that is useful in that process.

The process starts with the preparation of plans. These plans are made within the context of goals and strategies which have been decided on in the strategic planning process, and they take account of other relevant information that bears on the problem of how the organization can operate most effectively and efficiently to reach its goals. The plans are expressed as programs, budgets, objectives, and in other terms.

Each responsibility center uses the plans as a guide to operations. They

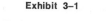

Exhibit 3–1

THE CONTROL PROCESS

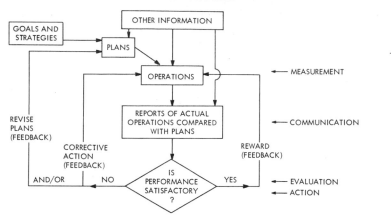

are, however, not a complete guide because operations are also influenced by other information, particularly current information from both external and internal sources. This information may suggest that operations should not proceed in exact conformance with the plan. If the production budget was based on a sales estimate of $1,000,000 and a current estimate is that sales will be $1,500,000, the actual production schedule should take account of this new information.

During the conduct of operations, actual performance is *measured*. Periodically, the results of these measurements are *communicated* to the manager who supervises the manager of the responsibility center, and this information is *evaluated*. The evaluation process starts with a comparison of reported actual performance with planned performance. Based on this comparison, and on other information which may help to explain why actual performance differed from planned performance, the manager makes a judgment on whether or not the performance was satisfactory.

The judgment gives rise to various types of *feedback*. If the performance was judged to be satisfactory, this is communicated to the responsibility center manager with appropriate commendation, and this signals to the responsibility center manager that he is judged to be performing in a way that is consistent with over-all goals. If the performance is judged to be unsatisfactory, either or both of two types of feedback signals are communicated: (1) the manager of the responsibility center may be motivated to take corrective action, and/or (2) the plans may be revised.

This diagram is given as a basis for pointing out some common misconceptions about the nature of control information:

1. Good performance does not necessarily mean that actual performance conforms to the plans. Information that becomes available after the plan was made

may indicate that departure from the plan is desirable. <u>Good performance is</u> <u>performance that is consistent with the organization's</u> *goals,* <u>and the plans may</u> <u>not reflect the actions that, under current conditions, are those best calculated</u> <u>to achieve these goals.</u> In other words, although the format of control reports typically indicates that actual performance is being compared with planned performance, the fundamental question is whether actual performance is consistent with the goals. In the usual situation, there is a presumption that planned performance does describe actions that are consistent with goals, but this is a rebuttable presumption.

2. Although the diagram indicates that feedback occurs *after* the person evaluating performance has made a judgment on it, the fact of the matter is that the feedback process is occurring within the responsibility center all during the conduct of operations. The responsibility center manager is reacting to new information and, if he is a good manager, is adjusting operations to take account of the new information received. If this new information indicates that a significant change in operations should be made, the manager communicates this need as soon as it is perceived; he does not wait for it to be communicated through the formal control reports.

It is often said that in a good control system the reports "should contain no surprises." This means that the competent manager has become aware of conditions that require a change of plans, has taken the necessary corrective action, and has informally informed his superior of the situation—all before the superior receives the formal control report. Thus, although the diagram indicates that corrective action is taken *after* the reports have been evaluated, the fact is that a competent responsibility manager has already taken the corrective action before the reports are published. If the report does communicate genuine news of unsatisfactory performance, the reason is likely to be that the manager has not kept his superior advised of what actually is going on.

3. Evaluation of performance always involves a comparison of actual performance with something. A statement that "Division A earned $100,000 last month," taken by itself, provides no basis for control. The report of actual performance is meaningful only when it is compared with a standard. Presumably, the budget and accompanying statement of objectives provide the best first approximation to such a standard, but performance can also be judged against other standards, including the person's intuitive judgment of what is an appropriate amount of profit under the circumstances. In any event, without a standard of some sort, there can be no control.

4. The management control process involves action. The communication of information is part of the process, but the process is obviously ineffective if nothing happens after the information has been evaluated. Control reports are feedback devices, but they are only one part of the feedback loop. Unlike the thermostat, which acts automatically in response to information about temperature, a control report *does not by itself* cause a change in performance. A change results only when managers take actions that lead to change. Thus, in management control, the feedback loop requires both the control report *plus* management action. (Of course, the information usually indicates that the situation is under control, in which case no action is required.)

5. Finally, although the process can, and often does, lead to a revision of plans, it does not ordinarily lead to a change in goals or strategies. Such changes

are made rarely, and they are outside of the management control process. A heating system is "in control" when the system keeps the temperature at the standard set in the thermostat. The corresponding standard in a management control system is the *goal* of the organization, which is not necessarily expressed in the budget or other control device.

Motivational Reports and Economic Reports

Control reports are of two general types. Ons is intended to report on *personal* performance, and the other to report on *economic* performance. Since the first type is intended to motivate managers, it is often called a motivational report. Essentially, such a report compares actual performance for a responsibility center with what performance should have been under the prevailing circumstances. Presumably, the budget states the responsibility manager's commitment to a certain level of performance, and reports show how well he has carried out this commitment. Behavioral considerations are important in using such reports.

An economic report is designed to show how well the responsibility center has performed as an economic entity. The content of such a report may be quite different from that of a motivational report. For example, an economic report would ordinarily include all the costs of the responsibility center, including allocated costs, whereas a motivational report may show only those elements of cost that the responsibility manager can influence. Economic reports are prepared much less frequently than motivational reports.

The motivational report may show that the responsibility manager is doing an excellent job, considering the circumstances, but if the economic analysis shows that the responsibility center is not earning an adequate profit, or otherwise is not making an adequate contribution to company goals, action may nevertheless be necessary. The manager of a downtown department store may be doing the best job possible, but if the economic report indicates that the store is operating at a loss (because, say, of the movement of business out of the the downtown area and into suburban shopping centers), the store may be closed. This action does not reflect unfavorably on the manager's performance.

Critics of a management control system sometimes overlook the fact that the system contains these two types of reports. Depending on their bias, they criticize reports because, for example, they report full costs including allocated costs, or alternatively because they do not report full costs. It must be appreciated that each type of cost construction has its place in a management control system.

Appropriate Standards

Standards used in control reports are of three types: (1) predetermined standards or budgets, (2) historical standards, or (3) external standards.

Predetermined standards or budgets, if carefully prepared, are the best formal standards; they are the basis against which actual performance is compared in many well-managed companies. The validity of such a standard depends largely on how much care went into its development. If the budget numbers were arrived at in a slipshod manner, they obviously will not provide a reliable basis for comparison.

Historical standards are records of past actual performance. Results for the current month may be compared with results for last month, or with results for the same month a year ago. This type of standard has two serious weaknesses: (1) conditions may have changed between the two periods in a way that invalidates the comparison; and (2) when a manager is measured against his own past record, there may be no way of knowing whether the prior period's performance was acceptable to start with. A foreman whose spoilage cost is $500 a month, month after month, is consistent, but we do not know, without other evidence, whether he is consistently good or consistently poor. Despite these inherent weaknesses, historical standards are used in many companies.

External standards are standards derived from the performance of other responsibility centers or other companies. The performance of one branch sales office may be compared with the performance of other branch sales offices, for example. If conditions in these responsibility centers are similar, such a comparison may provide a useful basis for judging performance. The catch is that it is not easy to find two responsibility centers that are sufficiently similar, or whose performance is affected by the same factors, to permit such comparisons on a regular basis.

Limitations on Standards. A variance between actual and standard performance is meaningful only if it is derived from a valid standard. Although it is convenient to refer to "favorable" and "unfavorable" variances, these words imply value judgments that are valid only to the extent that the standard is a valid measure of what performance should have been. Even a standard cost may not be an accurate estimate of what costs "should have been under the circumstances." This situation can arise for either or both of two reasons: (1) the standard was not set properly, or (2) although set properly in the light of conditions existing at the time, those conditions have changed so that the standard has become obsolete. An essential first step in the analysis of a variance, therefore, is an examination of the validity of the standard.

Engineered and Discretionary Costs. Engineered costs are items of cost for which the right or proper amount of costs that should be incurred can be estimated, for example, the direct material cost and the direct labor cost of a pair of shoes. Discretionary costs are items of costs whose amount can be varied at the discretion of the manager of the responsibility center; there is no scientific way of deciding what the "right" amount of cost should be. In evaluating control reports, engineered costs are viewed in an essentially different way from discretionary costs. With respect to engineered costs, the general rule is "the lower they are, the better." The objective is to spend as little as possible, consistent with quality and safety standards. The supervisor who reduces his engineered costs below the standard amounts usually should be congratulated. With respect to discretionary costs, however, the situation is quite different and much more complicated. Often, good performance consists of spending the amount agreed on, for spending too little may be as bad as, or worse than, spending too much. A factory manager can easily reduce his current costs by skimping on maintenance or on training; a marketing manager can reduce his advertising or sales promotion expenditures; top management may eliminate a research department. None of these actions may be in the over-all best interest of the company, although all of them result in lower costs on the current reports of performance.

Control of Information

In this book we focus on management control information. We do not discuss in any detail the techniques that are needed to control the cost and quality of the information system itself. Such techniques are obviously essential, but they are best discussed in a course designed for that purpose. In such a course, techniques for the efficient processing of information and for assuring that the information is reasonably reliable are discussed. Conceptually, the distinction between the two courses is that in the information processing course, the parameters of the desired information are taken as givens, whereas the management control course sets these parameters. In practice there is overlap between the two courses because one cannot understand techniques for processing information efficiently without some appreciation of the purpose for which it will be used.

SUGGESTED ADDITIONAL READINGS

BONINI, CHARLES P. *Simulation of Information and Decision Systems in the Firm*. Englewood Cliffs, N.J.: Prentice-Hall, Inc., 1963.

CAPLAN, EDWIN H. *Management Accounting and Behavioral Science*. Reading, Mass.: Addison-Wesley, 1971.

CHURCHMAN, C. WEST. *The Design of Inquiring Systems*. New York: Basic Books, Inc., 1971.

EMERY, JAMES C. *Organizational Planning and Control Systems*. New York: The Macmillan Company, 1969.

MURDICK, ROBERT G., and JOEL E. ROSS. *Information Systems for Modern Management*. Englewood Cliffs, N.J.: Prentice-Hall, Inc., 1971.

PRINCE, THOMAS R. *Information Systems for Management Planning and Control*. Homewood, Ill.: Richard D. Irwin, Inc., 1975.

RAIFFA, HOWARD. *Decision Analysis: Introductory Lectures on Choices under Uncertainty*. Reading, Mass.: Addison-Wesley, 1968.

Case 3-1

Empire Glass Company

ORGANIZATION

Empire Glass Company was a diversified company organized into several major product divisions, one of which was the glass products division. This division was responsible for manufacturing and selling glass food and beverage bottles. Each division was headed by a divisional vice-president who reported directly to the company's executive vice-president, Landon McGregor.

Mr. McGregor's corporate staff included three men in the financial area—the controller, the chief accountant and the treasurer. The controller's department consisted of only two men—Mr. Walker and the assistant controller, Allen Newell. The market research and labor relations departments also reported in a staff capacity to Mr. McGregor.

All the product divisions were organized along similar lines. Reporting to each product division vice-president were several staff members in the customer service and product research areas. Reporting in a line capacity to each individual vice-president were also a general manager of manufacturing and a general manager of marketing. The general manager of manufacturing was responsible for all the division's manufacturing activities. Similarly, the general manager of marketing was responsible for all the division's marketing activities. Both of these executives were assisted by a small staff of specialists. There was also a controller and supporting staff in each division. Exhibit 1 presents an organization chart of the glass product division's top management group. All the corporate and divisional management group were located in British City, Canada. Exhibit 2 shows the typical organization structure of a plant within the glass products division.

PRODUCTS AND TECHNOLOGY

The glass products division operated a number of plants in Canada producing glass food and beverage bottles. Of these products, food jars consti-

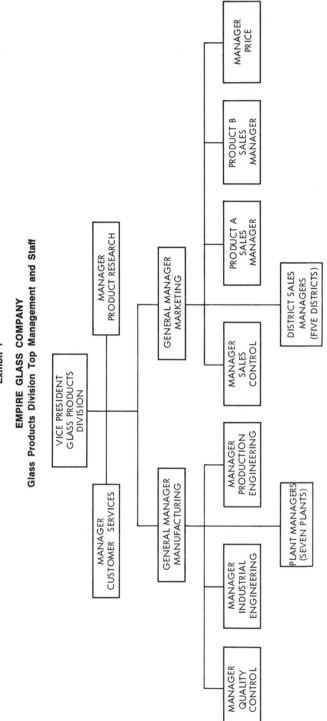

Exhibit 1

EMPIRE GLASS COMPANY

Glass Products Division Top Management and Staff

Exhibit 2

EMPIRE GLASS COMPANY
Typical Plant Organization—Glass Products Division

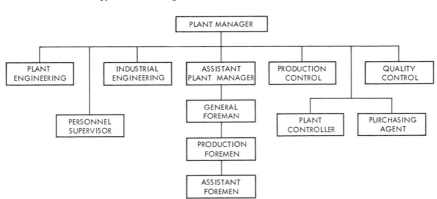

tuted the largest group, including jars for products like tomato catsup, mayon-
naise, jams and jellies, honey, and soluble coffee. Milk bottles and beer and
soft drink bottles were also produced in large quantities. A great variety of
shapes and sizes of containers for wines, liquors, drugs, cosmetics, and chemicals were produced in smaller quantities.

Most of the thousands of different products, varying in size, shape, color,
and decoration were produced to order. According to British City executives,
during 1963 the typical lead time between the customer's order and shipment from the plant was between two and three weeks.

The principal raw materials for container glass were sand, soda ash, and
lime. The first step in the manufacturing process was to melt batches of these
materials in furnaces or "tanks." The molten mass was then passed into
automatic or semiautomatic machines, which filled molds with the molten
glass and blew the glass into the desired shape. The ware then went through
an automatic annealing oven or lehr, where it was cooled slowly under carefully controlled conditions. If the glass was to be coated on the exterior to
increase its resistance to abrasion and scratches, this coating—often a
silicone film—was applied at the lehr. Any decorating (such as a trademark or
other design) was then added, the product inspected again, and the finished
goods packed in corrugated containers (or wooden cases for some bottles).

Quality inspection was critical in the manufacturing process. If the melt
in the furnace was not completely free from bubbles and stones (unmelted
ingredients or pieces of refinery material), or if the fabricating machinery
was slightly out of adjustment, or molds were worn, the rejection rate was
very high. Although a number of machines were used in the inspection process, including electric eyes, much of the inspection was still visual.

Although glassmaking was one of the oldest arts, and bottles and jars had been machine molded at relatively high speed for over half a century, the glass products division had spent substantial sums each year to modernize its equipment. These improvements had greatly increased the speed of operations and had substantially reduced the visual inspection and manual handling of glassware.

Most of the jobs were relatively unskilled, highly repetitive, and gave the worker little control over work methods or pace. The moldmakers who made and repaired the molds, the machine repairmen, and those who made the equipment setup changes between different products were considered to be the highest classes of skilled workers. Wages were relatively high in the glass industry. Production employees belonged to two national unions, and for many years bargaining had been conducted on a national basis. Output standards were established for all jobs, but no bonus was paid to hourly plant workers for exceeding standard.

MARKETING

Over the years, the sales of the glass products divisions had grown at a slightly faster rate than had the total market for glass containers. Until the late 1950's, the division had charged a premium for most of its products, primarily because they were of better quality than competitive products. In recent years, however, the quality of the competitive products had improved to the point where they now matched the division's quality level. In the meantime, the division's competitors had retained their former price structure. Consequently, the glass products division had been forced to lower its prices to meet its competitor's lower market prices. According to one division executive:

Currently, price competition is not severe, particularly among the two or three larger companies that dominate the glass bottle industry. Most of our competition is with respect to product quality and customer service. . . . In fact, our biggest competitive threat is from containers other than glass. . . .

Each of the division's various plants shipped their products throughout Canada to some extent, although transportation costs limited each plant's market primarily to its immediate vicinity. While some of the customers were large and bought in huge quantities, many were relatively small.

BUDGETARY CONTROL SYSTEM

In the fall of 1963, James Walker, Empire Glass Company controller, described the company's budgetary control system to a casewriter. Mr. Walker had been controller for some fifteen years. Excerpts from that interview are reproduced below.

To understand the role of the budgetary control system, you must first understand our management philosophy. Fundamentally, we have a divisional organization based on broad product categories. These divisional activities are coordinated by the company's executive vice-president, while the head office group provides a policy and review function for him. Within the broad policy limits, we operate on a decentralized basis; each of the decentralized divisions performs the full management job that normally would be inherent in any independent company. The only exceptions to this philosophy are the head office group's sole responsibilities for sources of funds and labor relations with those bargaining units that cross division lines.

Given this form of organization, the budget is the principal management tool used by head office to direct the efforts of the various segments of the company toward a common goal. Certainly, in our case, the budget is much more than a narrow statistical accounting device.

Sales Budget

As early as May 15 of the year preceding the budget year, top management of the company asks the various product division vice-presidents to submit preliminary reports stating what they think their division's capital requirements and outlook in terms of sales and income will be during the next budget year. In addition, corporate top management also wants an expression of the division vice-president's general feelings toward the trends in these particular items over the two years following the upcoming budget year. At this stage, head office is not interested in too much detail. Since all divisions plan their capital requirements five years in advance and had made predictions of the forthcoming budget year's market when the budget estimates were prepared last year, these rough estimates of next year's conditions and requirements are far from wild guesses.

After the opinions of the divisional vice-presidents are in, the market research staff goes to work. They develop a formal statement of the marketing climate in detail for the forthcoming budget year and in general terms for the subsequent two years. Once these general factors have been assessed, a sales forecast is constructed for the company and for each division. Consideration is given to the relationship of the general economic climate to our customers' needs and Empire's share of each market. Explicitly stated are basic assumptions as to price, weather conditions, introduction of new products, gains or losses in particular accounts, forward buying, new manufacturing plants, industry growth trends, packaging trends, inventory carry-overs, and the development of alternative packages to or from glass. This review of all the relevant factors is followed for each of our product lines, regardless of its size and importance. The completed forecasts of the market research group are then forwarded to the appropriate divisions for review, criticism, and adjustments.

The primary goal of the head office group in developing these sales forecasts is to assure uniformity among the divisions with respect to the basic assumptions on business conditions, pricing, and the treatment of possible emergencies. Also, we provide a yardstick so as to assure us that the company's overall sales forecast will be reasonable and obtainable.

The product division top management then asks each district manager what he expects to do in the way of sales during the budget year. Head office and the divisional staffs will give the district sales managers as much guidance as they request, but it is the sole responsibility of each district sales manager to come up with his particular forecast.

After the district sales managers' forecasts are received by the divisional top management, the forecasts are consolidated and reviewed by the division's general manager of marketing. Let me emphasize, however, that nothing is changed in the district sales manager's budget unless the district manager agrees. Then, once the budget is approved, nobody is relieved of his responsibility without top management approval. Also, no arbitrary changes are made in the approved budgets without the concurrence of all the people responsible for the budget.

Next, we go through the same process at the division and headquarters levels. We continue to repeat the process until everyone agrees that the sales budgets are sound. Then, each level of management takes responsibility for its particular portion of the budget. These sales budgets then become fixed objectives.

I would say we have four general objectives in mind in reviewing the sales forecast:

1. A review of the division's competitive position, including plans for improving that position.
2. An evaluation of its efforts to gain either a larger share of the market or offset competitors' activities.
3. A consideration of the need to expand facilities to improve the division's products or introduce new products.
4. A review and development of plans to improve produce quality, delivery methods and service.

Manufacturing Budgets

Once the vice-presidents, executive vice-president, and company president have given final approval to the sales budgets, we make a sales budget for each plant by breaking down the division sales budgets according to the plants from which the finished goods will be shipped. These plant sales budgets are then further broken down on a monthly basis by price, volume, and end use. With this information available, the plants then budget their gross profit, fixed expenses, and income before taxes. Gross profit is the difference between gross sales, less discounts, and variable manufacturing costs—such as direct labor, direct material and variable manufacturing overheads. Income is the difference between the gross profit and the fixed costs.

The plant manager's primary responsibility extends to profits. The budgeted plant profit is the difference between the fixed sales dollar budget and the sum of the budgeted variable costs at standard and the fixed overhead budget. It is the plant manager's responsibility to meet this budget profit figure, even if actual dollar sales drop below the budgeted level.

Given his sales budget, it is up to the plant manager to determine the fixed overhead and variable costs—at standard—that he will need to incur so as to meet the demands of the sales budget. In my opinion, requiring the plant managers to make their own plans is one of the most valuable things associated with the budget system. Each plant manager divides the preparation of the overall plant budget among his plant's various departments. First, the departments spell out the program in terms of the physical requirements, such as tons of raw material, and then the plans are priced at standard cost.

The plant industrial engineering department is assigned responsibility for developing engineered cost standards and reduced costs. Consequently, the phase of budget preparation covered by the industrial engineers includes budget standards of performance for each operation, cost center, and department within the plant. This phase of the budget also includes budgeted cost reductions, budgeted unfavorable variances from standards, and certain budgeted programmed fixed costs in the manufacturing area, such as service labor. The industrial engineer prepares this phase of the budget in conjunction with departmental line supervision.

Before each plant sends its budget into British City, a group of us from head office goes out to visit each plant. For example, in the case of the glass products division, Allen Newell, assistant controller, and I, along with representatives of the glass products division manufacturing staffs visit each of the division's plants. Let me stress this point: We do not go on these trips to pass judgment on the plant's proposed budget. Rather, we go with two purposes in mind. First, we wish to acquaint ourselves with the thinking behind the figures that each plant manager will send in to British City. This is helpful, because when we come to review these budgets with the top management—that is, management above our level—we will have to answer questions about the budgets, and we will know the answers. Second, the review is a way of giving guidance to the plant managers in determining whether or not they are in line with what the company needs to make in the way of profits.

Of course, when we make our field reviews we do not know about what each of the other plants is doing. Therefore, we explain to the plant managers that while their budget may look good now, when we put all the plants together in a consolidated budget the plant managers may have to make some changes because the projected profit is not high enough. When this happens, we must tell the plant managers that it is not their programs that are unsound. The problem is that the company cannot afford the programs. I think it is very important that each plant manager has a chance to tell his story. Also, it gives them the feeling that we at headquarters are not living in an ivory tower.

These plant visits are spread over a three-week period, and we spend an average of half a day at each plant. The plant manager is free to bring to these meetings any of his supervisors he wishes. We ask him not to bring in anybody below the supervisory level. Then, of course, you get into organized labor. During the half day we spend at each plant we discuss the budget primarily. However, if I have time I like to wander through the plant and see how things are going. Also, I go over in great detail the property replacement and maintenance budget with the plant manager.

About September 1, the plant budgets come into British City, and the accounting department consolidates them. Then, the product division vice-presidents review their respective divisional budgets to see if the division budget is reasonable in terms of what the vice-president thinks the corporate management wants. If he is not satisfied with the consolidated plant budgets, he will ask the various plants within the division to trim their budget figures.

When the division vice-presidents and the executive vice-president are happy, they will send their budgets to the company president. He may accept the division budgets at this point. If he doesn't, he will specify the areas to be reexamined by division and, if necessary, by plant management. The final budget is approved at our December board of directors meeting.

Comparison of Actual and Standard Performance

At the end of the sixth business day after the close of the month, each plant wires to the head office certain operating variances, which we put together on what we call the variance analysis sheet. Within a half-hour after the last plant report comes through, variance analysis sheets for the divisions and plants are compiled. On the morning of the seventh business day after the end of the month, these reports are usually on the desks of the interested top management. The variance analysis sheet highlights the variances in what we consider to be critical areas. Receiving this report as soon as we do helps us at head office to take timely action. Let me emphasize, however, we do not accept the excuse that the plant manager has to go to the end of the month to know what happened during the month. He has to be on top of these particular items daily.

When the actual results come into the head office, we go over them on the basis of exception; that is, we only look at those figures that are in excess of the budgeted amounts. We believe this has a good effect on morale. The plant managers don't have to explain everything they do. They have to explain only where they go off base. In particular, we pay close attention to the net sales, gross margin, and the plant's ability to meet its standard manufacturing cost. Incidentally, when analyzing the gross sales, we look closely at the price and mix changes.

All this information is summarized on a form known as the Profit Planning and Control Report No. 1 (see Exhibit 3). This document is backed up by a number of supporting documents (see Exhibit 4). The plant PPCR No. 1 and the month-end trial balance showing both actual and budget figures are received in British City at the close of the eighth business day after the end of the month. These two very important reports, along with the supporting reports (PPCR No. 2, PPCR No. 11) are then consolidated by the accounting department on PPCR-type forms to show the results of operations by division and company. The consolidated reports are distributed the next day.

In connection with the fixed cost items, we want to know whether or not the plants carried out the programs they said they would carry out. If they have not, we want to know why they have not. Here, we are looking for sound reasons. Also, we want to know if they have carried out their projected programs at the cost they said they would.

In addition to these reports, at the beginning of each month the plant managers prepare current estimates for the upcoming month and quarter on forms similar to the variance analysis sheets. Since our budget is based on known programs, the value of this current estimate is that it gets the plant people to look at their programs. Hopefully, they will realize that they cannot run their plants on a day-to-day basis.

If we see a sore spot coming up, or if the plant manager draws our attention to a potential trouble area, we may ask that daily reports concerning this item be sent to the particular division top management involved. In addition, the division top management may send a division staff specialist—say, a quality control expert if it is a quality problem—to the plant concerned. The division staff members can make recommendations, but it is up to the plant manager to accept or reject these recommendations. Of course, it is well known throughout the company that we expect the plant managers to accept gracefully the help of the head office and division staffs.

Sales-Manufacturing Relations

If a sales decline occurs during the early part of the year, and if the plant managers can convince us that the change is permanent, we may revise the plant budgets to reflect these new circumstances. However, if toward the end of the year the actual sales volume suddenly drops below the predicted sales volume, we don't have much time to change the budget plans. What we do is ask the plant managers to go back over their budgets with their staffs and see where reduction of expense programs will do the least harm. Specifically, we ask them to consider what they may be able to eliminate this year or delay until next year.

I believe it was Confucius who said: "We make plans so we have plans to discard." Nevertheless, I think it is wise to make plans, even if you have to discard them. Having plans makes it a lot easier to figure out what to do when sales fall off from the budgeted level. The understanding of operations

Exhibit 3

EMPIRE GLASS COMPANY

MONTH			Ref.		YEAR TO DATE		
Income Gain (+) or Loss (−) From		Actual			Actual	Income Gain (+) or Loss (−) From	
Prev. Year	Budget					Budget	Prev. Year
			1	Gross Sales to Customers			
			2	Discounts & Allowances			
			3	Net Sales to Customers			
%	%	/////	4	% Gain (+)/Loss (−)	/////	%	%
				DOLLAR VOLUME GAIN (+)/ LOSS (−) DUE TO:			
		/////	5	Sales Price	/////		
		/////	6	Sales Volume	/////		
			6(a)	Trade Mix	/////		
			7	Variable Cost of Sales			
			8	Profit Margin			
				PROFIT MARGIN GAIN (+)/ LOSS (−) DUE TO:			
		/////	9	Profit Volume Ratio (P/V)	/////		
		/////	10	Dollar Volume	/////		
%	%	%	11	Profit Volume Ratio (P/V)	%	%	%
		Income Addition (+)			Income Addition (+)		
			12	Total Fixed Manufacturing Cost			
			13	Fixed Manufacturing Cost−Transfers			
			14	Plant Income (Standard)			
%	%	%	15	% of Net Sales	%	%	%
		Income Addition (+) Income Reduction (−)			Income Addition (+) Income Reduction (−)		
%	%	%	16	% Performance	%	%	%
			17	Manufacturing Efficiency			
		Income Addition (+)			Income Addition (+)		
			18	Methods Improvements			
			19	Other Revisions of Standards			
			20	Material Price Changes			
			21	Division Special Projects			
			22	Company Special Projects			
			23	New Plant Expense			
			24	Other Plant Expenses			
			25	Income on Seconds			
			26				
			27				
			28	Plant Income (Actual)			
%	%	/////	29	% Gain (+)/Loss (−)	/////	%	%
%	%	%	30	% of Net Sales	%	%	%
			36A				
Increase (+) or Decrease (−)				EMPLOYED CAPITAL	Increase (+) or Decrease (−)		
			37	Total Employed Capital			
%	%	%	38	% Return	%	%	%
			39	Turnover Rate			

———————   ———————   ———————19———

Plant   Division   Month

Exhibit 4. EMPIRE GLASS COMPANY

Brief Description of PPCR No. 2—PPCR No. 11

Individual Plant Reports

Report	Description
Report	*Description*
PPCR No. 2	Manufacturing expense: Plant materials, labor, and variable overhead consumed. Detail of actual figures compared with budget and previous year's figures for year to date and current month.
PPCR No. 3	Plant expense: Plant fixed expenses incurred. Details of actual figures compared with budget and previous year's figures for year to date and current month.
PPCR No. 4	Analysis of sales and income: Plant operating gains and losses due to changes in sales revenue, profit margins and other sources of income. Details of actual figures compared with budget and previous year's figures for year to date and current month.
PPCR No. 5	Plant control statement: Analysis of plant raw material gains and losses, spoilage costs, and cost reductions programs. Actual figures compared with budget figures for current month and year to date.
PPCR No. 6	Comparison of sales by principal and product groups: Plant sales dollars, profit margin and P/V ratios broken down by end product use (i.e., soft drinks, beer). Compares actual figures with budgeted figures for year to date and current month.

Division Summary Reports

Report	Description
Report	*Description*
PPCR No. 7	Comparative plant performance, sales and income: Gross sales and income figures by plants. Actual figures compared with budget figures for year to date and current month.
PPCR No. 8	Comparative plant performance, total plant expenses: Profit margin, total fixed costs, manufacturing efficiency, other plant expenses and P/V ratios by plants. Actual figures compared with budgeted and previous year's figures for current month and year to date.
PPCR No. 9	Manufacturing efficiency: Analysis of gains and losses by plant in areas of materials, spoilage, supplies and labor. Current month and year to date actuals reported in total dollars and as a percentage of budget.
PPCR No. 10	Inventory: Comparison of actual and budget inventory figures by major inventory accounts and plants.
PPCR No. 11	Status of capital expenditures: Analysis of the status of capital expenditures by plants, months and relative to budget.

that comes from preparing the budget removes a lot of the potential chaos and confusion that might arise if we were under pressure to meet a stated profit goal and sales declined quickly and unexpectedly at year-end, just as they did last year. In these circumstances, we don't try to ram anything down the plant managers' throats. We ask them to tell us where they can reasonably expect to cut costs below the budgeted level.

Whenever a problem arises at a plant between sales and production, the local people are supposed to solve the problem themselves. For example, a customer's purchasing agent may insist he wants an immediate delivery, and this delivery will disrupt the production department's plans. The production group can make recommendations as to alternative ways to take care of the problem, but it's the sales manager's responsibility to get the product to the customer. The salesmen are supposed to know their customers well enough to judge whether or not the customer really needs the product. If the sales manager says the customer needs the product, that ends the matter. As far as we are concerned, the customer's wants are primary; our company is a case where sales wags the rest of the dog.

Of course, if the change in the sales program involves a major plant expense which is out of line with the budget, then the matter is passed up to division for decision.

As I said earlier, the sales department has the sole responsibility for the product price, sales mix, and delivery schedules. They do not have direct responsibility for plant operations or profit. That's the plant management's responsibility. However, it is understood that sales group will cooperate with the plant people wherever possible.

Motivation

There are various ways in which we motivate the plant managers to meet their profit goals. First of all, we only promote capable people. Also, a monetary incentive program has been established that stimulates their efforts to achieve their profit goals. In addition, each month we put together a bar chart which shows, by division and plant, the ranking of the various manufacturing units with respect to manufacturing efficiency.[1] We feel the plant managers are one hundred percent responsible for variable manufacturing costs. I believe this is true, since all manufacturing standards have to be approved by plant managers. Most of the plant managers give wide publicity to these bar charts. The efficiency bar chart and efficiency measure itself is perhaps a little unfair in some respects when you are comparing one plant with another. Different kinds of products are run through different plants. These require different setups, etc., which have an important impact on a position of the plant. However, in general, the efficiency rating is a good indication of the quality of the plant manager and his supervisory staff.

---

[1] Manufacturing efficiency $= \dfrac{\text{total actual variable manufacturing costs}}{\text{total standard variable manufacturing costs}} \times 100\%$

Also, a number of plants run competitions within the plants which reward department heads, or foremen, based on their relative standing with respect to a certain cost item. The plant managers, their staffs, and employees have great pride in their plants.

The number one item now stressed at the plant level is *quality*. The market situation is such that in order to make sales you have to meet the market price and exceed the market quality. By quality I mean not only the physical characteristics of the product but also such things as delivery schedules. As I read the company employee publications, their message is that if the company is to be profitable it must produce high-quality items at a reasonable cost. This is necessary so that the plants can meet their obligation to produce the maximum profits for the company in the prevailing circumstances.

The Future

An essential part of the budgetary control system is planning. We have developed a philosophy that we must begin our plans where the work is done—in the line organization and out in the field. Perhaps, in the future, we can avoid or cut back some of the budget preparation steps and start putting together our sales budget later than May 15. However, I doubt if we will change the basic philosophy.

Frankly, I doubt if the line operators would want any major change in the system; they are very jealous of the management prerogatives the system gives to them.

It is very important that we manage the budget. We have to be continually on guard against its managing us. Sometimes, the plants lose sight of this fact. We have to be made conscious daily of the necessity of having the sales volume to make a profit. And when sales fall off and their plant programs are reduced, they do not always appear to see the justification for budget cuts. Although I do suspect that they see more of the justification for these cuts than they will admit. It is this human side of the budget to which we have to pay more attention in the future.

QUESTION

Comment on the strong points and the weak points in the management control system of Empire Glass Company. What changes, if any, would you suggest?

Thurber Division*

The Parent Company

In the last decade, the International Gothic Company went through a planned transition from what was basically an automotive supply business to a broadly diversified company serving many industries and markets. This intensive and somewhat successful effort to broaden the base of Gothic's markets and to find new product lines was necessary to replace diminishing markets and outmoded product lines. New products added in this period included pneumated controls and actuators, aircraft landing gear, metal alloys, and instruments. By developing new products and purchasing other companies with different product lines, the following diversification was accomplished:

Product Group	Total Sales		Increase (Decrease)
	1967	1974	
Castings & forgings	44%	38%	(6%)
Automotive products	44	25	(19)
Aircraft products	3	22	19
Machine tools	9	15	6

Under each product group, Gothic had a number of divisions which totaled 19 (composed almost equally of foreign and domestic companies) in 1975. The largest product group in number of divisions was Aircraft Products with 8 divisions consisting entirely of companies purchased since 1967.[1] Foreign Aircraft Products companies were located in West Germany (2), France, England, Italy and Japan.

---

* This case was prepared by Professor Thomas Burns of Ohio State University.

[1] The function of this group is to create controlled pneumatic power to handle jobs in defense and other industries. Pneumatic means gas in motion—it is the process of

The Division

The Thurber Company was a manufacturer of electro-mechanical devices and sensitive instruments which are used in measuring the performance of missiles and in controlling automated industrial equipment. Since its founding in 1965 by an Ohio State University engineering professor, the company had developed rapidly. In December 1970, the company was purchased by Gothic and grouped with the Aircraft Products division.

Prior to its purchase by Gothic, only limited records were kept by Thurber. The reports prepared had been for tax, credit, or loan purposes. Even these apparently had been incomplete since Gothic found upon purchase that some Ohio taxes had not been paid for many years. Most of the accounts receivable purchased turned out to be worthless since they represented returned instruments for which no credit memos had been issued. There were so many discrepancies in the inventory records that they had little value. Plant records were practically nonexistent. In order to stay solvent, the founder and inventor had not been able to pay himself salary, royalties, or dividends. In its pre-Gothic period, the corporation had been barely able to meet a payroll which normally consisted of from 5 to 10 persons. The wife of an employee had been hired to do the record-keeping. A factory employee informally kept track of production.

Once Gothic took over in 1970 it attempted to improve Thurber's accounting by installing Gothic's system which was used in Aircraft Products divisions (see Exhibit 1). Due to the unavailability of any present Thurber or Gothic employee who could account adequately, the Gothic controller decided to hire a competent accountant for this purpose. Since Thurber had never been profitable for Gothic, it was anticipated that such an action (coupled with the starting of IBM accounting services for Thurber in 1973) might provide better controls which would result in substantial cost reductions, increased manufacturing efficiencies, and eventual profits.

In February 1974, an accountant, Mr. Christopher Fry, age 27, had been hired in Cleveland to become controller of the Thurber division. Gothic officials regarded themselves as fortunate in securing his services due to his college record, his excellent experience as a Navy auditor and supply officer, and especially because the labor market for accountants was very tight.

In September 1974, the university professor (who continued to be Thurber's chief executive) hired Thurber's first production manager, Mr. Charlie Brown, formerly employed at the Dayton factory of Thurber's chief competitor, to improve the manufacturing operation.

---

transmitting power, pressure or motion by means of gaseous force. In modern industrial and defense systems, pneumatic power is created by a pump or compressor much as a generator creates electric power and is under pressure as high as 3,000 pounds per square inch. If rotary motion is needed the gas is forced through a pneumatic turbine or motor. If linear motion or force is needed, the gas acts as a ram or pneumatic cylinder.

Exhibit 1

**ORGANIZATION CHART FOR THURBER DIVISION,
INTERNATIONAL GOTHIC CO.**

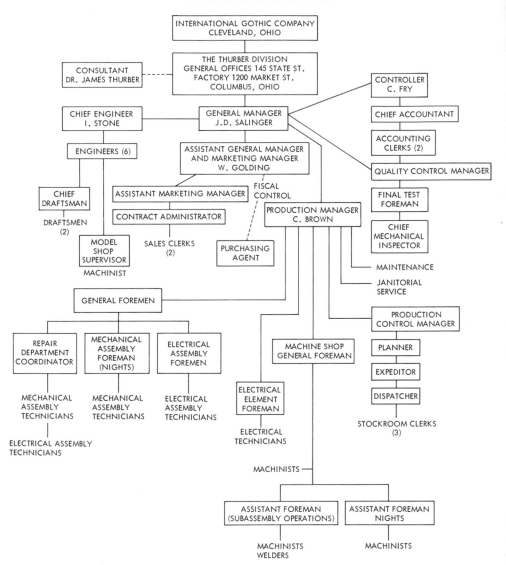

Meanwhile Gothic sales had increased from $110.7 million in 1967 to $158.2 million, the highest in history, in 1974. But net earnings in 1974 equaled $3 per share which was $.35 to $.50 less per share than it had been for many years.

As a result of this and several major management changes, Thurber found itself under increasing pressures to improve its operating situation. The long-time chairman of Gothic retired in 1974 after 37 years of company service. In addition to a new chairman, a new Gothic president and a new Gothic vice president for the Aircraft Products group of divisions were also appointed. At Thurber, the founder voluntarily relinquished his post as line executive in January, 1975.

Since Gothic had taken over, many new instrument models had been introduced and well accepted. For instance, in 1974 a very promising model for use in ground-testing rocket engine components was developed. Prices of Thurber products currently ranged from $200 to $700, with a few as high as $2,000. Due to a major change in production to manufacture parts previously purchased, the number of Thurber employees had increased from 79 in March 1974, to 144 in July, 1975. Of those currently employed, 117 were classified as factory employees; of these 106 were nonsalaried and 11 were salaried. Up until six months ago, all activities had been carried on in the same building. Now that the office operations were carried out in a separate building, production personnel did not run off the stencils, handle the mail, and furnish an employee part-time for accounting as they had done previously.

The Immediate Situation

On August 6, 1975, after having been in the hospital for eight weeks Thurber's general manager, Mr. J. D. Salinger,[2] returned to his office. Immediately he called in the assistant general manager (and marketing manager) Mr. William Golding, to consider the current state of company affairs. During this discussion, Mr. Golding said:

Our really acute problem is our production department. Information should flow out from production to sales to customers regarding the status of the jobs. It is our normal selling practice to quote the customer a price whereupon he may place an order immediately or within the next 60–90 days. In the sales-engineering-planning stages the order is under complete control but once it gets into the factory, control is nonexistent. If anything happens to the order in the factory, there is no feedback of such information to the sales force. For instance, if jobs run into production difficulties which might necessitate more engineering, literally nothing is done to keep the sales force informed. There have been numerous situations where jobs have been stopped for over two months; the only way the sales force finds out is when the customer complains.

Even then we can't always pacify the customer because we may not be able to track down the job in the factory for three or four days. Besides taking an inordinate amount of the time of a small sales force to find the job; even when found, there is still the problem of trying to establish when delivery will be made. If we want to stay in business, we must at least take our key orders and expedite

---

[2] Before becoming the first general manager in 1972, Mr. Salinger had been chief engineer.

them.[3] Even so, we continue to run the grave risk of permanently alienating our other customers.

We also must keep in mind our tremendous growth in the face of the increasing competitiveness of our industry. In the almost five years since Gothic came in and you and I started here, Thurber has grown over five times in annual sales going from $.4 million to $2 million despite increasing severe price competition. It used to be that only one instrument specification would be offered by a particular company; now some six or seven companies do. We face direct price competition on every job today. Consequently, our pricing must be based upon:

1. What has the instrument cost us in the past?
2. What economies can we make in the future?

Nowadays we pare off costs in the hope that we can come in with a price that will secure the order. It used to be that if you were 10% to 20% off on a bid it wasn't so important since you could adjust on the following order. This is not so today; instead every cent counts. There is presently a great need for more accurate cost information. Formerly the cost information that was available often really wasn't utilized.

I reiterate, we simply must be competitive costwise these days. Four years ago there were two or three firms sharing a $10 million sales market, nowadays there are 15 companies cutting up a $20 million sales market. And of these companies, two out of three are extremely capable.

It used to be that a customer had to stick with you. Now if he doesn't get the price and service he wants, there are any number of competent firms waiting in line to take the business. Another thing is that we must now bid to a much more precise set of specifications. All of these things influence our cost consciousness.

Our accounting department is working very hard. I am confident we will be getting better information from them but production must help them out.

We have helped out production by giving them many more large orders. The stuff they are making this summer is all this way. To make 800 of the same thing has been a rarity around here; last summer we had only 400 of this order. Sales have been very successful in increasing the size of orders from Republic and Douglas and others. For example, last year we got an order for 50 instruments. This year we got an order for 300. All of this makes for many economies but it all hinges on how production is handled.

As a company, our competitive advantage is engineering. In engineering, we are rated tops in the industry. In sales, we are considered as good as we ought to be perhaps.[4] It is commonplace for the industry to describe us as the firm that can make wonderful instruments if you can wait long enough for them. The word is that you can order with two months' quote but it will run a year or more before you get delivery.

We brought Brown in last fall to solve our production problems and I am still hopeful that he can solve them, given time.

---

[3] The maximum delivery time on a government order is 120 days.

[4] The company sells through: (1) manufacturers' agents and (2) telephone calls to customers. Manufacturers' agents are reasonably loyal to company if company is competitive in price and delivery.

After lunching with Mr. Golding, Mr. Salinger called a haggard-look-ing Mr. Brown into his office and asked him to report on Thurber production.

In order to stay in business nowadays, said Charlie Brown, you must "chop away at price" and take marginal orders since "pickings are slim." Salesmen "clutch at every straw" and pick up "garbage" in the way of orders. Meanwhile overhead keeps going up, etc.

Mr. Salinger interrupted to point out that was "the nature of their beast."

Well, anyway production is caught in a squeeze to produce more economically and standardize products more while the product is perpetually in the state of being improved. Last month, by actual count, we were producing some 42 models (out of a possible 55 models) each with some four to eight variations.

Another aspect of this is the size of the order. It is damn difficult trying to schedule production when the typical order has been two or three pieces. Ten pieces in an order is unusual and a 800-piece order like we have now is a rarity. And to complicate all of this now we face a shorter delivery schedule. Nowadays, if it takes more than 60 days' delivery time the customers go elsewhere.

When I came here we had a backlog of over a million dollars in orders while we were shipping orders out at the rate of $100,000 per month. On June 1, (1975) we had $450,000 of back orders—a sharp reduction from last September (1974) —but some $300,000 of this couldn't be scheduled until late August or Septem-ber. Some of the latter will be canceled before they can be produced while the one third which can be scheduled is insufficient production for our current quarter. The major sales effort is on government-oriented companies such as Martin, Fairchild, and Republic. The little customers, such as the universities, are ne-glected and go elsewhere. But government-oriented company contracts usually turn out to be long-range jobs which leaves a lack of immediate jobs to earn current profits.[5]

We still operate on two nominal eight-hour shifts, which really comes down to a shift-and-a-half since only the first shift is a full shop. We still have our problems with the night shift too. I was called to the phone at 3:30 this morning (after having put in a 15-hour day here yesterday) by the night foreman needing papers so he could ship out production to meet our closing deadline. Naturally nobody in accounting was available at that time.[6]

One must also keep in mind the complete reformation that production has undergone since my arrival. When I came in September, production purchased 70 percent of the parts; nowadays, we purchase about 7 percent. In short, we have converted an assembly shop into a truly producing one.

We still have to cope with our special inventory problem. We may not have any

---

[5] In a year, the total number of Thurber customers is about 200, but 15 customers account for 70% of sales, 8 for 60% and currently 2 for 40%.

[6] Each accounting month ends on the 20th so that accounting can prepare reports to be sent to Cleveland by the end of the month. The following reports are sent monthly: Comparative Balance Sheet (21 items), Details of Property, Plant & Equipment and In-tangible Assets (25 items), Comparative Summary of Operations (24 items), Com-parative Summary of Operating Results (30 items), Cost of Production and Burden Details. The applied burden normally is about 40% of the actual burden.

need for a certain item for an entire year, yet suddenly in a single day the engineers want a dozen. There are the 55 models with up to 10 variations apiece —I know I'm biased from the production point of view—but it's a real painful situation. . . .

I have worked out rather carefully that it takes 70 days on the average to produce an instrument with 60 days the absolute rock bottom minimum. Yet in order to get the order the salesmen will say, "I'll write it for 60 days, but I promise verbally to get it to you within 45 days." So, at the end of 45 days the customer will start inquiring and there never was any possibility that the cycle would be less than 60 days. This makes for very poor customer relationships. But you know instruments are not the type of product one can "crash" out. No clear-cut policy about this sort of thing has been worked out here as is true of so many of our arrangements. They should be in writing.

As Mr. Salinger started to speak, Brown hurried on:

Yes, I can shave this 60-day figure on some jobs if I want to have a hand-carry job but how many hand-carry jobs can I have at once out of the 1,000 jobs on the floor.

And to top it all off, there is absolutely no cost control. The accounting situation around here has often caused me to seriously think of giving up in despair. Presently an average markup is applied to a job whether it costs $45 or $450. I can't understand why we don't get a standard cost system in here. But of course, I am leery about using such information to quote jobs since we have gone from buy decisions to make decisions so recently.

All the pricing is still being done by hand by production. We do use the IBM reports and we don't have the situation we had when I came. But still there may be a two-or-three-week lag with sometimes as many as 1,000 documents waiting to be priced.

Under our accounting system, if we ship out 10 pieces from a 20-piece order accounting will hold out costs until the entire order is completed which plays havoc with both the inventories and the cost of goods sold. The Work-in-Process account is also off because if the quantity added hasn't been priced it is listed regardless so you have a situation where total quantities are compared to total partial prices. This results in only one correct balance which is one of quantities not of dollars.

The biggest problem around here is "people who don't know they don't know." Accounting around here is a headquarters function. The controller got his mandate from Cleveland and reports and budgets his time accordingly.

I have gotten into a number of heated discussions with them. If you ask for how many items on an order are left on the floor, where a partial shipment has been made, their answer is: "look at the packing slips." Their attitude is "This is accounting; you are production." If we are two screws off in the inventory, it is up to us to find them despite the fact that the accountants were the people who set up the system and made the counting errors in the first place.

The accounting department never has time to meet to discuss our mutual problems. I can understand that accounting is hard pressed at the end of the month but the controller surely could arrange to spend a few days with us in the middle of the month. Fry is not a factory accountant, but instead is an auditor. His approach too often is that the Navy way is the right way. He rejects our criticisms yet he never gets over to see how we do things. A few trips to the factory would help him (as much as us) by providing him with some on-the-job training regarding our stockroom and production scheduling.

Late in the afternoon, Mr. Salinger went over to talk to Mr. Fry whom he found out with his staff completing a payroll. While waiting, Mr. Salinger idly observed on a table in back of Fry's desk a number of Navy souvenirs and three accounting books.

When Fry came in, Salinger asked how the controller compared his present position to being a supply officer on a ship.

Really quite similar, Fry replied, except here you don't have to consider the personal life of the men as much as you did in the Navy but the general dealing with people is the same.

The controller mentioned he sometimes felt rather isolated in his job— that he "had nobody to talk to" and that the Gothic controller had only been able to manage two visits totaling a day and half in the year and a half since Fry had come to Thurber.

Our problems have continued while you were away. We still depend upon production to furnish us our information for about everything we do. For example, if production doesn't send over the information when they start a job, we can't open a job card to accumulate costs. If we don't receive information to open a job card, it is possible to pick up the discrepancy from the daily labor time cards but this is extremely awkward.

There was a problem with partial shipments also. If we ship out units (where overruns had been made), all the costs would continue in Work-in-Process most likely. I am now planning to minimize this in two ways: by taking a monthly check on the large inventory items, some 25 or 30 items, and also hereafter we will divide jobs into sublots according to the anticipated shipping dates.

Fry reminded Salinger that the practice of overruns (units produced for a job above sale order units) to provide for a high rejection rate had resulted in inflating inventory. Consequently this practice was being discontinued and this would eliminate much of the partial shipments problem since all the units produced would be shipped.

When Mr. Salinger asked why jobs weren't closed promptly in the first place, Fry gave two explanations:

1. Accounting has never emphasized sales and cost of sales as there is no pressure from Gothic to do so.
2. Production is responsible for sending over job close-out information. Such information is usually not sent promptly and sometimes not at all.

The controller reported that he was continuing to work with the IBM

Service Bureau Corporation in order to have all reports furnished promptly.[7] He mentioned that he had to deny Brown's request for a Work-in-Process report on a weekly basis because the cost would be prohibitive. In considering the possibility of a standard cost system some day, he had established cost centers. He concluded by mentioning that with the division's increase in business, his accounting staff was handicapped since production was doing less than they had done previously for accounting despite the increase in production employees.

QUESTIONS

1. Diagram the historical development of accounting controls for Thurber indicating how specific needs were satisfied by specific controls.

2. What should Mr. Salinger recommend, if anything, to:

> Mr. Fry
> Mr. Brown
> Mr. Golding
> International Gothic Company

giving particular attention as how these recommendations should be implemented?

3. Is Mr. Fry's role the same as that of the executive in charge of any staff function, ignoring technical differences?

---

[7] The following are made weekly: Payroll register, deduction register and year-to-date earnings totals; monthly; Work-in-Process detail and summary, closed jobs, closed work and inventory report, purchase balance listing, and direct-indirect labor report; and quarterly, the model analysis.

Chapter Four

GOALS AND STRATEGIES

The management control process takes place within the context of goals, and of strategies for achieving these goals, that have been decided upon in the strategic planning process. The management control process is concerned with the attainment of goals and the implementation of strategies, not with their formulation. A management control system is situational, that is, it is tailored to the particular goals and the particular strategies of the organization. In order to carry out the management control process managers must know what the company's goals and strategies are, and in particular, must understand how they influence the process. Moreover, the systems designer should insure that the control system is consistent with the organization's goals, whatever they are. It is appropriate, therefore, that we discuss the identification of goals and strategies and how they are communicated to those involved in management control, and this is the subject of the first sections of this chapter.

In implementing strategies, an important concept is that of the *key variable.* Key variables are those relatively few variables that must be watched with particular care if the company is to achieve its goals. This topic is discussed in the latter part of the chapter.

GOALS

Goals Distinguished from Objectives

As noted earlier, we use the term *goals* to mean broad, fairly timeless statements of what the organization wants to achieve and the term *objectives* for more specific statements of ends, the achievement of which is contemplated within a specified time period. Others use these terms as synonyms, and still others reverse the meanings given above. Our use is consistent with the etymology of these terms (although abridged dictionaries typically do not distinguish clearly between them), but more importantly, our meaning of "objectives" is consistent with its meaning in "management by objectives," which is a phrase used with increasing frequency in both business and government control systems.

Goals are developed in the strategic planning process, and objectives are used in the management control process. There is the possibility of confusion if a clear distinction between them is not made. They differ with respect to the time period and the degree of specificity.

1. *Time Period.* Goals are usually stated without reference to a time period, whereas objectives are intended to be accomplished by a specified date, sometimes in one year, sometimes in five years or longer. For example, a goal of government is to improve health; the government establishes objectives for medical education, research, insurance programs, construction of health care facilities and the like, each of which is to be attained by a certain time, and each of which presumably contributes toward the broad goal.

2. *Specificity.* Goals are stated in broad, general terms. Objectives are stated in more specific terms, preferably in such a way that there is some measurable basis for determining the extent to which the objective has been achieved. For example, an objective of McDonald's is to open a certain number of additional fast food outlets next year; indeed, its objective may be stated even more specifically in terms of the number of outlets that are to be opened in each geographical area. A company may set as an objective, the attainment of $X million sales volume five years from now. To the extent that objectives are stated in this way, the management control system can measure the degree of their attainment, but if they are vague or ill defined, no system can measure them.

Profitability as a Goal

It is safe to say that an important goal of most businesses is to earn a profit. This statement is too vague to be useful, however. Let us examine some of the possibilities for making it more specific.

A business is owned by its shareholders. They have invested money in the business, and they expect a return on this investment. Profit is a measure of this return. Presumably, the higher the profit, the better off are the shareholders. It follows that, in a general way, a goal of the business should be to earn as high a profit for the shareholders as is feasible. This is a somewhat more specific statement than that given in the preceding paragraph. We should make it even more specific by allowing for the fact that the amount of the shareholders' investment can change, and that the desirable amount of profit is related to the amount of investment at the time the profit is earned. This leads to the conclusion: The higher the profit in relation to the shareholders' investment, the better off are the shareholders. In brief, the name of the game is return on investment.

Two negative conclusions are implied by this relationship. First, it does *not* follow that the higher the *revenue* of the business, the better off are the shareholders. Additional revenue does not automatically generate additional profit for the shareholders. Secondly, it does *not* follow that the higher the *dollars of profit,* or the higher the *profit as a percentage of sales,* the better off are the shareholders. Neither of these measures of profit takes into account the amount of shareholders' investment that was employed in generating the profit.

As an example of these relationships, consider two businesses with results in a given year as follows:

	Business A ($000)	Business B ($000)
Revenue	$10,000	$100,000
Expenses	9,500	90,000
Profit	$ 500	$ 10,000
Investment	4,000	100,000
Return on sales	5%	10%
Return on investment	12.5%	10%

Business B has more revenue than business A, it has earned more dollars of profit than business A, its profit as a percentage of sales is higher than that of business A; but its return on investment is lower than that of business A. Business A has done a better job for its stockholders; it has earned 12.5 cents on every dollar that has been invested in it, while business B has earned only 10 cents.

Revenue, dollars of profit, and return on sales are *inadequate* statements of business goals. Other things being equal, it is desirable to have more revenue rather than less, more profit rather than less, and a higher profit margin rather than a lower one; however, an objective of a business should *not* be to increase revenue if the increase requires a more than offsetting increase in expenses (such as advertising) or in investment (such as inventory), and an objective should *not* be to increase profit or the profit margin, if the increase requires a more than offsetting increase in investment (as sometimes happens when a company acquires a subsidiary at too high a price). Put another way, the objectives of increasing revenue, or of increasing dollars of profit, or of increasing the profit margin are good if, but only if, they increase the return on investment.

It is often useful to think of the economics of a business in terms of the following equation:

$$\frac{\text{Revenue} - \text{Expenses}}{\text{Revenue}} \times \frac{\text{Revenue}}{\text{Investment}} = \text{Return on Investment}$$

For business A, above:

$$\frac{\$10,000 - \$9,500}{\$10,000} \times \frac{\$10,000}{\$4,000} = 12.5\%$$

In this equation, the first term is the profit as a percentage of revenue; for business A, the profit is $500, and the profit is 5 percent of revenue. The second term is called the *capital turnover* in that it shows the number of revenue dollars generated annually by each dollar of investment, in this case the capital turnover is 2.5 times (= $10,000 ÷ $4,000). Thus,

$$\text{Return on Revenue} \times \text{Capital Turnover} = \text{Return on Investment}$$
$$5\% \qquad \times \qquad 2.5 \qquad = 12.5\%$$

A business should try to increase its revenue if it can do so with less than a corresponding increase in expenses or in investment; it should try to reduce expenses if this can be done without decreasing revenue; it should add to its investment if there is a corresponding increase in profits; and so on. The point is that all elements in the equation are related to one another, and it is wrong to focus on one without considering the effect of actions on the others. The only measure that takes into account the net effect of movements in all the elements is return on investment.

Qualifications.   Several qualifications should be made to the foregoing general statement:

1. Regardless of the logic of the above analysis, some managements consciously strive to make their companies bigger, that is, to increase revenue, without too much attention to the ultimate effect of growth on profits. Sheer size is considered to be a measure of success in these companies; the name of the game in such a company is growth, and the management control system should be constructed so that it is consistent with this goal.

2. In some companies, the dominant goal is growth in reported earnings per share of common stock. This goal is similar to, but not necessarily identical with, return on investment. The choice among permissible accounting principles can affect reported earnings. A shift from accelerated depreciation to straight line depreciation in a growing company will ordinarily increase reported earnings, for example. Moreover, earnings per share will tend to be higher in a company that increases the amount of capital behind each share by retaining a relatively large fraction of earnings as compared with a company that pays out most of its earnings as dividends. In companies that seek growth in earnings per share, the management control system should give due regard to such effects.

3. Some companies state their financial goal in terms of "shareholder wealth" or the market price of its stock. This goal considers both earnings per share and the price/earnings multiple. The multiple in turn reflects (among other things) the rate of predicted growth in earnings per share and the stability (predictability) of that growth. Management control systems in such companies include the several variables that are presumed to affect stock prices.

4. Some managements are less willing to take risks than others, and this difference in the degree of risk aversion leads to differences in their actions. The return-on-investment objective is therefore qualified by the attitude toward risk.[1]

---

[1] For discussion of the implications of this point, see John Lintner, "The Impact of Uncertainty on the 'Traditional' Theory of the Firm" in *Industrial Organization & Economic Development,* J. W. Markham and G. F. Papanek, eds. (Boston: Houghton Mifflin Company, 1970), pp. 238–65.

5. The foregoing points are strictly matters of economics. Most companies have social, as well as economic goals, although these are usually difficult to state in a way that permits them to be incorporated in a management control system. They want to be a good place in which to work, they want to be responsible members of the community, they want to contribute to the development of the nation, and they want to behave ethically.

6. Although in the foregoing description "investment" was said to be the *shareholders' investment,* for many purposes it is more useful to think of the total capital supplied to the business, which includes debt capital supplied by creditors as well as the equity capital supplied by shareholders. The sum of debt capital and equity capital is called "capital employed," and return on capital employed is a basic control measure in many management control systems. By lumping both types of capital together, return on capital employed makes it possible to disregard the mix of debt and equity capital; this mix is not relevant in most business decisions relating to the operations of the company, as contrasted with decisions related to financing.

7. By focusing on capital employed, the foregoing implicitly assumes that capital is the single important resource that should govern the company's decisions. This assumption disregards the importance of human resources, the men and women that the company has hired, trained, and formed into a team. Few management control systems take into account the capital value of these human resources, but there is increasing interest in finding feasible ways of doing so. This topic is discussed in Chapter 14.

What Return on Investment?   Although the description of the profit objective is now much more specific than that given at the beginning of this section, it is not yet quite specific enough. Return on investment can be measured in any of several ways. In the illustrations above, it was expressed as a percentage. Actually, a conceptually better way of expressing it is by the number called "residual income." A more complete discussion of this subject will be found in Chapter 8; we do not need to go into it for the purposes of the present chapter.

The Trouble with Profit Maximization.   Most books on the principles of economics, although agreeing with the idea that the dominant goal of a business is return on investment, state this goal more specifically than has been done above. They say that the goal is to *maximize* the return on investment. By this, they have in mind a conceptual framework that is much more specific than the notion "the more profits, the better." According to this framework, businesses set their selling prices and make related output decisions by analyzing the difference between marginal revenue and marginal cost at various volume levels.

There is very little evidence to support the conclusion that businessmen actually behave in the way that the profit maximization model assumes. For example, according to this model, the only relevant costs in setting selling prices are estimates of future marginal costs, yet the General Motors Corporation pricing policy, described in a case accompanying this chapter, uses nonvariable costs, including historical depreciation, in arriving at its prices.

There are two basic reasons why the profit maximization model is not a valid representation of the situation in most companies. First, the model assumes that the business has information that most businesses cannot in fact obtain, principally the shape of the demand curve for its products, and the effect on profits of various amounts of spending for marketing, for research and development, and for other activities for which the causal relationship between effort and results is not known. Second, the model assumes that the businessman will act unethically, for example, that he will charge all that the traffic will bear, and this is an unrealistic assumption. Thus, the profit maximization model is neither feasible nor ethical; the businessman could not use the model if he wanted to, and he would not want to use it if he could.

Satisfactory Return on Investment.   An alternative to the profit maximization model is the *satisfactory return* model. This model is built on the premises that the purpose of a business is to use its resources as efficiently as possible in supplying goods and services to its customers and that the business will compensate equitably those who supply these resources, that is, the shareholders. The satisfactory return model is less precise than the profit maximization model, but the evidence suggests that it is a better reflection of what happens in the real world. It is important that the student consider carefully which of these models seems closer to reality, for each leads to a quite different management control system. For example, in a system based on the profit maximization model, there is no place for the allocation of overhead costs to products, nor for a "normal" profit margin that is added to costs in arriving at a first approximation of selling prices, but these elements are essential parts of a system based on the satisfactory return concept.[2]

The Increasing Return Fallacy.   Earnings per share can be made to increase indefinitely simply by retaining a portion of current profits and thereby providing a larger capital base for each share of stock. A constant increase in earnings per share is therefore a tenable goal. By contrast, some companies state that their goal is to increase the *rate* of return on shareholders' investment. As a short-range objective, in a company whose current rate of return is unsatisfactory, this is sound; but as a statement of a long-range goal, it is foolish. Economic, social, and political pressure set an absolute ceiling on the rate of return on investment, a ceiling which cannot be measured precisely, but which nevertheless exists. It can be breached temporarily by some companies under some unusual circumstances, but any company that sets a goal of a constantly increasing rate of return is kidding itself.

Statement of Goals

A statement about profitability, along the lines discussed above, and a statement about growth, express the *economic* goals of the organization. In

---

[2] For further discussion of this topic, see R. N. Anthony, "The Trouble with Profit Maximization," *Harvard Business Review,* November, 1960, pp. 126–34.

addition, although often unstated, an organization has the fundamental goal of *survival,* and therefore will not knowingly adopt strategies that are so risky that they threaten its very existence. The organization also has social goals which, although difficult to formulate in meaningful words, are appropriately part of its goals.

The list of goals is desirably short. The more numerous they are, the greater the possibility that one criterion will conflict with another when a proposed strategy is being discussed, and this conflict will hamper, rather than assist in, the resolution of the issue. To take an obvious example, if a company states its economic goals to be a 12 percent return on shareholders' investment, a 10 percent return on capital employed, a 10 percent annual increase in earnings per share, and a 10 percent increase in sales volume, a proposed strategy may be consistent with some of these goals, but not with others. Less obviously, some companies state a long list of goals, some of which are little more than platitudes, and a serious attempt to analyze proposed strategies in terms of these criteria can be frustrating. Actually, when the list is long and vague, the tendency is to disregard many of the stated goals when proposed strategies are being analyzed, and such a list therefore serves no useful purpose.

STRATEGIES

Although most companies have the goal of a satisfactory return on investment, each company selects its own paths that it hopes will lead to the achievement of this goal. These paths are its strategies. Although strategies can be classified in various ways, for our purposes, it is sufficient to call them either (1) charters or (2) policies.[3]

Charters   *— Business Definition*

Although most companies' legal charters are written in such broad terms that the company is permitted to engage in any type of lawful economic activity, in practice a company's management draws boundaries around the territory in which it will operate. In a conglomerate these boundaries may be very wide; at the extreme, a company may be willing to enter any industry in which it believes there are promising profit opportunities. One company states, for example, "Our policy is planned profitable growth in any market we can serve well." Few companies, including most conglomerates, have such wide boundaries, however. Most companies state, "We are in the steel business," "We are in the air transport business," or "We are in the food business." Such statements are a beginning for the delineation of the company's charter, but it is desirable that they be made more specific.

Within an industry, each company presumably tries to find the best

---

[3] Some authors include the determination of goals as one component of strategy. See Alfred D. Chandler, Jr., *Strategy and Structure* (Cambridge, Mass.: M.I.T. Press, 1962), p. 13.

niche for itself. (The current marketing term for this is "positioning.") Its decision in this regard is much affected by the personality of its chief executive officer, and is influenced by his background, his drive, and his attitude toward expansion and toward risk taking. The possible permutations are too large to enumerate, but to give an indication: The company can aim at the quality end of a market, at the low-price end, or at the whole spectrum; it can manufacture what it sells, or buy what it sells from vendors, or assemble components that it buys from vendors; it can seek a dominant market share, or accept a steady market share, and so on.

Divisional Charters.   Within the general boundaries set for the company as a whole, charters are established for each division or other principal operating unit. These divisional charters are an important factor in the management control process, for they set limits to divisional planning. In some companies, divisions are permitted to grow and to extend their activities without regard to a specific charter. When this happens, programs of two or more divisions may overlap in an undesirable way. Two divisions may compete against one another in the same market. Or, one division may be counting on orders from another division to fill its production capacity, without knowing that the other division has made plans to obtain its products from another source. Or, an important market segment may be overlooked by all the divisions. Under certain circumstances competition among the divisions is sound practice. For example, the various car divisions of General Motors Corporation compete vigorously with one another. The point is not that such competition be eliminated but rather that it be carried on knowingly, and as a part of the overall strategy of the corporation.

Although divisional charters are set by top management, divisional managers usually participate actively in the process. For various reasons, Division A may wish to invade the territory assigned to Division B, and the Division A manager will argue vigorously the case for doing so. Because the manager of Division B usually does not want his own boundaries to be constricted, he opposes such a move, and top management must then decide.

Policies

In addition to the corporate charter and divisional charters, the strategies also comprise the broad policies that are to govern corporate activities. These policies are essentially constraints within which subordinate managers are expected to operate. They include promotion, transfer, compensation, retirement, and other personnel policies; dividend, debt structure, short-term borrowing and other financial policies; capital investment criteria; quality levels and other product policies; and policies regarding discrimination, pollution, and other social issues. The formulation of policies that are specific enough so that they are more than platitudes, yet broad enough so that they do not unduly restrict the operating manager is a difficult task.

Formulating Strategies

Strategies are intended to remain in force for a reasonably long time. They must, however, be dynamic, for a company's environment changes, and its strategies must be adapted to the current environment. Thinking about strategy is an important top management activity, although not a time consuming activity. (A Cornell University study of how top managers spend their time reports that 2 percent is spent on formulating strategy.) Andrews says that the strategist considers four questions simultaneously: What *might* we do? What *can* we do? What do we *want* to do? and What *should* we do?[4] These questions are addressed in the context of the company's environment as it is currently perceived and taking account of the resources which are, or may be, available to the company. <u>Strategy is a match between environmental opportunities and organizational resources,</u> both as perceived by management.

A few companies have developed systematic approaches to the formulation of strategy. General Electric Company, for example, has developed a model that incorporates the principal factors that, according to its studies, govern return on investment and use this model both to search out strategic opportunities at the corporate level and also to analyze strategies proposed by division managers.[5] Aguilar describes companies that systematically re-examine their environment as a basis for making changes in strategy.[6] Most companies do not make systematic strategic studies. Instead when an opportunity or a threat is identified, it is studied, and the study may lead to a change in strategy. Some of the possibilities originate at corporate headquarters; others originate when a division perceives an opportunity that is outside of its existing charter.

In evaluating present and proposed strategies, the following questions are suggested:[7]

1. Is the strategy identifiable and has it been made clear either in words or practice? (The unstated strategy cannot be tested or contested and is likely therefore to be weak. If it is implicit in the intuition of a strong leader, his organization is likely to be weak and the demands his strategy makes upon it are likely to remain unmet.)

2. Does the strategy exploit fully domestic and international environmental opportunity? (Unless growth is incompatible with the resources of an organi-

---

[4] Kenneth R. Andrews, *The Concept of Corporate Strategy* (Homewood, Ill.: Dow Jones-Irwin, Inc., 1971), page 41.

[5] Sidney Schoeffler, Robert D. Buzzell, and Donald F. Heany, "Impact of Strategic Planning on Profit Performance," *Harvard Business Review,* March–April 1974, pp. 137–45.

[6] Francis J. Aguilar, *Scanning the Business Environment* (New York: The Macmillan Company, 1967).

[7] C. Roland Christensen et al., *Business Policy: Text and Cases* (Homewood, Ill.: Richard D. Irwin, Inc., 1973), pp. 114–17.

zation or the aspirations of its management, it is likely that a strategy that does not purport to make full use of market opportunity will be weak also in other respects. Vulnerability to competition is increased by lack of interest in market share.)

3. Is the strategy consistent with corporate competence and resources, both present and projected? (Although additional resources, both financial and managerial, are available to companies with genuine opportunity, the availability of each must be finally determined and programmed along a practicable time scale.)

4. Are the major provisions of the strategy and the program of major policies of which it is comprised internally consistent? (One advantage of making as specific a statement of strategy as is practicable is the resultant availability of a careful check on coherence, compatibility, and synergy—the state in which the whole can be viewed as greater than the sum of its parts.)

5. Is the chosen level of risk feasible in economic and personal terms? (Strategies vary in the degree of risk willingly undertaken by their designers, but the choice should be made knowingly.)

6. Is the strategy appropriate to the personal values and aspirations of the key managers? (Conflict between the personal preferences, aspirations, and goals of the key members of an organization and the plan for its future is a sign of danger and a harbinger of mediocre performance or failure.)

7. Is the strategy appropriate to the desired level of contribution to society? (Although it can be argued that filling any economic need contributes to the social good, it is clear that a manufacturer of cigarettes might well consider diversification on grounds other than his fear of future legislation.)

8. Does the strategy constitute a clear stimulus to organizational effort and commitment? (Some undertakings are inherently more likely to gain the commitment of able men of goodwill than others. Generally speaking, the bolder the choice of goals and the wider the range of human needs they reflect, the more successfully they will appeal to the capable membership of a healthy and energetic organization.)

9. Are there early indications of the responsiveness of markets and market segments to the strategy? (A strategy may pass with flying colors all the tests so far proposed, but if within a time period made reasonable by the company's resources and the original plan the strategy does not work, then it must be weak in some way that has escaped attention.)

KEY VARIABLES

A management control system is intended to facilitate planning to implement corporate strategies, to motivate managers to achieve corporate goals, and to measure performance toward the achievement of these goals. The system is structured to fit the situation in an individual company, so in its details the system will be unique to that company. Since profitability is a dominant goal in most companies, most systems are designed to measure profitability, but since companies differ as to the exact concept of profitability they find most useful, variations exist even in this basic measure.

In addition to measuring profitability, the system highlights certain variables that have a significant effect on profitability. These are called *key variables*. (Also "strategic factors," "key success factors," "key result areas," and "pulse points.") In most situations, there are relatively few such variables, six being the number most commonly cited. There will be key variables for the organization as a whole and other, perhaps different, key variables for the divisions or other organization units.

Nature of Key Variables

The identification of key variables requires a thorough understanding of the economics of the business. In some cases they can be found by constructing a model of the business and using it to discover the sensitivity of profits to various factors. Usually, however, the variables are uncovered by discussions with persons who have acquired a deep understanding of the business through long experience with it. These persons know intuitively the important things to keep an eye on, and these are the key variables. More specifically, a key variable has the following characteristics:

1. It is *important* in explaining the success or failure of the organization.
2. It is *volatile,* that is, it can change quickly, often for reasons that are not controllable by the manager.
3. *Prompt action* is required when a significant change occurs.
4. The change is *not easy to predict*.
5. The variable can be *measured,* either directly or via a surrogate. For example, *customer satisfaction* cannot be measured directly, but its surrogate, *number of returns* can be a key variable.

One way to attempt to isolate the key variables is to look at the *raison d'etre* of the industry itself, and of the particular firm within that industry. A useful question is, "Why, in a free-enterprise economy, should this company be able to operate at a satisfactory profit?" A hardheaded rethinking of this fundamental question should lead to a careful spelling out of just what functions the company is performing that its customers are willing to pay for. Further thought should then be devoted to the question of why this company, rather than its competitors, is able to attract profitable volume. Then, finally, it may be possible to pinpoint those activities that need to be done particularly well if the company is to enjoy even greater success.

Another approach that may be useful for an analyst who is trying to improve his understanding of the interplay of economic forces on a company is to examine the way in which decisions are made. What decisions does management regard as major ones? What are the factors that management is concerned about in making these decisions? And specifically, for many types of intangible, discretionary expenditures, what will be the source of revenue from which the company will recover this cost and earn a profit? Questions such as these should also eventually lead to the identification of those elements which are critical to the success of a company in a competitive environment.

Exception Variables

In addition to the relatively few key variables, the system provides information on a large number of other variables. A general characteristic of these variables is that no management attention need be paid to them unless they behave in an exceptional manner; thus, they may be called *exception variables*. The cost elements in a factory, both the direct material and direct labor cost and the many elements of overhead cost, normally can be expected to behave as planned. The system is set up so that it calls attention to an item only when there is a significant deviation from plan—the *exception principle*. Under normal circumstances the item need not even be examined or thought about. By contrast, the current behavior of key variables is always reported, and each is scrutinized by management.

Some Key Variables

As noted above, each company determines its own key variables. Nevertheless, some are common to companies generally, and many are common to companies in a given industry. An incomplete list of these is given below, for the purpose of making the key variable concept more concrete. The list is divided into categories, but it should be recognized that there is some overlap between categories. Also, there is no thought that a company selects one or two variables in each category; all the key variables in a given company may well be in the marketing category, for example.

Environmental Variables

The *state of the economy,* as measured by gross national product, leading indicators, or narrower measures that reflect conditions in the particular company's market is obviously significant. Many companies do not consider these measures as key variables *per se,* however. Instead they are used in connection with the marketing variables listed in the next section.

Marketing Variables

Some aspect of marketing effort is a key variable in most businesses, not only because of the need to take prompt action in the marketing area if results are unsatisfactory, but also because of the need to make prompt adjustments in production and other plans if a significant change in the volume of business seems to be on the horizon. Among the specific measures used are the following:

1. Sales.   This item is especially important in retailing and in other businesses in which the customer's action is immediately reflected in sales revenue.

2. Bookings.   In companies that manufacture for future delivery, the nature and volume of sales orders booked is more important than current sales volume, both as an indicator of marketing success and as a warning that other plans may require adjustment.

3. Market Share. Unless market share is watched closely, a deterioration in the company's competitive position can be obscured by a reported increase in sales volume that results from generally favorable business conditions. Automobile dealers report their sales to automobile manufacturers every ten days, and detailed information on market share is published a few days later. In some industries, however, market share is difficult to determine, or can be determined only several months after the fact.

4. Gross Margin Percentage. A change in the average gross margin percentage of a product line may signal a change in the sales mix of products, or in the proportion of sales that cannot be made at regular prices. Either situation can be cause for concern. An increase in off-price sales may be an indication of trouble in the production operation (resulting, e.g., from poor quality or from overproduction of certain styles) as well as in the marketing function itself.

5. Key Account Orders. In companies that sell to retailers, the orders received from certain important accounts—large department stores, discount chains, supermarkets, mail order houses—may provide an early indication of the success of the entire marketing effort. If the company does not get its "fair share" of the business from these accounts, this is a signal of grave trouble with its styling, its pricing, its promotional efforts, or other aspects of its marketing programs.

6. Lost Orders. A variation on the above is the number of customers who should be expected to place orders but who do not.

7. Promotional Indicators. The *renewal rate* on magazine subscriptions, the direct mail *response rate* for companies that rely on direct mail as a marketing tool, the *coupon returns* for companies that use advertisements with coupons, are all indicators of the success of marketing efforts. Because of the difficulty of predicting success and because of the importance of these efforts on profitability, in certain companies variables such as these are watched closely. Some of them, such as the subscription renewal rate for a magazine, may signal a basic weakness in the product rather than in the promotional effort *per se.*

8. New Customers. In organizations such as banks, newspapers, and service establishments that thrive by attracting new customers who, once acquired, tend to provide revenue for a long period of time, the number of such customers is a key variable. In automobile companies, the *owner body,* which is the number of people who now own the company's car, is a similar variable because there is a high probability that these owners will buy the same make of car again.

Production and Logistics Variables

In the ideal world, products would flow through a factory as smoothly and uneventfully as a river normally flows between its banks. But just as floods cause havoc in a watershed, so unexpected events can cause havoc in the factory, or in the distribution network that leads from factory to consumer. Some variables that may warrant special management attention and prompt action if an unsatisfactory situation develops are as follows:

1. Cost Control. In many companies, management can safely assume that actual costs will be in line with standard costs, and it need not pay attention to cost control unless a "red flag" is raised in accordance with the exception principle. In some companies, however, costs must be monitored all the time. This is particularly the case when the profit margin as a percentage of sales is small, as in the case of supermarkets; a small change in costs can have a major impact on profits. *Output per manhour* or *overtime* are indicators of cost control that are key variables in some companies.

2. Capacity Utilization. Unit costs, and hence profits, are strongly influenced by production volume, because of the impact of fixed costs. In part, volume fluctuations are the responsibility of the marketing organization, and are identified by variables listed above, but in part they reflect the ability of production people to schedule properly and to adjust capacity to current requirements. In a professional organization, *sold time,* which measures the percentage of the total available professional hours that is billed to clients, is a key measure of resource utilization. In a hotel, *occupancy rate,* the percentage of rooms occupied each day, is a similar measure. In these and certain other organizations, products cannot be produced for inventory; if available resources are not sold today, they are lost forever. Thus, a measure of capacity utilization is almost always a key variable in such organizations.

3. Backlog. This can be an important indication of the need to change production plans, either in total or for particular items.

4. Quality. In many companies, acceptable quality can be taken for granted. In some, such as aircraft or drug manufacture and the operation of transportation systems of all types, a departure from the highest quality standards can be catastrophic, and some measurement of quality is a key variable. In other companies, such as the manufacture of integrated circuits, the level of quality has a significant effect on unit costs. (If 10 percent of each batch of "chips" is of acceptable quality, unit costs are considerably higher than if the percentage is 90.) *Customer returns* is another measure of quality.

5. Yield. In many process industries, the yield, which is the amount of salable product that is obtained from a given input of raw material, has an important effect on profitability, and prompt action needs to be taken when unexpected changes are reported.

6. Raw Material Costs. If the company's raw materials tend to fluctuate widely in cost, their price movements need to be watched closely, so that appropriate management action can be taken to change inventory levels, change product prices, or adopt alternative product formulations. In such companies, raw material prices are a key variable all the time, and under unusual economic conditions (such as unforeseen inflation) they may temporarily become a key variable in most companies. By contrast, labor costs are rarely a key variable; changes in labor rates occur only annually or semi-annually; these changes can be foreseen, and their consequences can be taken account of without a special signalling system.

7. *On Time Delivery.* In companies in which fulfillment of delivery promises is important and in which delivery on time is difficult, the percentage of shipments that are late is a variable that may warrant special management attention.

Asset Management

Profitability is a function both of income and of the assets employed in generating that income. In some companies, special attention has to be paid to the behavior of assets, particularly current assets.

1. *Inventory.* A decrease in inventory turnover (i.e., inventory related to sales volume) not only is a signal that the return on investment may be decreasing, but it also may indicate the need for special financing, and more importantly it may be a symptom that something is basically wrong with the production process, with the communication between the sales and production departments, or with inventory control procedures. In some companies, *inventory writeoffs* may be a key variable; the amount and nature of the writeoffs can also be symptomatic of serious underlying problems.

2. *Accounts Receivable.* Accounts receivable, as measured by *days' sales on the books,* or in other ways, is a key variable in many companies, for reasons similar to those given to inventory; that is, an unfavorable change will not only have an obvious impact on financing requirements, but also may be a symptom of poor credit policies, financial difficulties of customers, or other more basic problems.

3. *Investment Return.* In banks, insurance companies, and other companies whose profitability is heavily dependent on their ability to make good investments, income earned on investments is a key variable. In banks, the *spread* between income earned and the cost of the money loaned is important. The measurement of investment return is complicated because of the necessity of combining both interest and dividend yield with the effect of market price fluctuations.

We emphasize that the above list is only indicative. Managers have other "pet" key variables that they have developed on the basis of years of experience. In some cases, they cannot even explain the reason why they believe these variables to be important, but if the key variable does the intended job of signalling the need for prompt management action, it is by definition satisfactory.

Pierce-Irwin Corporation

In early November, 1964, Mr. Frank Wood, manager of the Eastern Service Depot (ESD) of the Pierce-Irwin Corporation (PICOR) telephoned one of his former professors at a prominent graduate school of business. Mr. Wood indicated that he had a "measurement problem" and would like a second-year M.B.A. candidate to join his staff during the Christmas holidays to assist him in analyzing and resolving his problem.

Asked to outline the problem, Wood responded: "As you know, one of PICOR's basic objectives is to provide its customers with service second to none. The ESD, as an arm of the marketing function, has the responsibility of satisfying Eastern customer demand for replacement parts for PICOR equipments. We think that it is on the basis of our performance as a service depot that most of our customers evaluate the company's ability to minimize down-time on PICOR equipment and that outstanding service from ESD is crucial to attaining the corporate objective of unequaled service. Our problem, then, is to measure our performance against a stated objective; it's a basic problem in accounting (auditing)."

On December 14, 1964, Mr. Michael B. Allen, the M.B.A. candidate selected to work with PICOR's ESD, met with several members of Mr. Wood's staff. The first days of Allen's association with Picor were devoted to gaining a thorough understanding of the objectives, functions, and procedures of the ESD. Time for investigation and analysis was limited, since Allen was expected to complete his study before Christmas, but both Wood and Allen expected to work to produce fruitful recommendations on the information and analysis required to measure ESD performance against PICOR's stated objective.

PICOR HISTORY

PICOR was founded as a partnership in 1939 in Lowell, Massachusetts. The company's founders, Randolph Pierce and Oscar Irwin, had been impressed by the opportunities that seemed to exist in the field of electronics while they were taking their degrees at M.I.T. After forming the partnership, with assets of $312, Pierce and Irwin designed and built several basic test instruments on a part-time basis. A switch-over to full time production followed the introduction and demonstration of these instruments to several industries in the state of Massachusetts, Rhode Island, Connecticut, and New Hampshire.

The firm was incorporated in 1947, when sales reached $850,000; by 1950, sales reached $1,370,000; and, by 1961, sales totalled $49,600,000. During these first two decades of the company's life, expansion of the product line was Pierce's major interest. In 1964, PICOR had over 200 basic test instruments, principal among which were oscilloscopes, audio-oscillators, vacuum tube voltmeters, noise and distortion analyzers, signal generators, power meters, electronic counters, and waveguide and coaxial instrumentation for microwave work. A continuing objective of the firm was "to provide the market with instruments of the most advanced design and the finest craftmanship for the accurate measurement of electrical phenomena and to support its products with the utmost in customer service and technical service."

Manufacturing facilities were continually expanded to keep pace with the steady growth in volume. In the early 1960s, PICOR operated seven manufacturing facilities, which provided a total of almost 15 acres of floor space. Production facilities were located in Lowell and Holyoke, Massachusetts; Fullterton, California; Denver, Colorado; Dayton, Ohio; Renton, Washington; and Rotterdam, Holland. Marketing operations were carried out throughout the United States and in most of the industrialized countries of the free world.

CORPORATE ORGANIZATION

PICOR's operations were managed through the executive department, with headquarters in Lowell, Massachusetts. Two operating groups were responsible for Manufacturing and Marketing. Manufacturing was responsible for the operation of PICOR's seven plants. Marketing was split into two subdivisions: Sales and Service. The service division included the ESD (in Lowell, Massachusetts), the newly established Western Service Depot (WSD) in San Mateo, California, and the Technical Service Department. The ESD originally served as a centralized warehouse for all replacement parts and components, but, in August of 1964, the WSD was established. The service depots were then organized to satisfy demand for replacement parts and components for customers in their assigned regions. The field sales organization was broken into six regional divisions (see Exhibit 1 for a schematic diagram of the firm's functional organization): Western, Northeastern, Central, Southern, European, and Asia. Each of these six regional sales divisions had two or more sales offices located in key marketing cen-

Exhibit 1

PIERCE-IRWIN CORPORATION

Schematic Organization Chart

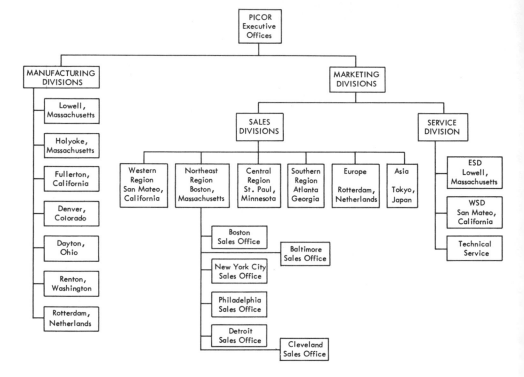

ters. There were 18 sales offices in the United States and six sales offices in Europe and Asia. The ESD filled replacement orders of customers served by the northeastern, central, southern, and European regional sales divisions; WSD served the western and Asia regional sales divisions.

During an average month, ESD would ship approximately $300,000 worth of parts in response to some 6,000 orders. The median order was for less than $40 and over 50 percent of the incoming orders requested only one line-item.

ESD OPERATIONS

Mr. Wood noted that though the ESD was considered a profit center and was partially evaluated by PICOR executives on the basis of its profitability, its prime function was to minimize the time lag between the point at which the customer recognized a need for a replacement part and the delivery of the replacement to the customer's plant. Expanding on this objective, Wood explained that "as long as the customer feels his down-time was at a reasonable minimum and less than would have been experienced in dealing with

PICOR's competition, we have fulfilled our function as a service depot. In other words, when we say our objective is to minimize the time lag, we really mean 'provide the minimum available time lag.' Now, in translating the corporate objective of service second to none into time minimization, we're making one crucial assumption about our customers: namely, that they order replacement parts on the basis of an immediate need."

Allen questioned the significance of this assumption: "Even if the bulk of ESD activity is occasioned by stocking orders, aren't we providing outstanding service by minimizing lead times, providing a stable lead-time history, and proving to our customers that they need not invest heavily in replacement parts for PICOR equipment?"

Asked about the tradeoff between functioning as a profit center and satisfying the service objective, Wood remarked: "We're prepared to lose money on individual transactions. Otherwise, we wouldn't bother filling the 35 cent orders. But we feel that overall, ESD can show a contribution to corporate profit and overhead and still provide the best service in the industry. The ESD is not, of course, a profit-maximizing division; our role is to provide the marketing function with a convincing, crucial sales argument in favor of PICOR instruments so as to improve the profitability of the company as a whole. When we budget our operation, there's no pressure to sacrifice service for divisional margins; the exercise is always based on the assumption that we are a service activity which, happily enough, more than covers its direct costs."

PICOR encouraged its customers to deal solely with their local sales offices. Orders for replacement parts were usually placed with the local sales office. The sales office prepared the PICOR documentation (see Exhibit 2, a flow chart of the order processing). The sales office handled all customer contact with almost no exceptions: (1) parts were shipped directly from the service depot to the customer's specified receiving location; (2) if an item were back ordered at the service depot, a note indicating delayed shipment would be sent directly from the service depot to the sales office; and (3) when back-ordered items were shipped, a shipping notice would be sent to the sales office. The service depot executed virtually all its actions on a PICOR invoice prepared at the sales office. In the event of a stock-out condition at the service depot, a back-order notice would be prepared in order to insure expediting of the restocking and shipment of the parts.

The service depot specified the mode of shipment in virtually all cases (the only exception was in the rare event the customer did specify mode of shipment) and bore all transportation charges. The decision as to mode of shipment was based on a standing policy of least-time delivery to the customer's specified receiving station. ESD and WSD used air freight in all instances in which other modes of shipment from their location were less rapid, except when the customer specified a delivery date that permitted use of low-cost shipping.

Stocking decisions at the service depots were based on analysis of demand

Exhibit 2

PIERCE-IRWIN CORPORATION

**Simplified Order Processing
Flow Chart**

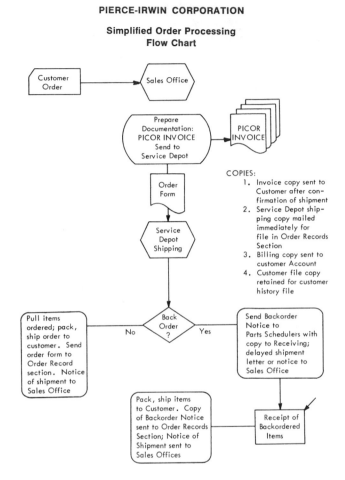

COPIES:

1. Invoice copy sent to Customer after confirmation of shipment
2. Service Depot shipping copy mailed immediately for file in Order Records Section
3. Billing copy sent to customer Account
4. Customer file copy retained for customer history file

history, demand forecasts, and EOQ calculations (which included estimated stock-out costs based on an ABC analysis of historical and forecast demand).

ESD PERFORMANCE SAMPLING

In attempting to measure the service level achieved by ESD, Wood had initiated the "Friday Sample" in 1962. The Friday Sample attempted to measure the percentage of orders shipped on the same day as the order was received. At the close of business each Friday, Wood assembled copies of the order forms received at ESD during the week. The number shipped same day was divided by total number received during the week to develop a "Same Day" performance index. Wood indicated that the index varied between

90 percent and 95 percent, indicating that ESD was shipping that percentage of orders on the same day the order was received. This ESD Performance Rating was prominently displayed throughout the ESD building.

On the first Friday with PICOR, Allen remained after normal closing hours, chatting with the manager of the shipping section. The full work force remained to work overtime for nearly an hour. Allen asked the shipping section manager about the overtime work, and received the following reply: "We work about an hour overtime every Friday to make sure that we don't have a backlog of leftover orders on Monday morning. If we had a big backlog, we'd have to clean that up before we started filling Monday's orders, and then the performance index would drop way down. Mr. Wood wants each week's work load to be 'normal,' whatever that means."

On Wednesday, December 16, Allen and Wood met to discuss Allen's project. In response to Allen's first question, Wood ruled out the possibility of directly contacting customers or PICOR competitors in any survey work. Wood indicated that he was interested in measuring (1) ESD's efficiency in processing orders that could be filled from stock (this was the purpose of the Friday Sample); (2) the impact of each link in the order processing chain (customer to sales office to ESD to customer) on the speed with which customer orders were filled; and (3) the significance of back-ordered items to PICOR customers and to PICOR. Wood indicated that he recognized the impact of nonrandom selection of the day for the ESD weekly performance survey.

Wood and Allen focused their attention on the different kinds of measures that might be used. Wood's performance rating had dealt with orders. Allen suggested alternative measures of efficiency, remarking that "counting the number of times separate line-items are requested gives us one measure of customer demand. Dollar value, or inventory cost, or number of units, or number of customers submitting an order may be equally significant measures of our activity. We may fill 90 percent of the orders received; but analyzing the 10 percent we back order, we may find 10 percent of the customers who submitted orders that day, or we might find the back-order delays running two weeks. These other indicators may provide a more meaningful measure of customer satisfaction. The percentage of requests filled the same day provides a good measure of ESD efficiency, but when I took this job, you indicated an interest in measuring the extent to which ESD met the objective of providing good service. Have we changed our minds? Or, have we made a simplifying assumption that internal efficiency is identical with providing good service as measured by customer satisfaction?"

"If we can't go to the customer and if we can't find out what kind of service the competition is providing, we at least ought to be able to develop some measure of the level of service—as opposed to the efficiency of the ESD."

Wood responded by saying, "Mike, you've got a good point. We want to operate efficiently, but our major objective is providing service. Perhaps it would be well if we both put our feet on our desk this afternoon and tried to figure out just what we can measure in order to evaluate our service level. Take back orders for instance: the customer is interested in how long he has to wait; if price has anything to do with value, service might be measured by the dollar value of back-ordered items; or, if we assume price and time are both relevant, we'd want a measure of the dollar-days back ordered, wouldn't we? Or, perhaps the percentage of customers who placed orders that receive back-order notices each day would be a good indicator, suggesting revision of our stock'ng policy if that number shows an uptrend. Now, that's useful because it not only tells us about our ability to fill orders for customers but it also gives us a place to look if we feel our performance is either below par or deteriorating."

Allen commented: "Are we agreed, then, that we want to evaluate both efficiency and service level? and that in measuring efficiency we can define an 'optimum' system and measure our through-put time against the optimum? and . . . "

Wood interrupted: "Wait a minute, Mike. I thought we were going to use some variation of the ESD Performance Rating to measure efficiency. Through-put is tough to define because we only operate on a one-shift basis."

Allen responded: "I guess that's right, Mr. Wood. But now, in evaluating our service level, we want to define service in such a way that it's measurable on the basis of internally available data. We've got a number of variables: days, customers, orders, dollars, units, line-items. And these can be put together in almost any variation or combination. I'm going to have to bat those combinations and variations around for awhile; but I'll see if I can't come up with some way to measure service, using those variables, against historical levels of service, measured the same way."

Wood concluded the discussion by commending Allen on the amount of insight he had gained and by offering one word of warning: "Watch out for the fallacy of looking at dollars too hard. The price of the part may be no measure of its value to the customer—remember the old arguments about 'for the want of a nail, a shoe was lost; for the want of a man, the battle was lost;' and so on. If our customer's electronic counter is out of commission, the opportunity cost may be many times the price of parts to repair it; and it's really the customer's opportunity cost we want to minimize."

QUESTION

As Allen, prepare the procedure(s) you will recommend to Mr. Wood to achieve his objectives.

Case 4–2

General Motors Corporation*

In an article in the *NACA Bulletin*, January 1, 1927, Albert Bradley described the pricing policy of General Motors Corporation. At that time, Mr. Bradley was general assistant treasurer; subsequently, he became vice-president, executive vice-president, and chairman of the board. There is reason to believe that current policy is substantially the same as that described in the 1927 statement. The following description consists principally of excerpts from Mr. Bradley's article.

GENERAL POLICY

Return on investment is the basis of the General Motors policy in regard to the pricing of product. The fundamental consideration is the average return over a protracted period of time, not the specific rate of return over any particular year or short period of time. This long-term rate of return on investment represents the official viewpoint as to the highest average rate of return that can be expected consistent with a healthy growth of the business, and may be referred to as the economic return attainable. The adjudged necessary rate of return on capital will vary as between separate lines of industry as a result of differences in their economic situations; and within each industry there will be important differences in return on capital resulting primarily from the relatively greater efficiency of certain producers.

The fundamental policy in regard to pricing product and expansion of the business also necessitates an official viewpoint as to the normal average rate of plant operation. This relationship between assumed normal average rate of operation and practical annual capacity is known as standard volume.

The fundamental price policy is completely expressed in the conception of standard volume and economic return attainable. For example, if it is the accepted policy that standard volume represents 80 percent of practical an-

---

* This case was prepared from published material.

nual capacity, and that an average of 20 percent per annum must be earned on the operating capital, it becomes possible to determine the standard price of a product—that is, that price which with plants operating at 80 percent of capacity will produce an annual return of 20 percent on the investment.

STANDARD VOLUME

Costs of production and distribution per unit of product vary with fluctuation in volume because of the fixed or nonvariable nature of some of the expense items. Productive materials and productive labor may be considered costs which are 100 percent variable, since within reasonable limits the aggregate varies directly with volume, and the cost per unit of product therefore remains uniform.

Among the items classified as manufacturing expense or burden there exist varying degrees of fluctuation with volume, owing to their greater or lesser degree of variability. Among the absolutely fixed items are such expenses as depreciation and taxes, which may be referred to as 100 percent fixed, since within the limits of plant capacity the aggregate will not change, but the amount per unit of product will vary in inverse ratio to the output.

Another group of items may be classified as 100 percent variable, such as inspection and material handling; the amount per unit of product is unaffected by volume. Between the classes of 100 percent fixed and 100 percent variable is a large group of expense items that are partially variable, such as light, heat, power, and salaries.

In General Motors Corporation, standard burden rates are developed for each burden center, so that there will be included in costs a reasonable average allowance for manufacturing expense. In order to establish this rate, it is first necessary to obtain an expression of the estimated normal average rate of plant operation.

Rate of plant operation is affected by such factors as general business conditions, extent of seasonal fluctuation in sales likely within years of large volume, policy with respect to seasonal accumulation of finished and/or semifinished product for the purpose of leveling the production curve, necessity or desirability of maintaining excess plant capacity for emergency use, and many others. Each of these factors should be carefully considered by a manufacturer in the determination of size of a new plant to be constructed, and before making additions to existing plants, in order that there may be a logical relationship between assumed normal average rate of plant operation and practical annual capacity. The percentage accepted by General Motors Corporation as its policy in regard to the relationship between assumed normal rate of plant operation and practical annual capacity is referred to as standard volume.

Having determined the degree of variability of manufacturing expense, the established total expense at the standard volume rate of operations can be estimated. A *standard burden rate* is then developed which represents the proper absorption of burden in costs at standard volume. In periods of low volume, the unabsorbed manufacturing expense is charged directly against profits as unabsorbed burden, while in periods of high volume, the over-absorbed manufacturing expense is credited to profits, as overabsorbed burden.

RETURN ON INVESTMENT

Factory costs and commercial expenses for the most part represent outlays by the manufacturer during the accounting period. An exception is depreciation of capital assets which have a greater length of life than the accounting period. To allow for this element of cost, there is included an allowance for depreciation in the burden rates used in compiling costs. Before an enterprise can be considered successful and worthy of continuation or expansion, however, still another element of cost must be reckoned with. This is the cost of capital, including an allowance for profit.

Thus, the calculation of standard prices of products necessitates the establishment of standards of capital requirement as well as expense factors, representative of the normal average operating condition. The standard for capital employed in fixed assets is expressed as a percentage of factory cost, and the standards for working capital are expressed in part as a percentage of sales, and in part as a percentage of factory cost.

The calculation of the standard allowance for fixed investment is illustrated by the following example.

```
Investment in plant and other fixed assets ...............$15,000,000
Practical annual capacity ...............................   50,000 units
Standard volume, per cent of practical annual capacity .....    80 %
Standard volume equivalent (50,000 × 80%) ..............   40,000 units
Factory cost per unit at standard volume .................    $1,000
Annual factory cost of production at standard volume
  (40,000 × $1,000) ....................................$40,000,000
Standard factor for fixed investment (ratio of investment
  to annual factory cost of production; $15,000,000 ÷
  $40,000,000) ........................................     0.375
```

The amount tied up in working capital items should be directly proportional to the volume of business. For example, raw materials on hand should be in direct proportion to the manufacturing requirements—so many days' supply of this material, so many days' supply of that material, and so on—depending on the condition and location of sources of supply, transportation conditions, etc. Work in process should be in direct proportion to the requirements of finished production, since it is dependent on the length of time required for the material to pass from the raw to the finished state, and the amount of labor and other charges to be absorbed in the process. Finished product should be in direct proportion to sales requirements. Accounts receivable should be in direct proportion to sales, being dependent on terms of payment and efficiency of collections.

THE STANDARD PRICE

These elements are combined to construct the standard price as shown in Exhibit 1. Note that the economic return attainable (20 percent in the illustration) and the standard volume (80 percent in the illustration) are long-run figures and are rarely changed;[1] the other elements of the price are based on current estimates.

Exhibit 1

ILLUSTRATION OF METHOD OF DETERMINATION OF STANDARD PRICE

	In Relation to	Turnover Per Year	Ratio to Sales Annual Basis	Ratio to Factory Cost Annual Basis
Cash	Sales	20 times	0.050	—
Drafts and accounts receivable. . .	Sales	10 times	0.100	—
Raw material and work in process	Factory cost	6 times	—	0.16⅔
Finished product	Factory cost	12 times	—	0.08⅓
Gross working capital			0.150	0.250
Fixed investment			—	0.375
Total investment			0.150	0.625
Economic return attainable, 20%			—	—
Multiplying the investment ratio by this, the necessary net profit margin is arrived at			0.030	0.125
Standard allowance for commercial expenses, 7%			0.070	—
Gross margin over factory cost			0.100	0.125
			a	b

$$\text{Selling price, as a ratio to factory cost} = \frac{1+b}{1-a} = \frac{1+0.125}{1-0.100} = 1.250$$

If standard cost = $1,000
Then standard price = $1,000 × 1.250 = $1,250

---

[1] A Brookings Institution Survey reported that the principal pricing goal of General Motors Corporation in the 1950's was 20 percent on investment after taxes. See Lanzillotti, "Pricing Objectives in Large Companies," *American Economic Review*, December, 1958.

DIFFERENCES AMONG PRODUCTS

Responsibility for investment must be considered in calculating the standard price of each product as well as in calculating the overall price for all products, since products with identical accounting costs may be responsible for investments that vary greatly. In the illustration given below, a uniform standard selling price of $1,250 was determined. Let us now suppose that this organization makes and sells two products, A and B, with equal manufacturing costs of $1,000 per unit and equal working capital requirements, and that 20,000 units of each product are produced. However, an analysis of fixed investment indicates that $10 million is applicable to product A, while only $5 million of fixed investment is applicable to product B. Each product must earn 20 percent on its investment in order to satisfy the standard condition. Exhibit 2 illustrates the determination of the standard price for product A and product B.

From this analysis of investment, it becomes apparent that product A, which has the heavier fixed investment, should sell for $1,278, while product B should sell for only $1,222, in order to produce a return of 20 percent on the investment. Were both products sold for the composite average standard price of $1,250, then product A would not be bearing its share of the investment burden, while product B would be correspondingly overpriced.

Differences in working capital requirements as between different products may also be important due to differences in manufacturing methods, sales terms, merchandising policies, etc. The inventory turnover rate of one line of products sold by a division of General Motors Corporation may be six times a year, while inventory applicable to another line of products is turned over thirty times a year. In the second case, the inventory investment required per dollar cost of sales is only one-fifth of that required in the case of the product with the slower turnover. Just as there are differences in capital requirements as between different classes of product, so may the standard requirements for the same class of product require modification from time to time due to permanent changes in manufacturing processes, in location of sources of supply, more efficient scheduling and handling of materials, etc.

The importance of this improvement to the buyer of General Motors products may be appreciated from the following example. The total inventory investment for the 12 months ended September 30, 1926, would have averaged $182,490,000 if the turnover rate of 1923 (the best performance prior to 1925) had not been bettered, or an excess of $74,367,000 over the actual average investment. In other words, General Motors would have been compelled to charge $14,873,000 more for its products during this 12-month period than was actually charged if prices had been established to yield, say, 20 percent on the operating capital required.

Exhibit 2

VARIANCES IN STANDARD PRICE DUE TO VARIANCES IN RATE OF CAPITAL TURNOVER

	Product A		Product B		Total Product (A plus B)	
	Ratio to Sales Annual Basis	Ratio to Factory Cost Annual Basis	Ratio to Sales Annual Basis	Ratio to Factory Cost Annual Basis	Ratio to Sales Annual Basis	Ratio to Factory Cost Annual Basis
Gross working capital	0.150	0.250	0.150	0.250	0.150	0.250
Fixed investment	—	0.500	—	0.250	—	0.375
Total investment	0.150	0.750	0.150	0.500	0.150	0.625
Economic return attainable, 20%	—		—		—	
Multiplying the investment ratio by this, the necessary net profit margin is arrived at	0.030	0.150	0.030	0.100	0.030	0.125
Standard allowance for commercial expenses, 7%..	0.070	—	0.070	—	0.070	—
Gross margin over factory cost	0.100	0.150	0.100	0.100	0.100	0.125
	a	b	a	b	a	b
Selling price, as a ratio to $\left.\begin{array}{c}\\\\\end{array}\right\} = \dfrac{1+b}{1-a}$ Factory cost	$\dfrac{1.+0.150}{1.-0.100} = 1.278$		$\dfrac{1.+0.100}{1.-0.100} = 1.222$		$\dfrac{1.+0.125}{1.-0.100} = 1.250$	
If standard cost equals		$1,000		$1,000		$1,000
Then standard price equals		$1,278		$1,222		$1,250

CONCLUSION

The analysis as to the degree of variability of manufacturing and commercial expenses with increases or decreases in volume of output, and the establishment of "standards" for the various investment items, makes it possible not only to develop "Standard Prices," but also to forecast, with much greater accuracy than otherwise would be possible, the capital requirements, profits, and return on capital at the different rates of operation, which may result from seasonal conditions or from changes in the general business situation. Moreover, whenever it is necessary to calculate in advance the final effect on net profits of proposed increases or decreases in price, with their resulting changes in volume of output, consideration of the real economics of the situation is facilitated by the availability of reliable basic data.

It should be emphasized that the basic pricing policy stated in terms of the economic return attainable is a policy, and it does not absolutely dictate the specific price. At times, the actual price may be above, and at other times below, the standard price. The standard price calculation affords a means not only of interpreting actual or proposed prices in relation to the established policy, but at the same time affords a practical demonstration as to whether the policy itself is sound. If the prevailing price of product is found to be at variance with the standard price other than to the extent due to temporary causes, it follows that prices should be adjusted; or else, in the event of conditions being such that prices cannot be brought into line with the standard price, the conclusion is necessarily drawn that the terms of the expressed policy must be modified.[2]

QUESTIONS

1. An article in the *Wall Street Journal*, December 10, 1957, gave estimates of cost figures in "an imaginary car-making division in the Ford-Chevrolet-Plymouth field." Most of the data given below are derived from that article. Using these data, compute the standard price. Working capital ratios are not given; assume that they are the same as those in Exhibit 1.

```
Investment in plant and other fixed assets ...................$600,000,000
Required return on investment.........30% before income taxes
Practical annual capacity ......................... 1,250,000
Standard volume—assume ........................   80%
```

---

[2] This paragraph is taken from an article by Donaldson Brown, then vice-president, finance, General Motors Corporation, in *Management and Administration*, March, 1924.

Factory cost per unit:
Outside purchases of parts ....$ 500*
   Parts manufactured inside 600*
   Assembly labor 75
   Burden 125
     Total $1,300

* Each of these items includes $50 of labor costs.

"Commercial cost," corresponding to the 7 percent in Exhibit 1, is added as a dollar amount, and includes the following:

Inbound and outbound freight ....$ 85
Tooling and engineering   50
Sales and advertising   50
Administrative and miscellaneous   50
Warranty (repairs within guarantee)   15
     Total ....$ 250

Therefore, the 7 percent commercial allowance in Exhibit 1 should be eliminated, and in its place $250 should be added to the price as computed from the formula.

2. What would happen to profits and return on investment before taxes in a year in which volume was only 60 percent of capacity? What would happen in a year in which volume was 100 percent of capacity? Assume that nonvariable costs included in the $1,550 unit cost above are $350 million; i.e., variable costs are $1,550 − $350 = $1,200. In both situations, assume that cars were sold at the standard price established in Question 1, since the standard price is not changed to reflect annual changes in volume.

3. In the 1975 model year, General Motors gave cash rebates of as high as $300 per car off the list price. In 1972 and 1973 prices had been restricted by price control legislation, which required that selling prices could be increased only if costs had increased. Selling prices thereafter were not controlled, although there was always the possibility that price controls could be reimposed. In 1975, demand for automobiles was sharply lower than in 1974, partly because of a general recession and partly because of concerns about high gasoline prices. Does the cash rebate indicate that General Motors adopted a new pricing policy in 1975, or is it consistent with the policy described in the case?

4. Is this policy good for General Motors? Is it good for America?

Case 4–3

General Electric Company (A)

The General Electric Company is a large, multilocation corporation engaged in the manufacture and marketing of a wide variety of electrical and allied products. In 1964, there were almost 400 separate product lines and over three million catalog items. Sales volume in that year totaled $4,941 million, and net income was $237 million. Total employment was about 262,000.

Early in the 1950's, General Electric initiated an extensive decentralization of authority and responsibility for the operations of the company. The basic unit of organization became the product department. As of 1964, there were over 100 of these departments.

The company recognized that if this decentralization was to be fully effective it would need an improved system of management control. It also recognized that any improved system of control would require better measures of performance. To meet this need, the company established a measurements project and created a special organizational unit to carry out this project. This case summarizes the main features of this project, with particular emphasis on measuring performance of the operating (i.e., product) departments.

THE MEASUREMENTS PROJECT

The measurements project was established in 1952. Responsibility for the project was assigned to accounting services, one of the corporate func-

---

NOTE: With the exception of the statistical information and publicly known facts presented in the introduction of this case, the sources for the facts making up the body of this case are William T. Jerome, III, *Executive Control—The Catalyst* (New York: John Wiley & Sons, Inc., 1961), pp. 217–37; and Robert W. Lewis, "Measuring, Reporting and Appraising Results of Operations with Reference to Goals, Plans and Budgets," *Planning, Managing and Measuring the Business,* A Case Study of Management Planning and Control at General Electric Company (New York: Controllership Foundation, Inc., 1955).

tional services divisions. A permanent organizational unit, initially called measurements service, was set up to carry out this project.

An early step in the measurements project was the development of a set of principles by which the project was to be governed. Five such principles were formulated:

1. Measurements were to be designed to measure the performance of *organizational components*, rather than of *managers*.

2. Measurements were to involve common *indexes* of performance, but not common *standards* of performance. (For example, rate of return on investment might be the index of performance common to all product departments, but the standard in terms of this index might be 12 percent for one department and 25 percent for another.)

3. Measurements were to be designed as aids to judgment in appraisal of performance, and not to supplant judgment.

4. Measurements were to give proper weight to future performance as well as current performance, in order to facilitate the maintenance of a balance between the long run and the near term.

5. Measurements were to be selected so as to facilitate constructive action, not to restrict such action.

The overall measurements project was divided into three major subprojects:

1. Operational measurements of the results of a product department.

2. Functional measurements of the work of engineering, manufacturing, marketing finance, employee and plant community relations, and legal components of the organization.

3. Measurements of the work of managing as such—planning, organizing, integrating, and measuring itself.

The first step in the subproject on operational measurements was to develop an answer to the following question:

What are the specific areas for which measurements should be designed, bearing in mind that sound measurements of overall performance require a proper balance among the various functions and among the aspects (planning, organizing, for example) of managing?[1]

In seeking an answer to this question, the organization made a careful analysis of the nature and purposes of the basic kinds of work performed by each functional unit with the purpose of singling out those functional objectives that were of sufficient importance to the welfare of the business[2] as a whole, to be termed "key result areas."

---

[1] Lewis, *op. cit.*, p 30.

[2] The word "business" is used here to refer to a product department, not to the whole company.

THE KEY RESULT AREAS

In order to determine whether an area tentatively identified according to the preceding analytical framework was sufficiently basic to qualify as a key result area, the organization established a criterion in the form of the following test question:

Will continued failure in this area prevent the attainment of management's responsibility for advancing General Electric as a leader in a strong, competitive economy, even though results in all other key areas are good?[3]

As an outcome of analysis and application of this test, eight key result areas were decided on. These were as follows:

1. Profitability.
2. Market position.
3. Productivity.
4. Product leadership.
5. Personnel development.
6. Employee attitudes.
7. Public responsibility.
8. Balance between short-range and long-range goals.

Each of these key result areas is described below.

Profitability

The key index used by General Electric to measure profitability was "dollars of residual income." Residual income was defined as net profit after taxes, less a capital charge. The capital charge was a certain percentage (say, 6 percent) of the net assets assigned to the department; it corresponded to an imputed interest charge. The criteria formulated to guide the development of a satisfactory measure of profitability were expressed as follows:

1. An index that recognized the contribution of capital investment to profits.
2. An index that recognized what human work and effort contribute to profits.
3. An index that recognized the "corporate facts of life" (e.g., one consistent with General Electric's needs and organizational objectives).
4. An index that served to make the operating decisions of individual managers in the company's best interests.

In the process of selecting and developing a measure of profitability, the measurements organization considered several more conventional indices, including rate of return on investment, ratio of profit to sales, and ratio of profit to value added. A weakness of these ratios or indices was stated in this way:

---

[3] *Ibid.*, p. 30.

. . . the acid test of an index should be its effectiveness in guiding decentralized management to make decisions in the best interests of the company overall, since operating managers' efforts naturally will be to improve the performance of their businesses in terms of the index used for evaluation. This test points up the particular weakness of rate of return and of other ratio indexes, such as per cent profit to sales. This weakness is the tendency to encourage concentration on improvement of the *ratios* rather than on improvement in *dollar* profits. Specifically, the business with the better results in terms of the ratios will tend to make decisions based on the effect the decisions will have on the particular business's current *ratio* without consideration of the *dollar* profits involved. This tends to retard incentive to growth and expansion because it dampens the incentive of the more profitable businesses to grow.[4]

Market Position

Performance in this key result area was measured in terms of the share of the market obtained during a given measurement period. The measurement was expressed as a percentage of available business in the market. Market, as used in this sense, was expressed in dollars or units, kilowatt-ampere, or other meaningful terms.

The first major consideration in designing market position measurements is a determination of what constitutes a product line and what constitutes the market for each product line of a business. A product line may be defined as a grouping of products in accordance with the purposes they serve or the essential wants they satisfy. The definition is somewhat misleading in that a product line may be a broad classification, such as clocks, or it may be a narrow classification, such as alarm clocks, kitchen clocks, or mantel clocks. In addition, product lines may overlap so that a particular product could be included in several product lines. Hence, the actual grouping of products by product lines must be accurately identified.

There may be wide variations in the interpretation of what constitutes the market for a given product line. Therefore, it is important that for each of their lines, our product departments identify such things as:

1. Whether the market includes not only directly competing products but also indirectly competing products (electric ranges versus electric ranges; electric ranges versus all types of ranges—electric, gas, oil, and others).
2. Whether the market includes sales by all domestic competitors or only those reporting to trade associations.
3. Whether the market includes imports, if foreign sellers are competing in the domestic market.
4. Whether the market includes export sales.
5. Whether the market includes captive sales.
6. Whether the market is considered to be represented by sales to distributors, or to retailers, or to ultimate users.

---

[4] *Ibid.*, p. 32.

In other words, in establishing measurements of market position there should be a clear understanding of precisely what comprises the product line and what comprises the market. The purpose of having sharp definitions of these two items is, of course, to avoid being misled into thinking we are doing better than we actually are simply because of failure to identify the nature and extent of our competition.[5]

Productivity

Although the concept of productivity is a relatively simple one—a relationship of output of goods and services to the resources consumed in their production—this concept proved a difficult one to make operational as a measure of performance. For the national economy as a whole, it has been the practice to look at productivity simply in terms of the amount of output per unit of labor input. In any given firm, however, labor is only one of the factors contributing to output. Therefore, the company sought to develop an index that would accomplish two things: (1) broaden the input base so as to recognize that capital as well as labor contributed to improvements in productivity, and (2) eliminate from the measure those improvements contributed by suppliers of materials.

On the output side of the productivity ratio, the company considered several refinements of sales billed. One such refinement was the use of value added (e.g., sales billed less the cost of goods or services acquired outside the company). On the input side, the company considered payroll dollars plus depreciation dollars. Payroll dollars were employed as the variable, rather than labor hours, so as to give effect to differences in the labor skills employed. The inclusion of depreciation charges constituted an attempt to include the consumption of capital resources. All factors were to be readjusted for changes in the price level, so that changes in the resulting ratio would more nearly reflect real changes in productivity.

Product Leadership

Product leadership was defined as "the ability of a business to lead its industry in originating or applying the most advanced scientific and technical knowledge in the engineering, manufacturing and marketing fields to the development of new products and to improvements in the quality or value of existing products."[6] To make this definition operational, procedures were established for appraising periodically the products of each department. These appraisals were directed at providing answers to the following questions:

1. How did each product compare with competition and with company standards?

2. Where within the company was the research conducted upon which the product was based?

---

[5] *Ibid.,* p. 33.
[6] *Ibid.,* pp. 35–36.

3. Who first introduced the basic product and subsequent improvements, General Electric or a competitor?

The appraisal procedures were based largely on qualitative rather than quantitative considerations. Appraisals were made by appropriate experts from the areas of engineering, marketing, accounting, and manufacturing. In general, these experts were located within the product department for which the appraisal was to be made. Standard forms were employed so as to facilitate as high a degree of consistency as possible. The trends revealed by these appraisals over a period of time were considered to be as significant as the specific information revealed by an appraisal for a particular period.

Personnel Development

For the purposes of measurement, personnel development was defined as "the systematic training of managers and specialists to fill present and future needs of the company, to provide for further individual growth and retirements and to facilitate corporate growth and expansion."[7] Management of General Electric defined personnel development as including "programs in each field of functional endeavor, such as engineering, manufacturing, marketing and finance, and broad programs aimed at developing an understanding of the principles of managing. Such programs must be designed to provide a continuous flow of potentially promotable employees in sufficient numbers to permit proper selection and development of individuals for each position. And, at the same time, these programs must encourage competition and initiative for further individual growth."[8]

Three steps were involved in the measurement of performance in this key result area. (1) The basic soundness of the various programs or techniques being sponsored by a product department for the development of its employees was appraised. (2) An inventory was taken of the available supply of trained men, as well as their qualifications, for the key positions that must eventually be filled within the department. (3) The effectiveness with which the department executed its personnel development programs was evaluated.

The first step consisted of judgments regarding the adequacy of the following elements in the development process.

Recruitment. How good a job was being done in the selection of candidates for the development process?

On-the-job training. What programs were available for training candidates, for providing information and knowledge about both general company matters and job particulars, and for advanced training for those who had been on the job for a while?

Review and counsel. Was there any provision for periodically reviewing the

---

[7] *Ibid.,* p. 37.
[8] *Ibid.*

performance of the men, for discussing with an individual the caliber of his work, for providing help and consultation, and for identifying especially promising talent?

Placement. What was being done to see that recruits were placed in jobs commensurate with their interests and abilities, that the more promising were rotated, and that promotions came to those who merited them?

The second step was accomplished with the aid of manning tables and related inventorying procedures. These procedures were directed primarily at determining the training background of each man in the inventory; i.e., graduates of company-sponsored programs, those hired from outside the company, and those who attained their positions without the benefit of a company-sponsored program.

The investigating group used two statistical measures in carrying out the third step. The first of these was the ratio of the number of men promoted (both within department and through transfer to another department) in a given period (usually a year) to the total number of men regarded as "promotable" during the same period. The second measure was tied in with the personnel rating procedure employed throughout the company. At the conclusion of each performance review cycle, the rating forms for a particular department were analyzed to determine the proportions of employees whose performance was considered to be (*a*) improving, (*b*) unchanged, and (*c*) deteriorating.

Employee Attitudes

For purposes of developing measurements of performance in this key area, the group defined an attitude as "a generalized point of view towards objects, events or persons which might serve to influence future behavior." It used two basic approaches to the measurement of attitudes. The first involved the use of statistical indicators, such as turnover rate, absenteeism, number of grievances, lateness, and accident experience. The second approach involved a periodic survey of employees through questionnaires.

Several shortcomings were recognized in the first approach. (1) The statistical indicators provided little or no information about underlying causes. (2) In general, the indicators told of trouble only after the harm had been done. (3) Because these indicators were traditionally associated with the personnel functions, managers tended to minimize their importance or else place responsibility for improvement on the personnel function. (4) Unfavorable trends in certain of these indicators might be due to external factors (e.g., short labor supply) rather than to some shortcomings of management.

The attitude survey made use of a standardized questionnaire designed to reveal the attitudes of employees in a number of broad areas. The survey was administered at intervals of about eighteen months. Results for each attitude area were tabulated in terms of proportion of responses that were favorable. Tabulations were made by work groups and not by individual employees; this practice helped protect the anonymity of responses, and thus the validity of the surveys.

Public Responsibility

This key result area evolved from General Electric's recognition of its obligation to conduct itself as a good citizen within society, complying faithfully with the laws and ethics governing business conduct. The company believed its progress required not only an active recognition of the broad public interest, but also a responsiveness to certain special publics who had a stake in the success of the business—namely, shareowners, customers, employees, vendors, dealers and distributors, the plant community, educational institutions, and government.

While the responsibility to certain publics such as shareowners, educational institutions, and the federal government could best be measured from an overall company viewpoint rather than departmentally, nevertheless, the actions taken by a product department (including the individual acts of employees of that department) could have an important impact on the whole company's reputation as a good corporate citizen. Accordingly, the company attempted to assure wholehearted observance of the legal and ethical standards of business by insisting that all managerial and professional employees at least once a year conduct periodical surveys of the activities of those who reported to them with respect to antitrust compliance, conflict of interest, and other areas of business practice. These matters were discussed with each individual, who then signed a statement affirming his understanding and compliance.

Other measurements related to the effectiveness of department action in strengthening the company's reputation and business relationships. With respect to fulfilling obligations to customers, it was determined that the previously mentioned product leadership and market position areas were the best indicators. For the remaining publics, the following measures were recommended.

Shareowners.   The total shares of General Electric Company stock were to be "allocated" to the various operating components that were assigned responsibility for preserving and enhancing "their portion" of the shareowners' investment in the company.

Vendors, Dealers, and Distributors.   Suppliers of raw materials and parts were to be surveyed periodically to determine their appraisal of the department's practices in conducting its business as compared with the practices of others who bought from them. Dealers and distributors were likewise to be interviewed from time to time to measure whether these important relationships were being responsibly maintained.

Plant Community.   Again, comprehensive reaction surveys were to be used, aimed at identifying the impact of the actions of a product department on the individuals who made up the community. These reactions disclosed by the opinion surveys were to be supplemented by use of trends developed from various types of data such as community wage rates, number of employment applications received, volume of purchases made locally, contributions to local charities, and participation in civic, church, and business organizations.

Balance between Short-Range and Long-Range Goals

This factor was set out separately as a key result area in order to emphasize the importance of the long-term survival and growth of the company. Short-range goals and performance had to be balanced against the need for satisfactory performance five, ten, fifteen years in the future, since undue pressure for current profits could, in effect, borrow from the future.

Various means were employed to experiment with suggested measures in this key result area. However, it is important to note that when the eight key result areas were established, each of the first seven had both short-range and long-range dimensions. The eighth area, balance between short-range and long-range goals, had been specifically identified to make sure that the long-range health of the company would not be sacrificed for short-term gains. The plans, goals, and actions in each of the other areas were, therefore, to be appraised in terms of both their short-term and their long-term implications.

During the period after the measurements project was established in 1952, deep research work was carried on to establish the specific measurements in each of the eight key result areas. Before communicating these measures to the product departments, the investigators reviewed the recommendations in each area with operating personnel and with officers, for their comments, suggestions, and final approval.

The company's business planning, budgeting, and forecasting program incorporated the use of selected key result areas in (1) reviewing the recent history and current status, (2) setting standards for each department, (3) planning to achieve the standards, and (4) periodic reporting and measurement of accomplishment. Since the first four key result areas lent themselves readily to numerical evaluations, they were a part of the planning, budgeting, forecasting, reporting, and measuring system. Building on this experience in using the key result areas to plan and measure performance, management at the General Electric Company made the search for effective business measurements a continuing, evolutionary process.

QUESTIONS

1. For the purpose described, how should profitability be defined? The definition should be specific enough so that a quantitative measure can be constructed from it.

2. What, if anything, do the factors other than profitability add to the proposed measurement system? Isn't the impact of the other factors reflected in the profitability measure if it is properly constructed?

Case 4–4

National Tractor and Equipment Company

National Tractor and Equipment Company, Inc., was a manufacturer of a number of products, including a wide line of farm tractors. Tractors were divided into several fairly well-defined types, according to their capacity, and National manufactured tractors of each type. This case deals with one of these types, here referred to as type X.

Fixed costs represented a relatively large share of total costs at National, and, therefore, achieving a strong sales position was an important means of reducing unit costs and improving profits. Consequently, a major objective of the company was to be the sales leader in each of the several types. If National was not the leader during a particular year, its goal was to surpass whoever was the leader. If National was the leader, its goal was to maintain the size of its lead.

The company had experienced a rather erratic showing in sales of type X tractors over the previous several years. Though National had been the sales leader in four of the previous six years (1970–75) its lead in 1973 and 1974 had been slim, and in 1975 its chief competitor took over first place. Meanwhile, profits of this division of its business had fluctuated widely. Accordingly, early in 1976 the controller's department made a sales analysis of the type X tractor division.

William Lawrence, who was given the job of making the analysis, decided to use the approach the controller had used for other analyses. Usually, these analyses started with a comparison of actual costs or actual profit with some bench mark, such as the budget or the figures for some prior year when performance was satisfactory. The analyst then sought to isolate and quantify the various causes of the difference between actual and the standard applied in that particular case.

In the case of tractors, since management's objective was to surpass the sales leader, unit sales of the leading competitor—here called competitor A—seemed to be the most logical standard. Competitor A had sold 13,449 type X tractors in 1975 compared with 10,356 for National—a deficiency of 3,093. (A copy of Mr. Lawrence's analysis as presented to management appears as an appendix to this case.)

Mr. Lawrence began his analysis by looking at the profits and return on assets of the type X tractor division. Both had improved significantly over the 1973 and 1974 levels. However, in 1975 National dropped from the first-place sales position it had held during 1973 and 1974 and this was of grave concern to management. Furthermore, its market share had decreased from 25.0 percent to 23.5 percent. Both of its major competitors had increased their market shares, and competitor A had outsold National for the first time in five years.

Mr. Lawrence next prepared the sales portion of the table that appears as Exhibit 1 in the appendix. This table compares sales of type X tractors by National and competitor A for the preceding three years, 1973–75. The major task, then—and this was the crux of the analysis—was to identify and analyze those factors that accounted for the volume difference in each of the three years.

After he had completed this initial analysis, Mr. Lawrence, representing the controller's department, met with representatives of the sales department and the product development department. Together, they discussed the various factors that might have accounted for the volume differences in each of the three years under review. Using their collective judgments and estimates, they broke down the volume difference into as many specific factors as they could agree on. All the remaining factors, they decided, must have accounted for the remaining difference, although they could not agree on the proportions; so they gave the total under other factors.

The first matter that Mr. Lawrence called to the attention of this group was that a major fire in one of competitor A's plants in the latter part of 1974 had severely limited production. He had compiled monthly production estimates for competitor A for 1974 and the two prior years. He then had gathered estimates of industry sales during those years and developed certain relationships that seemed to him to hold among estimated monthly sales, actual monthly sales, and actual monthly production for 1972 and 1973 by competitor A. When he applied these relationships to 1974 it seemed evident to him that competitor A had produced significantly fewer type X tractors than it normally would have during the months when its plant was shut down.

Mr. Lawrence then had looked at sales patterns during 1972 and 1973 so that he could make an estimate of how much this lost production had resulted in a shifting of demand from 1974 to 1975 he tried to estimate how many competitor A customers for type X tractors delayed purchase of a new type X tractor from 1974 to 1975 because of the fire. In addition to research with the data available in his office, Mr. Lawrence traveled around the country and talked to distributors and dealers. He became convinced that a large number of potential purchasers of tractors actually had deferred their purchases of new type X tractors. Some of competitor A's dealers had had no type X tractors in stock in the latter part of 1974 because of the fire, and others had had only a limited supply.

On the basis of Mr. Lawrence's analysis and the collective judgments of the other members, the group agreed that the fire caused a shift of 1,500 of competitor A's tractor sales from 1974 to 1975. This shift was recorded as a minus factor in 1975 and a plus factor in 1974.

Sales of type X tractors to government agencies was another factor studied by this group. Since government sales figures were published, the group ascertained that National outsold competitor A by 138 units. Government sales depended almost entirely on price; therefore, this was the type of business a tractor manufacturer could "buy" depending on how badly he wanted it.

Mr. Lawrence had done a considerable amount of research into the advantage that competitor A enjoyed because of its larger owner body.[1] National's owner body had always been smaller than competitor A's, but National had made sizable gains since 1967. There was a tendency for the owner of a tractor to buy the same make when he purchased a new tractor; thus, competitor A enjoyed an advantage. Mr. Lawrence wanted to know *how much* this advantage was. An annual survey made by the trade association of the industry indicated the behavior of a representative sample of buyers of new type X tractors. This survey indicated that owners of competitor A's tractors were more loyal than were National tractor owners (see page 160). Using these survey results, Mr. Lawrence was able to calculate the advantage to competitor A of its larger owner body. Although only the calculations for 1975 are shown, he applied the same methodology to 1973 and 1974. Members of the group were impressed with this analysis and agreed to accept Mr. Lawrence's figures—a net advantage of 700 units for competitor A in 1975.

The next factor he analyzed was product differences. National did not have so varied a product line as did competitor A. Because of this, National dealers were at a competitive disadvantage for certain models of type X tractors. The group was able to agree on the approximate extent of this disadvantage.

The last main heading for variances listed in Exhibit 1 was other factors, which the group thought accounted for the remaining difference between National's sales and competitor A's sales. Mr. Lawrence had prepared a thorough analysis of these factors, too. For example, he had heard that competitor A built a more efficient and more durable type X tractor. He tried

---

[1] Owner body is the number of tractors in the hand of owners.

to quantify the effect of these variables by use of the data shown on pages 159 and 161. He also requisitioned five National type X tractors and five competitor A type X tractors, and arranged to have these tractors tested at National's experimental farm to determine their operating characteristics, including power, performance, durability, reliability, and economy. Mr. Lawrence himself actually drove some of these tractors. He also inspected each tractor and its performance at the end of the testing period.

The group could not agree, however, on the quantitative effect on sales volume of these factors or of the remaining factors listed under other. Therefore, they were represented by one figure. The total variance of all the factors affecting market penetration, of course, equaled the difference in sales betweet National and competitor A.

QUESTIONS

1. Are analyses of this type within the proper scope of a controller's function?

2. Can you suggest a better way of making the analysis?

3. What action, if any, should be taken on the basis of this study?

Appendix

National Tractor and

Equipment Company

An Analysis of Type X Tractors

Prepared by the Controller's Department

PROFITS, ASSETS, AND AFTER-TAX RETURNS

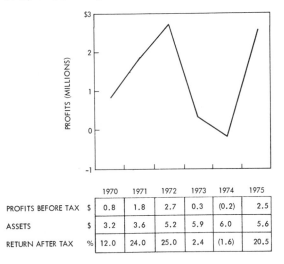

		1970	1971	1972	1973	1974	1975
PROFITS BEFORE TAX	$	0.8	1.8	2.7	0.3	(0.2)	2.5
ASSETS	$	3.2	3.6	5.2	5.9	6.0	5.6
RETURN AFTER TAX	%	12.0	24.0	25.0	2.4	(1.6)	20.5

This chart depicts National's profits, assets, and return on assets for the years 1970–75. Profits have ranged from a high of $2.7 million in 1972 to a loss of $200,000 in 1974 and a profit of $2.5 million in 1975. Return on assets employed in 1975 was 20.5 percent after taxes.

MARKET PENETRATION VERSUS COMPETITION

INDUSTRY PENETRATION

		1970	1971	1972	1973	1974	1975
NATIONAL	%	24.3	35.5	33.0	25.5	25.0	23.5
COMPETITOR A	%	27.9	21.8	22.8	24.5	23.1	30.5
COMPETITOR B	%	27.4	23.0	19.6	9.9	20.7	21.1

VOLUME (THOUSANDS OF TRACTORS)

	1970	1971	1972	1973	1974	1975
NATIONAL	10.9	12.8	15.6	10.6	8.4	10.4
COMPETITOR A	12.5	7.9	10.8	10.2	7.8	13.4
COMPETITOR B	12.3	8.3	9.3	4.1	7.0	9.3
OTHER	9.2	7.1	11.6	16.7	10.5	11.0
INDUSTRY TOTAL	44.9	36.1	47.3	41.6	33.7	44.1

This chart shows National's penetration of the domestic market for type X tractors from 1970–75 compared with its two major competitors.

National's penetration rose from 24.3 percent in 1970 to a peak of 35.5 percent in 1971. In 1975, National's penetration was 23.5 percent. Competitor A's penetration, which was 27.9 percent in 1970 fell to a low of 21.8 percent in 1971 and then increased to 30.5 percent in 1975. In four out of the last six years, National outsold competitor A in the type X tractor market. Competitor B's penetration moved from 27.4 percent in 1970 to 23.0 percent in 1971 but declined to 9.9 percent in 1973 rising to 21.1 percent in 1975.

Exhibit 1 sets forth those factors that account for the difference in market penetration between National and competitor A—its chief competitor in the type X tractor market. The upper portion of the table compares National's and competitor A's sales during the years 1973–75. The lower portion of the table shows the various factors that account for the differences between

Exhibit 1

SALES OF TYPE X TRACTORS AND FACTORS AFFECTING MARKET PENETRATION

National versus Competitor A, 1973 to 1975

	Jan.–Dec. 1973		Jan.–Dec. 1974		Jan.–Dec. 1975	
	Units	% of Market*	Units	% of Market*	Units	% of Market*
Sales:						
National	10,611	25.5%	8,431	25.0%	10,356	23.5%
Competitor A	10,246	24.5	7,828	23.1	13,449	30.5
National over/(under) A	365	1.0%	603	1.9%	(3,093)	(7.0%)
Factors affecting market penetration:						
Effect of major fire at one of competitor A's plants	—	—	1,500	4.5	(1,500)	(3.4)
Sales to government agencies	(3)	—	321	1.0	138	0.3
Competitor A's advantage in size of owner body	(850)	(2.0)	(660)	(1.9)	(700)	(1.6)
Product differences	(269)	(0.6)	(1,071)	(3.2)	(1,986)	(4.5)
Other factors:						
Customer attitudes toward National						
Operating cost						
Durability and quality						
National's price position	1,487	3.6	513	1.5	955	2.2
National's distribution system						
Sales administration						
Other factors						
Total Variance	365	1.0%	603	1.9%	(3,093)	(7.0%)

* These percentages were calculated from the rounded numbers given on the preceding page; if calculated from the exact number of units, they would be somewhat different.

National's and competitor A's share of the market in each of these years. National's volume was 10,611 units in 1973 compared to competitor A's 10,246. In 1975 National's volume was 10,356 units, representing a market penetration of 23.5 percent, compared with A's volume of 13,449 units and 30.5 percent of the market. In 1975 National was outsold by 3,093 units.

Turning to the specific factors that account for this volume difference, we have estimated that the effect of a major fire at one of competitor A's plants in the last half of 1974 which halted production for nearly five months, resulted in a deferral of demand for 1,500 of its type X tractors from 1974 to 1975. This estimate is based on our knowledge of competitor A's output in 1974 compared with other years, and represents our best estimate as to what sales might have been without the fire. In 1975 these 1,500 units represented 3.4 percent of market penetration. In 1975 National sold 138 more units to government agencies, equivalent to 0.3 percent of market penetration. We shall examine the effect on our market penetration of differences in the size of our respective owner bodies in subsequent tables.

The product differences result from gaps in our product line that prevent National from entering certain segments of the type X tractor market, thereby providing competitor A with a clear product advantage. For example, competitor A offers a larger variety of attachments and related equipment which increase the number of different jobs its tractor can perform. We have estimated, for each year, the net market advantage accruing to competitor A because of its broader product line.

Other factors, whose effects cannot be measured quantitatively, are summarized at the bottom of the table, including customer attitudes toward National with respect to operating cost, durability, quality, and similar factors. In 1975 these other factors, in total, represented a net advantage to National of 955 units, or 2.2 percent of market penetration.

BASIS FOR ESTIMATED ADVANTAGE TO COMPETITOR A OF OWNER BODY

The chart on Page 176 shows the estimated number of National and competitor A type X tractors in operation for the years 1967–1975.

In 1967, it is estimated that competitor A had approximately 88,000 type X tractors in operation, while National had approximately 27,000 units in use. By 1975 National units in operation had more than quadrupled to a level of approximately 127,000 units. Competitor A units, on the other hand, had increased by almost 100 percent to a level of 158,000 units. During this period, National units as a percent of competitor A increased from 31 percent in 1967 to 80 percent in 1975. At the same time, our variance, in terms of units, decreased from 60,700 in 1967 to 31,200 in 1975.

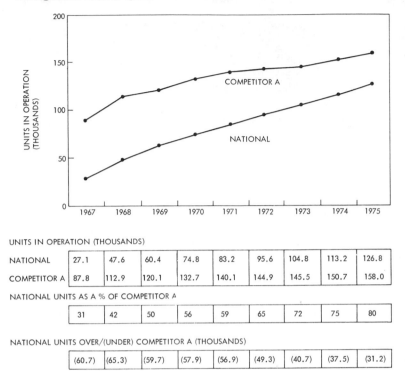

UNITS IN OPERATION (THOUSANDS)

NATIONAL	27.1	47.6	60.4	74.8	83.2	95.6	104.8	113.2	126.8
COMPETITOR A	87.8	112.9	120.1	132.7	140.1	144.9	145.5	150.7	158.0

NATIONAL UNITS AS A % OF COMPETITOR A

31	42	50	56	59	65	72	75	80

NATIONAL UNITS OVER/(UNDER) COMPETITOR A (THOUSANDS)

(60.7)	(65.3)	(59.7)	(57.9)	(56.9)	(49.3)	(40.7)	(37.5)	(31.2)

Because of the importance of owner loyalty, competitor A's advantage in owner body represents an automatic advantage in market penetration as indicated in the succeeding pages.

1975 Type X Replacement Patterns

	Make Purchased			
Make Replaced	National	A	Other	Total
National	48%	27%	25%	100%
Competitor A	13	73	14	100
Other	17	20	63	100

* Source: Replacement analysis published annually by trade association.

This table indicates the relative loyalty in 1975 of National and competitor A type X tractor owners. In this sample, 48 percent of the National owners who replaced a tractor bought a new National, 27 percent bought an A model, and 25 percent bought some other type X tractor. In contrast, 73 percent of A owners bought a new A, 14 percent bought some type X tractor other than National, and 13 percent of A owners purchased a National tractor when they reentered the market.

EFFECT OF DIFFERENCES IN OWNER BODY
ON 1975 TRACTOR PURCHASES

Make Purchased	Make Replaced (thousands of units)			Total Purchased
	National	A	Other	
National	5.0	2.8	2.6	10.4
Competitor A	3.6	6.4	3.4	13.4
Other	3.7	3.8	12.8	20.3
Total	12.3	13.0	18.8	44.1
Penetration	27.9%	29.5%	42.6%	100.0%
National (under) competitor A:				
Percentage points (1.6)				
Units (0.7)				

In this table, we have calculated the effect of owner bodies on type X tractor purchases in 1975. We have used actual figures for the size of National and competitor A owner bodies but have assumed that all other factors, including owner loyalty rates, are equal. In this calculation, we have applied National loyalty to both National and competitor A owner bodies. Based on these premises, one would expect National to have a deficiency in market penetration relative to competitor A of 1.6 percent solely as a result of the differences in the size of the two owner bodies, with National market penetration at 27.9 percent and competitor A penetration at 29.5 percent.

TYPE X TRACTOR WARRANTY EXPENSE[2]

	Model Year						1975 (over)/under 1970	
	1970	1971	1972	1973	1974	1975	Per Unit	Per-cent
Engine	$11.30	$ 7.56	$28.05	$28.40	$22.58	$12.76	$(1.46)	(13%)
Transmission	3.70	3.09	3.90	6.60	6.00	7.19	(3.49)	(94)
Hydraulic system. . .	.80	.46	.74	5.21	1.35	.57	.23	29
Electrical	.65	1.14	1.93	3.88	4.40	3.27	(2.62)	(403)
Other	5.03	4.20	5.20	10.97	8.90	7.59	(2.56)	(51)
Total	$21.48	$16.45	$39.82	$55.06	$43.23	$31.38	$(9.90)	(46%)

Some indication of National's type X tractor quality and durability problem is found in the level of our warranty expense as shown in the above table.

---

[2] Warranty Expense is the amount spent by National for replacements and repairs to tractors in use for which it had accepted responsibility. The company kept detailed records of such costs, broken down not only in the main classifications indicated above, but also for individual parts within each classification.

From 1970 to 1973 our warranty expense on the average type X tractor increased from $21.48 to $55.06, an increase of $33.58 per unit. Since 1973 warranty costs have declined to $31.38, a reduction of $23.68. Expense on all components, with the exception of the hydraulic system, has increased over 1970 levels. It seems clear that warranty costs of over $31 per unit are too high and represent an unsatisfactory level of quality as far as the user is concerned.

The following table indicates changes in warranty expense and design costs per unit on the N–50 tractor in the 1973, 1974 and 1975 models. In total, during this period, warranty expense has been reduced approximately $33, while design costs have increased $36. Engine warranty expense on this model has declined $40 per unit, while design costs have increased $24. In the case of the transmission, warranty expense has increased $3.30 per unit, despite an increase of $1.77 per unit in design costs.

NATIONAL N-50 TYPE X TRACTOR— WARRANTY AND DESIGN[3] COST

CHANGES BY YEAR

	1973 (over)/under 1972		1974 (over)/under 1973		1975 (over)/under 1974		1976 (over)/under 1975	
	Warranty	Design	Warranty	Design	Warranty	Design	Warranty	Design
Engine	$ 9.80	$(3.74)	$24.00	$(12.99)	$ 6.48	$ (7.62)	$40.28	$(24.35)
Transmission	(2.69)	(1.31)	.59	—	(1.20)	(.46)	(3.30)	(1.77)
Hydraulic system	(4.48)	(8.90)	3.87	.94	.77	(2.97)	.16	(10.93)
Electrical	(1.93)	—	(.53)	(1.09)	1.13	.32	(1.33)	(.77)
Other	(5.70)	4.17	2.00	(.50)	1.33	(1.73)	(2.37)	1.94
Total	$(5.00)	$(9.78)	$29.93	($13.64)	$ 8.51	$(12.46)	$33.44	$(35.88)

[3] Design cost refers to the costs of the tractor itself. These costs are a function of the way in which the tractor is designed. For example, the total standard cost of the 1973 model was $9.78 more than the total standard cost of the 1972 model; the designers had devised a more expensive tractor in 1973. In making the comparisons, wage rates and material costs are held constant.

PART II

The Management
Control Structure

In Chapter 1, management control was defined as "the process by which managers assure that resources are obtained and used effectively and efficiently in the accomplishment of the organization's goals." Depending on the situation in a given organization, this process may relate to either or both of two structures: (1) the organization structure and/or (2) projects. The discussion of management control as related to projects (e.g., research/ development projects, construction projects, production of motion pictures) is deferred to Chapter 16. In Part II we have limited the discussion to the type of management control that focuses on organization units.

A key concept in this discussion is that of the responsibility center. A responsibility center is any organization unit headed by a manager who is responsible for its activities.

Characteristics of a responsibility center that are relevant to the management control process are discussed in Chapter 5. All responsibility centers produce outputs (that is, they do something), and all have inputs (that is, they use resources). They can be classified on the basis of the measurement of inputs and outputs into one of four types: revenue centers, expense centers, profit centers and investment centers.

In a *revenue center,* outputs are measured in monetary terms, but inputs are not measured in monetary terms. These responsibility centers usually are part of the marketing organization. They are discussed briefly in Chapter 5.

In an *expense center,* the control system measures inputs in monetary terms, but does not measure outputs in monetary terms. Various types of expense centers are discussed in Chapter 5.

In a *profit center,* the management control system measures both inputs and outputs in monetary terms; that is, inputs are measured in terms of cost and outputs in terms of revenue. Profit is the difference between costs and revenues. Profit centers are discussed in Chapter 6. Many profit centers transfer products (either goods or services) to other profit centers within the company. The price used in measuring the amount of products transferred is called a transfer price. Because of its importance in the management control system of profit centers, a whole chapter, Chapter 7, is devoted to a discussion of transfer pricing.

In an *investment center,* the control system measures not only the inputs and outputs in monetary terms, but it also measures the investment that is employed in the responsibility center. Investment centers are discussed in Chapter 8. Chapter 8 also discusses some of the organizational considerations that are involved in deciding whether a responsibility center should, or should not, be treated as an investment center.

Chapter Five

RESPONSIBILITY CENTERS: REVENUE AND EXPENSE CENTERS

In the first part of this chapter we discuss the nature of responsibility centers in general. In the second part we discuss revenue centers and expense centers, which are two types of responsibility centers.

RESPONSIBILITY CENTERS

We have used the term "responsibility center" to denote any organization unit that is headed by a responsible manager. In a sense, an organization is a collection of responsibility centers, each of which is represented by a box on the organization chart. These responsibility centers form a hierarchy. At the lowest level in the organization there are responsibility centers for sections, work shifts, or other small organization units. At a higher level there are departments or divisions that consist of several of these smaller units plus overall departmental or divisional staff and management people; these larger units are also responsibility centers. And from the standpoint of top management and the board of directors, the whole company is a responsibility center. Although even these large units fit the definition of responsibility center, the term often is used to refer primarily to the smaller, lower level units within the organization.

Nature of Responsibility Centers

A responsibility center exists to accomplish one or more purposes; these purposes are its *objectives*. Presumably, the objectives of an individual responsibility center are intended to help achieve the overall goals of the whole organization. These overall goals are decided upon in the strategic planning process, and are assumed to have been established prior to the beginning of the management control process.

Exhibit 5–1 is a schematic diagram that shows the essence of any responsibility center. A responsibility center uses inputs, which are physical

Exhibit 5–1

NATURE OF A RESPONSIBILITY CENTER

quantities of material, hours of various types of labor, and a variety of services. It works with these resources, and it usually requires working capital, equipment, and other assets to do this work. As a result of this work, the responsibility center produces outputs, which are classified either as goods, if they are tangible, or as services if they are intangible. Presumably, these outputs are related to the responsibility center's objectives, but this is not necessarily so. In any event, whatever the responsibility center does constitutes its outputs.

The goods and services produced by a responsibility center may be furnished either to another responsibility center or to the outside world. In the former case, they are inputs to the other responsibility center; in the latter case, they are outputs of the whole organization.

Measurement of Inputs and Outputs

The amount of labor, material, and services used in a responsibility center are physical quantities: hours of labor, quarts of oil, reams of paper, kilowatt hours of electricity, and so on. In a management control system it is convenient to translate these amounts into monetary terms. Money provides a common denominator which permits the amounts of individual resources to be combined. The monetary amount is ordinarily obtained by multiplying the physical quantity by a price per unit of quantity (e.g., hours of labor times a rate per hour). This amount is called cost. Thus the inputs of a responsibility center are ordinarily expressed as costs. Cost is a measure of resources used by a responsibility center.

Note that inputs are resources *used* by the responsibility center. The patients in a hospital or the students in a school are *not* inputs. Rather, it is the resources that are used in accomplishing the objectives of *treating* the patients or *educating* the students that are the inputs.

Although inputs almost always can be measured in terms of cost, outputs are much more difficult to measure. In a profit-oriented organization, revenue is often an important measure of output, but such a measure is rarely a complete expression of outputs; it does not encompass everything that the organization does. In many responsibility centers, outputs cannot be measured at all. In many nonprofit organizations, no good quantitative measure of output exists. A school can easily measure the number of students graduated, but it cannot measure how much education each of them acquired. Although outputs may not be measured, or may not even be measurable, it is fact that every organization unit *has* outputs; that is, it does something.

Efficiency and Effectiveness

The concepts stated above can be used to explain the meaning of efficiency and effectiveness, which are the two criteria for judging the performance of a responsibility center. The terms efficiency and effectiveness are almost always used in a comparative, rather than in an absolute, sense; that is, we do not ordinarily say that Organization Unit A is 80 percent efficient, but rather that it is more (or less) efficient than Organization Unit B, or more (or less) efficient currently than it was in the past.

Efficiency is the ratio of outputs to inputs, or the amount of output per unit of input. Unit A is more efficient than Unit B either (1) if it uses less resources than Unit B, but has the same output, or (2) if it uses the same resources as Unit B and has a greater output than Unit B. Note that the first type of measure does not require that output be quantified; it is only necessary to judge that the outputs of the two units are approximately the same. If management is satisfied that Units A and B are both doing a satisfactory job and if it is a job of comparable magnitude, then the unit with the lower inputs, i.e., the lower costs, is the more efficient. The second type of measure does require some quantitative measure of output; it is therefore a more difficult type of measurement in many situations.

In many responsibility centers, a measure of efficiency can be developed that relates actual costs to some standard—that is, to a number that expresses what costs should be incurred for the amount of measured output. Such a measure can be a useful indication of efficiency, but it is never a perfect measure for at least two reasons: (1) recorded costs are not a precisely accurate measure of resources consumed, and (2) standards are, at best, only approximate measures of what resource consumption ideally should have been in the circumstances prevailing.

Effectiveness is the relationship between a responsibility center's outputs and its objectives. The more these outputs contribute to the objectives, the more effective the unit is. Since both objectives and outputs are often difficult to quantify, measures of effectiveness are difficult to come by. Effectiveness, therefore, is often expressed in nonquantitative, judgmental terms, such as "College A is doing a first-rate job, but College B has slipped somewhat in recent years."

An organization unit should be *both* efficient and also effective; it is not a matter of one or the other. Efficient managers are those who do whatever they do with the lowest consumption of resources; but if what they do (i.e., their output) is an inadequate contribution to the accomplishment of the organization's goals, they are ineffective. If a credit department handles the paperwork connected with delinquent accounts at a low cost per unit, it is efficient; but if it is unsuccessful in making collections or, if in the process of collecting accounts it needlessly antagonizes customers, it is ineffective. Drucker states that "there is a sharp clash today between stress on the efficiency of administration (as represented, above all, by the governmental administrator and the accountant) and stress of effectiveness (which emphasizes (results)."[1] There should not in fact be a "sharp clash" between efficiency and effectiveness, nor is there substantial evidence that such a clash exists. Management's emphasis should be on both these criteria.

The Role of Profits.   One important objective in a profit-oriented organization is to earn profits, and the amount of profits is therefore an important measure of effectiveness. Since profit is the difference between revenue, which is a measure of output, and expense, which is a measure of input, profit is also a measure of efficiency. Thus, profit measures both effectiveness and efficiency. When such an overall measure exists, it is unnecessary to determine the relative importance of effectiveness versus efficiency. When such an overall measure does not exist, it is feasible and useful to classify performance measures as relating either to effectiveness or to efficiency. In these situations, there is the problem of balancing the two types of measurements. For example, how do we compare the profligate perfectionist with the frugal manager who obtains less than the optimum output?

Although profit is an important overall measure of effectiveness and efficiency, it is a less than perfect measure for several reasons: (1) monetary measures do not exactly measure either all aspects of output or all inputs; (2) standards against which profits are judged may not be accurate; and (3) at best, profit is a measure of what has happened in the short run, whereas we are presumably also interested in the long-run consequences of management actions.

REVENUE CENTERS

In a revenue center, outputs are measured in monetary terms, but no formal attempt is made to relate inputs or costs to outputs (if costs were matched against revenues the unit would be a profit center). Revenue centers are found primarily in marketing organizations. Budgets, or sales quotas, are prepared for sales made, or orders booked, for the revenue center as a whole, and for the individual salesmen who work in it, and

---

[1] Peter F. Drucker, *The Age of Discontinuity* (New York: Harper & Row, 1969), p. 197.

records of actual sales or orders are compared with these budgets. In this book, we do not discuss revenue centers as such. The control of costs of these units is discussed below in the section on expense centers. We shall discuss the measurement of revenue as part of our discussion of profit centers.

EXPENSE CENTERS

Expense centers are responsibility centers for which inputs, or expenses, are measured in monetary terms, but in which outputs are not measured in monetary terms. There are two general types, engineered cost centers and discretionary expense centers. They correspond to two types of costs. Engineered costs are elements of cost for which the "right" or "proper" amount of costs that should be incurred can be estimated with a reasonable degree of reliability. The direct labor and direct material costs incurred in a factory are examples. Discretionary expenses are those for which no such engineered estimate is feasible; the amount of expense incurred depends on management's judgment as to the amount that is appropriate under the circumstances.

Engineered Cost Centers

Engineered costs are usually expressed as standard costs. If one can establish standard costs for a cost center, a measure of output can be determined by multiplying the physical quantity of the output by the unit standard costs for each of the products produced and summing the results. The total actual cost is compared to the total standard cost of the output and variances are analyzed. The manager of the cost center is evaluated on how well he keeps actual costs at or below these standard costs.

It should be emphasized that in engineered cost centers there are other important tasks that are not measured by costs alone. It is necessary to control the effectiveness of these aspects of performance. For example, a cost center supervisor is responsible for the quality of the products and for the volume of production, in addition to his responsibility for cost efficiency. It is necessary, therefore, to prescribe the type and amount of production and to set careful quality standards; otherwise, manufacturing costs could be minimized at the expense of quality or volume.

There are few, if any, responsibility centers in which all items of cost are engineered. Even in highly automated production departments, the amount of indirect labor and of various services used can vary with management's discretion. Thus, the term "engineered cost center" refers to responsibility centers in which engineered costs predominate, but does not imply that valid engineering estimates can be made for each and every cost item.

Control systems for engineered cost centers are described in cost accounting texts, and therefore are not discussed in detail in this book.

DISCRETIONARY EXPENSE CENTERS

Some organization units have outputs that are not measured in monetary terms. These are principally administrative staff units (e.g., accounting, legal, industrial relations), research and product development organizations, and some types of marketing activities.[2]

By definition, the efficiency or effectiveness of these organization units cannot be measured in monetary terms. Usually, the control system starts with an annual budget or plan that management approves. Subsequently, actual expenses are compared to budget. These comparisons compare *budget input* to *actual input*. Since they do not measure output in monetary terms, they do not provide a complete measure of performance and, therefore, cannot be used as a basis for overall evaluation of the manager. Such a system will motivate the manager only to keep his expenses equal to his budget.

General Control Characteristics

Budget Formulation. The decision that management must make with respect to a discretionary expense budget is different from the decision that it must make with respect to the budget for an engineered cost center, e.g., the budget for a manufacturing department. For the latter, management must decide whether the proposed operating budget represents a reasonable and efficient task for the coming period. Management is not so much concerned with the magnitude of the task because this is largely determined by the sales and production budgets. In formulating the budget for a discretionary expense center, however, management's principal task is to decide on the magnitude of the job that should be done.

In preparing a budget proposal for consideration by management, one should be careful not to include irrelevant data that might obscure the important information needed for this decision. Some budget proposals include a breakdown of the number of people by classification, the expense by each account, and a history of these costs for several years, all in great detail; but there may be little or no information that will aid management in making an intelligent decision, such as expenses classified by the tasks to be accomplished. If the proposal is of this nature, management must either rubber-stamp its approval, try to question individual expense items, or make arbitrary reductions. Questioning individual items is unlikely to be fruitful, for if a proposal has been prepared carefully, a reasonable rationale can be given

---

[2] There are activities within each of these categories for which financial standards may be set, for example, the handling of accounts receivable within the accounting department. These activities tend to be those with repetitive operations where the variables of performance can be controlled. Where this type of activity constitutes an important proportion of the total staff cost, it should be controlled by comparing actual costs against performance standards.

for any individual expense (whether or not it is really justifiable). If management reduces a budget arbitrarily in one year, it can expect to receive a budget proposal the following year that contains sufficient "water" so that a reduction creates no hardship. The following questions should be asked with respect to a discretionary expense budget proposal:

1. What are the precise decisions that management should make?
2. Does the proposal include all the available information pertinent to making these decisions?
3. Does the proposal include irrelevant information which, at best, will tend to obscure the real issues?

Type of Control.   The financial control exercised through a discretionary expense budget is quite different from the financial control exercised through an operating expense budget for a manufacturing department. The latter attempts to minimize operating costs by setting a standard and reporting actual costs against this standard. Costs are minimized by motivating line managers to maintain maximum efficiency and by giving higher management a means of evaluating the efficiency of departmental management. The main purpose of a discretionary expense budget, on the other hand, is to allow management to control costs by *participating in the planning.* Costs are controlled primarily by deciding what tasks should be undertaken and what level of effort is appropriate for each.[3]

Some authorities state that a tight budget is a good budget because a tight budget will result in more pressure to reduce costs than one that is easily attainable. While this philosophy may have merit for a standard cost budget, it is of questionable validity for a discretionary expense budget. The head of a discretionary expense center can easily cut costs. He simply reduces the magnitude of the job that is done. However, when this happens, the individual responsible for spending the money, instead of higher management, is making the decision as to the job to be done. Such decisions should properly be made by higher management.

The general rule, then, is that discretionary expense budgets should reflect as closely as possible the *actual costs* of doing the job. A deviation from this rule should be backed by adequate reasons and this condition should be known to management when the budget is presented for approval.

Measurement of Performance.   In discretionary expense budgets, the performance report is used to insure that the budget commitment will not be exceeded without management's knowledge. It is not a means for evaluating the efficiency of the manager. This is in contrast to the report in an engineered cost center, which helps higher management evaluate the efficiency of manufacturing management. If these two types of responsibility

---

[3] Management may, of course, set certain kinds of standards to be used companywide; for example, the ratio of secretaries to professionals or the relative amounts to be spent on professional societies, and so forth.

centers are not carefully distinguished, management may treat a report for a discretionary expense center as if it were an indication of efficiency. If this is done, the people responsible for spending may be motivated to spend less than budgeted. This pressure toward lower costs may possibly result in the same job being done for less money, but it is more likely that the lower spending will be accompanied by lower performance. In any event, since higher management can rarely gauge the efficiency of a discretionary expense center, there is little point in trying to increase the efficiency by such indirect methods as rewarding executives who spend less than budget.

Control over spending can be exercised by requiring that management approval be obtained before the budget can be overrun. Sometimes, a certain percentage of overrun (say, 5 percent) is allowed without additional approval. If the budget really sets forth the best estimate of actual costs, there is a 50–50 chance that it will be overrun, and this is the reason that some latitude is often permitted.

In the following paragraphs, we discuss three of the most common types of discretionary expense centers: administrative centers, research/development centers, and marketing centers.

ADMINISTRATIVE CENTERS

Administrative centers include the top management, divisional management, other managers who are responsible for several responsibility centers, and staff units.

Control Problems

The control of administrative staff expense is particularly difficult because of (1) the impossibility of measuring output, and (2) the frequent lack of congruence between the goals of the staff department and the goals of the company.

Difficulty in Measuring Output. Some staff activities, such as payroll accounting, are so routinized that they can be regarded as engineered cost centers. For others, however, the principal output is advice and service, and there are no realistic means of measuring the value, or even the amount, of this output. Since output cannot be measured, it is not possible to set cost standards and measure financial performance against these standards. A budget variance, therefore, cannot be interpreted as representing either efficient or inefficient performance. Even where the budget is subdivided into tasks, the results cannot be interpreted in terms of efficiency or inefficiency. For instance, if the finance staff was given a budget allowance to "develop a standard cost system," a comparison of actual cost to budgeted cost would in no way tell management how effectively and efficiently the job had been done. The job of development and installation might have been poor, regardless of the amount spent.

Lack of Goal Congruence. In most administrative staff offices, it is to the benefit of the manager to have as excellent a department as he possibly can have. Superficially, it may appear that the most excellent department is best for the company. Actually, a great deal depends on how one defines an "excellent department." For example, an excellent controller's department can answer immediately any question involving accounting data. The cost of a system to do this, however, might far exceed the benefits it provides. Similarly, an excellent legal staff never would permit the slightest flaws in any contract that it approves. However, the cost of making reviews that are thorough enough to detect all flaws is high. The potential loss from minor undetected flaws may be much less than the cost of insuring perfection. As another example, it is to the benefit of the manager of training to have the most complete and up-to-date visual aid devices; yet, the benefits received may not be worth the cost.

Thus, although the manager of a staff office may want to develop the "ideal" operation, such an ideal can cost more than the additional profits that it generates. There also can be a tendency to "empire build" or to "safeguard one's position," without regard for its value to the company.

The severity of these two problems—the difficulty of measuring output and the lack of goal congruence—is fairly directly related to the size and prosperity of the company. In small to medium-sized businesses, top management is in close personal contact with the staff units and can determine from personal observation what they are doing and whether it is worth the expense. Also, in a business with low earnings, discretionary expenses are often kept under tight control. In a large business, top management cannot possibly know about, much less evaluate, all the staff activities, and in a company that has satisfactory profits there is a temptation to go along with staff requests for constantly increasing budgets.

The severity of these two problems is also directly related to organizational level of the staff activity. For example, at the plant level, the administrative staff tends to be carefully controlled by the plant manager. Furthermore, there is less discretion in the tasks to be performed. At the divisional level, there is more discretion in the tasks to be performed by the staff than at the plant level. However, there is less discretion at the divisional level than at the corporate level. In general, the type of staff activity that is performed at the plant and divisional level are closely related to organizational objectives. Furthermore, most of the highly discretionary cost centers (e.g., public relations) are located at the corporate level.

Budget Formulation

The budget proposal for an administrative center often consists of the following components:

1. A section covering the basic costs of the department. This includes the costs of "being in business" plus the costs of all activities which *must* be

undertaken and for which no general management decisions are required.
2. A section covering all other activities of the department. This includes a description of the purposes and the estimated costs of each such activity. The quantity of detail depends upon the amount of money involved and the ability of management to make a decision about the activity. For example, a limited amount of detail may be enough for a financial analysis department because management does not need to review its functions each year.
3. A section explaining fully all proposed increases in budget.

In addition, some companies include a section explaining the activities that would be curtailed or cancelled if the budget were reduced 5 percent or 10 percent, and a section explaining the activities that would be increased or started if the budget could be increased 5 percent or 10 percent. Most companies, however, do not require such estimates; they prefer that departmental managers concentrate their efforts on preparing the best possible budget for the activities that they believe should be undertaken.

The amount of detail varies greatly among companies, and within a company among departments of various sizes and importance. In some situations, only the proposed costs are expressed in written form, and the other information is conveyed orally during the discussion of the proposed budget. The important point is that *if* management is expected to decide the level of administrative activity, the presentation should be aimed at providing the information needed for an intelligent decision.

Measurement of Performance

A monthly report comparing actual expenses with budget is usually prepared. As indicated earlier, this report is not designed to measure efficiency, but rather to keep management informed about any possible cost under- or over-runs. There are few accounting problems associated with such reports. The actual costs are usually recorded in at least the same detail as that required for reporting purposes. Detailed reports are designed for the most part to help the manager of the administrative unit control costs. Top management usually needs only summaries by department.

Management Considerations

The problem for management is that, even under the best circumstances, the budgeting and accounting systems are of limited help in determining the optimum level of expenses. Consequently, the decision on how much to spend must be based largely on executive judgment. These decisions become more difficult as staff offices become more numerous and specialized. It is not unusual to have a dozen staff groups reporting to the president. They include, among others, legal, treasury, controller, systems and operations research, industrial relations, community relations, government relations, personnel, and planning staffs. The president often has neither the time nor the specialized knowledge to exercise more than cursory control over these activities. Consequently, many of the larger companies appoint an administrative vice president, to whom all or most of these staff functions report. This hopefully assures an independent review and an appraisal by an executive with the time and expertise required to exercise the necessary control over these staff activities.

RESEARCH/DEVELOPMENT CENTERS

Control Problems

The control of research/development expense is difficult for the following reasons:

1. Results are difficult to measure quantitatively. As contrasted to administrative activities, research/development usually has at least a semitangible output in terms of patents, new products, new processes, and so forth. Nevertheless, these outputs and their relation to inputs are difficult to measure and appraise. The "product" of a research/development group may require several years of effort; consequently, inputs as stated in an annual budget may be unrelated to outputs. Even if an output can be identified, a reliable estimate of its value often cannot be made. Even if the value of the output can be calculated, it is usually not possible for management to evaluate the efficiency of the research/development effort because of its technical nature. The causal connection between the input and the output often cannot be established. A brilliant effort may fail, whereas a mediocre effort may, by luck, result in a bonanza.

2. The goal congruence problem in research/development centers is similar to that in administrative centers. The research manager typically wants to build the best research organization that money can buy, even though this might be more expensive than the company can afford. A further problem is that research people often may not have sufficient knowledge (or interest in) the business to determine the optimum direction of the research efforts.

3. Research/development cannot be controlled effectively on an annual basis. A research project may take years to reach fruition, and the organization must be built up slowly over a long period of time. The principal cost is for manpower. Scientific manpower is scarce, and a man working on a given project often cannot be easily replaced because only he has knowledge of the project. This means that it is inefficient to have short-term fluctuations in manpower and, consequently, in costs. It is not reasonable, therefore, to reduce research/development costs in years when profits are low and increase them in years when profits are high. Research/development must be looked at as a long-term investment, not an activity that varies with short-run corporate profitability.

Approach to Control

Management makes essentially three decisions concerning research/development cost. It must:

1. Decide on the amount of financial commitment to research/development over the next several years.
2. Decide on the direction of the research/development effort.
3. Evaluate the effectiveness of the research/development group.

Only the first of these decisions is related to the calendar year and then only when the program is viewed as part of a longer program; the annual budget is not governing in making any of these decisions.

A decision must be made by top management as to the amount of funds that will be made available for research/development over a period of years. This plan can, of course, be reviewed periodically and changed. The advantage of a long-range plan is that the change will be made in the *entire plan* and the total effect of these changes can be evaluated. When a research/development budget is approved on an annual basis, it is difficult to make intelligent changes because the impact of any change is not restricted to a single year.

This long-range plan can be used for two purposes:

1. As a guide to approving specific projects.[4]
2. As a guide to approving the annual budget.

Specific Projects

Except in the most unusual circumstances, top management must decide the general direction of the research effort. This is often accomplished by having a research committee review and approve individual projects (or groups of projects) before they are undertaken by the research staff. The research committee is usually composed of either the president or executive vice president, the director of research, the director of marketing, plus other executives who are likely to use the research results. The research committee does not have to concern itself with the availability of funds each time that it approves a specific project. Its concern is whether the amount of money requested should be spent on the particular research proposed, rather than in some other way. If the number of worthwhile projects increases to the point where the long-range plan will not provide enough funds, the plan should be reconsidered.

The management control of specific projects is discussed in more detail in Chapter 16.

---

[4] A project is a specific research task with a definite end or accomplishment. There can be wide variances in the size and type of task, but this is a technical problem. For our purposes, think of a project as a specific job to be done.

Annual Budgets

If a company has systematically developed a long-range research/development expenditure plan and implemented this plan with a system of project approval, preparation of the annual research/development budget is a fairly simple matter. The annual budget is the calendarization of the expected expenses for the budget period. If the annual budget is in line with the long-range plan and the approved projects (as it should be), the budget approval is routine, and its main function is in cash planning. Preparation of the budget does give management an opportunity for another look at the research/development plan. Management can ask the question: "Is this the best way to use our resources next year?" Also the annual budget insures that actual costs will not exceed budget without management knowing about it. Significant variances from budget must be approved by management *before they are incurred.*

Measurement of Performance

The reporting of research/development expense resembles that for administrative expense. Each month or each quarter, actual expenses are compared to budgeted expenses for all responsibility centers and also for projects. These are summarized progressively for managers at higher levels. The purpose of these reports is to assist the managers of responsibility centers to plan their expenses and to assure their superiors that expenses are within approved plans.

Two types of reports are provided to management. The first type compares the latest forecast of total cost with the approved project, for each active project. This is prepared periodically and given to the executive or group of executives that approve the research projects. The main purpose of this report is to help determine whether changes should be made in approved projects. The second type is a report of actual expenses compared with the budget. Its main purpose is to help the research executives in expense planning and to make sure expense commitments are being met. Neither report informs management about the efficiency or effectiveness of the research effort.

Although financial control reports are not of much use in evaluating performance, there should be *some* explicit evaluation of the research staff by top management periodically, using whatever relevant data are available. The entire future of the company could depend upon the ability of the research group.

Management Considerations

1. If a company depends upon research for its future products (and most large companies do), it is vital that the right amount of money be spent for

the right things and that the research effort be staffed by highly competent people. Information on planned and actual expenses can be of only limited help in assuring that the correct decisions on these matters are made.

2. Research/development expenses are similar to capital investments. Consequently, the annual budget is an unsatisfactory vehicle for making basic decisions with respect to research/development. Instead, these decisions should be made without the time constraints inherent in an annual budget. Subsequently, the impact of these decisions on the timing of expenses can be incorporated into the annual budget.

3. Research/development expenses are controlled in terms of projects. Consequently, it is vital to have a system of project approval and review. The accounting organization is responsible for maintaining a record of actual costs by project and presenting these results. The projection of the cost of completion of each project in process should be made by the research staff.

4. The impact of an error in judgment concerning either the amount or direction of expenditures can be much greater in research than in administration. It may take a much longer time to correct the effects of an error in research expenditures. Moreover, the impact on profits can be much greater, even if the error can be corrected quickly.

5. The problems described in this section apply more to research than to development. The closer a development project is to the production stage, the more practical it is to use, at least to some degree, industrial engineering measures of efficiency.

MARKETING CENTERS

In many companies the activities that are grouped under the heading of marketing consist of two quite different types, and the control that is appropriate for one type is quite different from the control that is appropriate for the other. One set of activities relates to filling orders, and they are called order-filling or *logistics* activities. The other type relates to efforts to obtain orders. These are the true marketing activities, and are sometimes labelled as such. Alternatively, they may be called order-getting activities. Thus, one set of activities takes place *after* an order has been received, and the other set takes place *before* an order has been received. In both types of activities, there are administrative functions that have the same characteristics as those discussed in a previous section, so no further mention of them will be made here.

Logistics Activities

Logistics activities are those involved in getting the goods from the company to its customers and collecting the amounts due from customers. The responsibility centers that perform these functions are fundamentally similar to manufacturing departments, and they are therefore not discussed separately here because of our basic plan to exclude matters that are covered in cost accounting courses.[5]

True Marketing Activities

True marketing activities—that is, those directed at obtaining orders—have two important characteristics that affect the control problem.

1. The output of a marketing organization can be measured; however, it is difficult to evaluate the effectiveness of the marketing effort because the environment in which it operates cannot be controlled. This environment changes in economic conditions, competitive action, customer tastes, and so on.

2. Meeting the budgetary commitment for selling expense will normally be a small part of the evaluation of marketing performance. For example, if a marketing group sells twice as much as its quota, no one is going to worry too much if it exceeded its budget by 10 percent. The impact of sales on profits is so great that it tends to overshadow the cost performance. Few companies evaluate a marketing organization primarily on its ability to meet its cost targets. The sales target is the critical factor in evaluation.

The control techniques that are applicable to logistics activities are generally not applicable to true marketing activities. Failure to appreciate this fact can lead to wrong decisions. For example, a manager, realizing that fixed budgets result in inequitable situations when the sales volume is high with a consequent high amount of sales commissions, may attempt to cure the problem by putting the entire sales budget on a flexible basis. Indeed, a reasonably good correlation may often be found between volume of sales and the level of sales promotion and advertising (and even the cost of sales staff). This may be taken to mean that sales expenses are variable with sales volume. Flexible budgets, however, cannot be used to control selling expenses that are incurred *before* the time of sale. Advertising or sales promotion expense, for example, should not be authorized on the basis of a flexible budget, unless, of course, management wishes to base its advertising expenses on the volume of sales, on the theory that the higher the sales volume, the more the company can afford to spend on advertising.

The apparent correlation between sales volume and advertising costs reflects either the overall growth of the company, which increases volume and costs alike, or the fact that advertising costs *cause* the increase in sales. It does not make sense to turn this around and act as though the sales volume *caused* the advertising expense.

---

[5] Some texts on cost accounting do not discuss logistics costs in any depth, but this is because cost accounting until recently was well developed only in connection with production activities.

Management Considerations

1. In deciding on how much to spend for marketing, the objective is to spend an additional dollar if it returns more than a dollar in contribution from additional sales. In advertising, for example, one of the principal decisions that management must make is *when to stop* advertising. This can be particularly complicated because there are many interrelated decisions. For example, there will be optimum points for media, for geographic locations, and for products. As in research, these are not decisions for which accounting data can provide much relevant information. The point is, however, that as much relevant information as possible should be provided (e.g., marginal contribution of products) and, where sufficient relevant information is not available, irrelevant data should not be substituted.

2. Management should be able to change planned order-getting expenses rapidly. Note that this is the opposite of the situation with research expense. Environmental conditions can change rapidly, and it is therefore necessary that sales and advertising plans be flexible enough to change with them. It is vital that the marketing budget not be a straitjacket that hampers necessary management action.

Case 5-1

New Jersey Insurance Company

On July 16, 1975, John W. Montgomery, a member of the budget committee of the New Jersey Insurance Company, was reading over the current budget report for the law division in preparation for a conference scheduled for the next day with the head of that division. He held such conferences quarterly with each division head. Mr. Montgomery's practice was to think out in advance the questions he wished to ask and the points he thought he should make about each division's performance.

The law division of the New Jersey Insurance Company was responsible for all legal matters relating to the company's operations. Among other things, it advised company management on current and prospective developments in tax and other legislation and on recent court decisions affecting the company, it represented the company in litigation, counseled the departments concerned on the legal implications of policies such as employee benefit plans, and it examined all major contracts to which the company was a party. It also rendered various legal services in respect of the company's proposed and existing investments.

As shown in Exhibit 1, the head of the law division, William Somersby, reported directly to top management. This relationship insured that Mr. Somersby would be free to comment on the legal implications of management decisions, much the same as would an outside counsel. The law division was divided into five sections. This case is concerned with only two of these sections, the individual loan section and the corporate loan section. It does not attempt to completely describe the work of these two sections or the professional service rendered by the lawyers.

INDIVIDUAL LOAN SECTION

The individual loan section was responsible for the legal processing of loans made to individuals and secured by mortgages on real property. The

Exhibit 1

NEW JERSEY INSURANCE COMPANY
Partial Organization Chart

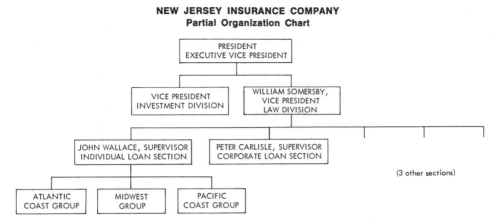

loan instruments were submitted by independent companies situated through-out the country. The company made no loans directly to individual borrowers, although at one time it had made direct loans in the New Jersey area. Most common among the loans submitted by the independent companies were FHA, VA, and conventional loans on homes, ranging in amounts from $10,000 to $50,000. These loans usually were made directly by banks or similar financial institutions organized for the purpose. They would batch together a number of loans and sell them to NJIC in a package. The insurance company purchased many thousands of such loans each year.

The investment division of the company was responsible for establishing the terms of these loans, including their amount, interest rate, and maturity. An independent company would submit to the investment division an offer to sell a mortgage loan. It was the function of this division to determine whether or not the property to be mortgaged and the mortgagor were acceptable to NJIC for a mortgage loan. After the proposed loan was approved and its terms worked out, the investment division would forward to the law division the note, mortgage, and related papers which it received from the seller.

The major function of the individual loan section was to perform the legal work necessary on all new loans purchased and on all existing loans. Among other things, it had to check all the loan instruments to make sure they did, in fact, protect the interests of NJIC as required by law and by the investment division. Organizationally, the section was divided into three groups, each headed by an attorney and each responsible for a geographical section of the country—Atlantic Coast, Midwest, and Pacific Coast. In addition to the three attorneys who headed regional groups, there were two other attorneys—one who helped out in busy spots and took over a group in case of sickness or vacation, and another who was in a training status.

Other than these five attorneys and a supporting secretarial staff, the section was comprised of 26 so-called mortgage examiners. These were persons who had had no formal legal training, but who had been carefully selected and company trained to check over and approve certain of the loan transactions that came into the section. Because of the repetitive nature of the routine loan transactions, management believed that properly selected and trained laymen could, under the supervision of lawyers, perform this task, which at one time had been performed only by lawyers. Problem cases were referred by the mortgage examiners to the attorneys. John Wallace, head of the individual loan section, estimated that it took about three months initially to train a person to do this type of work. It then took about a year and a half of on-the-job training and experience before the examiner achieved a satisfactory rate of output, and two to three years before the average examiner reached optimum performance.

Since the work performed by the mortgage examiners was repetitive, management felt that it could exercise considerable control over a substantial part of this section. Based on a time study, a work standard of 12 loan transactions per examiner per day had been established some years previously, and this standard later was raised to 15. Records were maintained within the section of the number of loan transactions received each day, the number processed by each examiner, and the backlog.

In evaluating the work of individual examiners, some judgment had to be exercised in applying this standard. For example, in the Atlantic Coast group, an examiner sometimes received a batch of loan transactions in which the mortgaged properties were in a single, large housing subdivision. The legal issues in these transactions tended to be the same. In other parts of the country, however, loans tended to come from scattered localities and thus would be quite different from one another in many respects. A supervisor, therefore, in applying the standard would have to be familiar with the type of work an examiner was doing.

BUDGET PROCESS

Although considerable control could be achieved over the output of individual examiners, control over the entire section was a more difficult problem. Each September, the budget committee of the company issued a memorandum to all division heads, asking them to prepare a budget for the operation of their division during the following year.

The basic intent of the budget process was to get division heads to plan and report in advance the scope of their operations for the following year. Usually, the budgets were prepared by anticipating first the changes in activity levels from the current year and then the cost implications of these changes. Management checked each individual budget for reasonableness, and also checked the total expected cost and revenue to insure that the overall anticipated profit was satisfactory. The budget was viewed as a device for informing management of the plans a division head had for the coming year so that management could appraise these plans in relation to what other divisional heads had planned and in relation to company policy. The budget was also considered to be a measure of a division head's ability to plan his division's operations and then to operate in accordance with that plan.

On receipt of the budget committee's memorandum in September, division heads began forecasting operations within their divisions for the following year. First, each section head made plans for his section. For example, the individual loan section obtained an estimate of the amount of money that the investment division would have available for individual loans in the following year. Based partially on this estimate and partially on its estimated needs for other activities, the individual loan section developed a budget. This estimate, along with the estimated budgets for the other sections of the law division, was reviewed by Mr. Somersby. The law division then sent its budget to the budget committee for review. Usually, the law division's figures were accepted. Each quarter during the year, actual performance to date was compared with budgeted performance. Heads of divisions were required to explain large deviations from projected estimates.

Although management within the law division could, in theory, vary the size of the staff in the individual loan section, in fact, there was great reluctance to increase or decrease the work force unless a definite trend in volume was apparent. One reason for this was company policy. The company felt a great responsibility toward its employees, and as a matter of policy would lay off or discharge employees only for serious offenses. This same policy made management reluctant to hire new employees unless there was assurance that the need for them was permanent. Therefore, the law division tended to maintain a staff sufficient to handle a minimum work load, and it supplemented this with overtime.

Another reason for the tendency to maintain a level work force of mortgage examiners was the cost of selecting and training them. Management went to great pains to select outstanding clerks for these jobs. This was followed by a thorough course of study and on-the-job training. Because of this large investment, management wanted to be sure that anyone trained for this job would be needed permanently in the section.

Management within the individual loan section, in attempting to achieve control over the section as a whole and yet in keeping with company policy, had devised several controls. Occasionally, when the work load lessened, supervisors would call the investment division to see if they could get some work that, although perhaps not quite ready to be sent over as a complete batch, could, nevertheless, be sent in parts. Also, since in periods when loan applications were low foreclosures tended to increase, the mortgage examiners were trained to handle some aspects of foreclosures, and this provided a degree of dovetailing in the work flow. Other than these measures, however, the division preferred to rely on overtime work. The use of outside law firms was out of the question for this type of work because of the far greater cost, even in comparison with overtime wages.

CORPORATE LOAN SECTION

The corporate loan section was a much different kind of operation. A corporate loan, generally for a much larger amount than an individual loan, was one made directly by NJIC to a borrower, such as an industrial or commercial enterprise or a public utility. The loan might be either secured or unsecured. An important advantage to a borrower of this type of loan, as compared with a loan evidenced by a bond issue sold to the general public, was that the borrower was not required to furnish a formal prospectus or file a registration statement with the SEC.

In this type of loan, financial determinations such as the amount of the loan, interest rate, timing of repayments, restrictive covenants, and so forth were made by the investment division, as was the case with individual loans, but by a different section in that division. Because of the size and complexity of corporate loans, the corporate loan section worked closely with the investment division people who made these financial determinations. This involved sitting in on the negotiations and rendering advice on all the terms of the transaction. It was the responsibility of the corporate loan section to insure that the final loan instruments protected the interests of NJIC in the manner intended by the financial people.

On this type of loan, for various reasons, the corporate loan section almost without exception retained well-known outside counsel. One important reason was that an opinion from such an independent law firm contributed to the marketability of the investment in the event of a sale at a later date. Further, in many of these transactions, a number of other investors were involved, and NJIC's law division could not appropriately represent these other investors. If NJIC was the leading investor, it did, however, select the outside counsel to be retained. In addition, it was not possible, without greatly increasing the size of the present staff, for company attorneys to handle all the legal work connected with this type of loan, especially at the time of peak loads. Under this system, any one lawyer had a large number of loan negotiations in process at all times with various outside counsel, and this was beneficial both to the individual and to the company in providing lawyers with a broad base of experience in a variety of situations. The background and experience of company attorneys assured the company of consistency of policy in the negotiation of direct placements.

A substantial part of the work in corporate loans consisted of drafting legal documents. The extent to which company attorneys relied on outside counsel to perform parts of this work depended on the complexity of the transaction (company attorneys tended to do more of the work on more complex transactions) and on how busy company attorneys were. In general, company attorneys handled as a minimum enough of the work to be thoroughly familiar with all aspects of the transaction. In many cases, they prepared the first drafts of all legal papers. But in the event that first drafts were left to outside counsel, company attorneys reviewed the work and redrafted it as necessary.

Borrowers were required to pay all expenses incurred in employing outside counsel. However, NJIC made clear to both prospective borrowers and to outside counsel that the counsel were representing NJIC and that their loyalty belonged to NJIC, much the same as for a company attorney. Even though the borrower paid the fee for outside counsel, the head of the corporate loan section, Peter Carlisle, checked closely on the fees charged by outside counsel. Over the years, a thorough tabulation of fees charged for different types of legal work throughout the country had been built up. Mr. Carlisle, simply by referring to this tabulation, could readily determine whether a particular fee was apparently out of line. If there was any substantial deviation, he looked into the case more closely to determine if there was some reasonable explanation; if not, he discussed the matter with the outside counsel and adjusted the fee. Over the years, NJIC had established excellent working relationships with many law firms throughout the country.

The control procedure in this section was substantially different from that in the individual loan section. At the initiation of each transaction, Mr. Carlisle was consulted by the attorney to whom it was referred. Reassignments to equalize the work load of the various attorneys were made as necessary. A degree of control also was achieved through weekly staff conferences with Mr. Carlisle. At this conference, lawyers raised individual problems they had encountered. In addition to keeping Mr. Carlisle informed in detail on what was going on, the conference provided an opportunity for each staff member to draw on the experience of other lawyers, and it served as a vehicle for developing a consistent policy on various matters. Also, the discussion of current negotiations made it more likely that in case of illness another lawyer would be prepared to take over the work.

Another control device was the current work assignment report which each attorney in the section submitted to Mr. Carlisle. Because corporate loan transactions took varying amounts of time to complete, ranging from several weeks to many months, it was found that daily and, in some cases, weekly reports were not feasible. Accordingly, each attorney submitted a report when his work situation suggested to him that a new one was desirable. Each report covered all the time elapsed since the preceding report.

At the top of this report the lawyer briefly indicated his current work status, such as "fully occupied" or "available." Although a detailed format was not prescribed, in general the report described briefly how the lawyer's present jobs were going, what kinds of problems were involved, and what he had completed since his previous report. These reports, in addition to supplementing Mr. Carlisle's knowledge of what was being done in this section, helped tell who was available for more work.

The amount of time a lawyer had to spend on a particular job was not predictable. Major variables were the number and complexity of restrictive covenants in an unsecured note, for example, and the terms and provisions of the security instruments in a secured transaction. The number and complexity of the various covenants in these security instruments did not necessarily vary with the size of the loan, but depended, rather, on the nature, size, and credit standing of the corporate borrower. Many times, a relatively small loan was more complicated than a larger one.

Also, even though the details of a loan had been worked out initially to the satisfaction of the borrower and NJIC, and even though the loan had been in effect for a considerable period of time, borrowers frequently came back to NJIC to ask for waivers or modifications; that is, they requested changes in the restrictive covenants, the terms, or other conditions or agreements. Such events increased the difficulty of planning in advance how a lawyer was to spend his time.

Unusually heavy work loads in the section were met not only by overtime but also by increasing to the extent feasible the amount of work given to outside counsel. Within limitations, the lawyer responsible for a particular job generally decided how much work would be assigned to outside counsel.

Although the corporate loan section followed the same budget procedure as the individual loan section, one of the variable factors—that is, the extent to which work was delegated to outside counsel—did not affect the budget, since the borrower paid for these services.

BUDGET REPORTS

Mr. Montgomery was thoroughly familiar with the background information given above as he began his review of the law division's budget performance for the first half of 1975. The report he had before him consisted of a summary page for the law division (Exhibit 2) and a page for each of the five sections, two of which are shown in Exhibits 3 and 4. The budget figures on the report were one-half the budget for the year.

QUESTIONS

1. In what ways does Mr. Somersby control the operations of the sections of his division? In what ways does top management control the operation of the law division?

2. What possibilities for improving control, if any, do you think should be explored?

3. As Mr. Montgomery, what comments would you make and what questions would you ask Mr. Somersby about the performance of the two sections of the law division for the first six months of 1975?

Exhibit 2

NEW JERSEY INSURANCE COMPANY

Budget Report, Law Division
First Six Months, 1975

Sections	Budget	Actual	Over Budget	Under Budget
Individual loans	$698,893	$753,154	$54,261	
Corporate loans	641,302	598,073		$43,229
(Three other sections omitted)	—	—	—	—
Total	$3,082,448	$3,107,822	$25,374	
Number of full-time employees	166	160		6

Exhibit 3

NEW JERSEY INSURANCE COMPANY

Budget Report, Individual Loan Section
First Six Months, 1975

Costs	Budget	Actual	Over Budget	Under Budget
Employee costs:				
Salaries, full time	$424,092	$432,201	$ 8,109	
Salaries, part time	—	—	—	
Salaries, overtime	2,500	31,610	29,110	
Borrowed labor	—	5,905	5,905	
Employee lunches	17,055	19,180	2,125	
Insurance, retirement, etc.	84,819	86,441	1,622	
Social security	21,205	21,610	405	
Total	$549,671	$596,947	$47,276	
Direct service costs:				
Photography	$ 9,205	$ 10,667	$ 1,462	
Tracing	370	690	320	
Mimeograph	407	587	180	
Reproduction	237	515	278	
Total	$ 10,219	$ 12,459	$ 2,240	
Other costs:				
Rent	$ 70,230	$ 70,230	$	
Office supplies	2,267	3,067	800	
Equipment depreciation and				
maintenance	11,940	11,940		
Printed forms	3,842	5,367	1,525	
Travel	2,835	3,155	320	
Telephone	7,577	8,690	1,113	
Postage	3,057	3,227	170	
Prorated company services	36,810	37,405	595	
Professional dues	50	100	50	
Miscellaneous	395	567	172	
Total	$139,003	$143,748	$ 4,745	
Grand Total	$698,893	$753,154	$54,261	
Number of full-time employees	46	46		

Exhibit 4

NEW JERSEY INSURANCE COMPANY

Budget Report, Corporate Loan Section
First Six Months, 1975

Costs	Budget	Actual	Over Budget	Under Budget
Employee costs:				
Salaries, full time	$438,720	$407,488		$31,232
Salaries, part time				
Salaries, overtime	3,000			3,000
Borrowed labor				
Employee lunches	10,325	9,355		970
Insurance, retirement, etc.	87,745	81,497		6,248
Social security	21,936	20,375		1,561
Total	$561,726	$518,715		$43,011
Direct service costs:				
Photography	$ 1,637	$ 1,353	$	$ 284
Tracing	730	265		465
Mimeograph		67	67	
Reproduction		35	35	
Total	$ 2,367	$ 1,720		$ 647
Other costs:				
Rent	$ 41,953	$ 41,953	$	$
Office supplies	1,850	2,955	1,105	
Equipment depreciation and				
maintenance	7,740	7,740		
Printed forms	445	915	470	
Travel	1,930	1,880		50
Telephone	2,275	2,835	560	
Postage	420	390		30
Prorated company services	20,213	18,357		1,856
Professional dues	200	200		
Miscellaneous	183	413	230	
Total	$ 77,209	$ 77,638	$ 429	
Grand Total	$641,302	$598,073		$43,229
Number of full-time employees	26	24		2

Case 5-2

Peterson Manufacturing Company

"For controlling direct labor and raw materials costs, we have had standard cost based on scientific measurements; for decisions on fixed asset investments, we have been using rather sophisticated return-on-investment calculations; but we have lagged behind in inventing even a most primitive technique for controlling such overhead items as advertising, research and development, and personnel, although these costs have grown in their relative importance over the recent years." Thus began Mr. Toomey, controller of the Peterson Manufacturing Company, in describing a control technique recently adopted by his company. He proceeded,

What makes the planning and control of these costs difficult, is, fundamentally, the difficulty in defining and measuring output—that is, benefit or result intended from the incurrence of these costs—and establishing predictable relationships between costs (input) and the result (output), if definable at all. For example, what is the benefit of adding another personnel man? How are advertising expenses related to sales volume? These questions cannot be meaningfully and operationally answered. If the research department or personnel department asks for an additional man, we have no way of judging whether the request is justifiable or not. More basically, we have no idea, in the first place, whether or not the current level of services rendered by these departments is adequate. Obviously, we need a reasonably objective standard in order to prevent constant haggling between those who request additional manpower or expenditure in these areas and those who must approve or deny such requests.

Briefly put, the standard on which our new technique is based is industry data—that is, how much other comparable companies are spending on advertising, R&D, personnel, etc. We are aware that what other companies do is not necessarily correct; nevertheless, such information provides a workable starting point of analysis. Suppose your company spends 20 percent of sales dollars on R&D, while a comparable company, company A, spends only 14 percent, the industry average being 16 percent. We would be curious to find out why our R&D effort is out of line in comparison with company A and with the industry. Is the difference a result of considered company policy, or is it something else?

SOURCE OF INDUSTRY DATA

A prerequisite for the effective use of the new technique of controlling these overhead costs at the Peterson company was the availability of reliable industry data. Fortunately, the company was a participant in the American Management Association's "Group Ten" project. Under this program, approximately 200 participating companies (in 1963) supplied Group Ten headquarters with detailed information on how many employees were doing what kind of work, and with supplementary financial information on such items as sales, operating expenses, and income. Group Ten headquarters processed the information on a computer, calculating industry averages and ratios for various functions, and sent each participant these tabulations in what is called the Red Book.

All participants were required to follow a uniform definition of functions so as to increase comparability. Exhibit 1 gives Group Ten's form for reporting information according to the prescribed functional groupings. A few examples of definitions and instructions on classification are given in the appendix. Although only code names were used for companies cited in the Red Book, each participant was supplied with a separate list of codes and actual company names so that it could identify companies with which it believed it could make useful comparisons. Frequently, one company would call another company to exchange more detailed information than that given in the Red Book. From time to time, at the request of participants, Group Ten carried out a special study for more detailed information on a specific function. The Group Ten membership fee was $675 a year.

According to Mr. Toomey, a major benefit of Group Ten participation came from the soul-searching self-appraisal that participants had to make in classifying employees into the uniform functions defined by Group Ten. Other benefits were limited to what the participants chose to do with the Red Book data. Mr. Toomey believed that Peterson was one of the companies that made good use of the data. Following are his descriptions of two examples of how Peterson used the information.

Example 1: Control of Personnel Function

"When we receive a new Red Book, we first compare the number of employees for our company with the industry average in each of the 60 functions defined by Group Ten. Then for further analysis we select a number of functional areas that seem out of line—that is, overstaffed.

"In September, 1959, the personnel function was selected as one of the over-

Exhibit 1

PETERSON MANUFACTURING COMPANY

Furnished by Group Ten

Manpower Utilization—Unit Report

DIVISION   UNIT:

Line	FUNCTIONAL GROUPING	Actual Number of Employees on Payroll as of:					C
		A (Exempt)	B (Non-Exempt)			TOTAL A+B	Outside Services
			Salaried	Hourly	Tot Non Ex		
1	EXTRACTING OR PRODUCING						
2	Production Workers						
3	Maintenance Workers						
4	1st Line Supervisors						
	A. Production						
	B. Maintenance						
	C. 1st Line Supv. Sub-Total (A+B)	( )	( )	( )	( )	( )	( )
5	Management and Staff						
	GROUP TOTAL						
8	MANUFACTURING OR PROCESSING						
9	Production Workers						
10	Maintenance Workers						
11	1st Line Supervisors						
	A. Production						
	B. Maintenance						
	C. 1st Line Supv. Sub-Total (A+B)	( )	( )	( )	( )	( )	( )
12	AUXILIARY SERVICE						
	A. Utilities and Waste Disposal						
	B. In-Plant Trans. & Material Handlg.						
	C. Inspecting or Testing						
	D. Receiving, Storing, Shipping						
	E. Prod. Planning, Sched. Expediting						
	F. Devising, Prod., Maint., Jigs. Etc.						
	G. Aux. Serv. Sub-Total (A – F)	( )	( )	( )	( )	( )	( )
13	Management and Staff						
14	GROUP TOTAL						
16	TRANSPORTING						
17	Marine						
18	Motor Truck						
19	All Other						
20	Management and Staff						
21	GROUP TOTAL						
23	Design, Creat. Devel., Research						
24	Oriented toward Extracting or Producing						
25	Oriented toward Processes or Mfg.						
26	Oriented toward Products or Marketing						
27	Oriented toward Facilities						
28	Oriented toward New Creations or Disc.						
29	Auxiliary Service						
30	Management and Staff						
31	GROUP TOTAL						
33	MARKETING						
34	Sales Representatives – Consumer						
35	1st Line Supervisors – Consumer						
36	Sales Representatives – Industry						
37	1st Line Supervisors – Industry						
38	Customer Servicing						
	A. Order Hand. Billing, Non-Tech. Serv						
	B. Serv. & Repair after Prod. Is Sold						
	C. Tech. Explan. of Existing Applic.						
	D. Cust. Serv. Sub-Total (A – C)	( )	( )	( )	( )	( )	( )
39	Advertising & Sales Promotion						
40	Market Research & Sales Statistics						
41	Management and Staff						
42	GROUP TOTAL						

Exhibit 1—Continued

Line	FUNCTIONAL GROUPING	A (Exempt)	B (Non-Exempt) Salaried	B (Non-Exempt) Hourly	B (Non-Exempt) Tot Non Ex.	TOTAL A+B	C Outside Services
44	GENERAL ADMINISTERING	/////	/////	/////	/////	/////	/////
45	Accounting and Auditing						
46	Finance, Insurance, Tax						
47	Economics, Budgeting						
48	Credit and Collections						
49	Personnel						
50	External Relations						
51	Purchasing						
52	Traffic						
53	Office Services	/////	/////	/////	/////	/////	/////
	A. Mail, Messenger, Repro, Etc.						
	B. Centralized Type & Steno Pools						
	C. Centralized Files & Archives						
	D. Office Serv. Sub-Total (A - C)	( )	( )	( )	( )	( )	( )
54	General Management Aux. Service						
55	Operations Improvement	/////	/////	/////	/////	/////	/////
	A. Industrial Engineering						
	B. Operations Research						
	C. Systems and Procedures						
	D. Scien. & Tech. Program & Coding						
	F. Op. Imp. Sub-Total (A - D)	( )	( )	( )	( )	( )	( )
56	Tabulating & Electronic Computing						
57	Legal and Secretarial						
58	General Management						
59	GROUP TOTAL						
61	Specific Accessory Functions						
62	TOTAL EMPLOYEES						

staffed areas that needed special management attention. According to the Red Book, our ratio of personnel staff to the number of employees served was the fourth highest among 35 companies that we think are roughly comparable to Peterson. The number of personnel staff per 1,000 employees was 22.0 for Peterson and 16.6 on the average for the 35 companies.

"Shortly thereafter, we received the result of a special, detailed study of personnel staff made under Group Ten sponsorship. In this study, the personnel function was further broken down into 10 subfunctions, and the interested companies supplied the figures for these subfunctions. After a careful analysis of all relevant information obtained from the special study and from our own investigation, we sent out the following memorandum to each operating division."

INTEROFFICE CORRESPONDENCE

February 10, 1960

TO: *Operating Division General Managers*
FROM: *Sean Toomey, Controller*
SUBJECT: *Manpower Utilization*
          Personnel Function

This report provides a further breakdown of the personnel function data distributed on October 5, 1959. The function has been exploded into 10 personnel activities to provide an opportunity for detailed comparisons and analysis.

Table 1 presents the suggested staffing ranges for the operating divisions in terms of the number of personnel staff per 1,000 employees. These ranges were developed by comparative analysis and judgment in conjunction with the personnel division. It is believed that they can be used effectively as guides for staffing divisions.

As used in the table, "personnel people" includes both individuals performing personnel functions in the operating divisions as well as an allocated portion of the individuals on the central personnel staff. (For the basis of allocation, see Table 2 and a paragraph below that explains the table.)

For the total company, it should be noted that the suggested ratio is lower in five of the ten categories, remains the same in four, and is up in one. The total shows a lowering of the ratio by 4.2 per thousand employees. This will drop our rank from fourth to sixth in the 35 companies.

Tables 2–9[1] show for the individual divisions the applications of the suggested staffing ratios.

Distribution of personnel staff of the central service divisions was based on the time spent on each operating division as estimated by the service division staff. Personnel staff by activity was supplied by you in November, 1959.

The ratio of personnel staff to 1,000 employees is shown, and the resulting ranking in the operating divisions.

The last two columns show the application to the division of the suggested staffing ratio. Although the *total* suggested ranges are the only figures of major significance, the detail by activity may give you clues as you apply the range to your division.

Mr. Toomey continued, "Dispatching this memorandum was virtually all we did, but the result was very pleasing. First of all, the availability of an objective standard put the burden of proof on the division. Second, the memorandum made

---

[1] Only Table 2 for division A is included in this case.

Table 1

PETERSON MANUFACTURING COMPANY

Suggested Staffing Ranges, February, 1960

(Ratio Personnel People per 1,000 Employees)

Personnel Activities	Empl. & Place.	Train & Educ.	Labor Rel.	Wages & Sal.	Ben. & Serv.	Health & Safe.	Pub. & Comm.	Sugg. Syst.	Per. Res.	Per. Adm.	Total
Present ratio (Sept. 1959)	2.9	.8	1.4	2.1	2.0	8.3	.8	.8	.3	2.6	22.0
Ranking in 35 companies*	6	7	8	4	6	1	8	4	9	6	4
Suggested ratio	2.4	.8	1.4	1.7	2.0	5.4	.8	.6	.4	2.3	17.8
The resulting ranking*	8	7	8	6	6	7	8	5	5	9	6
Present range:†											
Low	1.1	.1	.8	1.2	.9	3.3	.1	.3	0	1.2	13.2
	to	to	to	to	to	to	to	to	to	to	to
High	3.8	1.5	3.6	4.8	2.8	11.1	1.2	2.0	.5	3.1	26.3
Suggested range:†											
Low	1.1	.1	.8	1.2	.9	3.3	.1	.3	0	1.2	13.2
	to	to	to	to	to	to	to	to	to	to	to
High	2.8	1.5	2.3	2.2	2.4	6.3	0.9	1.0	.5	2.8	18.5

* Ranking: Highest Ratio = #1 rank.

† Ranges represent the highest and lowest among all Peterson divisions.

Table 2

PETERSON MANUFACTURING COMPANY
Personnel Function
Summary, September, 1959

Division A

Personnel Activities	Number of Personnel People				Personnel People Per 1,000 Employees	
	In Operating Division	From Central Serv. Div. for Oper. Div.	Total	Ratio	Present Operating Division Rank	Suggested Range
1. Employment and placement	1.2	.3	1.5	1.1	(8)	1.1 to 2.8
2. Training and education	.7	.1	.8	.6	(5)	.1 to 1.5
3. Labor relations	2.4	1.8	4.2	3.0	(3)	.8 to 2.3
4. Wage and salary administration	1.7	—	1.7	1.2	(8)	1.2 to 2.2
5. Benefits and services	2.7	1.1	3.8	2.7	(3)	.9 to 2.4
6. Health and safety	12.0	2.1	14.1	10.1	(2)	3.3 to 6.3
7. Publications and communications	.7	—	.7	.5	(5)	.1 to .9
8. Suggestion system	2.4	.1	2.5	1.8	(2)	.3 to 1.0
9. Personnel research	—	—	—	—	—	0 to .5
10. Personnel administration	1.2	.5	1.7	1.2	(8)	.8 to 2.8
Total	25.0	6.0	31.0	22.2		
Suggested range:						
Low			18		13.0	
High			26			18.5
Total employees in division: 1,400						

the division aware of and interested in the problem. Third, the divisions had detailed information if they cared to analyze further.

"To be sure, we heard a lot of complaints from the divisions. Typical were the comments that our company was different from the 'comparable' companies, and therefore the averages were without much meaning; that the divisions should not be charged for personnel staff of the central service divisions; and that one division was different from other divisions. To these, our answer was always that the data in the memorandum were to be taken only as 'guidelines', and it was up to the division managers to change the size of the personnel staff on the basis of the data. At any rate, whatever the feeling may have been, the important fact is that the divisions reduced personnel staff by 10 percent on the average in two years' time. The following is a progress report:"

INTEROFFICE CORRESPONDENCE

January 23, 1962

TO: *Operating Division General Managers*
FROM: *Sean Toomey, Controller*
SUBJECT: *Personnel Function—Progress Report*

This is a progress report aimed at showing how far we have come since the first study of personnel staff made in September, 1959. The result is gratifying to all of us. From September, 1959, to November, 1961, there was a reduction in personnel staff of 31 men, from 363 to 332, despite an increase, though slight, in the total number of employees of the company.

In 1960, we set the goal of a company-wide ratio of 17.8 personnel people for every thousand employees, and a range of 13.0 to 18.5 personnel people per thousand people for the operating divisions; the current figure was 22.0. In November, 1961, the company-wide ratio of personnel people per thousand employees was 20.0.

Table 3 summarizes the progress we have made and shows, in addition, how far we have to go in attaining the goals set up in the 1960 report.

Example 2: Control of Production Planning, Scheduling, and Expediting Function

The controller continued, "In Example 1, comparison with other companies led to a reduction of manpower, but it should not be inferred that the new technique is always aimed at economizing the number of employees. In many cases, seemingly overstaffed functions—compared to other companies—were left intact after a careful analysis; in a few cases, studies actually led to an increase in the number of employees.

"For instance, a few months ago Red Book data indicated that our production planning, scheduling, and expediting function might be overstaffed, since our company's ratio of sales to the number of employees engaged in these functions was low compared to that of other comparable companies. Accordingly, we initiated a special analysis. First of all, we had to determine what this particular staff function was contributing to the company. Of many indicators of the function's contribution, the most important, we decided, was inventory turnover—namely, the ratio of sales to inventories. Here, our company ranked among the top few of the comparable companies. The conclusion was that we were satisfied with the level of number of employees engaged in the function. I do not recall specifically, but our staff even did a fancy calculation of the cost of additional employees compared to the savings—chiefly in capital cost—from quick inventory turnover, and it was a considerable amount."

QUESTIONS

1. Is this approach useful in the Peterson Manufacturing Company?
2. Is it likely to be useful in companies generally?

Table 3

PERSONNEL FUNCTION COMPARISON
1959–61

| | Division Population | | Number of Personnel People | | | | | | Difference in Total Personnel Staff, 1959–61 | Reduction Required to Achieve Top of Range (18.5 per 1,000 employees) | |
| | | | September, 1959 | | | November, 1961 | | | | | |
	1959 Sept.	1961 Nov.	On Div. Payroll	Allocated	Total	On Div. Payroll	Allocated	Total		1959 Sept.	1961 Nov.
A	1,400	1,623	25	6.0	31.0	31	5.5	36.5	+5.5	5.0	6.5
B*											
C*											
D	3,117	3,096	64	9.6	73.6	52	7.8	59.8	−13.8	15.9	2.5
E*											
F*											
G*											
H*											
Totals	16,524	16,580	321	42.5	363.5	299	33.3	332.3	−31.2	57.8	25.6

* The figures for these divisions are omitted in order to make it more difficult to identify the divisions.

Appendix

Extracts from Group Ten
Definitions

*Examples of Definitions and Instructions on Group Ten Functional
Groupings Used in Manpower Utilization—Unit Report*[2]

. . . Report the manpower utilized for the various basic functions *without
regard* to our job titles or traditional names of our "departments," divisions,
etc. This is necessary because such varied departmental names are used to
describe the same work in other companies. Definitions of functional categories may be thought of as revolving around action-words. What *specific
work* does the employee *do* during his work day?

. . . If a person holds a position that falls into more than one functional
category, classify the employee according to the function that consumes the
greatest amount of time. Do not use additional categories.

NOTE: If the number of such employees has a significant effect on line
percentages, then the entire group should be allocated by percent to their
appropriate functions.

Occasionally difficulty has been reported with the classification of special
groups, task forces, and the like. Most of these difficulties disappear when
the group or task force unity is broken up and individuals are considered by
what they are doing. Departments, divisions, special groups, task forces, etc.,
rarely can be classified en masse. It is essential to carry out the functional
classification on an individual basis.

Column A generally is to be used to record the number of those employees
who are exempt from the U.S. Wage and Hour Law, or not covered by
it. . . .

Column B generally is to be used to record the number of those employees
who are *nonexempt*—that is, covered by the U.S. Wage and Hour Law. . . .

---

2 These examples refer to the form given in Exhibit 1.

Trainees are to be included in the functions for which the training is preparing them.

In collecting data this year, provision has been made for recording on *each line* where appropriate, an estimate of the number of people our company avoids having on its regular staff because of its purchase of outside services. For example, in the Personnel function outside medical practitioners are frequently used rather than staff doctors; in the operations improvement function outside industrial engineers may perform work in our company that is handled by its own staff in another company.

Line Definitions

Please read all line definitions and review the entire form before proceeding. . . .

1. *Extracting or Producing*
   A general heading controlling lines 1 thru 6. Employees concerned with prospecting for, extracting and producing materials for subsequent processing, refining and other manufacturing operations. Examples are exploring, mining, drilling, petroleum producing and farming.
2. *Production Workers*—Nonexempt—generally hourly employees in mining, drilling, farming and related occupations, except maintenance.
8. *Manufacturing or Processing*
   A general heading controlling 8 thru 14. Employees concerned with the processing, refining, fermenting, manufacturing, assembling, or packaging of products and the necessarily related occupations of storage, flow of products, materials and utilities.
11. *First Line Supervisors*—All positions in which the work is accomplished by the direct supervision of production and maintenance workers (lines 9 and 10). Exclude group leader, lead hand or others who spend more than half of their time doing the same work as those they supervise—Show supervisors' secretaries or clerks on line 13B.
12. *Auxiliary Service*—Employees performing service functions related specifically to manufacturing, fabricating, or processing. Include also all first line supervisors of auxiliary personnel in each line.
    A. Utilities and Waste Disposal. . . .
    E. Production planning, production scheduling and dispatching (including preparation of bill of materials and formulation), floor expediting and materials control. Typical titles: Inventory Clerk, Production Planning Manager, Perpetual Inventory Clerk, Expeditor, Scheduler, Job-Time or Machine Utilization Record Clerk. . . .
44. *General Administering*
    A general term controlling lines 44 thru 59. A group of general functions not specifically part of the functions of producing, manufacturing, transporting, creating and designing or marketing covered elsewhere. . . .

49. *Personnel*—Activities related to personnel or industrial relations including recruitment, employment and placement, training (except sales), education and development; labor relations; wage and salary administration; employee benefits and services; health, medical and safety; employee publications and communications; suggestion systems; personnel research; personnel administration and records. Certain apparently related items not specifically listed here belong on Line 61, for example, guards and firemen.

Case 5-3

Mercury Stores, Inc.*

Mercury Stores, Inc., is a drug chain that sells prescription and nonprescription drugs and a wide line of merchandise similar to that handled in "5 and 10 variety" stores. Customers can buy everything from vitamins to Pyrex coffeemakers, household mops, and hand luggage in any one of the company's 80 supermarket-type branches located in a fast-growing region of the United States.

The chain was founded 27 years ago and has grown steadily through merging, purchasing local drug stores, and rapidly increasing sales in an area characterized by local newspapers as one of "population explosion in America's finest economic and geographical climate."

Last year's sales of $68 million produced a net income before taxes of $4.8 million. Twelve new stores were opened during that period, and two small out-of-date facilities were closed. Average sales per store amounted to $844,000 per year, a figure the management would like to increase to over a million dollars. Present assets amount to $24 million.

The officers of the company have, from the very start, operated under the principle that mass advertising, public relations, and superior supermarket facilities are the keys to success over competition. They believe that the public wants fast, efficient, low-cost service in the most modern and up-to-date stores. Coupled with these top objectives, the officers have added another objective that is "almost as important." In the words of the president,

It's not enough to have low-cost, high-quality merchandise in fine stores, unless the public is kept constantly aware of our name and has a good feeling toward our organization. Especially since two other chains have arisen in our market area in the last ten years whose facilities and services are just as up-to-date as

* This case was written by Charles E. Summer, reprinted by permission from S. H. Newman and C. E. Summer, *The Process of Management: Concepts, Behavior and Practice.* © 1961, Prentice-Hall, Englewood Cliffs, N.J.

ours. We must have the additional objective of keeping the public informed of our facilities and services, and developing the feeling on the citizens' part that we too are a good citizen in the community.

Public Recognition and Public Good Will in "One-Store Cities"

This case concerns the problem faced by Mercury's top management in implementing that objective in cities where the company operates only one large store. Management feels that the problems of public awareness of the name and of public "good feeling" toward the organization are different in cities where five or ten stores are located.

There are 21 "one-store city" branches in the whole Mercury complex. The cities in which these stores are located range in population from 40,000 to 150,000. Each branch is headed by a store manager, who reports on the organization chart to a division manager. There are two division managers over the one-store city branches, one in the northern area and one in the southern area. These men report to the president.

Three years ago, D. M. James, Mercury president, called F. K. Simms, director of public relations for the company, into his office. He told Simms that the top management had never taken any steps to see whether branch managers are actually developing a public awareness of the company name or creating good feeling toward the company.

We have published a list of our corporate objectives, with this one included, and I assume that managers are running their internal store operations so that we do get a certain amount of good public recognition. We have no way of knowing, however, the *degree* to which this is happening: Is public feeling deficient? Is it adequate? Or is it actually very high, in relation to what can be done? Are the managers doing all they can? I am a little concerned because we've grown so big, and a manager has his hands full running the store, and some of these managers may not be as conscious of public opinion as others, and may not have an inherent interest in giving special attention to this area.

As a result of this conversation, Mr. Simms got an assignment to draw up a list of control reports that would give the top management some indication of the recognition of the company, and good feelings toward it, on the part of the public in one-store cities. James also told Simms that he was asking Bob Flood, a branch manager, to perform a similar assignment; he said, however, that he would like the two projects to be done independently, so that the two proposed report systems could be compared with an eye to drawing on the best features of each. Flood was to be given a short leave of absence from managing one of the largest one-branch city stores in order to prepare his report. The president also told the two men that he wanted (1) a general statement of what information management should get, (2) an indication of which executives should receive various kinds of information, and (3) a statement of how often control information should be sent in. The essential features of the proposals submitted by the two men appear in Exhibits 1 (Simms' proposal) and 2 (Flood's).

Exhibit 1

PROPOSED REPORT SYSTEM FOR PUBLIC RELATIONS
(Prepared by F. K. Simms)

1. The branch manager will be evaluated once a year on his ability to produce good public relations results. These evaluations will be performed by the director of public relations, on the basis of the reports and information described below.

2. By January 10 of each year, branch managers will submit a report for the preceding year showing:

a) The number of visits made by the manager with municipal or county officials in his city (three per year is satisfactory).

b) The number of newspaper articles in his city in which the company name was mentioned, either favorably or unfavorably (eight favorable articles per year is satisfactory).

c) The number of newspaper articles, other than paid advertising, written in city newspapers exclusively about the company or its branches (two per year is satisfactory).

d) The number of speeches made by the manager to local clubs, schools, or other organizations (two per year is satisfactory).

e) The number of training sessions which the branch manager holds with key store employees on the subject of courteous actions of store personnel (two per year is satisfactory).

f) The number of complaints received by the store because of poor service during the year.

g) The number of unsolicited written compliments to the store, its personnel, and the company as a whole, received during the year (30 is satisfactory).

h) The number of serious difficulties encountered with the public, other than minor complaints, during the year. This might include such things as threats of legal action, public criticism, and so on.

3. This report will be sent to the director of public relations, with a copy to the division managers for their information. The director of public relations will be responsible for visiting each branch manager during the year to discuss the results indicated on the reports. The public relations director will submit to the president a short summary of the statistics for all branches as a consolidated summary, and a verbal summary of the "state of public opinion" in the company.

4. Division managers will receive copies of yearly reports of branch managers, and yearly reports of the director of public relations.

Exhibit 2

PROPOSED PLAN FOR CONTROL OVER PUBLIC RELATIONS
(Prepared by Robert Flood)

1. Every three months, division managers should visit with branch managers in their area, in order that the latter can report verbally on what they have done to improve public recognition and public good will in their cities.

Exhibit 2—Continued

2. The store manager's performance in public relations will be deemed satisfactory when:

a) He can show an overall plan of what he expects to accomplish during the next three months in the way of public relations activities.

b) There is evidence that he has handled customer complaints in a friendly, courteous manner.

c) He shows that he has a systematic plan for various advertising and promotional activities, within a lump sum budget allocation of four per cent of sales.

d) He shows that he has participated in such outside relationships with the public as he deems advantageous in improving the prestige of the company.

e) Public satisfaction ratios fall in the ranges specified in the table below, as measured by Johnson and Leeds (this ratio is explained in point 4).

3. The first four items are to be reviewed by the division manager every three months in a personal discussion with the division manager. In addition, the store managers will send a brief written report of the four points once each year to the director of public relations to be used in discovering unique methods of public relations that might be of interest to other branch managers. The fifth point, results of the bi-annual Johnson and Leeds survey, will be sent to the president and public relations director.

4. Johnson and Leeds, public opinion consultants, should be employed to interview a random sample of citizens in one-store cities every two years. In order to keep cost down (the firm estimates that they will do the job for $4,500 per store per survey), one summary question will be asked:

"Considering all of the drug outlets in (name of city), which of the following statements most nearly describes your opinion of the store?"

a) "A highly satisfactory company—best in town"   (25)%

b) "A good company—I'm glad they are in   (65)%
(name of city)   (40)%

c) "I don't know. They are about the same as
other drug stores"   (30)%

d) "I believe they are not a satisfactory company   (35)%
to do business with"   (5)%

The figures in the right column show what percentage of total persons interviewed should check this answer. Branch managers' performance will be satisfactory if levels specified above are maintained. Cumulative totals of the top two and bottom two categories are also significant.

The President's Review of the Proposals

When both proposals were completed, Mr. James studied them with, he says, a "constructively critical attitude." Regarding Simms' proposal, he wondered why three, instead of two or four, was selected as the number of visits of branch managers with public officials. Simms replied that a definite, quantitative result, known in advance, would eliminate the otherwise inevitable gripes of branch managers. "If we simply appraised and judged them on their relations with officials in a general way, *we* would have to say they are 'good' or 'bad.' This way, both sides know what is satisfactory before-hand—they either do or don't carry out this task, and if they don't, all we do is point at the standard; we don't sit and argue about what 'satisfactory' is." Mr. James asked similar questions about some of the other standards (eight newspaper articles, two speeches, and so on), and Simms' arguments in support of the absolute standards were the same. Flood, who also was present at the meeting for studying the proposals, raised the question whether this arbitrariness might not stifle the initiative of managers who may want to make more visits or speeches, and who were inclined to produce more newspaper articles.

Regarding Flood's report, James expressed some reservation about the ability of branch managers to draw up their own programs for public rela-tions activities. He said that his long experience in operating stores and Simms' expertness in public relations practices were such that they should possibly lay out in specific terms just what activities managers should per-form. For example, he cited the kinds of things Simms had listed but said that even Simms had left out some important facets of public relations activities, such as membership on charity drives, membership in Rotary and other service clubs, and so on. James also expressed some concern that the director of public relations would receive reports only once a year under Flood's plan and that he himself would receive reports only every two years. Flood an-swered Mr. James' questions by saying that the situation in public relations is quite different from city to city, and that all managers need not, for in-stance, concentrate on visits to public officials in any one year if in one branch the relations with the city and county were already good, or if a manager's time was needed in training employees for courteous service instead.

Recognizing that there were certain pros and cons of each plan, all three men agreed that a two-year test in four selected stores—two using each plan —would be advisable. Four cities of about 100,000 population were chosen where store sales ran between $600,000 and $800,000 annually. During the two years the president asked all four branch managers, their two division managers, and the director of public relations, to forward to his office all problems that arose in connection with the systems. One of the president's administrative assistants kept a file of this correspondence and of memos the president dictated after he, from time to time, conferred personally with the various men involved.

There was, of course, a voluminous amount of material concerning prob-lems that arose during the two years. Following are some significant ex-amples of these problems, drawn from the experiences of the managers in various cities: Miller (City 1) and Jones (City 2), who operated under Simms' proposal; Fry (City 3) and Kesler (City 4), who operated under Flood's proposal.

Results under the Simms Plan

Miller complained to the president at the beginning of the study that his branch city had always shown public acceptance of the company, and that listing the number of speeches and "political calls" for him to make was going against the spirit of independence that the store managers had always been guaranteed. At the outset, Miller also said he thought getting newspaper articles, and reporting number of complaints and compliments, were good ideas and that he did not object to these points (*b, c, f, g* in Exhibit 1).

Jones made a number of statements throughout the two years in support of the system, stating that he was enthusiastic about it and thought the appraisal points were good. He did admit, privately to the president, that he had been "rubbed the wrong way" by Simms, who appeared only infrequently from company headquarters and did not seem to understand the pressure on a branch manager's time. Jones also said that "the system helped remind me, and even force me, to take the time to do things I've always known I should do but didn't always get around to." His principal complaint was that the newspaper editors in his town were very sensitive to efforts to try to get mentioned in the paper's news stories (as opposed to advertisements), and they took every precaution not to offend competing drug companies by appearing to show favoritism in free publicity. Therefore, he, Jones, thought he would be put at an unfair advantage with most branch managers when no such articles appeared in the paper.

At the end of the study, when the Johnson and Leeds figures were in (see Exhibit 2), Fry came to headquarters apparently upset and said to the president that though he did not know what the ratios were, he knew he was bound to show up poorly. He said he had come to City 3 only 26 months ago, following a long tenure by Mr. Forrest, a branch manager who was noted for his abrupt manner and lack of interest in community affairs. Mr. James knew this to be true, and agreed that the J&L survey results would include influences left as legacy by Forrest that would affect Fry's incumbency. James wondered how many other managers would be in the same position.

Another thing puzzled James when he saw the result of the survey. He noted that City 4 had 67 percent in the top two categories (highly satisfactory and good). He wondered, "How do I know what this means—are they doing their best in City 4? How do I know it couldn't be 75 percent . . . 80 percent. . . ? I haven't anything to measure it against."

Kesler, in City 4, reported to his division manager that, in carrying out appraisal point 1 (Exhibit 2) he expected to attend the meeting of his Chamber of Commerce each month and that this, with his very active role in the church to which he belonged, was as much as his work pressures, and genuine interests, would allow. He showed the division manager three letters registering minor complaints, together with his replies, as the evidence referred to in point 2.

Finally, Kesler reported that the standard four percent ratio of advertising to sales (see point 2–c in the Flood proposal) was an unjust measurement of his effectiveness in City 4. He said that City 4 had five large supermarket-type drug stores, three of which were operated by the strongest competitors of Mercury. It was his opinion that no other one-store city had such tough competition, and that he needed a larger advertising budget in the face of such strong competitors.

Future Course of Action

After reviewing all the materials in the experience file, the president decided that there should be another study of the control problem in the area of public relations, one that would (1) be creative in listing the public relations activities of branch managers that would benefit the company and that did not appear in the proposals; (2) strive to make these listings as precise as possible, yet keep them valid; (3) overcome some of the problems encountered in the experiments; and (4) give special attention to the problem of what information goes to which executives and how often.

Case 5–4

Westport Electric
Corporation

On a day in the late autumn of 1974 Peter Ensign, the Controller of Westport Electric; Michael Kelly, the Manager of the Budgeting Department (reporting to Ensign); and James King, the Supervisor of the Administrative Staff Budget Section (reporting to Kelly) were discussing a problem raised by King. In reviewing the proposed 1975 budgets of the various administrative staff offices, King was disturbed by the increases in expenditure that were being proposed. He believed that, in particular, the proposed increases in two offices were not justified. King's main concern, however, was with the entire process of reviewing and approving the administrative staff budgets. The purpose of the meeting was to discuss what should be done about the two budgets in question and to consider what revisions should be made in the approval procedure for administrative staff budgets.

ORGANIZATION OF WESTPORT

Westport Electric is one of the giant United States Corporations that manufactures and sells electric and electronic products. Sales in 1974 were in excess of $1 billion and profits after taxes were over $75 million. The operating activities of the corporation are divided into four groups, each headed by a group vice president. These groups are: the Electrical Generating and Transmission Group; the Home Appliance Group; the Military and Space Group; and the Electronics Group. Each of these groups is comprised of a number of relatively independent divisions, each headed by a divisional manager. The division is the basic operating unit of the corporation and each is a profit center. The divisional manager is responsible for earning an adequate profit on his investment. There are twenty-five divisions in the corporation.

225

At the corporate level there is a Research and Development Staff and six administrative staff offices, each headed by a vice president, as follows: Finance; Industrial Relations; Legal; Marketing; Manufacturing; and Public Relations. The responsibilities of the administrative staff offices, although they vary depending upon their nature, can be divided into the following categories:

1. *Top management advice:* Each of the staff offices is responsible for providing advice to the top management of the corporation in the area of its specialty. Also, all of the staff vice presidents are members of the Policy Committee, the top decision-making body of the corporation.
2. *Advice to operating divisions and other staff offices:* Each staff office gives advice to operating divisions and, in some instances, to other staff offices. (An example of the latter is the advice the Legal Staff might give to the Finance Staff with respect to a contract.) In theory, at least, the operating divisions can accept or reject the advice as they see fit. In most cases, there is no formal requirement that the operating divisions even seek advice from the central staff. In fact, however, the advice of the staff office usually carries considerable weight and divisional managers rarely ignore it.
3. *Co-ordination among the divisions:* The staff offices have the responsibility for co-ordinating their areas of activities among the divisions. The extent of this coordination varies considerably, depending upon the nature of the activity. For example, the Finance Staff has the greatest amount of this co-ordination to do because it is necessary to establish and maintain a consistent accounting and budgetary control system. On the other hand, the Legal and Public Relations Staffs have no direct representation in the activities of the divisions.

Exhibit 1 is an organization chart of the Westport Electric Corporation.

THE BUDGETING ORGANIZATION

Exhibit 2 provides a partial organization chart of the Finance Staff. As you can see from the chart, Ensign, the Controller, reports to the Finance Vice President. Reporting to him is Kelly, who is in charge of the Budgeting Department. Reporting to Kelly is King, who is in charge of the Administrative Staff Budget Section.

Approval Procedure

Information Submitted. In the early autumn of each year, the Budgeting Department issues instructions and timetables for the preparation, submission, and approval of the budgets for the coming year. Since we are concerned in this case with the administrative staff budgets, we will limit our description to the nature of the information submitted by each administrative staff office.

Each staff office completes the following schedule:

Budget by Expense Classification. This schedule shows the proposed

Exhibit 1

WESTPORT ELECTRIC CORPORATION

Organization Chart—January 1, 1975

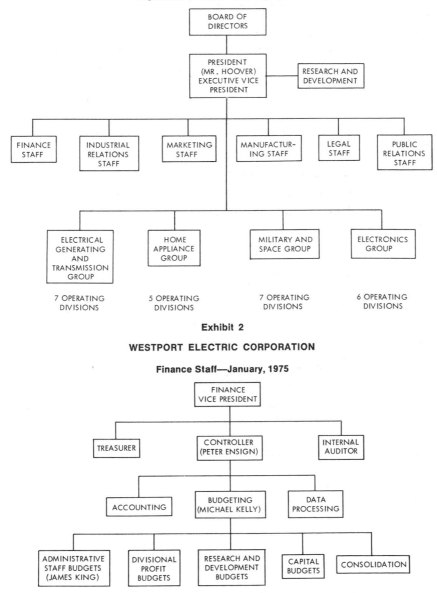

Exhibit 2

WESTPORT ELECTRIC CORPORATION

Finance Staff—January, 1975

budget, last year's budget, and the current year's expected actual costs, by expense classification (professional salaries, clerical salaries, supplies, consulting services, utilities, and so forth). The purpose of this schedule is to compare the new budget with the current year's budget and the current year's expected actual by expense categories.

Budget by Activity. This schedule shows the same information as the previous schedule except that the information is classified by organizational component. The purpose of this schedule is to show which activities are being increased, which decreased, and which new activities are being proposed.

Explanation of Changes. This schedule is really a letter that accompanies the budget proposal and explains the reasons for the proposed budget. Explanations are divided into the following categories: economic changes (i.e., changes in the general level of wages and materials); increases or decreases in existing activities; new activities added and old activities dropped.

These reports are submitted by each administrative staff office to the Budgeting Department two weeks before the office is to present its proposed budget.

Presentation of Budget Proposal

Each administrative staff office budget was approved by the President and the Executive Vice President in a "budget review meeting." The Finance Vice President sat in on all the budget presentations but had no official power to approve or disapprove.

On the day scheduled for presentation, the vice president of the administrative staff office whose budget was to be approved would make a presentation to the President and Executive Vice President. The presentation would be based on the budget schedules previously submitted, but the explanations justifying the proposals might go into much greater detail. For example, last year the Marketing Vice President used three-dimensional colored slides to describe a new activity that he was proposing to organize.

Attending these meetings were the President, the Executive Vice President, the administrative staff office vice president and his principal executives, the Finance Vice President, the Controller, the Budgeting Manager, and the particular budget supervisor involved.

Typically, a budget meeting would proceed as follows: The presentation would be made by the administrative staff vice president. During the presentation, questions would be raised by the President and the Executive Vice President. These would be answered by the administrative staff vice president or one of his executives. At the end of the presentation, the President and Executive Vice President would decide whether to approve the budget or whether to curtail some of the proposed activities. Before the final decision, the Finance Vice President would be asked to comment. In almost every case, he would agree with the decision of the President and Executive Vice President.

Once approved, the budget became authorization to undertake the budgeted activity for the coming year.

Function of Budgeting Department

The functions of the Budgeting Department with respect to administrative staff budgets has been to prescribe the schedules to be submitted and time-table for their submission and to "keep the presentations honest." In fulfilling the last function, the Budgeting Department analyzed the proposed budgets and made sure that the facts were correctly stated. For instance, they checked to make sure that the increases due to economic changes were accurate; or, if some present activity were to be dropped, they made sure that the cost of this activity was shown as a reduction, so that the cost savings could not be used to hide an increase in another activity. The details of the presentation were worked out beforehand between James King and the administrative assistant to the administrative staff vice president involved. When the presentation was made, the Budgeting Department would be asked to concur with the financial information being presented. The Budgeting Department, however, took no position on the appropriateness of the proposed budget or the efficiency of the activity. It was this situation that bothered James King.

BUDGET EVALUATION

This was James King's second year as Supervisor of the Administrative Staff Budget Section. Prior to that, he had been the Budget Manager in the Electric Stove Division. At the divisional level, the budget analysts exercised considerable influence over the level of efficiency represented in the operating budgets. For example, in the Electric Stove Division, the Divisional Controller attended every divisional budget meeting and argued long and hard for rejecting any budget that he believed was not sufficiently "tight." Because he had had a considerable amount of experience in the operations of that division, he was usually successful. King found it hard to reconcile the attitude of the Finance Vice President (who never seems to raise any objections to the proposed budgets) with his former boss, the Controller of the Electric Stove Division. Consequently, he asked to meet with Ensign and Kelley to see if something could not be done to improve the evaluation techniques for administrative staff budgets. Below is an edited version of the meeting between Ensign, Kelly, and King on this problem:

King: All we do about these budgets is to make sure that the accounting figures are correct. We don't do anything about the efficiency represented by the figures and I know for a fact that it is lousy in at least two cases and I have my suspicion about some of the others.

Kelly: Tell Peter about Legal.

King: Earlier this year, you remember, we hired a consultant to work with our Data Processing Group. We gave the contract to the Legal Staff to look over and it took them three months before they approved it. They had all kinds of nit-picking changes that didn't amount to a hill of beans, but which took up everybody's time.

Shortly after the contract was approved, I had a college friend of mine visiting who's a lawyer in one of the biggest New York firms. We discussed the matter and he looked over the original contract and the revised one and was astounded at the time that it had taken to get it approved. He said that a simple contract like that would be handled in a day or two by an outside lawyer. Since then, I find that everyone in the organization seems to feel the same about Legal. They take forever to do a five-minute job and they never stick their necks out in the slightest.

To add insult to injury, this year the Legal Staff is asking for a 30 percent increase in their budget to take care of the added cost resulting from the expansion of their workload. The trouble is that unless we do something, they will get this increase.

Ensign: If everyone feels that the Legal Staff is so inefficient, why should Mr. Hoover (the president) approve their budget?

King: I think that Mr. Hoover has neither the time nor the knowledge to evaluate the Legal Staff. Any time Mr. Hoover asks for anything from them, he gets superdeluxe treatment. Since none of us are lawyers we have a hard time proving inefficiency, but we know it is there.

Ensign: What is the other budget that you think is out of line?

King: Industrial Relations—especially management training: We are spending more money on senseless training that you can shake a stick at. It's not only costing us money, but it is wasting management's time. For instance, last month we all had to take a course in quality control. It was the most simple-minded course I have ever seen. They gave us a test at the end to see how much progress we have made. I gave a copy of the test to my secretary and she got a hundred percent, without taking the course, or really even knowing what quality control is. Out in the division, the training was even worse. At one time they had a slide film that was supposed to teach us economics in three lessons! The film consisted of "Doc Dollar" explaining to "Jim Foreman" about money markets, capitalism, and so forth. We all felt that it was an insult to our intelligence. In their new budget, Industrial Relations is proposing to increase training by nearly 50 percent and, because the general profit picture is so good, it will probably be approved.

Ensign: If the training program is so bad, why don't we hear more complaints?

King: I will have to admit that I feel more strongly than most of the other people, a lot of managers and supervisors just go along with these programs because to be against management training is like being against motherhood. Also, the personnel evaluation forms that Industrial Relations prescribes have a section on the performance of the individual in these courses. I guess people are afraid to rebel against them because it might hurt their chances of promotion. The point is, at best, they are not worth the money that they cost. No one seems to get much out of them as far as I can see, so we certainly don't want to *increase* the training budget.

The conversation continued for some time. Although he did not express it in exactly these terms, King's other concern was a lack of goal congruence between the activities of the administrative staff office and the earnings for the corporation. It seemed to him that each administrative staff officer, at best wanted to have the "best" operation in the country and, at worst, was simply interested in building an empire. Even the "best" operation, however, might cost much more than it was worth in terms of increasing profits. He was also concerned about the ability of the President and the Executive Vice President to evaluate the efficiency and the effectiveness of the staff offices or even to decide whether additional activities were really worthwhile. King, therefore, believed it was necessary for someone to evaluate the budget proposals critically as they did at the divisional level.

The meeting closed with Ensign asking Kelly and King to prepare a proposal that would solve the issue raised in the meeting.

QUESTION

What should Westport Electric do about the evaluation problem raised in the case?

Case 5-5

Seneca Steel Corporation

In November of 1967 Ted Cunningham, the production superintendent of the Charlestown Works of Seneca Steel Corporation met with the plant manager to discuss training and personnel development for the Production Department. At the end of the meeting the plant manager said that Cunningham had been selected to attend a four months' management development program, and the plant manager asked Cunningham to nominate a replacement during his absence. Cunningham suggested that he assemble some performance measurement data on the likely candidates before a final decision was made. The candidates to be considered were all in the Production Department, reporting to Cunningham.

Cunningham used a "management-by-objectives" system with the people reporting to him. The performance of each of the line superintendents was measured in four categories; in their department they had relatively complete responsibility and authority in these four areas. The table below shows the four areas of responsibility and the results or measurement methods used for performance appraisal:

Exhibit 1

SECTION SUPERINTENDENT RESPONSIBILITIES

Performance Item	Methods of Measurements
I. Safety	Monthly reports—safety experience and department report on program implementation.
II. Production losses	Monthly operating factor report
III. Costs	Monthly cost reports Superintendents' monthly budget cost analysis report
IV. Employee relations	Subjective measurement—jointly by section, production and industrial relations superintendents.

232

In the "management by objectives" system each section superintendent set specific objectives for his department for the coming year. These objectives were reviewed with the production superintendent, and if they were acceptable to him they became "published" objectives for that department for the next year. Objectives, and wherever possible, specific programs for achieving them, were developed on all items in Exhibit 1. The production superintendent stressed at least that achievement of these goals would represent "good" (or above average) performance. It was also understood that salary administration would be tied to this performance. Each item in Exhibit 1 would generally result in four or five programs for improved performance, and, in the case of costs, some five to ten programs were usually developed for each department. A typical budget sheet and cost reduction program summary are shown in Exhibits 2 and 3.

Exhibit 2

SENECA STEEL CORPORATION

Typical Cost Summary Sheet
1968 Budget
104—Open Hearth Spending—1968 Forward Plan

	1968 Plan*	Average Month 1967	1967 Standard†	1968 Standard (Predicted)‡
Services labor	$ 200	$ 290	$ 0	$ 290
Operating labor	15,700	21,890	21,100	15,000
General labor	3,000	5,274	3,350	2,500
Operating supplies	2,200	2,818	2,350	2,000
Power	2,800	3,706	3,600	3,600
Steam	126,600	132,344	129,574	116,000
Air	500	554	546	550
Total R & M	30,700	38,263	39,716	35,700
Subtotal	$181,700	$205,139	$200,236	$175,640
Major repair	4,500	9,000	14,800	14,800
Total	$186,200	$214,139	$215,036	$190,440

* The "1968 Plan" was the Superintendent's Plan (goal for the coming year), subject to the approval of the Production Superintendent.

† The "1967 Standard" represents the year's engineered standard costs. Seneca Steel plants used Industrial Engineering standards as well as the forward plan system.

‡ The standards were prepared at year end. The plan was prepared in October. Therefore, the next year's standard could only be estimated at the time the plan was done.

Comparison of the 1968 plan to 1967 average "actual" performance gave some indication of the degree of difficulty in achieving the plan on a historical basis.

Comparison to standard costs showed the effect of capital improvements. The distinction looked for in this comparison was how much of the improvement was the result of the department management.

The Previous System

In 1963 Cunningham had read several articles discussing the merits of management-by-objectives systems. Seneca had recently instituted a Forward Planning Program on a corporate-wide basis, and it seemed to Cunningham that these two programs could easily be combined into a single

Exhibit 3

SENECA STEEL CORPORATION

Cost Reduction Program

Summary

INTEROFFICE MEMORANDUM

To: T. E. Cunningham   Date: January 23, 1968
At: Charlestown   From: F. O. Berger
                              At: Charlestown
                              SUBJECT: 1968 Forward Plan Program

There are seven Cost Reduction Programs in the Open Hearth Department which should yield definite savings.

1. Coke Operator Elimination: $3600/month—reduction made 10/1/67.
2. OP* Facilities: $4750/month—savings are as promised in the RFI† except for steam which is the actual expected. (The RFI did not include provision for steam pump steam.)
3. General Labor Reduction: $1600/month—savings are generally OP-related, but are above those promised in the RFI.
4. Operating Supplies Reduction: $400/month—savings are generally OP-related, but are above those promised in the RFI.
5. Power Reduction: $1050/month—savings are generally OP-related, but are above those promised in the RFI. The power usage will have to be redivided after OP startup.
6. Maintenance Reduction: $400/month—savings are as follows:

Reduced Production	$ 600
OP-solved Problems (above RFI)	850
Problems Already Solved	2550
	$4000

There is also a program for optimization of steam usage. Actual savings are unknown because OP operating conditions are not definite. A reduction in steam cost of 2 percent, however, would yield an annual saving of $2500 per month.

* Ore Processing Facilities
† Request for improvement

system that could accomplish the planning purpose and simultaneously set up a system of management by objectives.

Up to this time the leadership style at Charlestown had been rather authoritarian, with close control by the production superintendent over the section superintendents in as many variables in the total "process cost-safety-technical" system as his personal ability and drive allowed. Cost control revolved around a standard cost system. Monthly cost meetings were held for the Production Department in which each section superintendent discussed the reasons for his variations from standard. The general atmosphere was one of pressure from the production superintendent to the section superintendent. Since the meeting focused on the variances, the general tone of the meeting was negative. Cunningham was never comfortable with this system and welcomed the opportunity to try a new system. The production superintendent was free to use whatever management control system he felt best. The plant manager intervened only when there was a deviation from generally expected normal performance (which always implied improvement over previous performance) in the areas of cost, safety or production.

Developing the New System

At first there was general reluctance by the section superintendents to take the new system seriously. Objectives for the first year were hammered out by the production superintendent after several meetings with each section superintendent. In most cases the production superintendent actually set the objectives since the section superintendents were reluctant to set an objective that represented a really significant improvement.

Changes were also made in the monthly reporting process. The cost meeting was eliminated and a written monthly report of progress towards objectives was substituted. This report was reviewed in a meeting between the individual section superintendent and the production superintendent. Emphasis was on problems that were preventing the superintendent from reaching his goal. Cunningham attempted to remove as much pressure as possible from these meetings.

In the second year the original objectives as set by the section superintendents were more nearly in line with Cunningham's estimate of feasible progress. On only two or three items did he feel it necessary to pressure the superintendent to raise an objective. By the third year Cunningham actually found it necessary to scale down some of the objectives submitted because he felt the were too optimistic. The new system seemed to be beginning to function as it was intended to function; throughout the past two years the overall performance of the Production Department was generally considered to be good.

Reporting to Cunningham were four section superintendents, the manager of technical services and the general labor superintendent.

The List of Candidates

Cunningham concluded that the manager of technical services was really not a qualified candidate. He did not have the right type of personality to be a line manager. He seemed to prefer the slower pace of technical work and did not appear to like working under pressure, which he would encounter in line work. Cunningham had discussed this point with him before.

Exhibit 4

SENECA STEEL CORPORATION

Section Superintendent—Personnel Background

Sup't	Total Years Experience	Years with Seneca	Years Present Job	Education	General Summary Comments	
					Strong Points	Weak Points
A	5	3	2	B. Chem. Eng.	High potential type Poised Personable Technically very good	Performance poor last year Interdep't cooperation poor Worries about wrong things
B	10	3	2	B.S. Chem. Engr.	Excellent performance Good managerial technique Well liked by subordinates	Expression, speech, poise need strengthening Left Seneca once (?????) Only "knows" Sec't B
C	8	8	5	B.S. Chem. Engr.	Experienced all sections Performance improving Technically adequate	No respect for peers Some years of poor performance Lacks long-range potential

Exhibit 5

SENECA STEEL CORPORATION

Performance Ratings*
Production Superintendents' Opinion of Long-range Potential

Superintendent	Safety	Cost Reduction	Production	Employee Relations	Range of Potential†
A	Below average	Below average	Average	Average	2–3
B	Average	Average	Average	Above average	1–2
C	Above average	Average	Above average	Above average	0–1

* Performance Ratings: Outstanding.
                        Above Average.
                        Average.
                        Below Average.
† Number of levels he has potential to advance to (above present level).

The general labor superintendent likewise was eliminated from consideration because of his lack of a technical background and a general feeling that he was approaching his maximum potential in his present job. Cunningham was reasonably sure that this man did not expect to be considered for the job. Cunningham also eliminated one of the four Section superintendents because of his lack of managerial experience; he also had serious doubts about the ability of this man to succeed even in his present position.

The Final Three Candidates

This narrowed the choice down to Superintendents A, B, and C. Cunningham assembled background data performance data for the previous two years on these three men as shown in Exhibits 4 and 5. Performance was rated in two ways: (1) against budget, and (2) versus the prior year. General rankings (average, above average, etc.) were used, as Cunningham did not feel the performance appraisal system could be quantified beyond this point at this time. The rankings were established jointly by the production and section superintendents at the conclusion of their individual monthly meeting on the prior month's goal results.

The performance data showed that Superintendent C had turned in the best performance, followed by B and A, in that order. In implementing the management-by-objectives system, Cunningham had often stressed to his men that "performance was the only thing that really counts." This approach had been followed by Cunningham in determining the amount of salary increase each man would get.

Cunningham became concerned. If he really believed his statements that "results count," Superintendent C was the logical candidate. He was also the most experienced man. At the same time, Cunningham was reluctant to recommend "C" for a promotion. The comments in Exhibit 4 and the "potential" ranking given to him by Cunningham in Exhibit 5 were not consistent with his very good performance in recent years.

Superintendent B was also a good performer, but also had some personality traits which did not seem to warrant promotion. For example, it still worried Cunningham that he had quit Seneca several years before only to return one year later.

Superintendent A was regarded as the man with the highest long-range potential by Cunningham. However, his performance to date definitely did not justify his high ranking.

It became obvious to Cunningham that his performance appraisal system just wasn't sufficient to evaluate his men for promotion.

Later he reviewed the above data with the plant manager and recommended that they look for a replacement at one of the other Seneca plants. Since he was not familiar with the men involved, the plant manager agreed to follow Cunningham's recommendation. Cunningham left the meeting wondering how he would tell Superintendent C that he would not get a chance at the new job.

QUESTION

Does this incident indicate that the management by objective system should be modified or abandoned?

Chapter Six

PROFIT CENTERS

When financial performance in a responsibility center is measured in terms of profit, which is the difference between revenues and expenses, the responsibility center is called a profit center. In this chapter, we discuss considerations involved in deciding whether profit centers should be created. The first part of the discussion focuses on major organization units, which are called divisions, and then other types of profit centers are discussed. We also discuss alternative ways of measuring the profitability of a profit center.

DIVISIONALIZATION

A functional organization is one in which each of the principal functions of manufacturing and marketing are separate organization units. When such an organization is converted to one in which each of the organization units is responsible for both the manufacturing and the marketing of a product or a family of products, the process is called "divisionalization."

As Solomons points out,

The terms "divisionalization" and "decentralization" are sometimes used as if they were interchangeable. They are, however, not synonyms, for the devolution of authority to make decisions, which is the essence of decentralization, is often carried to considerable lengths in businesses which are not divisionalized.[1]

There are wide differences in the extent of decentralization of authority among divisionalized companies and, even within the same company, there can be significant differences in the amount of authority delegated to different divisional managers. In general, however, a company divisionalizes because it wishes to delegate more authority to operating managers. If a manager has profit responsibility, it is practical to delegate further down

---

[1] David Solomons, *Divisional Performance: Measurement and Control,* Financial Executives Research Foundation, 1965, p. 3.

the line decisions involving trade-offs between costs and revenues. For example, a manager who is responsible only for marketing activities will be motivated to make sales promotion expenditures that maximize sales, where a manager who is responsible for profits will be motivated to make sales promotion expenditures that optimize profits. Further, the ability to measure performance in terms of profitability makes the delegation of responsibility more feasible. The comprehensiveness of the measure makes detailed decision making by headquarters management less necessary.

Thus, although divisionalization and decentralization are not synonyms, divisionalization is almost always accompanied by greater decentralization.

The advantages and disadvantages of divisionalization can only be considered meaningfully in the context of a particular organization. The size of a company, the number and diversity of its products, the type and geographical dispersion of its facilities can all have an important effect on whether divisionalization will improve a company's ability to earn profits. There are, however, general attributes of the profit center system of organization.

Advantages of Divisionalization

1. The *speed* of operating decisions should be increased because many decisions do not have to be referred to corporate headquarters.

2. The *quality* of many decisions should be improved because they can be made by the person most familiar with the situation.

3. Headquarters management will be *relieved of day-to-day decisions* and can, therefore, concentrate on higher level activities.

4. *Profit consciousness* is enhanced. Line managers, being responsible for profits, will be constantly looking for ways to improve them.

5. *Measurement of performance is broadened.* Profitability is a more comprehensive measure of performance than the measurement of either revenues or expenses separately. It measures the effects of management actions that affect *both* revenues and expenses.

6. Line managers, with fewer corporate restraints, are freer to use their *imagination and initiative.*

7. Divisionalization provides an excellent *training ground* for management. At the same time, it provides an excellent means for *evaluating* divisional management's ability for higher management jobs.

8. If a company is pursuing a *strategy of diversification,* divisionalization facilitates the use of different talents and expertise in different types of situations.

9. Divisionalization provides top management with information on the *profitability of components* of the company.

The first three advantages relate to the decentralization of decision making. Although it is possible to decentralize some decisions without divisionalization, it is difficult to decentralize certain cost/revenue trade-off decisions in a functional organization. In other words, the point in the organization where revenue and cost responsibilities come together is considerably higher in the functional organization, and many decisions involving

cost and revenue trade-offs cannot be made below this point. As a consequence, divisionalization will make greater decentralization possible.

Difficulties with Divisionalization

1. To the extent that decisions are decentralized, top management *loses some
control*. A series of control reports is not as effective as an intimate knowledge
of an operation. Top management must change its approach to control. Instead of
personal direction, top management must rely to a considerable extent on financial and control reports.

2. Competent *divisional managers* are needed, and they may not be available.

3. Operations that were once cooperative now may be *competitive*. An increase in one divisional manager's profits may decrease that of another's. As a
consequence, cooperation among divisions is likely to be adversely affected. This
decrease in cooperation may manifest itself in a manager's unwillingness to refer
sales leads to another division even though that division is better qualified to
follow up on the lead, to production decisions that have undesirable cost consequences on other divisions, or even to the hoarding of personnel or equipment,
which from the overall company standpoint, would be better off if assigned to, or
used in, another division.

4. *Friction* can increase. There can be arguments over the appropriate transfer price, the assignment of common costs, and the credit for revenues that were
generated jointly by the efforts of two or more divisions.

5. There may be too much emphasis on *short-run profitability,* at the expense
of long-run profitability. In the desire to report high current profits, the divisional
manager may skimp on research/development, training programs, or maintenance. This tendency is particularly prevalent when the turnover of divisional
managers is relatively high. In these circumstances, the manager has good reason
to believe that his actions may not "come home to roost" until after he has moved
to another job.

6. There is no completely satisfactory system for insuring that each division,
by optimizing its own profits, will *optimize company profits.* (This point is discussed in Chapters 7 and 8.)

7. If headquarters management is more capable or has more comprehensive
information than the average divisional manager, the *quality* of some of the
decisions may be reduced.

8. Divisionalization may cause *additional costs* in terms of management
salaries and the number and type of staff people.

Constraints on Divisional Authority

A divisional manager must be able to exercise control over the profitability of his division. In order to realize fully the advantages listed above,
the divisional manager would have to be as autonomous as the president of
an independent company. As a practical matter, however, such autonomy
is rarely feasible. If a company were divided into completely independent
units, the organization would be giving up the advantages of size or synergism.
Also, top management would be abdicating its responsibility if it delegated
to divisional management the amount of authority that a board of directors

gives to the corporate president. Consequently, all divisionalized organizations represent trade-offs between divisional autonomy and corporate constraints. The effectiveness of a divisionalized organization is largely dependent upon how well these trade-offs are made.

Constraints from Other Divisions. One of the greatest problems in decentralizing profit responsibility occurs when divisions must deal with each other. It is useful to think of managing a profit center in terms of control over three functions: (1) the product decision (which goods or services to make and sell); (2) the procurement decision (how to obtain the goods or services); and (3) the marketing decision (how, where, and for how much are these goods or services to be sold). If a divisional manager controls all three of these functions, there is usually no difficulty in assigning profit responsibility and measuring performance. In general, the greater the degree of integration within a company, the more difficult it becomes to assign complete responsibility to a single profit center for these three activities. If, for example, the product, procurement, and marketing decisions for a single product line are split between two or more divisions, it can be difficult to separate the contribution of each division to the overall success of the product.

Where the responsibility for a product line is divided among two or more divisions, it is necessary to establish some system to assign fairly the profits to the divisions that have contributed to its design, manufacturing, and marketing. This is the function of the transfer price, and, as is discussed in Chapter 7, transfer price problems may be difficult.

Constraints from Corporate Management. The constraints imposed by corporate management can be divided into three types: (1) those resulting from strategic considerations, particularly financing decisions; (2) those resulting because uniformity is required; and (3) those resulting from the economies of centralization. Each of these is discussed in this part of the chapter.

Most companies restrict the raising of capital to the corporate level, at least for domestic activities. Consequently, one of the major constraints on divisions results from corporate control over investments. Each division must compete with other company units for a share of the available funds. Thus, a division could find its expansion plans thwarted because another division has a more attractive program. In addition to financial constraints, corporate management exercises other strategic constraints. For example, restrictions on markets and products are often imposed.

Companies impose some constraints on divisions because of the necessity for conformity. One constraint that exists almost universally is that divisions must conform to corporate accounting and management control systems. Some companies require large amounts of planning and reporting information from each profit center. Another example of a major uniformity constraint is personnel and industrial relations policies.

Certain services are centralized at corporate headquarters because it is more economical to have a central unit provide a particular service to all divisions. To some extent, all staff offices provide service to divisions, and divisions are generally required to use these services; that is, they are not allowed to acquire the service from other sources. Examples of staff services are legal, public relations, government relations, data processing and systems and training.

In general, these corporate constraints do not cause severe problems in decentralization as long as they are dealt with explicitly. Divisional management understands the necessity for most of these constraints, and usually accepts them with good grace. The major problems seem to revolve around the service activities. Often divisions believe (sometimes rightly) that they can obtain a particular service more cheaply from an outside source. The problems of chaging divisions for corporate services is described in Chapter 7.

The Movement to Divisionalize

Although Dupont and General Motors divisionalized in the early 1920s,[2] most companies in the United States remained functionally organized until after the end of World War II. Beginning at that time a great many of the major United States' corporations divisionalized because these companies had become too large and complex to be managed effectively through a functional organization.[3]

These corporations can be classified into three categories:

First, the _diversified companies_ (conglomerates) such as International Telephone and Telegraph, Litton Industries, and Textron. For this type of company, divisionalization is ideal; it is difficult to see how they could operate in another way.

Second, the _single industry, multiproduct,_ company such as General Electric, Westinghouse Electric, Dupont, and Union Carbide. In this type of company, also, divisionalization is generally the most effective way of organizing, although the decision is not always as clearcut as with the diversified company. Also, there tends to be a lesser degree of decentralization in a single industry company than in a diversified company.

Third, the large _single product_ (or integrated) company such as the steel companies, the automobile companies, and the petroleum companies. In this type of company, the decision to divisionalize is less clearcut. Many major decisions are made centrally. Furthermore, this type of company tends to have large amounts of intracompany transfers because of its integrated nature. Also many of the transferred goods have no outside market

---

[2] See Alfred D. Chandler, Jr., _Strategy and Structure_ (Cambridge, Mass.: MIT Press, 1962), Chapters 2 and 3.

[3] For an excellent discussion of this process see "Evolution and Revolution as Organizations Grow," by Larry E. Greiner, _Harvard Business Review,_ July–Auust 1972.

source, which makes it difficult to arrive at a useful transfer price. However, the very size of some of these companies made divisionalization almost necessary. Also, most of these have operations not related to their principal products. (For example, General Motors produces and sells refrigerators and diesel engines.) When a company in this category is divisionalized, the delegation of authority is usually more restricted than in the case of the other two types of companies. For example in the automobile business, vehicle product and pricing decisions are made at the very top of the organization. Furthermore, many of the manufacturing divisions sell exclusively to other divisions, and the buying divisions are restricted either by the nature of the product or company rule to purchasing from inside sources.

To summarize, then, both size and diversity are important factors in the decision to divisionalize. Diversity, however, is more important than size because a diversified industry is more adaptable to the delegation of profit responsibility. Size alone is not a compelling reason to divisionalize. With increased size, however, there will almost always come some diversity, and it is the combination of the two that makes divisionalization desirable.

Personnel Matters

In considering the importance to its unique situation of the advantages and difficulties listed above, a company would do well to give special attention to the personnel problems involved in the establishment of profit centers. A divisionalized company requires certain types of personnel that may not be found in the typical organization where profit responsibility is centralized. If these people are not available within the organization, they must be trained or hired. If management is unable or unwilling to do this, then the company should not decentralize profit responsibility. There are three needs:

1. Top management must know how to use management control reports in planning, controlling and coordinating profit center operations.

2. A divisionalized company requires capable divisional managers. A functionally organized company may have few executives who are broad enough in their outlook to take on the responsibility for a division. A company should not divisionalize unless existing personnel are capable, with training, of handling new responsibilities, or until plans have been made to acquire new personnel.

3. A divisionalized company requires capable financial and budget analysts at both the central staff and the divisional levels. Such talent may be scarce.

One Major Activity. If a company has a single activity on which its success hinges, it is doubtful that divisionalization will be successful. Top management *cannot* delegate responsibility for the success of this activity to a divisional manager. In this circumstance, an attempt to decentralize profit responsibility merely results in a more expensive and cumbersome control and communications system. For example, a medium-size company with one major product line and several smaller and relatively unrelated products divided its activities into profit centers. Top management, however, continued to spend most of its time and energy on the major product line, making most of the decisions that normally would be made by the divisional manager. The company was in fact being operated in the same old way except that staff costs had risen and new communications problems had been created.

Similar Major Activities. Decentralized profit responsibility seems best adapted to companies that are composed of several *dis*similar businesses. In these companies, management is unable to be intimately acquainted with the relevant details of all of the businesses; therefore, it delegates the day-to-day decisions to different people in each activity who are familiar with the various problems. If, on the other hand, the activities of a company are similar, it may be desirable for one group to make many of the day-to-day decisions for *all* of the activities. For example, a central marketing group might make all of the advertising, sales promotion, and new product decisions for the entire company. When a central group does this, a divisional manager cannot, of course, be held responsible for that aspect of his profit performance. Hence, there may be no real decentralization of profit responsibility.

Any company whose major activities are related closely to one another should carefully consider alternative methods of control before decentralizing profit responsibility. Not only is it more expensive to have each division make its own decisions, but the quality of these decisions is likely to be inferior to those that would be made centrally. Furthermore, coordination among the activities is very important when they are related; this coordination is much more difficult to accomplish properly with a decentralized profit center system.

Indivisible Responsibility. As stated earlier, in order to be able to decentralize profit responsibility successfully, a company must find it practical to divide its operations into logical profit-determining units. The existence of serious transfer pricing problems is sometimes indicative of the fact that profit responsibility is not clearly segregated. To the extent that divisions buy from and sell to each other, two or more divisions are sharing in marketing, production, and product planning decisions. Transfer pricing problems also indicate sometimes that profit centers are not really independent. These problems occur principally when outside competitive prices are unavailable. When this happens, it can mean that there is no effective outside competition. This, in turn, indicates that the concept of the division as an independent company is fictional because, if there is no effective outside competition, the profit centers *must* deal with each other.

Alternatives to Divisionalization

Even large and complex companies need not necessarily divisionalize. There may be less drastic and less expensive methods of minimizing their problems. Here are four of them.

1. Split Executive Responsibility. One way to relieve the pressure on management is to divide the executive responsibilities among the top executives. For example, if long-range planning is a problem, then planning may be separated from administration, for example, the chairman of the board may be responsible for planning and the president for day-to-day management.

2. Decentralize Functional Responsibility. Delegation of certain functional responsibilities is an excellent way to relieve pressures on top management's time. For such delegation, management can select functional activities that have the most capable staff, or ones to which top management can make the least contribution, or ones that are less vital to the success of the company. For example, in a company that was largely marketing-oriented, the president delegated the responsibility for manufacturing to a vice president. The president was then able to devote most of his time to marketing and product decisions. Decentralization on this basis can be done with little additional cost and with no disruption to the current organization.

3. Strengthen the Staff. In some stiuations, the real problem is lack of adequate staff assistance, and this will not be solved by divisionalization. Some operating executives regard staff people as a type of parasite, and they keep the staff small. Divisionalization can be a very expensive substitute for an adequate central staff.

4. Decentralize Minor Activities. If a company has several, more-or-less minor activities which are unrelated to its main products, these activities might be set up as profit centers under the control of a central staff executive. Such an arrangement does not require the sophisticated control system that full decentralization would require. The responsible executive controls by personal observation, by direct communication with general managers, and by the usual accounting reports. In this way, top management is in a position to devote most of its time to its main business.

OTHER PROFIT CENTERS

So far in this chapter we have been considering the problem of divisionalization, which is the process of reorganizing a functional organization into profit centers. Divisionalization involves major changes in any company. It involves changing relationships among company executives. It often involves different ways of doing business, and it can involve considerable additional expense. As a consequence, the decision to divisionalize is one of the major decisions that any company makes.

There are, in addition to major divisions, other profit centers. Often these can be created without difficulty. Some examples are described below.

Marketing Organizations

Many marketing organizations can be made into profit centers by simply changing the accounting so that the organization is charged for the cost of the goods that it sells. It does not necessarily follow that the manager of such a profit center will be held strictly responsible for profits. If the marketing organization has little or no influence over the product design or procurement, and limited influence over pricing, its responsibility may be limited.

Service Organizations

Many service organizations are well suited to the profit center form of organization. Thus, consulting firms, public accounting firms, architectural firms, and engineering firms, for example, can be divided into profit centers by arranging the accounting system so that each unit is credited for the revenue it generates and is charged for the costs that it incurs. Such units have considerable control over the product (the type of service), the revenues, and the costs. Consequently, profitability can be an effective way of measuring performance. Top management must be careful, however, not to generate such pressure for profitability that the quality of the service declines. These organizations are discussed in more detail in Chapter 14.

Manufacturing Organizations

A manufacturing unit selling exclusively to other company units is principally responsible for manufacturing costs. In most companies, such units are treated as expense centers, and goods are transferred at standard cost. A manufacturing manager, however, can minimize his costs by reducing quality, refusing to change his production schedules to meet some special customer order, or using outside sources for products that are difficult to manufacture. Any of these actions could be contrary to the overall interests of the company. If the manufacturing manager is assigned profit responsibility, the expectation is that he will be concerned with quality, with customer demands, and with increasing his production by making as many products as he is able to do profitably.

The technique for assigning responsibility to the manufacturing unit is to transfer the goods at a price that includes a profit margin as well as cost. As explained in Chapter 7, this could be a market price, standard cost plus a profit, or the final selling price of the product reduced by the cost of marketing it. When this is done, the manufacturing manager is no longer concerned solely with costs. He is also concerned with volume and, thus, is interested in satisfying customers in both quality and delivery dates. Furthermore, he is interested in increasing the number of products he produces.

A manufacturing manager ordinarily cannot be held responsible for most of the volume fluctuations. He usually has nothing to do with setting the sales budget and little short-run influence on meeting it. Nevertheless, when a manufacturing manager is assigned profit responsibility, this often has a marked influence on the manager's perception of the importance of his job.

Other Organizations

A company that has branch operations, responsible for marketing the company's products in a particular geographical area, is often a natural for a profit center type of organization. Even though the branch managers have no product or procurement responsibilities, profitability is often the best single measure of their performance. Furthermore, the profit measurement is frequently an excellent motivating device. Thus, the individual stores of most retail chains are organized as profit centers, and the branches of many commercial banks are profit centers.

Some companies organize their customer service units as profit centers. Such units are responsible for product installation, for servicing equipment upon request of the user, and/or for making repairs required by warranty agreements or for other reasons. In such units, however, the profit center approach may be dysfunctional. It may lead the unit to skimp on its work in order to reduce costs, and thereby damage the company's reputation.

MEASURING PROFITABILITY

There are two types of profitability measurements in a profit center. There is, first, a measure of *personal performance,* in which the focus is on how well the manager is doing. This measure is used for planning, coordinating and controlling the day-to-day activities of the profit center, particularly as a device for providing the proper motivation to the manager. Second, there is a measure of *economic performance,* in which the focus is on how well the profit center is doing as an economic entity. The messages given by these two measures may be quite different.

These two measures may, or may not, require separate sets of accounts. In most cases, the necessary information for both purposes can be furnished from a single underlying set of data, by appropriate rearrangement. Since the personal measure is used frequently, but the economic measure only on occasions when economic decisions must be made, considerations relating to personal performance measurement have first priority in systems design; that is, the system is designed to measure personal performance routinely, and economic measures are derived from them.

Problems in Profit Measurement

Because a profit center is part of a company and its transactions with other parts of the company are not always at arms length, problems in measuring profits arise that are not present in organizations that are independent entities. There are three types of such problems: (1) transfer prices, (2) joint revenues, and (3) common costs. Transfer pricing is deferred to Chapter 7, and the other two problems are discussed below.

Joint Revenues. Although in most circumstances, the measurement of the revenues earned by a profit center is straightforward, there are some situations in which two or more profit centers participated in the work that gave rise to the sale, and ideally each should be given appropriate credit for its part in the transaction. For example, the principal contact between the company and a certain customer may be a salesman from Division A, but on occasion the customer may place orders with the Division A salesman for products carried by Division B. Although the Division A salesman should be motivated to seek such orders, he is unlikely to do so if all the revenue resulting from them is credited to Division B. Conversely, the customer of a bank may carry his account in Branch C, which is credited for the revenue generated by this account, but the customer may prefer to do some banking business with Branch D because it is more conveniently located or for other reasons; Branch D is unlikely to be anxious to provide services to such a customer if all the revenue is credited to Branch C.

Most companies have not given much attention to the solution of these joint revenue problems. They take the position that the identification of precise responsibility for revenue generation is too complicated to be practical, and that sales personnel must recognize that they are working not only for their own profit center but also for the overall good of the company. A few companies do attempt to untangle the responsibility for joint sales. They may, for example, credit the division that takes an order for a product handled by another division (Division A in the above example) with the equivalent of a "brokerage commission" or "finder's fee" on that order. In the case of a bank, the branch performing a service may be given explicit credit for that service, even though the customer's account is kept in another branch.

Common Costs. Goods or services that are furnished to one profit center by another profit center are valued at a transfer price, as discussed in Chapter 7. Services that are furnished by staff units and other common costs should be charged to profit centers on a basis that reflects the actual consumption of the service and on the basis of specific requests made by the responsibility center that wants the service, to the extent that this is feasible. In these circumstances, the services are controllable costs, and the profit center can be held responsible for incurring them.

When such direct charging is not feasible, the common costs can be allocated to profit centers on some reasonable basis. Such an allocation is necessary for the measurement of the economic performance of the profit center. Opinions differ as to whether or not allocated costs are useful in personal performance measurement, as will be discussed in the next section.

Types of Profitability Measures

The profitability of a profit center can be measured in essentially four different ways: (1) as the contribution margin, (2) as direct divisional profit, (3) as income before income taxes, or (4) as net income. The nature of these measures is indicated by Exhibit 6–1, and each is discussed below.

Contribution Margin. Measuring profits as the difference between revenue and variable costs is advocated by the so-called "direct costers," and is a

Exhibit 6–1

TYPES OF PROFITABILITY MEASURE

Income Statement		Measure
Revenue	$1,000	
Cost of sales	600	
Gross margin	$400	
Variable expenses	180	
Contribution Margin	$220	←⎯ ①
Other divisional expense $60		
Direct charges from other divisions 30	90	
Direct divisional profit	$130	←⎯ ②
Allocated corporate costs	30	
Income before taxes	$100	←⎯ ③
Income taxes	50	
Net income	$ 50	←⎯ ④

practice used in many companies. Their principal argument is that the fixed costs are noncontrollable by the profit center manager, and that the manager should focus his attention on maximizing the spread between revenue and variable costs. The fundamental weakness of this argument is that it assumes that fixed costs are noncontrollable, which is by no means the case. As discussed in Chapter 5, many items of cost, although not varying with the level of activity, can be changed at the discretion of the profit center manager. Presumably, top management wants the profit center to be concerned with these discretionary costs and to keep them in line with amounts agreed on in the budget formulation process. A focus on the contribution margin tends to direct attention away from this responsibility.

If the contribution margin is defined as the difference between revenue and *controllable* costs, there is much room for argument as to what items of cost are controllable and what are not. Insurance and property taxes, for example, are in some cases noncontrollable by the profit center manager because the insurance coverage is set by corporate policy and property taxes by the municipality; however, the profit center manager may be able to reduce insurance costs by reducing the amount of insured property (such as inventory and fixed assets), or by reducing fire or safety hazards. Disputes about whether an item is or is not controllable can be time consuming and unproductive.

Direct Divisional Profit. This measure shows the amount that the division contributes to the general overhead and profit of the corporation. It incorporates all costs incurred in or directly traced to the division, regardless of whether or not these items are controllable. The use of this measure eliminates the necessity of allocating general corporate costs to divisions. If general corporate costs are allocated on the basis of sales revenue, as is a common practice, the relative profitability of the several divisions would tend to be the same when measured by direct divisional profits as they would be as measured by net income before taxes.

The principal weakness of this measure is that it cannot be used as a reliable economic measure of performance. A division cannot be said to earn a profit until it has covered all costs, including a fair share of general corporate costs. Thus profits as measured on the direct division basis cannot be compared directly with published data, or trade association data that report the profits of other companies in the industry.

Income before Taxes. In this measure, all pretax costs are allocated to some division. Presumably, the basis of allocation reflects the relative amount of cost that is caused by each division, and the allocations are made more carefully than by the use of a single rate, such as a percentage of sales revenue. The sum of the profits of all the divisions equals the pretax profit of the company. Division managers are given the message that the division has not earned a profit unless all costs are covered, and they may be motivated to raise questions about the amount of corporate overhead, which can lead to desirable actions. (One company sold its corporate airplane because of complaints about its costs from profit center managers.) This measure can be used as a basis for comparison with published data and for other economic analyses of the inherent profit potential of the division.

Net Income. Not many companies measure performance of domestic divisions at the "bottom line," the amount of net income after income tax. There are two principal reasons for this: (1) In many situations, the income after tax is a constant percentage of the pretax income, so there is no advantage in incorporating income taxes; and (2) decisions that have an impact on income taxes are made at headquarters, and it is believed that divisional profitability should not affect, or be affected by, these decisions. Because of the variations in income taxes in foreign countries, foreign divisions are customarily measured on an aftertax basis.

Those companies that measure net income of domestic divisions on an aftertax basis do so in order to motivate divisional managers to be interested in the tax consequences of their decisions, and particularly to seek opportunities to minimize taxes.

Other Performance Measures

The foregoing discussion has been limited to measurements of a division's performance as measured by financial data. As pointed out in Chapter 3, financial data provides an incomplete measurement at best, and at worst it is seriously misleading. Nonfinancial measures of performance are therefore important in the management of profit centers, just as they are in the management of independent companies. This topic is discussed in subsequent chapters.

Case 6–1

Bultman Automobiles, Inc.

William Bultman, the part owner and manager of an automobile dealership felt the problems associated with the rapid growth of his business were becoming too great for him to handle alone. (See Exhibit 1 for current financial statements.) The reputation he had established in the community led him to believe that the recent growth in his business would continue. His long-standing policy of emphasizing new car sales as the principal business of the dealership had paid off, in Mr. Bultman's opinion. This, combined with close attention to customer relations so that a substantial amount of repeat business was available, had increased the company's sales to a new high level. Therefore, he wanted to make organizational changes to cope with the new situation. Mr. Bultman's three "silent partners" agreed to this decision.

Accordingly, Mr. Bultman divided up the business into three departments: a new car sales department, a used car sales department, and the service department. He then appointed three of his most trusted employees managers of the new departments: John Ward was named manager of new car sales, Marty Ziegel was appointed manager of used car sales, and Charlie Lassen placed in charge of the service department. All of these men had been with the dealership for several years.

Each of the managers was told to run his department as if it were an independent business. In order to give the new managers an incentive, their remuneration was calculated as a straight percentage of their department's gross profit.

Soon after taking over as the manager of the new car sales department, John Ward had to settle upon the amount to offer a particular customer who wanted to trade his old car as part of the purchase price of a new one with a list price of $3,600. Before closing the sale, Mr. Ward had to decide the amount of discount from list he would offer the customer and the trade-in value of the old car. He knew he could deduct 15 percent from the list price of the new car without seriously hurting his profit margin. However, he also wanted to make sure that he did not lose out on the trade-in.

Exhibit 1

BULTMAN AUTOMOBILES INC.

Income Statement for the Year Ended December 31, 1964

Sales of new cars			$764,375
Cost of new sales		$631,281	
Sales remuneration		32,474	
			663,755
			$100,620
Allowances on trade*			23,223
			$ 77,397
Sales of used cars		$479,138	
Appraised value of used cars $381,455			
Sales remuneration 18,312			
		399,767	
		$ 79,371	
Allowances on trade*		12,223	
			67,148
			$144,545
Service sales to customers		$69,502	
Cost of work		51,397	
		$ 18,105	
Service work on reconditioning			
Charge ....$ 47,316			
Cost 48,862	(1,546)		
			16,559
			$161,104
General and administrative expenses			98,342
Profit before taxes			$ 62,762

* Allowances on trade represents the excess of amounts allowed on cars taken in trade over their appraised value.

During his conversations with the customer, it had become apparent that the customer had an inflated view of the worth of his old car, a far from uncommon event. In this case, it probably meant that Mr. Ward had to be prepared to make some sacrifices to close the sale. The new car had been in stock for some time, and the model was not selling very well, so he was rather anxious to make the sale if this could be done profitably.

In order to establish the trade-in value of the car, the manager of the used car department, Mr. Ziegel, accompanied Mr. Ward and the customer out to the parking lot to examine the car. In the course of his appraisal, Mr. Ziegel estimated the car would require reconditioning work costing about $200, after which the car would retail for about $1,050. On a wholesale basis, he could either buy or sell such a car, after reconditioning, for about $900. The wholesale price of a car was subject to much greater fluctuation than the retail price, depending on color, trim, model, etc. Fortunately, the car being traded in was a very popular shade. The retail automobile dealers handbook of used car prices, the "Blue Book," gave a cash buying price range of $775 to $825 for the trade-in model in good condition. This range represented the distribution of cash prices paid by automobile dealers for that model of car in the area in the past week. Mr. Ziegel estimated that he could get about $625 for the car "as-is," (that is, without any work being done to it) at next week's auction.

The new car department manager had the right to buy any trade-in at any price he thought appropriate, but then it was his responsibility to dispose of the car. He had the alternative of either trying to persuade the used car manager to take over the car and accepting the used car manager's appraisal price, or he himself could sell the car through wholesale channels. Whatever course Mr. Ward adopted, it was his primary responsibility to make a profit for the dealership on the new cars he sold, without affecting his performance through excessive allowances on trade-ins. This primary goal, Mr. Ward said, had to be "balanced against the need to satisfy the customers and move the new cars out of inventory—and there was only a narrow line between allowing enough on the used car and allowing too much."

After weighing all these factors, with particular emphasis on the personality of the customer, Mr. Ward decided he would allow $1,200 for the used car, provided the customer agreed to pay the list price for the new car. After a certain amount of haggling, during which the customer came down from a higher figure and Ward came up from a lower one, the $1,200 allowance was agreed upon. The necessary papers were signed, and the customer drove off.

Mr. Ward returned to the office and explained the situation to Ronald Bradley, who had recently joined the dealership as accountant. After listening with interest to Mr. Ward's explanation of the sale, Mr. Bradley set about recording the sale in the accounting records of the business. As soon as he saw the new car had been purchased from the manufacturer for $2,500, he was uncertain as to the value he should place on the trade-in vehicle. Since the new car's list price was $3,600 and it had cost $2,500, Mr. Bradley reasoned the gross margin on the new car sale was $1,100. Yet Mr. Ward had allowed $1,200 for the old car, which needed $200 repairs and could be sold retail for $1,050 or wholesale for $900. Did this mean that the new car sale involved a loss? Mr. Bradley was not at all sure he knew the answer to this question. Also, he was uncertain about the value he should place on the used car for inventory valuation purposes.

Bradley decided that he would put down a valuation of $1,200, and then await instructions from his superiors.

When Marty Ziegel, manager of the used car department, found out what Mr. Bradley had done, he went to the office and stated forcefully that he would not accept $1,200 as the valuation of the used car. His comment went as follows:

"My used car department has to get rid of that used car, unless John (new car department manager) agrees to take it over himself. I would certainly never have allowed the customer $1,200 for that old tub. I would never have given any more than $700, which is the wholesale price less the cost of repairs. My department has to make a profit too, you know. My own income is dependent on the gross profit I show on the sale of used cars, and I will not stand for having my income hurt because John is too generous towards his customers."

Mr. Bradley replied that he had not meant to cause trouble, but had simply recorded the car at what seemed to be its cost of acquisition, because he had been taught that this was the best practice. Whatever response Mr. Ziegel was about to make to this comment was cut off by the arrival of William Bultman, the general manager, and Charlie Lassen, the service department manager. Mr. Bultman picked up the phone and called John Ward, the new car sales manager, asking him to come over right away.

"All right, Charlie," said Mr. Bultman, "now that we are all here, would you tell them what you just told me."

Mr. Lassen, who was obviously very worried, said: "Thanks Bill. The trouble is with this trade-in. John and Marty were right in thinking that the repairs they thought necessary would cost about $200. Unfortunately, they failed to notice that the rear axle is cracked, which will have to be replaced before we can sell the car. This will use up parts and labor costing about $150.

"Besides this," Lassen continued, "there is another thing which is bothering me a good deal more. Under the accounting system we've been using, my labor cost for internal jobs is calculated by taking the standard blue book[1] price for the labor required for a job and deducting 25 percent. Normally, the blue book price is about equal to the estimated time required to do the work, multiplied by twice the mechanic's hourly rate. On parts, an outside customer pays list price, which has about a 40 percent gross margin, but on internal work the parts are charged at cost plus 20 percent, which is less than half the margin. As you can see from my department statement, calculating the cost of parts and labor for internal work this way didn't even cover a pro rata share of my department's overhead and supplies. I lost fifteen hundred bucks on internal work last year.

"So," Lassen went on, "on a reconditioning job like this which costs out at $350, I don't even break even. If I did work costing $350 for an outside customer, I would be able to charge him about $475 for the job. The blue book gives a range of $460 to $490 for the work this car needs, and I have always aimed for the middle of the blue book range. That would give my department a gross profit of $125, and my own income is based on that gross profit. Since it looks as if a high proportion of the work of my department is going

---

[1] In addition to the blue book for used car prices, there is a blue book which gives the range of charges for various classes to repair work. Like the used car book, it is a weekly, and is based on the actual charges made and reported by motor repair shops in the area.

to be the reconditioning of trade-ins for resale, I figure that I should be able to make the same charge for repairing a trade-in as I would get for an outside repair job. In this case, the charge would be $450."

Messrs. Ziegel and Ward both started to talk at once at this point. Mr. Ziegel, the more forceful of the two, managed to edge Mr. Ward out: "This axle business is unfortunate, all right, but it is very hard to spot a cracked axle. Charlie is likely to be just as lucky the other way next time. He has to take the rough with the smooth. It is up to him to get the cars ready for me to sell."

Mr. Ward, after agreeing that the failure to spot the axle was unfortunate, added: "This error is hardly my fault, however. Anyway, it is ridiculous that the service department should make a profit out of jobs it does for the rest of the dealership. The company can't make money when its left hand sells to its right."

William Bultman, the general manager, was getting a little confused about the situation. He thought there was a little truth in everything that had been said, but he was not sure how much. It was evident to him that some action was called for, both to sort out the present problem and to prevent its recurrence. He instructed Mr. Bradley, the accountant, to "work out how much we are really going to make on this whole deal," and then retired to his office to consider how best to get his managers to make a profit for the company.

A week after the events described above, William Bultman was still far from sure what action to take to motivate his managers to make a profit for the business. During the week, Charlie Lassen, the service manager, had reported to him that the repairs to the used car had cost $387, of which $180 represented the cost of those repairs which had been spotted at the time of purchase, and the remaining $207 was the cost of supplying and fitting a replacement for the cracked axle. To support his own case for a higher allowance on reconditioning jobs, Lassen had looked up the duplicate invoices over the last few months, and had found other examples of the same work that had been done on the trade-in car. The amount of these invoices totalled $453, which the customers had paid without question, and the time and materials that had gone into the jobs had been costed at $335. As described by Lassen earlier, the cost figures mentioned above included an allocation of departmental overhead, but no allowance for general overhead or profit. In addition, Lassen had obtained from Mr. Bradley, the accountant, the cost analysis shown in Exhibit 2 on page 257. Lassen told Bultman that this was a fairly typical distribution of the service department expense.

Exhibit 2

BULTMAN AUTOMOBILES INC.

Analysis of Service Department Expenses for the Year Ended
December 31, 1964

	Customer Jobs	Reconditioning Jobs	Total
Number of jobs	183	165	348
Direct labor	$21,386	$19,764	$ 41,150
Supplies	7,412	6,551	13,963
Department overhead (fixed)	6,312	5,213	11,525
	$35,110	$31,528	$ 66,638
Parts	16,287	17,334	33,621
	$51,397	$48,862	$100,259
Charges made for jobs to customers or other departments	69,502	47,316	116,818
Profit (loss)	$18,105	($ 1,546)	$ 16,559
General overhead proportion			11,416
Departmental profit for the year			$ 5,143

Case 6–2

Universal National
Company

The Universal National Company was a large aircraft and missile manufacturer with a concentration of plants on the West Coast and a number of divisions in other parts of the country as well as overseas. (The basic organization of the company is indicated by the simplified organization chart, included as Exhibit 1.) Its Aircraft Division, the unit from which the company had developed, was located on the West Coast. In 1955 it was awarded a contract for the production and delivery of 100 Sky Haul Troop carriers. The contract was placed on a cost plus incentive fee basis which means that there was a negotiated target price with an incentive formula under which Universal and the government would share 50/50 any saving below this target. This was the largest award that the Aircraft Division had received in some time, because procurement of military aircraft had been declining with increasing emphasis on missiles. The Aircraft Division in the two previous years had been just breaking even. Management expected that the award of the Sky Haul contract would restore the division to its position as one of the major profit contributors in the company.

In fact, the company's executive vice president, Joseph Sullivan, was determined that the Aircraft Division would achieve its former profit position, and to this end he called in major management personnel from the division and lectured them in rather blunt terms about the need for a dramatic profit improvement. He told them that if they did not do it with the Sky Haul contract, they would never do it.

Fred Clark, the Aircraft Division manager, had recently developed a Profit Improvement Program (PIP). The idea behind it was to get people excited over profits; to get them to concentrate on profit improvement. The initials PIP were written over the walls in the plants and corridors. Each department was given a PIP mandate in terms of cost reduction goals; semi-

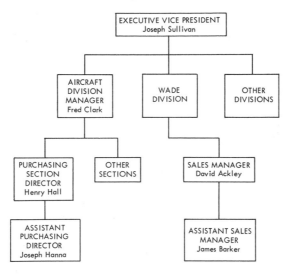

nars were held throughout the division; and special PIP announcements were made over the plant loudspeakers.

Henry Hall, divisional director of purchasing, made a comprehensive analysis of the material requirements for the Sky Haul contract. He recognized that, along with several other items, the automatic direction finder was extremely critical to the success of the program. Whereas the Sky Haul contract was let as a straight production contract, the model actually was an advanced one, calling for a number of basic improvements. In particular, the automatic direction finder had to meet requirements that, while within the state of the art, called for considerable improvement over previous production.

Hall determined that there were three logical sources for this radio direction finder: the Bolster Company located in New York, the Acme Radio Electronics Company of Chicago, and the Wade Division of Universal National located in the Midwest. On the basis of previous experience, Hall thought that the Bolster Company would probably be the best source. However, he was fairly sure that all three sources would be able to pass the facility survey. He was willing to make the award to whichever company made the best cost proposal, although he did not want the Wade Division to obtain the order.

Hall discussed the problem with Joseph Hanna, his assistant. Hanna felt that the Wade Division looked upon the Aircraft Division as a captive customer. On past jobs it had shown an unwillingness to respond quickly to changes, to keep the Aircraft Division informed of progress, and objectively to evaluate and adopt suggestions. There were times when the Wade Division sales manager, David Ackley, did not even return a critical call for several days. Hall agreed with this opinion. In fact, he wondered if Wade really could be considered a qualified supplier. Two years previously when he was head of quality control, the Aircraft Division had found unsatisfactory a radio transmitter that Wade had produced. Other sources that previously had produced similar radio transmitters had had serious difficulty also, but as Hall said: "The difference was that they did something about it. They didn't sit on their duff or submit long, cumbersome memos blaming everything on the Aircraft Division's specifications and inspection practices."

Hall thought that Wade really did not belong in the electronic business. It had been a small radio manufacturer that branched into electronics in a big way in World War II. Since the Middle '40's it had gained an increasingly large part of the market for electronics equipment for commercial aircraft. Hall believed that its chief trouble was that it was trying to cut cost and did not worry enough about quality. Hall said:

The automatic direction finder should cost somewhere around $1,500, but I am sure Wade, with its five and dime tactics, will bid considerably below that.

Hanna said:

If you let them bid, we're sunk. They'll come in with a low price and nobody will be able to get them out of here, but their people will never go out of their way to be helpful to us. We'll have to beg for the equipment. Also, it's nothing for them to make a change without even telling us about it. I have to admit some of the changes they have made in past products were pretty ingenious with regard to getting the cost down, but they raised havoc with the rest of the job. No interface at all.

Hall and Hanna spent a few hours reviewing their experience with the only prior order that they had placed with Wade for automatic direction finders. They concluded that there was no doubt about it—Wade's prices were low, but the rejection rate was high and the delivery rate was only fair. They admitted that there had been a number of specification changes on that job and that their own incoming inspection department had been going through a major crisis at that time. Thus, it might be unfair to blame Wade, but both Hall and Hanna still were convinced Wade was wrong for the direction finder job.

Also, they vividly remembered some of the clashes they had had with Mr. Ackley. Ackley refused to respond to urgent calls and refused to incorporate changes immediately. At one point he had refused to take back sets that had to be repaired because of damage during transit. He wanted a memo listing the exact nature of the damage, and a written admission that the Aircraft Division was responsible for filing any necessary claims.

Hall gave much thought to the Wade problem and finally decided that if Wade had not been a division of Universal National he would not consider it for the bid list. He mentioned the problem briefly to Clark, the division manager, who said:

Henry, if there is any way you can get rid of Wade, get rid of them. It's more difficult to do business inside than it is outside. They are a bunch of prima donnas; but just one thing, Henry, they are always running in to see Sullivan, so make sure you're right.

A month later the Aircraft Division released the request for bids to the two outside vendors. Both had been qualified previously on the basis of investigations including plant surveys.

Hall was not surprised that when the bids came in Bolster was low, but he was surprised that the bids ranged from $1,850 each to $2,200. As a result of fairly intensive negotiations with Bolster, Hall was able to negotiate the price down to $1,800 each. A patent problem proved to be more knotty than expected, and all in all it took a month to negotiate the proposed subcontract with Bolster.

Hall had just sent the subcontract to the company's contracting officer for the latter's approval in accordance with the terms of the prime contract, with a request for urgent action because of contract lead time, when he received a call from Clark, the division manager, who said:

Henry, I just came out of Sullivan's office. Sullivan is hopping mad and I am too. I thought I told you to see that Wade was taken care of on this finder. Ackley and some other clowns were there. They really burned us.

In summary, this is what the Wade people had told Sullivan during a two-hour meeting. They were not even asked to bid on the automatic direction finder, even though in the previous year the division had put something like $50,000 of independent research and development money into this product area. They said that troop carriers were going to be one of the biggest markets for the future. They claimed that they had now matched their reputation for low cost with technical proficiency and they were now the leader in the field. They said that they needed this job to start exploiting the independent research and development money the company had spent. They also said they badly needed it to absorb fixed overhead until the radio receiver market recovered—probably the following year. They claimed also that their reputation in the market place had suffered a staggering blow. Bolster was going all over the industry telling Wade's customers that Universal National would not even deal with Wade and that on the Sky Haul contract they were not even asked to bid. In fact, Ackley said he did not even know about this procurement until one of his customers asked him if there was any truth to the story that Wade was going out of the finder business. Sullivan was particularly incensed about what he called the waste of independent research and development money and the unabsorbed overhead. "Henry," Clark continued, "I want to talk to you later about how you made this mistake, but right now do one thing first—get a bid quotation from Wade."

Hall tried to remind Clark about their previous conversation. He wanted to give Clark reasons why he felt it was the wrong thing to go to Wade. He also wanted to tell Clark that it was too late. Although the subcontract with Bolster had not yet been executed, it had been written in final form and submitted to the contracting officer.

Hall called Bolster Company and told it that it would have to hold up on the direction finder order. He then put a call through to Sullivan's office for Ackley who he thought was there, but was unable to get through to Ackley. He left a message for Ackley to stop by. Not having heard from Ackley in two hours, he called Sullivan's office again and was told that Ackley had just left for Wade. He called Wade and talked to Ackley's assistant, James Barker. He explained the situation and said that the important thing was for Wade to get its estimate in right away. Barker pointed out that he needed the prints before he could make an estimate. He said it might take two or three weeks to evaluate the prints and to price the job. Hall replied, "That's not good enough. You make sure Ackley calls me as soon as his plane gets in." Hall then sent an expediter by plane to Wade with the prints.

Hall called again the next day, but he could not reach Ackley, nor could he reach Barker. However, the secretary to both men said that Ackley had left a message for him as follows:

Would you please touch base with Wade's regional representative on the West Coast?

This man would receive a commission for the sale and Ackley thought he should earn it. Ackley said they wanted Hall to make sure the company got its money's worth from this sales representative.

About this time, Hall received a call from David Ford, the sales manager of the Bolster Company. Ford wanted to know what to do with the $50,000 in anticipatory costs they had spent in order to meet the short delivery dates on the order. There ensued a long argument between the two men about who was responsible for incurring this expense. Ford said that all he wanted was the $50,000 the company had incurred in trying to help Hall—money that was spent with Hall's full knowledge and agreement.

At this point, Hall had a recurrence of an old ulcer attack and was hospitalized for a week. He had to stay in bed at home for an additional week. When he returned to his office he found that the quote had been received from Wade Division. The price was $2,500 and the quoted delivery was four weeks behind that required. And, if this were not enough, Wade had conditioned its bid on a number of waivers being made in the specification.

Hall went into Clark's office with the quotes from Wade. At this point Clark decided that he should take over the problem until it was finally resolved and a subcontractor was selected and a final price determined. He called Ackley and told him that if Wade received the order, he wanted to send a team of Aircraft Division personnel to the Wade plant to help expedite the order in order to meet the prime contractor's delivery requirements. Included in this team would be men from the Aircraft Division's engineering, production, purchasing, quality control, and inspection departments. Their assignment would be to help iron out problems on the spot with Wade personnel.

Ackley's reply to Clark was:

These panic visits never solve anything. They create more problems than they resolve. There is only one way of doing business and that is in an orderly fashion. As far as I am concerned, I am going to do business the right way. That means that we will perform in accordance with our quotation. If you want to make a change, you should issue a change order in accordance with the changes clause and I will process it like any other change and submit my quotation for an increase in price and delivery time as equitable under the circumstances. The one thing I do not want is a lot of oral communications that no one will remember later on. That's the trouble with doing business inside. People depart from proven business practices and the whole deal gets fouled up.

One week later, Clark got Ackley to agree on a new set of specifications and a compromise delivery date. Ackley also agreed to drop his price $5.32 to reflect the deletion of a fastener from the equipment.

About this time Clark got a call from the resident Air Force contracting officer wanting to know why his purchasing agent was considering a subcontract with Wade at $2,500, when he could get it from Bolster for $1,800.

Clark believed that he had negotiated as hard as he could to get the Wade Division to reduce its price. He felt that $2,494.68 was its rock bottom offer, and he believed that this represented an out-of-pocket expense to Wade of about $1,500 per unit for each of the 100 units he was ordering. He wanted to keep peace in the organization. He knew that Sullivan had his eyes on the Aircraft Division's profit figure for this contract. He also knew that he was in trouble for not calling in Wade earlier and that if he did not give it the order, Ackley would take the dispute back to Sullivan. He wondered whether he should present all the facts to Sullivan or let Wade have the contract and absorb part of the difference in his own profit and loss statement or let the Bolster Company go ahead with the order and just wait to see what happened. He wondered, further, what the decision and the consequences for him personally would be if he took the dispute to Sullivan.

Case 6–3

Thunderbolt Manufacturing
Company

Early in 1972, Mr. Ray Alexander, recently elected president of the Thunderbolt Manufacturing Company, was reflecting on the progress the company had made since 1964, when Mr. Earl Goodwin had become president. Annual sales had increased from about $30 million to nearly $80 million during this period and profits had risen from $1 million to about $3 million. The company had become a leading supplier in the automotive industry.

In Mr. Alexander's view, however, current operating practices were not satisfactory in several areas. There were an excessive number of disagreements between the plant managers and those in charge of marketing. There also were disagreements between plant managers and corporate management. The disputes centered upon transfer prices, out-of-stock position, and production mix. Many of the problems seemed to arise from the fact that performance was measured by profit and loss statements for three plants in the manufacturing group and for the marketing group.

Profit centers had been introduced in 1964. Thunderbolt had only two plants at that time, and each had its own product lines. Even though they both sold through a common sales force, it was relatively easy to think of each plant manager as the president of his own small company. In 1972 there were four plants, and product lines were no longer associated with particular plants. Also the company now had six profit centers, instead of just two.

It seemed to Mr. Alexander that, under the present organization, the managers of the various profit centers had relatively little control over the factors that influenced the profitability of their operations. He wondered whether conditions had changed enough since 1964 to call for reconsideration of the use of profit centers.

Mr. Alexander decided that this problem needed attention. Also, he thought it should be studied by someone not associated with the company, someone with an objective viewpoint. Consequently, he called in an acquaintance, Mr. James Smith. Mr. Smith was a management consultant, recognized as an authority on organization and management control.

Mr. Smith began his assignment by familiarizing himself with the company in general terms—its environment, its history, and its present organization. His notes from this familiarization phase are given in the Appendix.

Exhibit 1

THUNDERBOLT MANUFACTURING COMPANY

Organization Chart

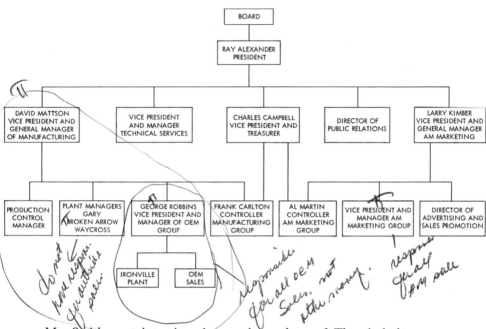

Mr. Smith next interviewed several members of Thunderbolt management to obtain their views on the company's use of profit centers. Summaries of these interviews follow.

Charles Campbell, Vice President and Treasurer

We've discovered that there are a number of problems with making profit centers work well, now that our company is quite a bit different from the way it used to be. In fact, it makes you wonder sometimes if the whole thing is still worthwhile, and if it might not be better to drop the profit center idea completely.

One of them is caused by the fact that measurement of performance tends to be unfair. A plant manager really has little control over some of the major factors that influence his profitability. Product mix, production volume, transfer price, all things he does not control, can make a plant manager show a low profit. Thus, a poor plant P&L may not necessarily mean poor performance. Of course, we try to recognize all this, because we compare profits to budget. But somehow, performance measurement always seems to get back to the profit figure alone. Even though a plant manager may be doing a tremendous job, he'll get discouraged if his profit is low for period after period. He figures that no matter how hard he tries he just can't improve profits. Worse yet is the opposite case, where a manager is not doing a good job but has a high profit figure. Whenever we try to question this guy on some of his variances from budgeted figures, the first thing he'll say is: "Yeah, but look at the profits I brought in." And it becomes somewhat difficult to motivate him to improve his performance because he is unwilling to give up this crutch.

Another problem we've found is that some managers tend to spend too much time worrying about the wrong things. For example, they'll often argue about the product mix assigned to them by the production scheduling group, or they'll grumble about transfer prices not being fair, or they'll complain that their assigned production volume is too low.

Of course, it is good to have some tension in an organization; it motivates people to produce. But it has to be aimed in the proper direction; that is, it should make managers worry about matters that they have some control over, not about things they can't influence.

Now, in our case, we sometimes get the feeling that we have too much tension, and tension aimed in the wrong direction. And that both are the result of profit centers.

There is another disadvantage to profit centers. As you know, we have a considerable number of product transfers between profit centers. But in order to figure out how the company as a whole is doing, we have to eliminate profits on these transfers from corporate financial statements. And this makes an awful lot of extra work for the accounting department. So, if we did away with profit centers, we probably would have a nice bundle of cash.

But I don't mean to paint too bleak a picture. If there were only disadvantages, we would have done away with profit centers some time ago.

Two advantages existed in 1964, when profit centers were installed. One was that managers received valuable training for top management jobs; the other was that they tended to become more profit conscious. These advantages still hold today.

There is another advantage, related to this greater profit consciousness. As we see it, the alternative to using profit centers is expense centers controlled by budgets. But holding a manager responsible only for variances from expense budgets is nit-picking; such an approach doesn't look at the major economic factors that make or break a business. Thus, despite all the problems I mentioned earlier, I feel that control by means of expense centers would not be as effective as with profit centers.

And then, I think we also should consider how the managers feel about profit centers before making a decision to drop them. Now that our managers are used to being measured on the basis of their profit contribution, they might not want to change to something else, despite the fact that this measurement by profits may not be fair to them. I think that they get quite a bit of satisfaction out of being held responsible for running their own show.

Frank Carlton, Manufacturing Group Controller

(As his title indicates, Mr. Carlton was mainly responsible for control functions within the manufacturing group. He reported directly to Mr. David Mattson, vice president and general manager of manufacturing. Because of his position, Carlton was described by other members of Thunderbolt management as being "able to present the plant managers' side of the situation." Since some of his comments were similar to those made by Mr. Campbell, only selected remarks representing additional points are reported here.)

Since there is no real market price for transfers between the plants and marketing, transfer prices are fictitious. Therefore, management is just playing games, and the managers know this.

If you are going to judge a man on the profits of his group, he's going to try to maximize these profits, even if this may not be in the best interest of the whole company. Let me give you a few examples of this here at Thunderbolt. Sometimes a plant manager will make production runs that are longer than scheduled, because this reduces his set-up costs. Now, you can't really blame him for doing this, because it increases his profits. But it also increases the finished goods inventory. And by deviating from his production schedule in order to have longer production runs, he may even increase the out-of-stock position of other items, a situation clearly not in the best interest of the company.

Another example. When it comes to new products, the marketing people like to include just about everything. As long as they can get even a small contribution from an item, they're willing to add it to their line, regardless of the volume they can get, because it will increase their profit figure. On the other hand, the boys in manufacturing lean in the opposite direction. Since there are start-up and capital costs associated with a new product, they need a certain volume before they reach the break-even point. The net result is that marketing tends to overestimate demand for new products, just to increase the chance that these will be added to the line. On the other hand, manufacturing tends to overestimate their costs, just to make sure that marginal products are not authorized by headquarters for production.

Actually, there's another reason why the boys in manufacturing tend to overestimate their costs. Cost estimates are used in setting the initial transfer prices, and, of course, the higher the transfer prices, the better their chance of showing a profit on any items added.

Another problem we have encountered with profit centers is that feelings between manufacturing and marketing run pretty high sometimes. Arguments may result over transfer prices, out-of-stock position, or whatever. And the result is that these two groups then become antagonistic, don't communicate well, and withhold information from each other.

Despite all I've said against profit centers, I'm still not sure that we should do away with them. We haven't really got anything that is *better* for management control purposes than our present profit center P&L reports.

And then, there's the fact that our managers don't want to do away with the profit center approach, despite all their complaints. And they feel quite strongly about this. In fact, one of our managers told me that he would quit if we eliminate profit centers at the plant level. And he may very well mean it. You know, there's quite a bit of prestige in being responsible for the whole operation. If we replace profit centers with expense centers, wer're reducing our plant managers to mere supervisors, mere foremen.

Al Martin, Marketing Group Controller

When you measure a manager's performance by profits, he's going to try to maximize this measure. And that may not always be the best thing for the company. Let me give you an example. You're aware that marketing is permitted to obtain products either from our plants or from the outside. But when they do buy outside, it usually turns out that they are not making a good decision from the company's standpoint. Of course, they're only looking at their own profits, so they don't recognize this. Now, even though my associates and I report to Mr. Kimber, we are also members of the treasurer's staff. Consequently, we have some information on our manufacturing costs, too, and we can usually figure out which way such decisions should go. And we've had to intervene time after time in situations like this, trying to convince marketing to buy from our own plants.

Now you may say that we could easily eliminate this problem by setting transfer prices in such a way that we would have "goal congruence," or whatever you call this animal. But before you do, let me tell you that it is impossible to set goal congruent prices on over 3,000 different items when manufacturing costs, and even selling prices, are constantly changing. About the only way we can eliminate this problem is by eliminating profit centers. . . .

. . . And there's another reason why I don't think that profit centers are a good idea here at Thunderbolt. Marketing people are sales oriented, and they perform best if they are measured in terms of sales. If you hold them responsible for profits, and costs, and inventories, and warehousing, and this and that, you're just confusing them and taking their attention away from the only thing that really means something to them, namely sales. . . .

Ray Alexander, President

In judging the performance of a plant manager, we use flexible budgeting. I know what each manager's costs should have been for the period in question, given a particular volume of activity. Then, all I need to do is look at his variances by industrial expense classifications to tell how well he has done his job.

Actually, I don't look at his profit figure on the P&L report and see how that compares with the budgeted profit. I feel it is more meaningful to look at the variances. Besides, if a manager's costs are in line with his particular volume, then his budgeted profit will result automatically.

I am considering the possibility of discontinuing the profit center approach at Thunderbolt. If we did, I think we would use expense centers. Each plant, for example, would become an expense center, and that would be about the only change here. We would still use a flexible budget, and we would measure performance by variances from the budget. As before, we would expect each plant manager to keep his out-of-stock position down. Also, we'd still judge him on intangibles, such as his labor relations and his community relations.

For the marketing group, we would use sales quotas instead of profit budgets. Sales is a more direct and more meaningful measure for marketing-oriented people. To control their selling expenses, we would use a flexible expense budget and measure their variances from that. Also, we would hold them responsible for keeping finished goods inventories at budgeted levels, similar to the way we do it now.

You see, what we would like to do is to hold each manager responsible only for items he can control. Of course, we probably will never be able to achieve this goal completely; however, I think that this system would be better in this respect than what we have now.

Of course, we'd probably have to pay a price for changing to expense centers. For example, we might lose some profit consciousness at the plant manager level.

However, I feel that there are two offsetting factors here. First, our plant managers would receive corporate financial statements on a monthly basis. Right now, they see these only once a year. For that reason, these corporate statements aren't too meaningful to them; that is, they can't trace the effect of their decisions on the corporate picture. But now, if they become familiar with and use the corporate statements, they will be able to see better the implications of their decisions on the company. And I feel that this will motivate them to act in the best interest of the company.

Second, we finally have our computer working well, and we expect this to give us at headquarters more and better information for decision making. Without such information available at headquarters, it is probably best to place a good bit of decision-making authority in the hands of those managers who are close to the day-to-day operations. However, with the right information available at headquarters, I don't see any good reasons why decisions can't be made there. And if they're made there, they are more likely to be in the best interest of the company, and so we get around the problem of profit consciousness at lower management levels.

Appendix

MANAGEMENT CONSULTANT'S NOTES

Nature of the Business

The Thunderbolt Manufacturing Company is in the automotive parts business and is a major supplier of ignition parts for both passenger cars and commercial vehicles. Other major product lines are carburetors and electric motors. Total company sales were about $80 million in 1971. Of this, about 70 percent was accounted for by ignition parts.

There are nine major classifications of ignition parts: coils, distributors, condensers, spark plugs, points, relays, switches, connectors, and fuses. Within each classification, there may be many different types of items. As a result of this variety of product lines and types, Thunderbolt manufactures over 3,000 different ignition items.

Market and Customers

The company sells its products both to automobile manufacturers (commonly referred to as original equipment manufacturer or OEM) and to the replacement market (called the aftermarket or AM).

The OEM Market. This market accounts for about one third of the total ignition parts volume. Sales are made to two different groups within the automobile companies: OEM production and OEM service. The first group concerns itself with the procurement of materials for the manufacture of automobiles, while the second deals with the parts requirements of the OEM dealers for service and repairs.

In this business, four major factors determine whether a parts manufacturer will be successful in establishing and continuing a relationship with an OEM. The most important factor is service, and there are two aspects to this: (1) The ability (*a*) to design ignition parts that meet OEM specifications and (*b*) to come up with innovations beneficial to the OEM, (2) the ability to meet OEM delivery requirements, even though these may change drastically from original estimates, (3) price, since very small differences in unit selling prices of parts can mean the difference between winning or losing a bid, and (4) quality.

The Aftermarket. This market accounts for the other two thirds of Thunderbolt's ignition parts volume. Whereas in OEM sales a relatively small number of sales engineers handle sales to only a few automobile companies, in the aftermarket a national sales force covers a large number of accounts. Also, in the aftermarket a chain of distributors is usually involved in getting the product to the ultimate consumer. A Thunderbolt salesman may sell to a wholesaler, who in turn sells to a jobber; from there the product moves to a retailer, who then sells it to the ultimate customer, the car owner.

As in the OEM business, service, price, and quality are essential for success in the aftermarket. Here, however, price is less important than either service or quality.

Competition

The automobile parts business is keenly competitive. There are other manufacturers who have product lines similar to those of Thunderbolt and strong marketing organizations with established contacts. In addition, there is a further pressure in the OEM market. The automobile companies have value analysis staffs that review a supplier's cost structure and manufacturing methods and, because of their huge purchasing power, often specify what they think his costs—and prices—should be.

Pricing Practices

Thunderbolt's OEM bid prices are calculated by the price estimating group, which is located at headquarters. For a particular item, this group obtains the estimated full manufacturing cost from the plant (or plants), making it. The group also gets an estimate from the sales people of what the product can be sold for. If this sales price estimate in view of estimated costs meets certain profit criteria (such as a 10 percent profit on sales), the estimate then becomes the bid price. If the estimate does not meet the profit criteria, the pricing decision is then usually made by Mr. David Mattson, vice president and general manager of manufacturing.

Because of competitive pressures and the negotiating power of the OEM, the profit criteria usually are not met, and thus top management quite frequently gets into OEM pricing decisions. Also, management may be especially interested in getting an item used in a particular automobile model, in the hope that "a foot in the door" will lead to increased sales later. As a result of these factors, profit margins are generally quite low in this area.

Another factor that complicates OEM pricing decisions is that there is a one to two year lag between the time a bid is submitted and the time the product is delivered. (As an example, in July 1972, Thunderbolt was quoting on parts for the 1974 model.) Even though there is a clause in each purchase contract that permits a renegotiation of the price if there have been increases in material or labor costs, the seller is not always successful in obtaining an increase in bid prices. Thus, it is desirable to take any foreseeable changes in costs into account at the time the bid price is determined.

In the aftermarket, parts suppliers such as Thunderbolt also have limited freedom in setting prices. This is because the OEM service divisions set the retail prices that are charged by automobile dealers for replacement parts that the OEM supplies them, and these prices, in turn, largely determine the retail prices that can be charged for similar parts by the independent dealers. With dealer prices fixed, the prices that a parts manufacturer is able to obtain are also relatively fixed, because all distributors involved in handling AM products receive standard mark-ups. About the only area where some pricing flexibility exists is in special designs, such as "hot" coils or special-purpose spark plugs. Even here, however, flexibility is limited by competitive pressures.

With this lack of flexibility in pricing, parts manufacturers' profit margins for a particular product are highly dependent on the level of manufacturing costs. Because of differences in cost structures among companies, some product items can be quite profitable for a particular manufacturer while others are not. Some products may even be loss items, carried only to provide a full line to the aftermarket. However, on the average, the profit margins for AM products are considerably larger than those in the OEM area. This difference in profit margins, however, may be partly due to the method of allocating costs. For example, whenever Thunderbolt manufactures a product for an OEM, the cost of tooling is charged completely to that part of the OEM business. Consequently, if no new tooling is required to produce the same item for the aftermarket, no tooling costs are charged against that part of the AM business.

Organization

In 1964, Thunderbolt had only two plants, one in Ironville, Ohio, the other in Gary, Indiana. The Ironville plant manufactured coils, condensers, and spark plugs, while the Gary plant concentrated on distributors, points, and relays. (Switches, connectors, and fuses were not produced by Thunderbolt at that time.) A single sales force dealt with both the OEM market and the aftermarket and handled the products of both plants.

Each plant was made a profit center in 1964. Under this concept, the plant manager was held responsible for the profits of his operation. The marketing group, however, was not made a profit center at that time. Thus, revenues on the plant P&L statements were shown at the dollar value of sales to the outside, rather than at some (lower) transfer price.

This organization by profit centers was initiated by Mr. Earl Goodwin, who joined Thunderbolt in 1964 as president. He had come from an automobile manufacturing company where profit centers had been used for some time with great success.

According to Mr. Charles Campbell, vice president and treasurer, there were essentially three reasons for introducing profit centers:

1. At the time Earl Goodwin joined Thunderbolt, its competitive position and profits had been dropping and there was considerable pressure for improvement. From his experience, Mr. Goodwin felt that holding operating managers responsible for profits, instead of just for costs, and giving them corresponding authority would improve the situation by inducing in them a strong profit consciousness.

2. There was need for an effective means of developing managers. Under the old approach, plant managers and their immediate subordinates were only supervisors—they just didn't have the opportunity to participate in decisions outside of their own limited areas of responsibility. As a result of this narrow exposure to business problems, they weren't ready to step into top management jobs. Yet Thunderbolt needed good managers. Mr. Goodwin believed that by holding them responsible for profits, and thus forcing them to deal with all phases of the business, they would receive the valuable training they needed to become top managers.

3. Mr. Goodwin had brought with him a number of top-flight managers from his previous employer. Some of these men came to the head office, others went to the plants. They were familiar with profit centers and Mr. Goodwin thought this would be of great help in introducing such centers at Thunderbolt.

Changes since 1964. Late in 1971 Mr. Earl Goodwin became chairman of the board and Mr. Ray Alexander was elected president. Mr. Alexander's background has been in finance.

The company has grown considerably. There are now four plants; one in Broken Arrow, Oklahoma, and one in Waycross, Georgia, in addition to the two original plants in Ironville, Ohio, and Gary, Indiana.

There has been a trend to specialization by market among the plants. In 1964, the plants were specialized by product line, emphasizing neither the OEM nor the AM business. Now, however, the Ironville plant produces almost eighty percent of its volume for the OEM market. The other three plants do about 90 percent of their business in the AM area. As a result of this market specialization, the plants are not limited to the manufacture of certain product lines. Rather, production scheduling by product lines is based mainly on economics with the goal of achieving the lowest total cost (which includes manufacturing, warehousing, and shipping costs) for the company. As a result, each plant now handles a wide mix of items—considerably wider than the original plants did in 1964.

Profit Centers. Currently there are six profit centers. All manufacturing under Mr. David Mattson (vice president and general manager of manufacturing) is treated as a profit center (see organization chart, Exhibit 1). The three plants reporting to Mr. Mattson (those at Gary, Broken Arrow, and Waycross) are also profit centers. These plants do not have responsibility for outside sales of their products, as they did in 1964.

The OEM group, under Mr. George Robbins (vice president and general manager of the group) is treated as a profit center. Mr. Robbins also reports to Mr. Mattson. The Ironville plant, which produces mainly for the OEM market, is part of this profit center. So also are the OEM sales engineers, who sell only to the automobile manufacturers. The responsibility of this profit center for sales extends to all products purchased by the automobile companies whether manufactured at Ironville or at the other plants. The responsibility of the center for manufacturing, however, includes only production at the Ironville plant.

The sixth profit center is AM marketing, with responsibility for all sales in the aftermarket regardless of which plant manufactured the products or whether they were acquired from outside suppliers. This center is headed by Mr. Larry Kimber, vice president and general manager of AM marketing.

Transfer Pricing

Because all four plants manufacture products for both the OEM and the replacement markets, and because AM marketing is a separate profit center, transfers of finished goods between profit centers are necessary. In addition, there are transfers between profit centers of materials in various stages of completion. For example, partly finished distributors are sometimes transferred from the Ironville plant (mainly OEM production) to the Gary plant (mainly AM production) for special processing and then back to Ironville for sale by the OEM sales engineers. Or, parts manufactured by one plant may be shipped to another for completion and eventual sale by AM marketing.

Transfers are based on standard costs plus a markup, as market prices are not readily available. Standard costs are set by headquarters, but are strongly influenced by the level of actual costs at the plants. In setting the prices for transfers of finished goods from the plants to AM marketing, the aim is to allocate the total margin equitably among the involved profit centers on the basis of their costs. (Total margin is the difference between the selling price to wholesalers and the standard cost.)

For ignition parts, transfer prices are determined for the nine product lines rather than for individual items. According to Mr. Campbell, it would be impractical to have a transfer price for each of the 3,000 different items. Transfer prices are reviewed at headquarters at least once a year, and a review may take several hours; thus, the total management time involved would be excessive if there was a separate price for each item. Instead, a percentage mark-up over standard costs is used for each product line. This mark-up is set by headquarters in such a way that the producing plant and the AM marketing group receive approximately equal profits after all expenses directly associated with the product are included.

Thus, in theory, only nine transfer mark-ups are needed, one for each product line. In practice, however, it has been necessary to make adjustments to these mark-ups for a few items. After agreeing in general with a particular product line mark-up, the AM marketing group has found instances in which some items could be purchased for less on the outside than from the plants. For these items, a below standard mark-up is used, so that the outside market price is equalled.

Similarly, for parts transferred between plants, the total margin is allocated between the affected plants. Here, also, a mark-up over standard costs is used. According to a member of management, this practice has been satisfactory mainly because the volume of parts so transferred is less than 5 percent of the company's total production.

Transfer prices are not necessary for transfers from OEM manufacturing to OEM marketing inasmuch as both are part of the same profit center.

Budgets

Measurement of performance at Thunderbolt is based on actual profit shown as compared to budgeted profit. Preparation of profit budgets for the coming fiscal year is initiated in July and the "big push" occurs during September, when the budgets are consolidated. Budgets are broken down by months. As a first step, monthly sales forecasts are made by the marketing groups on the basis of expected demand, industry trends, and the state of the economy. Because the forecasts are broken down by items, they take into account such factors as product mix and new products. These forecasts are reviewed by management and revised as necessary.

The approved sales forecasts are then converted into production schedules by the production scheduling group at headquarters. Anticipated changes in inventory levels are taken into account in this step. These schedules are then broken down by plants. Factors such as plant capacity, special manufacturing capabilities, freight costs, and manufacturing costs determine to a large extent which plant will produce what.

These individual plant schedules are used by the plants as a basis for developing their own budgets. For the volume of production scheduled, both revenues (based on transfer prices) and costs are developed. After corporate management has reviewed the completed budgets and agreement has been reached, they become the official budgets for the next year. The budgets for the OEM group and the AM marketing group are prepared in a way very similar to the plant budgets. The differences are that sales volume instead of production volume is the basis of the budget, and, of course, that revenues are derived from actual sales to the outside instead of from transfer prices. A further difference for marketing is that cost-of-goods sold is based on transfer prices.

In order to control the inventories and fixed assets that are related to a profit center, capital appropriations and monthly inventory budgets are determined at the same time as the profit budgets. These budgets are also developed by the "bottom-up" approach, by which the individual profit centers first arrive at tentative figures, which are then reviewed by top management, revised as necessary, and agreed to.

Responsibilities of Managers

Each manager of a profit center is responsible for achieving his budgeted profit. His performance is not judged on the basis of his profits relative to the investment required to achieve these profits. (However, one member of management stated that the company hopes to measure managers on the basis of return on investment in the future.)

Plant managers, furthermore, are expected to keep their acquisition of fixed assets within the limits set by the capital appropriation budget. Only plant managers have capital appropriation budgets, as the plants are the only profit centers with a continuing need for new investments. Also, they are responsible for the out-of-stock position of their plants. Since delivery is one of the critical success factors in the automotive parts business, it is important that out-of-stock position be kept at a minimum. In fact, an out-of-stock position of 2 percent is the allowed limit for the plant managers. Out-of-stock position of the plants is measured in units, and is judged with respect to the forecasts that were used in preparation of the plant production schedules, rather than with respect to sales volume. In this way, the plant managers are not held accountable for incorrect sales forecasts. Instead, if sales exceed scheduled production plus available inventory, such that a back-order position results, AM marketing is held accountable. The reason is that marketing makes the forecasts and is charged with selling the products.

AM marketing is also responsible for the finished goods inventory. This responsibility ranges from maintaining the inventory at the levels set forth in the monthly inventory budgets, through warehousing, physical security, and paperwork, to obsolescence. The basic reason for holding AM marketing responsible for the inventory is, again, that marketing makes the estimates that determine the inventory levels and is charged with selling the products.

There is a further reason for holding AM marketing responsible for finished goods inventory. Plants are also warehousing points to facilitate national distribution. Because the plants do not all produce the same items, there must be transfers of goods from plants at one location to warehouses at another. If manufacturing were responsible for the inventory, there would be complications. For example, who should be responsible for plant A's inventory at plant B? Should it be the plant that produced the item? Or the one that is warehousing it? Under the present system, this problem does not arise.

As part of its responsibility for the warehousing of the finished goods inventory, the marketing group is charged with warehousing expenses. One reason for this is to discourage marketing from exceeding budgeted inventory levels. Because competition is on the basis of delivery (among other factors), marketing has a tendency to stockpile inventory so that products will be available for immediate delivery. Corporate management, of course, does not like to see an already large inventory increase even further; and for that reason, marketing gets charged with these costs. (Finished goods inventories account for almost one-third of total current assets, and for almost 20 percent of total assets.)

Degree of Latitude

Even though managers are held responsible for the profits of their groups, they do not have complete control over all the factors that influence profitability. Plant managers, for example, do not have direct control over their production volume; they are told by the production scheduling group at headquarters what and how much to produce. They cannot refuse to produce an item, nor may they sell to the outside directly.

Similarly, plant managers have no control over their product mix; this also is fixed by the production schedule determined at headquarters. Yet this factor alone can have a large impact on a plant's profitability as there is a large variation in margins for different products.

Plant managers do have control over their manufacturing costs, and thus partly control their profit margins. Even though standard costs are set at headquarters for all operations, a plant manager can, for example, reduce his material costs by reducing scrap and rejects. Or he can reduce his labor costs by increasing output per man-hour.

In addition, plant managers have some control over factors such as quality of product and service. As discussed earlier, these factors are important in competing in this business, and, thus, plant managers actually do have some indirect control over their volume in the long run.

The AM marketing group also does not have complete control over the important factors that influence its profitability. Although it does have considerably more latitude than the plants in determining sales volume, this element depends to a large degree on external factors, such as competition, number of cars on the road, and the rate at which parts need to be replaced. In addition, another factor that has a direct effect on sales volume is the out-of-stock position at the warehouses.[1] Yet this factor is mainly under the control of the plant managers.

As far as margins are concerned, AM marketing has little control. As pointed out earlier, selling prices for parts are essentially predetermined by the OEM service divisions. Similarly, product costs for AM marketing are relatively fixed. These are determined by transfer prices, which, although reviewed at least once a year, are changed only when conditions change.

---

[1] A member of top management estimated that about one-half of the back-ordered AM business is lost. He was unable to provide a similar estimate for the OEM business, as here the buyer/seller relationship is of longer term than in the AM business.

On the other hand, AM marketing does have control over its selling and administrative expenses. However, these are relatively small when compared to cost-of-goods sold.[2]

Another opportunity for the AM marketing group to influence its profits arises from the fact that it is permitted to purchase products outside of the company. This can be done either when the prices charged by the plants are too high or when the plants cannot meet delivery requirements.

Because the OEM manufacturing/marketing group is just one profit center, its degree of control over sales volume is slightly greater than that of the three plants supplying AM marketing. Volume, of course, is determined largely by automobile manufacturers and by the vagaries of the automobile market. An OEM will ask Thunderbolt to supply a certain portion of its requirements for an ignition part for a particular model. Then, if demand for that model rises beyond expectations, Thunderbolt will be expected to increase delivery proportionately. If demand is lower than expected, the reverse will be true. However, by being able to develop a particularly good OEM part, the OEM group can gain an advantage over competitors and increase its portion of the OEM requirements.

With respect to margins, the degree of latitude for the OEM group is about the same as for the other three plants. Where negotiated transfer prices determine revenues in their case, negotiated product prices fix revenues for the OEM group; and because of the great purchasing power of the automobile manufacturers, pricing flexibility is limited. Similarly, since manufacturing methods are essentially the same for the Ironville plant as for the other three, flexibility with respect to costs is about the same. However, if the need arises, the OEM group may purchase products from the outside, which is a freedom the other plants do not have.

---

[2] S&A expenses for the AM marketing group amount to about 15 percent of net sales, while cost-of-goods sold is over 60 percent. (The remaining 25 percent is made up of items such as R&D expense, interest expense, taxes, and profits.)

Chapter Seven

TRANSFER PRICING

As pointed out in Chapter 6, one of the principal problems in operating a profit center system is to devise a satisfactory method of accounting for the transfer of goods and services from one profit center to another. Since in most companies there are significant amounts of intracompany transactions, this problem is a common one. In this chapter we discuss various approaches to arriving at transfer prices for transactions between profit centers and the system of negotiation and arbitration that is essential when transfer prices are used. We also discuss the pricing of services that corporate staff units furnish to profit centers.

OBJECTIVES OF TRANSFER PRICES

A sound transfer price system should accomplish the following objectives:

1. It should motivate the division manager to make sound decisions, and it should communicate information that provides a reliable basis for such decisions. This will happen when actions that the division manager takes to improve the reported profit of his division also improves the profit of the company as a whole.
2. It should result in a report of divisional profits that is a reasonable measure of the economic performance of the division.

These objectives cannot be achieved perfectly. In striving to increase the profits of his division, the division manager may make decisions that hurt the profits of other divisions and thus hurt the company as a whole; the transfer price system can minimize, but it probably cannot eliminate, this tendency. Up to a point, the system should motivate division managers to act as if they were the heads of independent companies; but division managers must, beyond this point, act for the good of the corporation as a whole, even at the expense of the reported profitability of their own divisions. Furthermore, as we shall see, there are transfer price systems that are good in accomplishing the first objective but that result in distorted measurement of divisional performance.

TRANSFER PRICING METHODS

Some writers use the term "transfer price" to refer to the amount used in accounting for *any* transfer of goods and services between responsibility centers. We use a somewhat narrower definition and limit the term "transfer price" to the value placed on a transfer of goods or services among two or more *profit centers*. Such a price would normally include a profit element because an independent company would not normally transfer goods or services to another independent company at cost or less. The term "price," as used here, has the same meaning as the word has when it is used in connection with transactions between independent companies.

When divisions of a company buy and sell from each other, there are two decisions that must be made periodically for each product that is being produced (or that may be produced) by one division and sold to another. First, it must be decided *where* the product is to be produced, that is, whether it is to be produced inside the company or purchased from an outside vendor; this is the *sourcing* decision. Second, it is necessary to determine a *transfer price*.

Market Prices

Under most circumstances, if market prices exist, current market prices are an ideal basis for transfer prices. When transactions are recorded at market prices, divisional pofitability represents the real economic contribution of the division to the total company profits. (If the selling division did not exist, presumably the products would be purchased from outside sources at current market prices.) Consequently, divisional profitability can be compared directly to the profitability of outside companies in the same type of business. Moreover, divisional managers are subject to the same competitive pressures on cost as they would be if they were the heads of independent companies. There is a constant incentive for the selling division to review make-or-buy decisions and produce and sell only the profitable products.

Independent Sourcing. If the selling division can sell its products to an outside market and the buying division can purchase material and services from an outside source, it is feasible to make the divisions independent of each other. When divisions have such independence, the sourcing and pricing decisions are resolved simultaneously by the divisions involved. There need be little or no involvement by the central staff or top management. If the selling division does not meet competition with respect to prices and other conditions, it is not awarded the business. Conversely, if production capacity is limited, the buying division must compete with outside companies for the scarce supply. This system, in effect, uses the outside market-price mechanism as a basis for setting internal prices by letting the divisions determine from whom they will buy or to whom they will sell.

Clearly, this system provides accurate competitive prices and requires little time of the central staff in settling pricing or sourcing disputes between divisions. The system does not necessarily assure optimum total company profits, however. In order to recognize a division's obligations to the overall corporate welfare, certain restrictions on its freedom to deal with the outside world are desirable. Among these are:

1. If the price offered by the inside division is the same as the outside market price, and other conditions are equal, the product should be made internally.
2. A distress price, that is, a temporarily low price, offered by an outside vendor should ordinarily be disregarded in arriving at the transfer price for products made internally.
3. Either the buying or the selling division should be able to request a headquarters review of a proposed source change that is believed not to be in the best overall interests of the company.

Sourcing Constrained. In many instances, freedom of sourcing is not feasible. There may not be appropriate outside sources for some products. Also, where the volume is significant, or the product is a key component, top management may be unwilling to run the risk of relying on an outside source.

In some situations in which divisions must deal with each other, it is possible to obtain market prices. For products such as steel, glass, and petroleum, lists of market prices are available. Even if formal price lists do not exist, it may be possible to approximate market prices if divisions deal with outsiders as well as insiders. For example, if Part A is purchased from an outside source and a similar Part B produced by an inside source, it is possible to estimate the price of B by adjusting the price of A for the effect of the differences in design. Another method of approximating market prices is to adjust a former market price for changes in price levels since the date that it was actually purchased. Also market prices might be obtained through quotations from outside suppliers. One has to be very careful with this practice, however, if the chance of awarding the business to the outside source is small. Not only is it unfair to ask for quotations under such circumstances but, after a few instances in which quotations did not lead to orders, the reliability of the quotations is likely to deteriorate.

The outside market price would, of course, be adjusted for any differences in the conditions of sale or delivery between the outside supplier and the inside sale.

Cost-Based Transfer Prices

If market prices are not available or cannot be estimated, then it may be necessary to have the transfer price based on the costs of the selling division.

In setting up a cost-based transfer price system, it is necessary to decide two things: First, how should the costs be calculated, and second, what type of profit margin should be added to the costs. Each is discussed below.

The Cost Component. In general, transfer prices should be based on standard costs. If the prices of material and services fluctuate, it may be appropriate to make adjustments in standard costs for changes in price levels. The principal consideration is that the selling division should not be allowed to pass on inefficiencies to the buying division in the form of higher prices, which could easily happen if transfer prices were based on actual costs. If standard costs are not available, a price should be established that is not changed for a relatively long period of time, except for changes in wage rates and material costs.

One of the problems with cost-based transfer prices is that the selling divisions have little incentive to improve efficiency if these improvements are immediately reflected in reduced standard costs and hence in lower transfer prices. This problem must be taken into account in an effective transfer price system. One solution is to give the selling division the benefit of improved efficiency for a specified period of time, such as a year or two, by not reducing the transfer price during that period.

The Profit Component. If the selling division sells both to outside customers and to inside divisions, one method of arriving at the profit component of the transfer price would be to apply the outside average markup percentage to the standard cost of goods transferred. If the equipement and processing methods used for the outside products are similar to those used for the inside products, such a markup on cost would be appropriate. However, if there is a difference in the type of equipment used or the degree of automation, it would be preferable to use a markup percentage that is related to the assets employed in making the product, rather than to costs. Assume, for example, that the outside products were produced in relatively low volumes on general purpose equipment, while the inside products were made on highly automatic special purpose equipment. Standard costs of the inside products would be lower than those for comparable outside products, but the investment in equipment would be greater. It would be unfair to apply the lower profit markup of the outside products to the lower costs of the inside products.

If the selling division does not sell to outside customers or if the outside sales are not comparable with inside sales, it is necessary to estimate a competitive markup. This can be based on a knowledge of typical markups in the industry or the profitability of similar products made by other divisions. (As in the case just cited, it is important that, if this markup is to be applied to costs, it should be calculated on a basis consistent with the equipment and automation to which it is to be applied.)

One of the problems with using a markup related to investment is that a division can increase its profits by adding new equipment. Equipment added for cost savings purposes, therefore, should not be a reason to increase transfer prices. As mentioned above, in order to provide an incentive for the selling division to increase its efficiency, the savings from new equipment should be retained for a period of time, and not passed along in the form of a reduced transfer price.

Two-Step Pricing

Problems with Cost-Based Prices. When a transfer price is based on cost, as described in the preceding section, it becomes a variable cost to the buying division even though it contains fixed elements. If excess capacity exists, subsequent analysis of costs by the buying division for short-run marketing decisions may result in incorrect conclusions. If the buying division treats this cost as a variable cost, the divisional variable cost will be different from the company's variable cost. For example, assume division A sells a product to division B for a price of $100, which consists of three elements, as follows:

```
Variable cost  . . . . . . .   $ 50
Fixed cost  . . . . . . . . . .     30
Profit  . . . . . . . . . . . . .     20
          Price  . . . . . . . .   $100
```

To the manager of division B, the entire $100 price is a variable cost. To the company, however, the variable cost is $50. The transfer price system, therefore, may obscure the relevant cost to the decision maker.[1]

Even if the manager of division B was aware of the true variable cost, he would be affecting his profit performance adversely by making decisions on the basis of this cost if he was paying the $100 transfer price. These decisions include: (1) a change in price that affects sales volume; (2) a change in costs (e.g., advertising or sales promotion) that affects sales volume; or (3) a change in product mix. If these decisions were made in such a way as to optimize division B's profit, total company profits could be less than optimum.

Although this problem exists any time goods are transferred between divisions at unit transfer prices, it is particularly acute in companies that have divisions primarily engaged in marketing products that are manufactured by other divisions within the company.

It should be noted that variable manufacturing cost will equal company marginal cost only when capacity is available and the option to sell to an outside customer does not exist. If, by selling to an inside buyer, a manager foregoes the opportunity to sell to an outside buyer, the marginal cost

---

[1] This assumes that the variable costs approximate the marginal costs. While this may not always be true, in the short run variable costs will be much closer to marginal costs than to the transfer price.

to the company is the competitive market price. This is so because the *opportunity cost* to the company is the amount of cash given up by selling to the inside source.

When a division sells exclusively (or nearly exclusively) to other divisions of the same company, the divisional manager rarely has any significant marketing responsibility. He is, in effect, a captive supplier, whose principal responsibilities are controlling costs, quality, and production schedules. The profits of such a division can be affected to a much greater extent by the volume of sales, over which the manager has relatively little control, than by the cost performance that he can control. Under these circumstances, divisional profitability can be a poor measure of managerial performance. Even if a division sells to outside customers, as well as to internal divisions, profitability can be affected adversely by the failure of another division to market adequately.

Solutions to These Problems. There are a number of possible adjustments to the transfer pricing mechanism to mitigate the problems just described, in addition to the alternative of eliminating the problem by operating the division as a cost center.

Fixed Monthly Charge. One alternative would be to charge the standard variable cost for each unit transferred plus a fixed amount each month to cover fixed costs. The amount of fixed costs would cover the costs associated with the capacity reserved for the buying division. A profit margin can also be added. For example, assume the following condition:

DIVISION X

(Manufacturer)

	Product A	Product B
Expected sales to division Y	$ 100,000	$ 100,000
Variable cost per unit	$ 5.00	$ 10.00
Total annual fixed costs		
assigned to product	$ 480,000	$ 480,000
Investment in working capital		
and facilities to produce products	$1,200,000	$1,500,000
Competitive return on investment	10%	10%

The transfer price for product A would be $5 for each unit that division Y purchases plus $40,000 per month (480,000 ÷ 12) for fixed cost + $10,000 per month $\left(\dfrac{1,200,000}{12} \times .10 \right)$ for profit.

The transfer price for product B would be $10 for each unit that division Y purchases plus $40,000 per month for fixed costs plus $12,500 $\left(\dfrac{1,500,000}{12} \times .10 \right)$ for profit.

The fixed cost calculation is based on the capacity that is reserved for the production of each of the products that is sold to division Y. The investment represented by this capacity is then allocated to each of these products. The return on investment that division Y earns at standard cost on competitive (and, if possible, comparable) products is calculated and multiplied by the investment assigned to the product.

In the example just given, we have calculated the profit allowance as a fixed amount. It would be appropriate under some circumstances to divide the investment into variable (e.g., receivables and inventory) and fixed (physical assets). Then, a profit allowance based on a return on the variable assets would be added to the standard variable cost for each unit sold.

Following are some points to consider about this method of pricing:

1. The monthly charge for fixed costs and profits would be negotiated periodically and would depend on the capacity reserved for the buying division.

2. Some objections may be raised to the accuracy of the cost and investment allocation. Actually, in most situations there is no great difficulty in assigning costs and assets to individual products. In any event, approximate accuracy is all that is needed. The principal problem is usually not the allocation technique but rather the decision as to how much capacity is to be reserved for the various products. Incidentally, if capacity is reserved for a group of products sold to the same division, there is no need to allocate fixed costs and investments to individual products in the group.

3. Standard variable costs are not always the same as marginal costs. Where there is a real possibility that marginal costs might vary significantly from standard variable costs, some system should be developed for monitoring the costs and communicating to management when such differences develop.

4. Under this pricing system, the manufacturing division's profit performance is not affected by the volume of sales. Thus, this system solves the problem described earlier that arises when other divisions' marketing efforts affect the profit performance of a purely manufacturing division.

5. There could be some conflict between the interests of the manufacturing division and the interests of the company. If capacity is limited, the manufacturing division can increase its profit by selling outside because the outside selling price will be higher than the standard variable cost. Consequently, if a divisional manager has the choice of using his capacity to produce parts for outside sale, it will be to his advantage to do so.

Profit Sharing.   As described above, in those instances where one division markets products produced by another, the transfer price becomes the variable cost to the marketing division in the typical transfer price system. Where the two-step pricing system just described does not appear to be appropriate, a profit sharing system might be used to insure congruence of divisional interest with company interest. This system operates somewhat as follows:

1. The product is transferred to the marketing division at standard variable cost.
2. After the product is sold, the divisions share the contribution earned, which is the selling price minus the variable manufacturing and marketing costs.

This method of pricing is often appropriate when the demand for the manufactured product is not steady enough to warrant the permanent assignment of facilities, as in the two-step method. In general, this method accomplishes the purpose of making the marketing division's interest congruent with the company's. There can be, however, practical problems in calculating the contribution, finding an equitable method to divide it, and in administering the system. Note that under this method the profits of the manufacturing division *are* affected by the volume of sales.

Two Sets of Prices. A third possible solution to the problem of the manufacturing division that sells only to a marketing division is to have two sets of transfer prices. The manufacturing division's revenue is credited at the outside sales price minus a percentage to cover marketing costs. The buying division is charged the variable standard costs (or, sometimes, the total standard cost). The difference is charged to a headquarters account and eliminated when the divisional statements are consolidated.

This method gives the manufacturing division an incentive to help maximize profits rather than simply minimizing costs. The marketing division is motivated to make correct short-term product and pricing decisions. The method has the disadvantage, however, of making divisional profits greater than company profits. Consequently, top management must be aware of this situation in evaluating divisional profitability.

ADMINISTRATION OF TRANSFER PRICES

Most transfer price systems require formal administration procedures to operate successfully. They are described in this section.

Negotiation among Divisions

In most companies, divisions negotiate transfer prices with each other; that is, transfer prices are not set by a central staff group. Perhaps the most important reason for this is the belief that one of the primary functions of line management is to establish selling prices and to arrive at satisfactory purchase prices. If control of pricing is left to the headquarters staff, line management's ability to affect profitability is reduced. Also, many prices represent compromise positions by both buyer and seller. A headquarters group would have to rationalize the prices that it established. If the central staff group cannot defend the prices it sets, division managers can argue that their low profits are due to the arbitrariness of the prices. A third reason for having the divisions negotiate their prices is that they usually have the most information on markets and costs and, consequently, are best able to arrive at reasonable prices.

If the divisions are to negotiate prices, they must know the ground rules within which these negotiations are to be conducted. In a few companies, headquarters informs divisions that they are free to deal with each other or with outsiders as they see fit. Where this is done and there are outside sources and outside markets, no further administrative procedures are required, assuming that top management really means that the divisions are free to deal outside the company. As we described earlier, the market sets the price and, if divisions cannot agree on a price, they simply buy from or sell to outsiders. In most companies, however, some administrative procedures are established. If divisions are required to deal with one another, they do not have the threat of doing business with competitors as a bargaining point in the negotiation process. Consequently, the headquarters staff must develop a set of rules that govern both pricing and sourcing of intracompany products.

Sourcing and Transfer Pricing Rules.   The extent and formality of the sourcing and transfer pricing rules will depend to a great extent on the amount of intracompany transfers and the availability of markets and market prices. The greater the amount of intracompany transfers and the less the availability of market prices, the more formality and specificity of rules will be required. In some instances, all that is required is to tell the divisions that goods will be transferred at prevailing market prices. If such prices are readily available, there is little problem. Sourcing can be controlled by having headquarters review make-or-buy decisions that affect revenues in excess of a specified amount.

If there are significant amounts of intracompany transfers and if competitive prices are not available for all products, guidelines similar to the following have been found to be useful.

1. Divide products into two main classes:
    Class I includes all products for which top management wishes to control the sourcing. These would normally be the large volume products, products where no outside sources exist, and products where for quality or secrecy reasons the company wishes to maintain control over manufacturing.
    Class I products are further classified as follows:

    Class IA are products for which no outside, competitive prices are available. *Class IB* are products for which outside competitive prices are available.
    Class II are all other products. In general, these are products that can

be produced outside the company without any significant disruption to present operations. These are products of relatively small volume, produced with general purpose equipment.
2. The sourcing of Class I products can be changed only with permission of central management.
3. The sourcing of Class II products is determined by the divisions involved. Both the buying and selling divisions are free to deal either inside or outside the company.

Under this arrangement it is possible to concentrate on the sourcing and pricing of a relatively small number of high volume products. A list of products by classification should be provided as well as specific instruction as to how the prices of each product should be established. There should be rules for establishing market-based prices and rules for establishing cost-based prices. It is not unlikely that all of the different methods described in the preceding section would be used. If divisions are to negotiate, they must know how each product is to be priced, and this is the purpose of the set of rules.

It is important that line managers spend as little time as possible on transfer price negotiations and that the guidelines for these negotiations be specific enough so that skill in negotiations is not a significant factor in the determination of the transfer price. Without such rules, the most stubborn manager will negotiate the most favorable prices.

Arbitration

No matter how specific the pricing rules are, there may well be instances where divisions will not be able to agree on a price. For this reason, there should be some procedure for arbitrating transfer price disputes.

There can be widely different degrees of formality in transfer price arbitration. At one extreme the responsibility for arbitrating disputes is assigned to a single executive, for example, the financial vice president or the executive vice president, who talks to the division manager involved and then announces the price orally.

The other extreme is to set up a committee. Usually such a committee will have three responsibilities:

1. To settle transfer price disputes.
2. To review sourcing changes.
3. To change the transfer price rules where appropriate.

The degree of formality employed depends on the extent and type of transfer price disputes. In any case, transfer price arbitration should be the responsibility of a high level headquarters executive or group, since arbitration decisions can have an important effect on divisional profits.

There are a number of ways in which arbitration can be conducted. With a formal system, both parties submit a written case to the arbitrator. The arbitrator, with the assistance of the appropriate staff, reviews both positions and decides on the price. In doing so, he usually obtains the assistance of other staff officers. For example, he might have the purchasing department review the validity of a proposed competitive price quotation or the industrial engineering department review the appropriateness of a disputed standard labor cost. As indicated above, in less formal systems, the presentations may be largely oral.

It is important that relatively few disputes should be submitted for arbitration. If a large number of disputes are arbitrated, this indicates that the rules are not specific enough, the rules are difficult to apply, the divisional organization is illogical, or divisionalization should not have been adopted. In short, it is a symptom that something is wrong. Not only is arbitration time-consuming to both line managers and headquarters executives, but also arbitrated prices often satisfy neither the buyer nor the seller.

In some companies, there is such an onus involved in submitting a price dispute to arbitration that very few are ever submitted. If, as a consequence, legitimate grievances do not surface, the results are undesirable. Preventing disputes from being submitted to arbitration will tend to hide the fact that there are problems with the transfer price system.

TRANSFER PRICING AND COST-TYPE CONTRACTS

In some instances, a division that is working on a cost-type government contract may purchase material or parts from another division of the company. The problem occurs as to what cost will be allowed under the contract: the selling division's cost or a transfer price that includes a profit margin. Clearly, in most instances, it will be to the company's benefit to use the transfer price.

Government regulations state that transfers from other divisions, subsidiaries, or affiliates will be at cost except under the following conditions:

1. The transfer price is based on an established catalogue or market price of commercial items sold in substantial quantities to the general public.
2. It is the result of adequate price competition and is the price at which an award was made to an affiliated organization after obtaining quotations on an equal basis from such organizations and one or more outside sources which normally produce the item or its equivalent in significant quantities.[2]

The price calculated above must not be in excess of the selling division's current sales price to its most favored customer. Also, the transfer price should be adjusted, when appropriate, to reflect the quantities being procured and may be adjusted for the actual costs of any modifications required by the contract.

---

[2] Armed Services Procurement Regulations, Chapter XV, Sec. 202. (These regulations are used by many government agencies.)

Even where all of the requirements above are met, the contracting officer may determine that a particular transfer price is unreasonable. If he so determines, however, he must support this position with appropriate facts.

The implication of these transfer price regulations for managers is that special care should be taken in establishing transfer prices for divisions working on government contracts. Otherwise, the company may suffer a real economic loss.

PRICING CORPORATE SERVICES

In this section we describe some of the problems associated with charging divisions for services furnished by corporate staff units.

It is useful to classify central services in the following three types:

1. Those central services over which the division has no control.
2. Those central services that the division must accept, but for which the amount of the service is at least partially controllable by the division.
3. Those central services over which the division has the discretion of using or not using.

No Control by the Division

Divisions ordinarily cannot control the services rendered by such staff offices as accounting, public relations, industrial relations and legal. The divisions must accept these services and have little, if anything, to say about the amount that is spent on them.

The principal problem with these services is whether to allocate the costs to the operating divisions. As indicated in Chapter 6, the main reasons given for allocating them are:

1. If an operating manager pays for a service whether he uses it or not, he will be more likely to use it.
2. An operating manager will be more likely to exert pressure to keep down those costs (by complaining) if he must pay for them.
3. Divisional profits will be more realistic and comparable to outside firms because, presumably, the outside firm would have to pay for comparable services.

The main argument against allocation is that it is not controllable by the operating manager and, therefore, may only annoy him.

If top management does decide to allocate these costs, the usual cost accounting techniques for estimating the "fair share" applicable to each profit center are satisfactory. However, when costs are allocated, the *budgeted* costs, not the actual costs, should be allocated. In this way, the allocation will not affect the comparison between budgeted and actual divisional profit performance, and variances will appear in the reports of the responsibility center that incurred the costs. An exception to this generalization might occur if personnel costs or prices for purchased services increase significantly during the budget period; it would seem appropriate to pass on these increased costs to the users.

Control over Amount of Service

In some cases, divisions must accept a central service, but the amount of the service that it accepts may be controllable. Data processing and research/development are two examples. There are three schools of thought about such services.

One school holds that a division should pay the *marginal costs* of the discretionary services. If it pays less than this, it will be motivated to use more of the service than is economically justified. For example, if a divisional manager did not have to pay for his reports, he might request reports from the data processing department even though these were of little value to him. If, on the other hand, a divisional manager pays more for a service than the marginal cost to the company, he might not elect to use certain services because the value to him was not equal to the cost. If the value of the service was more than the marginal cost to the company, it might be a mistake for the operating manager to reject this service.

A second school advocates a price equal to the full cost, that is, marginal cost plus a fair share of the fixed costs. It is argued that if the divisions do not believe that the services are worth at least their full cost, then there is something wrong with either the quality or the efficiency of the service unit. Furthermore, as described, divisions may be permitted to obtain services from an outside source if they can do so at a price that is lower than the company's full cost. If services are in fact procured from an outside source, this is another signal that something may be wrong with the company's service unit. It is also argued that full costs represent the company's long-run costs and this is the amount that should be paid. If full costs are used, they should be *budgeted* costs, with the exception stated above.

A third school of thought advocates a price that is equivalent to the market price, or to full cost plus a profit margin. The market price would be used if one is available (e.g., the costs charged by a computer service bureau); if not, the price would be full cost plus a return on investment. The rationale for this position is that the capital employed by the service unit should earn a return just as much as the capital employed by manufacturing divisions. Said another way, the divisions would incur the investment if they provided their own services. Xerox Corporation uses this approach as indicated by the following:

Xerox is an example of one of the companies that is beginning to tap the potential of the pricing mechanism. Xerox has implemented a "standard cost" type system for processing computer-based applications. Each application was subjected to an industrial engineering study to establish its standard cost. The standard costs used market based prices for computer resources. The company then charges users the standard cost for processing their applications throughout the year and actual costs are also tracked and available to users on request. Where several users share the benefits of a computer application the processing costs are allocated between them. Users decide upon a "fair" appropriation of the costs. If one user decides to eliminate his report, the other users must pick up the added costs. The intent is to provide accountability to those that benefit from computer resources, and to provide feedback information so those that benefit can more effectively behave as responsible users.[3]

The decision on pricing depends to a considerable extent on the wishes of management. If management wants to encourage divisions to use a central service (e.g., operations research or computer systems), it might provide them at marginal cost, or even less, at least for a period of time. On the other hand, if management believes that the profit centers should pay a price that approximates the cost of an outside service, it might charge full cost or even more.

Discretionary Use of Services

In some cases, management may decide that the use of a central service is optional to the operating divisions. The divisions may use an outside service, develop internal capability, or simply not use the service at all. This type of arrangement is most often found in such activities as data processing or internal consulting groups. The reason for making these services independent is to have them "stand on their own feet." If these services are not used by the divisions, the scope of their activity will be contracted or they may even be eliminated entirely. In effect, management is delegating the responsibility for supporting these particular central services to the users.

In some instances, service groups of this type are made into profit centers. To the extent that they are treated as profit centers, the transfer price is set according to the considerations described earlier.

Simplicity of the Pricing Mechanism

The prices charged for corporate services will not accomplish their intended result unless they are sufficiently straightforward so that division managers understand their significance. Computer experts are accustomed to dealing with complex equations, and the computer itself provides information on the use made of it on a second-by-second basis and at low cost. There is sometimes a tendency, therefore, to charge computer users on the basis of rules that are so complicated that the user cannot understand them. Often the user cannot understand what the effect on his costs would be if he decided to use the computer for a given application, or alternatively, to discontinue a current application. These rules are self defeating.

---

[3] "A Panel Session—Charge-out System for Management Acceptance and Control of the Computer Resource." *Proceedings, National Computer Conference, 1974,* Session Chairman, Richard L. Nolan, p. 1013.

Appendix

Some Theoretical Considerations

There is a considerable body of literature on theoretical transfer pricing models. Few, if any, of these models are used in actual business situations, however, and, for reasons explained below, we doubt they ever will be widely used. Consequently, we have omitted reference to these models in the body of this chapter. Although these models are not directly applicable to real business situations, they are useful in conceptualizing transfer price systems. The purpose of this appendix is to give a brief description of some of these models and to provide references for the interested student.

Transfer pricing models may be divided into two types: (1) models based on classical economic theory, and (2) models based on mathematical programming.

Economic Models

The classic economic model was first described by Jack Hirschliefer in a 1956 article. Professor Hirschleifer developed a series of marginal revenue, marginal cost, and demand curves for the transfer of an intermediate product from the transferor (the selling division) to the transferee (the final processing division). He used these curves to establish transfer prices, under various sets of economic assumptions, that would optimize the total profit of the two divisions. Using the transfer prices thus developed, the two divisions would produce the maximum total profit by optimizing their divisional profits. The two-step pricing system described in the chapter is an adaptation of this type of model.

The difficulty with the Hirschleifer model is that it can be used only when a narrowly specified set of conditions exist: It must be possible to estimate the demand curve for the intermediate product, the assumed conditions must remain stable, there can be no alternative uses for the facilities used to make the intermediate product, and the model is applicable only to the situation in which the selling division makes a single intermediate product, which it transfers to a single buying division which uses that intermediate product in a single final product. Such conditions exist rarely, if at all, in the real world.

Mathematical Programming Models

In contrast with the marginal cost approach of the economic models, the mathematical programming models are based on an opportunity cost approach. These models also incorporate capacity constraints. They develop a linear program that calculates an optimum company-wide production pattern, and using this pattern they calculate a set of values that impute the profit contribution of the scarce resources. These are called *shadow prices,* and the process of calculating them is called "obtaining the dual solution" to the linear program. If the variable costs of the intermediate products are added to their shadow prices, a set of transfer prices result that should motivate divisions to produce according to the optimum production pattern for the entire company. This is so because if these transfer prices are used, each division will optimize its profits only by producing in accordance with the patterns developed through the linear program.

If reliable shadow prices could be calculated, they would indeed be useful in arriving at transfer prices. However, in order to make the programming model manageable, even on a computer, many simplifying assumptions must be incorporated in it. It is assumed that the demand curve is known, that it is static, that the cost function is linear, and that alternative uses of production facilities and their profitability can be estimated in advance. As is the case with the economic model, these conditions rarely exist in the real world.

Practical Problems with Models

The theoretical models have limitations that prevent their use in real world situations:

1. As already noted, the models are based on simplifying assumptions that do not exist in the real world.
2. The model assumes the availability of information that usually cannot be obtained.
3. In general, the model assumes that transfer prices will be imposed by the central staff, and denies the importance of negotiation among divisions. As indicated in the body of the chapter, division managers usually have better information than is available to the central staff. Indeed, if the central staff could determine the optimum production pattern, the question arises as to why this pattern is not imposed directly, rather than attempting to arrive at it indirectly via the transfer price mechanism.

SUGGESTED ADDITIONAL READINGS

ABDEL-KHAIIK, A. RASHAD and EDWARD J. LUSK. "Transfer Pricing—A Synthesis," *The Accounting Review,* January 1974.

BAUMAL, W. J. and T. FABIAN. "Decomposition, Pricing for Decentralized and External Economies," *Management Science,* September 1964.

DOPUCH, N. and D. DRAKE. "Accounting Implications of a Mathematical Approach to the Transfer Pricing Problem," *Journal of Accounting Research,* Spring 1964.

GOULD, J. R. "Economic Price Determination," *Journal of Business,* January 1964.

HIRSCHLEIFER, JACK. "On The Economics of Transfer Pricing," *Journal of Business,* July 1956.

ONSI, MOHAMED. "A Transfer Price System Based on Opportunity Cost," *The Accounting Review,* July 1970.

RONEN, J. and G. MCKINNEY, III. "Transfer Pricing for Divisional Autonomy," *Journal of Accounting Research,* Spring 1970.

SOLOMONS, DAVID. *Divisional Performance: Measurement and Control,* Homewood, Ill.: Richard D. Irwin, Inc., 1968, Chapter VI.

Case 7-1

Birch Paper Company

"If I were to price these boxes any lower than $480 a thousand," said James Brunner, manager of Birch Paper Company's Thompson division, "I'd be countermanding my order of last month for our salesmen to stop shaving their bids and to bid full-cost quotations. I've been trying for weeks to improve the quality of our business, and if I turn around now and accept this job at $430 or $450 or something less than $480, I'll be tearing down this program I've been working so hard to build up. The division can't very well show a profit by putting in bids that don't even cover a fair share of overhead costs, let alone give us a profit."

Birch Paper Company was a medium-size, partly integrated paper company, producing white and kraft papers and paperboard. A portion of its paperboard output was converted into corrugated boxes by the Thompson division, which also printed and colored the outside surface of the boxes. Including Thompson, the company had four producing divisions and a timberland division, which supplied part of the company's pulp requirements.

For several years, each division had been judged independently on the basis of its profit and return on investment. Top management had been working to gain effective results from a policy of decentralizing responsibility and authority for all decisions except those relating to overall company policy. The company's top officials believed that in the past few years the concept of decentralization had been successfully applied and that the company's profits and competitive position had definitely improved.

Early in 1957, the Northern division designed a special display box for one of its papers in conjunction with ·the Thompson division, which was equipped to make the box. Thompson's staff for package design and development spent several months perfecting the design, production methods, and materials to be used. Because of the unusual color and shape, these were far from standard. According to an agreement between the two divisions, the Thompson division was reimbursed by the Northern division for the cost of its design and development work.

When all the specifications were prepared, the Northern division asked for bids on the box from the Thompson division and from two outside companies. Each division manager was normally free to buy from whatever supplier he wished; and even on sales within the company, divisions were expected to meet the going market price if they wanted the business.

In 1957, the profit margins of converters such as the Thompson division were being squeezed. Thompson, as did many other similar converters, bought its paperboard, and its function was to print, cut, and shape it into boxes. Though it bought most of its materials from other Birch divisions, most of Thompson's sales were made to outside customers. If Thompson got the order from Northern, it probably would buy its linerboard and corrugating medium from the Southern division of Birch. The walls of a corrugated box consist of outside and inside sheets of linerboard sandwiching the fluted corrugating medium. About 70 percent of Thompson's out-of-pocket cost of $400 for the order represented the cost of linerboard and corrugating medium. Though Southern had been running below capacity and had excess inventory, it quoted the market price, which had not noticeably weakened as a result of the oversupply. Its out-of-pocket costs on both liner and corrugating medium were about 60 percent of the selling price.

The Northern division received bids on the boxes of $480 a thousand from the Thompson division, $430 a thousand from West Paper Company, and $432 a thousand from Eire Papers, Ltd. Eire Papers offered to buy from Birch the outside linerboard with the special printing already on it, but would supply its own inside liner and corrugating medium. The outside liner would be supplied by the Southern division at a price equivalent of $90 a thousand boxes, and it would be printed for $30 a thousand by the Thompson division. Of the $30, about $25 would be out-of-pocket costs.

Since this situation appeared to be a little unusual, William Kenton, manager of the Northern division, discussed the wide discrepancy of bids with Birch's commercial vice-president. He told the vice-president: "We sell in a very competitive market, where higher costs cannot be passed on. How can we be expected to show a decent profit and return on investment if we have to buy our supplies at more than 10 percent over the going market?"

Knowing that Mr. Brunner had on occasion in the past few months been unable to operate the Thompson division at capacity, it seemed odd to the vice-president that Mr. Brunner would add the full 20 percent overhead and profit charge to his out-of-pocket costs. When asked about this, Mr. Brunner's answer was the statement that appears at the beginning of the case. He went on to say that having done the developmental work on the box, and having received no profit on that, he felt entitled to a good markup on the production of the box itself.

The vice-president explored further the cost structures of the various divisions. He remembered a comment that the controller had made at a meeting the week before to the effect that costs which were variable for one division could be largely fixed for the company as a whole. He knew that in the absence of specific orders from top management Mr. Kenton would accept the lowest bid, which was that of the West Paper Company for $430. However, it would be possible for top management to order the acceptance of another bid if the situation warranted such action. And though the volume represented by the transactions in question was less than 5 percent of the volume of any of the divisions involved, other transactions could conceivably raise similar problems later.

QUESTIONS

1. In the controversy described, how, if at all, is the transfer price system dysfunctional?

2. Describe other types of decisions in the Birch Paper Company in which the transfer price system would be dysfunctional.

Case 7-2

Strider Chemical Company

On December 9, 1970, the president of the Strider Chemical Company, which had sales of around $75 million, announced that on January 1, 1971, the company would be reorganized into separate divisions. Until that time, the company had been organized on a functional basis, with the manufacturing, sales, finance, and research departments each under one man's responsibility. Six divisions were to be set up—four by product group and two by geographical area. Each division was to have its own production, sales, and accounting staff, and a general manager who would be responsible for its operation. The division's operating performance was to be judged by the profit it produced in relation to the investment assigned to it. It was anticipated that the procedure for computing the investment base and the return thereon would have to be carefully worked out if the resultant ratio was to be acceptable to the new division managers as a reasonable measure of their performance.

One of the biggest obstacles to the establishment of the desired monthly profit and loss statement for each division was the pricing of products for transfer from one to another of the various divisions. At the time the divisions were established, the company's president issued a policy statement upon which a pricing procedure was to be based. The president's statement follows.

STATEMENT OF POLICY

The *maximum,* and usual, price for transfers between profit units is that price which enables the producing unit to earn a return on the investment required, consistent with what it can earn doing business with the *average* of its customers for the product group concerned.

Established prices will be reviewed each six months or when a general change in market prices occurs.

DISCUSSION

Pricing policy between operating units is particularly important, because to the extent that the price is wrong, the return on one segment of the business is understated, and the return on another is overstated. This not only gives a false measure of how well individuals are performing, but also may make for bad decisions on the business as a whole, which will affect everyone.

Certain elements of expense that may not be found in intracompany relations are:

1. Deductions for cash discounts, freight, royalties, sales taxes, customer allowances, etc.
2. Usual selling expenses and, in many cases, order and billing services.
3. Certain customer services by the research laboratories, such as sales services where this applies.

The producing division that acts as a supplier will establish a price by discounting its *regular price* structure for the elements listed above which apply.

In case the buying division disagrees with the price as computed above, it will explain the basis of its disagreement to the president, who will decide what is to be done.

We are hopeful that this policy will work out equitably, giving each division a fair basis for the business they do. If, in practice, it is found that the policy is not working properly, is complicated in its application or calculation, or is working a hardship, the policy will have to be changed.

The largest of the newly formed divisions, the Williams division, was strongly affected by the problem of transfer prices, since about 23 percent of its sales would be to other divisions.

With only three weeks before the separation into divisions, it was important that a schedule of prices be quickly established for the transfer of products between divisions. The Williams division's task was complicated by its large number of products. There were several hundred different compounds and materials for which a price had to be fixed. It was, therefore, partly for the sake of expediency that the Williams division chose to set the prices on the basis of direct manufacturing cost. The figures used in this method were more readily available than those used in setting a price based on the current market price.

A week after the president's policy statement on transfer pricing had been distributed, the Williams division issued an interpretation of the policy which stated its proposed method for setting prices for the sale of products by the Williams division to other divisions. The key paragraphs from this statement were as follows:

The Williams Division will charge the same price to another division as it charges to the average of its existing customers, less an allowance for those expenses incurred with average customers but not with interdivisional customers.

These non-comparable expenses to be deducted include Sales Deductions and a part of Selling Expenses. The prices will be calculated in terms of a markup or multiplier factor on Direct Manufacturing Cost. A markup will be recalculated each six months, based on the prior twelve months' experience with regular customers.

The markup for the first six months of 1971 will be 1.41 times Direct Manufacturing Cost as shown by the following computation which uses actual data for the 12 month period ended October 31, 1970:

		Dollars	Percent
Gross sales to outside customers		$5,126,328	
Less: Amounts not applicable to internal sales:			
a) Freight, royalties, sales taxes	$ 58,625		
b) Selling expenses	260,123		
Total Deductions		318,748	
Adjusted sales		$4,807,580	100
Direct manufacturing cost		3,404,923	71
Margin		$1,402,657	29
Computation: 100 ÷ 71 = 1.41 times			

By the end of March, 1971, the president had received a number of letters from division managers, raising questions about transfer prices. Three of these are summarized below.

1. The Williams division questioned the price which the Johnson division had established for compound A, a raw material for the Williams division. The Johnson division had initially calculated a markup of 1.33, computed in the same way the Williams division computed its markup of 1.41. At a markup of 1.33, however, the Johnson division would show a net loss, since the division had not operated at a profit in the preceding 12 months. It therefore raised its markup to 1.41, the same as that used by the Williams division. At this markup, it would show about the same profit as that of the Williams division. The Williams division argued that this markup violated company policy.

2. The International division questioned the transfer price of several products it purchased from the Williams division for sale abroad. It said that at these prices the International division could not meet competitive prices in European markets and still make a profit.

3. The Western division purchased chemical B from the Williams division for resale to its own customers. It submitted data to show that at the computed transfer price the Western division would be better off to manufacture chemical B in one of its own plants. Rather than do this, it proposed that the transfer price be cut by 15 percent, which would still leave a margin over direct manufacturing cost for the Williams division.

As of the end of March, the president had not acted on any of these letters, other than to reply that existing relationships between divisions should be continued until further notice, and that after the questions had been decided, adjustments in transfer prices would be made retroactive to January 1.

In view of the numerous questions that had already arisen about the markup, the president was considering the possibility of transferring all products at cost, without any markup.

QUESTION

What changes, if any, should be made in the transfer price practices of Strider Chemical Company?

Case 7-3

Zemblan Electronics Corporation

In April, 1973, S. C. Halloway, corporate controller of the Zemblan Electronics Corporation, received the following memorandum from J. D. Walcott, controller of the circuits division:

INTEROFFICE MEMORANDUM

April 5, 1973

To: *S. C. Halloway*
FROM: *J. D. Walcott*
SUBJECT: *Recommendation on the method of determining the divisional share of cost-based government contract fees*

When one of our equipment or systems divisions that has a cost-reimbursable government contract engages a sister components division to produce necessary components for the contract, it is only fair that the components division be given a fair share of the total fee receivable from the government.

At present, fees are shared among the divisions through after-production negotiations without regard to the initial estimate of the fee. I propose, with our division managers' approval, that regardless of whether the actual production cost is over or under the estimated cost the components divisions should be given the fee credit as originally estimated. The following two examples illustrate the present and suggested methods.

Example 1. A year ago, the Santa Ana systems division asked from us a "bid" for 7,000 units of a certain type of ceramic part. We estimated the total production cost of $294,000 and added a 10 percent profit of $29,400 for the part, and on this basis obtained the order from the systems division. When the job was completed and the parts delivered, we billed the systems division for the amount of $256,900, as calculated below:

Actual total production cost	$227,500
Originally estimated profit	29,400
Total Price	$256,900

But the systems division has written back to us that we would be allowed a credit of only $245,700, as calculated below:

Actual total production cost		$227,500
Allowable profit		18,200
Total cost	$227,500	
Actual profit % earned on the contract	8%	
	$ 18,200	
Total Price Allowable		$245,700

The systems division and we are still negotiating as to what fee we are entitled to. The systems division argues that it cannot allow any more profit than 8 percent, instead of 10 percent as originally agreed on, because actual costs on the overall contract exceeded the initial cost estimate on which the overall fee on the contract was based. We feel, however, that we are entitled to 10 percent profit, because decrease in total profit on the contract was caused by the systems division itself or other subcontracted divisions, not by our division. If anything, we should be rewarded for being efficient enough to show a cost underrun. If my proposal is adopted, we shall automatically receive the originally estimated profit of $29,400 without going through meaningless after-production negotiations.

Example 2. We have recently finished producing 1,000 units of KTN 21 circuit for the La Jolla equipment division. Our original bid was based on the following estimate:

Estimated total production cost	$1,250,000
Estimated profit ($1,250,000 $\times$ 7%)	87,500
Estimated Total Price	$1,337,500

Unfortunately, however, our actual cost has turned out to be $350,000 above our estimate, that is, $1,600,000. We have billed the Equipment Division as follows:

Actual production cost	$1,600,000
Originally estimated profit (see above)	87,500
Total Price	$1,687,500

Despite a cost overrun of $350,000, we have asked as our share of the fee only $87,500 as originally estimated by us and accepted by the equipment division.

The proposed method of fee determination would eliminate uncertainty and unnecessary after-production negotiations.

It had been Mr. Halloway's practice to answer as soon as possible all inquiries, recommendations, and memoranda from any individuals in the company, and he wanted in this instance, too, to express his opinion promptly on Mr. Walcott's memorandum. Before a final ruling on the specific recommendation, however, he wanted to be sure that his decision would be consistent with Zemblan's management philosophy of decentralization, policies governing interdivisional relationships, and other aspects of interdivisional pricing.

Zemblan, a fast growing, large electronics company with sales of $400 million in 1973, consisted of six highly decentralized divisions—three equipment divisions and three components divisions. The equipment divisions were the Santa Ana systems division, the La Jolla equipment division (mostly for government contracts), and the commercial (nongovernmental) apparatus and equipment division. The circuits division, of which Mr. Walcott was the controller, was one of the three components divisions. Approximately 70 percent of the total outside sales of the company were made by the equipment divisions, and 30 percent from the components divisions. Although policy with respect to operating components divisions was nowhere written or otherwise made explicit, at least one executive thought the divisions were indispensable for the long-run survival and continued growth of the company, because technological advances in the equipment divisions—the basis of the company's success—were made possible largely through inventions and breakthroughs originating in the components divisions.

The divisions were allowed or encouraged to lead their own lives, with minimum interference from the top management. A major criterion in the evaluation of the divisional performance was the return on investment. The elements in the return-on-investment calculation were materially controllable by the division management.

A list of products made by each division was drawn up and approved by top management; a division could not make the products listed by other divisions. Otherwise, the divisions could manufacture and sell almost any products within their capabilities. The equipment divisions were free to purchase their component needs either internally or externally, that is, either from their sister components divisions or from outside suppliers. The components divisions were also free, in general, to sell their products internally or externally, except for a few classified items. The volumes of internal and external purchases were significant for all equipment divisions; the volumes of internal and external sales were significant for all components divisions.

Prices for the interdivisional transactions not covered by government contracts were determined through arm's-length negotiations between the divisions concerned. Therefore, all transfers from the components divisions to the commercial apparatus and equipment division were so priced. For the transactions covered by government contracts—that is, transactions between the government equipment divisions and the components divisions—the determination of transfer prices was more complex. If the contract held by the buying division was noncost-recoverable—that is, of the fixed-price type—the procedure was the same as that involving nongovernment contracts.

If the contract was of cost-recoverable type—e.g., cost plus a fixed fee (CPFF)[1]—the process was as follows: First, the buying division would ask

---

[1] In a CPFF contract, the company is reimbursed for its actual cost (in accordance with a detailed definition of cost) plus a fixed dollar amount of fee. The dollar amount of the fee is determined when the contract is signed, and is based on a percentage (from 3 percent to 12 percent, depending on the risks involved) of the *estimated* cost. The CPFF contract is used only when the uncertainties involved in contract performance are of such magnitude that it is not possible to establish a firm price or an incentive arrangement at any time during the life of the contract.

the selling division to submit a bid. Second, the selling division would estimate its recoverable production cost (the cost elements included in the government's definition of cost), and the profit or fee percentage anticipated by the buying division on the overall contract, and submit the price thus determined to the buying division. Sometimes, the buying division adjusted downward the fee percentage allowable to the selling division according to the additional risk it was taking as the "prime contractor." Third, if this bid was acceptable, the buying division would award an order to the selling division. Fourth, the selling division would produce and deliver the parts and invoice the buying division. Fifth, the buying division would either accept the amount in the invoice, or would protest and begin negotiations with the buying division.

If a dispute arose, it might be over the fee or profit element alone, as in Example 1 of the above memorandum. In other cases, it might be over the cost element also, if the actual cost substantially exceeded the estimated cost of the original bid. If the actual cost was below the estimate, Mr. Halloway said, "the buying division had to be charged at the actual cost (plus profit element), because the government agency would not allow any more than the actual cost." Thus a dispute over the cost element arose only when the actual was above the estimate. The divisions, according to Mr. Halloway, were encouraged to resolve disputes between themselves; the corporate management intervened rarely and only with reluctance.

"Of course, if the buying division could recover the actual cost from the government," Mr. Halloway said, "it was for the good of the company that the buying division should be charged at the actual cost and try to recover it." But when a cost overrun could not be wholly recovered because a maximum price ceiling was specified in the contract, "the dispute was real"; according to Mr. Halloway, "neither the selling nor the buying division likes to absorb the loss." The cause of cost overrun could be inefficiency, carelessness, wrong forecast, unforeseen technical difficulties, error in the buying divisions' specifications, or any combination of these.

Mr. Halloway felt that he had been greatly restricted by government procurement regulations in choosing the best method of transfer pricing. He preferred, he said, negotiated prices based on market as transfer prices, but the government tended to prefer the cost-based transfer prices.

If an equipment division first asked for bids both from its sister division and from an outside supplier, but finally decided to award the subcontract to the sister division, government auditors would require "costs" as transfer prices, although an objective outside market price was available in the bid made by the outside supplier. Likewise, if a components division was asked to make a bid by its sister equipment division and by an outside equipment manufacturer (the last two competing for the same government contract), and if the sister equipment division was awarded the contract and gave the components division the job, the transfer price had to be based on cost. On the other hand, if the outside equipment division obtained the contract and subcontracted with the Zemblan components division, the price would be a negotiated market price. Mr. Halloway had been asking government auditors to broaden their interpretation of the clause and to allow transfer pricing based on the negotiated market price.

Mr. Walcott made the following comments in relation to his memorandum.

My proposal is fair to everyone concerned. Under the recommended method, we are not always the winner: We will be rewarded if we are efficient; we will be penalized if we are inefficient.

We are willing to go further than the proposal. We would be happy if we were held responsible for the estimates of both cost and profit—not just the estimate of profit, as suggested in the present proposal. Penalize us if we couldn't meet the bid price, including both cost and profit element; reward us if we economize on our costs.

In connection with Example 2 in my memorandum, I don't know exactly how the La Jolla equipment division made the decision to give us the KTN 21 job, but it is possible that it had asked a couple of outside suppliers to make a bid, and the suppliers' bid price might have been higher than ours. If the suppliers' bid had been lower than $1,600,000 it would have been unfair for the La Jolla division to be charged $1,600,000 by us. The best way would be to make the initial bid price final, no matter what the actual cost is.

QUESTION

What should the transfer price policy be?

Case 7-4

Medoc Company

The Milling Division of the Medoc Company milled flour and manufactured a variety of consumer products from it. It's output was distributed as follows:

1. Approximately 70 percent (by weight) was transferred to the Consumer Products Division and marketed by this division through retail stores. The Consumer Products Division was responsible for these items from the time of packaging; that is, it handled warehousing, shipping, billing, and collections as well as advertising and other sales promotion efforts.

2. Approximately 20 percent was sold by the Milling Division as flour to large industrial users.

3. Approximately 10 percent was flour transferred to the Consumer Products Division and sold by that division to industrial users, but in different industries than those serviced directly by the Milling Division.

Counting each size and pack as one unit, there were several hundred products in the line marketed by the Consumer Products Division. The gross margin percentage on these products was considerably higher than that on flour sold to industrial users.

Wheat was purchased by the Grain Department, which was separate from the Milling Division. The price of wheat fluctuated widely and frequently. Other ingredients and supplies were purchased by the Milling Division.

The Milling Division and Consumer Products Division were two of 15 investment centers in the Medoc Company.

In 1969, products were transferred from the Milling Division to the Consumer Products Division at a unit price that corresponded to actual cost. There was a variation among products, but on the average, this cost included elements in the following approximate proportions:

Flour	30%
Other ingredients and packaging material	25
Labor and variable overhead	20
Nonvariable overhead	25
	100%

Also, 75 percent of the Milling Division's investment was charged to the Consumer Products Division in computing the latter's return on investment. This investment consisted of property, plant, equipment, and inventory, all of which was "owned and operated" by the Milling Division.

This transfer price resulted in friction between the Milling Division and the Consumer Products Division, primarily for three reasons:

1. As in many process industries, unit costs were significantly lower when the plant operated at capacity. Indeed, the principal reason for accepting the low-margin industrial business was to permit capacity operations. There was general agreement that acceptance of such business at a low margin, or even at something less than full cost, was preferable to operating at less than capacity. In recent years, the Milling Division had operated at at least 98 percent of capacity.

The Milling Division alleged that the Consumer Products Division was not aggressive enough in seeking this capacity-filling volume. The Milling Division believed that the Consumer Products Division could increase the volume of consumer sales by increasing its marketing efforts and by offering more attractive special deals, and that it could do more to obtain industrial business at a price which, although not profitable, nevertheless would result in a smaller loss than that which the Milling Division incurred from sales made to the industry it served. This additional volume would benefit the company, even though it reduced the average profit margin of the Consumer Products Division. The Consumer Products Division admitted that there was some validity in this argument, but pointed out that it had little incentive to seek such business when it was charged full cost for every unit it sold.

2. The Consumer Products Division complained that although it was charged for 75 percent of the investment in the Milling Division, it did not participate in any of the decisions regarding the acquisition of new equipment, inventory levels, etc. It admitted, however, that the people in the Milling Division were technically more competent to make these decisions.

3. The Consumer Products Division complained that since products were charged to it at actual cost, it must automatically pay for production inefficiencies that were the responsibility of the Milling Division.

A careful study had been made of the possibility of relating the transfer price either to a market price or to the price charged by the Milling Division to its industrial customers. Because of differences in product composition, however, this possibility had been definitely ruled out.

The Consumer Products Division currently earned about 20 percent pretax return on investment, and the Milling Division earned about 6 percent.

Top management of the Medoc Company was convinced that, some way or other, the profit performance of the Milling Division and the Consumer Products Division should be measured separately; that is, it ruled out the simple solution of combining the two divisions for profit-reporting purposes.

One proposal for solving the problem was that the transfer price should consist of two elements: (*a*) a standard monthly charge representing the

Consumer Products Division's fair share of the nonvariable overhead, plus (b) a per-unit charge equivalent to the actual material, labor, and variable overhead costs applied to each unit billed. Investment would no longer be allocated to the Consumer Products Division. Instead, a standard profit would be included in computing the fixed monthly charge.

The monthly nonvariable overhead charge would be set annually. It would consist of two parts:

1. A fraction of the budgeted nonvariable overhead cost of the Milling Division, corresponding to the fraction of products that was estimated would be transferred to the Consumer Products Division (about 80 percent). This amount would be changed only if there were changes in wage rates or other significant noncontrollable items during the year.

2. A return of 10 percent on the same fraction of the Milling Division's investment. This was higher than the return that the Milling Division earned on sales to industrial users. The selection of 10 percent was arbitrary because there was no way of determining a "true" return on products sold by the Consumer Products Division.

QUESTIONS

1. Is the general approach to transfer pricing proposed here—namely, a nonvariable dollar amount per month, plus a variable amount per unit—better than the present method in this situation? Why?

2. Suggest improvements in the details of the proposed method.

Case 7–5

Chadwick Company

Several divisions of the Chadwick Company used parts and subassemblies produced by other divisions of the company. In some instances finished products were manufactured by one division and sold by another. Each division was treated as a profit center for control purposes, and a division general manager was compensated in part on the profits which his division made and the return realized on the capital employed by his division. Consequently, the price at which goods were transferred from one division to another was a matter of substantial concern to the divisional general manager. The company control system had been reorganized in 1958 and the present system of profit centers was instituted at that time. Corporate management was aware that the problem of transfer pricing was a difficult one and had devoted considerable time and effort to it during the past several years.

The policy statement pertinent to this problem was: "It is the policy of Chadwick Company to utilize more fully its current and potential manufacturing capabilities. To the extent economically justified, all of the company's productive facilities shall be used in the manufacture of the end products of all divisions." The purpose of this policy was to maximize the over-all profits of the company by increasing the value added in all of its end products. The primary responsibility for execution of the policy lay with divisional management. The vice president-manufacturing had responsibility for identifying areas of possible integration and aiding operating managements in the application of the policy to specific areas. In effect, he acted as an arbitrator in the process of interdivisional bargaining.

A supplement to the policy statement read as follows: "Every division of Chadwick Company will consider every other division of the company as the primary source for products or services which such other division is capable of supplying. Assuming equal quality and delivery, such reports or services will be purchased from an outside vendor *only when the vendor's price is lower than the out-of-pocket cost of the Chadwick division.*"

This statement did not imply that interdivisional transfer prices were based on out-of-pocket costs. In general, transfer prices were determined as follows: For any product or service for which there was an established market price, the transfer price was the same as the market price, less an allowance for the average selling expense incurred by the supplying division on sales to outside customers. In other cases the transfer price was determined by computing the cost to the supplying division in accordance with the procedures normally followed in establishing total costs to outside customers, except that no allowance for selling expenses was allowed to be included. An allowance for profit was added to this cost, 10 percent of total costs in the case of products, and 25 percent in the case of services. In no event could the transfer price be greater than the price for which the buying division could purchase the item, or a usable substitute item, from an outside supplier.

Mr. Spofford, the director of finance, was responsible for establishing appropriate cost procedures and financial guides to assure sound transfer prices for all transactions. The suggest method of computation which he had circulated to the divisions is shown in the Appendix.

By 1964 it had become obvious that the guidelines set for interdivisional billings were inadequate and were becoming a source of frictions between divisions. Mr. Spofford enumerated some of the difficulties. He pointed out that the present policies really only served as a "make or buy" decision tool. Generally, a buying division had no alternative source of supply since components were always made to Chadwick specifications. Thus, the purchasing division did not have the buying power to obtain quantity discounts. Even in the case of standard parts there was still the question of what constituted like quality and delivery. In the case where finished goods were manufactured by one division and sold by another, it was often impossible for both divisions to make a "target profit." The target profit was that profit which each division regarded as satisfactory. It was usually measured as a percentage of sales and not as a return on assets because of the difficulty in measuring the assets employed in the production of one specific product. When a product was being introduced into a new market (for the company) where competition was already well established, the latter problem was sometimes particularly acute. Indeed, in some instances the two divisions could not even recover full cost during the initial stages, let alone recover a normal profit.

Finally, when parts or assemblies were being transferred between countries, there arose the question of duty payable. Most countries allowed goods to be transferred at standard cost and charged duty on that amount. Clearly, it was to the company's advantage to do this and not to transfer at standard cost plus profit; otherwise, a higher duty would have to be paid.

Mr. Spofford did not favor the accumulation of duplicate profits on the books of separate divisions. However, he was aware that the transfer of goods at standard cost could lead a division manager to make a decision which would be contrary to the best interests of the company as a whole.

By the middle of 1965, Mr. Spofford had drafted a proposal for new guidelines in setting transfer prices. These proposed guidelines were based on the existing policy statement. They were designed to benefit the over-all interests of the company by providing adequate information and motivation for short-range and long-range planning and by encouraging decisions which led to the sound development of potentially profitable products and markets, and the maximization of overall corporate profits. The proposed procedures were as follows:

1. When normal over-all profit over the combined costs of the two divisions could be made, the transfer price was to be established so that the profit would be shared by the divisions in approximate proportion to the capital investments (receivable, inventories, and plant facilities) required to manufacture and sell the product. Capital investment was to be computed on the basis of normal utilization of plant facilities (eliminating significant excess capacity) and reasonable turnover rates for receivables and inventories.

2. When a normal over-all profit over combined costs could not be made, the transfer price was to be set with due regard to the total costs and the out-of-pocket costs of the two divisions. If the manufacturing division had available capacity to produce the items required by the selling division without impairing its ability to handle its regular business, the transfer price was to be established so that the total profit *over out-of-pocket costs* was shared by the two divisions in approximate proportion to the capital investment required to manufacture and sell the product. If the manufacturing division could produce the items only by using capacity that might otherwise be devoted to more profitable regular business, the formula suggested in the preceding sentence was modified so that the manufacturing division recovered not less than its full costs. In such situations there was a strong suggestion that additional manufacturing facilities should be acquired by one of the two divisions involved.

3. In billing to foreign subsidiaries, the prices established by the foreign customs authorities as the basis for duty charges were to be used for transfer pricing unless the cost formulas, developed as suggested in the preceding paragraph, demonstrated that such a basis would work a substantial hardship on one of the two divisions. This rule was suggested primarily because any attempt to use transfer prices which differed from the prices established for duty purposes might create significant accounting (and possibly legal) problems.

For the purposes of the procedure, "full cost" was defined as the sum of the following elements:

a) Standard manufacturing costs based on the current material and labor specifications and current wage rates, plus overhead at standard normal rate, computed at a reasonable percentage of plant utilization.

b) Reported variances from standard costs as follows:
Material price variances to reflect current prices.
Material usage variances, spoiled work and direct labor variances based on actual experience over a period of at least one year.

c) A reasonable provision for unreported variances, based on experience over a three-year period adjusted for known changes in reporting practices.

d) A proportionate share of other manufacturing costs and credits applicable to the product billed (e.g., purchase discount, scrap income, etc.).

e) Shipping costs, allocated in accordance with regular divisional practice, but with adjustment for special conditions (e.g., lower cost of bulk packing, excess costs of packing for export, etc.).

f) Product engineering and research costs.

Regular product—prorated share of total divisional costs excluding special projects not related to the regular product line.

Specially designed product—the additional direct cost of such design.

g) Costs of order handling and invoicing, whether classified as *selling* or *administrative* expense.

h) A prorated share of that portion of administrative expense not included in *g*) which was applicable to the administration of the manufacturing function. In the absence of any contrary indication it will be assumed that 50 percent of the administrative expense is applicable to manufacturing and 50 percent to selling.

Items excluded from the computation of costs thus defined were overhead absorption variance, advertising and sales promotion expense, selling expense except as noted in *g*), branch warehouse expense, bad debts, and nonoperating income and expense. Major nonrecurring expenses and excess costs due to temporary conditions (plant startup or relocation, etc.) were also excluded.

The proration of costs not directly chargeable to the product billed were to be made as percentages of standard manufacturing cost.

"Out-of-pocket cost" for the purpose of the procedure was to be determined by reviewing each of the elements of "full cost," as enumerated above, and estimating its percentage variability with sales or plant activity. The following percentages of variability were to be assumed unless there was evidence that a special study was necessary to establish more accurate percentages.

Standard material, direct labor, reported and unreported variances (except unreported overhead variance), and other manufacturing costs and credits	100%
Standard manufacturing overhead and provision for unreported overhead variance	40
Shipping	85
Product engineering and research	
General	15
Special	100
Cost of order handling and invoicing	85
Administrative expense	15

On the request of either division the corporate controller's office was available to assist in the computation of costs compiled by the divisions and to make recommendations as to any adjustments which might be in accordance with the principles outlined.

Appendix

CHADWICK COMPANY

Current Procedure for Computing Transfer Price
Summary of Costs

Item: *X-12*   Date: *9-25-61*

		Cost per 100 Pcs.		Illustrative
			Out-of	Schedule
Cost Element		*Total*	*Pocket*	*Number*
Direct material		$ 54.66	$ 54.66	1
Direct labor		15.65	15.65	2
Direct labor variances		2.04	2.04	2
Other direct costs:				
a) Tooling		16.51	16.51	3
b) etc.		—	—	
Manufacturing overhead:				4

		O. H. Rate			
		(percent)			
Dept.	*D.L.*	*Std.*	*Var.*		
A	$9.78	350	133.7	34.23	13.08
B	5.87	370	129.4	21.72	7.60
	Cost to manufacture			$144.81	$109.54

Shipping expense:		
2.2 percent of cost to manufacture	3.19	
1.2 percent of cost to manufacture		1.31
Product engineering and research		
2.5 percent of cost to manufacture	3.62	
Other costs and credits		
0.01 percent of cost to manufacture	—	—
Scrap sales		
1.7 percent of material	(.93)	(.93)
Selling and administrative expense		
21.7 percent of cost to manufacture	31.42	
Total	$182.11	$109.92
Selling expense (credit)		
13.4 percent of cost to manufacture	(19.40)	5
Cost basis of transfer price $162.71		

Schedule 1

CHADWICK COMPANY

Direct Material Work Sheet

Item No. *X-12*

Amount per 100 Pcs.

Material (from bill of
  material) .... —— $50.702

Material variances
  a) Purchase price (if material
     is at standard) ....

	Percent	Material	*Amount of Variance*
b) Spoilage 3.1			
c) Other reported variances			
d) Current provision for unreported variances 4.7			
Total material variances...7.8		$50.702——	$ 3.955

Total Material (place on
  line 1 of Summary of Costs) $54.657

Schedule 2

CHADWICK COMPANY

Direct Labor Work Sheet

Item No. *X-12*

Amount per 100 Pcs.

Labor (from estimates
  or planning paper)
    Department A .... $ 9.782
    Department B 5.866
      Total labor (place on line 2
        of Summary of Costs) $15.648

Labor variances (current percentage
  to standard direct labor)

Department A	%	*Labor*	*Amount of Variance*
Efficiency 5.8			
Spoilage 2.6			
Total 8.4	$ 9.782		$ .822
Department B	%		
Efficiency 5.3			
Spoilage 2.9			
Total 8.2	$ 5.866		.481
Current provision for unreported variances 4.7	$15.648		.735
Total labor variances (place on line 3 of Summary of Costs)			$ 2.038

Schedule 3

CHADWICK COMPANY

Specimen Calculation of Tooling Cost

Item No. *X-12*

1. Tool cost $578.00
2. Estimated total parts producible
   (tool life)   5000
3. Estimated parts to be produced   3500
4. Unit cost of tooling:
   Cost ÷ line 2 or 3, whichever
   is smaller ....$ .1651
5. Applicable tooling cost:
   line 4 × 100
   (place on line 4a of Cost Summary) ......$ 16.51

Schedule 4

CHADWICK COMPANY

Specimen Calculation of Departmental Overhead

Department A

	Total	*Variable*
Department Direct Labor	$53,000	$53,000
Departmental Expenses:		
Salaries and wages:		
Supervisory and technical ....$	11,500	$ 1,150
Factory clerical	5,000	1,000
Sweeping	500	50
Material handling	9,000	9,000
Set-up	15,000	15,000
Hourly rate guarantee	1,000	1,000
Allowed time (various reasons)	250	250
Down time (various reasons)	550	550
Repairs and maintenance	6,500	6,500
Repair and maint. labor—GMP	5,500	5,500
Plant rearrange. labor—GMP	7,000	—
Overtime premium	1,200	1,200
Shift premium	300	300
Taxes—FICA	2,500	2,500
Taxes—UCI	2,500	2,500
Repair and maintenance mat'l.	4,000	4,000
Supplies	4,500	4,500
Heat, light and power	5,000	3,000
Depreciation	18,000	—
Applied O. H. intradiv.	3,700	—
Allocated GMP & Gen'l Co. O. H.	8,200	—
Labor trans. out (capital, etc.)	(400)	—
	$111,300	$58,000

Overhead Rate:
  Departmental—Standard 210.0%

Schedule 4—Continued

Departmental—Variable		109.4%
*General Factory—Standard	140.0%	
*General Factory—Variable		24.3%
Total	350.0%	133.7%

* Computation not illustrated.

Notes:

The personnel complement of a department whose salaries and wages are reported on lines 1, 2, and 3 is largely nonvariable in nature. Ten percent variability is reflected in this example.

The indirect labor reported on lines 4 thru 9 will normally vary rather directly with manufacturing activity and is considered here to be fully variable.

General Main Plant maintenance performance in a department will vary rather directly with that department's manufacturing activity. However, General Main Plant incurred costs will probably not. As an expedient, General Main Plant direct charges (line 10) are considered fully variable but General Main Plant and General Company allocated charges (line 21) are considered fixed. These assumptions may fairly reflect Chadwick Company's expense variability, which is what is wanted.

Power is considered fully variable and is estimated here as 60% of the heat, light, and power account.

Schedule 5

CHADWICK COMPANY

Specimen Calculation of Selling Expense

Sales		$4,866,000
5X00 accounts*—Advtg. and Sales Promotion expense		$ 112,000
6X00 accounts*—Selling expense		610,000
7X00 accounts*—Administrative expense ...		334,000
Total selling and administrative expense		$1,056,000
Percent to sales 21.7		
Less:		
Administrative expense $334,000		
Order entry (account 6X93*) 47,000		
Order processing (account 6X96*) 21,000		
		402,000
Selling expenses not applicable to interdivisional activity		$ 654,000
Percent to sales 13.4		

* Main plant account code. 6X93 and 6X96 are hypothetical account numbers.

Case 7-6

General Appliance Corporation

ORGANIZATION

The General Appliance Corporation was an integrated manufacturer of all types of home appliances. As shown in Exhibit 1, the company had a decentralized, divisional organization consisting of four product divisions, four manufacturing divisions, and six staff offices. Each division and staff office was headed by a vice-president. The staff offices had functional authority over their counterparts in the divisions, but they had no direct line authority over the divisional general managers. The company's organization manual stated: "All divisional personnel are responsible to the division manager. Except in functional areas specifically delegated, staff personnel have no line authority in a division."

The product divisions designed, engineered, assembled, and sold various home appliances. They manufactured very few component parts; rather, they assembled the appliances from parts purchased either from the manufacturing divisions or from outside vendors. The manufacturing divisions made approximately 75 percent of their sales to the product divisions. Parts made by the manufacturing divisions were generally designed by the product divisions; the manufacturing divisions merely produced the parts to specifications provided to them. Although all the manufacturing divisions had engineering departments, these departments did only about 20 percent of the total company engineering.

TRANSFER PRICES

The divisions were expected to deal with one another as though they were independent companies. Parts were to be transferred at prices arrived at by negotiation between the divisions. These prices were generally based on the actual prices paid to outside suppliers for the same or comparable parts.

319

Exhibit 1

GENERAL APPLIANCE CORPORATION

Organization Chart

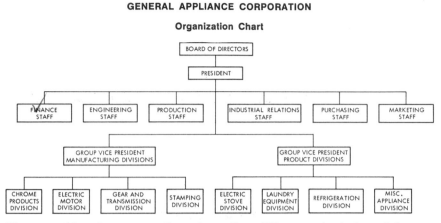

These outside prices were adjusted to reflect differences in design of the outside part from that of the inside part. Also, if the outside price was based on purchases made at an earlier date, it was adjusted for changes in the general price level since that date. In general, the divisions established prices by negotiation among themselves, but if the divisions could not agree on a price they could submit the dispute to the finance staff for arbitration.

SOURCE DETERMINATION

Although the divisions were instructed to deal with one another as independent companies, in practice this was not always feasible, because a product division did not have the power to decide whether to buy from within the company or from outside. Once a manufacturing division began to produce a part, the only way the product division buying this part could change to an outside supplier was to obtain permission of the manufacturing division or, in case of disagreement, appeal to the purchasing staff. The purchasing staff had the authority to settle disputes between the product and manufacturing divisions with respect to whether a manufacturing division should continue to produce a part or whether the product division could buy outside. In nearly every case of dispute, the purchasing staff had decided that the part would continue to be manufactured within the company. When the manufacturing divisions were instructed to continue producing a part, they had to hold the price of the part at the level at which the product division could purchase it from the outside vendor.

In the case of new parts, a product division had the authority to decide on the source of supply. Even for new parts, however, a manufacturing division could appeal to the purchasing staff to reverse the decision if a product division planned to purchase a part from an outside vendor.

STOVETOP PROBLEM

The chrome products division sold to the electric stove division a chrome-plated unit that fitted on the top of the stove; the unit had to be resistant to corrosion and stain from spilled food. It was also essential that the unit remain bright and new-looking. The chrome products division had been producing this unit since January 1, 1974; prior to that time, it had been produced by an outside vendor.

The unit in question was produced from a steel stamping. Until June 1975, the stamping was processed as follows:

Operations	Processes
1	Machine buffing
2	Nickel plating
3	Machine buffing
4	Chrome plating
5	Machine buffing

About the middle of 1974, the president of General Appliance Corporation became concerned over complaints from customers and dealers about the quality of the company's products. A customer survey appeared to indicate quite definitely that in the previous year the company's reputation as a producer of quality products had deteriorated. Although this deterioration was believed to have been caused principally by the poor performance of a new electric motor, which was soon corrected, the president had come to the conclusion that the overall quality of the company's products had been decreasing for the past several years. Furthermore, he believed that it was essential for the company to reestablish itself as a leader in the production of quality products. Accordingly, early in 1975 he called in the manufacturing vice-president (i.e., the director of the manufacturing staff office) and told him that for the next six months his most important job was to bring the quality of all products up to a satisfactory level.

In the course of carrying out this assignment, the manufacturing vice-president decided that the appearance of the chrome-plated stovetop was unsatisfactory. Until now, the bases for rejection or acceptance of this part by the quality control section of the chrome products division were a corrosion test and an appearance test; appearance was largely subjective and, in the final analysis, dependent on the judgment of the quality control man. In order to make the test more objective, three tops were selected and set up as standards for the minimum acceptable quality. Because better than average units were selected, rejects increased to over 80 percent. Personnel from the chrome products division and the manufacturing staff jointly studied the manufacturing process to find a way of making the stovetops conform to the new quality standards. They added copper plating and buffing operations at the beginning of the process, and a hand-buffing operation at the end of the manufacturing cycle. The total cost of these added operations was 40 cents a unit. As soon as the new operations were put into effect in June 1975, the rejection rate for poor quality declined to less than 1 percent.

increase p.

In July 1975, the chrome products division proposed to increase the price of the stovetop by 45 cents; 40 cents represented the cost of the added operations, and 5 cents was the profit markup on the added costs. The current price, before the proposed increase, was $5.00 a unit. This price had been developed as follows:

Price charged by an outside producer (12/31/73) $4.50
Design changes since 12/31/73 .... .25
Changes in raw materials and labor prices since 12/31/73 ...... .25
Price as of June 30, 1975 .... $5.00

The electric stove division objected to the proposed price increase, and after three weeks of fruitless negotiations it was decided that the dispute should be submitted to the finance staff for arbitration. The positions of the parties to the dispute are summarized below.

Chrome Products Division

arguments

In a letter to the vice-president for finance, the general manager of the chrome products division stated that he believed he was entitled to the increased price because:

1. He had been required by the manufacturing staff to add operations at a cost of 40 cents a unit.
2. These operations resulted in improved quality that could benefit only the electric stove division.
3. The present price of $5.00 was based on old quality standards. Had the outside supplier been required to meet these new standards, the price would have been 45 cents higher.

Electric Stove Division

The general manager of the electric stove division, in appealing the price increase, based his position on the following arguments.

1. There had been no change in engineering specifications. The only change that had taken place was in what was purported to be "acceptable appearance." This was a subjective matter that could not be measured with any degree of precision. Further, both the particular case and the possible effects of establishing a precedent were objectionable. "If we were to pay for any change in quality standards, not accompanied by a change in engineering specification, we would be opening up a Pandora's box. Every division would request higher prices based on giving us better quality based on some subjective standard. Every request by this division to a manufacturing division to improve quality would be accompanied by a price increase, even though we were requesting only that the quality be brought up to competitive levels."

2. The electric stove division had not requested that quality be improved. In fact, the division had not even been consulted on the change. Thus, the division should not be responsible for paying for a so-called improvement that it neither requested nor approved.

3. Whether there was any improvement in quality from the customer's viewpoint was doubtful, although to the highly trained eye of the quality control personnel there may have been an improvement. The customer would not notice a significant difference between the appearance of the part before and after the change in quality standards.

4. Even if there were an improvement in quality perceptible to the consumer, it was not worth 45 cents. By adding 45 cents to the cost of the stove, he could add features that would be far more marketable than the quality improvement.

5. Any improvement in quality only brought the part up to the quality level that the former outside producer had provided. The cost of the improved quality, therefore, was included in the $5.00 price.

Finance Staff Review

The finance staff reviewed the dispute. In the course of this review, the engineering department of the production staff was asked to review the added operations and comment on the acceptability of the proposed cost increases. The quality control department of the manufacturing staff was asked to verify whether quality was actually better as the result of the added operations and whether the new units were of higher quality than the units purchased from the outside vendor 18 months ago. The engineering department stated that the proposed costs were reasonable and represented efficient processing. The quality control department stated that the quality was improved and that the new parts were of superior quality to the parts previously purchased from outside sources.

THERMOSTATIC CONTROL PROBLEM

One of the plants of the electric motor division produced thermostatic control units. The laundry equipment division bought all its requirements for thermostatic control units (about 100,000 a year) from the electric motor division. The refrigeration division used a similar unit, and until 1972 it had purchased all its requirements (20,000 a year) from an outside supplier, the Monson Controls Corporation. In 1972, at the request of the electric motor division, the refrigeration division purchased 25 percent of its requirements from the electric motor division. In 1973, this percentage was increased to 50 percent, and in 1974 to 75 percent. In July 1974, the refrigeration division informed the Monson Controls Corporation that beginning January 1, 1975, it would buy all its thermostatic control units from the electric motor division. The refrigeration division made these source changes as a result of electric motor division requests which were, it said, "in the best interests of the company." The units made outside and inside were comparable in quality, and the price paid to the electric motor division was the same as the price paid to the Monson Controls Corporation. The laundry division also paid this same price to the electric motor division.

In 1971, the demand for this kind of thermostatic control unit was high in relation to the industry's production capacity. Between 1972 and 1974, several appliance companies, including the General Appliance Corporation, built or expanded their own facilities to produce this unit, so that by the middle of 1974 the production capacity of the independent companies considerably exceeded the demand. One of the results of this situation was a declining price level. Prices of the Monson Controls Corporation had been as follows:

1971	$3.00
1972	2.70
1973	2.50
1974 (January–June)	2.40

As a result of these price reductions, which the electric motor division had met, the profits of the electric motor division on this product had dropped from a before-tax profit of 15 percent on its investment in 1971 to nearly zero in 1974.

In August 1974, after being told it could no longer supply the refrigeration division, the Monson Controls Corporation reduced its price to the refrigeration division by 25 cents, retroactive to July 1. The price reduction was not reflected immediately in the intracompany price, because the three divisions involved had agreed to use $2.40 for the entire year.

In October 1974, the electric motor division and the refrigeration division were negotiating 1975 prices. The refrigeration division proposed a price of $2.15, the price paid to the Monson Controls Corporation. The electric motor division, however, refused to reduce its prices below $2.40 to either the refrigeration division or the laundry equipment division. After several weeks of negotiations, the disagreement was submitted to the finance staff for settlement.

Electric Motor Division

The electric motor division based its refusal to accept the last price reduction of the Monson Controls Corporation on the premise that it was made as a last, desperate effort to continue supplying General Appliance Corporation with this part. (Monson Controls Corporation continued to supply General Appliance Corporation with other products, although this control unit had been the major item.) As support for this premise, the electric motor division indicated that at the lower price it would lose money. Since it was as efficient as the Monson Controls Corporation, it concluded that Monson must also be losing money. The price was, therefore, a distress price and not a valid basis for determining an internal price. To support its case further, the electric motor division pointed out the downward trend in the price of this part as evidence of distressed pricing practices growing out of the excess capacity in the industry.

The general manager of electric motor division stated that it was going to take all his ability and ingenuity to make a profit even at the $2.40 price. At $2.15, he could never be in a profit position; and if forced to accept a price of $2.15, he would immediately make plans to close the plant and let outside suppliers furnish all the thermostatic control units.

Laundry Equipment Division

The laundry equipment division based its case for a $2.15 price on the intracompany pricing rules that required products to be transferred between divisions at competitive prices. The general manager pointed out that his annual volume was 100,000 units a year, compared to a total of only 20,000 for the refrigeration division. He believed that with his higher volume he could probably obtain an even more favorable price if he were to procure his requirements from outside the corporation.

Refrigeration Division

The refrigeration division based its case on the fact that the division not only could, but did, buy the thermostatic control unit from a reliable outside supplier for $2.15. The division was sure that the Monson Controls Corporation had capacity to produce all its requirements and would be happy to do so for $2.15 a unit. Since patronage had been transferred to the electric motor division only as a favor and to benefit the company as a whole, the refrigeration division believed it was unjust to make it pay a higher price than it would have paid if the division had never allowed the business to be taken inside the company.

As further evidence to support its case, the refrigeration division pointed to an agreement made with the electric motor division at the time it had agreed to purchase all its requirements of the thermostatic control unit from that division. This agreement read, in part: "In the event of a major pricing disparity, it is agreed that further model requirements will be competitively sourced [i.e., sourced to the lowest bidder]."

The refrigeration division stated that in the light of the major pricing disparity it should be allowed to request quotations from outside suppliers and place the business outside should such a supplier bid lower than the electric motor division.

Finance Staff Review

In the course of arbitrating this transfer price dispute, the finance staff asked the purchasing staff to review the outside market situation for the thermostatic control unit. The purchasing staff replied that there was excess capacity and that, as a result of this, prices were very soft. Eventually, the prices would rise either when the demand for comparable units increased or when some of the suppliers went out of business. The purchasing staff had no doubt that the refrigeration division could purchase all its requirements for the next year or two for $2.15 a unit, or even less. The purchasing staff believed, however, that if all the corporation's requirements for this unit were placed with outside suppliers, the price would rise to at least $2.40 because this action would dry up the excess capacity.

TRANSMISSION PROBLEM

The laundry equipment division began production of automatic washers shortly after the end of World War II. Initially, it had purchased its transmissions from two sources—the gear and transmission division and the Thorndike Machining Corporation. The transmission had been developed and engineered by the Thorndike Machining Corporation. In consideration of an agreement to buy one half of its transmissions from the Thorndike Machining Corporation, the General Appliance Corporation had been licensed to produce the transmission. The agreement ran from 1965 to 1975; at the expiration of the 10 years, General Appliance would have the right to use the design without restrictions.

In early 1973, nearly two years before the end of the agreement, the management of the General Appliance Corporation decided that it would not extend the agreement when it expired, but that it would expand the facilities of the gear and transmission division enough to produce all the company's requirements. Accordingly, in March 1973, the Thorndike Machining Corporation was notified that beginning January 1, 1975, the General Appliance Corporation would manufacture all its own transmissions and, consequently, would not renew the current agreement.

This notification came as a surprise to the Thorndike Machining Corporation; furthermore, its implications were very unpleasant, because the General Appliance Corporation took its major share of the output of an entire plant, and there was little likelihood that the lost business could be replaced. The Thorndike Machining Corporation consequently faced the prospect of an idle plant and a permanent reduction in the level of profits.

In April 1973, the president of the Thorndike Machining Corporation wrote to the president of the General Appliance Corporation, asking that the decision not to extend the current agreement be reconsidered. He submitted a proposed schedule of price reductions that would be made if the current agreement was extended. He stated that these reductions would be possible because (*a*) Thorndike would be better off to obtain a lower price than to abandon the special-purpose machinery used for transmissions and (b) it expected increases in productivity. These proposed reductions were as follows:

Present price	$14.00
Price effective 7/1/73	13.50
Price effective 1/1/74	13.00
Price effective 7/1/74	12.50
Price effective 1/1/75	12.00

The letter further stated that the corporation had developed a low-cost transmission suitable for economy washers; this transmission was designed to cost $2.00 less than the present models, and could be made available by January 1, 1975.

On receiving a copy of the letter, the general manager of the laundry equipment division reopened the issue of continuing to buy from the Thorndike Machining Corporation. He had been interested in adding to the line a low-cost automatic washer, and the possibility of a $10 transmission appealed to him. The general manager of the gear and transmission division, however, was interested in expanding his production of transmissions, and to satisfy the laundry equipment division he offered to develop a unit that would be comparable in price and performance to the proposed Thorndike Machining Corporation's economy unit. The offer was set forth in a letter signed by the general manager of the gear and transmission division, dated April 22, 1973. The general manager of the laundry equipment division accepted this offer, and no further question was raised about continuing to buy from the Thorndike Machining Corporation.

During the next two months, the engineering departments of the gear and transmission and the laundry equipment divisions jointly determined the exact performance features needed for the economy transmission; some of these features were different from those of the proposed Thorndike transmission. In June 1973, the general manager of the gear and transmission division wrote a letter to the general manager of the laundry equipment division, outlining the agreed-on engineering features and including the following price proposal:

Proposed selling price of Thorndike model		$10.00
Probable cost (assuming 10% profit)		9.00
Add:		
Cost of added design features	$ .85	
Increased cost of material and labor since date		
of quotation	.75	1.60
Total Cost		$10.60
Profit		1.06
Adjusted Price of G & T Unit		$11.66

The letter went on to say: "Because a price of $11.66 will not give us our objective profit, we propose to sell you this unit for $12. We believe that this is a fair and equitable price, and decidedly to your benefit."

This letter was never acknowledged by the laundry and equipment division.

In October 1973, the gear and transmission division submitted a project proposal to the top management of the corporation, requesting money to build facilities to produce the new economy transmission. The project proposal included a profit projection based on a $12 price. The laundry equipment division was quoted in the project proposal as agreeing to the price. There was no objection to this statement from the laundry equipment division personnel who were asked to comment on the proposed project. The project was approved, and the gear and transmission division proceeded to buy and install the equipment to produce the new transmission.

In the latter part of 1973, the gear and transmission division opened negotiations with the laundry equipment division on the price of the new transmission, proposing $12 plus some minor adjustments for changes in cost levels since the previous year. The laundry equipment division refused to accept the proposed price and countered with an offer of $11.21, developed as follows:

Proposed selling price of Thorndike model		$10.00
Adjustments:		
Cost of added design features	$ .85	
Cost of eliminated design features	(.50)	
Increased cost of material and labor since date of quotation	.75	
Net cost change	$1.10	
Profit on added cost	.11	
Total Price Increase		1.21
Proposed Price		$11.21

The gear and transmission division refused even to consider this proposal, and after several days of acrimonious debate both divisions decided to submit the dispute to the finance staff for arbitration.

Laundry Equipment Division

The laundry equipment division based its case on the following argument:

1. The division could have purchased a transmission, comparable in performance characteristics to the gear and transmission division's unit, from the Thorndike Machining Corporation for $11.21.

2. The gear and transmission division had agreed to this price in consideration of being allowed to produce all the transmissions.

3. The intracompany pricing policy was that the supplying divisions should sell at competitive prices.

The general manager of the laundry equipment division stated that it would be unfair to penalize him for keeping the transmission business inside the corporation as a benefit to the gear and transmission division, particularly in the light of the promise made by the general manager of the gear and transmission division.

The general manager also stated that he had not protested the price proposal included in the May 1973, letter because he believed that it was then too early to open negotiations. His cost analysts had not evaluated the proposal, but he assumed that the gear and transmission division was approximately correct in its evaluation of the cost differences from the Thorndike unit. His position was that the difference of 34 cents between the adjusted Thorndike price and the quoted gear and transmission price was not worth negotiating until nearer the production date. The laundry equipment division had naturally assumed that the gear and transmission division would live up to its agreement, and therefore regarded the request for $12 as just a negotiating gimmick.

Gear and Transmission Division

The gear and transmission division based its case on two arguments.

1. The $10 quotation of the Thorndike Machining Corporation was invalid because it represented a final desperate effort to keep a share of the transmission business. A price of this nature should not form a long-term intracompany pricing base. If the Thorndike Machining Corporation had received the business, it would have eventually raised its price.

2. The laundry equipment division did not object to the gear and transmission division's price proposal until after the facilities to build the transmission were already in place. The $12 price was used in the calculations that showed the profitability of the project, and on which the project approval was based. If the laundry equipment division wished to object, it should have done so when the project was presented to top management. Because facilities were purchased on the assumption of a $12 price, the laundry equipment division should not be allowed to object after the money has been spent.

Finance Staff Review

A review by the finance staff disclosed the following.

1. If the Thorndike Machining quotation of $10 were adjusted for the cost effect of changes in performance characteristics and the increase in general cost levels since the original quotation, the price would be $11.25, or approximately the same as that proposed by the laundry equipment division. The price of $11.66 developed by the gear and transmission division was in error because it failed to allow for a design elimination that would reduce the cost of the Thorndike unit by 50 cents.

2. At $12, the gear and transmission division could expect to earn an after-tax profit of 15 percent on its investment; this was equal to its profit objective. At the $11.25 price, the division would earn about 6 percent after taxes.

3. The purchasing staff stated that in its opinion the transmission could be obtained from the Thorndike Machining Corporation at the quoted price level for the foreseeable future.

QUESTIONS

1. As a member of the finance staff, how would you settle these intracompany disputes? How would you explain your decision to the general managers involved?

2. Should the company's intracompany price policy and its procedure for negotiating differences be changed?

Case 7-7

The Warren Corporation

The Warren Corporation is a large conglomerate that is in many types of businesses. A significant portion of its business, however, is in electronics. In this area, the Warren Corporation is quite integrated. There are 15 profit centers in electronics and most of these profit centers deal with each other. More than 50 percent of the sales in some of these divisions are to internal units. As a consequence, it has been necessary to establish specific procedures to govern intracompany relationships. The Central Finance staff of the Warren Corporation has developed a manual that dictates company policy with respect to intracompany relationships and describes precisely how transfer prices are to be established under a variety of circumstances. This manual changes frequently when decisions of the Price Arbitration Committee make it evident that the manual is incomplete or that policy has been changed. In some respects, the process is like the codification of common law. The decisions of the Price Arbitration Committee are constantly being incorporated into the transfer pricing procedures in the same way that court decisions affect legal procedures.

The *Price Arbitration Committee* (called hereafter the PAC), as the name implies, is a committee that has been set up to arbitrate intracompany pricing disputes. It consists of three staff vice presidents—finance, manufacturing, and purchasing. The secretary of this committee is the manager of the Price Analysis Department of the Finance staff. This department has the responsibility for providing staff service to the PAC.

This case presents three disputes that were submitted to the PAC by divisional managers of the Warren Corporation. In each instance, the revelant transfer pricing rules are stated. The problem is to decide how each of these disputes should be settled, keeping in mind that any settlement could establish a precedent for future intracompany relationships.

PRODUCT DEVELOPMENT

The X Division produces a low-volume but high-grade series of electronic products. Its engineering group spent $300,000 developing a new type of unit to be attached to one of the major products. When the development was completed, a marketing survey showed that the number of units that was likely to be sold would not warrant the expenditure required for the tooling and facilities to produce the new unit. The total number of units likely to be sold by the X Division was only 2,500 annually. Consequently, the project was shelved.

The Y Division sells an electronic product, with a much higher sales volume, that could use the new unit. Six months after the project was shelved, at a company-wide meeting of certain research personnel, a research manager of the Y Division learned of this new unit and requested a copy of the blueprints. This was provided to him, since the company policy on research was that all divisions should cooperate and that there should be no secrecy among divisions.

Within the next nine months, Division Y decided to produce the new unit and proceeded to purchase the necessary tools and facilities. About three months later (a year and a half after the X Division had shelved the project) the general manager of the X Division heard that the Y Division was going to produce the unit that had been developed by his division. He immediately called in his controller and told him to send the Y Division a bill for $300,000. He was particularly interested in receiving payment because the X Division's profits were less than budget. Since the costs of development had been written off in the previous year, the $300,000 would be a direct increase in profitability.

The Y Division refused to pay and the X Division brought the matter to the PAC. The Intracompany Pricing Manual said nothing about the transfer of research.

The X Division based its case on a statement in the manual that said: "In general, divisions will deal with each other in the same way that they deal with outside companies." The X Division's position was that, if it was independent, it could have sold the blueprint for a least $300,000 to an outside company. (Company rules forbade the sale of research findings to outside companies by divisions.)

The position of the Y Division was that the product was marginal. If they had had to pay $300,000 for the blueprints, they would not have gone ahead with the project.

SPLIT SOURCING

The A Division buys a complex electronic component; 50 percent is purchased from an outside source and 50 percent is purchased from Division B.

The outside source developed the component and licensed the B Division to produce it in consideration of a five-year contract to produce half of Warren's requirements. The contract with the outside source established an initial price, with provision for annual negotiations. These negotiations were to determine the amount that the price should be reduced as the manufacturing efficiency increased. The A Division requested detailed information from the B Division on the manufacturing processes in order to be able to negotiate with the outside source more effectively. If the engineers from the A Division knew precisely in what ways and the extent to which the B Division was increasing its efficiency, it could pinpoint precisely the amount of the price reduction that it should obtain. The B Division refused to provide this information and the A Division submitted the dispute to the PAC.

The Intracompany Pricing Manual stated that split-sourced products should be transferred within the company at the same price as the outside source. Nothing else was said about split-source pricing.

The B Division based its refusal on the statement that "Divisions deal with each other in the same way that they deal with outside companies." Under no conditions, it stated, would we provide our customers with details of our production processes. Furthermore, Division B pointed out that they were "cutting their own throats." The greater the price reduction that Division A negotiated, the lower would be the profits of Division B.

Division A based its case on company welfare. The company profits would be maximized by division B cooperating with Division A.

RESERVED CAPACITY

Division S is essentially a marketing division. It buys most of its products from Division M. The transfer price agreement is that products are sold at the standard variable cost per unit plus a monthly charge equal to the fixed costs and 10 percent of the investment assigned to the products produced for Division S. By agreement half the capacity of one plant (Plant M–1) is reserved for Division S. The other half of the capacity of the plant is used by Division M to produce products that it sells to outside customers. The facilities in Plant M–1 are quite similar. Consequently, the plant can produce either Division S products or Division M products on its facilities.

During 1971, the demand for Division S products declined, while the demand for Division M products increased. As a result, about 75 percent of the capacity of Plant M–1 was used to produce products for Division M and only 25 percent was used for products of Division S. Division S objected to paying for 50 percent of the capacity of Plant M–1. The M Division refused to reduce the price and the case was submitted to the PAC.

The Intracompany Pricing Manual stated that products of the type produced by Division M for Division S should be priced at "the standard variable cost per unit plus a monthly charge equal to the fixed costs and 10 percent of the book value of the assets assigned to the capacity reserved for the products of the buying division."

The M Division stated that they were reserving 50 percent of the capacity of Plant M–1 for the S Division. The S Division, however, was not using this capacity this year. Because the demand was sufficiently strong for M Division products, the M Division could utilize this excess capacity. It would be foolish to leave it idle. If, however, the S Division had needed the capacity, the M Division would have been able and willing to provide it.

The S Division felt that it was unfair to pay Division M for capacity that the M Division was using. They were being paid for the capacity and yet utilizing it themselves. The S Division felt that it should pay just for the capacity that it was using, or, at a maximum, for the capacity it used plus any excess capacity up to a total of 50 percent of Plant M–1's capacity.

QUESTIONS

1. How would you settle these disputes?
2. In each case, how would you change the manual?

Chapter Eight

INVESTMENT CENTERS

In a profit center, the focus is on profit as measured by the difference between revenues and expenses. In an investment center this profit is compared with the assets employed in earning it. Many people consider an investment center as a special type of profit center, and use the term "profit center" for both. Our reason for treating them separately is primarily pedagogical; that is, there are so many problems involved in measuring the assets employed in a profit center that the topic warrants a separate chapter.

In this chapter we first discuss each of the principal types of assets that may be employed in an investment center. The sum of these assets is called the *investment base*. We then discuss the two methods of relating profit to the investment base: (1) the percentage return on investment (ROI), and (2) residual income. Finally, in view of the problems involved in measuring assets employed, we discuss the question of whether a division should or should not be set up as an investment center, and, if not, the alternative methods that can be used to control assets employed.

STRUCTURE OF THE ANALYSIS

The purpose of measuring assets employed are analogous to those discussed for profit centers in Chapter 6, namely:

1. To provide information that is useful in making decisions about assets employed and to motivate divisional managers to make sound decisions, that is, decisions that are in the best interests of the company.

2. To measure the performance of the division as an economic entity.

In examining the several alternative treatments of assets and in comparing ROI and residual income—the two ways of relating profit to assets employed—we are primarily interested in how well the alternatives serve these two purposes.

It should be recognized at the outset that a focus on profits without consideration of the assets employed to generate those profits is an inadequate basis for control. Except in certain types of service organizations in which the amount of capital is insignificant, an important objective of a profit-oriented company is to earn a satisfactory return on the capital which its investors have supplied. An increase in profits does not represent improved performance if it is accompanied by a more than proportional increase in the assets employed in generating those profits.

Unless assets employed are considered, it is difficult for top management to compare the profit performance of one division with another division or with similar outside companies. Comparisons of absolute differences in profits are not meaningful if the divisions use different amounts of resources; clearly, the greater the resources used, the greater should be the profits. Such comparisons are used both to judge how well divisional managers are performing and also as a basis for deciding how resources should be allocated.

In general, divisional managers have two performance objectives. First, they should generate adequate profits from the resources at their disposal (subject of course to legal and social constraints). Second, they should invest in additional resources only when such investment will produce an adequate return. Conversely, they should disinvest if the expected annual profits of any resource divided by its selling price is less than the company's cost of capital. The purpose of combining profits and investments is to motivate the divisional manager to accomplish these objectives. As we shall see, however, there are significant practical difficulties involved in creating a system that focuses on both profits and assets employed.

Exhibit 8–1 is a hypothetical, simplified set of divisional financial statements that will be used throughout this analysis. (In the interest of simplicity, income taxes have been omitted from this exhibit and will generally be omitted in the discussion of this chapter. Inclusion of income taxes would change the magnitudes in the calculations that follow, but would not change the conclusions.) The exhibit shows the two ways of relating profits to assets employed, namely, return on investment and residual income.

Return on investment is a *ratio*. The numerator is income, as reported on the income statement. The denominator is assets employed. In Exhibit 8–1, the denominator is taken as the corporate equity in the division. This amount would correspond to the sum of noncurrent liabilities plus shareholders' equity in the balance sheet of a separate company. It is mathematically equivalent to total assets less current liabilities, and also to noncurrent assets plus working capital. (This statement can be easily checked against the numbers in Exhibit 8–1.)

Residual income is a dollar amount, rather than a ratio. It is found by subtracting an interest charge from the reported income. This interest charge is found by multiplying the amount of assets employed by an interest rate, which in Exhibit 8–1 is 10 percent. We shall discuss the derivation of this interest rate in a later section.

Exhibit 8–1

DIVISIONAL FINANCIAL STATEMENTS

Balance Sheet
(000 omitted)

Current Assets:		Current Liabilities:	
Cash	$ 50	Accounts payable	$ 90
Receivables	150	Other current	110
Inventory	200		
Total current assets	$400	Total current liabilities	$200
Fixed Assets:			
Cost	$600	Corporate equity	500
Depreciation	−300		
Book value	300		
Total Assets	$700	Total Equities	$700

Income Statement

Revenue		$1,000
Expenses, except depreciation	$850	
Depreciation	50	900
Income before taxes		$ 100
Interest ($500 × 10%)		50
Residual Income		$ 50

$$\text{Return on Investment} \frac{\$100}{\$500} = 20\%$$

For reasons to be explained later, residual income is conceptually superior to return on investment, and we shall therefore generally use residual income in our examples. Nevertheless, return on investment is widely used in business practice, probably more widely than residual income.

MEASUREMENT OF ASSETS EMPLOYED

In this section, we shall discuss alternative ways of measuring the principal items that constitute the investment base in a division and evaluate these alternatives in accordance with the two purposes given earlier.

Cash

Most companies control cash centrally because central control permits the total cash to be smaller than would be the case if each division held cash balances sufficient to provide the necessary buffer for the unevenness of cash inflows and cash outflows. Divisional cash balances may well be only the "float" between daily receipts and daily disbursements. Consequently, the actual cash balances at the division level tend to be much smaller than would be required if the division were an independent company. Most companies, therefore, calculate the cash to be included in the investment base by means of a formula. For example, General Motors is reported to use 4½ percent of annual sales; Dupont, two months' cost of sales minus depreciation. The formula is designed to approximate the amount of cash the division would have if it were an independent company.

There are two reasons for including cash at a higher amount than the nominal balance normally carried by divisions. First, the higher amount is necessary to permit comparability among divisions or with outside companies. Second, if only the actual cash were shown, the return shown by internal divisions would be abnormally high and might be misleading to top management.

Some companies omit cash from the investment base on the theory that the investment base consists of working capital plus fixed assets. These companies reason that the amount of cash approximates the current liabilities; if this is so, the sum of the accounts receivable and the inventories will approximate the amount of working capital.

Receivables

Division management can usually influence the level of receivables, not only indirectly by its ability to generate sales, but also directly by establishing credit terms, by approving individual credit accounts and credit limits, and by its vigor in collecting overdue amounts. In the interest of simplicity, receivables are often included at the actual end-of-period balances, although the average of intraperiod balances is conceptually a better measure of the amount that should be related to profits. If the division does not control credits and collections, receivables may be calculated on a formula basis. This formula should be consistent with the credit terms, for example, one month's sales where credit terms are 30 days.

Inventories

Inventories are ordinarily treated in a manner similar to receivables; that is, they are often recorded at end-of-period amounts even though intraperiod averages would be conceptually preferable. If the company uses Lifo for financial accounting purposes, a different valuation method is ordinarily used for divisional profit reporting because in periods of inflation, the Lifo inventory balances tend to be unrealistically low. In these circumstances, inventories would be valued at standard costs or average costs, and these same costs would be used to measure cost of sales on the divisional income statement.

If work-in-process inventory is financed by *advance payments* or *progress payments* from the customer, as is typically the case with goods that require a long manufacturing period, these payments are usually subtracted from the gross inventory amounts.

Some companies subtract *accounts payable* from inventory on the grounds that the amount of accounts payable represents financing of part of the inventory by vendors, at zero cost to the division; the corporate capital required for inventories is only the difference between the gross inventory amount and accounts payable. If the division can influence the payment period allowed by vendors, the inclusion of accounts payable in the calculation encourages the manager to seek the most favorable terms. In times of high interest rates or credit stringency, the manager would be encouraged to consider the possibility of foregoing the cash discount in order, in effect, to have additional financing provided by vendors.

Working Capital in General

As can be seen from the above, there is considerable variation in how various working capital items are treated. At one extreme, companies include all current assets in the investment base, with no offset for any current liabilities. This is sound from a motivational standpoint if the divisions have no influence over accounts payable or other current liabilities. It overstates the amount of corporate capital required to finance the division, however, because the current liabilities are a source of capital. At the other extreme, all current liabilities (except current obligations to the corporation) may be deducted from current assets, as was done in calculating the investment base in Exhibit 8–1. This provides a good measure of the capital provided by the corporation, on which it expects the division to earn a return. It may, however, imply that the division manager is responsible for certain current liabilities over which he has no control.

Property, Plant, and Equipment

In financial accounting, fixed assets are initially recorded at their cost, and this cost is written off over the asset's useful life by the depreciation mechanism; no attempt is made to record the current value of the asset. Most companies use a similar approach in measuring divisional profitability in the division's asset base. This causes some serious problems in using the system for its intended purposes. In this part of the chapter, we shall examine these problems.

Acquisition of New Equipment. Suppose a division has an opportunity to acquire a new machine at a cost of $100,000. This machine is estimated to produce cash savings of $27,000 a year for five years. If the company has a required return of 10 percent, such an investment is attractive, as shown by the calculations in Section A of Exhibit 8–2. The proposed investment has a net present value of $2,400, and therefore should be undertaken. However, if the machine is acquired, and if the division measures its asset base as shown in Exhibit 8–1, the reported residual income of the division in the first year will decrease, rather than increase. The income statement without the machine and the income statement if the machine is acquired are shown in Section B of Exhibit 8–2. It should be noted that with the acquisition of the machine, income before taxes has increased, but this increase is more than offset by the increase in interest expense. Thus, the residual income calculation signals that profitability has decreased, whereas the eco-

Exhibit 8–2

INCORRECT MOTIVATION FOR ASSET ACQUISITION

A. *Economic Calculation* (000 omitted)

Investment in machine $100
Life, 5 years
Cash inflow, $27,000 per year
Present value of cash inflow ($27,000 × 3.791*) 102.4

Net present value .... $ 2.4

Decision: Acquire the machine

* 3.791 is the present value of $1 per year for five years at 10%.

B. *As Reflected on Divisional Income Statement*

(000 omitted)

	As in Exhibit 8–1		First Year with Machine	
Revenue		$1,000		$1,000
Expenses, except depreciation	$850		$823	
Depreciation	50	900	70	893
Income before taxes		$ 100		$ 107
Less interest at 10%		50		60
Residual income		$ 50		$ 47

* Interest on the new machine is calculated at its beginning book value, which for the first year, is $100 × 10% = 10. We have used the beginning-of-the-year book value for simplicity. Many companies use the average book value ($\frac{100 + 80}{2}$ = 90). The results will be similar.

nomic facts are that profitability has increased. Under these circumstances, the division manager is not motivated to purchase this machine.

Note that in Exhibit 8–2, depreciation was calculated on the straight-line basis. If it had been calculated on an accelerated basis, which is not uncommon, the discrepancy between the economic facts and the reported results would have been even greater.

In later years, the amount of residual income will increase, as the book value of the machine declines, as shown in Exhibit 8–3, going from −$3,000 in year 1 to $5,000 in year 5. The increases in residual income each year do not represent real economic changes. They apparently indicate constantly improving profitability, whereas, the facts are that there has been no real change in profitability subsequent to the time the machine was acquired. Generalizing from this example, it is evident that divisions that have old, almost fully depreciated assets will tend to report larger residual income than divisions that have newer assets.

If profitability is measured by return on investment, the same inconsistency exists, as shown in the last column of Exhibit 8–3. Although we know from the present value calculation that the true return is about 11%, the divisional financial statement reports that it is less than 10 percent in the first year, and that it increases from year to year. Furthermore, the average

Exhibit 8-3

EFFECT OF ACQUISITION ON REPORTED ANNUAL PROFITS

(000 omitted)

Year	Book Value at Beginning of Year (a)	Income* (b)	Interest† (c)	Residual Income (b−c)	ROI (b÷a)
1	100	7	10	−3	7%
2	80	7	8	−1	9
3	60	7	6	1	12
4	40	7	4	3	18
5	20	7	2	5	35

* $27,000 cash inflow — $20,000 depreciation = $7,000
† 10% of beginning book value
Note: True return = approximately 11%.

of the five annual percentages shown is 16 percent, which far exceeds what we know to be the true annual return.

It is evident that if depreciable assets are included in the investment base at net book value, divisional profitability is misstated, and division managers may not be motivated to make correct decisions on acquiring new assets.

Gross Book Value. The fluctuations in residual income and return on investment from year to year in the above example can be avoided by including depreciable assets in the investment base at gross book value, rather than net book value—and some companies do this. If this were done, the investment each year would be the $100,000 original cost, and the additional income would be $7,000 ($27,000 cash inflow minus $20,000 depreciation). The residual income, however, would be decreased by $3,000 (= $7,000 minus $10,000 interest), and the return on investment would be 7 percent (= $7,000 ÷ $100,000). Both of these numbers indicate that the division's profitability has decreased, which is not in fact the case. Return on investment calculated on gross book value always understates the true return.

Equipment Replacement. If a new machine is being considered as a replacement for an existing machine that has some undepreciated book value, we know that the undepreciated book value is irrelevant in the economic analysis of the proposed purchase (except indirectly as it may affect income taxes). Nevertheless, in the calculation of divisional profitability, the book value of the old machine can have a substantial effect. Gross book value will increase only by the difference between the cost of the new machine and the cost of the old. Net book value will increase only by the difference between the cost of the new machine and the net book value of the old. In either case, the relevant amount of additional investment is understated, and the residual income is correspondingly overstated. Managers are therefore encouraged to replace old equipment with new equipment, even in situations in which such replacement is not economically justified. Furthermore, divisions that are able to make the most replacements will show the greatest improvement in profitability.

Disposition of Assets. If assets are included in the investment base at their original cost, then the division manager is motivated to get rid of them, even if they have some usefulness because the division's investment base is reduced by the full cost of the asset.[1]

Annuity Depreciation. If, instead of straight-line depreciation, depreciation is calculated by the annuity basis, the divisional profitability calculation will show the correct residual income and return on investment, as demonstrated in Exhibits 8–4 and 8–5. This is because the annuity depreciation

Exhibit 8–4

PROFITABILITY USING ANNUITY DEPRECIATION

Smoothing Residual Income
($000)

Year	Beginning Book Value	Cash Inflow	Residual Income*	Interest†	Depreciation‡
1	$100.0	$ 27.0	$0.6	$10.0	$ 16.4
2	83.6	27.0	0.6	8.4	18.0
3	65.6	27.0	0.6	6.6	19.8
4	45.8	27.0	0.6	4.6	21.8
5	24.0	27.0	0.6	2.4	24.0
		$135.0	$3.0	$32.0	$100.0

* The reason for using annuity depreciation is to make the residual income the same each year by changing the amount of depreciation charged. Consequently, we must estimate the total residual income earned over the five years. A 10 percent return on $100,000 would require five annual cash inflows of $26,378. The actual cash inflows are $27,000. Therefore, the residual income (the amount in excess of $26,378) is $622 per year.

† This is 10 percent of the balance at the beginning of the year.

‡ Depreciation is the amount required to make the residual income (profits after interest and depreciation) equal $622 per year (rounded here to $600). This is calculated as follows:

$$\$27.0 - \text{Interest} - \text{Depreciation} = \$.6$$

therefore

$$\text{Depreciation} = \$26.4 - \text{Interest}$$

method exactly matches the recovery of investment that is implicit in the present value calculation. Annuity depreciation is the opposite of accelerated depreciation in that the annual amount of depreciation is low in the early years when the investment values are high and increases each year as the investments decrease; the rate of return remains constant.

The examples in Exhibit 8–4 and Exhibit 8–5 show the calculations when the cash inflows are level in each year. The equations can derive the deprecia-

---

[1] For a complete analysis of this and other problems of accounting for depreciable assets, see John Dearden, "Problem in Decentralized Profit Responsibility," *Harvard Business Review,* May–June 1960.

Exhibit 8–5

PROFITABILITY USING ANNUITY DEPRECIATION

Smoothing Return on Investment
($000)

Year	Beginning Book Balance	Cash Inflow	Net Profit*	Depreciation†	Return on Beginning Investment
1	$100.0	$ 27.0	$11.0	$ 16.0	11%
2	84.0	27.0	9.2	17.8	11
3	66.2	27.0	7.3	19.7	11
4	46.5	27.0	5.1	21.9	11
5	24.6	27.0	2.4	24.6	10‡
		$135.0	$35.0	$100.0	

* A return of $27,000 a year for 5 years on an investment of $100,000 provides a return of approximately 11% on the beginning of the year investment. Consequently, in order to have a constant 11% return each year, the net profit must equal 11% of the beginning of the year investment.

† Depreciation is the difference between the cash flow and the net profit.

‡ Difference results because the return is not exactly 11%.

tion for other cash flow patterns, such as a decreasing cash flow as repair costs increase, or an increasing cash flow as a new product gains market acceptance.[2]

Very few managers accept the idea of a depreciation allowance that increases as the asset ages, however. They visualize accounting depreciation as representing physical deterioration or loss in economic value. They therefore believe that accelerated or straight-line depreciation is a valid representation of what is taking place, while annuity depreciation is not. Conseqently, it is difficult to convince management to use the annuity method for divisional profit measurement.

Annuity depreciation also presents some practical problems. For example, a depreciation schedule is developed on the basis of an estimated cash flow pattern. If the actual cash flow pattern differs from that assumed, even though the total cash flow might result in the same rate of return, some years would show higher than expected profits and others would show lower. Do you change the depreciation schedule each year to conform with the actual pattern of cash flow? This would not seem to be practical. Annuity depreciation would not be desirable for income tax purposes, of course, and although, as a "systematic and rational" method, it clearly is acceptable for financial accounting purposes, few companies use this method in their financial reporting. Indeed, surveys of company practice in measuring divisional profitability show no use of the annuity method.[3]

---

[2] See Harold Bierman, Jr., "ROI as a Measure of Managerial Performance," *Financial Executive,* March 1973.

[3] John J. Mauriel and Robert N. Anthony, "Misevaluation of Investment Center Performance," *Harvard Business Review,* March–April 1966.

Other Valuation Methods.   A few companies depart from the use of either gross book value or net book value in calculating the investment base. Some use net book value but set a lower limit, usually 50 percent, as the amount of original cost that can be written off; this lessens the distortions that occur in divisions with relatively old assets. A difficulty with this method is that a division with fixed assets that have a net book value of less than 50 percent of gross book value is, in effect, on the same basis as if it used gross book value; that is, the division can decrease its investment base by scrapping perfectly good assets. Other companies depart entirely from the accounting records, and use an approximation of the current value of the asset. They arrive at this amount by a periodic appraisal of assets (say, every five years or when a new division manager takes over), by adjusting original cost by an index of changes in equipment prices, or by using insurance values.

A major problem with using nonaccounting values is that they tend to be subjective, as contrasted with accounting values which appear to be objective and generally not subject to argument. Consequently, accounting data have an aura of reality for operating management. Although the intensity of this sentiment will vary with different managers, the further one departs from accounting figures in measuring financial performance, the more the system seems like playing a game of numbers to many divisional managers and, often, to higher levels of management also.

A second problem with the economic value approach is deciding how the economic values are to be determined. Conceptually, the economic value of a group of assets is equal to the present value of the flow of funds that these assets will generate in the future. As a practical matter, it is not possible to determine this amount with the tools we have available. For plant and equipment, it is possible to use published indices of replacement costs. This, however, solves only the easiest part of the problem, because this method provides no means for valuing the intangible assets. Also, price indices are not entirely relevant because they make no allowance for the impact of changes in technology.

Summary.   The great majority of companies include fixed assets in their investment at their net book value. They do this for the simple reason that this is the amount at which the assets are carried in the financial accounts and therefore represents, according to the accounts, the amount of capital that the corporation has employed in the division. Managements recognize the fact that this method gives misleading signals, but they argue that it is the responsibility of users of the divisional profit reports to make allowances for these errors in interpreting the reports, and that alternative methods of calculating the investment base are so subjective that they are not to be trusted. They reject the annuity depreciation approach on the grounds that it is inconsistent with the way in which depreciation is calculated for financial statement purposes.

Leased Assets

Suppose the division whose financial statements are shown in Exhibit 8–1 sold its $300,000 of fixed assets, returned the proceeds of the sale to corporate headquarters, and then leased back the assets at a rental rate of $60,000 per year. As shown in Exhibit 8–6, the division's income before

Exhibit 8–6

EFFECT OF LEASING ASSETS

Income Statement
(000 omitted)

	As in Exhibit 8–1		If Assets Are Leased	
Revenue		$1,000		$1,000
Expenses other than below	$850		$850	
Depreciation	50	900		
Rental expense			60	910
Income before taxes		$ 100		$ 90
Interest $500 × 10%		50		
$200 × 10%				20
Residual Income		$ 50		$ 70

taxes would be reduced because the new rental expense would be higher than the depreciation charge that has been eliminated. Nevertheless, residual income would be increased because the higher cost would be more than offset by the decrease in interest cost. Because of this tendency, division managers will be induced to lease assets, rather than own them, under any circumstances in which the interest charge that is built into the rental cost is less than the interest rate that is applied to the division's investment base. (Here, as elsewhere, this generalization is an oversimplification because in the real world the impact of income taxes must also be taken into account.)

Many leases are financing arrangements; that is, they provide an alternative way of obtaining the use of assets that otherwise would be acquired by funds obtained from debt and equity financing. Financial leases are usually viewed as being similar to debt. Financing decisions are usually made by corporate headquarters. For these reasons, restrictions are usually placed on the division manager's freedom to lease assets. If a division acquires assets through a financial lease (i.e., a long-term, noncancellable lease), the assets are usually capitalized and included in the investment base as if they had been purchased.

Idle Assets

If a division has idle assets that can be used by other divisions, often the division is permitted to exclude them from the investment base. The purpose of this is to encourage division managers to release underutilized assets to divisions that may have some better use for them. However, if the fixed assets cannot be used by other divisions, removing these assets from the investment base could result in some dysfunctional actions on the part of divisional management. For example, it would encourage the division manager to idle partially utilized assets that are not earning a return equal to the division's profit objective. If there is no alternative use for the equipment, *any* contribution from this equipment will improve company profits.

Noncurrent Liabilities

Ordinarily, a division receives its permanent capital from the corporate pool of funds. The corporation obtained these funds from debt securities, from equity investors, and from retained earnings. To the division, the total amount of these funds is relevant, but the sources from which they were obtained are irrelevant. In unusual situations, a division's financing may be peculiar to its own situation. For example, a division that builds or operates residential housing uses a much larger proportion of debt capital than is the case with typical manufacturing and marketing divisions. Since this capital is obtained through mortgage loans on the division's assets, it is appropriate to account for the borrowed funds separately and to compute a residual income based on the assets that were obtained from general corporate sources, rather than on total assets.

The Interest Rate

The rate used to calculate the interest charge is set by corporate headquarters. It should be higher than the corporation's rate for debt financing because the funds involved are a mixture of debt and higher-cost equity. Usually, the rate is set somewhat below the company's estimated cost of capital (assuming that a company can calculate its cost of capital, which rarely is the case) so that the residual income of an average division will be somewhat above zero.

Although conceptually a good argument could be made for using different rates for divisions with different risk characteristics, in practice this is rarely done; that is, the same rate is used for all divisions. Some companies do use a lower rate for working capital than for fixed assets. In some cases, this represents a judgment that working capital is less risky than fixed assets because the funds are committed for a shorter period of time. In other cases the lower rate is a way of compensating for the fact that the company included inventory and receivables in the investment base at their gross amount, that is, without a deduction for accounts payable; the lower rate is an implicit recognition of the fact that funds obtained from accounts payable have a zero cost.

Summary of the Investment Base

As can be seen from the foregoing description, a large number of alternatives exist for calculating the investment base. Some are better than others for the purposes for which divisional residual income or return on investment are used. No practical method provides a perfect measure of the profitability of the division. Considerable thought is warranted in deciding on the best set of rules for a given situation.

RESIDUAL INCOME VERSUS ROI

Many companies, probably a large majority, evaluate divisions on the basis of the return on investment percentage. They do this because the meaning of ROI is well understood, and ROI data are available for other companies or industries that can be used as a basis of comparison. The dollar amount of residual income does not provide such a basis for comparison. Nevertheless, the residual income approach has some inherent advantages over ROI.

The most important advantage of residual income over ROI is that all divisions will have the same profit objectives for comparable investments, while the ROI approach provides an erroneous incentive for investments. Since each division is expected to meet an ROI objective, a division manager will not be likely to propose a capital investment unless it is expected to earn a return at least as high as this objective. Thus, a division with an objective of 20 percent ROI would not want to invest at less than this rate, while a division with an objective of 5 percent ROI would benefit from anything over this rate. Since the profit objectives of some divisions are higher than the company's overall rate of return for capital expenditures, and the profit objectives of other divisions are lower, this situation can cause seriously inconsistent capital investment actions. For similar reasons, inventories in one division will have a different implicit carrying charge from identical types of inventories in another division which has a different profit objective.

A second advantage of residual income is that different interest rates may be used for different types of assets. For example, a relatively low rate can be used for inventories while a higher rate can be used for investments in fixed assets. Furthermore, different rates can be used for different types of fixed assets to take into account different degrees of risk. In short, the measurement system can be made consistent with the decision rules that affect the acquisition of the assets. It follows that the same type of asset can be required to earn the same return throughout the company, regardless of the profitability of the particular division. Thus, divisions should act consistently in decisions involving investments in new assets.

The difference between ROI and residual income is shown in Exhibit 8–7.

Exhibit 8–7

DIFFERENCE BETWEEN ROI AND RI

($000 omitted)

ROI Method

Division	ROI Objective	Cash	Receiv- ables	Inven- tories	Fixed Assets	Total Invest- ment	Budgeted Profit
A	20%	$10	$20	$30	$60	$120	$24.0
B	12	20	20	30	50	120	14.4
C	10	15	40	40	10	105	10.5
D	5	5	10	20	40	75	3.8
E	(5)	10	5	10	10	35	(1.8)

Residual Income Method

Div.	(1) Profit Potential	Current Assets			Fixed Assets			Budgeted Residual Income (1) − [(4) + (7)]
		(2) Amount	(3) Rate	(4) Required Earnings	(5) Amount	(6) Rate	(7) Required Earnings	
A	24.0	$60	4%	$2.4	$60	10%	$6.0	$15.6
B	14.4	70	4	2.8	50	10	5.0	6.6
C	10.5	95	4	3.8	10	10	1.0	5.7
D	3.8	35	4	1.4	40	10	4.0	(1.6)
E	(1.7)	25	4	1.0	10	10	1.0	(3.7)

Assume that the company's rate for investing in fixed assets is 10 percent after taxes and that the companywide cost of money tied up in inventories and receivables is 4 percent after taxes. The top section of Exhibit 8–7 shows only one division (C) where the ROI objective is consistent with the cutoff rate, and none where the objective is consistent with the cost of carrying current assets. Division A would decrease its chances of meeting its profit objective if it did not earn at least 20 percent on added investments in either current or fixed assets, whereas divisions D and E would benefit from a much lower return.

The residual income method corrects these inconsistencies in the following manner: The profit potential of each division is calculated. The investments, multiplied by the appropriate rates (representing the companywide rules), are subtracted from this profit potential. The resulting amount is the budgeted residual income. Periodically, the actual residual income is calculated by subtracting from the actual profits the actual investment multiplied by the appropriate rates. The lower section of Exhibit 8–7 shows how the budgeted residual income would be calculated.

For example, if division A earned $28,000 and employed average current assets of $65,000 and average fixed assets of $65,000, its actual residual income would be calcuated as follows:

$$RI = 28{,}000 - .04(65{,}000) - .10\,(65{,}000)$$
$$= 28{,}000 - 2{,}600 - 6{,}500$$
$$= 18{,}900$$

This is $3,300 (18,900 − 15,600) better than its objective. Note that if any division earns more than 10 percent on added fixed assets, it will increase its residual income. (In the case of C and D the additional profit will decrease the amount of negative residual income, which amounts to the same thing.) A similar result occurs for current assets. Inventory decision rules will be based on a cost of 4 percent for financial carrying charges. (There will be of course additional costs for physically storing the inventory.) In this way, the financial decision rules of the divisions will be consistent with those of the company.

The residual income method solves the problem of differing profit objectives for the same asset in different divisions and the same profit objective for different assets in the same division. Residual income makes it possible to incorporate in the measurement system the same decision rules that are used in the planning process. The more sophisticated the planning process, the more complex can be the residual income calculation. For example, assume that the capital investment decision rules called for a 10 percent return on general-purpose assets and 15 percent return on special-purpose assets. Divisional fixed assets could be classified accordingly and different rates applied when measuring performance. (For example managers may be reluctant to make new nonprofitable investments that improve working conditions, reduce pollution, or meet other social goals. Investments of this type would be much more acceptable to the divisional manager if he were expected to earn a reduced return on them.)

Uses of Return on Investment

Although ROI has severe limitations as a measure of divisional performance, it is useful for diagnosing areas of profit deficiency and, thus, directing management's attention to potential areas of improvement. Areas for analysis could include divisions, product lines, geographical areas, and so forth. The analyst would start with the accounting results which would be adjusted if accounting conventions resulted in unrealistic amounts. Fixed assets might be adjusted to economic values, Lifo inventories increased to current market value, and depreciation adjusted to reflect a realistic amount based on the economic value of the assets. The life of the asset could be adjusted to the best estimate of its actual life, if this is different from that used in the accounting records. Profits could be adjusted for unusual or nonrecurring items. After these adjustments, the return on investment can be calculated for all meaningful activities. Those showing less than a satisfactory return are candidates for further study to find out how profits can be improved or to decide whether the activity should be discontinued. Note, however, that this analysis would be merely for diagnosis. Any action must be based on an evaluation of future cash flows for alternative courses of action.

Using ROI as a diagnostic tool does not result in the problems created by using ROI as a measurement tool because:

1. The analyst can make such adjustments to the accounting data as he believes are necessary to make them meaningful. Consequently, it is not necessary to convince a divisional manager of the appropriateness of the adjustments because he is not held accountable for them.

2. The results of the analysis are used to pinpoint areas that need attention. The action taken would depend on the circumstances; however, this action would not be aimed at improving ROI, but rather at improving profitability.

3. If the analysis is incorrect because of the inability to calculate economic values or to assign investments, no great harm has been done. It means only that time has been spent unnecessarily on an analysis of an area for which no analysis was warranted.

ALTERNATIVES TO INVESTMENT CENTERS

The residual income method does not solve all the problems of measuring profitability in an investment center. In particular, it does not solve the problem of accounting for fixed assets discussed above unless annuity depreciation is also used, and this is rarely done in practice. If gross book value is used, a division can increase its residual income by taking action contrary to the interest of the company as shown in Exhibit 8–2. If net book value is used, residual income will increase simply from the passage of time. Furthermore, residual income will be temporarily depressed by new investments because of the high net book value in the early years. Residual income does solve the problem created by differing profit potential. All divisions, regardless of profitability, will be motivated to increase investments if the rate of return from a potential investment exceeds the required rate prescribed by the measurement system.

Another problem of measuring the investment base is that some assets tend to be undervalued when they are capitalized, and others are omitted altogether. Many elements of investment are expensed rather than capitalized. Although the purchase cost of fixed assets is ordinarily capitalized, an equal amount of investment in start up costs, new product development, dealer organization, and so forth may be written off as expenses and therefore not appear in the investment base. This situation applies especially in marketing divisions. Often in these divisions the accounted investment is limited to inventories, receivables, and office furniture and equipment. In a purely marketing division the understatement of true investment is usually clear; consequently, residual income is often ignored. However, when a group of divisions with varying degrees of marketing responsibility are ranked, the division with the relatively smaller manufacturing operations will tend to have the highest residual income.

In view of all these problems, many companies have decided not to create investment centers. The alternative is to make an interest charge for controllable assets only, and to control fixed assets by separate devices.

Controllable assets are, esentially, receivables and inventory. Divisional management can make day-to-day decisions that affect the level of these assets; if these decisions are wrong, serious consequences can occur quickly. For example, if inventories are too high, unnecessary capital is tied up in them and the risk of obsolescence is increased; whereas if inventories are too low, production interruptions or lost customer business can result from the stockouts. In order to focus attention on these important, controllable items, some companies include an interest cost for them in the divisional income statement. This acts both to motivate divisional management properly and also to measure the real cost of resources committed to these items.

Investments in fixed assets are controlled by the capital budgeting process before the fact and by postcompletion audits to determine whether the anticipated cash flows in fact materialized. This is far from completely satisfactory, of course, because often it is not possible to measure precisely how actual results compare with those predicted in the original projects. In most cases, however, serious deviations can be ascertained.

The argument for evaluating profits and investments separately is that this is consistent with what top management wishes the divisional manager to accomplish; namely, to obtain the maximum long-run cash flow from the investments that he controls and to add investments only when they will provide a net return in excess of the company's cost of providing that investment.

Investment decisions are controlled at the point where these decisions are made. Consequently, the capital investment analysis procedure is of primary importance in investment control. Once the investment has been made, it is largely a sunk cost and should not influence future decisions. Nevertheless, management wants to know when capital investment decisions have been made incorrectly for two reasons:

1. Some action may be appropriate with respect to the person responsible for the mistakes.
2. Some safeguard to prevent a recurrence may be appropriate.

Even at best, residual income will not provide accurate information on the effectiveness of new investment decisions because divisional profits are affected by many factors other than the consequences of new investments. Companies that use ROI or residual income, therefore, must also use some form of postcompletion audit if they are to control capital investments adequately.

Students of management control systems disagree on whether it is better to use residual income or whether it is better to evaluate profit performance and investment performance separately. Most seem to favor residual income. The main reason is the belief that it is important to have a single measurement of financial performance. For example, if the profit performance was better than objective and the investment performance worse, how does management measure the overall financial performance? Residual income weighs the impact of the poorer investment performance against the improved profit performance and provides this single measure. Another reason for using residual income its that it might motivate managers to be more careful about adding investments that may not be profitable.

Case 8-1

Investment Center Problems

1. The ABC Company has three divisions—A, B, and C. Division A is exclusively a marketing division; Division B is exclusively a manufacturing division; and Division C is both a manufacturing and marketing division. Listed below are some financial facts for each of these divisions.

	Division A	Division B	Division C
Current assets	$100,000	$ 100,000	$100,000
Fixed assets (cost)	—	1,000,000	500,000
Total assets	$100,000	$1,100,000	$600,000
Profits before depreciation and market development costs	$200,000	$200,000	$200,000

Required

Assume that the ABC Company depreciates fixed assets on a straight-line basis over ten years. In order to maintain its markets and productive facilities it has to invest $100,000 per year in market development in Division A and $50,000 per year in Division C. This is written off as an expense. It also has to replace 10 percent of its productive facilities each year. Under these equilibrium conditions, what are the annual rates of return earned by each of the divisions?

2. The D Division of the DEF Corporation has budgeted after-tax profits of $1,000,000 for 1975. It has budgeted assets as of January 1, 1975, of $10,000,000, consisting of $4,000,000 in current assets and $6,000,000 in fixed assets. Fixed assets are included in the asset base at gross book value. The net book value of these fixed assets is $3,000,000. All fixed assets are depreciated over a 10-year period on a straight-line basis.

Note: In solving these problems, ignore income taxes. Most of the problems state that savings or earnings are "after taxes." Assume that the amount of income taxes will not be affected by alternative accounting treatment.

The manager of the D Division has submitted a capital investment project to replace a major group of machines. The financial details of this project are as follows.

New equipment:

Estimated cost	$2,000,000
Estimated after-tax annual savings*	300,000
Estimated life	10 years

Old equipment to be replaced:

Original cost	$1,500,000
Original estimate of life	10 years
Present age	7 years
Present book value ($1,500,000–$1,050,000)	$450,000
Salvage value	0

* These are cash inflows, disregarding depreciation and capital gains or losses (except for their tax impact.)

Required

The capital investment project was approved and the new machinery was installed on January 1, 1975. Calculate the rate of return that is earned on the new investment, using the divisional accounting rules, and calculate the revised 1975 and 1976 budgeted rate of return:

a) assuming that the investment and savings are exactly as stated in the project; and

b) assuming that the investment is overrun by $500,000 and the annual savings are only $200,000.

3. Assume that everything is as stated in Problem 2, except that the fixed assets are included in the divisional assets base at their net book value at the end of the year. Answer the questions in Problem 2 for 1975 and 1976.

4. The G Division of the GHI Corporation proposes the following investment in a new product line.

Investment in fixed assets	$100,000
Annual profits before depreciation but after taxes	
(i.e., annual cash flow)	25,000
Life	5 years

The GHI Corporation uses the time-adjusted rate of return, with a cut-off rate of 8 percent in evaluating its capital investment proposals. A $25,000 cash inflow for five years on an investment of $100,000 has a time-adjusted return of 8 percent. Consequently, the proposed investment is acceptable under the company's criterion. Assume that the project is approved and that the investment and profit were the same as estimated. Assets are included in the divisional investment base at the average of the beginning and end of the year's net book value.

Required

1. Calculate the rate of return that is earned by the G Division on the new investment for each year and the average rate for the five years, using straight-line depreciation.
2. Calculate the rate of return that is earned by the G Division on the new investment for each year, and the average for the five years using the sum-of-the-year's-digits depreciation.

5. A proposed investment of $100,000 in fixed assets is expected to yield after-tax cash flows of $16,275 a year for ten years. Calculate a depreciation schedule, based on annuity-type depreciation, that provides an equal rate of return each year on the investment at the beginning of the year, assuming that the investment and earnings are the same as estimated.

6. The JKL Company uses the residual income method for measuring divisional profit performance. The company charges each division a 5 percent return on its average current assets and a 10 percent return on its average fixed assets. Listed below are some financial statistics for three divisions of the JKL Company.

	Division		
	J	K	L
Budget data ($000s):			
1975 Budgeted profit	$ 90	$ 55	$ 50
1975 Budgeted current assets	100	200	300
1975 Budgeted fixed assets	400	400	500
Actual data ($000s):			
1975 Profits	$ 80	$ 60	$ 50
1975 Current assets	90	190	350
1975 Fixed assets	400	450	550

Required

1. Calculate the ROI objective and actual ROI for each division for 1975.
2. Calculate the RI objective for each division for 1975.
3. Calculate the actual RI for each division for 1975 and calculate the extent that it is above or below objective.

7. Refer to the budgeted profits and assets of the three divisions of the JKL Company provided in Problem 6. Listed below are four management actions, together with the financial impact of these actions. For each of these situations, calculate the impact on the budgeted ROI and RI for each division. (Another way of looking at this problem is to calculate the extent to which these actions help or hurt the divisional managers in attaining their profit goals.)

Situation 1. An investment in fixed assets is made. This action increases the average fixed assets by $100,000 and profits by $10,000.

Situation 2. An investment in fixed assets is made. This action increases the average assets by $100,000 and profits by $7000.

Situation 3. A program to reduce inventories is instituted. As a result inventories are reduced by $50,000. Increased costs and reduced sales resulting from the lower inventory levels reduce profits by $5000.

Situation 4. A plant is closed down and sold. Fixed assets are reduced by $75,000 and profits from reduced sales are decreased by $7500.

Case 8-2

Diversified Products Corporation*

The Diversified Products Corporation manufactured consumer and industrial products in more than a dozen divisions. Plants were located throughout the country, one or more to a division, and company headquarters was in a large eastern city. Each division was run by a division manager and had its own balance sheet and income statement. The company made extensive use of long- and short-run planning programs, which included budgets for sales, costs, expenditures, and rate of return on investment. Monthly reports on operating results were sent in by each division and were reviewed by headquarters executives.

The Able division of the Diversified Products Corporation manufactured and assembled large industrial pumps, most of which sold for more than $1,000. A great variety of models were made to order from the standard parts that the division either bought or manufactured for stock. In addition, components were individually designed and fabricated when pumps were made for special applications. A variety of metalworking machines were used, some large and heavy, and a few designed especially for the division's kind of business.

The division operated three plants, two of which were much smaller than the third and were located in distant parts of the country. Headquarters offices were located in the main plant, where more than 1,000 people were employed. They performed design and manufacturing operations as well as the usual staff and clerical work. Marketing activities were carried out by sales engineers in the field, who worked closely with customers on design and installation. Reporting to Mr. Allen, the division manager, were men in charge of design, sales, manufacturing, purchasing, and budgets.

* Although not previously copyrighted, this case was written by Professor William Rotch, University of Virginia, published by Intercollegiate Case Clearing House (ICH4C53R), Soldiers Field, Boston, and reproduced here with the permission of the author.

The division's product line had been broken down into five product groups, so that the profitability of each could be studied separately. Evaluation was based on the margin above factory cost as a percentage of sales. No attempt had been made to allocate investment to the product lines. The budget director said this not only would be difficult in view of the common facilities, but also such a mathematical computation would not provide any new information, since the products had approximately the same turnover of assets. Furthermore, he said it was difficult enough to allocate common factory costs between products, and even margin on sales was a disputable figure. "If we were larger," he said, "and had separate facilities for each product line, we might be able to do it. But it wouldn't mean much in this division right now."

Only half a dozen men ever looked at the division's rate of return, for other measures were used in the division's internal control system. The division manager used shipments per week and certain cost areas such as overtime payments to check on divisional operations.

THE DIVISION MANAGER'S CONTROL OF ASSETS

During 1957, the total assets of the Able division were turned over approximately 1.7 times, and late that year they were made up as follows:

Cash	12%
Accounts receivable	21
Inventory:	
Raw material	7
About 3% metal stock	
About 4% purchased parts	
Work in process	11
About 7% manufactured parts	
About 4% floor stocks	
Finished goods	2
Machinery (original cost)	29
Land and buildings (original cost)	18
	100%

Cash (12 Percent of Total Assets)

The Able division, like all divisions in the Diversified Products Corporation, maintained a petty cash account in a local bank to which company headquarters transferred funds as they were needed. This local working account was used primarily for making up the plant payroll and for payment of other local bills. Payment of suppliers' invoices as well as collection of accounts receivable was handled by headquarters for Able as well as for most of the other divisions.

The division's cash account at headquarters was shown on the division's balance sheet as cash and marketable securities. The amount shown as cash had been established by agreement between top management and the division manager, and was considered by both to be about the minimum amount necessary to operate the division. The excess above this amount was shown on the division's balance sheet as marketable securities, and earned interest from headquarters at the rate of 3 percent a year. It was this account which varied with receipts and disbursements, leaving the cash account fixed as long as there was a balance in the securities account. It was possible for the securities account to be wiped out and for cash to decline below the minimum agreed on, but if this continued for more than a month or two, corrective action was taken. For Able division, the minimum level was equal to about one month's sales, and in recent years cash had seldom gone below this amount.

Whether or not the company as a whole actually owned cash and marketable securities equal to the sum of all the respective divisions' cash and security accounts was strictly a headquarters matter. It probably was not necessary to hold this amount of cash and securities, since the division accounts had to cover division peak needs and, from headquarters' point of view, not all the peak needs necessarily occurred at the same time.

The size of a division's combined cash and marketable securities accounts was directly affected by all phases of the division's operations that used or produced cash. It also was affected in three other ways. One was the automatic deduction of 52 percent of income for tax purposes. Another was the payment of "dividends" by the division to headquarters. All earnings that the division manager did not wish to keep for future use were transferred to the corporation's cash account by payment of a dividend. Since a division was expected to retain a sufficient balance to provide for capital expenditures, dividends were paid generally only by the profitable divisions that were not expanding rapidly.

The third action affecting the cash account occurred if cash declined below the minimum, or if extensive capital expenditures had been approved. A division might then "borrow" from headquarters, paying interest as if it were a separate company. At the end of 1957, the Able division had no loan and had been able to operate since about 1950 without borrowing from headquarters. Borrowing was not, in fact, currently being considered by the Able division.

Except for its part in the establishment of a minimum cash level, top management was not involved in the determination of the division's investment in cash and marketable securities. Mr. Allen could control the level of this investment by deciding how much was to be paid in dividends. Since only a 3 percent return was received on the marketable securities and since the division earned more than that on its total investment, it was to his advantage to pay out as much as possible in dividends. When asked how he determined the size of the dividends, Mr. Allen said that he simply kept what he thought he would need to cover peak demands, capital expenditures, and contingencies. Improving the division's rate of return may have been part of the decision, but he did not mention it.

Accounts Receivable (21 Percent of Total Assets)

All accounts receivable for the Able division were collected at company headquarters. Around the twentieth of each month, the accounts were run off and the report was forwarded to the division. Though, in theory, Mr. Allen was allowed to set his own terms for divisional sales, in practice it would have been difficult to change the company's usual terms. Since Able division sold to important customers of other divisions, any change from the net-30-days terms would disturb a large segment of the corporation's business. Furthermore, industry practice was well established, and the division would hardly try to change it.

The possibility of cash sales in situations in which credit was poor was virtually nonexistent. Credit was investigated for all customers by the headquarters credit department, and no sales were made without a prior credit check. For the Able division, this policy presented no problem, for it sold primarily to well-established customers.

In late 1957, accounts receivable corresponded to 45 average days of sales. This exceeded the 30-day credit period as a result of a slight increase in shipments the month before, coupled with the normal delay caused by the billing and collection process. Mr. Allen could do almost nothing directly to control the level of accounts receivable. This asset account varied with sales, lagged behind shipments by a little more than a month, and departed from this relationship only if customers happened to pay early or late.

Inventory, Raw Material Metal Stock (about 3 Percent of Total Investment)

In late 1957, inventory as a whole made up 20 percent of Able division's total assets. A subdivision of the various kinds of inventory showed that raw material accounted for 7 percent; work in process, 11 percent; and finished goods and miscellaneous supplies, 2 percent. Since the Able division produced to order, finished goods inventory was normally small, leaving raw material and work in process as the most significant classes of inventory.

The raw material inventory could be further subdivided to separate the raw material inventory from a variety of purchased parts. The strictly raw material inventory was composed primarily of metals and metal shapes, such as steel sheets or copper tubes. Most of the steel was bought according to a schedule arranged with the steel companies several months ahead of the delivery date. About a month before the steel company was to ship the order, Able division would send the rolling instructions by shapes and weights. If the weight on any particular shape was below a minimum set by the steel company, Able division would pay an extra charge for processing. Although this method of purchasing accounted for the bulk of steel purchases, smaller amounts were also bought as needed from warehouse stocks and specialty producers.

Copper was bought by headquarters and processed by the company's own mill. The divisions could buy the quantities they needed, but the price paid depended on corporate buying practices and processing costs. The price paid by Able division had generally been competitive with outside sources, though it often lagged behind the market both in increases and in reductions in price.

The amounts of copper and steel bought were usually determined by the purchasing agent without recourse to any formal calculations of an economic ordering quantity. The reason for this was that since such a large number of uncertain factors continually had to be estimated, a formal computation would not improve the process of determining how much to buy. Purchases depended on the amounts on hand, expected consumption, and current delivery time and price expectations. If delivery was fast, smaller amounts were usually bought. If a price increase was anticipated, somewhat larger orders often were placed at the current price. Larger amounts of steel were bought, for example, just before the 1956 steel strike, when steel negotiations were expected to result in a price increase, and perhaps also in a delay in deliveries.

The level of investment in raw material varied with the rates of purchase and use. Mr. Allen could control this class of asset within a fairly wide range, and there were no top management directives governing the size of his raw material inventory.

Inventory, Purchased Parts and Manufactured Parts (about 11 Percent of Total Assets—4 Percent from Raw Material, 7 Percent from Work in Process)

The Able division purchased and manufactured parts for stock to be used later in the assembly of pumps. The method used to determine the purchase quantity was the same as that used to determine the length of production run on parts made for work-in-process stocks.

The number of parts bought or manufactured was based on a series of calculations of an economical ordering quantity (EOQ). Since several thousand different items were bought and manufactured, these calculations had been made routine so that most of the work was done by clerks with the aid of an inventory control work sheet, Exhibit 1. This sheet had been prepared by headquarters staff personnel, and was used throughout the company in conjunction with two tables drawn up by each division. To show how this procedure worked, an actual computation is shown in Exhibit 1 for a hypothetical part called a gremlet.

Section I of the worksheet shows two methods of calculating the value of future quarterly requirements. In the first method, the clerk considered two quarters of past activity and, with the aid of the first of the two tables, filled in the estimated requirements for the next quarter. This table is simply an automatic method of weighting the average of the two quarters, applying a weight of three to the most recent quarter and a weight of one to the quarter before. In the example furnished, 83 dozen gremlets were used last quarter

Exhibit 1

INVENTORY CONTROL WORK SHEET
Order Quantity and Review Point
(Long Form)

Item Style No. Size	P D S	Ledger Codes	PROBABILITY ACCOUNTS SINGLE DELIVERY	
			[✓] Purch.	PROTECTION
Description Blue Gremlets	End Use fasten box top	Unit Measure dozen	[ ] I.W.R. [ ] Self Mfd.	1 Stock out in 2 yrs

I. A. PAST ACTIVITY

Past six month activity (from ledger)

1st	53	/most \	4th	28
2nd	12	(recent)	5th	6
3rd	18	\ past /	6th	20

3 Mo. Total __83__ - - - - - ▶ 83

X $ 1.77 Std. Cost   6 Mo. Total __137__

- $ 147 (L) Val.   X $ 1.77 Std. Cost Val.

- $ 242 (M)

From Requirements Table where (L) & (M) intersect read indicated $ 133 (N) future quarterly requirements

OR _____

B. PAST ACTIVITY AND FUTURE TREND

Past three months activity (from ledger)

1st _____ (most recent past)
2nd _____ | % Rate should not exceed
3rd _____ | (+) (-) 25%. When quarter to
3 Mo. _____ | quarter changes are erratic,
Total _____ | consider the Planned Approach.

X _ _ _ _ % Rate of future trend

- _____

X $_ _ _ _ Standard Cost

- [$] (P) Value of future quarterly requirements

II.
1. Quarterly requirements (I. (N) or (P)) $ 80
2. Set up value (if self mfd.) $ -
3. EOQ (from OQ Table) $ 149
4. No. times/yr. stock is ordered   2.1
5. EOQ Units $\frac{\text{Line 3 } \$ \ 149}{\text{Std. Cost } \$ \ 1.77}$ = [84] 75   EOQ Units

III.
1. No. demands during expected delivery time

No. demands past 3 mos. $\frac{\text{(from ledger)} \quad 8}{\text{Calendar Days} \quad 90}$ = _ _.09 _ _ (S) No./Day

x E.D.T. (from Delivery Time Schedule) 30 (F)

= No. Demands during E.D.T. 2.7 (T)

2. From O.R.P. table where No. demands (line 1 (T). above) intersect with No. times/yr. stock is ordered (II. line 4) read O.R.P.   O.R.P. Dem. [3.8]

3. O.R.P. in Units
a. Average size of demands Past 3 mos. activity
$\frac{\text{(I. A or B) - Units} \quad 83}{\text{No. demands past 3 mos.}} = 10.4$ (U)
(Line 1, before division)   8

x O.R.P. demands (line 2) _ _ = _ _3.8 _ _

b. O.R.P. - Units = [40]

NOTE: Post O.R.P. in units on ledger record and reset signal devices.

IV.
1. Present Stock Balance — 0
2. On Order — 0
3. Total Stock   24 issued 3/19 — 0
4. O.R.P. (III. line 3b) — 40
5. Difference
   a. Total under ORP (line 4-3) - _____
   b. Total over ORP (line 3-4) + _____
6. If the difference under or over, (5a or b above) is within 10% (±) of the O.R.P. (4 above) follow this general rule: (Q) place a requisition for the E.O.Q.(*) (II. line 5) and schedule delivery for the E.D.T. (III. line (F)) in this case.

_____ days from today's date _____

Equals order schedule date [3/28/58] Short date

7. If a positive difference and the difference (5b above) is greater than 10% (±) do not place a requisition now. Wait until new O.R.P. is reached and recalculate.

8. If a negative difference and the difference (5a above) is greater than 10% (±) place the requisition for the E.O.Q. (II. line 5) and calculate the length of time total stock (3 above) will last.

$\left(\frac{\text{Size Dem.}}{\text{(III. 3 (U))}} \right)$ _ _ _

X $\left(\frac{\text{Dem./Day}}{\text{(III. 1 (S))}} \right)$ Days Total Stock Will Last

(Units/Day)_____) _ _ _ _ _ (Line 3)   Total Stock

Refer to EDT (III. line 1 (F) and schedule requisition for the shortest time. In this case.

_____ days from today's date _____

± Equals Order Schedule Date [   ]

Subject to change based upon local policy.

Ø See operating procedure (Part IV. Sec. 7A) for exception.

* If the new order quantity plus the total (3 above) does not exceed the O.R.P. (4 above) place an additional requisition(s) for the economical order quantity and schedule as required.

Subject to Quantity Discount	If special information is considered, check here and record on other side.
[ ] YES [ ] NO	[ ]

Ordering & Storage Limitations, etc.	Minimum Quantities
[ ] YES [ ] NO	[ ] YES [ ] NO

Work Sheet By & Date	Reviewed By & Date

and 54 dozen the quarter before. The clerk located the dollar value (standard cost) of the most recent quarter on the left side of the table ($147), moved across that line to the column corresponding to the value of gremlets used in the last half year ($242), and read off the estimated future quarterly requirements ($133). The alternative method for estimating future activity was used when only three months' activity was known, or when a definite trend was anticipated. In such cases, instead of using the table to weight past activity, the clerk applied a percentage rate of change, not to exceed ±25 percent.

In transferring the indicated quarterly requirements from section I to section II, a clerk in the Able division made the first of the two special adjustments by the application of a factor of .6 to the indicated requirements ($133), thereby reducing them to the $80 shown on line 1 of section II. The factor had been established at .75 by the division manager sometime before 1957 and was changed to .6 late that year. By changing this factor, the division manager could reduce or increase across-the-board inventories of both purchased and manufactured parts.

In section II of the work sheet, the quarterly requirements are converted into an economical ordering quantity with the aid of the order-quantity table. In this table, two constants were combined with the estimated requirements— the incremental cost of handling an additional order and the inventory carrying charge. The order cost used by the Able division was a constant of $3.14 for outside orders, but for manufactured parts it varied with the cost of machine setup. The carrying charge was 9 percent of the average value of the inventory; this covered the cost of capital tied up—considered to be about 4.5 percent—and the cost of insurance, inventory taxes, and obsolescence. When quarterly requirements were $80 worth of gremlets, the table said that $149 worth should be ordered, or 84 dozen. This, then, was the economical order quantity for gremlets if the future requirements were expected to be only 60 percent of past requirements.

In determining what the actual order would be, the inventory control supervisor applied the second special adjustment, ranging from 0 to 75 percent or more. He based this on his judgment of what would be needed and the speed of delivery. In special situations, he asked the advice of his superior, the superintendent of production, and on rare occasions the decision actually was made by the division manager. In this particular case, the economical order quantity of 84 dozen gremlets was revised downward to 75 dozen because the division manager had made a general request that inventory be reduced. The remainder of the work sheet concerned the order review point and scheduling of the order.

A second work sheet was used for making an analysis of quantity discounts when they were available. Exhibit 2 shows a copy of a work sheet filled out for widgets, of which the division used 21,000 each year. The economical order quantity for widgets as calculated on the order quantity work sheet was 1,500 at 19 cents each. One half-cent per unit could be saved if orders

Exhibit 2

INVENTORY CONTROL WORK SHEET
Quantity Discount Analysis

				DWG. & ITEM PART OR STYLE NO.	PDS	UNIT MEAS.	DESCRIPTION		
				Widgets					
(A) ANNUAL REQUIREMENTS	21,000		UNITS	SUPPLIER					
					Staple Co.				
	(B) ORDER QUANTITY	(C) UNIT PRICE	(D) ORDERS PER YEAR (A ÷ B)	(E) MATERIAL COST PER YR. (A X C)	(F) DECREASED MATERIAL COST (IE - IIE)	(G) ADDITIONAL ORDERING & CARRYING COSTS (FROM TABLE)	(H) DECREASE OR INCREASE IN COST (G - F)		
I E.O.Q. DATA	1,500	.19	14	3990.00	XXXXX	XXXXXXX	XXXXXX		
II DISCOUNT SCHEDULE 1.	5,000	.185	4	3885.00	105.00	50.20	54.80		
2.									
3.									
4.									
5.									

III COST REDUCTION AND RETURN ON ADDITIONAL INVESTMENT	6.	COST REDUCTION -	LARGEST NEGATIVE VALUE IN COLUMN (H)		-$ 54.80
	7.	ADDITIONAL INVESTMENT -	DISCOUNT QTY. 5,000 X DISCOUNT PRICE .185 / 2 E.O.Q. -1500 X STANDARD PRICE .19		-$ 320.00
	8.	RETURN ON ADDITIONAL INVESTMENT -	COST RED. X 100 / ADD. INVEST.		- 17%
APPROVALS		PURCHASING	DATE	INVENTORY CONTROL	DATE

of 5,000 were placed, making a total annual saving of $105. From this saving was subtracted the net increase in ordering and carrying costs, which was taken from a table, leaving a net increase or decrease in cost as a result of the larger orders. In the example, $54.80 is the net cost reduction, which is a 17 percent return on the $320 average increase in investment.

Whether 17 percent was a sufficient return to prompt the ordering of larger quantities depended in the Able division on other related factors. The inventory control supervisor who made the decision considered general business conditions, the time required to use up the larger order, the specialization of the particular part, and any general directives made by the division manager concerning inventory levels. A return below 15 percent was probably never acceptable, more than 20 percent was required in most instances, and any quantity discount yielding 25–30 percent or more usually was taken, though each case was judged individually. In the example shown, 17 percent was considered not sufficient, both because it was on the borderline of acceptability and because the division manager had requested a general reduction in inventories.

The level of purchased and manufactured parts inventory in the Able division varied with changes in rate of consumption and purchase. If the rules for calculating economical order quantity were adhered to, inventory levels increased with usage; and for all items whose annual requirements were above $4.36,[1] the rate of inventory change was less than the rate of usage change. Thus, an increase in sales yielding the same percentage profit on sales would, under strict application of the rules, provide a higher return on investment. However, application of the two adjustments in determining economical quantities destroyed this relationship. In times of anticipated downturn, the adjustments tended to accelerate inventory reduction; in times of expanding sales, relaxing the adjustments tended to accelerate the buying and production of parts. Thus, the division manager, by setting the first adjustment factor and the general tone of the second adjustment, controlled the level of his parts inventory with considerable flexibility.

Inventory, Floor Stocks (about 4 Percent of Total Investment)

Floor stock inventory consisted of parts and components being worked on and assembled. Items became part of the floor stock inventory when they were requisitioned from the storage areas, or when delivered directly to the production floor. Pumps were worked on individually, so that lot size was not a factor to be considered. Mr. Allen could do little to control the level of floor stock inventory, except to see that there was no excess of parts piled around the production area.

Inventory, Finished Goods (2 Percent of Total Investment)

As a rule, pumps were made to order and for immediate shipment. Finished goods inventory consisted of those few pumps on which shipment was delayed. Control of this investment was a matter of keeping it low by shipping the pumps as fast as possible.

Land, Buildings, and Machinery (47 Percent of Total Investment)

Since the Able division's fixed assets, stated at gross cost, comprised 47 percent of total assets at the end of 1957, the control of this particular group of assets was extremely important. Changes in the level of these investments depended on retirements and additions, the additions being entirely covered by the capital budgeting program.

Diversified Products Corporation's capital budgeting procedures were described in a planning manual. The planning sequence was as follows:

1. Headquarters forecasts economic conditions.   (March)
2. The divisions plan long-term objectives.   (June)
3. Supporting programs are submitted.   (September)   These are plans for specific actions, such as sales plans, advertising programs, and cost-reduction pro-

---

[1] If ordering costs were $3.14 per order, and carrying costs were 9 percent of average inventory, and the average inventory was considered to be one-half of the ordering quantity, then average inventory when economical-size orders were made equaled $4.175 \sqrt{A}$, where A is the annual requirements in dollars. By differentiating this equation, it can be found that average inventory increased faster than A until A was equal to $4.36; thereafter, average inventory increased more slowly.

grams, and include the facilities program which is the capital expenditure request. The planning manual states under the heading, "General Approach in the Development of a Coordinated Supporting Program," this advice:

Formulation and evaluation of a supporting program for each product line can generally be improved if projects are classified by purpose. The key objective of all planning is return on assets, a function of margin and turnover. These ratios are, in turn, determined by the three factors in the business equation— volume, costs, and assets. All projects, therefore, should be directed primarily at one of the following:

> To increase volume.
> To reduce costs and expenses.
> To minimize assets.

4. Annual objective is submitted. (November 11, by 8:00 A.M.) The annual objective states projected sales, costs, expenses, profits, and cash expenditures and receipts, and shows pro forma balance sheets and income statements.

Mr. Allen was "responsible for the division's assets and for provision for the growth and expansion of the division." Growth referred to the internal refinements of product design and production methods as well as to the cost-reduction programs. Expansion involved a 5- or 10-year program, including about two years for construction.

In the actual capital expenditure request there were four kinds of facilities proposals:

1. Cost-reduction projects, which were self-liquidating investments. Reduction in labor costs was usually the largest source of the savings, which were stated in terms of the liquidation period and the rate of return.
2. Necessity projects. These included replacement of worn-out machinery, technical changes to meet competition, and facilities for the safety and comfort of the workers.
3. Product-improvement projects.
4. Expansion projects.

Justification of the cost-reduction proposals was based on a comparison of the estimated rate of return (estimated return before taxes divided by gross investment) with the 20 percent standard, as specified by headquarters. If the project was considered desirable and yet showed a return of less than 20 percent, it had to be justified on other grounds and was included in the necessities category. Cost-reduction proposals made up about 60 percent of the 1958 capital expenditure budget, and in earlier years these proposals had accounted for at least 50 percent. Very little of Able division's 1958 capital budget had been allocated specifically for product improvement and none for expansion, so that most of the remaining 40 percent was to be used for necessity projects. Thus, a little over half of Able division's capital expenditure was justified primarily on the estimated rate of return on the investment. The remainder, having advantages that could not be stated in terms of the rate of return, was justified on other grounds.

Mr. Allen was free to include what he wanted in his capital budget request, and for the three years that he had been division manager his requests had always been granted. However, no large expansion projects had been included in the capital budget requests of the last three years. Most of the capital expenditures had been for cost-reduction projects, and the remainder were for necessities. Annual additions had approximately equaled annual retirements.

Since Mr. Allen could authorize expenditures of up to $100,000 per project for purposes approved by the board, there was, in fact, some flexibility in his choice of projects after the budget had been approved by higher management. Not only could he schedule the order of expenditure, but in some circumstances he could substitute unforeseen projects of a similar nature. If top management approved $50,000 for miscellaneous cost-reduction projects, Mr. Allen could spend this on the projects he considered most important, whether or not they were specifically described in his original budget request.

For the corporation as a whole, about one quarter of the capital expenditure was for projects of under $100,000, which could be authorized for expenditure by the division managers. This proportion was considered by top management to be about right; if, however, it rose much above this fraction, the $100,000 dividing line would probably be lowered.

QUESTIONS

1. For each asset category, discuss whether the basis of measurement used by the company is the best for the purpose of measuring divisional return on investment. If, in your opinion, it is not the best, suggest an improvement.

2. Comment on the general usefulness of the return-on-investment measure. Could it be made a more effective device?

Case 8–3

Long Manufacturing Company

The Long Manufacturing Company, with 1956 sales of just over $100 million, operated six plants which produced different but related products for sale to other companies or consumers. Each plant was operated independently by a plant manager whose performance was judged by several factors, one of the most important being the return the plant made on the investment that had been allocated to it.

The investment figure used in the calculation had, since the system was started, included all the investment over which each plant manager had control. Until the spring of 1957, two classes of investment were not included in the division's investment base—headquarters investment and research investment. The first was small (.2 percent of the company's total net investment), since most of the headquarters facilities were rented. Until recently, research investment had also been small, but by the spring of 1957 had grown to just over 1 percent of the company's total net investment, and it was expected that more money would be invested in research facilities in the near future.

In late 1956, the president of Long Manufacturing Company asked that all the company's investment be distributed in some way to all the operating divisions. This would, he stated, make the reported return on investment by the plants more realistic as indicators of how well the company as a whole was doing.

The recommended method of distribution of investment was to be based initially on the allocation of expenses. Distributed investment would bear the same relationship to total investment as allocated expenses bore to total expenses. If a division had 20 percent of total research expenses allocated to it, it would carry 20 percent of total research investment. The allocation of expenses for both research and headquarters activities was, in turn, according to a simple average of three weighting factors: net realization or sales less freight and discounts; net book value of the property assigned to the plant;

and payroll or total salaries and wages. Thus, if a division had 10 percent of the company's total net realization, 9 percent of total net book value of property, and 14 percent of the directly assignable payroll, the division would be allocated 11 percent of the headquarters and research expenses. It would also now be allocated 11 percent of the research and headquarters investment. One exception to the allocation of research expenses by formula occurred in the case of expenses in the nature of technical service costs. These were charged directly to the plant for which the work was done. In theory, this exception had seemed reasonable; in practice, however, the line separating technical service from research was difficult to define.

A memorandum was issued to all plants early in 1957, explaining the forthcoming allocation of headquarters and research investment. The memorandum made the following statements about the allocation of research investment.

Allocation of Total Gross Investment to Plants

Currently, the plants do not include in their operating investment base any of the facilities that serve the entire company, e.g., research. Inclusion of these facilities will mean that the operating return on investment should now measure the performance of the total assets in the company.

Recommended Method of Allocation of Research Investment to Plants

Distribution on the Basis of Research Expenses. This makes use of readily available figures and adds a measure of flexibility, for distribution depends on the annual budgeted research expenses. This incorporates a measure of their value received from research during the year. Over a period of time, allocation of the research gross investment will be improved as more precise expense figures are developed.

Soon after this memorandum was issued, the financial analysis manager received from one of the division managers a letter which said, in part:

. . . I question the advisability of allocating research investment to the divisions. As you know, we exercise no direct control over research expenditures; consequently, we are unable to control the effect of increased research investment on our return. It seems to me the return on investment concept will be a more meaningful tool to the divisions if our investment base includes only those items over which we have some degree of control. . . .

The financial manager knew that though it was the company's research director who actually planned what was to be worked on by his research staff, the plant managers did have some influence on the research director's decisions through periodic discussions with him. Furthermore, two of the plant managers were on the board of directors, and in directors meetings they could exercise some influence over the choice of research projects.

With these facts in mind, the financial analysis manager wrote an answer to the plant manager's letter. This read, in part, as follows:

Letter to a Division Manager from Financial Analysis Manager

. . . The major item that had not formerly been carried by the plants in their investment base is the investment in research. This is now included so that returns will be based upon the *total* investment in the company. We do not believe that the company could long exist without research. And we believe that the plants and products they produce benefit from the research and should, therefore, carry their share of such investment.

Your point on exercising direct control over research investment is well taken. However, I do not feel that this is an issue, and I do question the implication that a plant manager has no degree of control over research.

Return on investment is an anlytical tool that we have tried to make uniformly applicable to as many general and specific problems as possible. We have attempted to make it equally applicable in measuring past performance and providing a guide for current problems, as well as in giving a basis for decisions affecting the future. It is not a perfect yardstick, but it does come close.

There is no reason why this tool cannot be designed by plant management to serve its particular purposes at any level within the plant. I am thinking here of plant managerial control and would be glad to work with you on this. . . .

QUESTION

Assume that you are administrative assistant to the president, and that he has asked you to comment on the question(s) raised in the case. What would you say to him?

Case 8–4

The Cheetah Division
Cougar

The Cheetah Division of the Multi-National Motors Corporation designs and sells Cheetah automobiles and parts to dealers throughout the United States and Europe. The division is responsible for designing, engineering, and marketing its products but the automobiles are manufactured by other divisions of the company and the Cheetah Division buys its automobiles from the Assembly Division.

Each division of Multi-National Motors is responsible for earning a return on its investment. Investment in Multi-National is calculated as follows:

Cash: 10 percent of the cost of sales.
Receivables
Inventories } Average end-of-the-month actual balances.
Fixed assets: Average actual gross book value at end of the month.

Profits are the accounted profits, calculated in accordance with the company's accounting system. Because of its relatively low asset base (few fixed assets) and its high profit potential, the Cheetah Automotive Division had a profit objective of 45 percent after taxes.

INVENTORY CONTROL PROBLEM

In addition to marketing automobiles, the Cheetah Division is responsible for supplying repair and replacement parts and accessories to its dealers throughout the country. This requires an extensive warehouse system since parts are supplied for automobiles up to 15 years old. The system handles over 20,000 different parts, with annual sales in excess of $25 million.

In 1975, the corporation established an operations research group, with responsibility for reviewing inventory control procedures throughout the company. In carrying out their assignment, members from the group visited the Cheetah Division.

An important inventory control problem was one involving buying current model parts at the end of a model year. At the end of each model year, any parts to be discontinued with the new model became past model service parts. A past model service part was usually much more expensive to produce (and consequently buy) than a current model part because of set-up time and the short length of the run on the past model parts. For example, at the end of the 1975 model year, the front fenders were to be changed. During regular production, fenders are run continuously over an automated line. There is no set-up cost and production is very efficient. Consequently, the manufacturing cost of a 1975 fender is low during the 1975 model year. Once the part has been discontinued, however, the costs of production can become quite high. It is necessary to pull the dies out of storage, clean them, place them in presses, try them out (usually involving spoiling a certain amount of material) and, then, run off the required number of parts without any automation. Thus, the cost of a past model service part can be several times higher than what it was as a current model part.

As a result of this cost differential, it is usual to order, at the end of a model year, a relatively large supply of those parts that are to be discontinued. A formula has been developed that provides the economic order quantity. This formula determines the point where the added cost of carrying the inventory is equal to the cost savings from buying at current model prices. The formula is quite complex and need not be considered here. An important feature of the formula, however, is that the cost of carrying inventory includes a return on the capital tied up in the inventory. The operation research group reviewed the formula and agreed that it was a reasonable method for calculating the economic order quantity. The group, however, were surprised to find that the Cheetah Division used a 45 percent cost for carrying inventory. Other divisions used between 5 and 10 percent in their inventory decision formulas and, currently, the corporation had over a half billion dollars invested in government securities that were earning less than 5 percent before taxes (2½ percent after taxes).

The operations research group raised two questions concerning the economic order quantity formula:

1. They questioned whether 45 percent was not much too high a percentage for the capital charge of carrying inventories. Their estimate was that it should be no more than 10 percent.
2. They questioned the fact that the Cheetah Division used their purchase price to calculate the investment in the inventory. The company's out-of-pocket cost of most parts was between 50 percent and 60 percent of the purchase price.

The controller of the Cheetah Division met with the operations research group and told them bluntly that he had no intention of changing the formula. This formula, including charging 45 percent on his purchase price for carrying inventory, was the one that optimized his rate of return. If he followed their suggestions, he would be lowering the rate of return that his division earned. He stated that, if it was really to the benefit of the company for him to use a 10 percent cost of investment on 60 percent of his purchase price, he would be glad to comply, if he (the Cheetah Division) were given the benefit of the increased profit that the company would earn. Otherwise, he would continue to do as he was instructed and that was to maximize the division's return on investment.

THE PARTS WAREHOUSE PROBLEM

In 1974 the Cheetah Division was in the process of building two new parts warehouses on the West Coast. At that time, the Sparrow Division of Multi-National requested that Cheetah provide some space in those warehouses for Sparrow parts. Sparrow was a much smaller division than Cheetah and could not justify economically a new warehouse. The location on the West Coast, however, of two new supply points would improve the effectiveness of their distribution system. Sparrow asked for space equal to about 10 percent of the total.

After the warehouses had been completed and both the Cheetah and Sparrow parts systems were placed in operation, the question of charging for the service came up. Cheetah proposed that Sparrow pay a proportionate share of the cost of running the warehouse plus a return on their proportionate share of the investment. The calculation was made as follows:

```
10% of cost of operating warehouses ......$ 20,000
10% of the investment in warehouses:
   $200,000
   90% of $200,000 ...................... 180,000
      Total annual charges ............. $200,000
```

The Sparrow Division was astounded with the charge. It was several times higher than the highest price for available leased warehouse space. They agreed with the $20,000 but disagreed violently with paying $180,000 for the return on investment. The Cheetah Division pointed out that they had invested $200,000 at the request of Sparrow and that they had to earn $180,000 before taxes on this investment in order to earn 45 percent after taxes. The Sparrow Division said that they could lease space anywhere on the West Coast for a fraction of Cheetah's charge and that was what they proposed to do. They stated that Cheetah may have a 45 percent return but Sparrow was lucky to break even *without the exorbitant rental.*

Case 8–5

Antol Company

The Antol Company consisted of a central corporate office and 20 operating divisions scattered throughout the United States. Each operating division produced and marketed a line of products unrelated to those of the other divisions. There was little interaction among the divisions. Personnel were moved from one division to another only in exceptional circumstances. Interdivisional transfers of products were insignificant.

Although primary responsibility for managing a division rested with the division president, the central corporate management made basic policy decisions, provided permanent capital for the divisions, and approved capital expenditures, long-term financing, and salaries of division presidents and vice-presidents. Major tools of top management control of the activities of the divisions were the balance sheet and income statement prepared monthly by each division. The corporate controller regularly summarized and analyzed these financial statements in a report prepared for the executive committee. In this report, he described the causes of significant deviations from the budgets, and showed the percentage return on net worth for each division.

This percentage was viewed as a key indication of divisional performance. It was found by dividing divisional earnings by divisional net worth. Divisional earnings was defined as the net earnings of the division after all charges properly allocable or attributable to the division, including depreciation, an administrative service charge equal to 1 percent of net sales of the division (which for all divisions was about equal to the cost of the central corporate organization), plus a net worth capital charge equal to .5 percent per month of divisional net worth. Divisional net worth was defined as net total assets less total liabilities as shown on the divisional balance sheet, Exhibit 1. For the purpose of determining the net total assets, cash was fixed at an amount agreed on between the division and the corporate management as necessary for day-to-day operation; inventories were valued at the lower of Fifo cost or market; and property, plant, and equipment were included at

374

Exhibit 1

FORM OF DIVISIONAL BALANCE SHEET
ASSETS

	End of this Month	Beginning of Year
Current Assets:		
Cash		
Accounts and notes receivable, less: Reserves		
Inventories		
Raw material and supplies		
Work in process and finished goods		
Other		
Inventory reserves		
Total Inventories		
Prepaid and deferred expenses		
Other current assets		
Total Current Assets		
Notes receivable, noncurrent		
Property, Plant, and Equipment:		
Land and buildings		
Machinery and equipment		
Other property		
Less: Reserves for depreciation and amortization..		
Property, plant, and equipment, Net		
Other assets		
Total Assets		

LIABILITIES AND NET WORTH

Current Liabilities:		
Notes payable, banks		
Current portion of long-term debt		
Accounts payable		
Accrued liabilities		
Accrued federal taxes on income		
Other current liabilities		
Total Current Liabilities		
Long-term debt		
Other liabilities and deferred income		
Total Liabilities		
Net worth		
Total Liabilities and Net Worth		

net book value after allowance for depreciation. All divisions used the unit, double-declining-balance method of depreciation.

QUESTIONS

1. Assuming that Antol top management wished to calculate one overall ratio that related earnings to investment, as a measure of a division manager's performance, do you think the formula described above is probably as good as any? If not, in what respects should it be changed?

2. If you need more information before definitely recommending a change, what information would you seek? Why?

3. Do you think top management was basically correct in regarding percentage return on net worth (as possibly modified by your answer to Question 1) as an important figure? Is some other single indicator of performance even more important?

4. Antol Company paid a substantial bonus to division managements. The bonus was based in part on a calculated measure of performance, but the bonus so calculated was subject to change in accordance with the judgment of corporate top management. To the extent that a calculated figure is used, would you recommend the percentage return on net worth as the best figure to use? Presumably, the bonus would be calculated on the basis of the excess of the actual return over some agreed-on budgeted return. If you think some other figure would be preferable, please describe it.

Case 8–6

Lemfert Company

Lemfert Company was a large manufacturing company organized into divisions, each with responsibility for earning a satisfactory return on its investment. Division managers had considerable autonomy in carrying out this responsibility. Some divisions fabricated parts; others—here called end-item divisions—assembled these parts, together with purchased parts, into finished products and marketed the finished products. Transfer prices were used in connection with the transfer of parts among the various fabricating divisions and from the fabricating divisions to the end-item divisions. Wherever possible, these transfer prices were the lowest prices charged by outside manufacturers for the same or comparable items, with appropriate adjustments for inbound freight, volume, and similar factors.

Parts that were not similar to those manufactured by outside companies were called type K items. In most fabricating divisions, these items constituted only 5 to 10 percent of total volume. In division F, however, approximately 75 percent of total volume was accounted for by type K items. Division F manufactured 10 such items for various end-item divisions; they were less than 5 percent of the total cost of any one of these end-item divisions. The procedure for arriving at the transfer price for type K items is described below.

First, a tentative transfer price was calculated by the value analysis staff of the corporate purchasing department and was submitted to the two divisions involved for their consideration. This price was supposed to be based on the estimated costs of an efficient producer plus a profit margin. An "efficient producer" was considered to be one conducting its purchasing and using modern equipment in a manner that could reasonably be expected of the company's principal competitors.

The material cost portion of the total cost was based on current competitive price levels. Direct labor cost was supposed to reflect efficient processing on modern equipment. Overhead cost represented an amount that could be expected of an efficient producer using modern equipment. Depreciation expense, expenditures on special tooling, and a standard allowance for administrative expense were included in the overhead figure.

The profit margin was equal to the divisional profit objective applied to the cost of the assets employed to produce the product in question. Assets employed was the sum of the following items:

Cash and receivables—18 per cent of the total manufacturing cost.

Inventories—the value of the optimum inventory size required at standard volume.

Fixed assets—the depreciated book value (but not less than one-half original cost) of assets used to fabricate the part, including a fair share of buildings and other general assets, but excluding standby and obsolete facilities.

The percentage used for cash and receivables was based on studies of the cash and receivable balances of the principal outside manufacturers of parts similar to those manufactured in the fabricating divisions. The standard volume was an estimate of the volume that the plants should *normally* be expected to produce, which was not necessarily the same as current volume or projected volume for the next year.

For an average division, the budgeted profit objective was 20 percent of assets employed, but there were variations among divisions. The divisional budgeted profit objective multiplied by the assets employed, as calculated above, gave the profit margin for the item. This profit was added to the cost to arrive at the suggested transfer price, which then was submitted to the two divisions. If either the buying or the selling division believed that the price thus determined was unfair, it first attempted to negotiate a mutually satisfactory price. If the parties were unable to agree, they submitted the dispute to the controller for arbitration. Either party might appeal the results of this arbitration to the executive vice-president.

QUESTIONS

1. Are these the best transfer price practices for the Lemfert Company? If not, how should they be revised?

2. For what types of companies would the revised policy not be best? Why?

3. Do you think the attempt to measure profitability in division F is worthwhile? If not, how would you measure performance in this division?

Schoppert Company

Mr. P. A. Franken, Controller of Schoppert, was considering the appropriateness of available means for appraising the annual operating results for each of the company's product lines. Schoppert Gereedschapfabrieken, N.V., located near Leiden in the Netherlands, manufactured a variety of hand tools, such as wrenches, screwdrivers, chisels, and so forth. The company produced several hundred different products, but from the point of view of sales and production these could be grouped into five quite different product lines or groups.

Mr. Franken was interested in applying the concept of return on investment to the evaluation of the company's individual product lines. He stated his reasons for this as follows:

When a company sells a number of different product groups there is a danger that the relative position of each product group in the total is judged by the profit made on the turnover of each separate group. There is a tendency to judge the yield of each group by comparing these percentages. In doing so, one forgets that the first purpose of a business is to make a profit on its employed capital, and that making a profit on the turnover is only a means to that purpose. As some of our product groups for a given turnover need a much higher employed capital than others, I think it is necessary to take these differences into account, by showing the profit in each product group as a percentage of the employed capital.

PRODUCT-LINE PROFIT

The company regularly prepared product-line income statements based on what was known as a cost price calculation. The profit for each product line was obtained by deducting product costs from turnover (sales) for the product line. There were four elements of cost in the product line income statements, as follows:

1. *Variable cost.* These included raw materials, direct labor, paint, solder, and the like. These were standard costs which were based on time studies,

product specifications, and so forth, and could be traced directly to individual products. They tended to vary more or less proportionately with volume of production. These variable costs accounted for about 74 percent of total costs at normal volume levels.

2. *Direct fixed costs.* These included costs of operating and maintaining factory buildings (allocated on a square meter basis), costs of maintenance of machinery, machine depreciation, interest, cleaning, and so forth. All of these except the building costs could be readily traced to small groups of products. They were allocated to individual products on the basis of machine hours. These costs accounted for about 12 percent of total costs at normal volume levels.

3. *Plant costs.* These included such things as maintenance, operation, and depreciation of forklift trucks, salaries, and wages of supervisory and clerical staffs, and maintenance of office buildings. These costs were allocated to product lines on a value-added basis; that is, the total of the costs included in groups 1 and 2 above, less the costs of raw material. At usual operating levels they amounted to about 8 percent of total costs.

4. *Head office expenses.* These included wages and salaries of head office personnel and of management, maintenance and depreciation of head office buildings and equipment, and laboratory expense. They were allocated to products on the basis of the ratio of these costs to the total of costs in groups 1, 2, and 3, including raw material. They usually amounted to about 6 percent of all other costs.

These cost calculations provided a basis for overall evaluation of product lines and for selling price calculations. For control purposes the company had a system of manufacturing expense budgets and standards for the variable and traceable costs in each department.

PRODUCT-LINE INVESTMENT

Evaluation and appraisal of the results of each of the product lines was traditionally made by comparing this profit with sales. Mr. Franken, for reasons given earlier, felt that this product-line profit should be compared with

Exhibit 1

ANALYSIS OF PRODUCT-LINE PROFITS

	Product Line					
	A	B	C	D	E	Total
Investment	fl. 56.0	fl. 11.8	fl. 1.6	fl. 1.0	fl. 0.6	fl. 71
Sales	118.0	18.5	3.3	1.2	1.0	142
Profits	4.5	.6	.4	.2	.2	5.5
Profit as percent of investment ..	8.0%	5.1%	25.0%	20.0%	33.3%	7.7%
Profits as percent of sales	3.8%	3.2%	12.1%	16.7%	20.0%	3.9%

Monetary amounts are in millions of Dutch guilders.

the investment necessary to support production and sale of the product line.

In order to do this it was necessary to determine what the investment in each product line actually was. Mr. Franken made an analysis of product-line investments, which he regarded only as a preliminary step. His procedures are described below and the results, for the five product groups, are shown in Exhibit 1.

Current Assets

In the case of current assets, it was possible to trace the investment in stocks (inventories) directly to the product groups. Accounts receivable could also be traced to the product groups which gave rise to them. Mr. Franken deducted accounts payable (also traceable to product lines) from accounts receivable in determining product-line investments.

Mr. Franken felt that it was not possible to relate cash to individual product groups; that the amount of cash required by any particular product group could not be determined accurately. Consequently, he excluded cash from his calculations of product-line investments.

Fixed Assets

In dealing with fixed assets, Mr. Franken used replacement value less accumulated depreciation rather than net book value based on historical cost. He felt that the use of historical cost would make it impossible to compare departments with each other if some utilized older machinery purchased when price levels were lower, while others worked with machinery which had a much higher cost as a result of price inflation.

Mr. Franken initially used insured values as an estimate of replacement value, but he expected to develop a system of price indices which would permit a more precise determination of replacement value. From insured value an allowance of 40 percent (of insured value) was deducted to give an approximation of replacement value less accumulated depreciation. In the case of depreciation, as in the case of replacement value, Mr. Franken looked forward to the development of more refined procedures for determining the amounts involved.

Most buildings, machinery, and equipment could be traced directly to individual product groups. In a great many cases, the machinery used by Schoppert was quite highly specialized and was used only for manufacturing certain specific products.

In the case of buildings and other facilities utilized by more than one product group and in the case of such things as the company's head office and its research laboratory, the problem was considerably more complex. Mr. Franken simply allocated these costs to product lines on the basis of the costs which were traceable to the product lines.

The value of current assets (less accounts payable) and of machinery and equipment traced directly to product lines amounted to about 90 percent of

total assets (not including cash and less accounts payable and depreciation).
Thus the allocated portion of product-line investment represented about 10
percent of the total.

QUESTIONS

1. What were Mr. Franken's objectives in designing the new product-line
income statements?

2. Are the statements likely to meet these objectives in their present form
or would you suggest some improvements?

Case 8–8

General Electric Company (B)

In early May 1974, Mr. Standley Hall,* Manager of the Business Analysis and Cost Accounting Operation in the Comptroller's Department of General Electric Company (GE), was trying to identify and evaluate alternative procedures for assigning interest expense to the operating components of the company. His investigation had been instigated by Mr. R. H. Smith, Chairman and Chief Executive Officer, when, at the end of 1973, Mr. Smith had discovered that the total amount of corporate interest expense was substantially under-liquidated in terms of assignment to operating units. The problem had wound up on Mr. Hall's desk for analysis and recommendation because he was the staff executive responsible for the design of all internal financial measurements used within the company.

BACKGROUND

In 1974, GE was the largest diversified industrial organization in the world. (Summary financial data are presented in Exhibit 1.) In the early 1950s, as sales volume passed the three billion dollar level and the prospects for continued growth were good, management had adopted a decentralization philosophy. The corporation was reorganized into product departments, each one small enough and cohesive enough to be analogous to a separate business and headed by a general manager who was responsible for running it in a manner consistent with overall corporate objectives.

By 1974, there were approximately 160 product departments in GE. Department general managers reported to division general managers, numbering about 40, who were also vice presidents of the company. Division managers reported to one of ten vice presidents and group executives who, in turn, reported to one of three vice-chairmen and executive officers. The

---

* The names of individual executives in this case have been disguised.

Exhibit 1

GENERAL ELECTRIC COMPANY

Ten Year Financial Summary

(in millions of dollars)

	1973	1972	1971	1970	1969	1968	1967	1966	1965	1964
Sales of products and services	$11,575.3	$10,239.5	$9,425.3	$8,726.7	$8,448.0	$8,381.6	$7,741.2	$7,177.3	$6,213.6	$5,319.2
Operating margin	954.8	814.7	737.0	548.9	486.6	647.8	640.9	632.0	645.5	388.6
Interest and other financial charges	(126.9)	(106.7)	(96.9)	(101.4)	(78.1)	(70.5)	(62.9)	(39.9)	(27.4)	(21.2)
Net earnings after taxes	585.1	530.0	471.8	328.5	278.0	357.1	361.4	338.9	355.1	219.6
Earnings per common share (a)	3.21	2.91	2.60	1.81	1.54	1.98	2.00	1.88	1.97	1.22
Dividends declared per common share (a)	1.50	1.40	1.38	1.30	1.30	1.30	1.30	1.30	1.20	1.10
Earnings as a percentage of sales	5.1%	5.2%	5.0%	3.8%	3.3%	4.3%	4.7%	4.7%	5.7%	4.1%
Earned on share owners' equity	18.1%	18.0%	17.6%	13.2%	11.5%	15.4%	16.5%	16.2%	18.0%	11.7%
Cash dividends declared	$ 272.9	$ 254.8	$ 249.7	$ 235.4	$ 235.2	$ 234.8	$ 234.2	$ 234.6	$ 216.7	$ 197.7
Shares outstanding—average (in thousands) (a)	182,501	182,112	181,684	181,114	180,965	180,651	180,266	180,609	180,634	179,833
Market price range per share (a)	75⅞	73	66½	47¼	49⅛	50¼	58	60	60⅛	46¾
(b)	55	58¼	46½	30⅛	37	40⅛	41¼	40	45½	39⅜
Price/earnings ratio range	24–17	25–20	26–18	26–17	32–24	25–20	29–21	32–21	31–23	39–32
Plant and equipment additions	$ 598.6	$ 435.9	$ 553.1	$ 581.4	$ 530.6	$ 514.7	$ 561.7	$ 484.9	$ 332.9	$ 237.7
Depreciation	334.0	314.3	273.6	334.7	351.3	300.1	280.4	233.6	188.4	170.3
Employees—average worldwide	388,000	369,000	363,000	397,000	410,000	396,000	385,000	376,000	333,000	308,000
—average U.S.	304,000	292,000	291,000	310,000	318,000	305,000	296,000	291,000	258,000	243,000
Cash	296.8	267.0	250.1	190.8	201.6	285.6	240.3	228.3	289.8	245.3
Marketable securities	25.3	27.3	35.9	15.0	127.7	87.7	96.8	100.3	353.3	365.7
Receivables and inventories	4,163.3	3,685.0	3,353.0	3,129.0	2,958.5	2,937.8	2,870.5	2,684.4	2,199.3	1,932.8
Total Current Assets	4,485.4	3,979.3	3,639.0	3,334.8	3,287.8	3,311.1	3,207.6	3,013.0	2,842.4	2,543.8
Short-term borrowings	665.2	439.4	569.8	658.1	340.7	280.6	266.9	286.3	120.6	120.6
Payables and accruals	2,827.2	2,430.3	2,270.6	1,992.2	2,026.0	1,823.7	1,710.5	1,596.9	1,446.2	1,218.3
Total Current Liabilities	3,492.4	2,869.7	2,840.4	2,650.3	2,366.7	2,104.3	1,977.4	1,883.2	1,566.8	1,338.9
Working Capital	993.0	1,109.6	798.6	684.5	921.1	1,206.8	1,230.2	1,129.8	1,275.6	1,204.9
Plant and equipment (net)	2,360.5	2,136.6	2,025.7	1,749.4	1,815.0	1,677.7	1,495.0	1,259.3	1,037.0	943.5
Investments and other asset	1,478.3	1,285.9	1,223.1	1,114.3	904.8	755.0	644.6	579.4	421.0	348.7
Long-term borrowings	917.2	947.3	787.3	573.5	673.3	749.1	724.1	476.5	364.1	320.8
Other liabilities	492.1	456.8	415.9	379.8	385.3	356.8	265.5	235.8	221.0	174.5
Minority interests	50.1	43.4	42.4	41.3	42.3	40.1	38.0	44.5	41.5	57.6
Stockholders equity	3,372.4	3,084.6	2,801.8	2,553.6	2,540.0	2,493.5	2,342.2	2,211.7	2,107.0	1,944.0
Prime interest rate range (c)	6–10	4½–6	5¼–6¾	6¾–8½	6¾–8½	6–6¾	5½–6	5–6	4½–5	4½

(a) Amounts have been adjusted for the two-for-one stock split in April 1971. (b) Represents high and low market price on New York Stock Exchange for each year. (c) Represents high and low rate charged by most commercial banks during the year.

vice-chairmen and Mr. Smith, collectively referred to as the Corporate
Executive Office, were assisted by six senior vice presidents who comprised
the Corporate Executive Staff. In addition, the Corporate Administrative
Staff consisted of about two dozen vice presidents with functional or technical responsibilities.

At the time of the reorganization, corporate management realized that
effective decentralization would require appropriate and comprehensive
measures of the performance of the operating units down to the product department level. A measurements project was established to design and install
a new set of internal operating reports (see the General Electric (A) case).
"Profitability" was identified as one of eight "key result areas" for which the
performance of a product department should be measured. Profitability was
to be measured in terms of "dollars of residual income," where residual income was defined as net income (after taxes) less a capital charge equal to
5 percent (after taxes) of the net assets assigned to the department. At about
this same time, the shareholders of GE approved a new incentive compensation plan: the total bonus pool each year would be 10 percent of corporate
net income after deducting 5 percent of total invested capital. The distribution of this pool among GE executives was not specified by formula.

As the new reporting system evolved in its early years, corporate management found it desirable to use two measures of the profitability of operating components, residual income as defined above and net income before
deducting the capital charge. In Mr. Hall's opinion, "Top management needs
to look at net income on a monthly basis because it measures what they are
responsible for and is reported to the stockholders quarterly and at the end
of the year. If corporate net income doesn't meet budgeted goals, top management needs to be able to identify the components that are responsible
for the variance."

IMPUTED INTEREST EXPENSE

"The new reporting system worked pretty well for the first ten years or
so," Mr. Hall continued, "but in the middle sixties the net amount of cor-
porate-level adjustments turned red. Up until then, other income, like dividends from investments, had about equaled net interest expense. But our rate
of growth was accelerating and, increasingly, we had to use debt as a source of
funds for expansion. Total borrowings have increased by more than a
billion dollars in the last ten years. Realizing that interest expense would
become a significant cost of doing business, we had to find a way to assign
it to the operating components so that their net income would continue to
approximate the corporate net income."

The approach we finally adopted in late 1967 was intended to reflect the situation we were coping with. Our businesses were growing faster than we could
generate funds internally to finance the growth. So we established January 1,

1966 as a retroactive starting point and told the department managers that, from that point on, there would be no more free money from the Treasurer's office. We referred to it as cash flow approach to financial management.

The imputed interest calculation was performed at the end of each month. Using the balance sheet maintained for each component, the change in the corporation's investment in the component was readily determinable. All cash was managed centrally in GE, so the component balance sheets contained only working capital items (receivables and inventories less payables and accruals) plus the net book value of plant and equipment. A component's monthly cash flow analysis typically showed two sources of cash: component net income and depreciation. The typical uses of cash were an increase in working capital and the cost of new investments in plant and equipment. The net difference of these four items represented cash that the component had provided to or drawn from the corporate treasury.

"In order to make the whole thing work," Mr. Hall went on, "we also had to assess dividends paid to stockholders as a use of funds at the component level. Not all our net income can be invested in financing expansion, only the retained earnings. The net effect was that a department manager would not be charged any imputed interest as long as he was able to finance his own growth out of his retained earnings plus the cash flow from depreciation. If he needed more funds, we'd provide them, but he'd have to pay interest on the excess. If he was throwing off more cash than he needed then he was really helping to finance other units, and we'd credit him with imputed interest income. The interest rate, either way, was a four-year rolling average of the actual cost of all money borrowed by the corporation."

The calculation of imputed interest was a little complex, so it took a while for all the general managers to understand it, and some of them complained that the starting date was arbitrary. But there's no question that it worked. First, over the next several years, this routine did succeed in assigning the increase in the corporate interest expense to the components. That made top management happy. Second, and probably more important, the general managers had to learn a lot about financial management. During the first five years after the routine was installed, working capital at the component level increased less than 10 percent, even though sales volume rose over 30 percent. That made top management even happier.

THE PROBLEM IN 1973

"The magnitude of the underliquidation in 1973," Mr. Hall said, "came as something of a surprise. The amount of net interest expense that we actually charged to the components was only about 55 percent of the amount that should have been liquidated. If we define the problem narrowly, then a simple variance analysis can explain the shortfall. There are two causes: the interest rate we use and the investment base to which it's applied. In 1973, the formula rate was 6 percent and that was also the prime rate at the start of the year. But the prime skyrocketed to 10 percent before the year was out and we've got a few hundred million dollars of bank debt and commercial paper that moves with the prime. Our actual average interest rate on short- and long-term debt in 1973 was about 7½ percent."

"The bigger cause of the variance, though, was in the deterioration of our investment base during recent years. The total increase in the company's investment in the operating components since the beginning of 1966 is about a billion dollars. During those years, however, we've launched a lot of new products and ventures, some of which have failed, and we've also discontinued some of our old product lines. The Comptroller adopted a policy a few years ago of 'forgiving' the cumulative investment in product lines that were abandoned; it didn't seem fair to continue to impute an interest expense to a defunct line of business. By 1973, such abandonments had wiped out about 30 percent of our base.

"Well," Mr. Hall continued, "the large, sudden underliquidation sure got Smith's attention. In discussions with my boss, Maurice Mott, the Comptroller, and his boss, Al Woods, the Vice President—Finance, we've decided that maybe we shouldn't define the problem narrowly as: How do we fix the formula to eliminate the variance? Given the magnitude of the problem, fixing the formula might involve bending it out of shape in any event. Instead, we've decided to use this problem as an opportunity to review the fundamental philosophy behind our imputed interest procedure and, perhaps, adopt a whole new approach. A problem like this can make people more receptive to a major change than would be feasible in the normal course of events, and there are some aspects of the current procedure that are troublesome, quite apart from the underliquidation.

"First, several of us think that charging interest as we do may make it harder to implement GE's broad strategy for continued growth. Mr. Smith has made the strategy quite explicit: The allocation of corporate resources must be biased in favor of our high-growth, high-potential, newer businesses even if that means a reduction in the resources available for our mature businesses that are growing more slowly. Making such allocation decisions is always tough, and one important criterion is the trend in the bottom line for each business; they look at the net income over the last three years and the forcast for the next three. One effect of the way that we imput interest expense is that it makes the net income of the mature businesses appear to be growing faster than it really is, and it dampens the apparent growth rate of our high-growth businesses.

"Another aspect of this same effect," Mr. Hall went on, "is the protection that imputed interest income provides for the net income of mature businesses. We're fortunate in having several highly profitable businesses that aren't growing very fast anymore so they have a substantial cash throwoff. Last year, the largest of these earned more than a million dollars of interest income, and that figure grows each year. Theoretically, the day might come when the imputed interest income of such a business will exceed its operating income. To the extent that there's a problem in that, it's compounded by the fact that our general managers tend to get new assignments every three or four years and a new man coming into such a business has two things going for him—a fine business and an annuity from prior cash flow—not just one."

ALTERNATIVE SOLUTIONS

"So," Mr. Hall said, "we're in the midst of a review of the whole procedure. Without being too academic about it, Al Woods, Maurie Mott and I have tried to identify the criteria that our recommendation to Smith should fulfill. First, the procedure should be as simple as possible, not just to facilitate computation but to make it easy for the general managers to understand. Second, the procedure should be effective in liquidating corporate interest expense into the components, although a modest over- or under-liquidation would be tolerable. Finally, the procedure should help to increase the awareness of our general managers about the major increase in the cost of borrowing money. Prime interest rates [inserted by the casewriter at the bottom of Exhibit 1] have really climbed and stand at 11 percent today. That may come down a little, but we think high rates are going to be with us for several years.

"At the moment, we're trying to conceptualize alternative procedures that might meet these criteria, focusing really on what investment base to use. We also have to decide on what rate to use and there's a nest of issues there—whether to use one rate or several different ones; whether the rate should be a 'policy' rate, a cost-based rate, or a current market rate; and how often the rate should be changed—but we've decided to defer dealing with that until we get some resolution on the conceptual issue. So far, we've identified four main alternatives, although a couple of them are rather theoretical.

No Capital Change

"Any exhaustive list of alternative ways to assign interest expense," Mr. Hall said, "would have to start with the question of why do it at all? The basic reason, I think, is that a capital charge of some sort is required by criterion number three. Also, our general managers have gotten used to the idea of having their net income be a "realistic" number. They know that interest is a cost of doing business and believe that it should appear on their operating statement. The primary argument against liquidation of the actual corporate interest expense is that it is a function of GE's capital structure and dividend policy, and the component general managers really don't control that."

Complete Capital Charge

"That brings us to the second alternative," Mr. Hall continued. "Why not charge for the total corporate investment in each component, rather than just for its cumulative cash flow requirements since 1966? That brings us right back to residual income, of course, so it would be the simplest of all procedures. The rationale for residual income is that it's the total investment in a component—not just the portion of it that the corporation finances with borrowed money—that is important, and the general manager is the person who is responsible for the total investment.

"The major problem with this approach is that the components' net income would not be realistic—there'd be a major overliquidation at the corporate level. Nevertheless, I've given this approach some thought. If we could agree to just change the name—to call residual income at the component level 'net income'—and to adjust our thinking to accept a positive variance between corporate net income and component net income—it would be a big step forward. As a practical matter, however, I'm sure this is too revolutionary a change. It just won't happen."

Modified Cash Flow Approach

"Some modification of our existing procedure is clearly the most feasible alternative," Mr. Hall went on. "It's now widely accepted because it's been applied for several years and everyone is used to it and understands it more or less. This is a huge company with a great diversity of businesses and when you finally get something that works you don't change it lightly—and sometimes you can't change it even if you want to.

"If we do keep it, then criterion number two dictates that we'll have to modify it immediately, and I'm not sure how to do that in any way that isn't totally arbitrary. Also, when we make a modification this time, we ought to build some flexibility into the formula so that it will continue to be effective. For example, in explaining the need for a change, we'll have to disclose that, in part, it was caused by the Comptroller's forgiveness of the investment in abandoned product lines. Now, most general managers didn't realize that such forgiveness was possible, but when they find out I think that Maurie will get a lot more requests. Any change in the procedure ought to anticipate the need to deal with that issue on a continuing basis."

Net Working Capital Approach

"Finally," Mr. Hall said, "I can only think of one other way to deal with the problem. The idea is simple, and my calculations indicate that it would achieve a reasonable liquidation of corporate interest expense. The big problem is that it's a totally different approach, and, as I'll describe in a moment, some managers will be upset.

"You know, once you get a new idea, it's hard not to get enamored with it. At first blush, this idea looked flawless. The proposal is simply to charge each component for the investment in net working capital shown on its balance sheet. I see two big advantages to this approach. First, it focuses on that part of the component investment that the general manager really can control on a current basis. Through our capital budgeting procedures, we already have explicit controls on new investments in plant and equipment, and this approach would provide a decentralized control over working capital. Second, this new approach would treat all components in exactly the same way on a current basis, no matter whether it's a new business or an old one. That would mean that no component would earn imputed interest income, but that any unit could lower its interest expense by reducing working capital. Product abandonments under this proposal would be adjusted for automatically; if you closed out a product line, the working capital supporting it would be eliminated and so would the interest expense.

"So," Mr. Hall continued, "I took the idea to Maurie and then to Al. They thought it was interesting enough to be explored further, but both were concerned about how it might be accepted in the components. I agreed that I ought to try the idea on a few Managers of Finance in the operating units—and did I get an earful.

"I've only talked to a handful so far, but I haven't yet found anyone who likes it. A variety of concerns have been expressed, but some patterns are emerging. First, everyone I've talked to is worried about what it would do to the pattern of their net income. Even if we recast the imputed interest calculation for the last five years—and that could be done—they can't predict how the recast—and their forecast—using the new method would be affected. The components with interest income know that they'd be hurt, but it's not the drop in net income that bothers them as much as the caprious ways that the new approach might change the earnings trend.

"Another worry is with the general fairness of the new approach. As one finance manager in a profitable, mature business put it, 'It doesn't seem right that, with all the cash we throw off that we should also have to pay interest expense. In effect, we get no credit for our cashflow, and it is used to pay for plant and equipment that is built—interest-free—for a growing business.' A similar criticism but expressed a little more broadly is that this approach is just another type of corporate assessment, like corporate overhead but assessed on a different basis, and that it will fail to get and keep the general manager focused on financial management the way that our cash flow method does.

"So, I went back to the drawing board to search for a way to modify the cash flow approach. One idea, that one of my assistants suggested, would be to adopt a banker's method of doing business. A savings bank, for example, accepts deposits and pays, say, 6 percent interest on them and then turns around and loans the money to borrowers at, say, 8 percent. We might try something like that, paying a lower rate of interest to components that provide cash than we charge to components that use it.

"An alternative set of modifications would be to charge components interest on their beginning-of-the-year "long term debt" and charge (or credit) them for their cumulative use or generation of cash during the year at the current monthly prime rate of interest. This proposal would retain the cash flow approach although it would eliminate January 1, 1966, as the starting date. In addition, the use of one rate to apply to past as well as current uses of cash would be replaced by a long and short term rate concept.

"The beginning-of-the-year "debt" for each component would be established by multiplying the corporation's investment in that component by the parent Company's ratio of debt to debt plus equity. In recent years, this ratio has been roughly 30 percent. By resetting the debt each year, the need to adjust for abandonments will no longer be necessary. A conventional cash flow analysis, as we do it now, would calculate the net cash provided or used during the current year, to which the monthly prime rate would be applied."

"I don't know," Mr. Hall concluded, "what the reactions will be to either of these modifications, but I'm not very optimistic. Some part of the negative reactions to the working capital approach could be labeled simply as resistance to change, but the resistance is real nonetheless. Beneath that there may also be substantive concern that any new proposal won't have the effect on managers that we expect or want. I admit that a change in the measurement system can affect behavior, and that it might affect one manager differently than another because the people as well as the businesses are different. But we've got over 200 component general managers and the same measurement procedure has to be applied to all of them. How could we tailor it to the personalities of each one—particularly when they keep changing jobs? About all I can hope to do is to find the right answer—whatever that is."

PART III

The Management
Control Process

A management control system, like any system, consists of both a structure and a process. In Part II we focused on the main elements of the control *structure,* that is, on the various types of responsibility centers and on the techniques that were appropriate for measuring performance in each of them. In Part III we focus on the main steps in the management control *process.* Because one cannot discuss structure without some mention of how the structure works, there is some overlap between Parts II and III.

The principal steps in the control process are, in chronological order: programming, budget preparation, and the analysis and appraisal of performance. Programming is discussed in Chapter 9, budget preparation in Chapter 10, and the analysis and appraisal of performance in Chapters 11 and 12.

Chapter Nine

PROGRAMMING

Programming is the process of deciding on the nature and size of the several programs that are to be undertaken in order to achieve an organization's goals. In an industrial company, the programs are structured essentially by products or product lines.

The process of programming involves three related, but separable, activities. The first activity involves the preparation and analysis of proposals for new programs, and making decisions on these proposals. The second is the analysis of ongoing programs with the objective of improving the profitability of these programs. The third is the system for coordinating the separate programs so as to optimize the functioning of the company as a whole. An organization should do a good job at all three of these activities, but many organizations do not. Some organizations are effective at formulating and analyzing individual program proposals, but they have no formal programming system; other organizations have a well-developed programming system, but they do an inadequate job of analyzing the individual proposals for new programs that flow through the system, or they are overly complacent about the status quo of existing programs. Each of these three aspects of programming is discussed in this chapter.

RELATION TO OTHER PROCESSES

Programming is to be distinguished from strategic planning, which precedes it in time, and from budget preparation, which follows it.

Relation to Strategic Planning

In Chapter 1 we drew a line between two management processes, labelled respectively strategic planning and management control. Programming, although part of management control, is close to the line dividing these two processes, and it is therefore of some importance to distinguish between them. The distinction is not crucial, however, and, as is the case in most matters relating to organizations, the line is not a sharp one. In fact, some authors use the term "long-range planning" to encompass both strategic planning and programming.

In the strategic planning process, management decides on the goals of the organization and the main strategies for achieving these goals. Conceptually, the programming process takes these goals and strategies as given and seeks to identify programs that will implement them effectively and efficiently. The decision by an industrial goods manufacturer to diversify into consumer goods is a strategic decision. Having made this basic decision, a number of programming decisions then must be made: whether to implement the strategy by acquisition or by building a new organization, what product lines to emphasize, whether to make or to buy, what marketing channels to use, and so on.

In practice, there is a considerable amount of overlap between strategic planning and programming. Studies made during the programming process may indicate the desirability of changing goals or strategies. Conversely, strategic planning usually includes a preliminary consideration of the programs that will be adopted as means of achieving goals.

An important reason for making a separation in practice between programming and strategic planning is that the programming process tends to become institutionalized, and this tends to put a damper on purely creative activities. Segregating strategic planning as a separate activity, either organizationally or at least in the thinking of top management, can provide an offset to this tendency. Strategic planning should be an activity in which creative, innovative thinking is strongly encouraged.

In many companies goals and strategies are not explicitly stated or communicated clearly to the managers who need to use them as a framework within which program decisions are made. Thus, in a formal programming process an important first step often is to formulate descriptions of these goals and strategies. This may be a difficult task, for although top management presumably has an intuitive feel for what they are, the goals and strategies may not have been verbalized with the specificity that is necessary if they are to be used in making program decisions. This topic was discussed in more detail in Chapter 4.

Relation to Budget Preparation

Both programming and budget preparation involve planning, but the types of planning activities are different in the two processes. The budgeting process focuses on a single year, whereas programming focuses on activities that extend over a period of several years. A budget is, in a sense, a one-year slice of the organization's programs although, for reasons discussed in Chapter 10, this is not a complete description of a budget; the budgeting process involves more than simply carving out such a slice.

Programming precedes budgeting, and in the budget process the approved program is essentially taken as a given. Thus, having decided on its consumer product lines and on the arrangements for manufacturing and marketing these products, the company mentioned in the preceding section would prepare a budget showing planned revenues and expenses for the forthcoming year.

Another difference between a program and a budget is that the former is essentially structured by product lines or other programs while the latter is structured by responsibility centers. This rearrangement of the program so that it corresponds to the responsibility centers charged with executing it, is necessary because the budget will be used to motivate performance before the fact and to appraise performance after the fact, and motivation and appraisal are activities that must be related to organizational responsibilities.

Many organizations do not make an explicit, formal distinction between the programming process and the budgeting process. Since the two processes are conceptually different, it is useful to think about these differences even if no formal distinction is made.

ANALYSIS OF PROPOSED PROGRAMS

Ideas for new programs can arise anywhere in the organization. They can originate with the chief executive, with a headquarters planning staff, or in various parts of the operating organization. Some units are a more likely source than others, for fairly obvious reasons. The research/development organization is expected to generate ideas for new products or processes, the marketing organization for marketing innovations, and the production engineering organization for new equipment and manufacturing methods. Proposals for programs are essentially either *reactive* or *proactive,* that is, they arise either as the reaction to a perceived threat to the company, such as rumors of the introduction of a new product by a competitor, or they represent an initiative designed to capitalize on a newly perceived opportunity.

Because a company's success depends in part on its ability to find and implement new programs, and because ideas for these can come from a wide variety of sources, it is important that the atmosphere be such that these ideas do come to light and that they receive appropriate management attention. A highly structured, formal system may lead to exactly the wrong atmosphere for this purpose, and it is therefore important that the system be flexible enough and receptive enough so that good new ideas do not get killed off before they come to the attention of the proper decision maker.

It is also important that, wherever possible, the adoption of a new program be viewed not as a single all-or-nothing decision, but rather as a series of decisions, each one involving one relatively small step in testing and developing the proposed program, with full implementation and its consequent significant investment being decided upon if, but only if, the tests indicate that the proposal has a good chance of success. Most new programs are not like the Edsel, which involved the commitment of several hundred million dollars in a single decision; rather, they involve many successive decisions: agreement that the initial idea for a product is worth pursuing, then examining its technical feasibility in a laboratory, then examining production problems and cost characteristics in a pilot plant, then testing consumer acceptance in test markets, and only then making a major commitment to full production and marketing. The system must provide for these successive steps, and for a thorough evaluation of the results of each step as a basis for making the decision on the next step.

Capital Investment Analysis

Most proposals require significant amounts of new capital. Techniques for analyzing such proposals are described in many sources and are not repeated here.[1] In general, the techniques attempt either to (a) measure whether the present value of the estimated cash inflows of a project exceeds the amount of investment required, with present value being determined by discounting the flows at a rate that the company believes to be a satisfactory return on investment, or, (b) to find the internal rate of return implicit in the relationship between inflows and outflows. An important point is that these techniques are not in fact used in a great many situations in which, conceptually, they are applicable.[2] There are at least four reasons for not using present value techniques in analyzing certain types of proposals:

1. The proposal may be so obviously attractive that a calculation of its net present value is unnecessary. A newly developed machine that reduces costs so substantially that it will pay for itself in a year is an example.

2. The estimates involved in the proposal are so uncertain that making present value calculations is believed to be not worth the effort—one can't make a silk purse out of a sow's ear, nor draw a reliable conclusion from unreliable data. This situation is especially common when the results are heavily dependent on estimates of sales volume of new products for which no good market data exist.

3. The rationale for the proposal is something other than increased profitability. The present value approach assumes that the "objective function" is to increase profits in some sense, but many proposed investments are justified on the grounds that they improve employee morale, improve the company's image, or are needed for safety reasons.

---

[1] See, for example, Robert N. Anthony and James S. Reece, *Management Accounting Principles* 3d ed. (Homewood, Ill.: Richard D. Irwin, Inc., 1975), Chapters 18 and 19; and John Dearden, *Cost Accounting and Financial Control Systems* (Reading, Mass.: Addison-Wesley Publishing Company, 1973), Chapter 13.

[2] See the following surveys: J. William Petty et al., "The Capital Expenditure Decision-Making Processes of Large Corporations," *The Engineering Economist,* Vol. 20, No. 3, pp. 159–72; James M. Fremgen, "Capital Budgeting Practices: A Survey," *Management Accounting,* May 1973, pp. 19–25, and other surveys cited in these sources.

4. There is no feasible alternative to adoption of the proposal. An investment that is required to comply with antipollution legislation is an example.

The management control system must provide an orderly way of reaching a decision on these proposals, which may well amount to half the funds that the company commits to capital projects. In particular, the fact that these proposals do exist means that systems that attempt to rank projects in order of profitability are likely not to be practical because many projects do not fit into a mechanical ranking scheme.

Analytical Techniques

Instead of, or as a part of, the conventional approach to capital investment analysis, several analytical techniques have been proposed as an aid to decision making. Some of these are discussed briefly in this section, but no attempt is made to describe them in detail.[3]

Probabilistic Estimates. The idea of expressing estimates of future events in stochastic terms rather than as single numbers is not new. "Optimistic/best guess/pessimistic" budgets were described in textbooks in the 1950s and probably earlier. The largest effort involving probabilities was the PERT system, which is a control system that was at one time required to be used on all major Defense Department contracts. Conditions favored the adoption of the PERT system: A genuine need for a better system existed, large amounts of money were at stake, top management in the Department of Defense backed the system vigorously, and an elaborate education program was set up. Nevertheless, although a type of PERT system continues in widespread use, the probabilistic feature has largely been abandoned. The essential reason for its failure was that people did not trust the validity and/or the weighting of the probabilistic estimates. Thus, widespread use of these techniques depends on whether confidence in the validity of the estimates is warranted and on whether, even if warranted, decision makers will in fact have enough confidence in the data to use them.

Risk Analysis. If probabilistic estimates of even rough validity can be made, they can be used not only as an improved estimate of a variable (by means of the calculation of its *expected value*), but also as raw material for a new type of information, the amount of risk inherent in a project. If the estimate involves only one variable, such as sales volume, the easily computed *standard deviation* provides a good measure of the amount of risk—or more accurately, of uncertainty—in the estimate. If, as is usually the case, several variables are involved in the problem and some of these are interdependent, the problem is more complicated. The risk or uncertainty in such a situation can be measured by what is called the *Monte Carlo* method. In this method, the estimated profitability of a project is computed by using one set

---

[3] For an excellent collection of articles describing new approaches, see Alfred Rappaport, ed., *Information for Decision Making,* 2d ed. (Englewood Cliffs, N.J.: Prentice-Hall, Inc., 1975).

of revenue or cost estimates, with each number in this set being selected at random from the probability distribution of each variable. This process is repeated many times, sometimes a thousand times, by a computer. A frequency distribution of the results of these separate trials is computed, and the standard deviation, or other measure of dispersion, of this frequency distribution indicates the uncertainty of the project.

Sensitivity Analysis.   Another approach to measuring the riskiness of a proposed project is called *sensitivity analysis*. It does not require that a probability distribution be estimated and thus can be used in situations in which such estimates are not feasible. It simply involves varying the estimates of one of the variables by a stated amount, say 5 percent or 10 percent, and calculating what this does to the profitability of the project. Doing this calculation for each variable in succession shows which of them have the most influence on the overall profitability of the project and therefore which need to be considered most carefully when the decision on the project is being made.

Decision Theory.   The assessment of probabilities can be combined with certain other techniques into a complete mathematical framework for analyzing a proposed project.[4] Of these other techniques, a central one is called the *decision tree*. In its simplest form, a decision tree is a diagram that shows the several decisions or *acts* and the possible consequences of each act; these consequences are called *events*. In a more elaborate form, the probabilities and the revenues or costs of each event's outcomes are estimated, and these are combined to give an *expected value* for the event.

Since a decision tree is particularly useful in depicting a complicated series of decisions, any brief illustration is highly artificial. Nevertheless, the decision tree shown in Exhibit 9–1 will suffice to show how the technique works.

The assumed situation is this. A company is considering whether to develop and market a new product. Development costs are estimated to be $100,000, there is a 0.7 probability that the development effort will succeed and that the product will be marketed, and it is estimated that:

a. If the product is highly successful, it will produce differential income of $400,000 (or a net $300,000 after subtracting the development cost);
b. if the product is moderately successful, it will break even, that is, its income of $100,000 will just offset the development cost;
c. if the product is a failure, it will lose $100,000 (or a total loss of $200,000 after taking account of the development cost).

The estimated probability of high success is 0.4; of moderate success, 0.4; and of failure, 0.2.

---

4 For a description of this approach which, unlike most other descriptions, can be studied by a person who understands only elementary algebra, see Howard Raiffa, *Decision Analysis: Introductory Lectures on Choices under Uncertainty* (Reading, Mass.: Addison-Wesley, 1968).

Exhibit 9–1

SIMPLE DECISION TREE

	INCOME	PROBA-BILITY	EXPECTED VALUE
HIGHLY SUCCESSFUL + $400,000	$300,000	0.28	$84,000
(p = 0.4) MODERATELY SUCCESSFUL + $100,000	0	0.28	0
FAILURE − $100,000	−$200,000	0.14	−$28,000
	−$100,000	0.30	−$30,000
EXPECTED VALUE, IF DEVELOP		1.00	$26,000
EXPECTED VALUE, IF DON'T DEVELOP	$0	1.00	$0

The expected value of each outcome is the monetary income or loss times the probability of that outcome's occurrence. Thus,

1. If development fails, the expected value is the development cost times the probability of failure: −$100,000 × 0.3 = −$30,000, i.e., a $30,000 loss.
2. If development succeeds, but the product is a failure, the loss is $100,000 development cost plus $100,000 marketing costs, a total loss of $200,000. The total probability of development success *and* product failure is 0.7 × 0.2 = 0.14. The expected value of this outcome is 0.14 × −$200,000 = −$28,000.
3. If development succeeds and the product is moderately successful, the probability is 0.28 (0.7 × 0.4) and the differential net income is zero; hence the expected value is 0.28 × $0 = $0.
4. If development succeeds and the product is highly successful, the net income is $400,000 − $100,000 development costs, or $300,000, and the probability is again 0.28; hence the expected value of this outcome is 0.28 × $300,000 = $84,000.

The *total* expected value of the act "Develop Product" is the algebraic sum of the expected values of all possible outcomes on the "Develop Product" branch of the tree, that is, $26,000. This amount is then compared with the expected value of the other alternative act, "Don't Develop." If the development is not undertaken, there is a 100 percent chance (1.0 probability) that the incremental income will be $0; hence the expected value of "Don't Develop" is zero. Because the act "Develop Product" has the larger expected value, the decision would be to proceed with the development effort. This does not mean, of course, that the ultimate outcome is "guaranteed" to be differential income of $26,000; rather it means that based on the estimates that have been made in considering this decision, management should "gamble" and go ahead with the development, because the *expected* payoff from this gamble is positive, whereas if the gamble is not taken there will be zero payoff.

This approach to decision making is a powerful one if, *but only if,* the probabilities can be estimated. As stated above, there are relatively few situations in the real world where such estimates can be made with sufficient reliability that the decision maker will trust them.

Overall Corporate Models. If the behavior of each important variable in a company could be estimated and the relationships among the variables could be expressed as mathematical equations or inequalities, the decision maker would have a powerful tool for analyzing proposed projects. Various alternatives could be fed into this overall corporate model, and the effect of each alternative on profitability could be easily computed. In a 1974 survey of member companies of the Financial Executives Institute (whose members tend to be large companies), about 50 percent of the respondents, including 80 percent of respondents with a sales volume of over $500 million, reported that they prepared financial models. Of the companies that modelled, at least one third prepared overall corporate models, and the remainder used more specialized models. The typical company incorporated 90 input variables in its corporate model.[5]

Companies are experimenting with two approaches to an overall corporate model, the optimization approach and the heuristic approach.

In the *optimization* approach, the objective is to make a single model that encompasses all variables and that explains the profitability of the company under a given set of circumstances. This approach requires the use of *linear programming,* which is a device for finding the optimum combination of variables when there are constraints (such as production capacity limitations) on the amount of resources available. Eseimating the behavior of variables and of the interaction among them is so complicated that no reports of success have yet appeared in the literature, nor do we know of any successful model that exists in practice. Nevertheless, many companies are working to develop such a model.

The *heuristic* approach is a less ambitious, and therefore more practical, one. Instead of attempting to model all variables in the company at once, the mathematical expressions are developed only for certain segments of the company for which reliable estimates can be made. The overall company model is, in effect, the conventional income statement and balance sheet, and those items not encompassed by the heuristic models, or *blocks,* are estimated in the conventional way. In the Sun Oil Company model, for example, one block estimates the investment required for new service stations to achieve a specified market share for the coming year. Another block estimates the amount of crude oil and other raw materials that will be produced

---

[5] Jeffrey W. Traenkle et al., *The Use of Financial Models in Business* (New York: Financial Executives Research Foundation, 1975).

in the coming year on the basis of the number of wells available and the estimated output of each. The outputs of each of these blocks are combined with those of other blocks to provide an estimate of net income and of balance sheet amounts.[6]

Program Analysis Systems

Whether or not a formal analysis is made, there must be some systematic way of considering individual program proposals. The system is usually referred to as a capital budgeting system since the proposals usually require the commitment of capital funds. The system has these main elements:

1. The originator of a proposal prepares a description of it and a justification for it, or he has such a justification prepared by an appropriate staff unit. If the proposal is amenable to formal analysis, the justification includes a summary of this analysis.

2. The proposal is sent up the organization. If it involves a relatively small investment, it may be acted on by the person's immediate superior. If it is of significant size, it gets considered at successively higher levels in the organization, and, assuming that the manager at each level judges it to be attractive, it becomes a part of the corporate capital budget. For important projects, this stage of the process may require a long time—sometimes a year or more—during which questions are raised and answered, alternatives are explored, and all possible effort is made to examine the soundness of the proposal. Much informal discussion and persuasion and much staff work on details of the proposal occur during this stage.

3. A capital budget is prepared, usually once a year. The capital budget is usually prepared separately from the operating budget, and in many companies it is prepared at a different time and cleared through a capital appropriations committee that is separate from the budget committee. In the capital budget, projects are often classified under headings such as the following

a) Cost reduction and replacement.
b) Expansion of existing product lines.
c) New product lines.
d) Health and safety.
e) Other.

Within these classifications, the projects are often listed in what is believed to be the order of their desirability, and the estimated expenditures are broken down by years, or by quarters, so that the funds required for each time period are shown. Important projects are listed individually; a blanket amount is included for the total of smaller projects.

4. The budget is considered, revised if necessary, and approved. Usually final approval is made at the board-of-director level. In preparing the capital

---

[6] George W. Gershefski, "Building a Corporate Financial Model," *Harvard Business Review,* July, 1969.

budget, management must appraise not only the individual projects but also the total amount of funds requested. It may happen that the funds required for desirable projects total more than the amount of money that management thinks should be spent for additional fixed assets. In this event, a worthwhile project might not be approved simply because the funds are not available.

5. Approval of the capital budget usually means approval of the projects *in principle,* but does not constitute final authority to proceed with them. For this authority, a specific authorization request is prepared for the project, spelling out the proposal in more detail, perhaps with firm bids or price quotations on the new assets. These authorization requests are approved at various levels in the organization, depending on their size and character. For example, each foreman may be authorized to buy production tools or similar items costing not more than $100 each, provided the total for the year does not exceed $1,000; and at the other extreme, all projects costing more than $500,000 and all projects for new products, whatever their cost, may require approval of the board of directors. In between, there is a scale of amounts that various echelons in the organization may authorize without the approval of their superiors.

6. Work to accomplish the project is begun. The control system used in this connection is discussed in Chapter 16.

7. In some companies, there is a procedure designed to follow up on capital projects once they have gone into operation. Its purpose is to find out whether the original estimates of costs and earnings in fact work out in practice. In many situations, however, it is not feasible to identify earnings with specific projects, so such a follow-up cannot be made.

ANALYZING ONGOING PROGRAMS

There is a natural human tendency to assume that the future is going to resemble the past. Consequently, long-range plans are often prepared simply by extrapolating from the current situation. In the dynamic environment within which most businesses operate, such extrapolations are likely to be unrealistic, and reliance on them is dangerous. A preferable approach is to make a thorough analysis of each major segment of the company and to adopt programs that are consistent with the opportunities that exist for that segment.

A natural focus for such an analysis is an individual product or product line. In a divisionalized company, each division tends to represent one product line, so the analysis often can be made by divisions. An approach to such an analysis, suggested by Robert V. L. Wright of Arthur D. Little, Inc., is described briefly in the following paragraphs.[7]

A product line is classified in terms of the maturity of its industry and the

---

[7] Adapted from Robert V. L. Wright, *A System for Managing Diversity* (Cambridge. Arthur D. Little, Inc., 1974).

company's competitive position within the industry. Four stages of maturity are identified:

An *embryonic* industry (for example, laser measuring devices) is normally characterized by rapid growth, changes in technology, great pursuit of new customers, and fragmented and changing shares of market; a *growth* industry is one that is still growing rapidly, but customers, market shares, and technology are better known and entry into the industry is more difficult (as illustrated by RCA's attempt to enter the computer business); a *mature* industry (like automobiles or paper in this country) is characterized by stability in known customers, technology, and in shares of market, although the industries may still be market-competitive; and *aging* industries (such as men's hats) are best described by falling demand, a declining number of competitors, and, in many such industries, a narrowing of the product line.[8]

The product line is also classified according to its competitive position, as either dominant, strong, favorable, tenable or weak.

As a basis for these classifications, and for thinking about desirable courses of action, the staff assembles data on the size, strengths and weaknesses of each major competitor, the size and composition of the market and expected changes in it, and company data on the product line. Wright says that after staff has assembled the appropriate basic data, management usually can classify a product line unambiguously and in a short time.

This two-way classification suggests a 4×5 matrix, and different practices are appropriate for product lines that are in each cell in such a matrix. The characteristics for each stage of maturity are listed in Exhibit 9–2. Management's task is then to examine the division's activities and, if necessary, plan changes in these activities so that they are consistent with those appropriate for the stage of maturity and competitive position. If a formal programming system, as described in the next section, is used, these plans provide the starting point in formulating the program for the product line.

The foregoing is only one of several possible approaches to the analysis of ongoing programs. The essential idea behind any good approach is that it motivates management to think constructively and in new ways about the product line and thus overcome the tendency to make straight extrapolations.

Analyses of existing product lines are often made by the divisions concerned, following guidelines furnished by corporate headquarters and with some staff assistance from corporate headquarters. Such staff assistance may include training in the use of techniques such as those outlined above. Not only is divisional management in the best position to make such an analysis, because of its intimate knowledge of the product and the market, but also the analytical process is a useful device for stimulating divisional thinking about the future, a stimulus that would be lacking if the effort were regarded as being merely a "headquarters exercise."

---

[8] Ibid., p. 7.

Exhibit 9–2

MANAGEMENT CHARACTERISTICS BY STAGE OF INDUSTRY MATURITY

Management Activity or Function	Embryonic Industry	Growth Industry
Managerial Role	Entrepreneur	Sophisticated market manager
Planning Time Frame	Long enough to draw tentative life cycle (10)	Long-range investment payout (7)
Planning Content	By product/customer	By product and program
Planning Style	Flexible	Less flexible
Organization Structure	Free-form or task force	Semi-permanent task force, product or market division
Managerial Compensation	High variable/low fixed, fluctuating with performance	Balanced variable and fixed, individual and group rewards
Policies	Few	More
Procedures	None	Few
Communication System	Informal/tailor-made	Formal/tailor-made
Managerial Style	Participation	Leadership
Content of Reporting System	Qualitative, marketing, unwritten	Qualitative and quantitative, early warning system, all functions
Measures Used	Few fixed	Multiple/adjustable
Frequency of Measuring	Often	Relatively often
Detail of Measurement	Less	More
Corporate Departmental Emphasis	Market research; new product development	Operations research; organization development

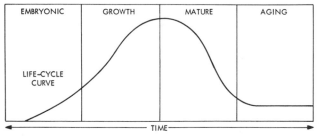

Source: Robert V. L. Wright, *A System for Managing Diversity* (Cambridge: Arthur D. Little, Inc., 1974) p. 10.

Following is a summary of one company's list of the areas that corporate management wants stressed in such a review:

1. New customers and new markets
2. New products
3. Cost control

Mature Industry	Aging Industry
Critical administrator	"Opportunistic milker"
Intermediate (3)	Short-range (1)
By product/market/ function	By plant
Fixed	Fixed
Business division plus task force for renewal	Pared-down division
Low variable-high fixed group rewards	Fixed only
Many	Many
Many	Many
Formal/uniform	Little or none, by direction
Guidance/loyalty	Loyalty
Quantitative, written, production oriented	Numerical, oriented to written balance sheet
Multiple/adjustable	Few/fixed
Traditionally periodic	Less often
Great	Less
Value analysis Data processing Taxes and insurance	Purchasing

4. Cost reduction (at least 3 percent of cost of goods sold annually)
5. Low profit product review
6. Purchasing strategy
7. Pricing analysis
8. Capital investment.
9. People involvement (better communication and team effort)
10. Management accountability (well defined responsibility centers)
11. Contingency planning (for lower than budgeted sales volume)[9]

The completed analysis and the resulting program should be the subject of a thorough discussion between divisional management and top management because it should set forth a course of action that will govern the operations of the division for some time to come. Even if the program is judged to be optimum from the standpoint of the division, it nevertheless is subject to change if it does not fit into the overall corporate program. For example,

---

[9] Eltra Corporation, 1973 annual report.

a division may contemplate an expansion of its product lines into markets that are better served by some other division; decisions on divisional "charters"—that is the boundaries within which each division is supposed to operate—are clearly the province of top management. Also, the divisional estimates of its capital requirements may be inconsistent with the overall corporate financial plan. A mature product line is usually treated as a "cash cow"; that is, it is milked to the maximum feasible extent so as to provide the funds needed by the growth divisions. The manager of a cash cow may not be happy about such a policy; he may feel that at least a certain percentage of the funds generated "belongs" to the division. Corporate management may well decide otherwise. One company, for example, specifically outlined its policy as follows, in guidelines funished to divisions:

> The primary role of those profit centers which are in mature industries will be to provide funds to the corporation. While we will be prepared in special circumstances to invest in these units for a limited period of time for specific purposes, they should be taking steps to improve their cash flow through the rationalization of their marketing, distribution, product line and/or production methods.

> Any investment, be it fixed or working capital, in profit centers in mature industries will be expected to produce a significantly improved ROI over the unit's previous performance.

> Where we feel that profit centers do not have a high probability of meeting stated objectives, will not hestate to divest ourselves of them.

> For those profit centers where the risk of not achieving planned performance is high, we will be looking for a commensurately higher rate of return.

> We will only invest in those aging businesses where there is an immediate prospect of additional high cash flow.

Zero-Base Review

The type of analysis described above is focused on a product line in relation to its market. Other approaches are necessary for staff units and other activities whose profitability cannot be measured directly. Some companies have a systematic plan for reviewing all these aspects of their operations over a period of years. This approach has come to be called a "zero-base review." According to a regular schedule, each ongoing activity is studied intensively, perhaps once every five years. In contrast with the usual budget review, which takes the current level of spending as the starting point, this more intensive review starts from scratch and attempts to build up, *de novo,* the resources that actually are needed by the activity. It may even challenge the need for having the activity at all. These studies are especially important when costs are of the discretionary cost type. Basic questions are raised, such as: (1) Should the function be performed at all? (2) What should the quality level be? Are we doing too much? (3) Should it be performed in this way? (4) How much should it cost?

As a part of this approach, it is desirable to compare costs and, if feasible, output measures for similar operations. Such comparisons may identify activities that appear to be out of line, and thus lead to a more thorough examination of these activities. Such comparisons can be useful even though there are problems in achieving comparability, finding a "correct" relationship between cost and output in a discretionary cost situation, and danger in taking an outside average as a standard. They often lead to the following interesting question: If other organizations get the job done for $X, why can't we?

Although sometimes called a "zero-base budget," such a review actually is not part of the annual budgeting process, for these isn't enough time to conduct it during that process. A zero-base review is time consuming, and it is also likely to be a traumatic experience for the managers whose operations are being reviewed. This is one reason why such a review is scheduled, not annually, but periodically so that all responsibility centers are covered once every four or five years. This review establishes a new base for the budget, and the annual budget review attempts to keep costs reasonably in line with this base for the intervening period until the next review is made.

Zero-base review is difficult. Managers under scrutiny will not only do their best to justify their current level of spending, but they may also do their best to torpedo the entire effort. They consider the annual budget review as a necessary evil, but zero-base review as something to be put off indefinitely in favor of "more pressing business." If all else fails, they attempt to create enough doubts so that the findings are inconclusive and the status quo prevails.

FORMAL PROGRAMMING SYSTEMS

Although most large organizations have a system for analyzing and deciding on individual program proposals, along the lines described in the preceding sections, fewer companies have a formal method of bringing together all programs into an overall plan for the company. The development of such formal long-range plans has been rapid in the last decade, however. A formal long-range plan provides top management with a better basis for making judgments about the overall balance among the different parts of the company. By showing the future implications of decisions that have already been made, it provides a starting point in the analysis of proposed new programs. It provides a frame of reference for the preparation of the annual budget. And it encourages managers at all levels to think more deeply and more systematically about the future, thus offsetting the natural tendency to focus on immediate, fire-fighting problems. Offsetting these advantages is the fact that the process is expensive, especially in its use of management time, since it is successful only if managers, including top management, devote a considerable amount of time to it.

Time Period

The long-range plan typically covers a period of five future years, of which the first year is the year for which the next budget will be prepared. Its end products are a set of financial statements for this period, together with clarifying information on the actions that are implied by the accounting numbers. These statements are not necessarily prepared for each of the five years; in order to save paperwork, some companies prepare statements only for the budget year, the following year, and the fifth year, omitting the third and fourth years. Even though complete plans are prepared for only a five-year period, some aspects of the program may be extended for a longer interval, such as ten or even twenty years. For example, electrical generating and distribution companies customarily make plans for new generating facilities and for revisions in their power distribution networks for twenty years or more into the future, and timber companies make plans for the full cycle of the growth of trees, which may be 40 years.

Steps in the Process

The principal steps in a formal programming process are as follows:

1. Preparation of assumptions and guidelines.
2. Preparation of the divisional plans.
3. Review and approval of plans.

The process requires several months. If it is to be completed in time to serve as the starting point in the preparation of an annual budget for a year beginning January 1, it must be completed by some time in October, and perhaps earlier. In order to meet this deadline, it must be started in the spring of the year. The timetable is particularly long if provision is made for recycling the plans, that is, for a sequence that involves the submission of one plan, discussion of it with top management, and a revision of this plan based on the top management discussion. Such recycling is especially desirable in the first few years of a formal programming system because of the unfamiliarity of managers and their staffs with the process.

Assumptions and Guidelines

The process starts with the preparation of guidelines and assumptions that are to govern the preparation of the program. The analytical work leading to these guidelines is done by a headquarters staff, which is either a separate planning staff reporting to top management or is a part of the controller organization. The decisions, however, are made by top management.

The guidelines issued by corporate management include a statement of goals, assumptions about the external environment and a statement of policies that are to be followed in preparing the program.

The statement of goals includes:

1. Financial goals, expressed as earnings per share, return on investment, or similar numbers, specified year by year if feasible.
2. Inventory goals, expressed as turnover rates, and receivables goals, expressed as days' sales or comparable ratios.
3. Growth goals, usually expressed in terms of sales revenue.

Environmental assumptions include:

1. The trend of growth in gross national product, and an assumption about cyclical movements in GNP in the next year or two.
2. The rate of inflation in general, and the changes in labor rates, prices of important raw materials, and selling prices in particular.
3. Interest rates and, if relevant, currency exchange rates.
4. Market conditions, including the growh in principal markets the company serves, changes in the relative importance of distribution channels, anticipated government legislation or other action affecting the product, competitive influences, and profit margins.
5. Production factors, including probable new technology and other factors affecting production.

Statements regarding corporate policy include:

1. The amount of new capital likely to be available either from retained earnings or from new financing.
2. Divisional charters, including the products that each division can make, the products it can sell, the extent to which one division is expected to use the production facilities of other divisions for products it sells but does not make, and the marketing facilities of other divisions for products it makes but does not sell, and the markets the division can serve.
3. Policy on acquisitions and divestments.
4. Personnel policies, compensation policies, and policies on training, promotion, and rotation of managers.

These guidelines and assumptions, together with instructions on the format and content of the planning document itself, are sent to the divisions. In some companies, the first statement is regarded as tentative, and divisional managers are asked to comment on it and to suggest revisions. After discussion between division managers and top management, a revised set of assumptions and guidelines is disseminated.

The preliminary discussion may take the form of a "summit conference" in which corporate management and divisional managers meet, usually for several days and usually at a location which isolates participants from day-to-day pressures. The summit conference may lead to a rethinking of the goals and strategies of the company, and thus to a revision of the guidelines. Discussions at this stage may also lead to changes in divisional charters.

It is essential that the product, production, and marketing boundaries within which each division is expected to operate be clearly set forth in advance of the preparation of the plans; otherwise overlaps and consequent wasted effort can occur.

Preparation of the Plan

Based on the guidelines and assumptions, the divisions and other operating units then prepare their five-year plan. As a starting point, they have the plan that was prepared the previous year, but changes in the environment often require considerable revision in this plan. Many decisions that will affect the division during the next five years have already been made in the capital budgeting process, and the implications of these decisions, both on capital outlays and the consequent impact on operations, are incorporated in the plan.

As is the case with the preparation of guidelines, much of the analytical work in the preparation of the plan is done by the divisional staff, but the final judgments are made by divisional management. Members of the headquarters staff often visit the divisions during this process, for the purpose of clarifying the guidelines, assumptions, and instructions, and in general to assist in the planning process.

The end product of this process may be a fairly bulky document. It typically has the following parts:

1. A *summary,* written personally by the division manager, giving his overview of the plan.

2. A *marketing plan,* describing for each product line and market: the planned penetration, the tactics to be used in achieving this share of market, pricing policies, anticipated actions of competitors and how they will be dealt with, technological developments and their implementation, advertising and other promotional efforts, and the size and nature of the marketing organization.

3. A *production plan,* including changes in plant capacity, inventory levels, warehousing and other logistics activities, and staffing levels, wage and salary schedules, and other aspects of the personnel program.

4. A *staff plan,* describing the nature and size of the several staff units, with reasons for changes in them.

5. A *research/development plan,* identifying major research/development projects individually as well as the total size of the research/development effort.

6. A *capital expenditure plan,* in which capital expenditures that have already been approved are identified separately from those that will subsequently be submitted for approval.

7. *Financial statements,* including balance sheets, income statements, and funds flow statements, usually accompanied by historical data in order to show trends.

Review and Approval of Plans

When the divisional plan reaches headquarters, the staff makes a preliminary examination of it to insure that it conforms to instructions, that the division has not strayed outside the boundaries set by its charter, that the assumptions have been incorporated properly, and that the document is internally consistent. Problems uncovered during this examination are discussed with the divisional staff and are resolved. This discussion does not directly address the question of the adequacy of the plan in achieving the corporate goals; such matters are discussed at the management level, not the staff level. As a basis for this discussion, headquarters staff notes matters that top management should discuss with divisional managers.

The discussion between top management and divisional managers is the heart of the formal programming process. If the plan submitted by the division is judged to be either overly optimistic or an inadequate contribution to corporate goals, top management raises questions about it. Such discussions usually require several hours, and often go on for a day or more for each division.

As a part of the headquarters review, the staff combines the plans for the several divisions into an overall plan for the company as a whole. The "first cut" of such an overall plan may reveal that the sum of divisional plans does not equal the corporate goals; for example, that earnings per share is inadequate. This situation is called a *planning gap*. There are only three ways to close a planning gap: (1) Find opportunities for improvements in the divisional plans; (2) plan on making acquisitions, and (3) revise the corporate goals. The easiest alternative is often viewed as that of making acquisitions, but this possibility may be unrealistic. Opportunities to boost sales revenues by acquiring other companies always exist, but finding acquisitions that will improve earnings per share is a much more difficult matter. In any event, the company's general policy on searching for acquisition opportunities is often governed by the need for additional earnings, as revealed by the planning gap.

The approved program that emerges from this discussion is the starting point in the preparation of the budget, but it is not by itself a budget. The budget is a fairly detailed statement of operations, is structured by responsibility centers and is a bilateral commitment between the responsibility center manager and his superior. The program is much less detailed, is structured by product lines or other programs, and cannot have the force of a commitment because of the uncertainties that are inherent in predicting events that are to occur at some considerable distance in the future.

Organization Relationships

In the foregoing description, we have referred to corporate management and division managers as if these were the only two managerial levels involved in the programming process. If the company has a large number of divisions, the chief executive officer does not have the time to carry on these discussions with each of them. In this case, the divisions are usually organized into groups, and a group vice president is responsible for leading the discussions with the managers of the division in his group and for then discussing the group's plans with the chief executive officer. The divisional managers usually participate in these discussions.

If the company is organized functionally, rather than by divisions, the programming process is more complicated. Instead of treating each division and its product lines as semi-independent entities, the plans must recognize the interdependence of the several functional units. As an obvious example, staffing and material procurement plans of the production organization must be consistent with the sales program of the marketing organization. In order to achieve this consistency, the headquarters staff necessarily plays a more prominent role than is the case in a divisional type of organization.

As emphasized above, programming is a line management activity. A primary purpose is to improve the communication between corporate and divisional executives by providing a sequence of scheduled activities through which they can arrive at a mutually agreeable set of objectives and plans. Staff planners can greatly facilitate this process, but will usually be frustrated if they attempt to intervene in it too strongly.

The staff planner's role in a divisionalized corporation is best conceived of as that of a catalyst. He is attempting to help corporate management do a better job of resource allocation among the divisions, and one way to do that is to assist the division managers in doing a better job of developing plans for their businesses. If the division managers view the staff planner as someone influential in the corporate decision-making process, they will be reluctant to use him as a source of assistance in developing their own plans.

Divisional plans must be subjected to critical review at the corporate level, but the staff planner at that level can rarely serve as both an adviser to the divisions and as a critic of their proposals. Instead, he tries to design the formal part of the planning process in such a way that corporate management, dealing directly with each divisional manager, can perform its own analysis and critique of divisional proposals.

Designing a formal planning system for a divisionalized corporation is still a relatively mystical activity. Few corporations have had more than a few years' experience in formal planning, and thus far the only safe generalization about such systems is that they tend to change fairly rapidly over time. The first year or two of a formal planning effort tends to be confused and frustrating for both corporate and divisional managers. It is clear, however, that in those corporations that have accumulated several years of experience, a mature planning system can be valuable. Formal planning can help division managers to become more creative in identifying environmental opportunities and more explicitly rational in their analysis of strategic alternatives. Corporate management gains increasing confidence in the allocation of resources among the divisions. And both groups of managers benefit from the groundwork developed in the programming process as they engage in the next process, which is the preparation of the budget.

Top Management Style

Programming is a management process, and the way in which it is conducted, if at all, in a given company is heavily dependent on the style of the chief executive officer of that company. Some chief executives prefer to make decisions without the benefit of a formal planning apparatus. If the controller of such a company attempts to introduce a formal programming system, he is likely to be wasting his time and that of the line managers. No system will function effectively unless the chief executive actually uses it as part of his way of managing, and if other managers perceive that the system is not a vital part of the management process, they will give only lip service to it.

In other companies, the chief executive wants some overall planning apparatus for the reasons given earlier, but by temperament he has an aversion to paperwork. In such companies, the system should contain all the elements described in earlier sections, but with a minimum amount of detail in the written documents, and relatively greater emphasis on informal discussion. In still other companies, top management prefers extensive analysis and documentation of plans, and in these companies the formal part of the system should be relatively elaborate.

In designing the system, it is important that the style of top management be correctly diagnosed and that the system be appropriate for that style. This is a difficult task, for formal programming has become somewhat of a fad, and some managers think they may be viewed as being old fashioned if they do not embrace all its trappings. Thus, they will instruct that an elaborate system be installed, or permit one to be installed, even though they later are uncomfortable with it.

SUGGESTED ADDITIONAL READINGS

HERTZ, DAVID B. "Risk Analysis in Capital Investment," *Harvard Business Review,* January–February 1964, pp. 95–106.

LIVINGSTONE, JOHN L. *Management Planning and Control: Mathematical Models.* New York: McGraw-Hill, 1970.

RAIFFA, HOWARD. *Decision Analysis: Introductory Lectures on Choices under Uncertainty.* Reading, Mass.: Addison-Wesley, 1968.

RAPPAPORT, ALFRED (ed.) *Information for Decision Making,* 2d ed. Englewood Cliffs, N.J.: Prentice-Hall, Inc., 1975.

STEINER, GEORGE A., *Top Management Planning.* New York: Macmillan, 1969.

Case 9-1

Hastings Electronics Company

"Now that our decentralization and profit center set-up is beginning to shake down, I would like to devote some attention to developing a more uniform way of appraising our research and development projects and new business ventures." The speaker was Warren Long, recently appointed president of Hastings Electronics. "It's fairly difficult," he continued, "to compare proposals from the four product divisions and the research division for the purpose of allocating our limited resources. Some of the proposals I get are backed up by estimates of cost savings, others by predictions of new business, and still others by nothing more than an interest on the part of some members of one of the various laboratories."

"I agree," replied Arnold Green, executive vice president, "but we have to be careful about how much control we try to exert over these division managers. After all, they have only been in office two or three years and are just beginning to act like all-around businessmen. It wouldn't do to hit them with a set of detailed procedures at this point that might be viewed as encroaching on their prerogatives as managers."

"That's right, but we do need some way of choosing between research projects or other opportunities in businesses as diverse as those represented by our current product lines and the several potential ones that have been suggested already by our new business development group."

For several months Long and Green had been aware of the necessity of doing something about this situation, but both clearly recognized (and were continually reminding each other about) the potential dangers of interfering directly in the decision making of their division managers. The profit-center arrangement, backed up by a substantial bonus system, appeared to be working very well and they were anxious to avoid anything that would interfere with its efficient operation.

Pressures had been building up, however, to make certain choices between proposed business ventures—some generated from within the company's laboratories and some from acquisition opportunities. As long as the choices involved alternatives within an existing line of business, management could rely fairly well on the company's experience in that line of business to provide clues to the better bets. Where the alternatives involved radically different lines of business, however, there was no systematic way of choosing projects.

The new business development group had come up with a number of acquisition possibilities as well as some suggestions for extensions of existing product lines into new markets and for developing new products to fit existing company markets. Several dozen such proposals were being examined currently, but the company lacked an adequate set of criteria or systematic method of comparing them and assigning priorities.

Some preliminary analysis of the profit and share-of-the-market trends in several of Hastings' current lines of business had revealed radical differences between product lines even within a given division. Instruments Division, for example, had found that one of its major product lines was in a declining market that offered little opportunity for increases in profits. Price competition—a phenomenon this product line had not faced before—was becoming severe. New models of these instruments did little except to compete with Hastings' own existing models and to decrease the margin through heavy development expenses.

In another product line in the same division, it was clear that a larger expenditure for research and development could help the company stay in the lead in a growing market where radically new instruments could command a high enough price to pay for R&D expenses in a very short period.

The problem in these two situations was that the older, declining product line was still profitable and could apparently support heavy R&D costs, while the new product line was not yet at break-even and could not support a heavy R&D load based on current volume or profits. At least this is the way the situation appeared when viewed through the eyes of the division managers who had to report profitability on their current operations on a quarterly basis.

Hastings Electronics had always depended on a strong R&D program to keep it ahead of competition. It had traditionally spent 4 to 5 percent of sales on R&D, on a sales volume of $50–$75 million. When the company had been decentralized, the research division had been established to ensure that the long-run possibilities for technological progress would be looked after. It was recognized in the company that the product division managers, operating close to the current market and evaluated primarily on the basis of current earnings, might not be in a position to carry on much long-range research. In addition, it was recognized that the company currently operated in only a fraction of the potential markets open to a company with its background and potential, and that the most promising future lines of business might not evolve logically from any of the existing product lines or divisions.

In addition to the establishment of the research division, several other moves had been made to help deal with these problems. The first had been a new business development group which was charged with investigating the various merger and acquisition possibilities that were continually popping up in this dynamic industry. Several of these had survived initial screening and were being analyzed for their potential technical and economic impacts on Hastings Electronics.

A second device had been tried in the specific area of new product development. A task force composed of members of two of the product division laboratories and the research division were using "brain-storming" and other idea-generation techniques to develop a list of ideas for new products which, upon screening, might provide the basis for new product lines or whole new areas of business.

A third group—the Product Planning Task Force—had been assigned to examine the existing product lines of the company and to evaluate their strengths and weaknesses. This activity was also generating some ideas for potential research and development projects.

All of these ad hoc groups, plus the several division labs and the research division, were actively generating ideas for R&D projects. The proportion of the R&D budget available for initiating new projects was limited, due to the continuing nature of much of the work in the laboratories—studies of materials, product improvement studies, programs of testing and evaluating components, and so forth. This was not the major concern of the company management, however, for Hastings had always been able to find some extra R&D money for very promising projects. The primary concern was with the more expensive, later phases of those projects which would prove successful in their initial R&D phases and which would look promising for full-scale exploitation.

Both Long and Green were anxious to find or develop a systematic method for estimating the long-run profit potential of projects that had been and would be proposed as part of the R&D or acquisition program. In order to satisfy themselves that a particular project A was more desirable than another project B, they wanted to have some idea of what would be involved in A and B if they were successful in the long-run and actually succeeded in establishing a new product, a greatly improved one, a brand new product line, or a new market for their existing products or technology. One of the problems which kept arising was that some of the most appealing ideas for research projects were often proposed by the operating departments least able to afford them from the viewpoint of budget and available technical skill. Top management wanted to be sure that, from the overall company standpoint, the best ideas were getting adequate backing and the ideas that were not so good were being dropped.

Although each division manager was autonomous, in the sense that he could spend his own budget in the manner he considered best, top management was responsible for overall coordination of the expenditures on technology and new ventures in the company. They wanted to have available a systematic method of comparing the many proposals from the divisions and the various task forces. They would then be in a better position to advise division managers on their R&D programs, and to make better decisions in the allocation of capital funds for exploitation of research results and expansion of facilities for current product lines. They felt that some continuing programs in all of the laboratories could stand some economic review to see whether they were contributing to the long-run profit position of the company.

Green had had an opportunity to discuss one particular aspect of the problem with several of the division managers, and found them quite willing to admit that sometimes they were not making "cut-off" decisions on a long-run, company-wide basis. Will James, of Industrial Equipment, had been frank, "It is certainly not a matter of failing to recognize the importance of longer range research, aimed at entirely new products and businesses. But our bread and butter comes from a program of continual minor improvements in our present equipments, and we must devote a major share of our technical effort to customer service and helping to keep their equipment operating." George Leahy, of Components, replied to Green's question by saying, "When we have to watch profits closely, we don't do so much long term work. Right now, I am concerned about profits in the current quarter and I have had to terminate a long-term project my lab director had his heart in. If things look better next year, I may reinstate it."

Bob Gordon, of Instruments, was even more direct. "It takes guts to cut off a project that still shows some promise. In the absence of a systematic way of evaluating the potential of such projects, the easier way out is to accede to the pressures from my laboratory people, who are competent in their fields, and let them drift on another few months. I would welcome a better way of reviewing current projects that would make the cut-off decision more objective and get me off the hook with my people."

In two of the divisions (including Bob Gordon's, despite his comments) some straightforward economic evaluation was being applied with an increasing ability to kill off really bad projects and to spot new ones with high potential. The methods used were not uniform and were unknown to the other divisions. In addition, the situation in the research division was very unsystematic. Most of the people in the research division (which included most of the PhD.'s in the company) were not particularly interested in economic and management problems and were not reluctant to say so. They had been impatient with several previous attempts to develop a "project selection formula." One such formula had turned out to be both mathematically wrong and conceptually unattractive to them. They continued to argue for project proposals primarily on their technical merits.

Management was faced, on the one hand, with a researcher whose only argument for a new project was, "This has great potential for a major technical breakthrough," and, on the other, with a salesman who could "sell a million of them." Neither of them generally tried to determine how much profit could be made from a particular project. Under these conditions, the need for more systematic methods was clear. What was needed was a procedure, not necessarily a formula, which would take into account all of the important considerations in project selection, and would generate the kind of information necessary for a good decision.

As an initial step, Green asked Hastings' controller, George Horn, to set up a committee to look into the possibilities of evolving a project selection procedure. Initially the committee consisted of ten members: Horn; Don Edwards, the Market Research Director; Paul Baird, Assistant to the President (who had been doing some economic analysis of company operations); Sam Davis, head of New Business Development; and representatives of the four divisional laboratories and the research division. (Exhibit 1 gives the names of the five laboratory representatives.)

Exhibit 1

HASTINGS ELECTRONICS COMPANY

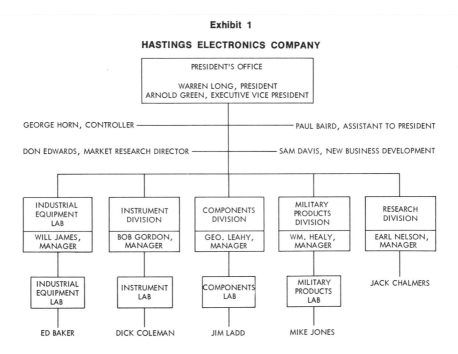

After two meetings of this committee, it was agreed that it was too large to accomplish specific results, and that it would tie up a large number of man-hours in general discussion. In the two sessions, however, a general discussion was held on the problems of project selection and some of the approaches to it. The discussion followed a lecture by a faculty member from the local university who had been active in the field of research economics for some time.

The discussion brought out the differences in practice between the several divisions and also some of the technical differences between their business and the kinds of R&D projects they customarily carried on.

Following the second meeting, George Horn reported back to Arnold Green and suggested that a working group of four people who would devote a significant portion of their time to the project over a few weeks might be the best approach. He further suggested that the work of the four-man group could benefit from several more, carefully focused, lecture-discussions with Professor Royce. Following these sessions, the group would work out procedures and formulations for project selection. When the group was satisfied that it had a workable and useful system developed, the original committee of ten would be called in and asked to comment and suggest improvements. After that, a method would have to be worked out for introducing the new system to the operating divisions and for follow-through to see that the procedures and formulas were properly adapted to the circumstances of each division. There was some uncertainty at the outset as to the best method of doing that, due to the decentralization of the company and the strong autonomous position of the operation divisions. In George Horn's words, "A real selling job would have to be done in presenting the new system to the operating divisions."

The working group of four was established within the next two weeks. It included George Horn, as chairman: Paul Baird, Assistant to the President; Dick Coleman, of the Instruments Division laboratory; and Jack Chalmers, of the Research Division. The four had been with Hastings for a total of over 30 years and combined a broad knowledge of the company's lines of business, its technical programs, and its financial situation. After several more sessions with Professor Royce, the group met several times a week for the next two months. In their first few sessions they discussed a number of aspects of the general project selection problem as well as the specific circumstances in Hastings that would affect the success of any given system. Among the topics covered in these discussions were:

General criteria for the size of an R&D budget

Formulas that had been presented in the literature for selecting between technically feasible projects

Specific criteria for comparing projects

The "pay-off period" and the rate of profit

The return on investment concept

The discounted cash flow method of determining present value

Methods for after-the-fact evaluation of the results of specific projects

Check lists for factors that should be considered, regardless of whether they could be inserted into a formula

The combination of qualitive criteria into "project worth profiles"

Procedures necessary to generate the information needed for project selection

Throughout the discussions, it was emphasized that a workable procedure must be acceptable to the operating divisions, as well as reasonable and valid mathematically. Several objectives of a project selection procedure were stressed, in addition to the original one of providing a better basis for top management choice of business opportunities:

A stimulus to careful estimates and re-estimates of the probabilities of factors such as technical success and particular sales volumes

The integration of such estimates and all other relevant information into a company-wide framework, related to the company's business objectives.

The opportunity to learn by experience, through constant reexamination of estimates and ultimate checking of estimates against actual results

A decision program for generating estimates, re-estimates, and investment decisions

At the end of the two months, the working group had drawn up a procedure which included a "Project Evaluation Check List" for use by people proposing new projects and for use in periodical reevaluations of existing projects. The other major aspect of the procedure was the recommended use of the Discounted Cash Flow method for evaluating the economic returns from a project and for comparing alternative projects or business opportunities. These two devices, plus an outline for stating business objectives and the group's suggested plan for selling the new techniques in the company, were presented to Arnold Green for the approval of top management.

"This looks fine," said Green, as he examined the portfolio of material presented to him by Horn. "Now all we have to do is to sell it to the operating people."

Case 9-2

Geebold Company (A)

Richard Monroe, controller of Geebold Company, sent the article which is abridged below to his assistant, Thomas Ritzman, with a memorandum in which he requested Ritzman to recommend whether the approach should be considered for adoption by the Geebold Company, either as presented or in some modified form.

Geebold Company was considerably larger than the company used as an illustration in the article. Its capital budgeting procedure required that all projects involving expenditures over $100,000 be approved by the president and Board of Directors. In the preceding year, there had been 15 such projects. A net present value was estimated for most of these projects, but in some cases the estimates were quite rough.

The article was entitled "Capital Budgeting: A Pragmatic Approach," and is reproduced in abridged form below.[1]

The utilization of a theoretically optimal investment criterion, such as (1) accept any investment proposal which has a net present value greater than zero, or (2) accept those projects with the highest rate of return until the cutoff rate is reached, does not directly consider many practical constraints. Furthermore, a pragmatic approach such as "accept those projects that appear desirable" is equally unpalatable. One possible method of treating both theoretical and practical considerations is to examine all possible combinations of investment alternatives to determine the effect of each combination on all of the corporate objectives. Although this method will certainly work, the computational task becomes huge when a large number of projects is considered. Thus, a more efficient and operational method is required.

A possible approach to this problem is to use the technique of linear

---

[1] By Alexander A. Robicheck, Donald G. Ogilvie and John D. C. Roach. Abridged, by permission from *Financial Executive*, April 1969.

programming to determine the optimal set of investment proposals. The objective of the approach would be to maximize the IRR (Internal Rate of Return) or the NPV (Net Present Value) of those investment alternatives under consideration subject to a set of constraints. The constraints, in addition to the supply of capital available, would be those factors, such as earnings per share, ROI (Return on Investment), dividends per share, R&D expenditures, and so forth, which management feels should be considered as operational or practical objectives of the firm.

It should be pointed out that ours is not the first attempt to apply linear programming techniques to the capital budgeting decision. In a doctoral dissertation published in 1963, H. Martin Weingartner attempted to utilize linear programming and integer programming in analyzing certain traditional problems of capital budgeting: namely, investment planning under capital rationing and under imperfect capital markets.

Other authors, such as Van Horne and Charnes, have also attempted to apply linear programming to capital budgeting problems. More recently, in a parallel study less broad in scope, Lerner and Rappaport describe an approach using linear programming and the net present values of projects. All of these authors have been influential in their attempt to introduce linear programming to the realm of capital budgeting decisions.

Capital Budgeting as a Linear Programming Problem

Linear programming (LP) is a mathematical technique that provides optimal solutions to certain classes of problems. The problem must meet the following requirements: (1) the objective to be maximized must be stated in mathematical form; (2) the maximization of the objective must be subject to constraints or limits on certain resources or variables in the problem; (3) all relationships must be linear in character; and (4) there must be more than one way of solving the problem.

In a typical practical capital budgeting situation, the objective may be to maximize IRR or NPV, subject to constraints on the amount of cash available for investment, required earnings per share, limitations for particular projects, and so forth.

Perhaps the best way to illustrate how LP can be applied in practice is to present a simple case example. The example is intended merely to illustrate the methodology and is not necessarily representative of a real life situation.

Case Illustration

The Company, Its Current Status, and Its Objectives. The relevant information for this hypothetical company is shown in Exhibit 1. The company is relatively small, with after-tax earnings of $500,000 for the year just ended. Since there are 100,000 shares outstanding, the earnings per share (EPS) were $5.00. Management estimates earnings for the current year before any new investments to be $470,000 or $4.70 per share. Total cash

Exhibit 1

COMPANY INFORMATION

A. *Current Data:*

Actual earnings after taxes last year	$ 500,000
Number of shares outstanding	100,000
Earnings per share	5.00
Cash available for investments and dividends	1,200,000
Estimated earnings for current year without new investment	470,000
Estimated cash flow for current year without new investment	1,130,000

B. *Goals and Requirements for Current Year:*

Earnings per share—minimum (6% increase)	$	5.30
Total earnings required		530,000
Less estimated earnings without new investment		470,000
Incremental earnings required from new investment		60,000
Cash flow required—minimum		1,300,000
Less estimated cash flow without new investment		1,130,000
Incremental cash flow required from new investments		170,000
Minimum R&D expenditures		300,000
Minimum "necessary" expenditures		60,000
Minimum dividends on last year's earnings		
(40 percent of earnings)		200,000
Cash available for new investments		1,200,000
Less: R&D expenditures	$300,000	
Necessary expenditures	60,000	
Dividends	200,000	560,000
Net cash available for new investments	$	640,000

currently available is $1.2 million, and estimated cash flow for the current year from existing projects without any new investment is $1.13 million.

Exhibit 1B summarizes the factors that the management feels reflect the company's operational goals. Desirous of a 6 percent growth in EPS, next year's goal is earnings of at least $5.30 per share, or $530,000 total. Management feels a 40 percent dividend payout ratio is appropriate. Therefore a dividend of $2.00 per share ($200,000) is expected to be paid soon based on last year's earnings. Management estimates that $300,000 should be expended for R&D projects, and $60,000 is required for certain other necessary projects. Since the total capital available is $1.2 million, the amount available for new projects is $640,000. A minimum cash flow of $1.3 million is considered desirable for the current year.

Investment Opportunities. With this company background information in mind, we can now analyze the investment opportunities open for consideration. Exhibit 2 summarizes five possible investment alternatives. The data for these projects are presented so that both the accounting income and the cash flow for each year are evident. The calculations in Exhibit 2 assume that the revenues and expenses estimated for determining the marginal accounting income are identical to the marginal revenues and marginal expenses necessary for calculating the cash flows. Under traditional accounting practices, this equality is not always maintained. Also for the sake of sim-

Exhibit 2

INVESTMENT OPPORTUNITIES

(all figures in $000)

Period (1)	Investment (2)	Revenues (3)	Expenses (4)	Depreciation (5)	Operating Income (6) = (3) − (4 + 5)	Taxes (50%) (7) = .5(6)	Accounting Income (8) = (6) − (7)	Cash Flow (9) = (3) − (4) − (7)
				Project A				
1	100	140	85	25	30	15	15	40
2		175	100	25	50	25	25	50
3		175	100	25	50	25	25	50
4		175	100	25	50	25	25	50
				Project B				
1	300	100	80	60	(40)	(20)	(20)	40
2		400	200	60	140	70	70	130
3		1100	600	60	440	220	220	280
4		900	400	60	440	220	220	280
5		1500	800	60	640	320	320	380
				Project C				
1	200	300	140	100	60	30	30	130
2		200	80	100	20	10	10	110
				Project D				
1	300	230	105	75	50	25	25	100
2		300	125	75	100	50	50	125
3		350	145	75	130	65	65	140
4		400	165	75	160	80	80	155
				Project E				
1	200	200	110	40	50	25	25	65
2		200	110	40	50	25	25	65
3		220	120	40	60	30	30	70
4		240	130	40	70	35	35	75
5		270	140	40	90	45	45	85

plicity, straight-line depreciation is assumed for all projects for both tax and reporting purposes.

Exhibit 3

SUMMARY OF INVESTMENT OPPORTUNITIES

	Project				
	A	B	C	D	E
Initial investment ($000's)	100	300	200	300	200
First year's accounting income ($000's)	15	−20	30	25	25
First year's cash flow ($000's)	40	40	130	100	65
Internal rate of return	30.4%	45.6%	13.5%	24.2%	22.2%

Exhibit 3 shows the initial investment required, the first year's accounting income, the first year's cash flow, and the computed internal rate of return for each of the five projects. In calculating the rate of return, the investment cost was assumed to have been incurred on the first day of the first year, and all of the revenues and expenses were assumed to occur at the end of the respective periods.

Application of the LP Procedure. For this particular example, the assumption will be made that management wishes to maximize the average IRR subject to the various constraints noted above. The formulation of the problem is as follows:

Maximize:

$$Z = .304\,X_1 + .456\,X_2 + .135\,X_3 + .242\,X_4 + .222\,X_5,$$

where the X_j's represent the amount of funds (in thousands of dollars) committed to project j and the coefficients preceding each X_j stand for the project IRR's shown in Exhibit 3. Average IRR is obtained by dividing Z by 640, the total funds available.

Subject to:

1. Budget Constraint

$$X_1 + X_2 + X_3 + X_4 + X_5 \leq 640.$$

The amount allocated to all projects cannot exceed $640,000, the total amount available.

2. Project Constraints

$$0 \leq X_1 \leq 100.$$
$$0 \leq X_2 \leq 300.$$
$$0 \leq X_3 \leq 200.$$
$$0 \leq X_4 \leq 300.$$
$$0 \leq X_5 \leq 200.$$

The commitment of funds to any one project cannot exceed the project's maximum required funds or be negative.

3. Earnings Constraint

$$\frac{15}{100} X_1 + \frac{20}{300} X_2 + \frac{30}{200} X_3 + \frac{25}{300} X_4 + \frac{25}{200} X_5 \geq 60.$$

The first year's earnings contributions from the accepted new project must be at least $60,000.

4. Cash Flow Constraint

$$\frac{40}{100} X_1 + \frac{40}{300} X_2 + \frac{130}{200} X_3 + \frac{100}{300} X_4 + \frac{65}{200} X_5 \geq 170.$$

The first year's cash flow from the new projects must be at least $170,000.

The results of this capital budgeting model are given in Exhibit 4. As indicated in these results, the optimal solution is to accept all of Projects A and E, place $55,500 into Project B and $284,500 in Project D. No funds are committed to Project C. If this optimal allocation is made, the average IRR will be 26.4 percent. This is the highest obtainable average IRR given the management constraints on the allocation process. (It should be noted that our formulation permitted acceptance of fractional projects. Should such fractional projects not be feasible, a technique called integer programming may have to be substituted for LP.)

Exhibit 4

RESULTS OF THE LINEAR PROGRAMMING MODEL

X_1 = Project A = 100.0
X_2 = Project B = 55.5
X_3 = Project C =   0
X_4 = Project D = 284.5
X_5 = Project E = 200.0
Z = Objective = 168.97

$$\text{Average IRR} = \frac{Z}{640} = \frac{168.97}{640} = 26.4\%$$

If the management of this company is convinced that no additional capital can be raised, and if they are unwilling to reduce any of their requirements for earnings, dividends, R&D, or necessary expenditures, then the usefulness of the LP model is exhausted. The optimal allocation has been determined. However, we seriously doubt that any management is so totally recalcitrant that they will not even question these requirements. This is where the additional information made available by LP becomes invaluable.

Dual Variables. In addition to the data shown in Exhibit 4, the LP solution provides values for the so-called dual variables. These values are not reproduced here, but they provide the basis for testing the sensitivity of the solution to the changes in the various management-imposed restraints. For example, we can determine that the addition of $1,000 to cash available for new projects would increase Z by .360; that is, the IRR on the marginal $1,000 would be 36.0 percent. With this type of evidence confronting management, a decision may well be made either to raise additional capital from outside sources or to reduce the originally planned level of expenditures for R&D, necessary projects, or dividends.

Even more striking is the value of the dual variable for the earnings constraint,—1.42. This means that if management were to reduce their earnings requirement by $1,000 (from $60,000 to $59,000) the value of Z would increase by 1.42 and the average IRR would rise from 26.40 percent to 26.73 percent. This increase is accomplished by switching $6,667 from Project D to Project B. In other words, the reduction in earnings requirements permits a shift of funds from a project with a relatively low IRR but an attractive first-year earnings to a project that offers a very high rate of return, but reports an accounting loss in the first year. Although ours is not the job to judge the validity or reasonableness of this earnings requirement, the LP solution points out the dramatic and severe opportunity cost associated with this policy.

On the other hand, analysis of the LP solution indicates that the minimum cash requirement presents no problems and that for practical purposes the minimum cash constraint has no effect on the allocation procedure.

This analysis in depth of the LP solution illustrates the value that can be obtained from utilizing a linear programming procedure to solve capital budgeting problems. It forces management to question the real worth of their various "practical" goals of constraints. Furthermore, it gives them a number, the value of the dual variable, against which they can compare, analyze, and question their own set of objectives.

Conclusion

The state of the art of capital budgeting has come a long way in the last 15 years. Corporate management has grown increasingly aware of the overwhelming importance of financial decisions on the future growth and profitability of the firm. A great deal of valuable theoretical work has been done in identifying and evaluating the critical variables in the firm's investment and financing decision, and some of this work has been adopted on a practical basis.

However, we are a long way from having the theory provide the answers to all the questions of the modern financial manager. The contemporary financial executive is painfully aware of the multiplicity of corporate goals and objectives which he must keep in a delicate balance. The model proposed in this article is designed to help bridge the gap between theory and practice. We do not propose it as the ultimate solution to these difficult problems, but we do believe it is a step in the right direction.

Case 9–3

Copley Manufacturing Company

Copley Manufacturing Company had begun formal, corporate-wide planning in 1966. Its planning system was modified in 1967 and modified again in 1968. Company executives reviewed the experiences of these three years to see what lessons could be learned that would lead to an improved planning system.

Copley had grown fairly steadily in size and profitability since its founding in 1902; its growth was particularly rapid in the late 1950s and the 1960s. For most of its history, it was primarily a manufacturer of a wide line of cutting tools and related parts and supplies, and the cutting tool division in 1968 was the largest division. In 1968 there were eight other operating divisions, each making and selling a line of industrial products. Some of these divisions were the outgrowth of acquisitions; others had their origin in products developed by the corporate research department. Divisions had considerable autonomy. Sales volume in 1968 was $350 million, net income was $21 million, and there were 17,000 employees.

Introduction of Formal Planning

J. L. Albert, at that time Executive Vice President, said in early 1967:

The need for planning occurred only recently. Five years ago we were a one-product company. Cutting tools constituted 90 percent of our sales, and we instinctively understood our product's future. We'd been in the business for a lifetime. But now the case is quite different. Cutting tools are only about 64 percent of our business.

We started to diversify several years ago. The cutting tool industry was not growing very rapidly, and we decided that we weren't properly utilizing our resources for growth. Now we are in new businesses and have many product lines. There is a new demand for capital. We have gone from being a cash-rich to a borrowing company. Now, no man can grasp all the details. Planning helps us understand the alternatives in resource allocation for optimum results. We started our planning none too soon.

The formal planning effort at the corporate level was an outgrowth of work initiated by Russell A. Wilde, in mid-1962. Mr. Wilde had been head of the Precipitator Division's Commercial Development Department, and as such had been deeply involved in the division's efforts beginning early in 1962 to "plan ahead." Mr. Wilde's effort at the corporate level actually began as a search for companies to acquire, since Copley's top management saw the key question to be, "How should we diversify?" Within six months, Mr. Wilde was arguing that the crucial questions to be asked really were: "What are our objectives?" and "What is our potential?"

One result of the dialogue that followed was a request by Stanley Burton, President of Copley, for the divisions to look ten years ahead and to predict sales, profit, cash flow and return on investment. Mr. Wilde composed the actual questions asked of the divisions and coordinated collection of the data. The resulting consolidated growth projection was not ideal in the eyes of top management, but no imminent crisis was seen.

The ten-year look indicated that many of Copley's markets were mature, that its profits were indeed sensitive to cyclical swings, and that a large cash flow could be expected in the coming years. Before the end of 1963, Charles N. Sagan was appointed Director of Corporate Development, reporting to Mr. Burton. Mr. Sagan was to be mainly concerned with growth through acquisition and merger.

Late in 1965, Mr. Sagan began reporting to Mr. Albert, Executive Vice President. The two easily agreed that regular formal planning should become part of management's way of life at Copley. They were encouraged to work towards this end when Samuel K. Savage, Chairman of the Board, suggested that Copley should do some five-year sales forecasting.

The 1966 Effort

A Corporate Planning Committee was set up in February 1966 by Mr. Albert to guide the move toward a regular, formal planning process. The planning committee comprised the Vice President for Research, the Controller, the Corporate Economist, Mr. Albert, and Mr. Sagan. The latter was named chief coordinator of the committee.

The planning committee met almost weekly for the next few months, and attacked two major questions:

1. By what process should formalized planning be ingrained into life at Copley?
2. What are appropriate corporate goals for Copley?

A year later, in early 1967, no answer had yet been given to the second question, but decisions were made concerning the first.

A March 21, 1966, memorandum from Mr. Albert to division general managers cited a need for regular formal planning and outlined a plan and schedule for starting such an effort. The basic idea was to survey divisional planning history and attitudes and, after discussions, to issue guidelines for the preparation of divisional "provisional plans."

Visits by Corporate Groups

The concept of formal planning activities was introduced to the organization through a series of visits to the divisions by corporate groups beginning June 6. The composition of the groups varied somewhat, but always included Mr. Albert and Mr. Sagan. In these introductory meetings, Mr. Albert explained the importance of the planning effort, and Mr. Sagan explained the details. Divisions were asked to produce a five-year plan by October 1, 1966. It was left to the divisions to decide exactly who would do what in the process and in what format the final plans would be presented. Corporate staff groups were also instructed to submit plans.

By June 24, the corporate economist had issued his annual domestic five-year economic forecast. On July 25 he issued a set of "corporate assumptions" which had been agreed upon by the planning committee. Corporate goals, although continually debated within the planning committee, had not been reduced to writing.

The criteria selected and the general approach to formal planning at the divisional level were undoubtedly influenced by earlier experiences with budgets. Budgeting on an annual basis had long been well established at Copley. The mechanics for compiling the budget (called the financial plan) were the responsibility of the controller organization. In 1966 a position with the title "Manager of Financial Planning and Control" was created in the controller's department to be responsible for the formulation of capital budgeting procedures. One outcome of this development was a request for a five-year capital requirements forecast from each division. It was anticipated that this information would be prepared in the future as part of the quantitative phase of the planning cycle. The controller also described the financial data to be submitted in the five-year plan in a memorandum dated July 19, 1966 (Exhibit 1).

Exhibit 1

A MEMORANDUM FROM THE CORPORATE CONTROLLER

July 19, 1966

Tentative Five-Year Financial Planning

The planning meetings held thus far have mentioned the need for rough financial data as part of the initial phase of the five-year planning program. The following is meant to be only a guide for your consideration in developing the provisional financial plan for five years. Each division will wish to tailor its data to suit its own particular needs and characteristics; however, we wish to stress the need for thinking through the projection of a five-year plan so that some perspective will be available as indicated below:

Exhibit 1—Continued

Sales—Please state past and future sales at 1966 prices and also in actual $, in total, by major product group, and by market group (e.g., domestic customers, export customers, inter-company).

Profit before Taxes—Analyze projected $ profit in terms of variance from projected 1966 $ profit. The four significant areas of variance should be:

Price Realization—The change in profit due to prices being higher or lower than 1966.

Volume and Product Mix—The change in profit contribution due to changes in physical volume and product mix. This is calculated by applying 1966 contribution ratios to the change in physical volume, by product line.

Cost Variances—Changes in unit variable costs or aggregate fixed costs should be stated. These aggregate changes should be separated into *price* (wage & material rates) variances and *efficiency* (all other) variances.

Profit after Taxes—Translate pretax to after-tax profit dollars for future years at the 1966 tax rate. Show income taxes and investment credit separately.

Cash Flow—The following should be shown by years in total and by product line where a determination can be made. *Full* product line data is not required, but some indication of cash flow, say inventories and capital expenditures, by product line will be helpful.

    Profit after taxes
    Depreciation
    Accounts receivable
    Inventories
    *Capital expenditures
    Other working capital items:
        Cash (working balance only)
        Prepaid expense
        Accounts Payable and Accruals
        etc.
    All other
        Total Cash Flow

Do not project overdraft or debt of any kind.

* Detail by projects over $100,000, *if possible* at this stage.

Excluding profit after taxes, the above projection can be used to project the change in divisional net assets. This can be used, in turn, to project percent return on net assets.

           COPLEY MANUFACTURING COMPANY
           K. C. Steele
           Controller

Planning Review Meetings

Meetings to review divisional plans were held in November and December. As was expected, the format of the divisional plans and presentations varied widely. Attendance at the planning reviews varied also. The planning committee always attended, as did the head of the division being reviewed. In addition, members of the Executive Committee attended on occasion. Divisions were free to bring whomever they wished to their planning review. Representatives of divisions other than the one being reviewed on a given day were not invited to attend.

Planning Response Meetings

A second series of meetings was started December 28, 1966. In these meetings, the planning committee commented on the divisional presentation to the division general managers. The divisions had been expecting some reaction by corporate management ever since the planning reviews, and these planning responses were designed to meet this expectation. Typical of these meetings was that of the Cutting Tool Division, whose General Manager, Mr. Tyler, had recently become a member of the planning committee. The Cutting Tool Division discussion lasted three hours, with Mr. Tyler and the rest of the committee openly evaluating the Cutting Tool Division's plans and its planning review.

Mr. Albert sent a memorandum to the general manager of each division after its "planning response" meeting. Each memorandum summarized the major points agreed upon in the meeting, thanked the participants for their effort in 1966, and expressed the desire for continued progress in making planning a way of life for the Copley manager.

The 1966 Effort: Cutting Tool Division

"Planning must become a way of life," said Mr. Tyler. "When we got the planning assignment, our first move was to try and excite people. This was done by both group and individual discussion on what benefits to expect, and how to go about planning.

"One person should be accountable for all this," he added, explaining the appointment of Bradley A. Volante (Director of Process Development) as coordinator for planning within the Cutting Tool Division. "I was too busy in 1966," said Mr. Tyler, "but in 1967 I will have to be more involved. I couldn't have done it as well as Mr. Volante did, considering all the other things I had to do." Several sources commented that the Cutting Tool Division had done one of the best jobs in planning.

On the subject of goals, Mr. Tyler indicated that this was still an unresolved area. "The corporate management wanted to see what would come from the bottom up." Mr. Tyler also indicated that during the period of charter formation there had been much lively debate and that he had ultimately felt obliged to settle the debate by fiat in order to meet the deadline.

"Management by results" was a recent undertaking by Mr. Tyler, and he felt that planning made an excellent fit with this. Indicating a notebook, he explained that his subordinates had submitted written plans of action, with check-up and completion dates, for correcting the divisional problems noted in the five-year plan.

Mr. Tyler had appointed Mr. Volante and three other staff men to serve for 1966 as a four-man, divisional planning committee. According to Mr. Volante, the planning committee decided that the line should do the planning; and this intention was communicated to the line managers in a meeting convened for that purpose.

"We had some trouble keeping everyone on schedule," said Mr. Volante, "but by September 15 we had the data in and began to consolidate it. The paperwork on something like this is tremendous." By the end of September, the consolidation was ready for Mr. Tyler's approval. Mr. Tyler had a weekend to review the plans. "On the next Monday," said Mr. Volante, "we hand-carried the finished document over to Mr. Sagan, on time, with great satisfaction." The plan formed a notebook about three quarters of an inch thick.

According to Mr. Volante, time pressures had prevented any extensive discussion of departmental problems, and he admitted that "some grey areas went into the plan grey." He added, however, that these problems subsequently formed the basis of a list of areas for immediate action with target solution dates.

Another member of the planning committee, who was Assistant to the Divisional Vice President of Sales, further described the process. He explained that each line manager had turned in a report on what specific action he would take over the next year. He mentioned that the 1962–63 effort (which he considered mostly a forecast, as distinguished from planning) had produced a list of divisional strengths and weaknesses, and that the planning committee had had the line managers update the list for inclusion in the five-year plan.

This member was of the opinion that the "numbers game" had been played a little bit, in order to meet deadlines. He expressed some concern over the tendency of managers to worry more about deadlines than plans. He hoped aloud that 1967 would see more emphasis on strategies.

Mr. William French, a product line sales manager, explained his part in planning. "My group had to develop marketing strategies," he said, "We had to figure out how to get where we claimed we were going to be." Mr. French was of the opinion that the discipline imposed by the planning process had been very beneficial. He further stated that concrete actions regarding manpower and pricing strategy had already been motivated by the planning effort. "Otherwise, we wouldn't have made those decisions at this time."

The superintendent of one of the division's plants stated dissatisfaction with the various forecasts. As evidence, he pointed out that several individual products had already had their forecasts altered. In his opinion, Copley's internal data were generally inadequate to meet his needs. He conceded, however, that the people making the forecasts had to deal with a great many uncertainties.

On several occasions in the Cutting Tool Division, comments were made to the effect that the five-year plan had, in fact, resulted in actions being taken that would not otherwise have been taken. In addition, Mr. Albert indicated that in one of Copley's other divisions a significant materials position had been taken as a result of planning intelligence.

The Cutting Tool Division was the first Copley division to present its plan to corporate management. The presentation, using copies of the five-year plan and charts projected on a screen, took more than two hours. Mr. Volante, who helped Mr. Tyler and the Cutting Tool Division's department managers prepare their presentation for the planning committee, commented: "Since we were the first division, we were sort of guinea pigs, but we found the response disappointing. We were ready with a lot of information and expected difficult and probing questions. Perhaps we expected too much of the corporate group. But I heard from Charlie Sagan that later meetings with other divisions were much better."

The results of the first planning cycle were judged as mixed by Mr. Sagan and by members of top management. It was generally felt that the divisions had made a good beginning, but that they had only begun to dent the planning task. Divisional plans were seen generally to be optimistic extrapolations of past operating trends. Some members of management criticized the effort as having been a numbers game. Others countered that these results were a necessary first step. Most agreed that the plans had been helpful in providing information that would aid top management in understanding better the various business activities of the corporation.

1967 Organizational Changes

1967 witnessed a number of organizational changes that were to affect planning in major ways. Chief among these was the elevation of Mr. Albert to president in March. The corporate planning function moved up with Mr. Albert, continuing to report directly to him.

Several other important organizational changes followed shortly after. Two corporate staff functions were created, one for marketing, and the other for research/development. Operating responsibility was further delegated: the International Division was to report to the new Executive Vice President, John A. Tyler, the former General Manager of the Cutting Tool Division. The Cutting Tool Division was divided along product lines to become two separate divisions.

Two Group Vice Presidents were named, each responsible for three divisions, with the remaining four divisions reporting directly to Mr. Tyler.

Beginning of the 1967 Planning Activities

As a result of the "numbers" orientation of the 1966 planning efforts, Mr. Sagan recommended an increased emphasis on strategic concepts in 1967. After some discussion, the planning committee decided to separate the formal planning cycle into three phases. The first phase, to be held in the spring, was termed the "Strategy Development" phase. The second, or "Quantitative," phase would summarize, during the fall, the financial and manpower implications of the strategies selected in the first phase. The final, or "Action," phase would aim to translate the results of planning into specific programs for action.

In mid-March, the new president, Mr. Albert, sent a letter to each division manager outlining the planning cycle for 1967 and the objectives for the planning efforts that had been agreed to by the planning committee. This letter, reproduced in Exhibit 2, pointed out that while members of the planning committee would participate in the review meetings, actual approval of divisional plans was to be strictly a line function.

Exhibit 2

PRESIDENT'S LETTER, MARCH 15, 1967
To Division General Managers

1967 Planning Cycle

The 1966 formal planning cycle produced some excellent thinking and communication on major issues of concern to Copley. As a result of the planning, we are better informed on the problems and opportunities facing us, and we also see considerable action resulting from the plans.

During 1967, our major objectives are to complete the corporate steps required for planning, to improve attention to the strategy development phase, and to extend planning to all parts of Copley. The attachment gives details of our 1967 objectives.

The program planned for this year is described in Exhibit B [not included in this case.] Major milestones in the program are as follows:

1. Strategy Review Meetings. These will be scheduled from May 15 to June 15 (approximately). They will focus only on the strategy phase.
2. Plans Review Meetings. These will be scheduled from September 15 to November 15 (approximately). They will focus on the numerical results of the planning process.
3. Interaction Meeting. December or later. We hope to have a meeting with all division managers in attendance where each division can briefly present the key elements of its plan. The idea is to provide communication and encourage interaction among divisions.

I should like to make a comment about the review meetings planned in order to help clarify the roles of line and staff. I have chosen to include members of the Planning Committee to participate in the review of divisional plans because they have specialized skills which should be represented in an in-depth review. I want to make it clear, however, that the approval of divisional plans is a strictly line function and, therefore, is not done by the Planning Committee.

I should be pleased to hear from you concerning your reactions to our program and/or your ability to mesh your planning with the corporate schedule this year. I am hopeful that we can build upon the good beginning we made last year in planning and make significant progress this year in improving this valuable management tool to serve better both divisional and corporate ends.

/s/   J. L. Albert
President

Exhibit 2—Attachment

Objectives for 1967 Planning

General Objective

To improve the utility, efficiency, and acceptance of planning.

Specific Objectives

    I. Improve attention to strategy development phase.

        A. Separate "strategy development" and "quantitative summary."

        B. Encourage explicit statements of strategy for each division and/or product line/markets.

            1. Our present strategy and proposed strategy.

            2. Strategy of each major competitor.

        C. Encourage competitive analysis—resources, strengths, and weaknesses.

    II. Extend coverage to whole company.

    III. Complete corporate steps.

        A. Goals.

        B. Assumptions.

        C. Environment.

        D. Strategy.

        E. Identify "gap."

    IV. Improve planning techniques.

        A. Extend historical information back 10–15 years (to include business cycle).

        B. Provide more planning aids.

        C. Planning committee assistance.

    V. Promote divisional interaction.

    VI. Emphasize role of action steps (programs).

    VII. Establish progress reviews.

    VIII. Think about management climate for change.

    IX. Evolve structure appropriate to new strategies.

In April, the economist issued the annual five-year economic forecast which included environmental assumptions and projections of economic growth rates for the industries which constituted Copley's markets. Later that month Mr. Sagan issued a forecast of the social environment to 1975 which he had compiled from Stanford Research Institute data. The purpose of this report was to familiarize division planners with anticipated long-term developments in the general environment and in the marketplace. Also, around that time, a corporate goals committee comprising Messrs. Albert, Tyler, Sagan, and two other executives was attempting to develop a statement of corporate goals.

The divisions' strategic plans were presented to corporate management by each division in a review meeting and subsequently evaluated in a response meeting. Unlike 1966, when they were held a month apart, these meetings in 1967 followed each other on the same day.

Further Developments in 1967

Several developments were to impede progress of the planning efforts in 1967. As already mentioned there was a new president, who introduced seven men into new corporate executive positions. These changes in top management were temporarily disruptive to the planning effort.

Also, considerable management effort was required in assimilating a recently acquired large company and in working out the split-up of the old Cutting Tool Division into the two new divisions.

In 1966, the company had reported its highest sales and earnings ever. The annual report stated that prospects were for a strong 1967. But the machine tool industry was to suffer from depressed market conditions. Sales were down 1.6 percent from 1966; earnings per share declined 35.8 percent. Efforts to counter the unfavorable business conditions became a dominant preoccupation for key line executives.

On July 11, after completion of the strategy development phase of the planning cycle, the planning committee met to consider the planning efforts for the remainder of 1967. In view of the developments noted above, it decided against proceeding with the quantitative phase originally scheduled for the fall. It did, however, recommend that staff departments begin the planning process by analyzing past results and identifying resources, strengths, weaknesses, major problems, and major opportunities of their divisions. Mr. Albert approved the recommendations. The Corporate Goals Committee also lessened its efforts to prepare a statement of corporate goals.

In view of the disruption of formal planning at Copley, top management made special efforts to declare that long-range planning was there to stay. In a letter to division managers dated October 24, Mr. Albert explained the decision to curtail formal planning and emphasized that nothing would be allowed to stand in the way of doing the complete planning job in 1968. He reaffirmed his intention to emphasize planning at Copley in his president's statement in the 1967 annual report: "Long-range planning will become a way of life at our Company. By this medium we will set specific goals, allocate resources of talent and money, and measure our progress. There will be increased emphasis on the delegation of responsibility and in the measurement of performance against predetermined goals."

Situation in 1968

The Copley Company recovered financially in 1968 with a 6.2 percent improvement in net sales and a 58-cent gain in earnings per share. The year also witnessed recovery from many of the organizational pressures: The newly assembled top management team had become increasingly seasoned in its task; the fission of the Cutting Tool Division into two divisions had strengthened those operations; and the problems of assimilating the recently acquired company were generally under control. In his review of the year

1968, Mr. Albert renewed his commitment to planning: "We are continuing to emphasize long-range planning by constantly refining and updating our objectives and strategies for the future."

The Corporate Goals Committee held several informal dinner meetings during the first half of 1967 to discuss a framework developed by Mr. Sagan for arriving at corporate goals. Although a definite statement of corporate goals was not drawn up, the members generally felt that much progress had been made and that it had been a useful and educational experience for all who had participated. The committee as originally constituted was inactive in late 1967 and early 1968, but Mr. Sagan continued to work independently with Mr. Albert on the task. In line with these activities, Mr. Albert was quoted in the business press as stating corporate expectations to include a minimum annual profit growth of 10 percent and a return on equity of 12.5 percent.

Product Line Evaluation

One result of the planning review meetings held in May and June of 1967 was the conclusion that Copley had numerous unpromising product lines. Accordingly, a committee chaired by John Tyler, Executive Vice President, was established to prepare "position papers" on each of the approximately 75 product lines. The Product Line Study Committee (PLSC) planned to report its findings to the Executive Committee in the spring of 1968.

As Mr. Tyler later explained, "We tried to see if the product fit our picture of Copley five years out. If it did not, we made a decision on how and when it should be phased out. We examined the possibility of regrouping the product lines to take advantage of any synergistic benefits and also were concerned with identifying weaknesses in our present lines which could be rectified through acquisition."

Decisions reached by the PLSC were forwarded to the divisions, and each general manager had the opportunity to challenge the committee's opinion if he did not agree. According to Mr. Tyler, the PLSC did not make any in-depth market studies; therefore, subsequent discussions with some of the general managers brought out new information which resulted in changes to the recommendations.

In advance of this study, each division was requested by the controller's office to furnish product line data for 1966 and 1972 including sales, profits after taxes, net assets, market share, principal market, and a qualitative statement of the risks involved. The controller saw this effort as a one-shot study and not part of the formal planning cycle. He noted that many divisions were unable to come up with all the numbers, and in some cases could only report net sales.

Formal Planning in 1968

In 1968, the planning process in large part came to be influenced and administered by Mr. Tyler. Mr. Tyler, who had moved up from head of the

Cutting Tool Division when Mr. Albert assumed the presidency of Copley, enjoyed the reputation among his colleagues as a hard-driving, no-nonsense line manager who had little patience for elaborate staff support. He felt strongly that planning should be an integral part of line management's regular duties and that the existing format and structure tended somehow to separate planning from a line manager's central concern. The major thrust of change in Copley's planning activities was to cut down on details and to make planning a part of regular line activities.

In Mr. Tyler's opinion, division managers had been planning in previous years largely to satisfy the requirements set by the planning staff and had failed to become committed to the plans. He saw voluminous documentation required in 1967 to present a divisional strategy and financial plan as one reason for this failure to identify with the planning output. Thus, in 1968, division managers were asked to present each product group strategy in a statement of two pages or less and the related financial five-year plan on only one page.

The divisional strategy statements were to cover information on such items as industry trends, market size, competition, and major opportunities or threats as well as a description of the proposed strategic response. For the financial plan, divisions were required to submit figures for only the first, second and fifth years of the five-year plan. The purpose of this abbreviation was to reduce the time spent on the numbers, thereby allowing divisional management more time for strategic considerations. Exhibit 3 contains a

Exhibit 3

EXECUTIVE VICE PRESIDENT MEMORANDUM

March 6, 1968

Long-Range Planning 1968

The 1967 formal planning cycle effectively focused on the strategy development phase of planning and resulted in better communication concerning major issues facing Copley. Although the work on the quantitative phase was postponed last fall, we assume you and your division management have continued to develop and refine your projections of the future.

Considerable thought has been given to how our planning program should be structured and implemented during this year. In outlining our plans, it may be helpful to think of the planning program as serving two purposes. First, there is certain basic divisional information which is required at headquarters in order to establish and monitor a corporate program. Second, there is that planning which must be done by and for the divisions in order to insure proper management and adequate growth.

I. *The Quantitative Phase*

The quantitative phase for figures required at corporate headquarters is described on the sample report attached. [Omitted; the report called for the following data for 1968, 1969, and 1972: net sales, net income, receivables, inventories,

Exhibit 3—Continued

plant and equipment, net funds generated, capital expenditures, depreciation, interdivision net sales, and three ratios derived from the above.] It constitutes a minimum number of figures. You already have developed them for 1968. We believe that in a four-hour meeting with your key managers, you could make the adjustments necessary to arrive at a pretty accurate forecast or financial plan for 1969.

When it comes to 1972, we would expect you to plug in the effect of major shifts in direction or performance and to extrapolate and use historical ratios to arrive at the 1972 figures. Done thoughtfully, it will provide us with what we need and preclude your building up in every product line all the detail calculations that you performed in making your 1968 forecast.

II. *The Strategic Development Phase*

The qualitative phase of this request includes your submitting a statement on each major product line grouping. This statement should include your current strategies. We would expect you would want to include comments on such items as industry trends, market size, market share, competition, research effort, capacity, major problems or opportunities you see, and any unusual requests for capital that are predicted.

We ask that you also submit a description of those related opportunities that you are pursuing or might wish to pursue and which you believe will be compatible with our corporate objectives as you now understand them.

It is important that the statements on the strategy development phase be kept to a minimum necessary for effective communication to corporate management. While we recognize that more detail normally would be useful within the divisions for product line planning, please keep the material submitted succinct. A statement on each major product line grouping of two pages or less should be adequate.

Please feel free to consult with any members of our corporate staff whom you think may be helpful in providing format suggestions. Rigid uniformity in preparing these statements is not a criterion. However, your planned strategies should be clearly understandable and believable to be helpful for our purposes.

We hope the information requested in I and II can be in our hands no later than May 1, but please submit when ready and sooner than that date if possible.

III.   Between May 15 and June 30, each division manager will be asked to come to Hartford to review his plans. This will be an informal meeting. You may come alone or bring any members of your staff. It will enable us to ask questions and evaluate progress. Such a series of meetings would take place at this time each year.

IV.   The meetings we have held in early January each year with the Executive Committee to present the year's financial plan will be pushed ahead and held in December starting in 1968.

At that time, you will be asked to cover the coming year and then forecast a second year and fifth year.

To this same meeting you would be asked to bring the same summary statements described under the qualitative phase in paragraph II. This would give management a second time during the year to evaluate progress.

/s/   John A. Tyler

memorandum to divisional managers in which Mr. Tyler lays out the new approach to planning in 1968.

The management review process was also altered. Divisional presentations before the planning committee were replaced by two other meetings. The first of these was a one-hour "pre-meeting" attended by Mr. Albert, Mr. Tyler, the division general manager, and the responsible group vice president. In this pre-meeting Albert and Tyler explained Copley's strategy and acquisition policy, and reviewed the findings and conclusions of the Product Line Study. During the remainder of the hour, the division manager had to explain and to defend the division's strategy for the coming year. At the end of the one-hour meeting the president gave his decision on the division's plans. This review was immediately followed by a three-hour meeting in which the division manager and his staff presented their plans for the first time to the remaining members of the Executive Committee and to selected members of the corporate staff.

Mr. Sagan, Director of Corporate Development, became visibly disturbed by the recent turn of events in planning. He felt himself increasingly limited to corporate merger and acquisition studies. He was fearful that the company would revert to a short-term orientation if it continued along the present path. In voicing these objections to Mr. Albert, he realized that the formal planning system that he had worked so hard to develop was at stake. As a result of these discussions, he felt that he still had the full confidence and support of the chief executive. At the same time, Mr. Albert publicly acknowledged the benefits of getting increased line involvement in planning.

Recent Developments

In an interview in late 1969, Mr. Tyler described recent developments:

As was John Albert's desire, we believe planning is now a way of life at Copley. There just does not appear to be as much need today for a structured management of the process with a planning department per se at the corporate level. This is not to say that all line managers develop plans and strategies to the same degree of effectiveness. But the actual responsibility for planning has been placed directly on the line—that is, the Executive Vice President, the Group Vice Presidents, and in turn, their various Division Managers.

For various reasons, Charlie Sagan left the Company earlier this year. Fred Fisher has been appointed director of corporate development, but his job description was rewritten to put the emphasis on the planning and execution of growth through acquisition.

The planning process in 1968 followed pretty well the steps outlined in my memorandum of March 6 [Exhibit 3]. Of course, long-range planning ultimately involves setting down forecasts and goals. Our experience showed that we had trouble with the definitions of goals, forecasts, financial plans, and objectives. Therefore, it was necessary in early 1968 to get everybody on the same wave length with definitions.

In January 1969 we changed the format for the divisional planning presentations. My letter of January 30 [Exhibit 4] describes our current system of informing all key managers within the company of each division's long-range plans and broad strategies.

Exhibit 4

LETTER ANNOUNCING A SERIES OF EXECUTIVE MEETINGS
(Excerpts)

January 30, 1969

It is always difficult to draw lines across an organization, but those to whom this letter is addressed are either managing profit centers or are directing broad staff functions vital to Copley's operations and to its future growth.

We believe it is important to provide the means for keeping each person in this group better informed of the plans and progress of each division and each staff function as well as the total corporate programs.

The method selected to provide better communications will be tested over the next twelve months and will involve a series of nine meetings; the time and place of each are listed on the attached schedule. Each meeting will start at 1:30 P.M. on the first Monday of the month. They will end at 5:00 P.M. A different division will host each meeting on a rotating basis.

An agenda is planned as follows. From 1:30 to 2:00 P.M. five or six prepared talks of five minutes' duration will be given on subjects of current and general interest selected by the chairman in consultation with others. The following half hour (2:00–2:30) will be devoted to announcements from both the floor and the chairman.

At 2:30, the Division Manager serving as host will take charge of the meeting. He will have a total of two and one half hours during which he is asked to present his long-range plans, allow time for questions and comments, and complete a plant tour of some portion of his facilities.

The group of key executives in attendance does not make up a decision-making committee or a review board in the general sense. They are, however, encouraged to ask questions for interpretation and better understanding. The long-range plans presented by the Division Manager will previously have been approved by the President, Executive and Group Vice President. The Division Managers are asked to present their plans in simply written reports using an expanded outline technique. Copies will be reproduced by the Division Manager following the meeting on a request basis.

This test period will last through the February 1970 meeting. If it is felt these meetings cannot be made to serve their original intention, they will be discontinued.

/s/ John A. Tyler
Executive Vice President

This technique of communicating divisional plans was preceded in December of 1968 by a two-day conference in Bermuda with essentially the same group in attendance. At that conference, we reviewed all of the divisional plans up until that point and announced the broad corporate goals and strategies.

In the same interview Mr. Tyler furnished a copy of a recent talk in which he stated his personal beliefs about management:

I believe that corporate planning is *the* major responsibility of top management. It involves the direction of the whole company (not the parts) in deciding specifically what businesses the company wants to be in, in determining what rate of growth is desirable, in determining what method of growth is intended (research, acquisition, merger). I am a believer in decentralization; in delegating a great deal of authority; giving people their head; permitting some experiments and some mistakes; but sink or swim is the theory.

I do not believe in too many specialized staff functions to clutter up an organization. I avoid "assistant to's" and "administrative assistants" except for short term projects or as training spots in someone's career.

I believe a good manager by definition must put out the daily fires, improve the current quarter's earnings, and at the same time be a long-range planner. If a manager cannot do both, I do not believe the solution lies in shoring him up via a corporate planning department. I *do* believe it lies in using the talent of both line and specific staff personnel who surround him.

I believe in using the talents already present in marketing, finance, research, and manufacturing—and the head of each of these areas must be a planner himself or *he* will fail. I am opposed to separating the division managers from the top management by allowing any staff group to represent or speak for them—or to take their cues from them.

I believe there is fun in managing but the greatest enjoyment people find in managing comes from the variety and complexity of the problems. The broader the challenge, the greater the satisfaction. Division managers want to call the shots on marketing, manufacturing, research, and even control. They certainly do not enjoy someone else thinking through their future for them.

I believe there are many situations that call for specialized knowledge and objectivity that can only come from outside the company. We have used consultants to some extent in developing corporate strategy. But the corporate planning function, by our definition, involves the most vital decisions a company makes. Therefore, it seems to me that corporate introspection, analysis, and conclusions should involve the best all-around talent wherever it exists in the company.

I believe that America's greatest companies succeeded because one man or group of individuals with strong convictions made things happen. They had vision and used intuition in varying degrees but they did their own planning and monitoring of results. I may be overgeneralizing, but normally a company has its best all-around talent in top line positions. They are there because they have a good balance of talents and experience. For that reason, their judgment should have the greatest influence in strategy formation as well as final decision making. By this, I do not mean to imply that line personnel think more strategically than staff personnel. The opposite may, in fact, be true. There are often individuals way down the organization in both line and staff who are thinking persons.

Finally, I strongly believe there is a great tendency in American business to overmanage, overplan, overstaff, and overorganize, which is contributing in a major way to our declining ability to compete in world markets. Our fixed costs in staff and management are often a larger factor than factory labor in making us noncompetitive.

QUESTIONS

1. How do you appraise the formal planning efforts at the Copley Company?
2. What do you predict will occur with respect to formal planning at Copley?
3. How would *you* handle formal planning at Copley?

Case 9-4

Lakeside Oil Company*

In January, 1958, Mr. Karsten, treasurer of the Lakeside Oil Company, received a memorandum from Mr. Bocatelli, manager of the service station division. A few days earlier, Mr. Bocatelli had opposed a plan to lease and operate a chain of service stations and restaurants. The capital investment committee, of which Mr. Karsten was chairman, had tentatively approved this proposal on the ground that it showed an adequate return on the investment. In his memorandum, Mr. Bocatelli set out to explain and support his belief that the plan did not, in fact, show an adequate return.

The proposal referred to was operation of a chain of ten service stations and four restaurants to be built on a new automobile turnpike. When the offer first came to Lakeside's attention, it had been suggested that Lakeside lease the properties from the Turnpike Authority for 25 years, agreeing to pay a flat minimum annual rental of $782,300, plus an additional annual rental based on sales of gasoline and food. In the course of negotiations, the flat minimum rental was increased by a supplemental annual amount of $474,800 to be paid during the first five years only. The supplemental amount was occasioned by an unexpected increase in the estimated costs of building the properties. These minimum rental figures were equal to the level repayment schedule needed to amortize loans of $10 million and $2 million over 25 and 5 years, respectively, both including interest at 6 percent. The Turnpike Authority—the corporation set up by the state to borrow funds, and to construct and operate the toll highway—intended to borrow these amounts.

The calculations originally made by the capital investment committee to evaluate this proposal are summarized in Exhibit 1. The committee considered that from Lakeside's standpoint the lease was a form of investment, since it committed the company to a fixed financial burden over a number of years in the future, and they calculated the amount of the investment by

Exhibit 1

CAPITAL INVESTMENT COMMITTEE'S APPRAISAL

Capital Investment

Annual flat rental $782,300
(Amortizes $10 million 6% bank loan over 25 years)
Capitalized at 16% (782,300 × 6.10*) $4,772,000

Annual supplemental rental $474,800
(Amortizes $2 million 6% bank loan over 5 years)
Capitalized at 16% (474,800 × 3.27*) 1,553,000

Equipment and fittings 150,000

Total Capital Investment $6,475,000
* Present value of $1.00 per year for n years at 16 percent.

Calculation of Annual Cash Income

Gross margins:	¢ Per Gallon of Motor Fuel	$ Per Year at 40 Million Gallons Motor Fuel
Motor fuel	11.1	4,440,000
Motor oil	1.5	600,000
Service and labor	.6	240,000
Miscellaneous sales	1.1	440,000
Restaurant sales	3.7	1,480,000
Total Gross Margin	18.0	7,200,000
Less: Variable expense	5.2	2,080,000
Pretax profit before fixed expense	12.8	5,120,000
Less: Fixed expense		444,000
Pretax profit before gallonage sales rental		4,676,000

Gallonage sales rental	Rental Base	$ Per Year
Motor fuel, 40,000,000 gal.	4.4¢ gal.	1,760,000
Motor oil, (sales of $2,000,000)	4%	80,000
Service and labor (sales of $400,000)	4%	16,000
Miscellaneous sales (sales of $1,800,000)	4%	72,000
Restaurant sales (sales of $8,960,000)	10%	896,000
Total		2,824,000
Pretax profit before annual rental expense		1,852,000

	Years 1–5	Years 6–25
Pretax profit before annual rental expense	$1,852,000	$1,852,000
Annual rental expense	1,257,100	782,300
Pretax profit after rental expense	$ 594,900	$1,069,700
Income taxes at 50%	297,450	534,850
Annual cash income	$1,554,550	$1,317,150

Calculation of Rate of Return

Present value of $1 per year for years 1–5 at 22% $2.86
Present value of $1,554,550 cash income for years 1–5 .... $4,450,000
Present value of $1 per year for years 6–25 at 22% $1.65
Present value of $1,317,150 cash income for years 6–25 .... $2,170,000

Present value of total cash income at 22% $6,620,000
Since this is slightly more than the present value of the capital investment, the rate
of return is a little better than 22%.

taking the present value of all the flat annual payments guaranteed by Lakeside. For this calculation, they used a discount rate of 16 percent, which was the weighted before-tax cost of capital to Lakeside.

The revenue from the investment, from Lakeside's viewpoint, was the profit expected to be derived from sales of gasoline and food, less the additional rental based on sales volume. Past experience with similar projects had shown the profit ratios and operating costs that might be expected. The committee applied these estimates to traffic forecasts supplied by the Turnpike Authority. These forecasts indicated that Lakeside could conservatively expect to sell an average of 40 million gallons of motor fuel per year. This would result in annual cash income of $1,554,550 in the first five years, and $1,317,150 thereafter. The discount factor that made this stream of cash income over 25 years equal the original investment was approximately 22 percent, and therefore the committee concluded that the project had a rate of return of 22 percent.

On the basis of some informal discussion, Mr. Bocatelli gathered that at least one or two members of the capital investment committee, along with himself, did not agree with the majority opinion. Mr. Bocatelli's calculations are summarized in Exhibit 2. He reasoned that this lease represented a fixed financial burden over a number of years, somewhat the same as long-term debt. Since Lakeside had recently sold $215 million of its 25-year bonds at 4.5 percent, he thought that a discount rate of 2.25 percent would be appropriate in that this was equivalent to the current after-tax cost of borrowing

Exhibit 2

SUMMARY OF MR. BOCATELLI'S FIRST APPRAISAL

Capital Investment

Annual flat rental $782,300

Capitalized at a discount rate of 2.25% over 25 years after taxes of 50%
on the rental (782,300 × 50% × 19.03*) $7,444,000

Annual supplemental rental $474,800
Capitalized at a discount rate of 2.25% over 5 years and after taxes at 50%
on the rental (474,800 × 50% × 4.68) 1,111,000

Equipment and fittings   150,000

      Total Capital Investment $8,705,000

Calculation of Rate of Return

Pretax profit before annual rental expense (from Exhibit 1) $1,852,000
Income taxes at 50%   926,000

After-tax income for *appraisal* purposes
  (does not include lease expense) .... $ 926,000
Present value of $1 per year for 25 years at 10% $9.077
Present value of $926,000 annual income for 25 years ($926,000 × 9.077).. $8,405,000
Since $8,405,000 is slightly less than the investment of $8,705,000, the rate of return
is slightly below 10%.

  * Present value of $1.00 per year for n years at 2.25 percent.

to Lakeside. Since Mr. Bocatelli had taken account of the after-tax cash flow resulting from the lease payments in calculating the capital investment, the appropriate income figure for appraisal purposes in his calculation would be $926,000. The discount factor that made this stream of earnings over 25 years equal the original investment was a little below 10 percent. "This is a far cry from a 22 percent return," said Mr. Bocatelli, "and I'm sure we can find far more profitable projects than this one."

However, before any formal action could be taken on the matter, an unexpected problem arose. In the original plan, the Turnpike Authority intended to borrow the funds needed for construction of the property from the Trowton National Bank, using the long-term lease from Lakeside as security. In December, however, the authority's legal counsel ruled that such a loan would be illegal. By state legislation, the authority had been set up as a special corporation, wholly owned by the state. The legislation clearly defined limits on the type and amount of funds the authority could borrow. In December, 1957, the top limit on bank loans had been reached, and a further extension of credit was, therefore, not possible.

Another member of the committee, Mr. Lewis, thereupon conceived the idea of creating a special corporation that would act as an arm's length intermediary, thereby overcoming the legal restrictions on financing. This corporation, temporarily called X Company, would lease the properties directly from the Turnpike Authority, and immediately sublease them to Lakeside. Using the sublease as security, X Company would borrow the funds needed, which it would then advance to the Turnpike Authority. The money would be borrowed by X Company from the Trowton National Bank under exactly the same conditions as had been previously arranged for the Turnpike Authority. Two separate loans were to be made—for $10 million and for $2 million, each at 6 percent. The $10 million would be repaid over each of the next 25 years, including interest, by equal annual payments of $782,300; the $2 million would similarly be repaid over each of the next 5 years by equal annual payments of $474,800. Lakeside would pay exactly the same annual rent as previously arranged, but in this case payments would be made to X Corporation instead of to the Turnpike Authority.

Since the proposed investment was now tied more closely to this particular scheme of financing, Mr. Bocatelli was prompted to make a new study, which is summarized in Exhibit 3, and to use a different discount rate in calculating the present value of the lease. In his opinion, all other costs were identical with those in his original study. He used a rate of 3 percent, because this was the after-tax cost of this particular piece of credit. The use of this new rate changed the total investment cost to $8,111,000, and consequently resulted in a rate of return of less than 11 percent. "This new development, along with a fictitious corporation and a fancy scheme for financing, makes very little difference in my appraisal," said Mr. Bocatelli. "I'm still very much opposed to this proposal."

Exhibit 3

SUMMARY OF MR. BOCATELLI'S SECOND APPRAISAL

Capital Investment

Annual flat rental $782,300

Capitalized at a discount rate of 3% over 25 years and after taxes of 50%
on the rental $782,300 × 50% × 17.572*) $6,873,000

Annual supplemental rental $474,800

Capitalized at a discount rate of 3% over 5 years and after taxes at 50%
on the rental (474,800 × 50% × 4.582) 1,088,000

Equipment and fittings 150,000

    Total Capital Investment $8,111,000

Calculation of Rate of Return

After-tax income for appraisal purposes (from Exhibit 2) (does not include
lease expense) .... $ 926,000
Present value of $1 per year for 25 years at 10% $9.077
Present value of $926,000 annual income for 25 years ($926,000 × 9.077).. $8,405,000
Since $8,405,000 is slightly more than the investment of $8,111,000, the rate of return
is slightly higher than 10%.

   * Present value of $1.00 per year for n years at 3 percent.

At this point, Mr. Jones, another member of the investment committee, offered a completely different argument in favor of the plan. Mr. Jones said he could not for the life of him see why there was so much argument over the proposal. "After all," he said, "we pay out $1,257,100 ($782,300 + $474,800) in rentals before taxes, or $628,550 after taxes. We take in $926,000 after taxes. We therefore have a profit of almost $300,000 after taxes for the first five years, and considerably more thereafter. What is all the argument about?"

As there seemed to be some confusion among members of the capital investment committee, Mr. Karsten adjourned the meeting until the next morning, when a final decision would have to be made. He asked each member to carefully reconsider his position on the matter. It was important that there should not be such a wide difference of opinion among the senior executives of the company on such a basic matter. Mr. Karsten wondered what position he should take at the following day's meeting of the capital investment committee.

QUESTION

What position should Mr. Karsten take at the meeting of the capital investment committee? Be prepared to back up your recommendation with appropriate figure work and justification for any assumptions you have made.

Chapter Ten

BUDGET PREPARATION

This chapter provides an overview of the budgeting process, and focuses on the preparation of budgets. The description of this process is continued in Chapters 11 and 12. In Chapter 11 we describe budget reporting techniques, with particular emphasis on analyzing profit budget variances. In Chapter 12, we describe the role of the profit budget in the evaluation of divisional management.

BUDGETS VERSUS FORECASTS

A budget differs in fundamental respects from a forecast. A budget is a management plan, with the implication that positive steps will be taken to make actual events correspond to the plan; whereas, a forecast is merely a prediction of what will happen, carrying no implication that the forecaster will attempt to shape events so that the forecast will be realized.

A budget has the following general characteristics:

1. It is stated in monetary terms, although the monetary amounts may be backed up by nonmonetary amounts (e.g., units sold or produced).
2. It covers a period of one year.[1]
3. It contains an element of management commitment, in that managers agree to accept the responsibility for attaining the budgeted objectives.
4. The budget proposal is reviewed and approved by an authority higher than the budgetee (the person responsible for the budget).
5. Once approved, the budget can be changed only under specified conditions.
6. Periodically, actual financial performance is compared to budget and variances are analyzed and explained.

A *forecast* differs from a budget in several important ways:

---

[1] In businesses that are strongly influenced by seasonal factors, there may be two budgets per year; for example, apparel companies typically have a fall budget and a spring budget.

1. It may or may not be stated in monetary terms.
2. It can be for any period of time.
3. The forecaster does not accept responsibility for meeting the forecast results.
4. Forecasts are not usually approved by higher authority.
5. A forecast is updated as soon as new information indicates there is a change in conditions.
6. Variances from forecast are not analyzed formally or periodically. (The forecaster does some analysis, but this is in order to improve his ability to forecast.)

An example of a financial forecast is one that is made by the treasurer's office to help in cash planning. Such a forecast includes estimates of sales, expenses, capital expenditures and so forth. The treasurer, however, has no responsibility for making the actual results conform to the forecast. He does not clear it with top management; he may change it weekly or even daily, without approval from higher authority; and usually he does not analyze variances between actual and forecast.

From a management point of view, a financial forecast is exclusively a planning tool; whereas a budget is both a planning and a control tool. All budgets include elements of financial forecasting, in the sense that the budgetee cannot be held responsible for certain events that affect his ability to meet budgeted objectives. In fact, many so-called budgets are really merely financial forecasts. For example, if a budgetee can change his budget each quarter without formal approval (or, if the formal approval is perfunctory), the budget is essentially a financial forecast. It cannot be used for evaluation and control since by the end of the year, actual results will always equal the revised budget.

If one thinks of a spectrum with a pure budget system at one end and a pure financial forecasting system at the other, most budgetary control systems fall somewhere between these two extremes. The approximate location of a particular budgetary control system on this spectrum can be estimated by comparing the characteristics of the system with the characteristics just described. If a particular system happens to have more of the characteristics of a financial forecast than of a budget, this is not necessarily bad. It simply means that management must realize that it has a planning tool, not a control tool.

TYPES OF BUDGETS

In this section, we describe some of the more common types of budgets. These budgets closely parallel the types of responsibility centers described in earlier chapters.

Expense Budgets

Expense budgets can be divided into two types:

a. Budgets involving engineered costs in responsibility centers in which output can be measured.

b. Budgets involving discretionary costs in responsibility centers in which output cannot be measured.

Engineered Cost Budgets.   Manufacturing plants typically have engineered cost budgets, and they are also used in other organization units whose output is measurable. The basis for a manufacturing budget is the standard cost system. An annual production schedule is developed from the sales budget (to be described later), and the standard cost of material and direct labor for each element of cost is applied to each item of production. This is normally done by responsibility centers so that each department has a standard budgeted material amount (often by type of material) and a standard budgeted direct labor amount.

Next, overhead is estimated at the budgeted production volume and all overhead costs are charged directly or allocated to productive departments. Standard overhead rates are developed, usually by dividing the total overhead by a measure of activity, such as total standard direct labor dollars or hours.

Finally, overhead is divided into its variable and fixed elements, and budget equations are developed so that the budgeted overhead costs can be adjusted to the actual volume of production. These equations constitute the flexible budget. This provides the means for separating the spending variance, which is normally the responsibility of the operating manager, from the volume variance, which is normally not the responsibility of the operating manager. (Techniques for calculating spending and volume variance are described in Chapter 11.)

Engineered cost budgets have the following characteristics:

1. They are designed to measure efficiency. Normally, an unfavorable variance means that production costs are greater than they should have been (although this may not necessarily be the fault of the operating manager).

2. In general, operating management accepts almost complete responsibility for attaining budgeted goals. This is because most of the performance variables are under the control of the operating manager. The impact of the principal uncertainty, variances in sales volume, is eliminated through the flexible budget.

Discretionary Cost Budgets.   Techniques for budgeting discretionary cost centers were described in Chapter 5. To review, discretionary expense budgets have the following characteristics:

1. They are *not* designed to measure efficiency or inefficiency.

2. The budgetee is responsible for spending no more than budget (with perhaps some leeway), without obtaining new approval.

Revenue Budgets

Revenue responsibility centers prepare two types of budgets. First, there is a cost budget, which was described in Chapter 5. Second, there is a revenue budget, as described below.

A revenue budget consists of unit sales projections multiplied by expected selling prices. Of all of the elements of a profit budget, the revenue budget is the most critical, yet, at the same time it is the element that is subject to the greatest uncertainties. The degree of uncertainty differs among companies, and within the same company the degree of uncertainty is different at different times. Companies with large backorders or companies where the sales volume is constrained by production capacity will have less uncertainty in sales projections than companies where the sales volume is subject to the uncertainties of the market place. The important management consideration of the revenue budget is that it usually contains forecasts of some conditions for which the sales manager cannot be held responsible. For example, the state of economy or competitive pricing action are conditions which must be anticipated in preparing a revenue budget, yet the marketing manager has little control over them. Nevertheless, the manager does have a considerable degree of control over sales volume. Effective advertising, good service, good quality, and well trained salesmen influence sales volume, and he does control these factors.

Revenue budgets have the following characteristics:

1. The budget is designed to measure effectiveness in marketing. Unfavorable variances from budget means that sales volume or prices are lower than top management believed was a reasonable goal.
2. The marketing manager can be held much less responsible for meeting the budgeted objectives than is the case with cost budgets. Many of the uncertainties of the market place are completely beyond his control, particularly in the short run. This fact limits the use of a revenue budget in managerial evaluation.

In using actual performance compared with a revenue budget as a basis for evaluation, it is helpful if controllable variances can be separated from noncontrollable variances. Chapter 11 describes techniques for doing this.

The Profit Budget

Where a manager has control over both revenues and costs, the cost and revenue budgets can be combined into a profit budget. Because of their importance, and because the profit budget includes the other budgets described above, we will be concerned almost exclusively with profit budgets in the remainder of this chapter and in Chapters 11 and 12.

A profit budget is an annual profit plan. It consists of a set of projected financial statements for the coming year with appropriate supporting schedules. A profit budget, sometimes called a "master" budget, has the following uses:

1. For a whole company, and for its individual profit centers, it is used:
    a) For planning and coordinating the overall activities of the company or

division. For instance, the profit budget can be the basis for assuring that production facilities are in line with sales forecasts and that cash availability is in line with proposed capital expenditures.

b) As a final gauge in evaluating the adequacy of the expense budgets. For example, even though top management has reviewed and tentatively approved all of the expense budgets, after the profit budget is prepared it may become evident that the expense budgets are too high because the projected profit is too low. A further review and revision of the expense budgets will then be made to bring them into line with projected revenues.

c) For assigning to each manager the responsibility for his share of the financial performance of the company or division. For example, the marketing activity is assigned responsibility for the revenue budget. This budget can be further subdivided into regions and districts. The responsibility for meeting cost standards is assigned to the plants, and within plants, to departments. In this way, each manager will know what is expected of him. Subsequently the manager's actual financial performance can be compared to budgeted performance as stated in the overall plan.

2. Divisional profit budgets are used by top management:

a) To review expected total company financial performance for the coming year and to take action where this performance is not satisfactory.

b) To plan and coordinate the overall activities of the company.

c) To participate in divisional planning.

d) To exercise at least partial control over the divisions.

A profit budget has the following characteristics:

1. The extent that it is used to measure managerial performance varies greatly among companies. It can be anywhere from a firm commitment of management to a "best estimate" of what will happen, with little responsibility for making it happen.

2. Closely associated with the above, is the degree of responsibility assigned to the profit center manager for attaining budgeted results. This can vary considerably among companies.

REVIEW AND APPROVAL OF BUDGETS

The annual profit budget is initially prepared by the budgetee and is reviewed and approved by management prior to the beginning of the year. There are several reasons for this review. First, each divisional plan must be consistent with the overall company plan, and plans among divisions must be consistent with each other. The review and approval procedure gives management the capability of changing divisional budgets to obtain this consistency. Second, if the divisional profit budgets are to be used to evaluate the divisional manager, top management must be satisfied that each profit budget represents a reasonable task. In many situations the problem of ascertaining that each profit budget does represent a fair task is very difficult, and sometimes it is impossible. In these instances the profit budget has limited use in evaluation. Even in these situations, however, top management should review the divisional profit plans so as to learn about the changes in expected profitability from the previous year and the reasons for these changes. As a result, the typical profit budget analysis compares the current year's operating results with the coming year's budget and analyzes the reasons for the changes.

The amount of detail presented in a profit budget varies greatly from company to company. At one extreme, the budget proposal consists of summary financial projections with a few supporting financial schedules. At the other extreme, the proposal might run into hundreds of pages and include much detail on marketing, production, personnel, and capital investment plans. In general, the larger, more diversified and geographically dispersed the company, the more detail is required. A second important variable is the importance placed by management on the budgets and subsequent performance reports. The more reliance that management places on the profit budget as a control tool, the more detail is required.

General Considerations for Profit Budget Proposals

The organization and content of the profit budget varies greatly among companies. In general, proposed budgets should have the following features:

1. They should start with the actual profit performance for the current year. (Because budget proposals are prepared in the latter part of the year, it may be necessary to use ten months' actual and two months' forecast of profit performance.)

2. Proposed changes from the current year's actual profit performance should be described in terms that management can understand.

3. Changes in profit performance that are attributable to actions of operating management should be identified in such a way that top management will be able to see what actions the operating manager is proposing to take and what effect these actions are expected to have on profits. Changes in profits resulting from events that can be only partially controlled by divisional management should be identified separately. For example, the effect of a change in wage rates as a result of a corporate union agreement should be separated from an improvement in the efficiency of direct labor costs resulting from better methods and equipment, and changes in sales volume as a result of general economic conditions should be separated from changes resulting from an increase in advertising.

There are two basic methods of presenting the profit budget proposal. One method focuses on the overall causes of changes in profits and perhaps investments; the other method shows the changes to all of the items in the income statement. Exhibits 10–1 and 10–2 show simplified examples of the two methods.

Exhibit 10–1

BUDGET PROPOSAL, FOCUSING ON OVERALL CHANGES

	After-Tax Profits ($000)	Invest-ment ($000)	Rate of Return
1975 actual	$1,500	$12,000	12.5%
Projected increases/(decreases):			
Increased sales volume and mix	500		
Increased costs from changes in			
price levels and wage rates	(300)		
Increased efficiency in direct			
labor and overhead	200	500	
Net change	400	500	
1976 profit budget	$1,900	$12,500	15.2%

Advocates of the overall method (as in Exhibit 10–1) state that it is easier for management to understand the simpler presentation and that management is interested primarily in the overall amount of profits rather than in the detailed accounts that are affected. Advocates of the more detailed method (as in Exhibit 10–2) state that this method gives management more information on which to base decisions, and that with this method management can approve the specifics of the budget, as well as the total.

The choice of a method depends on management's wishes. If the overall approach is used, the detail nevertheless should be available as backup during the budget review.

It is sometimes desirable to group and subtotal related items. For example, changes in the general level of salaries and wages, in the general level of material prices, and in the level of selling prices may be grouped together if the policy of a company is to try to recoup in selling prices the increased costs from rising prices.

The profit effect of any change is influenced by the order in which it is considered in the analysis. For example, a decrease in variable cost will increase the contribution from additional sales and, at the same time, savings in variable cost will be greater if calculated after a projected increase in volume than if calculated before this change. The usual procedure is to list the changes in order of their controllability by management. This means that normally the changes resulting from management actions will come first.

In most cases it is desirable to combine less important items, at least for the presentation to management. Otherwise, the budget presentation will become unnecessarily complicated. In combining items, care should be taken not to mislead management by combining important factors that offset one another. For example, a general reduction in the material costs of scien-

Exhlbit 10–2

BUDGET PROPOSAL, FOCUSING ON DETAIL

Increase/(Decrease) in Profits
($000)

	1975 Actual	Sales Volume and Mix	Price Levels and Wage Rates	Manufac-turing Cost Efficiency	Total Changes	1976 Profit Budget
Sales	$15,000	$2,800			$2,800	$17,800
Material	5,500	(1,000)	(300)		(1,300)	6,800
Direct labor	1,700	(320)	(100)	$200	(220)	1,920
Variable overhead	2,600	(480)	(100)	200	(380)	2,980
Contribution	$ 5,200	$1,000	$(500)	$400	$ 900	$ 6,100
Fixed overhead ..	1,000					1,000
Selling expense ..	500		(25)		(25)	525
Research and development ...	400		(50)		(50)	450
Administrative expense	300		(25)		(25)	325
Net profit before taxes	$ 3,000	$1,000	$(600)	$400	$ 800	$ 3,800
Income tax	1,500	500	(300)	200	400	1,900
Net income	$ 1,500	$ 500	$(300)	$200	$ 400	$ 1,900
Investment Working capital .	$ 6,000	—	—	—	—	$ 6,000
Fixed assets	6,000	—	—	500	500	6,500
	$12,000			$500	$ 500	$12,500
Rate of return	12.5%					15.2%

tific equipment should not be included in the same column as an increase in the number of people employed in the research department. The former is a change in price levels; the latter is the result of management action.

BUDGET ADMINISTRATION

There are two aspects of budget administration: (1) the organization and procedural apparatus for processing the budgeting information; and (2) top management's approach to the use of the budget information. We discuss management's approach to the use of budget information in Chapter 12. In the following section we discuss the organization and procedural framework of budget systems.

The Budget Department

The information flow of a budgetary control system is usually adminis-tered by the budget department. This department normally (but not always) reports to the corporate controller. The budget department performs the following functions:

1. It publishes procedures and forms for the preparation of the budget.
2. It coordinates and publishes each year the basic corporate-wide assumptions that are to be the basis for the budgets (e.g., assumptions about the economy).
3. It makes sure that information is properly communicated between interrelated organization units (e.g., sales and production).
4. It provides assistance to budgetees in the preparation of the budgets, when they request such assistance.
5. It analyzes the proposed budgets and makes recommendations to top management.
6. It analyzes reported performance against budget, interprets the results, and prepares summary reports for top management.
7. It administers the process of making changes or adjustments to the budget during the year.
8. It coordinates and functionally controls the work of budget departments in lower echelons (e.g., divisional budget departments).

The Budget Committee ← Review

The budget committee usually consists of the top management (president, executive vice presidents) and the financial vice president. (The latter may be a nonvoting member.) Sometimes the president, alone, performs the duty of the budget committee. Regardless of its composition, the budget committee performs a vital role in budget approval. This committee meets annually to review and either approve or adjust each of the budgets. In a large, diversified company, the budget committee might meet only with the top operating executives to review the budget for a division or group of divisions. In some companies, however, each profit center manager meets with the budget committee and present individual budget proposals.

Usually, the budget committee must approve any budget changes made during the year. Sometimes, however, budget changes may be made without formal approval by the budget committee.

Budget Revisions

One of the principal considerations in budget administration is the procedure for revising a budget after it has been approved. Clearly if it can be revised at will by the budgetee, there would be no point in reviewing and approving the budget in the first instance. On the other hand, if the budget assumptions turn out to be so incorrect that the budget reports are meaningless, budget revisions would appear to be desirable.

There are two general types of procedures for budget revisions:

1. Procedures that provide for a systematic (say quarterly) up-dating of the budgets.
2. Procedures that allow revisions under special circumstances.

The first type of procedure is generally used where management uses the budgets essentially as a planning tool. If the budget is to be used for control and evaluation, a revision procedure that is as detailed and thorough as the original preparation process would be required. In most instances, this is impractical. Consequently, if a company frequently up-dates its budgets, it really has a forecast system, not a budget system.

If, however, budget revision is limited only to unusual circumstances, such a revision can be adequately reviewed. In general, permission to make such budget revisions should be difficult to obtain; that is, budget revisions should be limited to those circumstances where the approved budget is so unrealistic that it no longer provides a useful control device.

It should be noted that a revised budget is not necessary for an up-to-date forecast of expected financial results. As we shall describe in Chapter 11, good budget reporting systems include a current forecast of the expected annual results. Variance reports, however, analyze differences from the approved budget.

Reporting

Subsequent to the approval of the budgets, actual financial results are periodically (monthly or quarterly) compared to budget and variances analyzed. This process is described in Chapters 11 and 12.

BEHAVIORAL ASPECTS OF BUDGETS

One of the purposes of a management control system is to *motivate* the manager to be effective and efficient in attaining the goals of the organization. Although a detailed treatment of motivational considerations is outside of the scope of this book, some of these are mentioned briefly below.[2]

Degree of Difficulty

There appears to be general agreement that the ideal budget is one that is difficult to attain, but that *is* attainable. If the budget is unattainable, the budgetee may be discouraged from trying. If it is too easy, and represents an inadequate challenge, it will not be a motivating force. An easy budget may even be dysfunctional; the budgetee may perform less well than he is capable of doing because he does not wish to show too large a favorable variance. This might be particularly true if he believes that a large favorable variance would result in his being assigned a more difficult task in the following year.

One of the most difficult problems facing the budget committee is to maintain the right degree of difficulty in the approved budgets.

---

[2] A very good description of the behavioral problems associated with budget systems can be found in *The Game of Budget Control* by G. H. Hofstede, (New York: Barnes and Noble, 1968). Other references are listed at the end of this chapter.

Top Management Participation

Top management participation is necessary for any budget system to be effective in motivating budgetees. Management must participate in the review and approval of the budgets, and the approval should not be a rubber stamp. If it is, the budgets will be almost meaningless to the budgetee. Without this active participation in the approval process, there will be a great temptation for the budgetee to "play games" with the system; that is, some managers will submit easily attained budgets or budgets that contain excessive allowances for possible contingencies. In fact, even where there is adequate review and participation, there will always be "game playing" by some budgetees.

Management must also follow-up on budget results. If there is no top management feedback (both positive and negative) with respect to budget results, the budget system will probably not be effective in motivating the budgetee.

Fairness

For a budget to be effective, the budgetee must believe that his budget is a fair one. This means that the budget system will normally be a bottoms up system with the budgetee preparing an individual budget proposal. This makes the review and approval process critical. If top management changes the budgeted amounts, it must somehow convince the budgetee that such a change is reasonable. This is not always possible. Budgetees frequently express concern about the alleged arbitrariness of top management changes. At the least, top management should listen to the budgetee's position and explain the reasons for its decisions.

Another important consideration in the budgetee's perception of fairness is that the degree of difficulty in attaining the budget should be consistent among the budgetees. A manager who was satisfied initially that he or she had a reasonable budget might change that opinion if other budgetees are perceived to have easier tasks. This is one reason why the top management review is so important. There is nothing more disruptive to an effective budgetary control system than substantial inequalities in the budget task.

The Budget Department

The budget department has a particularly difficult behavioral problem. It must analyze the budgets in detail, and it must be sure that budgets are properly prepared and presented and that reports are accurate. To accomplish these tasks, the budget department sometimes must act in ways that line managers perceive as threatening or even hostile. For example, the budget department must try to insure that the budget does not contain excessive allowances (or "water") for possible unfortunate events. In doing so, it may find itself in direct opposition to the line manager. In other cases, the explanation of budget variances provided by the budgetee might hide or minimize a potentially serious situation. In such circumstances the budget department should "tell it the way it is," which may place the line manager in an uncomfortable position. As a consequence, the budget department often must walk a fine line between helping the line manager and insuring the integrity of the system.

In order to perform its function effectively, the members of the budget department must have a reputation for absolute integrity. If there is any question about their integrity, it beomes difficult, if not impossible, for them to perform the tasks necessary to maintain an effective budgetary control system. In addition to integrity, of course, the members of the budget department should have the personal skills that are required in dealing effectively with people.

NONFINANCIAL OBJECTIVES

In this chapter, we have limited budgets to formal financial documents. Other nonfinancial objectives are usually included in the annual review. For example, market share, new product introduction, training programs and so forth. These objectives should be defined in such a way that management can tell at the end of the year to what extent they have been met. Most of these objectives would be included in the profit budget but not necessarily all of them. Also, these nonfinancial objectives are commitments *in addition* to the financial commitment. For example, if a manager has a market penetration objective, he is expected to meet this objective in addition to his profit objective. Nonfinancial objectives are considered further in Chapter 12.

QUANTITATIVE TECHNIQUES

In the past few years, there have been numerous articles on the use of mathematical techniques and the computer in the budgetary control process. These articles fall into four general categories:

1. The use of computer models that simulate the financial process.
2. The use of mathematical techniques to optimize costs or profits.
3. The use of probability estimates in the budgetary process.
4. Statistical forecasting.

These techniques can also be regrouped into four categories according to their impact on the budgetary process:

1. Of general usefulness to management in planning and control.
2. Of use only in limited situations.
3. Of no practical direct use but useful in conceptualizing problems.
4. Of academic interest only.

In general, we believe that although mathematical and computer techniques improve the budgetary process, they will not change it significantly because none of the techniques solve the critical problems of budgetary control. The critical problems in budgeting tend to be in the behavioral area where mathematical solutions are difficult, if not impossible.

Simulation

Simulation is a method of approaching a problem by constructing a model of a real situation, and then manipulating this model in such a way as to draw some conclusions about the real situation. Simulation, therefore, is not a specific technique but an approach to a problem. The preparation and review of a profit budget is a simulation process. One difficulty with a budget prepared manually is that it is time-consuming to manipulate it. Also, because of computation constraints, a great many simplifying assumptions must be made. Both of these constraints can be significantly reduced if the budget is converted into a computer model. Two activities that a computer model of the budget made practical are:

1. Management can ask what the effect of many different types of changes would be and receive almost instantaneous answers. This gives management a change to participate more fully in the budgetary process.
2. A budget consists of many point estimates. That is, each estimate is the single "most likely" amount. For example, sales estimates include a forecast of the specific number of units of each type of product to be sold. Point estimates are necessary for control purposes. For planning purposes, however, a range of probable outcomes is more helpful. After a budget has been tentatively approved, it is possible with a computer model to substitute a probability distribution for each major point estimate. The model is then run a number of times and a probability distribution of the expected profits can be calculated and used for planning purposes. Simulation is probably the most useful of the mathematical techniques advocated for the budgeting process.

Optimizing Techniques

Optimizing techniques are mathematical methods for finding a best solution where there are one or more independent variables. A number of optimizing techniques have been adapted to the budgetary process. In this part of the chapter, we will describe two of these.

Linear Programming. In some respects, the budgetary process is used as a means for resource allocation. Techniques for combining linear programming with the budget preparation process make it possible to define a desirable end-of-the-year financial position and, then, determine the optimum way to reach this position. For a description of such a model see the Ijiri, Levey, and Lyon article in the bibliography.

Variance Analysis. One problem in budgeting systems is to decide when a variance is significant. A related problem is to decide when a variance requires managerial action. (Not all significant variances require management action, because some arise from uncontrollable causes.) Mathematical solutions have been developed to solve this type of problem. For example, using probability distributions, it is at least theoretically possible to decide whether a variance was most likely caused by the actual situation being different from budget or whether it was caused by the inherent inaccuracies of the point estimate. Other mathematical models have been used to determine the point where the cost of interference by the manager when a variance occurs is less than the potential benefits from such interference.

Optimizing models are rarely used in actual practice in the budgetary process. They are primarily useful in conceptualizing problems. Most actual business situations are too complex and the necessary information is too approximate to warrant the use of optimizing mathematical techniques in the budgetary process.

Probability Estimates

We described earlier the use of probability estimates for planning purposes, after budget approval. It has been proposed (see Geebold Company (B) Case) that budgets be prepared using probability distributions instead of point estimates. That is, the budget committee would approve a number of probability distributions, rather than specific amounts. Subsequent variance analysis would be based on these probability distributions.

Forecasting

The budgeting process requires a considerable amount of forecasting. Although statistical forecasting preceded the computer by a great many years, the computer has made improved forecast techniques practical. Some of these techniques involve economic forecasting. Economic forecasts may be developed internally by large businesses or purchased from outside (e.g., from Data Resources, Inc.) by other businesses. Other techniques are used to predict conditions within a company. For example, multiple regression may be used to forecast cost-volume relationships.

Applications of statistical forecasting techniques are likely to improve the budgetary process. Even with the best of these techniques, however, there will always be considerable uncertainty in most business budgets.

SUGGESTED ADDITIONAL READINGS

Quantitative Articles

DYCKMAN, T. R. "The Investigation of Cost Variances," *Journal of Accounting Research,* Autumn 1969.

FERRARA, WILLIAM L., and JACK C. HAYYA. "Towards Probabilistic Profit Budgets," *Management Accounting,* October 1970.

GERSHEFSKI, GEORGE W. "Building a Corporate Model," *Harvard Business Review,* July–August 1969.

IJIRI, Y., J. C. KINARD, and F. B. PUTNEY. "An Integrated Evaluation System for Budget Forecasting and Operating Performance with a Classified Budgeting Bibliography," *Journal of Accounting Research,* Spring 1968.

———, F. K. LEVY, and R. C. LYON. "A Linear Programming Model for Budgeting and Financial Planning," *Journal of Accounting Research,* Autumn 1963.

JAEDICKE, R. K. and A. A. ROBICHEK. "Cost-Volume-Profit Analysis under Conditions of Uncertainty," *The Accounting Review,* October 1964, pp. 917–26.

MATTESSICH, RICHARD. *Simulation of the Firm through a Budget Computer Program,* Homewood, Ill.: Richard D. Irwin, Inc., 1964.

RAYMOND, R. C. "Use of Time Sharing Computers in Business Planning and Budgeting," *Management Science,* April 1966.

Behavioral Articles

BECKER, SELWYN W. and DAVID GREEN, JR. "Budgeting and Employee Behavior," *Journal of Business,* October 1962.

DECOSTER, D. T. and J. P. FERTAKIS. "Budget Induced Pressure and Its Relationship to Supervisory Behavior," *Journal of Accounting Research,* Autumn 1968.

HEPWOOD, ANTHONY G. "Leadership Climate and the Use of Accounting Data in Performance Evaluation," *Accounting Review,* July 1974.

SCHIFF, MICHAEL and AVIE Y. LEWIN. "The Impact of People on Budgets," *Accounting Review,* July 1970.

SEARFOSS, D. G. and R. M. MONCZKA. "Perceived Participation in the Budget Process and Motivation to Achieve Budgets," *The Academy of Management Journal,* December 1973.

SWIERINGA, R. J. and R. H. MONCUR. "The Relationship between Managers' Budget-Oriented Behavior and Selected Attitude, Position, Size and Performance Measures," *Empirical Research in Accounting: Selected Studies 1972,* University of Chicago, 1974.

WALLACE, MICHAEL E. "Behavioral Considerations in Budgeting," *Management Accounting,* August 1966.

Case 10–1

National Motors, Inc.

William Franklin, controller of the Panther automobile division of National Motors, a manufacturer of numerous products including a wide line of automobiles and trucks, was faced with a difficult decision in August, 1975. Four months previously, the manufacturing office had submitted a supplemental budget in which it had requested additional funds for increased administrative costs in its operations control department. The controller's office had written a memorandum in reply, explaining why it thought this request was not justified, and the manufacturing office had now answered this memorandum.

Mr. Franklin now had three possible courses of action: (1) to concur with the manufacturing office's position, in which case the request would undoubtedly receive the necessary approval of the general manager; (2) to continue his opposition, in which case his views and those of the manufacturing office would be placed before the general manager, who would decide the issue; and (3) to reply with a further analysis, in the hope that the manufacturing office would become convinced of the soundness of his position.

During the last quarter of 1974, the Panther automobile division had absorbed the manufacturing activities of the Starling automobile division. Prior to this, the Starling division had a mechanized system of parts control in its operations control department. The Panther division, on the other hand, had been using a manual system in its corresponding department.

In December, 1974, a study was made to determine which system would serve the division best. On the basis of an estimated reduction of 23 salaried people and of $138,000 in salary and other costs in the operations control department because of mechanization, the decision was made to completely mechanize the Panther division system of parts control. The results of this study were concurred in by the manufacturing office of the Panther division. The appendix explains National Motors' method of controlling administrative expenses in general.

MANUFACTURING OFFICE'S PROPOSED
SUPPLEMENTAL BUDGET

In April, 1975 the manufacturing office proposed in a supplemental budget that the Panther operations control department, now servicing both Starling and Panther automobiles, be allotted for 1975 a personnel ceiling of 109 people to handle the combined work load. Its proposal and reasoning are summarized in Exhibit 1 and in the following paragraphs.

Exhibit 1

PERSONNEL CEILINGS FOR OPERATIONS CONTROL DEPARTMENT IN 1975

Proposed by Manufacturing Office

Positions	Starling Commitment 12/31/74	Starling Savings	Proposed Levels Starling	Panther	Totals
Manager and secretary	2	2	—	2	2
Specifications control	20	12	8	17	25
Design parts control	31	12	19	48	67
Planning and control	7	3	4	11	15
Total	60	29	31	78	109

Exhibit 1 shows the Starling division's personnel ceiling commitment as of December 31, 1974 the expected saving in numbers resulting from the consolidation, and the proposed ceiling for 1975. Since the manufacturing office believed that the new consolidated system of parts control in the operations control department was going to be about the same as the Starling division's mechanized system, the standards that it used to develop the proposed personnel requirements were based on the Starling division's work load and authorized personnel levels for 1974.

Specifications Control Section (25 people)

The work load determinant used in this activity was the number of specifications requests to be processed. In the previous year, 20 employees had been approved in the Starling division's specifications control section: 5 were clerical and supervisory, 10 processed specifications requests, and 5 were involved in specifications follow-up. The specifications control procedure currently used in the Panther division operations was generally the same as that used by Starling. But in the future, the specifications follow-up procedure would no longer be done in this section or, for that matter, in the operations control department.

In 1974 the 10 analysts in the Starling specifications control section had processed 2,964 specifications requests, or an average of 296 specifications each.

In the Panther division, 3,680 specifications requests had been processed during 1974. The manufacturing office believed that a comparison of both Starling and Panther data, as shown in Exhibit 2, indicated that there was a definite relationship between the number of specifications requests processed and the number of unique, new model parts.

On the basis of the above calculations, the manufacturing office estimated the total number of specifications requests for 1975 for both Panther and Starling automobiles, and the personnel required to handle this work load as in Exhibit 3.

Exhibit 2

RELATIONSHIP OF NUMBER OF PARTS TO SPECIFICATION REQUESTS

Division	Number of Unique Parts	Number of Specifications Requests	Specifications Requests per Unique Part
Panther	8,810	3,680	.42
Starling	6,584	2,964	.45
Total	15,394	6,644	.43

Exhibit 3

ESTIMATES OF PERSONNEL REQUIREMENTS FOR SPECIFICATIONS CONTROL SECTION, 1975

A. Specifications Requests and Equivalent Personnel

Division	Estimated Number of Unique Parts*	× Specifications Requests per Unique Part	÷ Actual Output per Man =	Equivalent Personnel
Panther	11,600	.42	296	16.5
Starling	4,800	.45	296	7.3
Total	16,400			23.8

B. Salaried Personnel Requirements

Division	Equivalent Personnel	Less Planned Efficiency (approx. 10%)†	Less Planned Overtime (approx. 5%)	Salaried Ceiling Required
Panther	16.5	1.7	.9	14
Starling	7.3	.8	.4	6
Total	23.8	2.5	1.3	20

C. Other Personnel Requirements

Position	Panther	Starling	Total
Section supervisor and secretary	2	—	2
Unit supervisor	1	1	2
Clerk-typist	—	1	1
Total Fixed	3	2	5‡
Total Salaried and Other			25

* The Panther division had added a new car to its line, and the Starling division had dropped one.

† "Planned efficiency" reduces the calculated personnel requirements to a level approximately consistent with the lowest work load level anticipated during the coming year. In order to handle periodic work load increases during a year, the department is forced to improve its efficiency and, if necessary, to utilize overtime or temporary clerical help from outside agencies.

‡ Same as Starling commitment of December 31, 1974.

Design Parts Section (67 people)

The number of unique parts to be processed was used as the general work load determinant in this section. In 1974 for 6,584 parts there were 27 specifications coordinators in the Starling division budget for an average of 242 parts per coordinator. According to Exhibit 4, which was drawn up in the manufacturing office, 58 specifications coordinators would be required to handle the combined work load in 1975 plus nine supervisors and clerical workers.

Exhibit 4

ESTIMATES OF PERSONNEL REQUIREMENTS FOR DESIGN PARTS SECTION, 1975

A. Specifications Coordinators Requested

Division	1975 Parts Count	Estimated Output per Man	Equivalent Personnel Required	Less Planned Efficiency (approx. 10%)	Less Planned Overtime (approx. 5%)	Ceiling Required
Panther	11,600	242	48.0	4.7	2.3	41
Starling	4,800	242	19.8	1.9	.9	17
Total	16,400		67.8	6.6	3.2	58

B. Supervisory and Clerical Workers Requested

Position	Panther	Starling	Total
Section supervisor and secretary	2	—	2
Unit supervisors	2	1	3
Clerk-typists	3	1	4
Total	7	2	9
Unit supervisors to coordinators	1:20	1:17	1:19
Clerk-typists to coordinators	1:13	1:17	1:15
Total for the Section			67

Exhibit 5

ESTIMATE OF PERSONNEL REQUIREMENTS FOR PLANNING AND CONTROL SECTION, 1975

Position	Starling Personnel	Number of Unique Parts for Starling, 1974	Parts per Person
Programming computer	3	6,584	2,195
Programming timing and coordination	2	6,584	3,292

	Number of Unique Parts, 1975		Estimated Output per Person	Equivalent Personnel		Personnel Ceiling Requested		
	Panther	Starling		Panther	Starling	Panther	Starling	Total
Program timing and coordination ..	11,600	4,800	3,292	3.5	1.5	4	2	6
Programming	11,600	4,800	2,195	5.3	2.2	5	2	7
Total				8.8	3.7	9	4	13
Section supervisor and secretary								2
Total for the Section								15

Planning and Control Section (15 people)

The requirements for this section were determined by the manufacturing office as shown in Exhibit 5, based on an overall work load indicator of number of parts to be handled.

Manager's Office (2 people)

A personnel ceiling of two was requested: the manager and his secretary.

Estimated Dollar Requirements

The manufacturing office estimated that a total of $1,458,000 would be needed to operate the consolidated operations control department for 1975. This figure was broken down as follows:

Personnel	$1,160,000
Material and supplies	45,000
Computer services	245,000
Miscellaneous	8,000
Total	$1,458,000

Personnel Expenses. This estimate was based on the figure for actual salaries plus approved fringe benefits, in accordance with the level of requested salaried personnel ceilings.

Materials and Supplies. This expense was about $10,000 higher than the 1974 Starling actual. According to the manufacturing office, the job to be accomplished now was about two-and-one-half times the job accomplished by the Starling division in 1974 but the expense was only 30 percent greater. This was a result of efficiencies in programming and reporting, which, in turn, would result in savings in materials and supplies.

Computer Services. Starling had spent $190,000 in 1974 to accomplish a job that was about 40 percent as great as the combined Starling-Panther job. Included in the proposed amount was $34,000 for start-up cost associated with the conversion of the manual Panther system to a mechanized system. Therefore, the real cost was $211,000, or only about 10 percent more than the 1974 Starling actual. The manufacturing office was proposing to do a job 150 percent greater than that done at Starling for only 10 percent more money. This was said to be the result of efficiencies in programming and reporting.

ANALYSIS BY THE CONTROLLER'S OFFICE

The controller's office did not concur with the manufacturing office's proposal. It summarized both the 1975 Panther division's budget and the Starling division's budget as approved prior to the consolidation, and compared these figures with those proposed by the manufacturing office. This summary is shown in Exhibit 6 and is explained in the following paragraphs.

Exhibit 6

BUDGET COMPARISON FOR SALARIED PERSONNEL PREPARED BY CONTROLLER

Budget Status	Panther Division		Starling Division		Total	
	Number	Dollars (000)	Number	Dollars (000)	Number	Dollars (000)
Approved	76	$722	55*	$668	131	$1,390
Proposed	78	974	31	484	109	1,458
Net change ....(2)		($252)	24	$184	22	($ 68)
	Explanation of Changes					
Savings from mechaniza- tion of Panther system	23†	$138†	—	$ —	23	$ 138
Savings from consoli- dation	—	—	24	184	24	184
Proposed increase to Panther budget	(25)	(390)	—	—	(25)	($ 390)
Net change ....(2)		($252)	24	$184	22	($ 68)

( ) = Adverse effect on profit.
* Reflects the transfer of five specifications follow-up personnel out of the specifications control system.
† Based on study of December, 1974, concurred in by manufacturing office.

Although the proposed combined Panther and Starling budgets for 1975 showed a decrease of 22 salaried personnel, there was an increase in cost of $68,000.

The manufacturing office had referred to a saving of 24 people and $184,000 in the Starling division. This reduction, according to the controller, was the result of (a) a reduction in the 1975 parts count and (b) a reduction of supervisory and clerical personnel. This saving of 24 people, therefore, had nothing to do with mechanization and would have occurred under either a mechanized or a manual system.

Although the main reason for mechanizing the Panther division's system of parts control had been financial savings, the controller calculated what the combined budget would have been if, in fact, the Starling division's system had been changed to a manual one comparable to the one in use by the Panther division prior to the consolidation. The budget requirement for the Panther division, of course, would not change. However, 35 people and $406,000 would be required for the Starling division, on the basis of Panther division's standards as developed in the manufacturing office's analysis. Thus, a comparison between the manual system and the mechanized system was as shown in Exhibit 7.

According to Exhibit 7, the effect of the mechanization and the consolidation on the 1975 Panther budget, which was based on a manual system, was to increase the 1975 salaried personnel level by two people and to increase costs by $252,000. The controller was at a loss to know why these increases should result from mechanization. Moreover, the manufacturing office had committed itself to a saving of 23 people and $138,000 in the

Exhibit 7

CONTROLLER'S REVISED BUDGET COMPARISON FOR SALARIED PERSONNEL, 1975

System	Panther Division		Starling Division		Total	
	Number	Dollars (000)	Number	Dollars (000)	Number	Dollars (000)
Combined manual systems	76	$722	35	$406	111	$1,128
Proposed mechanized systems	78	974	31	484	109	1,458
Difference between cost of mechanized system and manual system	(2)	($252)	4	($ 78)	2	($ 330)

Panther division, whereas the current proposal was 25 people and $390,000 *over* the levels committed.

The controller believed that budget figures under a *combined mechanized system,* instead, should be as shown in Exhibit 8.

Exhibit 8

CONTROLLER'S PROPOSED BUDGET, 1975

Salaried Personnel	Panther	Starling	Total
Number	53	31	84
Budget dollars (000)	$584	$484	$1,068 ✓

In this calculation, the Panther division's number of salaried personnel was based on the premechanization figure (76) minus the saving agreed to by the manufacturing office as a result of mechanization (23). The Panther division's budget dollars were based on the same sort of analysis—$722,000 minus $138,000. Starling division's figures were those used in the preceding table, based on a reduced parts count, supervisory savings, and the functional transfer of personnel. The budget figures for the new division have been 84 pepople and $1,068,000.

On the basis of its analysis, the controller's office recommended that the manufacturing office at least not increase its 1975 costs for the operations control department over the level that would have occurred under a combined manual system. This meant a dollar budget of $1,128,000. Personnel reductions would be required to contain costs within recommended levels; these were set forth in Exhibit 9.

PROTEST FROM THE MANUFACTURING OFFICE

The manufacturing office did not accept the controller's recommendation of a reduction of 25 salaried people and $330,000, though it agreed that, generally speaking, a mechanized operations control system should not be any more costly than the previously used manual system.

Exhibit 9

DETAIL OF CONTROLLER'S RECOMMENDED BUDGET, 1975

	Panther		Starling		Total	
Proposals	Number	Dollars (000)	Number	Dollars (000)	Number	Dollars (000)
Manufacturing office's request ...	78	$974	31	$484	109	$1,458
Controller's recommended reductions:						
Salary mix	—	85	—	—	—	85
Overtime	—	27	—	21	—	48
Required personnel (to meet financial objective)	25	197	—	—	25	197
Total Recommended Reductions	25	$309	—	$ 21	25	$ 330
Total Recommended Level	53	$665	31	$463	84	$1,128

Work Load Content and Volume Adjustments

One of the arguments of the manufacturing office was that its proposed Starling–Panther budget included additional people to handle actual work load volume increases over the estimated levels used in developing the 1975 Panther budget for a manual system. The parts counts estimates used in developing the 1975 manual budget and the proposed consolidated mechanized budget were as shown in Exhibit 10.

Exhibit 10

REVISED ESTIMATES OF NUMBER OF UNIQUE PARTS

Division	1975 Original Budget Estimates	Current Known Conditions
Panther	10,200	11,600
Starling	——	4,800
Total	10,200	16,400

According to the manufacturing office, in addition to increased work as a result of the added work load of the Starling division there had been an increase of 1,400 parts in the Panther division as a result of understated original estimates. This increased parts count would have resulted in a requirement for at least 10 more people under the manual system, at a cost of about $90,000, plus an estimated $4,000 for operating expenses.

Unavoidable Increases in Salary Mix

As a result of Starling–Panther consolidation and the consequent personnel changes, the average salary per employee retained in the operations control department had increased significantly. This resulted from the retention of employees on the basis of seniority. The approved budget provided for an average annual salary of $7,044. The Starling–Panther budget proposed by the manufacturing office for 1975 based on actual salaries, provided for an average annual salary in excess of $7,800. Therefore, if average salaries had remained unchanged after the consolidation, the manufacturing office's budget proposal would have been $91,560 less, as shown in Exhibit 11.

Exhibit 11

BUDGET INCREASE DUE TO SALARY MIX

Salary Base	Proposed Ceiling	×	Average Annual Salary	=	Total Annual Salaries
At approved budget rates	109		$7,044		$767,796
At proposed budget rates	109		7,884		859,356
Difference					($ 91,560)

Association with Integrated Data Processing Plan

By implementing the mechanized operations control system, the manufacturing office contended that it had taken an inevitable step included in the company's integrated data-processing plan, which provided for eventual establishment of a completely mechanized master parts control system. This step would make it possible to significantly reduce the original expense estimates associated with setting up this master system.

The original proposal, submitted prior to the consolidation of the two divisions, contained cost estimates of $94,887 during 1975 and $104,672 each year thereafter for providing a master parts control system to preproduction control. According to the manufacturing office, these cost estimates would have been increased to $111,872 and $159,241, respectively, as a result of the consolidation if a manual system were used. As a direct benefit of implementing a mechanized operations control system, however, the manufacturing office believed that it could show a saving of $103,000 during 1975 and $98,000 for each year thereafter. See Exhibit 12.

Exhibit 12

EFFECTIVE COST DECREASE DUE TO MECHANIZATION

Revised Cost Factors	1975	1976 Going Level
Original cost estimates	$ 94,887	$104,672
Cost of consolidation and revised assumptions based on manual system	16,985	54,569
Total cost estimates to include effect of consolidation based on a manual system	$111,872	$159,241
Reduction in cost estimates to give effect to consolidation based on mechanized system	8,700	61,010
Savings directly associated with a mechanized versus manual system	$103,172	$ 98,231

Nonrecurring Cost Penalties

The manufacturing office's proposed budget included a nonrecurring cost penalty of $112,305, resulting from the change in organization and procedure. This was compromised of $72,305 in salaries and wages, and $40,000 in computer expense. If work volume remained at the same levels in future years, the manufacturing office felt that its budget could be revised as follows:

Exhibit 13

FUTURE SAVING OF NONRECURRING COSTS

Budget Items	1975	Future Years	Reductions
Average personnel ceiling	117	109	8
Personnel costs $1,158,876		$1,086,571	$ 72,305
Computer expense	245,000	205,000	40,000
Other operating costs	54,136	54,136	—
Total $1,458,012		$1,345,707	$112,305

Functional Improvements and Advantages

The manufacturing office contended, furthermore, that a mechanized operations control system offered certain other advantages over a manual system.

1. It provided a single and better integrated program progress report that reflected the status of engineering, manufacturing, and purchasing actions against schedules on a more timely basis than did a manual system.

2. It provided a master file that, once stored in the computer, could be used to produce other useful information.

3. It was compatible with the objective to mechanize the issuance of specifications and would result in a more efficient method of handling this activity. The manufacturing office said that it could not put a dollar value on these advantages, but that it was reasonable to expect them to yield cost savings.

Summary

A cost comparison for a manual versus a mechanized operations control system, based on the above adjustments, was as shown in Exhibit 14.

The manufacturing office concluded its arguments by pointing out that the mechanized system cost only $41,000 a year more than a manual system, as shown in the preceding table, rather than $330,000 more, as stated by the controller.

QUESTION

Take a position on the problem stated in the second paragraph of the case. In order to make a judgment on this problem, you should make a careful analysis of the arguments advanced by the controller's office and by the manufacturing office.

Exhibit 14

MANUFACTURING OFFICE'S SUMMARY OF ADJUSTED COST ESTIMATES

	1975 Cost Comparison (000)	
	Manual	Mechanized
Costs	System	System
Unadjusted costs:		
Panther division ....$ 722		$ 974
Starling division 406		484
	$1,128*	$1,458†
Increases:		
Parts count .... (94)		—
Average salaries .... (92)		—
Implementation of mechanized operations control system in accordance with company's integrated data processing plan .... (112)		(9)
Total Adjusted Costs $1,426		$1,467

* Estimated by controller's office.
† Proposed by manufacturing office.

Appendix

Summary of Controller's Description of the Control of Administrative Expenses

Administrative expenses included such expense items as salaries and wages, operating expense, program expense, and assessments for certain divisional activities. Controlling administrative expenses in many ways is similar to the control of manufacturing costs. It is one of the most unpopular and sensitive jobs in the divisional controller's office, because it involves the exercise of control over the addition and elimination of people.

Annual Budgets

Annual budgets are submitted by all divisions and serve as the basis for the control system, performance evaluation, and forecasting of expenses. These budgets are commitments by the individual divisions that they will contain their spending within the committed levels unless they receive approval from the general manager for a supplemental budget.

Personnel Ceilings

A second means of controlling expense is that of setting personnel ceilings, which are limits on the number of people employed. This system of control is useful in reducing to a meaningful size the problem of establishing, analyzing, and controlling budget levels.

Supplemental Budgets

Using supplemental budgets is a technique of continuing budget adjustments. They must be justified on the basis of changed conditions from those existing when the original budget was approved. Through this system, the division reaps the advantage of a detailed review and management approval of all programs prior to the spending of funds. Many companies permit the expenditure of funds, and then ask the spending departments to justify, on an after-the-fact basis, any unfavorable variances. Our system provides more opportunity for coordinated and informed management decision-making.

Management Reports

To make any control system effective, there must be a meaningful system of management reports. Only through usable management reports can management be kept informed and be provided with the basis for performance evaluation, forecasts of costs, and the pinpointing of troubled areas.

DETAILS OF THE ADMINISTRATIVE
EXPENSE CONTROL SYSTEM

Annual Budgets

Assumptions.   Probably one of the most important things in an annual budget review is the establishment of a realistic timetable and the *development of budget assumptions* by the budget section of the controller's office. Divisions will tend to base their budget proposals on different assumptions unless instructed otherwise.

Objectives.   With these assumptions, the next step is to *establish budget objectives*. Objectives are realistic forecasts of next year's administrative expenditures based on known assumptions. To develop objectives, the budget section of the controller's office must normally begin with the current budget, including all supplemental budgets of a continuing nature, and then adjust for any known changes, such as projected cost reductions, increases based on new programs, and so forth. The objectives are then reviewed and approved by the general manager who, in turn, informs the divisions that this is to be the basis for their budget planning. These objectives become the primary bench mark against which the division's proposals are reviewed. If a division's proposal is within the objective, the proposal is usually approved as submitted. However, if a proposal is over the objective, the division must explain in detail the reasons for variance.

Instructions.   With the assumptions and the objectives established, the *issue of budget instructions* to the divisions is a routine job. It is very important, however, that a complete and clear set of instructions be issued. It is important that a budget analyst go through them personally with each division and make certain they are understood. The budget section does not save money. It is primarily a "back pressure" on the divisions that are, in fact, the money savers. Therefore, a close working relationship with the divisions and a good selling job by the personnel of the budget section are essential.

Standards.   As opposed to the majority of the manufacturing budgets, administrative expense budgets are primarily fixed budgets. Through years of reviewing these budgets, however, it has been found that work load standards, quite similar to those employed in variable budgets, can be established for most fixed positions. For instance, in the general manufacturing office, work load in the plant management staff can be partially measured by the number of automobile lines and the number of assembly plants; or in the production scheduling department, work load can be measured by the number of unique parts weighted by the number of plants to which they are released.

Budget Analysis and Review.   With the receipt of the budget submission from the divisions, a detailed analysis is performed by the budget section. One of the significant determinations is the appropriate bench mark from which to measure overall changes in work load. Objectives, of course, are of primary importance. However, actual spending performance in the current year is also used as a bench mark. Probably the single most important tool used in reviewing the detail of budgets is a complete organization chart and statement of functions. This tool is the basis of personnel evaluations and serves to isolate duplication and overstaffing. The organization and systems departments assist the achievement of this goal by giving the controller's office a list of recommended system changes with resulting personnel reductions.

Presentation of Final Budgets for Management Approval.   When the controller's analysis of the budgets is completed, his comments and recommendations are made available to the divisions. If appropriate levels can be agreed on through conferences with the divisions, the budget proposals are submitted to the general manager. If the controller's offices and a division cannot reach agreement, the budget proposal is submitted to the general manager together with a clear, concise statement of the area of disagreement. Recommendations of the divisional controller's office carry a great deal of weight with the general manager, and in a substantial majority of cases our position, when different from that of a division, is upheld. Budgets are not considered just as bench marks, but as actual commitments by divisions.

Personnel Ceiling

Numbers. One of the primary advantages of utilizing a salaried personnel ceiling control is that dealing with numbers of people, as opposed to dollars, brings the problem to a more manageable size. Understanding the need for, and justification of, 8,000 people is clearly much easier than that for the vague figure of $136 million. Moreover, once the justification for the number has been established, the budget dollars follow with very little added analysis.

Time Element. Another significant feature of the personnel ceiling control system is the time advantage it provides. Departments cannot hire or transfer people in excess of the authorized ceiling, and this rule provides a firm before-the-fact control on these administrative expenses. In the case of budget dollars, on the other hand, inappropriate spending cannot be determined until a budget performance report is issued, approximately a month after the expenditure has been made. This feature of the personnel ceiling control puts teeth into the principle of management approval on a before-the-fact basis.

Discipline. Under our budget system, if salary in a division is under budget in total the division is generally not required to explain an overrun in an individual account. On the other hand, by having a personnel ceiling control as well as a budget control a division cannot use up underruns in other accounts by *adding* people over authorization. This adds much more discipline in administrative expenditures, and prevents unauthorized increases in personnel, which in the long run are the source in one way or another of most administrative costs.

Supplemental Budgets

Purposes. Another important feature of the control system is the concept of supplemental budgets. The annual budgets established each fall are outdated almost before they are submitted. The continual changes in plans and programs caused by the volatile nature of the automobile industry do not permit fixed commitments. Moreover, the process of justifying budget supplements by the operating divisions requires them to take time to plan in detail how they propose to spend money. In addition, the system of supplemental budgets provides the general manager with a continuing source of information as to what changes are taking place and what new programs are being planned. It also provides him with a means of altering direction or giving directions to a division before expenditures have been committed.

Variable Adjustments. These are automatic adjustments to a division's budget, and include such changes as functional transfers between departments, division-wide changes in fringe benefits or wage rates (such as a change in the cost-of-living allowance), and volume and work loads in areas that operate under an approved variable budget. Divisions are not required to anticipate these items.

Approval by Management. The supplemental budget system provides for controller's office concurrence and general manager's approval for all proposals on a before-the-fact basis.

Planning and Justification by Activities. The supplemental budget system requires operating management to plan and justify expenditures in terms of benefits to the division.

Commitments. Through the supplemental budget procedure, divisions are asked to demonstrate the financial desirability of new programs. Then it becomes our job to identify and establish these proposed benefits as commitments. For instance, the establishment of the Auburn sales district was proposed by the sales office. Obviously, in the administrative area there are only increased costs associated with a new district. However, we specifically obtained a commitment for additional volume from the sales office. This commitment, if met, will result in substantial added sales to the division, and these incremental sales will more than offset the added administrative costs.

Management Reports

As with any control system, the key to its success is the information it provides to management. Without meaningful and concise reports to management, good analytical work can be wasted.

Performance Reporting. On a monthly basis, each activity's performance against budget is reported to the general manager. Also, on a semimonthly basis, the performance of each activity with respect to its salaried ceiling commitment is reported. Each of these reports is accompanied by a brief letter, pointing out any problem areas that need management attention.

Forecast Reporting. All forecasts are developed by the individual divisions and then reviewed by the budget section. These forecasts are then consolidated and included in the division's profit reporting system.

Product Line Reporting. As the division's profit reporting is segregated by product line, the administrative area is required to allocate its cost by product line. Although the majority of our costs are not specific to individual product lines, we do determine specific costs in the case of new product programs.

Forward Model Program Reporting. With the many new forward model programs in existence or being planned, reporting in this area has become a particularly important part of our reporting job. Administrative expense, particularly in the manufacturing and purchasing areas, can be substantial during the preactivation period of a new program and requires adequate visibility to insure its proper control.

Financial Review.   This is another tool to direct management attention to a problem area. It can deal with either a specific problem or a general problem. For example, financial reviews have been prepared that analyze a particular truck line and all the problems peculiar to it. Also, financial reviews have been made which study a sudden increase in administrative costs. The only requirement for preparing a financial review is that the problem be significant for management attention and action.

Case 10–2

Northwest Aggregates Corporation

In May 1961, Mr. William Markey, the manager of the budget and analysis department at the Northwest Aggregates Corporation, was trying to decide whether to attempt to introduce a flexible budget into the company's divisions. Mr. Markey believed that flexible budgeting would improve the usefulness of the division budgets for management decision-making since it would provide a method for adjusting the monthly targets according to fluctuations in output.

The Northwest Aggregates Corporation was formed in September 1956 as a merger of several companies, one of which was the Seattle Stone Company. Between 1957 and 1960, a number of other companies were acquired. Mr. Robert P. Stearns, the former president of the Seattle Stone Company, served as president of Northwest Aggregates Corporation until April 1959 when Mr. Leroy Cunningham succeeded him. Mr. Cunningham had first become associated with the company as the law partner in charge of the Stearns family account.

As each company was acquired, it was organized as an operating division of the Northwest Aggregates Corporation. In each instance where a family- or owner-controlled company was purchased, no changes in the operating management were made.

Early Budgeting Activities

In September 1958, while still serving as executive vice president, Mr. Cunningham told Mr. Van Sickle, the vice president and controller, that he felt that a corporatewide budgeting process should be instituted so that an operating budget for the year 1959 could be constructed. Mr. Van Sickle asked William Markey to supervise the preparation of the first budget. Mr. Markey had served as controller of a dry cleaning chain in Seattle before

Table 1

NORTHWEST AGGREGATES CORPORATION

Year	Sales	Net Income	Earnings Per Share	Common Stock Price High & Low
1955	$ 65,571,466	$6,194,462	$1.05	18½ — 15¼
1956	83,974,392	7,709,202	1.31	12¾ — 10¼
1957	88,571,260	5,778,000	0.92	20⅞ — 10¾
1958	101,433,062	6,786,340	1.13	17⅛ — 9¾
1959	115,897,199	6,191,455	0.86	20⅜ — 12⅝
1960	120,652,798	5,925,606	0.82	15⅝ — 7⅞

joining Northwest Aggregates as manager of its corporate tax department. They agreed that it would be difficult for the division operating officers to compile even a rough budget and that it might hamper budgeting effectiveness in the future if they attempted to gather too ambitious a budget at the first pass. They decided, however, that two of the primary goals of the budgeting program should be to make the division operating managements more aware of the over-all problems of running their businesses as well as to make them more sensitive to the benefits of careful operations planning. For these reasons they determined that the divisional budgets should not be prepared by the division controllers alone but rather that widespread participation by sales and operating executives should be stressed.

For the 1959 budget, William Markey decided that no new forms should be developed by the budget department and that all budgets should be prepared on the forms used for submitting the regular monthly operating reports to the Seattle office.

The budget that resulted from this directive was, for the most part, very general. At most of the divisions the division controller prepared the budget with minor assistance from the sales and operating vice presidents. In all cases the division personnel remarked that the paperwork and calculation burden in preparing a budget of this kind was tremendous. Although William Markey was responsible for consulting with the various divisions and suggesting methods to them for improving their forecasting and reporting methods, the limited amount of time available for preparing the budget prevented him from spending much time at the divisions. Nevertheless, by December 16, 1958, each of the divisions had consulted with Mr. Van Sickle, and Mr. Markey had submitted all the budgets to Mr. Cunningham and received approval from him. By the last week in December, William Markey's staff had succeeded in compiling these finalized divisional budgets into an operating plan for the entire company which was submitted to the board of directors.

Development in 1959

By April 1959, Mr. Cunningham was completely convinced that the budget could make an important contribution to the quality of the company's management. He realized, however, that William Markey was splitting his time between his tax duties and his budgeting duties and could not devote sufficient time to either. For this reason, Mr. Cunningham asked Mr. George Rudd, a staff procedures specialist who had spent a full year installing a cost accounting system at the Wilson Stone Company, to become assistant controller in charge of budgets.

During the first months in his new job, George Rudd concerned himself with two major projects. The first of these was to formalize a procedure for preparing monthly divisional operating reports and for circulating them among the company's top executives.

In addition to these changes, Mr. Rudd began developing forms to guide the divisions in the preparation of their 1960 budgets. On August 3, 1959, he formally initiated the 1960 budget by sending copies of the forms he had developed to each of the divisions and explaining some of the goals for the 1960 budget. A copy of the form he issued to be used for summary operating statements by product line is shown in Exhibit 1 (product budget). Mr. Rudd asked each division to support this statement with an operating budget, subdivided into variable and fixed costs, for every operating quarry. He also expected that each division would prepare a detailed budget of its selling, general, and administrative expenses (Exhibit 2).

On November 24, 1959, Mr. Rudd presented to the company's board of directors the completed budget for the year 1960. For each division, the budget was compared with actual results for 1958 and 1959 and with the 1959 budget figure. Before each of the divisional budgets was reviewed by Mr. Cunningham, Mr. Rudd had spent at least one day with the heads of each division discussing the forecasts for the coming year. He hoped by this action to make the division personnel more ready to answer the questions that Mr. Cunningham would ask when he completed the final review. In all cases, Mr. Rudd had consulted with the division controllers and presidents before this final meeting.

Mr. Cunningham's review of the divisional budgets for 1960 was considerably influenced by earnings objectives that he and Mr. Van Sickle had agreed upon in advance. In arriving at these objectives, the basic yardstick used was a satisfactory over-all earnings per share after taxes figure. Preferred dividend requirements, federal and state taxes and general corporate costs were added to this figure to obtain the total required divisional earnings. This figure was then allocated among the divisions according to their gross book investment. In each case, however, adjustments were made to the divisional objective according to the personal assessments of these two men of what each division could earn. These assessments were made in light of the

Exhibit 1

PRODUCT BUDGET

DIVISION — Seattle Stone Division / P & L by Product – Final YEAR 1960

	JANUARY AMOUNT	PER UNIT	FEBRUARY AMOUNT	PER UNIT	DECEMBER AMOUNT	PER UNIT	YEAR AMOUNT	PER UNIT
NET SALES BY PRODUCTS								
Slag	301,865		300,965		309,720		4,423,830	
Stone	102,900		102,900		156,900		2,300,700	
Sand and Gravel	69,300		69,300		84,700		1,037,580	
Readymix	192,320		195,455		191,575		3,002,510	
Concrete Block	244,247		240,257		165,748		2,855,999	
Asphalt	16,125		16,125		13,425		1,332,175	
Trucking	59,623		58,675		58,380		905,609	
Other Sales	55,750		61,000		52,750		1,003,000	
TOTAL NET SALES	1,042,130		1,044,677		1,033,198		16,861,393	
LESS: INTRA-DIVISION SALES	36,800		36,900		36,500		594,800	
1. NET SALES	1,005,330		1,007,777		996,698		16,266,593	
VARIABLE COST OF SALES BY PRODUCTS								
Slag	166,472		167,724		173,965		2,407,227	
Stone	47,640		47,170		80,780		1,053,520	
Sand and Gravel	42,806		38,792		46,647		573,218	
Readymix	154,966		156,179		153,752		2,385,287	
Concrete Block	156,585		152,167		105,093		1,791,418	
Asphalt	12,811		12,808		10,287		1,028,296	
Trucking	35,730		35,203		35,252		533,647	
Other Sales	41,235		45,635		37,778		761,543	
TOTAL VARIABLE COST OF SALES	658,245		655,678		643,554		10,534,556	
LESS: INTRA-DIVISION SALES	36,800		36,900		36,500		594,800	
2. NET VARIABLE COST OF SALES	621,445		618,778		607,054		9,939,756	
VARIABLE GROSS PROFIT:								
Slag	135,393		133,241		135,755		2,016,603	
Stone	55,260		55,730		76,120		1,246,780	
Sand and Gravel	26,494		30,508		38,053		464,362	
Readymix	37,354		39,276		37,823		617,223	
Concrete Block	87,662		88,090		60,655		1,064,571	
Asphalt	3,314		3,317		3,138		303,879	
Trucking	23,893		23,472		23,128		371,962	
Other Sales	14,515		15,365		14,972		241,457	
3. TOTAL VARIABLE GROSS PROFIT	393,885		388,999		389,644		6,326,837	
4. LESS: FIXED PLANT EXPENSES	203,451	SALES	207,921		215,314		2,556,950	
5. GROSS PROFIT	190,434		181,078		174,330		3,769,887	
SELLING EXPENSES								
GENERAL EXPENSES								
ADMINISTRATIVE EXPENSES								
6. TOTAL S.G. & A. EXPENSES	100,604		98,914		99,605		1,192,480	
7. OPERATING PROFIT	79,830		82,164		74,725		2,577,407	
8. ADD: OTHER INCOME	(2,900)		(3,200)		1,800		31,300	
9. LESS: OTHER EXPENSE	1,825		1,825		1,825		21,900	
10. PRE-TAX NET EARNINGS	75,105		77,139		74,700		2,594,807	
INVESTMENT		PER						
% RETURN ON INVESTMENT		CENT						
SALES TO OTHER DIVISIONS								
Wilson Stone	2,500		2,500		2,500		30,000	
Concrete Pipe	1,500		1,500		1,500		18,000	
Klamath Falls Rock	1,000		1,000		1,000		12,000	
TOTAL INTER-DIVISION SALES	5,000		5,000		5,000		60,000	

Exhibit 2

1960 BUDGET

Division: Seattle Stone
Selling, General and Administrative Expenses

	January		February		December		Year	
	Amount	Percent of Sales	Amount	Percent of Sales	Amount	Percent of Sales	Amount	Percent of Sales
801–Salaries—Administrative	23,830		23,830		23,985		286,890	1.7%
802–Salaries—Professional & Technical	14,770		14,770		14,825		177,570	1.1%
803–Salaries & Wages—Clerical	9,361		9,361		9,361		112,332	.7%
804–Salaries & Wages—Other	-		-		-		-	-
806–Overtime Premium Pay	45		45		45		540	-
807–Sales Office Expense	439		439		439		5,268	.1%
810–Automobile Expense	3,355		2,867		2,769		38,234	.2%
811–Travel Expense	2,775		2,968		2,313		33,049	.2%
812–Entertainment Expense	1,420		1,291		1,500		18,063	.1%
813–Professional & Club Dues	1,711		115		121		3,233	-
814–Meetings Expense	1,907		2,324		464		12,901	.1%
815–Collection Expense	100		100		100		1,200	-
816–Rejected Sales	20		20		20		240	-
817–Bad Debt Expense	-		-		-		-	-
818–Commissions	2,350		2,350		2,350		28,200	.2%
819–Advertising	1,455		1,455		1,455		17,460	.1%
820–Subscriptions	215		215		215		2,580	-
821–Association Dues	1,375		1,375		1,375		16,500	.1%
823–Communications (Telephone, Telegraph & Postage)	2,500		2,500		2,500		30,000	.2%
825–Printing & Office Supplies	1,208		1,208		1,209		14,500	.1%
826–Rental—Office Equipment	-		-		-		-	-
827–Maintenance—Furn. & Fix.	236		58		59		1,684	-
828–Payroll Department	600		600		600		7,200	-
829–Tabulating Department	3,800		3,800		3,800		45,600	.3%
830–Exploration Department	5,575		5,525		5,475		66,150	.4%
831–Office Rental Expense	1,445		1,445		1,445		17,340	.1%
832–Pension Fund Contributions	8,200		8,200		8,200		98,400	.6%
833–Payroll Taxes	1,060		1,060		1,060		12,720	.1%
834–Workmen's Compensation	740		740		740		8,880	-
835–Group Insurance	2,150		2,150		2,150		25,800	.2%
836–Other Insurance Expense	400		400		400		4,800	-
837–Depreciation—Office Equip.	2,502		2,568		2,120		29,326	.2%
838–Depreciation—Automobile	-		-		-		-	-
839–Automobile Lease Expense	1,500		1,575		1,950		20,700	.1%
841–Internal Professional Serv.	-		-		3,000		12,000	.1%
842–Consulting Fees	1,700		1,700		1,700		20,400	.1%
843–External Auditing	-		-		-		-	-
844–Legal Fees	100		100		100		1,600	-
845–Taxes & Licenses	160		160		160		1,920	-
846–Contributions	1,250		1,250		1,250		15,000	.1%
848–Research & Experimental Expense	-		-		-		-	-
849–Employee Transfer Expense	-		-		-		-	-
850–General Expense, N.O.S.	350		350		350		4,200	-
895–Contra to Exploration Expense	-		-		-		-	-
	100,604		98,914		99,605		1,192,480	7.8%

historical profit data available and the general business outlook for each division. Mr. Cunningham refused to give his approval to four of the divisions' budgets after the initial review because he felt that objectives were not set high enough. He required each of these divisions to revise its budget and to resubmit it to him.

Reports

Mr. Rudd was not satisfied with the quality of the summaries that the divisions were sending to the budget and analysis group. For this reason, he sent a letter to each of the division controllers on March 3, 1960, specifying the form that he wished each division controller to utilize in sending his monthly summary of results compared with the budget to his division president. At the same time and at Mr. Rudd's suggestion, Mr. Gilbert Goodman, who served as administrative assistant to Mr. Cunningham, wrote to all the division presidents and specified what information they were to include in their monthly comment sheets that were added to the controllers' monthly summaries. Mr. Goodman and Mr. Rudd structured their requests in such a way as to insure that each division president utilized his controller's report to answer the questions on the president's summary sheet. Representative copies of the monthly divisional operating reports, prepared jointly by the division president and controller, are shown in Exhibits 3 and 4 for the Seattle Stone and Farrell Brothers Divisions. The controllers' monthly summaries are shown as Part I of these Exhibits while the presidents' letters of comment are included as Part II.

In addition to the monthly summary reports prepared for the budget and analysis group, each of the divisions regularly prepared operating statements for distribution to its own executives. Exhibit 5 shows the operating statements that were circulated for June 1960 within the Farrell Brothers division.

Exhibit 3

MONTHLY OPERATING REPORT—SEATTLE STONE DIVISION

Part I

DATE: July 19, 1960

To: *George Rudd*
FROM: *George Franking, Controller*
SUBJECT: *Seattle Stone Division Operating Results—June 1960*

Division margin was in excess of budget by as follows: $81,800

> Gross profit on sales volume variance $78,900
> Price variance 14,500
> Production variance 5,000
> S.G. & A. expenses .... (6,300)
> Other income and expense .... (10,300)

Sales Volume

Slag sales were $79,000 over budget due to operating two shifts at the cold slag dump, thereby increasing production to meet sales demand.

Stone sales were $171,000 over budget resulting from customer requirements on booked orders and switching slag orders to stone.

Exhibit 3—Continued

Our portable plants are above budget due to favorable quarrying and weather conditions.

Ore block sales were off $90,000 due to reduced demand from mills. Tonnage shipped was 56 percent of budget.

Concrete block sales were $26,000 under budget resulting from the depressed level of activity in the southern Washington area.

The increase on all product sales amounted to $62,000, from which, due to changes in product mix, we realized an increase in gross profit of $78,900, as noted above.

July 19, 1960

Price Variances

Slag reflected the increases, not fully anticipated, resulting from tonnage switches between road aggregates and ballast, as well as price increases effected the first of the year...................... $15,000

Stone had an unfavorable variance due to increased shipments under a low price contracts obtained in prior years. In addition, we were required to furnish stone absorbing a substantial freight differential. .... ($25,000)

Sand and gravel price variances were favorable due to a change in product mix resulting from several large contracts............. $15,000

Asphalt prices reflected shipments under road maintenance contracts where a high price had been obtained.................... $ 9,000

Production Variances

Variances less than 1 percent.

S. G. & A. Expense

Variance of 6 percent of budget due principally to clerical salaries not budgeted and printing expense of new sales invoice forms.

Other Income and Expense

Income from partnerships was $5,000 under budget due to consulting expense in connection with supervision. An item of income was reclassified into the operating section, having been improperly treated as rental income in prior month.

General

Our stone quarry near Bolton started shipping this month, replacing slag orders placed at our Matero City Plant.

It is not expected that any marked improvement will be noted in the southern part of the state for the rest of this year.

The reduction in ore block tonnage was expected during the last half of the year but more drastic reductions than were anticipated were made.

The pattern of sales and profits by product line will continue during the balance of this year. The Division will, in the next few weeks, develop a profit figure that will more accurately reflect the expected 1960 results.

Exhibit 3—Continued

DIVISION CONTROLLERS SUMMARY REPORT
ON
OPERATING RESULTS AND ACTIVITIES
(000 omitted)

Month of _____ June _____   Division _____ Seattle Stone _____

	This Month			Year-to-Date		
	Actual	Budget	Better or (Worse)	Actual	Budget	Better or (Worse)
Sales	1,665	1,589	76	8,391	7,915	476
Cost of Sales:						
Variable cost of sales	951	963	12	4,970	4,819	151
Fixed plant expense	232	216	(16)	1,253	1,245	8
Production variance	27	—	27	20	—	20
Total Cost of Sales	1,156	1,179	23	6,203	6,064	139
Gross Profit	509	410	99	2,188	1,851	337
Expenses:						
Selling	44	40	(4)	238	234	(4)
Administrative	64	62	(2)	381	365	(16)
Total Expenses	108	102	(6)	619	599	(20)
Operating Profit	401	308	93	1,569	1,252	317
Other income	1	10	(9)	72	18	54
Other expense	3	2	(1)	20	11	(9)
Pretax Profit	399	316	83	1,621	1,259	362

Part II

To: *Leroy Cunningham*   Date: July 12, 1960
From: *John L. Stearns, President*
Subject: *Monthly Review—Seattle Stone Division*
Cash:

	June	Year-to-Date
Transferred to N.A.C.	$1,864,000	$9,056,500
Transferred from N.A.C.	$1,747,000	$7,683,500
Net cash to N.A.C.	$ 117,000	$1,373,000
Estimate of transfers to N.A.C. in July	$1,800,000	
Estimate of net cash to N.A.C. in July	$ 500,000	

Accounts Receivable:

	6/30/60	5/31/60
Balance	$2,941,200	$2,879,800
90-day accounts	$ 572,300	$ 515,600
Percent	19.5%	17.9%
Days' sales in receivables	55	56

Ace Construction—$33,900
   Check for less than full amount received but not deposited.
   To bonding company if not settled by 7/20/60.
J. F. Block—$121,500
   Check due week of 7/11/60
Floyd Mountain—$33,200
   Retainage due within 30–45 days. Did not keep promise to
   pay 50 percent on June 10, but we are holding off on this

Exhibit 3—Concluded

account pending our closing a rather large sale.
J. R. Grant—$74,000
Paying per schedule.

Note: The remainder of the report, six single-spaced pages, is not reproduced. It contained detail on personnel changes, backlog of orders, operating
activities, visits from headquarters, and the like.

Exhibit 4

MONTHLY OPERATING REPORT—FARRELL BROTHERS DIVISION

Part I

To   George Rudd   Date   July 14, 1960

From   Edward Overton, Controller

Subject   June Actual versus Budget (Old)

	Month of June			Year-to-Date		
	Actual	*Budget*	*Better or (Worse)*	*Actual*	*Budget*	*Better or (Worse)*
Sales	1,029,755	1,001,499	28,256	3,741,244	3,477,237	264,007
Cost of sales	686,201	668,018	(18,183)	2,765,064	2,356,712	(408,352)
Gross profit	343,554	333,481	10,073	976,180	1,120,525	(144,345)
Selling expenses ...	33,178	21,468	(11,710)	153,339	130,527	
G & A expenses	40,257	38,001	(2,256)	243,032	229,083	
Operating profit	270,119	274,012	(3,893)	579,809	760,915	(181,106)
Other income	40,322	43,038	(2,716)	66,566	202,325	(135,759)
Other expense	3,096	3,000	(96)	11,116	15,000	3,834
Pre-tax profit	307,345	314,050	(6,705)	635,209	948,240	(313,031)

Sales .... Large portion of sales increase attributed to Bristol delivering more than
anticipated ($32,500). Balance of increase made up from variances at other
plants.

Cost of sales .... Practically all of increase this item caused by $17,496 in setting up of un-
budgeted cost for portable in Portland.

Gross profit .... Remarks above will explain.

Selling expenses .... Increase in commissions $8,936 and bad debts charged off $2,127, plus
other minor items.

G & A expenses .... Increase $1,551 salaries, $1,041 General Operating Expense NOS less small
reductions in other items.

Operating profit .... Decrease caused by increases in S G & A.

Other income .... Partnership incomes down. Pine Stone Co. crushing and stockpiling for a
job supposedly to start in July. When deliveries do start, this joint venture
should show more profit than original budget since it developed after
making up budget.

Other expense .... No comment.

MONTHLY REPORT—FARRELL DIVISION

Part II

To   Leroy Cunningham   Date   July 13, 1960

From   J. B. Farrell, President

Subject   Monthly Review Letter

Cash and Receivables
1. Cash:

To Seattle	$2,951,676	Year-to-date
From Seattle	2,862,635	Year-to-date
Excess to Seattle	89,041	Year-to-date

Exhibit 4—Continued

2. Receivables:

	June 30, 1960	May 31, 1960
Balance month end	$2,233,504	$1,924,581
Over 90 days	292,289	385,494
Days sales in receivables ...	65.1	58.1

Note: The remainder of this report, two single-spaced pages, is not reproduced. It contained data on overdue accounts, personnel changes, backlog
of orders, labor turnover, and miscellaneous matters.

Exhibit 5

FARRELL BROTHERS DIVISION

Summary of Gross Profit by Operation
for the Month of June 1960

Stone	Tons Sold	Sales	Cost	Gross Profit
Q1	79,795	$ 114,134	$ 48,168	$ 65,966
Q2	50,976	61,418	12,501	48,917
Q3	38,280	51,608	27,385	24,223
Q4	22,483	39,052	19,006	20,046
Q5	17,240	22,071	13,664	8,407
Q6	–0–	–0–	18	(18)
Q7	46,697	62,814	45,729	17,085
Q8	17,021	21,786	10,752	11,034
Q9	48,260	47,471	29,657	17,814
Q10	24,510	30,145	20,547	9,598
Q11	–0–	–0–	–0–	–0–
Q12	48,126	63,004	49,271	13,733
Q13	1,557	1,895	1,572	323
Q14	–0–	–0–	51	(51)
Q15	46,249	67,323	47,850	19,473
Q16	39,690	52,067	29,721	22,346
Q17	32,387	42,717	39,435	3,282
Q18	–0–	–0–	–0–	–0–
Q19	30,720	40,373	21,812	18,561
Q20	27,020	34,623	31,975	2,648
Q21	–0–	–0–	467	(467)
Q22	42,218	54,164	40,914	13,250
Q23	–0–	–0–	–0–	–0–
Q24	1,086	1,629	5,297	(3,668)
Q25	65,154	86,231	84,101	2,130
Q26	–0–	–0–	245	(245)
Q27	–0–	–0–	–0–	–0–
Q28	–0–	–0–	17,496	(17,496)
Total Stone	679,469	$ 894,525	$597,634	$296,891
Readymix				
Q29	6,678*	71,644	55,449	16,195
Sand and Gravel				
Q30	28,662	45,915	30,500	15,415
Q31	570	913	(1,856)	2,769
Slag				
Q32	4,389	6,419	2,150	4,269
Trucking				
Q29		17,662	10,709	6,953
Commercial Products				
Miscellaneous		10,999	7,215	3,784

Exhibit 5—Continued

Other Operations				
Service Departments:				
Maintenance shop			(4,954)	4,954
Maintenance shop			558	(558)
A Warehouse			(1,965)	1,965
B Warehouse			9	(9)
Mobile equipment			(6,334)	6,334
Aircraft operation			(1,270)	1,270
Fort Project		–0–	–0–	–0–
Unallocated Costs:				
Idle plant and facilities...			13,335	(13,335)
Equipment repairs			(537)	537
Other costs			3,880	(3,880)
Totals 713,090		$1,048,077	$704,523	$343,554
Less Inter-Plant Sales .... (13,256)		(18,322)	(18,322)	
Net Totals 699,834		$1,029,755	$686,201	
Gross Profit from				
Operations				$343,554

* Units omitted from total tons sold

The 1961 Budget

By July 1960, Mr. Rudd was making preparations for the 1961 budgeting program. He believed that the format used for presenting the 1960 budget had been a good one and that no major changes in the forms issued by his group to the division managements were necessary. He asked that each budget letter include certain calculations which he believed would give the division managements a clue as to which aspects of their businesses could be most effectively controlled by means of measurement against the budget. Among these specific calculations were over-all dollar variance due to sales quantities, over-all dollar variance due to sales prices, and gross profit comparisons by plant locations. In addition, Mr. Rudd asked that dollar variances due to sales volume, sales prices, variable production costs, and fixed plant expenses be calculated for each plant location.

After the 1961 budget was completed and the final budget had been approved by the company's board of directors, George Rudd announced to Mr. Van Sickle that he intended to resign from the company to accept a higher level management position at another corporation located in Seattle. Although most members of the home office management group claimed that Rudd had done a good job of transforming the first attempt at budgeting into a workable and fairly sophisticated system, it was generally felt that Rudd's personal relationships with some members of the home office group were not especially good and that his prospects for advancement to a higher management position might be better at a different company.

Upon Mr. Rudd's resignation, Mr. Cunningham and Mr. Van Sickle agreed that William Markey, who had been responsible for the initial budgeting effort in late 1958 and who had since returned to his former position as manager of the corporation's tax department, was the logical person to become manager of the budget and analysis department. On February 1, 1961, therefore, Mr. Markey again assumed responsibility for the Northwest Aggregates Corporation's budgeting activity.

Proposed Variable Budget

In Mr. Markey's opinion, the major decision that confronted him was whether the time was appropriate to attempt the installation of a variable budget. He did not feel that any major improvements in the reporting system currently used were necessary or that the budget, as it was presently prepared, could be much more useful to the division managers than it was. He believed, however, that a major changeover to a variable budgeting system would improve the usefulness of the budget tremendously for decision-making within the division and had observed that most division managers felt that the primary shortcoming of the budget was the fact that no allowance was ever made for the fact that actual production varied considerably from budgeted production. Mr. Markey was eager to go ahead with variable budgeting for 1962, but he was not sure that the divisions were ready for it. Specifically, the Farrell and L'Esperance divisions appeared to have made slow progress in using the budget and there was some doubt as to whether personnel at these divisions paid any attention at all to the budget figures when making internal decisions. At most of the other divisions, the budget was used more extensively but Markey was not sure whether the personnel there were really ready to use a variable budget. Furthermore, he was not sure whether the standard cost data that was available at these divisions was accurate enough to base a variable budget on.

While attempting to reach a decision on the variable budget, Mr. Markey reviewed some notes that he had made of conversations he had had, or overheard, with some of the divisional executives. He recalled some remarks made by Mr. John L. Stearns, president of the Seattle Stone division, on the usefulness of the corporate budget. Mr. Stearns had said:

When this corporation was formed our family was faced with the prospect of a tremendous inheritance tax problem. All the stock in Seattle Stone was owned by members of our family and practically all the assets these people had were tied up in Stone stock. Furthermore, we knew that a tremendous road building program was coming along in this area and we estimated that we would need between $10 million and $20 million in cash to buy equipment and support the necessary inventories so that we could cash in on this development. The merger with Titan Detinning and the listing on the stock exchange had tremendous advantages for us because it gave us a way of disposing of small amounts of our stock at reasonable prices if the necessity arose as well as providing a medium for raising new funds for corporate purposes.

The trouble with the whole thing was that some of the managements that came into this corporation at various stages of its development were concentrating only on the tax and financing benefits of the merger. They never really stopped to consider the fact that life might be different for them once they were part of a large publicly held corporation. For example, before the merger, we were used to ordering equipment any old time we wanted it. There was no necessity for filling out capital justification forms and calculating returns on the additional investment which were reviewed by everyone in management. We just sat down, decided we needed some equipment and went out and got it. We didn't worry about all the formalities that we have to go through now that the home office takes care of approving capital expenditures.

In any case, there's little doubt in my mind that the headquarters staff plays an important role in the functioning of this company and I believe that that's the way it should be. For example, a company like Northwest must have a uniform and coordinated accounting system. The corporate staff also should coordinate equipment purchases and get better deals for us. They've done a lot of this lately and it's worked out well.

But these programs are puny in importance when compared to the budgeting program that Leroy has installed. Before the budget, we really had no way of controlling the operations of the divisions. Each one was operating in just the same fashion as it had before it became a part of the Northwest corporation and no one had any sound way of judging what was going on at any of these companies. In addition, most of our management people, and this includes me, were brought up in quarries. We didn't know anything about fancy budgeting methods or textbooks ways of analyzing stone crushing operations. We had a great deal of experience and made most of our decisions on the basis of past experience and a store of rough yardsticks that had been developed over the years.

Now we've got a real budget and it's extremely useful to us. I won't try to tell you that it's perfect—it sure is a lot of paperwork and, of course, you've always got to make allowances for things that you know exist but that don't show up in the figures. For example, sometimes you get bad weather and your production volume is way off and the targets don't mean that much. But nevertheless, it's got us thinking about our business and it gives us a sounder basis on which to make decisions.

Now at the Stone division, we investigate every product, on a monthly basis, to see how close we came to our sales goals, selling price goals, and variable and fixed expense predictions. When we see that a variance exists, we try to find out exactly what caused it. We know what's going on now—we can't be sloppy with a budget—when you're off, there's no two ways about it and you've got to find out the reason why. You've got to be on your toes. This awareness has filtered down through my organization. The vice presidents for sales and operations, for example, are completely involved with the budget here, as is, of course, the controller. But we don't stop at this level. Salesmen are asked, at the beginning of each year, to forecast their sales. Although they may not be very accurate, this still gets them thinking about what they are going to do, what they can do, and what problems they might run into. Our operating people, by the same token, get a monthly statement comparing their actual and budgeted variable costs. They are not only asked to analyze these but they must send back to George Franking a statement explaining the reasons for any variances.

One statement that I would honestly make is this. If the head office stopped asking for budgets and there was no necessity to go through the detailed calculations for the board, I believe we'd still continue to use them in this division. Frankly, I don't see now how one could manage a business of this size without some form of operations planning.

At the Farrell Brothers Division, by contrast, the budget was not given much credit for helping to improve operating efficiency. Several months ago, Mr. Markey had heard John W. Farrell, Northwest's executive vice president for construction materials and former president of Farrell Brothers, Inc, say:

To be very frank with you, I don't think the budget helps us much here at the Farrell division. Sure, a business always has to have a budget but we always had a budget. Now we just have an awful lot more paperwork. In the old days, we had a budget but we didn't know it as such. We always controlled our costs at Farrell —we always prepared monthly operating statements for every one of our quarries. We just never bothered to go through the whole routine of wildly guessing at our sales and expenses and then making a whole mess of calculations against these guesses. I tell you—we ran our business damn well before the budget was ever installed and we made a lot of money doing it.

My brothers and I started in the sand and gravel business without a penny in our pockets. All we had was a big stone pit and a lot of energy. Let me tell you that we didn't grow so big as we are by neglecting to budget. We just never bothered to spend so much money on paper to do it.

Naturally, I realize that a company the size of Northwest has to have some kind of over-all budget to pull things together so that those on top can get some kind of picture of what's going on. There's no doubt that Leroy's budgeting program has been a great help in this. You can't just expect the home office to sit around and let the divisions run wild. But sometimes, I tell you, the guys from the home office really get me.

Now Jack Van Sickle, for instance, is a guy who knows his figures but who doesn't understand the stone business. He's always on my back to reduce inventories at Farrell. He reads the budgets and sees that inventory ratios are a lot higher in our business than they are in other businesses with which he is familiar and he gets the idea that inventories should be reduced. Now let me tell you something about the sand and gravel business—the customers for your products can buy the same thing from plenty of other producers. The only thing that makes your product any better than the next guy's is your service. If you can deliver the gravel exactly when it's needed, you get the business. If you don't have it on hand, that's tough luck, because your customer can send his trucks over to your competitors who will have the stuff ready for him. Now Jack doesn't understand this. He doesn't think that it's good business to run the quarries overtime during the spring when we're just putting the stuff into stockpiles. But I know better—and I'm not interested in inventory ratios. I know that when spring comes I've got to get those stockpiles high. I know this business and I and my brothers got big by using these methods. All these guys with their fancy budgets just don't seem to understand the elements of what is involved.

Well, anyway, I don't think that the budget does a thing for us at the division. We always analyzed our costs and we still do. I personally could go out there and operate any of our quarries more efficiently than our superintendents can. I know this business. It's all a question of knowing men and knowing how to make them work. That's how we got big. My superintendents are good men but they just don't know as much about the business as we do. You've got to expect that, though, when you hire a man. A man that you hire just won't be as good as a man who is in business for himself. If he were as good, he'd be in business for himself and he wouldn't be working for someone else. But when you get big, you can't run everything yourself and you've got to put other men in charge.

Don't you let any one fool you—I know how my men put together that sales budget. They make believe that they are putting together a real estimate of what is going to happen this year but actually all they're doing is looking at last year's figure and making a little adjustment. No one knows what is going to happen and don't let them tell you that they do.

The only really positive benefit that I can see for the divisions out of this whole system comes in when you buy big equipment. Now in the old days, my brothers and I would bid on a job and if we got it and found we needed more equipment, we would sit down and talk it over. More often than not our discussions lasted for 10 minutes and we'd go ahead and place the order. As a matter of fact, I once placed an order for more than $400,000 worth of equipment right from this telephone after only a 15 minute talk with my brothers. This is the way we used to operate and, frankly, I think that it's done better now. First of all, we never really gave much thought to whether we'd have the cash around on time to pay for our equipment orders. Sometimes we'd get stuck with rising inventories and equipment bills coming due at the same time. Now, Leroy and his boys are really trying to coordinate this through the budget and I believe sincerely that they are doing a good job of it. Second of all, we never knew whether buying the equipment was a good deal. Sometimes, we gambled that the equipment would pay itself off in the future after the particular job that we were buying it for ended. Now, Leroy and Van Sickle tried to make some kind of comparison between our demands for equipment and those that the other divisions send in. Of course, we don't have to worry too much about being turned down on our equipment requests because the company has set up a slush fund to take care of worthwhile purchases that are above and beyond the budgeted amount.

Now let's face it, though. How can you budget costs in this business? The most crucial factor affecting your unit costs in this business is your output. If the weather is good and construction is high, you can sell all the stone and gravel in the world and you can produce it cheap. On the other hand, if the weather goes against you, you're in trouble because you've got certain fixed labor requirements that you just can't get around. So I can't honestly say that the budgeting program has really helped us in controlling our costs—we always did that and we still do it—but we do it in the way that we know. Now maybe you could say that the sales forecast has helped our quarry output schedules a little. I guess it has but we always had good communication between the quarry shipping clerks and the sales force. Whenever orders came in, or whenever big orders were on the horizon, the people at the quarries were informed. No, I don't think the budget has done very much for us there either. I'd positively state, though, that it has helped in ordering big equipment and that it is probably a tremendous help to the boys at Seattle who are sitting up there trying to figure out what's going on.

Mr. Markey intended to review carefully all these remarks as well as the reports currently prepared by the divisions before reaching a decision on the installation of a flexible budget. He was convinced, however, that flexible budgeting would help to eliminate the inaccuracies which resulted from not being able to adjust the budget figures according to output. Furthermore, he was aware that a number of company executives believed this inability to be the most severe weakness in the current budget program. On the other hand, Mr. Markey was not certain whether all the divisions were ready to make good use of a flexible budget and he wished to consider all the ramifications of the new system before introducing it at the company.

Case 10–3

Geebold Company (B)

Thomas Ritzman, assistant to the controller of Geebold Company, received from his boss an article, "Toward Probabilistic Profit Budgets,"[1] to which was clipped this note: "Do you think we should seriously consider adopting the approach described in this article? If so, why? What additional information do we need in order to make up our minds? If not, why not? There is no urgency, but let's discuss this whenever you are ready to do so."

As he read the article for the first time, Mr. Ritzman saw that the company used as an example was essentially similar to the Geebold Company. The article is reproduced below:

TOWARDS PROBABILISTIC BUDGETS[2]
by William L. Ferrara and Jack C. Hayya

Practical techniques have recently been developed for business applications of probability concepts so that they can be easily integrated with profit planning. This paper shows how some of these techniques can be used in the construction of probabilistic profit budgets, i.e., budgets that display expected values and a probability interval for every item.

The intent of this paper is to integrate three probabilistic techniques suggested in the literature with profit budgets. The PERT-like and probability-tree approaches used here emphasize most likely and mean values as well as measures of variability for each item in the income statement. Monte Carlo is used to simulate probability intervals for complex distributions that are too difficult to treat analytically.

---

[1] By William L. Ferrara and Jack C. Hayya. From *Management Accounting,* October 1970. Used with permission.

[2] The authors are indebted to Joseph Mackovjak (now with General Electric), who provided simulation expertise and other valuable assistance. From *Management Accounting,* October 1970.

Exhibit 1

PROFIT BUDGET FOR YEAR ENDING JUNE 197X

Sales (100,000 units @ $10)		$1,000,000
Variable costs		
Manufacturing ($5 per unit)	$500,000	
Marketing ($.50 per unit)	50,000	550,000
Marginal contribution		$ 450,000
Managed fixed costs		
Manufacturing	$ 20,000	
Marketing	10,000	
Administrative	40,000	70,000
Short-run margin		$ 380,000
Committed fixed costs		
Manufacturing	$180,000	
Marketing	40,000	
Administrative	60,000	280,000
Net income before tax		$ 100,000
Tax—50%		50,000
Net income after tax		$ 50,000

The Typical Profit Budget

Let us assume that the profit budget in a single product company is as shown in Exhibit 1. The direct-costing format of Exhibit 1 facilitates the use of break-even and cost-volume-profit analysis. Fixed costs are classified into managed and committed costs. Managed fixed costs are those costs which can be modified in the short run. Committed fixed costs are those which cannot be modified in the short run. The distinction between variable, managed and committed costs in this model is not only useful, it is particularly appropriate (as will become clear) in the preparation of probabilistic budgets.

The segregation of fixed costs into managed and committed fixed costs gives rise to the "short run margin." This margin is the contribution to earnings for which managers can be held accountable in a given budget period. The short-run margin further shows that committed costs are an obstacle which must be hurdled before a net profit is realized.

The weakness of Exhibit 1, and other models like it, is that they give no indication of the potential variability of the various estimates used. It is clear that the items in the budget are subjective estimates of most likely values, i.e., estimates of what is most probable in terms of revenues, costs and profits. The function of probabilistic profit budgets is to extend such models to indicate the variability of each budget item.

Optimistic, Pessimistic and Most Likely Values

Consider first the "three-level" estimates referred to as optimistic, pessimistic and most likely values. Such a "three-level" profit budget can be easily prepared, as shown in Exhibit 2.

Exhibit 2*

PROFIT BUDGET FOR YEAR ENDING JUNE 197X

	Pessimistic	Most Likely	Optimistic
Sale (10 per unit)	$800,000	$1,000,000	$1,100,000
Variable costs			
Manufacturing	408,000	500,000	528,000
Marketing ($.50 per unit)	40,000	50,000	55,000
Marginal contribution	$352,000	$ 450,000	$ 517,000
Managed fixed costs			
Manufacturing	10,000	20,000	30,000
Marketing	10,000	10,000	10,000
Administrative	25,000	40,000	40,000
Short-run margin	$307,000	$ 380,000	$ 437,000
Committed fixed costs			
Manufacturing	180,000	180,000	180,000
Marketing	40,000	40,000	40,000
Administrative	60,000	60,000	60,000
Net income before tax	$ 27,000	$ 100,000	$ 157,000
Tax—50%	13,500	50,000	78,500
Net income after tax	$ 13,500	$ 50,000	$ 78,500

* The data are based on Exhibit 1 with optimistic, most likely, and pessimistic values for sales volume and variable costs being 110,000, 100,000, 80,000 and $4.80, $5.00, $5.10, respectively. Unit variable costs are assumed to vary inversely with volume. Committed costs and unit variable marketing cost are assumed to be certain; some managed costs are modified to reflect changing volume levels.

It is evident that the three-level estimates of Exhibit 2 are more informative than the most likely one of Exhibit 1. For example, Exhibit 2 shows that net income after tax may be as low as $13,500 or as high as $78,500. The lone use of the most likely estimate of $50,000, as in Exhibit 1, can therefore be misleading.

From the data of Exhibit 2, one can calculate means and standard deviations for sales, variable costs, and marginal contribution by using the PERT formulas[3] or through probability-tree analysis. If we are to use the PERT formulas, the person who is providing the estimates must be made aware that a most likely estimate is a mode rather than a mean, and that the pessi-

---

[3] The PERT formulas for the standard deviation (σ) and the mean (μ) are:

$$\sigma = \frac{b - a}{6}$$

$$\mu = \frac{1}{3}[2m + \frac{1}{2}(a + b)]$$

Where b is the optimistic estimate, a is the pessimistic estimate and m is the most likely estimate.

mistic and optimistic estimates are assumed to be six standard deviations apart.

Probability-Tree Analysis: General

A more useful method for the preparation of probabilistic profit budgets is probability-tree analysis.[4] Probability-tree analysis is a generalization of the PERT method.

In using probability-tree analysis, probability estimates must be made for every level of volume and variable manufacturing cost considered. Thus, in our case, probabilities are assigned to each of the three sales and variable manufacturing cost levels as indicated in Exhibit 3. The probabilities (the p's and q's) assigned to each level are usually applicable to ranges whose midpoints are used in the calculations.

The budget variables under consideration in Exhibit 3 are sales, variable manufacturing cost, variable marketing cost, managed costs, committed costs, and net income after tax. The nine combinations in the Exhibit result by considering the three sales estimates to be independent of the three variable manufacturing cost estimates.[5]

In Exhibit 3 variable marketing costs, managed costs and committed costs are assumed to be non-probabilistic. The Exhibit shows net income after tax (NIAT) for each of the nine combinations and the expected value (the average or mean value) of NIAT.

The expected value of NIAT in Exhibit 3 [$\Sigma(NIAT)JP$] is \$44,710. On the other hand, the corresponding result for Exhibit 2 as calculated by use of the PERT formula for the mean turns out to be \$48,666. The two results differ because they are based on two different models.

Probability-Tree Analysis and Profit Budgets

In Exhibit 4 the expected value (μ) and the standard deviation (σ) of every item in the income statement is presented. The normal distribution and probability intervals[6] of $\pm 2\,\sigma$ or $\pm\,3\,\sigma$ from the mean cannot be used here since the probability distributions under consideration are not normal. They are discrete probability functions, i.e., functions where the random variable must assume distinct values.

It may be preferable to use the coefficient of variation rather than a probability interval in describing variability for discrete probability distributions of the type shown in Exhibits 3 and 4. The coefficient of variation is

---

[4] The probability-tree analysis used in this study differs from formal decision-tree analysis in that all nodes in the probability-tree are chance event nodes.

[5] Exhibits 2 and 3 represent different models. The model of Exhibit 2 assumes that volume and variable manufacturing costs are inversely related. The model of Exhibit 3 assumes them to be independent.

[6] Referred to as confidence intervals when the parameter to be estimated is not known.

Exhibit 3

THREE DIAGRAM OF BASIC PROBLEM INCLUDING EXPECTED VALUES

Volume (price = $10)	Variable Manufacturing Cost	Variable Marketing Cost	Managed Costs	Committed Costs	Net Income After Tax-50% (NIAT)	Joint* Probability (JP)	Combination	JP × NIAT
	$5.10	$0.50	$45,000	$280,000	$13,500	0.06	1	$ 810
$800,000 p = .3	q = .2 $5.00	$0.50	$45,000	$280,000	$17,500	0.18	2	3,150
	q = .6 $4.80	$0.50	$45,000	$280,000	$25,500	0.06	3	1,530
	q = .2							
	$5.10	$0.50	$70,000	$280,000	$45,000	0.10	4	4,500
$1,000,000 p = .5	q = .2 $5.00	$0.50	$70,000	$280,000	$50,000	0.30	5	15,000
	q = .6 $4.80	$0.50	$70,000	$280,000	$60,000	0.10	6	6,000
	q = .2							
	$5.10	$0.50	$80,000	$280,000	$62,000	0.04	7	2,480
$1,100,000 p = .2	q = .2 $5.00	$0.50	$80,000	$280,000	$67,500	0.12	8	8,100
	q = .6 $4.80	$0.50	$80,000	$280,000	$78,500	0.04	9	3,140
	q = .2							

Expected Value of Net Income after Tax $44,710

* Joint probabilities are calculated by multiplying the probabilities on the path (the succession of branches) moving toward each outcome.

Exhibit 4

CALCULATION OF EXPECTED VALUES, STANDARD DEVIATIONS AND COEFFICIENT OF VARIATION FOR ALL INCOME STATEMENT ITEMS
Combination (Dollars in Thousands)

	1	2	3	4	5	6	7	8	9
Joint probability	.06	.18	.06	.10	.30	.10	.04	.12	.04
Sales	$800	$800	$800	$1,000	$1,000	$1,000	$1,100	$1,100	$1,100
Variable costs:									
Manufacturing	408	400	384	510	500	480	561	550	528
Marketing	40	40	40	50	50	50	55	55	55
Marginal contribution	352	360	376	440	450	470	484	495	517
Managed costs:									
Manufacturing	10	10	10	20	20	20	30	30	30
Marketing	10	10	10	10	10	10	10	10	10
Administrative	25	25	25	40	40	40	40	40	40
Short-run margin	307	315	331	370	380	400	404	415	437
Committed costs	280	280	280	280	280	280	280	280	280
Net income before tax	$ 27	$ 35	$ 51	$ 90	$ 100	$ 120	$ 124	$ 135	$ 157
Tax @ 50 percent	13.5	17.5	25.5	45	50	60	62	67.5	78.5
Net income after tax	$ 13.5	$ 17.5	$ 25.5	$ 45	$ 50	$ 60	$ 62	$ 67.5	$ 78.5

	Expected Value*	σ^2†	σ	Coefficient of Variation‡
Sales	$960,000	$12,400,000,000	$111,400	11.6%
Variable costs:				
Manufacturing	478,080	3,164,913,600	56,300	11.8%
Marketing	48,000	31,000,000	5,560	11.6%
Marginal contribution	433,920	2,623,033,600	51,200	11.8%
Managed costs:				
Manufacturing	19,000	49,000,000	7,000	36.8%
Marketing	10,000	0	0	—
Administrative	35,500	47,250,000	6,870	19.4%
Short-run margin	369,420	1,462,363,600	38,250	10.4%
Committed costs	280,000	0	0	—
Net income before tax	89,420	1,462,363,600	38,240	42.8%
Tax @ 50 percent	44,710	365,590,900	19,120	42.8%
Net income after tax	44,710	365,590,900	19,120	42.8%

* $\Sigma\, x_1\, p(x_1)$ where the x_1 are the values of each combination and the $p(x_1)$ are the joint probabilities assigned to each x_1.

† $\Sigma\, [x_1^2\, p(x_1)] - \mu^2$ where μ is the expected value (mean).

‡ $\dfrac{\Gamma}{\mu}$, the % that Γ is the mean.

the percentage relationship between the standard deviation and the mean. The calculated values of this coefficient are presented in Exhibit 4 for each item in the income statement.

The coefficient of variation is a useful tool for planning and control purposes. From the point of view of planning, the coefficient of variation predicts the potential variability of budgeted items. A high coefficient of variation, for example, indicates that an outcome (e.g., actual sales) has relatively large variations about the budgeted value. From the point of view of control, differences between budgeted and actual outcomes are understood more meaningfully when they are related to the coefficient of variation.

Exhibit 5 summarizes Exhibit 4 in the format of an income statement. The three columns provide the mean, the standard deviation and the coefficient of variation.

Exhibit 5

PROFIT BUDGET FOR YEAR ENDING JUNE 197X

	Expected Value	Standard Deviation	Coefficient of Variation
Sales	$960,000	$111,400	11.6%
Variable costs			
Manufacturing	478,080	56,000	11.8
Marketing	48,000	5,560	11.6
Marginal contribution	$433,920	51,220	11.8
Managed fixed costs			
Manufacturing	19,000	7,000	36.8
Marketing	10,000	0	0
Administrative	35,500	6,870	19.4
Short-run margin	$369,420	38,240	10.4
Committed fixed costs			
Manufacturing	180,000	0	0
Marketing	40,000	0	0
Administrative	60,000	0	0
Net income before tax	$ 89,420	38,240	42.8
Tax—50 percent	44,710	19,120	42.8
Net income after tax	$ 44,710	19,120	42.8

An alternative format is presented in Exhibit 6, which displays the 100 percent and the 90 percent probability intervals (or ranges) for the budget items. As the terms imply, the 100 percent probability interval includes all the elements in the distribution, whereas a 90 percent probability interval excludes five percent in each of the two tails of the distribution. Probability intervals are obtained from Exhibit 4 by inspection as explained below.

Clearly the highest and lowest possible values for an item would contain a 100 percent probability interval. This can be obtained readily from Exhibit 4. The 90 percent range, on the other hand, is arbitrarily chosen in this instance

Exhibit 6

PROFIT BUDGET FOR YEAR ENDING JUNE 197X

	Expected Value	100 Percent Range	90 Percent Range
Sales	$960,000	$800,000—$1,100,000	not applicable
Variable costs			
Manufacturing	478,080	384,000— 561,000	400,000—550,000
Marketing	48,000	40,000— 55,000	40,000— 55,000
Marginal contribution ...	$433,920	352,000— 517,000	360,000—495,000
Managed fixed costs			
Manufacturing	19,000	10,000— 30,000	10,000— 30,000
Marketing	10,000	—	—
Administrative	35,500	25,000— 40,000	25,000— 40,000
Short-run margin	$369,420	307,000— 307,000	315,000—415,000
Committed fixed costs		—	
Manufacturing	180,000		—
Marketing	40,000	—	—
Administrative	60,000	—	—
Net income before tax ..	$ 89,420	27,000— 157,000	35,000—135,000
Tax—50 percent	44,710	13,500— 78,500	17,500— 67,500
Net income after tax	$ 44,710	13,500— 78,500	17,500— 67,500

because it fits the distribution of the nine possible values for each item shown in Exhibit 4. The highest value for each item has a probability of 0.04, while the lowest value for each item has a probability of 0.06. Thus the 90 percent range is determined by excluding the highest and lowest values for each item (with the exception of sales). By definition, the 90 percent probability interval as it has been presented here is slightly off center.

The probabilistic income statements of Exhibits 5 and 6 provide more information than the three-level format of Exhibit 2. The improvement results from attaching probabilities to sales and unit variable manufacturing cost. The choice of any of these formats, however, depends on managerial needs and preferences.

A Model with Continuous Distribution

Thus far we have considered two general approaches to preparing probabilistic income statements, i.e., the three-level and the probability-tree approaches. We now consider the construction of a probabilistic income statement for a model with continuous probability distributions.

Description of the Model. The assumptions of the model are listed in Exhibit 7. Note that basic data (e.g., price, mean volume, or mean unit variable manufacturing cost) similar to the previous illustrations are adopted. Again the model is for a single-product firm. The main variables (volume and unit variable manufacturing cost) are normally distributed and statistically independent with known means and standard deviations. A relevant

Exhibit 7

ASSUMED ONE-PRODUCT COMPANY MODEL

1. Volume (Q) is normally distributed with estimated mean, $\mu Q = 100{,}000$ units, standard deviation, $\sigma Q = 10{,}000$ units, and relevant range $80{,}000 \leq Q \leq 120{,}000$.
2. Sales price is constant at $10 per unit.
3. Unit variable manufacturing cost (v) is normally distributed with estimated mean, $\mu_v = \$5.00$ and standard deviation, $\sigma_v = \$0.20$.
4. Volume (Q) and unit variable manufacturing cost (v) are statistically independent.
5. Managed manufacturing cost (Cm mfg) has the following linear relationship with volume (Q):

$$\text{Cm mfg} = \$20{,}000 + \frac{1}{2}\,(Q - 100{,}000),$$

within a relevant range: $80{,}000 \leq Q \leq 120{,}000$.
6. Managed administrative cost (Cm ad) has the following quadratic relationship with volume (Q):

$$\text{Cm ad} = \$40{,}000 + 0.25\,Q + 0.64\,(10^{-5}\,Q^2)$$

within a relevant range: $80{,}000 \leq Q \leq 120{,}000$.
7. All other costs are constant: managed marketing ($10,000), committed manufacturing ($180,000), committed marketing ($40,000) committed administrative ($60,000), and variable marketing ($0.50 per unit).

range for volume $(80{,}000 \leq Q \leq 120{,}000)$, but not for unit variable manufacturing cost, is assumed. In addition, two costs are functions of volume. These are managed manufacturing cost and managed administrative cost. The former has a linear and the latter a quadratic relationship with volume. The other costs, and also unit price are constant.

The model presented may not be representative of the typical firm. Nevertheless, it is useful for gaining insight into the construction of probabilistic profit budgets.

Difficulties associated with the construction of probability intervals when the probability distributions are not readily identifiable. To estimate a 95 percent probability interval for the various budget items, we must know how these items are distributed.[7] If these items are normally distributed, or if they belong to distributions that are tabulated, it would be a simple matter to obtain the desired distribution limits. However, in spite of the simplifying assumptions of our model, difficulties associated with identifying the proper distributions occur.

These difficulties increase as one progresses from the top to the bottom of

---

[7] The probability interval could be set at whatever level desired if 95 percent is considered inappropriate.

the income statement. This is especially true with regard to the "short-run margin" and the "net income before and after tax" since these items are functions of a product of two normal variables, a linear function of a normal variable and a quadratic function of a normal variable.[8] Without knowing the specific or approximate distribution of these functions one cannot hope to obtain a probability interval for the items under consideration.

The distribution of these functions can be derived with involved numerical and mathematical techniques. By using simulation, however, we can more easily derive such probability intervals.

Probabilistic Intervals through Simulation

The model described in Exhibit 7 was simulated by computer, and the mean and a 95 percent probability interval for each budget item was determined. The result is the profit budget of Exhibit 8.

Exhibit 8

PROFIT BUDGET FOR YEAR ENDING JUNE 197X

	Expected Value	95 Percent Probability Interval*	
Sales	$1,002,146	$807,746—	$1,195,900
Variable costs			
Manufacturing	500,452	406,370—	600,546
Marketing	50,123	40,387—	59,795
Marginal contribution	$ 451,571	366,022—	548,412
Managed fixed costs			
Manufacturing	20,111	10,387—	29,795
Marketing	10,000†	—	
Administrative	49,937	20,825—	70,049
Short-run margin	$ 371,523	314,057—	433,914
Committed fixed costs			
Manufacturing	180,000†	—	
Marketing	40,000†	—	
Administrative	60,000†	—	
Net income before tax	$ 91,523	34,057—	153,914
Tax—50 percent	45,762	15,682—	75,870
Net income after tax	$ 45,761	15,682—	75,870

* Determined by dropping the upper and lower 2½ percent of the 1,000 iterations.
† Costs which are constant do not have a probability interval since they are considered "certain."

The simulation program involved 1,000 iterations; for in this type of problem, experience indicated that 1,000 iterations yields a reasonable approxi-

---

[8] The Short-Run Margin, $SRM = 60,000 + Q(8.75 - v) - .64(10^{-5})Q^2$, where Q is the volume, v is the unit variable manufacturing cost, and Q and v are independently and normally distributed. Net income before and after tax is of the same form.

mation to the theoretical distribution.[9] We have partially verified this in our case as test runs of 3,000 iterations did not produce significantly different results.

Summary and Conclusions

This paper presents three methods for the construction of probabilistic profit and loss statements: the three-level, the probability-tree and the continuous distribution approaches.

The paper begins with a typical profit and loss statement which displays most likely values. Valuable information, however, is added to budgeted profit and loss statements if every item in those statements displays a mean and a probability interval. The mean is an expected value—what the value of the item would be on the average if we are afforded a large number of trials. The probability interval, on the other hand, tells us that a stated percentage of the distribution of a budget item falls within a given range. Thus the probability interval serves as a measure of variability for the budget item. Other indices of variability suggested are, of course, the standard deviation and the coefficient of variation.

In models with continuous distributions, it is recommended that Monte Carlo simulation be used where the probability distributions in question are difficult to handle analytically. One thousand iterations usually yield an accurate approximation of the desired distributions.

---

[9] Additional information concerning how many iterations are appropriate in this type of problem is available in:

R. W. Conway, "Some Tactical Problems in Digital Simulation," *Management Science,* October 1963, p. 49.

Daniel Teichroew, "A History of Distribution Sampling Prior to the Era of the Computer and its Relevance to Simulation," *Journal of the American Statistical Association,* March 1965, pp. 27–49.

Chapter Eleven

ANALYZING AND
REPORTING FINANCIAL
PERFORMANCE

This chapter describes techniques for analyzing and reporting financial performance in companies that have a profit budget system. Since cost and revenue budgets are part of profit budgets, the discussion automatically includes these budgets as well.

CHARACTERISTICS OF A GOOD REPORTING SYSTEM

A good profit budget reporting system has the following characteristics:

1. It identifies separately the variances of actual performance from the budget according to the factors that caused them.
2. It includes an annual forecast.
3. It includes an explanation of:
   a) The reason for variances;
   b) The action being taken to correct any unfavorable variances;
   c) The time required for any corrective action to be effective.

Each is discussed in this part of the chapter.

Variance by Causal Factor

A variance analysis is not meaningful unless the variances are reported separately in terms of the factors that caused them. In particular, revenue variances should be separated from cost variances. Revenue variances, in turn, should be separated into price, mix, and volume variances, and cost variances should identify the causes of departures from budgeted standards.

Many companies simply place the actual results next to the profit budget

Exhibit 11–1

ABC DIVISION

Performance Report, January 1975
(000 omitted)

	Actual	Budget	Actual Better (Worse) Than Budget
Sales	$875	$600	$275
Variable costs of sales	583	370	(213)
Contribution	$292	$230	$ 62
Fixed overhead	75	75	—
Gross profit	$217	$155	$ 62
Selling expense	55	50	(5)
Administrative expense	30	25	(5)
Profit before taxes	$132	$ 80	$ 52

for the period and show the difference between them, as illustrated in Exhibit 11–1.

Such a statement shows that the profit is $52,000 higher than budgeted, principally because sales are higher than budgeted, but this is about all that it shows. The only other meaningful figures on the report are the fixed cost comparisons because these are not affected by the volume of sales. The reasons for the revenue increases are not shown. Further, the profit impact of the revenue variance is not shown, nor can the variable cost performance be evaluated. A report of this kind has little meaning; it may even be confusing. An effective report shows the causes for the variances and the impact of each of them on profits. Techniques for calculating profit budget variances are described later in this chapter.

Annual Forecast

Budget performance reports should, if feasible, show a current annual forecast for two principal reasons:

1. Management needs to know the significance of the variances. For example, management needs to know if a small variance in a current report is expected to develop into a large variance by the end of the year. Such a variance would be more important than a large variance that is expected to be reversed to zero by the end of the year. In short, top management can best judge the seriousness of a variance by its expected impact on profits for a period longer than the current month or quarter.
2. Management needs an up-to-date estimate of annual profits for planning purposes.

In some companies, particularly in times of great economic uncertainty, annual forecasts are so unreliable that management decides the effort required to make them is not worthwhile, but these are exceptional.

Reasons, Action and Timing

If top management is to use the budget performance report as a basis for controlling company activities, it must know the reasons for significant variances, the action being taken to correct unfavorable situations, and the expected timing of each action. The annual forecast provides some information on the timing of corrective action. The annual forecast, however, is restricted to the budget year. Management needs to know the total expected impact of variances where the correction time goes beyond the end of the current budget year.

The information for this part of the budget report must be obtained from the responsible operating manager. Much of this information is subjective and, consequently, there is the possibility of bias. No operating manager wishes to admit that a variance was the result of his mistakes. The integrity of the budgetary system is dependent upon the accuracy of this part of the budget report, however. One of the most difficult problems in budgetary control is ensuring this accuracy. In some companies, the divisional controller (as well as the manager) is held responsible for the accuracy of the entire budget report.

ANALYSIS OF VARIANCE—DIRECT COST SYSTEM

This section describes techniques for analyzing variances between the actual financial results and the budget. There are several different methods for calculating variances, depending upon the cost accounting system that is used. We will describe two: variance analysis where a standard direct cost system is used and variance analysis where a standard full cost system is used. Although techniques differ, they should all lead to similar results. Differences in techniques generally result from the type of information that is available and the degree of sophistication that is desired.

A direct standard cost system is one that assigns only variable manufacturing cost to products. Fixed manufacturing costs are charged as expenses of the current period.

Exhibit 11–2 provides details of the budget shown in Exhibit 11–1.

Revenue Variances

In this section, we describe how to calculate the price, volume, and mix variances. In all cases, the calculation is made for each product separately, and the separate results are then added algebraically to give the total variance. A positive result is favorable (in the sense that it indicates that actual profit exceeded budgeted profit), and a negative result is unfavorable.

Actual sales for January 1975 were as shown in Exhibit 11–3.

Exhibit 11–2

ABC DIVISION

Annual Profit Budget 1975

(000 omitted)

	Product A 1,200*		Product B 1,200*		Product C 1,200*		Total Profit Budget	
	Unit	Total	Unit	Total	Unit	Total	Annual	Monthly
Sales	$1.00	$1,200	$2.00	$2,400	$3.00	$3,600	$7,200	$600
Standard variable cost:								
Material	.50	600	.70	840	1.50	1,800	3,240	270
Labor	.10	120	.15	180	.10	120	420	35
Variable overhead	.20	240	.25	300	.20	240	780	65
Total variable cost	$ .80	$ 960	$1.10	$1,320	$1.80	$2,160	$4,440	$370
Contribution	$ .20	$ 240	$ .90	$1,080	$1.20	$1,440	$2,760	$230
Fixed costs:								
Fixed overhead		$ 300		$ 300		$ 300	$ 900	$ 75
Selling expense†		200		200		200	600	50
Administrative expense		100		100		100	300	25
Total fixed costs		$ 600		$ 600		$ 600	$1,800	$150
Profit before taxes		$ (360)		$ 480		$ 840	$ 960	$ 80

* Standard volume (units).
† For this example, selling expenses are fixed; in most business situations, there is usually a variable element to be considered.

Exhibit 11–3

ABC DIVISION

Actual Sales for January 1975
(000 omitted)

Product	Unit Sales	Selling Price	Dollar Sales
A	100	$ .90	$ 90
B	200	2.05	410
C	150	2.50	375
Total	450		$875

Price variance. The price variance is calculated by multiplying the difference between the actual price and the standard price by the actual volume. The calculation for the ABC Division is shown in Exhibit 11–4. It shows that the price variance is $75,000, unfavorable.

Exhibit 11–4

CALCULATION OF PRICE VARIANCE, JANUARY 1975
(000 omitted)

	A	B	C	Total
Actual volume (units)	100	200	150	
Actual price .... $	.90	$ 2.05	$ 2.50	
Budget price	1.00	2.00	3.00	
Actual over/(under) budget	(.10)	.05	(.50)	
Favorable/(unfavorable) price variance	$(10)	$10	$(75)	$(75)

Mix and Volume Variance. Often the mix and volume variances are not separated. The combined mix and volume variance is:

Mix and Volume Variance = (actual volume − budget volume)
× (budgeted unit contribution).

The calculation of mix and volume variance for the ABC Division is shown in Exhibit 11–5. It shows that the mix and volume variance combined is $150,000, favorable.

The volume variance results from selling more units than budgeted. The mix variance results from selling a different proportion of products from that contained in the budget. Since most products earn a different *contribution* per unit, selling a different proportion of products from budget will result in a variance. The division has a "richer" mix if the actual profit is higher than budgeted and a "leaner" mix if the profit is lower. Since the

Exhibit 11–5

MIX AND VOLUME VARIANCE, JANUARY 1975
(000 omitted)

(1) Product	(2) Actual Volume	(3) Budgeted Volume	(4) Difference (2) − (3)	(5) Contribution	(6) Variance (4) × (5)
A	100	100	—	$ —	$ —
B	200	100	100	.90	90
C	150	100	50	1.20	60
Total	450	300			$150

volume and mix variances are interrelated, the techniques for separating them must be somewhat arbitrary. (Because of this, some companies do not separate mix and volume variances.) One such technique is described below. Other ways of making this calculation are equally acceptable.

Mix Variance.   The mix variance for each product is found from the following equation:

Mix Variance = [(total actual volume of sales × budgeted %)
     − actual volume of sales] × budgeted unit contribution

The total mix variance is the algebraic sum of these variances.

The calculation of the mix variance for the ABC Division is shown in Exhibit 11–6. It shows that a higher proportion of Product B was sold and a

Exhibit 11–6

CALCULATION OF MIX VARIANCE, JANUARY 1975
(000 omitted)

(1) Product	(2) Budgeted Proportion	(3) Actual Volume at Budgeted Mix	(4) Actual Sales	(5) Difference (3) − (4)	(6) Unit Contri- bution	Variance (5) × (6)
A	1/3	150*	100	(50)	$.20	$(10)
B	1/3	150	200	50	.90	45
C	1/3	150	150	—		
Total		450	450			$ 35

* 1/3 × 450

lower proportion of Product A. Since Product B has a higher contribution than Product A, the mix variance is favorable, by $35,000.

Volume Variance.   The volume variance can be calculated by subtracting the mix variance from the combined mix and volume variance. This would be $150,000 minus $35,000 or $115,000. It can also be calculated for each product as follows:

Volume Variance = [(total actual volume of sales × budgeted %)
— <u>budgeted sales</u>] × budgeted unit contribution

The calculation of the volume variance for the ABC Division is shown in Exhibit 11–7.

Exhibit 11–7

CALCULATION OF VOLUME VARIANCE, JANUARY 1975
(000 omitted)

(1) Product	(2) Actual Volume at Budgeted Mix	(3) Budgeted Volume	(4) Difference (2) − (3)	(5) Unit Contribution	(6) Volume Variance
A	150	100	50	$ .20	$ 10
B	150	100	50	.90	45
C	150	100	50	1.20	60
Total	450	300	150		$115

Other Revenue Analyses. Where information is available, revenue variances may be further subdivided. For example, revenue variances can be calculated by market area, by product line, or by both market area and product line. In our example, we have not provided information on market area. We do, however, have the information by product. An analysis of the revenue variances by product for the ABC Division is shown in Exhibit 11–8.

Exhibit 11–8

CALCULATION OF REVENUE VARIANCES BY PRODUCT, JANUARY 1975
(000 omitted)

	Product			
	A	B	C	Total
Price variance	$(10)	$ 10	$(75)	$ (75)
Mix variance	(10)	45	—	35
Volume variance	10	45	60	115
Total	$(10)	$100	$(15)	$ 75

Market Penetration and Industry Volume. One common variation in revenue analysis is to separate the mix and volume variance into the amount caused by differences in market penetration and the amount caused by differences in industry volume. The principle is that the divisional manager is responsible for market penetration, but he is not responsible for the industry volume because this is largely influenced by the state of the economy. To make this calculation, industry sales data obviously must be available, and many companies cannot obtain such data. This calculation is described below.

Exhibit 11–9 provides details with respect to the assumptions made in the

Exhibit 11–9

ABC DIVISION

Analysis of Budgeted Sales Volume
(000 omitted)

		Product		
	A	B	C	Total
Estimated industry volume				
Annual	10,000	6,000	20,000	36,000
Monthly	833	500	1,667	3,000
Budgeted market				
penetration	12%	20%	6%	10%
Budgeted (standard) volume				
Annual	1,200	1,200	1,200	3,600
Monthly	100	100	100	300

original budget shown in Exhibit 11–2, and Exhibit 11–10 provides details on industry volume and market penetration for the month of January 1975.

Exhibit 11–10

ABC DIVISION

Analysis of Actual Sales, January 1975
(000 omitted)

		Product		
	A	B	C	Total
Industry Volume	1,000	1,000	1,000	3,000
Actual Sales	100	200	150	450
Market Penetration	10%	20%	15%	15%

The following equation is used to separate the effect of market penetration from industry volume on the mix and volume variance.

Market Penetration Variance = [actual sales − (industry volume ×
budgeted market penetration)] ×
budget unit contribution

The calculation for market penetration variance for the ABC Division is shown in Exhibit 11–11.

This means that $104,000 of the favorable mix and volume variance of $150,000 resulted from the fact that market penetration was better than

Exhibit 11–11

CALCULATION OF VARIANCE DUE TO MARKET PENETRATION, JANUARY 1975
(000 omitted)

	Product			
	A	B	C	Total
(1) Actual sales (unit)	100	200	150	450
(2) Budgeted penetration at industry volume	120	200	60	380
(3) Difference (1−2)	(20)	—	90	70
(4) Unit contribution (budget)	$.20	$.90	$1.20	
(5) Variance due to market penetration (3×4)	$ (4)	—	$ 108	$104

budget. The remaining $46,000 resulted from the actual industry volume being higher than budget.

The $46,000 industry volume variance can also be calculated as follows:

Industry Volume Variance = [(actual industry volume − budgeted industry volume) × budgeted market penetration] × budgeted unit contribution

This calculation of variance due to industry volume for the ABC Division is shown in Exhibit 11–12.

Exhibit 11–12

CALCULATION OF VARIANCE DUE TO INDUSTRY VOLUME, JANUARY 1975
(000 omitted)

	Product			
	A	B	C	Total
(1) Actual industry volume	1,000	1,000	1,000	3,000
(2) Budgeted industry volume	833	500	1,667	3,000
(3) Difference (1 minus 2)	167	500	(667)	—
(4) Budgeted market penetration	12%	20%	6%	
(5) (3) × (4)	20	100	(40)	
(6) Contribution—unit	$.20	$.90	$1.20	
(7) —total (5×6)	$ 4	$ 90	$ (48)	$46

Notes on Revenue Variances

Note that revenue variances in the above examples are calculated using the *budgeted* unit contribution. Any difference between the budgeted unit contribution and actual unit contribution is shown as a cost variance. This assumes that it is not expected that selling prices will change during the period *because* of changes in cost. If it is the marketing department's responsibility to change selling prices as costs change, then the price variance as computed in Exhibit 11–4 (page 515) would not reflect this responsibility. In these circumstances, a different set of calculations would be made. Instead of the price variance, the difference between budgeted and actual gross margins, or between budgeted and actual unit contributions would be computed.

Revenue variances are interrelated and variance equations are somewhat arbitrary. Other methods than shown in the text will therefore result in different amounts. However, the magnitude of the differences are not usually significant.

There are many types of revenue variances. This chapter has included some of the most common. Other kinds of revenue variances may be calculated. The question to ask is: "What types of variances will be most useful to management?"

Cost Variance

Fixed Costs. Variances between actual and budgeted fixed costs can be obtained simply by subtraction, since these costs are not affected by either the volume of sales or the volume of production. In the example given in Exhibit 11–1, this is shown in Exhibit 11–13.

Exhibit 11–13

CALCULATION OF FIXED COSTS VARIANCES, JANUARY 1975
(000 omitted)

	Actual	Budget	Favorable/ (Unfavorable) Variances
Fixed overhead	$ 75	$ 75	$ —
Selling expense	55	50	(5)
Administrative expense	30	25	(5)
Total	$160	$150	$(10)

Variable Costs. Variable costs are those costs that vary directly and proportionately with volume. Consequently the budgeted variable manufacturing costs must be adjusted to the actual volume of production. Assume the January production was as follows: Product A, 150,000 units; Product B, 120,000 units; Product C, 200,000 units. Assume also that the variable costs incurred in January were as follows: Material, $470,000; labor, $65,000; variable manufacturing overhead, $90,000. Exhibit 11–2 shows the standard unit variable costs.

The budgeted manufacturing expense is adjusted to the amount that should have been spent at the actual level of production by multiplying each element of standard cost for each product by the volume of production for that product. This calculation is shown for the ABC Division as Exhibit 11–14.

Exhibit 11–14

**CALCULATION OF VARIABLE MANUFACTURING EXPENSE VARIANCES,
JANUARY 1975**
(000 omitted)

	Product			Total	Actual	Favorable/ (Unfavorable) Variances
	A	B	C			
Material........	$ 75	$ 84	$300	$459	$470	$(11)
Labor.........	15	18	20	53	65	(12)
Overhead (variable)	30	30	40	100	90	10
Total ...	$120	$132	$360	$612	$625	$(13)

This exhibit shows that net variable manufacturing costs had an unfavorable variance of $13,000 in January. This is called a "spending" variance because it results from spending $13,000 in excess of the adjusted budget. It consists of unfavorable material and labor variances of $11,000 and $12,000 respectively. These are partially offset by a favorable overhead spending variance of $10,000.

Reporting Variances

The separate revenue and cost variances are assembled into a report for management. There are two principal methods of reporting variances: (1) a report that summarizes variances only; and (2) a report that compares the actual and budgeted figures. In some systems both types of reports are used. Each is illustrated below.

Summary of Variances Only. Using the information developed in the preceding section, the variance report for ABC Division would be as shown in Exhibit 11–15.

Comparison of Actual with Budgeted Costs. The same variance information could be shown in the format illustrated in Exhibit 11–16.

ANALYSIS OF VARIANCE—FULL COST SYSTEM

Under a full cost system, both the variable and fixed manufacturing cost are assigned to the products produced. The unit standard full costs for Products A, B, and C would be as follows (from Exhibit 11–2):

	Product		
	A	B	C
Material	$ .50	$ .70	$1.50
Labor	.10	.15	.10
Variable overhead	.20	.25	.20
Fixed overhead*	.25	.25	.25
Total	$1.05	$1.35	$2.05

* $300 total fixed overhead for each product divided by 1200 units.

Exhibit 11-15

THE ABC DIVISION, Performance Report, January 1975
(000 omitted)

Actual profit	$132
Budgeted profit	80
Variance	$ 52

Analysis of Variance—Favorable/(Unfavorable)

Revenue Variances

Price	$(75)
Mix	35
Volume	115
Net revenue variances	$ 75

Variable Cost Variances

Material	$(11)
Labor	(12)
Variable overhead	10
Net variable cost variances	$(13)

Fixed Cost Variances

Selling expense	$ (5)
Administrative expense	(5)
Net fixed cost variances	$(10)
Net variance	$ 52

Exhibit 11-16

THE ABC DIVISION, Performance Report, January 1975
(000 omitted)

	Actual	Budget*	Actual Better/ (Worse) Than Budget
Sales	$875	$950	$ (75)
Standard variable cost of sales	570	570	—
Material variance	11		(11)
Labor variance	12		(12)
Variable overhead variance	(10)		10
Total variable cost	$583	$570	$ (13)
Contribution	$292	$380	$ (88)
Fixed manufacturing cost	75	75	—
Gross profit	$217	$305	$ (88)
Selling expense	55	50	(5)
Administrative expense	30	25	(5)
Profit at actual volume and mix	$132	$230	$ (98)
Mix variance			35
Volume variance			115
Net variance			$ 52

* Budgeted prices and costs at actual sales volume and mix.

Assuming that everything was the same except that the budget and actual data were prepared using full costs rather than variable costs, the budget report that corresponds to Exhibit 11–1 would be as shown in Exhibit 11–17.

This part of the chapter describes the method of analyzing variances when a full cost system is used.

Exhibit 11–17

THE ABC DIVISION

Performance Report, January 1975
(000 omitted)

	Actual	Budget	Actual Better (Worse) Than Budget
Sales	$875	$600	$ 275
Cost of sales	653	445	(208)
Gross profit	$222	$155	$ 67
Selling expense	55	50	(5)
Administrative expense	30	25	(5)
Net profit	$137	$ 80	$ 57

Revenue Variances

Price Variance. The price variance is the same as under the direct cost system. It is $75,000 unfavorable.

Mix and Volume Variances. The method of calculating the mix and volume variance is the same as described in the first part of the chapter except that the standard unit gross profit is substituted for the standard unit contribution. Since the fixed cost per unit is $.25 for each product, the unit contribution will be $.25 less than the amounts used in the preceding calculation. Mix and volume variances are calculated in Exhibit 11–18.

Cost Variances

Selling expense and administrative expenses are not affected by the type of cost system used. Consequently, the variances for these two expense categories will be identical to those calculated for the direct cost system. Also, the material and labor variances will be the same as in the direct cost system. It is only the overhead expense variances that are different.

Absorbed Cost. Absorbed cost is the cost of the goods that are transferred to inventory. These goods are transferred at their standard cost. In the example, the ABC Division produced 150,000 units of Product A, 120,000 units of Product B, and 200,000 units of Product C. These units were transferred to finished goods inventory. The cost of goods produced and transferred to finished goods inventory is $729,500, as calculated in Exhibit 11–19.

Exhibit 11–18

MIX VARIANCE

January, 1975
(000)

(1)	(2) Actual Volume at Budgeted	(3) Actual	(4) Difference	(5) Gross	(6) Mix Variance
Product	Mix	Sales	(2) − (3)	Profit	(4) × (5)
A	150	100	$ (50)	$ (.05)	$ 2.5
B	150	200	50	.65	32.5
C	150	150	—		
Total	450	450			$35.0

VOLUME VARIANCE

(1)	(2) Actual Volume at Budgeted	(3) Budgeted	(4) Difference	(5) Gross	(6) Volume Variance
Product	Mix	Volume	(2) − (3)	Profit	(4) × (5)
A	150	100	50	$ (.05)	$ (2.5)
B	150	100	50	.65	32.5
C	150	100	50	.95	47.5
Total	450	300	150		$77.5

Exhibit 11–19

CALCULATION OF STANDARD COST OF GOODS PRODUCED
JANUARY, 1975
(000 omitted)

	150 Product A		120 Product B		200 Product C		
	Unit	Total	Unit	Total	Unit	Total	Total
Material	$ .50	$ 75.0	$ .70	84.0	$1.50	$300.0	$459.0
Labor	.10	15.0	.15	18.0	.10	20.0	53.0
Overhead*	.45	67.5	.50	60.0	.45	90.0	217.5
Total	$1.05	$157.5	$1.35	162.0	$2.05	$410.0	$729.5

* Variable overhead cost plus $0.25 per unit fixed cost.

Budgeted Cost. For material and labor, the budgeted cost is the unit budgeted cost multiplied by the units produced. The budgeted overhead cost is calculated by the following formula:

Budgeted Overhead Costs = total budgeted fixed costs + (units produced) (budgeted variable overhead cost per unit)

In our example, this would be as follows:

Budgeted overhead $= 75 + (150 \times .20) + (120 \times .25) + (200 \times .20) = 175$

Variances. The actual manufacturing costs were (as given above):

Material	$470
Labor	65
Overhead	165*
Total	$700

* This is the $90,000 variable cost plus $75,000 fixed.

The total overhead variance is equal to the absorbed cost minus the actual cost or $729,500 − $700,000 = $29,500. This means that in the month of January, the ABC Division spent $29,500 less than budgeted in producing products A, B, and C.

This variance is the result of two factors. First, the division could have spent more or less than budget in producing products A, B, and C. This is called the *spending* variance. Secondly, the division could have produced more or less than standard volume in January. This is called the *volume* variance. It is necessary to separate these variances for management because each has a different cause and may be the responsibility of different people. These two variances are calculated as follows:

Spending Variance = budgeted cost (at actual volume) minus actual cost.

Volume Variance = absorbed cost minus budgeted cost.

Spending Variance = $175	− 165	= $10	favorable
Volume Variance = $217.5 − 175.0 =		42.5	favorable
Total overhead variance		$52.5	favorable
Material variance (from Ex. 11–14)		(11.0)	unfavorable
Labor variance (from Ex. 11–14)		(12.0)	unfavorable
Net manufacturing variance		$29.5	favorable

Reporting Variances

The variance report in the full cost system is shown in Exhibit 11–20. Note that the total variance differs from that shown in Exhibit 11–16. This difference (between $57,000 and $52,000) arises because, in a direct cost system, fixed costs are charged as current period expenses, whereas in a full cost system they become part of product costs and are carried into inventory. Since production volume exceeded sales volume in the illustration, $5,000 of fixed costs remain in inventory. (Actual production of 470,000 units exceeded actual sales of 450,000 units by 20,000 units. These 20,000 units are in inventory carrying a fixed overhead cost of $.25 each, or $5,000 in total.)

Exhibit 11–20

THE ABC DIVISION
Analysis of Variances, January 1975
(000 omitted)

	Actual	Budget*	Actual Better/(Worse) Than Budget
Sales	$875.0	$950.0	$ (75.0)
Standard cost of sales	682.5†	682.5†	—
Spending variances	(13.0)		(13.0)
Volume variance	42.5		42.5
Gross profit	$222.0	$267.5	$ (45.5)
Selling expense	55.0	50.0	(5.0)
Administrative expense	30.0	25.0	(5.0)
Profit	$137.0	$192.5	$ (55.5)
Mix variance			35.0
Volume variance (revenue)			77.5
Net variance			$ 57.0

* Budgeted prices and costs at actual sales volume and mix.
† Standard unit costs multiplied by the actual volume of sales:

Product	Units Sold	Standard Unit Costs	Standard Cost of Sales
A	100	$1.05	$105.0
B	200	1.35	270.0
C	150	2.05	307.5
Total	450		$682.5

Note that there are two volume variances. The revenue volume variance results from *selling* a greater number of units than was budgeted. The cost variances result from *producing* a greater number of units than was budgeted.

Case 11–1

ABC Division

In this case you are asked to analyze the February and March financial performance of the ABC Division as compared with its budget which is shown in Exhibit 11–2 (see page 514).

PART A—FEBRUARY 1975

Below is the data describing the actual financial results for the ABC Division for the month of February 1975:

Sales	$781
Variable cost of sales	552
Contribution	$229
Fixed manufacturing costs	80
Gross profit	$149
Selling expense	57
Administrative expense	33
Net profit	$ 59

SALES

Product	Unit Sales	Price	Dollar Sales
A	120	$ .95	$114
B	130	1.90	247
C	150	2.80	420
Total	400		$781

PRODUCTION

			Manufacturing Cost		
Product	Units Produced	Material	Labor	Variable Overhead	Total
A	150	$ 80	$20	$ 40	$140
B	130	91	21	35	147
C	120	190	15	30	235
Total	400	$361	$56	$105	$522

QUESTIONS

1. Prepare an analysis of variance from profit budget assuming that the ABC Division employed a direct standard cost accounting system.

2. Prepare an analysis of variance from profit budget assuming that the ABC Company used a full standard cost accounting system. Under this assumption the cost of sales amount would be $632,000. (Can you derive this figure?)

3. Industry volume figures are presented below. Separate the mix and volume variance into the variance resulting from differences in market penetration and variance resulting from differences in industry volume. Make the calculation for the direct cost system only.

Industry volume, February, 1975:

	Units (000)
Product A	600
Product B	650
Product C	1,500

PART B—MARCH 1975

Below is the data describing the actual financial results for the ABC Division for the month of March 1975:

INCOME STATEMENT

Sales	$498
Variable cost of sales	278
Contribution	$220
Fixed manufacturing costs	70
Gross profit	$150
Selling expense	45
Administrative expense	20
Net profit	$ 85

SALES

Product	Unit Sales	Price	Dollar Sales
A	90	$1.10	$ 99
B	70	2.10	147
C	80	3.15	252
Total	240		$498

PRODUCTION

| | | | Manufacturing Costs | | |
Product	Units Produced	Material	Labor	Variable Overhead	Total
A	90	$ 40	$ 8	$17	$ 65
B	80	55	10	18	83
C	100	150	8	19	177
Total	270	$245	$26	$54	$325

QUESTIONS

Answer the same questions included in Part A. The actual cost of sales using full standard costing would be $340.5 in March. Industry volume for March was:

	Units (000)
Product A	500
Product B	600
Product C	1,000

Case 11–2

EFGH Company

The profit budget for the EFGH Company for January 1975 was as follows:

	(000)
Sales	$2,500
Standard cost of sales	1,620
Gross profit	$ 880
Selling expense $250	
Research and development expense 300	
Administrative expense 120	
Total expense	$ 670
Net profit before taxes	$ 210

The product information used in developing the budget is as follows:

	E	F	G	H
Sales-units (000)	1,000	2,000	3,000	4,000
Price per unit	$ .15	$ .20	$ .25	$ .30
Standard cost per unit				
Material	.04	.05	.06	.08
Direct labor	.02	.02	.03	.04
Variable overhead	.02	.03	.03	.05
Total variable cost	.08	.10	.12	.17
Fixed overhead ($000)	$ 20	$ 60	$ 60	$ 160
Total standard cost per unit	.10	.13	.14	.21

The actual revenues and costs for January 1975 were as follows:

530

Sales		$2,160
Standard cost of sales		1,420
Net standard cost variances		160
Actual cost of sales		$1,580
Gross profit		580
Selling expense	$290	
Research and development expense	250	
Administrative expenses	110	
Total expense		650
Net loss		$ (70)

Operating statistics for January 1975 were as follows:

Sales (units)	1,000	1,000	4,000	3,000
Sales—Price	.13	.22	.22	.31
Production	1,000	1,000	2,000	2,000
Actual manufacturing costs ($000)				
Material $360				
Labor 200				
Overhead 530				

QUESTION

Prepare an analysis of variance between actual profits and budgeted profits for January, 1971.

Case 11–3

Wellington Corporation

The machining department of the Wellington Corporation produced two metal parts that were subsequently incorporated into the company's finished products. In January 1975 the plant superintendent was reviewing the cost performance of the department for the preceding year. A summary of the historical data relating to productivity, labor cost, and material cost is shown below:

	1974
Number of good parts produced:	
Part No. 683	4,451,328
Part No. 845	975,744
Total	5,427,072
Pounds of steel rod used	1,770,739 lbs.
Cost of steel rod used	$ 460,392
Number of labor hours	34,500 hrs.
Labor cost	$ 103,500

The machining department operated two types of automatic screw machines: the Acme model 106 machines were used to produce Part #683, while the Detroit model X7 machines were used for Part #845. The Acme machines were faster and more efficient in that they could produce 60 pieces per hour and one operator could serve four machines. The department had 48 Acme machines and during 1974 these machines had been operated at full capacity (40 hours per week for 50 weeks) because of a strong demand for the product which used this part. During the year, therefore, twelve men had always been assigned to the Acme machines and, in order to achieve maximum output, the foreman had always assigned his most highly skilled operators to this equipment. The Detroit machines had a theoretical capacity of 40 units per hour of Part #845 and a skilled operator could serve only three of these machines. While there were 24 Detroit machines in the department, full utilization had not been necessary during 1974. The department's normal total work force was 17 men, but this number varied from day to day depending on the production of Part #845 required. Some workers might be temporarily assigned to or from another department to handle these fluctuating requirements. Wellington's contract with the labor union specified that all men assigned to the machining department were to receive the same wage ($3 per hour); for this reason, the payroll accounting department kept track of all temporary transfers, and the machining department was charged only for the time spent by men actually assigned to the department.

A study of the labor efficiency in the machining department, conducted in the fall of 1973 indicated that the machines normally operated about 90 percent of the time. Half of the 10 percent down time was due to regularly scheduled rest periods for the machine operators, the other 5 percent was the time required by a worker of average skill to make adjustments to the machine settings.

Both parts produced by the department were made from the same type of tempered steel rod. Wellington's major domestic supplier had announced a list price for this rod, f.o.b. Wellington's plant, of 28¢ per pound in late 1972. During 1974 however, Wellington's purchasing agent had found that imported rod of equal quality could be purchased on similar terms for 24¢ per pound. By the end of 1974 all of Wellington's rod was being supplied by the foreign producer.

Part #683 was smaller than Part #845; a finished piece of the smaller part weighed .20 pounds, while a finished unit of the larger part weighed .40 pounds. Because some material was wasted in the machining process, .45 pounds of rod were required to produce one piece of Part #845, while .24 pounds were needed for one piece of #683. In addition, some of the finished pieces were scrapped because the machine settings tended to become out of adjustment. The company's historical experience had been that Part #683, the more complex part, incurred a 20 percent scrappage rate while #845 had only a 10 percent scrappage rate. According to the foreman in the department, however, the actual scrappage on Part #683 during 1974 had been lower than normal—only 16 percent—because the more skilled workers on the Acme machines were better able to keep the machines in adjustment. The proceeds (10¢ per pound) received from the sale of both metal shavings and scrapped parts were regarded by Wellington's management as "Other Income," and were not credited to the materials cost account of the machining department.

QUESTIONS

1. Prepare a statement of estimated or standard prime costs for each part, as of the beginning of 1974. Prime cost is the sum of direct material cost

plus direct labor cost. Analyze the actual results for that year in terms of these standards, and compute quantity and price variances in as detailed a manner as is possible with the information available.

2. Wellington's management was considering an opportunity to enter into a one-year supply contract with a major mail-order house for the product which used Part #845. The contract would require at least 15,000 units of the part each month. As part of the analysis in deciding what price to offer on this contract, management has asked you to prepare an estimate of prime costs for the coming year which you think would be relevant for this bid.

Case 11-4

Cotter Co., Inc.

In preparing its profit plan for 1975, the management of the Cotter Co., Inc., realized that its sales were subject to monthly seasonal variations, but expected that for the year as a whole the profit before taxes would total $240,000, as shown below:

1975 BUDGET

	Amount	Percent of Sales
Sales	$2,400,000	100
Standard cost of goods sold:		
Prime costs	960,000	40
Factory overhead	840,000	35
Total standard cost	$1,800,000	75
Gross profit	$ 600,000	25
Selling and general overhead	360,000	15
Profit before taxes	$ 240,000	10

Management defined "prime costs" as those costs for labor and materials which were strictly variable with the quantity of production in the factory. The overhead in the factory included both fixed and variable costs; management's estimate was that, within a sales volume range of plus or minus $1,000,000 per year, variable factory overhead would be equal to 25 percent of prime costs. Thus, the total factory overhead budgeted for 1968 consisted of $240,000 of variable costs (25 percent of $960,000) and $600,000 of fixed costs. All of the selling and general overhead was fixed, except for commissions on sales equal to 5 percent of the selling price.

Mr. Cotter, the president of the company, approved the budget, stating that, "A profit of $20,000 a month isn't bad for a little company in this business." During January, however, sales suffered the normal seasonal dips, and production in the factory was also cut back. The result, which came as some surprise to the president, was that January showed a loss of $7,000.

OPERATING STATEMENT, JANUARY 1975

Sales		$140,000
Standard cost of goods sold		105,000
Standard gross profit		$ 35,000
Manufacturing variances:		
	Favorable or (Unfavorable)	
Prime cost variance	$ (3,500)	
Factory overhead:		
Spending variance	1,000	
Volume variance	(12,500)	(15,000)
Actual gross profit		$ 20,000
Selling and general overhead		27,000
Loss before taxes		$ (7,000)

ASSIGNMENT

Explain, as best you can with the data available, why the January profit was $27,000 less than the average monthly profit expected by the president.

Case 11-5

Bondsville Manufacturing Company

"Let's face it," said William Haywood, controller of the Bondsville Manufacturing Company to Frederick Strong, the manager of the budget department. "Our budgetary control program is considerably less than a roaring success. As far as I can tell, no one in top management takes any action from our monthly analyses of actual profit performance against budget. Jim [James Smith, Bondsville's president] told me this afternoon that he really cannot use these reports to control the divisions. He said that the variance from budgeted profits always seem to be large, but there always appeared to be reasonable explanations. Further, he pointed out that once a division started to miss its budget, the variances seemed to get larger each month. And Jim wasn't concerned only with unfavorable variances. He says that some divisions are showing favorable variances when he knows darn well that they are doing a poor job."

Frederick Strong was crestfallen. He had come to the Bondsville Manufacturing Company three years before from a large automobile manufacturer where he had been a budget analyst in one of the divisions. He was responsible for developing and installing the present profit budget system. The system had gone into effect 18 months ago. For the first year, it was considered experimental. Beginning with the current year (1975) the profit budget was officially installed as the basic tool of management control. Now, after six months, the president of Bondsville was questioning the utility of the budgetary control system and the controller was evidently agreeing.

"I don't understand it," said Strong to Haywood. "The system is similar to the one we used at Universal Motors and they sure paid attention to it. If we missed our budget, we were called on the carpet to explain—and the explanation had to be good."

"Well, it may have worked at Universal," said Haywood, "but it isn't working here. I'll arrange for you to talk with Jim about it. Then, I want you to go over the system and either modify it so that it will work or scrap it and develop something that will." With this last comment, Strong was dismissed to ponder his problems.

HISTORY OF THE COMPANY

The Bondsville Manufacturing Company started during World War I as a family-owned manufacturer of cotton textiles for the United States Army. The original plant was located in the town of Bondsville, a small village in western Massachusetts. The company's early growth was slow and it remained a one-plant manufacturer of cotton textiles until the outbreak of World War II. (With difficulty, Bondsville had managed to weather the economic shoals of the Depression.)

By the beginning of World War II, the company was taken over from the original family by a group of investors. This group renovated the Bondsville plant, built a knitting plant in nearby Ware, Massachusetts, and purchased a woolen plant in Monson, Massachusetts. During the war, the company prospered and grew until, at the cessation of hostilities, its annual profit was $3 million on a sales volume of nearly $28 million. After World War II, the company again went into somewhat of a decline. Sales increased very slowly and profits declined. By 1965, the stockholders (who had changed from the group who bought out the original family business) together with a Springfield, Massachusetts bank that held a large loan forced out the incumbent president and appointed James Smith to the post. Smith had been marketing vice president of a large southern textile company where he had developed a reputation for "getting things done."

Since 1965, the company had prospered. Sales in the three current lines (cotton, knitted goods, and woolens) grew, and by 1970 the company had added two new lines of goods: artificial fiber products (dacron and nylon hosiery, underwear, blouses, etc.) in a plant in Dedham, Massachusetts; and artificial leather in a plant in Milton, Massachusetts. These plants were both acquired by buying the companies that had been operating them. In each case the acquisition was made by a combination of exchange of stock and cash.

By mid-1975 (the date of the events described earlier in the case), Bondsville's sales were approaching $100 million a year. The profits, however, still were only about $3 million.

PRODUCTS

The Bondsville Manufacturing Company has five product lines. Each line is produced in a separate plant and is marketed by a separate organization. Each line is described below.

Cotton Textiles. The Bondsville plant produces gray goods that are sold directly to jobbers and converters (about 50 percent of the volume) and printed cotton fabrics that are sold to jobbers and also directly to clothes manufacturers.

Knitted Goods. The Ware plant produces knitted fabrics and converts these fabrics into clothes. Part of the production is of such standard items as underware and pajamas. Over 50 percent of the production is in women's clothes, which are style items and seasonal. These are sold directly to department stores by company salesmen.

Artificial Fibers. The Dedham plant produces products made of artificial fibers (principally dacron and nylon). The yarn is purchased but the plant weaves the cloth and manufactures the garments. These are sold to jobbers and also directly to buyers from the large department stores.

Woolen Goods. The Monson plant produces woolen cloth of various types. About three quarters of the cloth is sold to finishers by company salesmen. The company finishes (dyes) the remaining one quarter of its production and sells this cloth to manufacturers of clothes.

Artificial Leather. The Milton plant produces artificial leather for automobile and furniture upholstery. About 50 percent of the production is for automobiles; the remainder is used in a variety of furniture. Artificial leather is sold exclusively by company salesmen directly to manufacturers.

The following are the 1974 sales and gross profits (sales minus manufacturing costs) of each of the product lines.

	Sales (000)	Gross Profit (000)
Cotton textiles	$42,581	$ 463
Knitted goods	27,862	4,068
Artificial fiber	13,733	716
Woolen goods	10,429	(28)
Artificial leather	5,216	1,582
	$99,821	$6,801

ORGANIZATION

Exhibit 1 is an organization chart of the Bondsville Manufacturing Company. Each of the five operating divisions is headed by a divisional manager who is responsible for the profits that the division earns. Theoretically, the staff is responsible only for helping the divisions when needed and to coordinate the functional activities. In fact, the sales staff vice president and the manufacturing staff vice president had been senior operating people before taking up the staff positions. Consequently, they exercise considerable direct control over their functional areas in the divisions. The president also spends several days a month visiting the divisional offices and counselling

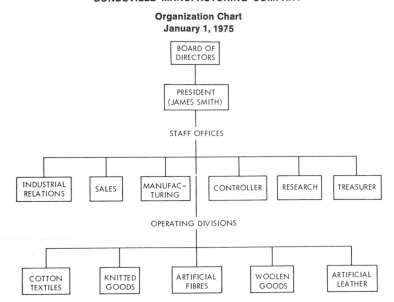

Exhibit 1

BONDSVILLE MANUFACTURING COMPANY

Organization Chart
January 1, 1975

the managers on their various problems. Exhibit 2 shows the organization of the cotton textiles division; this is typical of the other divisions.

The company's research efforts have been quite modest (about $500,000 a year) and all formal research is done at the central office level. Some informal research is done at the divisional level.

The president and all of the staff work in a two-story office building and laboratory located in Worcester, Massachusetts. This location is very close to the geographic center of the operating plants.

THE CONTROLLER'S OFFICE

Exhibit 3 is the organization chart for the controller's office, showing the budgeting department organization through the second level.

The basic accounting records are maintained at the divisional offices. Each month the divisional balance sheet and profit and loss accounts are submitted to the central office. The central office's accounting department prescribes the company's accounting systems, maintains the central office accounting records, consolidates monthly all of the accounts, and publishes a companywide balance sheet and profit and loss statement on the tenth working day after the end of the month.

Each division has its own accounting department. Reporting to the divisional accountant, the divisional budget manager is responsible for the bud-

Exhibit 2

BONDSVILLE MANUFACTURING COMPANY

Organization Chart—Cotton Textile Division—January 1, 1975

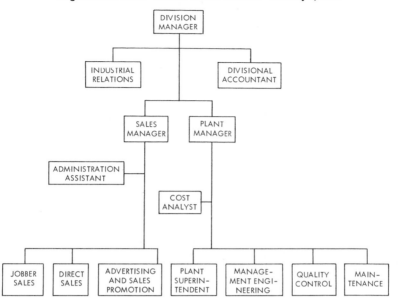

get reports in the division. Each plant manager has a cost analyst who reports directly to him and whose job is to assist the manager by interpreting budget and cost reports and obtaining any cost information that he needs. In addition, the cost analyst is responsible for providing the analysis of budget variances to the divisional budget manager.

At the plant level, the company uses a standard cost system to control material and labor and a flexible budget to control manufacturing overhead.

THE BUDGETARY CONTROL SYSTEM

Divisional Profit Budgets

Each divisional manager is responsible for preparing and submitting a profit budget in December to cover the succeeding year. The sales department first prepares an estimate of annual sales. This is reviewed and approved by the divisional manager. After sales volume approval, everyone reporting to the divisional manager is responsible for preparing his budget, based on the indicated volume of sales. The plant budget is based on standard costs for material and direct labor and the flexible budget for manufacturing overhead. Other departments budget in accordance with their estimated requirements for the coming year. The divisional manager reviews

Exhibit 3

BONDSVILLE MANUFACTURING COMPANY

Organization Chart—Controller's Office
January 1, 1975

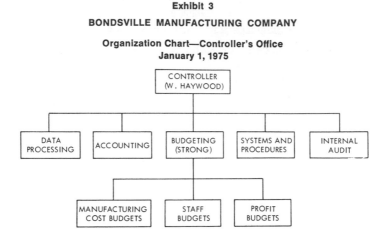

each budget and approves or adjusts it if he thinks the proposed budget is out of line.

The divisional manager next meets with the president, the manufacturing staff vice president, the sales staff vice president, and the controller. [This is the budget approval committee.] The divisional manager presents his proposed budget. In evaluating the proposed budget, differences from the current year's actual performance are carefully explained. (Since the current year's results are not usually known at the time of budget submission, 10 months' actual and two months' forecast is used as the basis of comparison.) The committee discusses the proposed budget with the divisional manager and either approves it, adjusts it, or sends it back to be partially redone.

After final approval, the budget becomes the basis for evaluating actual profit performance.

Staff Budgets

Each staff vice president also presents his budget for the coming year to the president. After discussion, the budget is either approved or adjusted.

Company Budget

The controller's office combines the divisional and staff budgets into a companywide profit budget which is presented to the president for final approval. (The president could call for a change in previously approved budgets if the total company profits were not satisfactory.)

Budget Reports

Each month a report is prepared for each division showing actual profits compared to budget. Exhibit 4 is an example of a budget performance report.

These budget performance reports are prepared by the divisions and sub-

Exhibit 4

BONDSVILLE MANUFACTURING COMPANY

Woolen Goods Division
Profit Budget Performance Report
April, 1975
($000)

	Month of April	Year-to-Date
Actual profit	$(12)	$ (43)
Budgeted profit	42	150
Actual over/(under) budget	(54)	(193)

Analysis of Variance
Favorable/(Unfavorable)

Revenue items	Month	Year-to-date
Sales volume	$(65)	$(240)
Selling prices	15	(25)
Product mix	2	10
Cost items		
Material prices	$ 4	$ 10
Material usage	(3)	6
Direct labor	10	45
Variable overhead	5	30
Advertising and sales promotion	(16)	(35)
Other selling	(1)	(9)
Administration	(5)	15
	$(54)	$(193)

Note: This exhibit was backed up with schedules showing the details of the variances and explanations of the reasons for the variances. The explanations were provided by the various operating executives responsible for these variances.

mitted to the central staff on the twelfth working day after the end of the month. After review by the central budget department, copies are distributed to the president, the sales staff vice president, and the manufacturing staff vice president. The central budget department prepares a brief analysis of each report, indicating points that should be brought to management's attention.

The central budget department prepares a "Company Profit Budget Report" on the fifteenth working day after the end of the month. This is a consolidation of the five operating divisions and the six staff offices. Copies of this go to the three executives indicated above.

DISCUSSION WITH SMITH

Strong made an appointment to talk to the president, James Smith, about the profit budget system. Following is a partial transcript of Smith's statements to Strong:

"Frankly, your profit budget performance reports are just about worthless to me. For one thing, we just cannot budget sales revenue with any degree of certainty. All of the budgets show large variances, but what do I do with them? The big variances are almost always in revenue. Either volume has been higher or lower than budget or prices have gone up or down. Furthermore, once a division starts having problems with sales or prices, it might take several months to change the situation. You might have to change your product line, wait until your competitors get tired of losing money and raise prices, or wait until the economy improves. In other words, I look at the budget performance report and say 'so what?'

"Another thing, I really get no surprises from the budget reports because I know when something has happened long before the budget report reaches me. I get weekly sales reports from each division and I can easily see those divisions that are having trouble with volume or prices. Costs do not usually vary much from month to month. The few times that our costs have gone to hell temporarily, I have known it ahead of time. What I need is a report that will tell me what is going to happen, not one that tells me what I have known for several weeks.

"There's a third thing that bothers me, but I'd like you to keep this under your hat. I know for a fact that John Bennett [the manager of the Artificial Leather Division] has been doing a poor job with that division this year, even though his budget performance is the best of the five divisions. Because of quality problems in his plant, he lost one of our best customers in the furniture business. Yet, because automobiles are selling far better than we anticipated, Bennett shows a large favorable sales volume variance. On the other hand, the most capable manager that I have shows the poorest budget performance.

"There you are, Fred—three complaints. I can't do anything with the reports: they contain no important information that I did not already know; they do not reflect the true performance of the managers. I had hopes of using profit budget performance as a basis for paying bonuses to the managers. You can see that I can't do this with your system.

"You will have to do something about these complaints or discontinue this fancy profit budget system. As it is now, it may have been all right for the big automobile firms but it's no good for us."

QUESTIONS

1. What do you think should be done about Bondsville's profit budgeting system?

2. If you believe it should be discontinued, what are company characteristics that have made it unworkable? With what should the system be replaced?

3. In what type of company does a profit budget system work effectively?

Chapter Twelve

THE APPRAISAL OF
PERFORMANCE

In Chapter 10, we stated that a budget is both a planning and a control tool, and we discussed its use for planning purposes. In this chapter we discuss its use in the control process. The profit budget is used for control by top management in two ways:

First, budget reports, comparing actual results with budget, together with accompanying analysis of variances, current annual forecast, and explanation of actions, are used to keep management informed on what is happening in the divisions. Management can, when necessary, take appropriate action on the basis of these reports.

Second, the budget system is used to appraise the performance of the divisional manager. The profit budget is his commitment, and he can be judged according to how well he meets this commitment.

Many things can be happening in a division that are not reflected in reports of current profitability. Consequently, top management cannot be assured that all important events will be adequately communicated through the profit budget system. The same limitation affects the use of the profit budget in performance appraisal. Not only are certain events not reflected in the current accounting results, but also the divisional manager may have little control over many events that *are* reflected in profits.

In this chapter we describe the problems that businesses experience in controlling divisional operations by means of the profit budget, and describe some of the actions companies can take to solve these problems.

THE PROFIT BUDGET IN PERFORMANCE APPRAISAL

Profit budgets can be an inadequate basis for evaluating managerial performance for several reasons.

First, profits are affected by so many complex variables that it is impossible to provide an exact answer to the question: How much should this profit center earn this year? Consequently, subjective judgment is required in setting an annual profit objective for a profit center. It follows that annual profit objectives will represent a considerable range of difficulty among profit centers, even in the best of circumstances. In the usual review process, where a dozen or more divisional budgets might be reviewed in less than a month, time does not permit a thorough analysis. Often the most persuasive manager ends up with the easiest profit objective. In general, the profit objectives of the various profit centers are likely to vary considerably with respect to the ease or difficulty of attaining them.

Second, in arriving at a profit objective, it is necessary to predict the conditions that will exist during the coming year, many of which are almost entirely beyond the control of the profit center manager. Two of the most important conditions are the economic climate and the competitive situation. If the predictions of these are incorrect, the profit objectives will also be incorrect. Thus, even if one started with a completely equitable profit objective, as soon as the assumptions on which it was based turned out to be incorrect, the profit objective would no longer be equitable.

This situation can be particularly frustrating in that the assumptions that affect revenues usually are much more uncertain than the assumptions that affect costs: yet changes in revenues usually have a much greater impact on profits than changes in costs. More than one manager has found that the results of successful cost reduction programs have been overshadowed by unfavorable variances from budget in the volume or mix of sales. What this amounts to is that the variance between actual and budgeted profit is often affected more by the ability to forecast than by the ability to manage.

Factors Affecting Performance Appraisal

The ability of a division to set equitable annual profit goals and to perform so as to attain these goals depends on four factors:

1. The degree of discretion that the divisional manager can exercise.
2. The degree to which the critical performance variables can be controlled by the divisional manager.
3. The degree of uncertainty that exists with respect to the critical performance variables.
4. The time span of the impact of the manager's decisions.

Degree of Discretion. The degree of discretion that a manager can exercise depends on two things:

1. The nature of the job. The more complex the job, the greater the discretion required to manage it effectively.
2. The degree of delegation. The greater the degree of delegation, the greater the discretion that the divisional manager can exercise.

The greater the degree of discretion that a divisional manager can exercise, the more difficult it is to set precise goals. This is because the greater the number of alternative courses of action that are open to a manager, the more difficult it is to determine ahead of time which particular courses of action are best and what the financial impact of these actions should be. For example, if a plant manager is held responsible for keeping actual costs in line with standard costs, but has relatively little discretion as to what will be produced, how it will be produced, and how much the labor force will be paid, it is a relatively simple task to set a reasonable financial objective. By contrast, a divisional manager who is responsible for product development, marketing, production, and procurement and development of personnel, has a large number of variables that he controls directly or indirectly. It is clearly very difficult to judge ahead of time how he should exercise his discretion with respect to each of these variables.

Degree of Controllability. The greater the degree of control that a divisional manager can exercise over the critical performance variables, the easier it is to develop an effective budgetary control system. The difficulty in measuring the performance of a divisional manager is directly related to the number and type of noncontrollable or semicontrollable performance variables that exist. In general, external marketing variables are much more difficult to control than internal production variables because a divisional manager has limited control over competitive activity or the general level of the economy. Thus, it is much easier to set a profit objective and to judge performance against this objective for a division where sales are limited by production capacity (i.e., everything that can be produced can be sold) than for a division that sells in a highly competitive or volatile market and has ample production capacity.

Degree of Uncertainty. The degree of uncertainty has an important impact on the effectiveness of a budgetary control system. The greater the uncertainty, the more difficult it is to set satisfactory goals and to measure performance against these goals. Like controllability, uncertainty is much greater with respect to external variables than to internal variables. Also, the degree of uncertainty tends to be related to the degree of innovation. The more innovative the division, the greater will be the uncertainty of its annual profitability.

Time Span. If a budget system is to provide a valid basis for judging performance, it must measure the real accomplishments of the manager during the period under review. This never happens. Many decisions that a manager makes today may not be reflected in profitability until some future period. Conversely, current profitability reflects in part the impact of decisions made in some past period. If the profit budget system were perfect, it would take into account the impact of past decisions, but this cannot be done accurately. If it could be done, budgeted profit would reflect satisfactory managerial performance, given the situation that existed at the beginning of the year, and the performance reports would measure the effectiveness of those managerial decisions that affect current profitability. The performance measurement would still be incomplete, however, because it would not measure the soundness of current decisions that affect future profits; such decisions are often extremely important.

In summary, the limitations of the financial control system to measure accomplishment in the short run are less serious when the following conditions exist:

1. The degree of discretion exercised by the divisional manager is limited.
2. The number and degree of either noncontrollable or uncertain variables are limited.
3. The time span of the manager's job is relatively short.

For example, divisions that sell established products or services in established markets and produce these products or services with established facilities can, with considerable confidence, use a profit budget system as a means for evaluation and control. The further divisional characteristics differ from those listed above, the less effective the control exercised through the profit budget is likely to be. Product, market, and facility innovations increase the degree of uncertainty, and increase the time span.

TIGHT VERSUS LOOSE DELEGATION

In order to exercise effective control over divisions, top management needs to receive information on all significant events that occur in the division, and it also needs a way of appraising divisional performance. In part, the formal reports of actual performance compared with budget meet these needs, but other control devices are also necessary. The relative importance of the formal system and the other devices depends on top management's preference for what might be called "tight delegation" versus "loose delegation."

Tight Delegation

Tight delegation is based on the management philosophy that:

1. Divisional managers work most effectively when they are required to meet specific short-term (e.g., one-year) goals; and
2. Top management can assist divisional management in solving many day-to-day problems. Or put another way, divisions make better day-to-day decisions if top management participates in the decision-making process.

Under tight delegation, the profit goal of a divisional manager is considered to be a firm commitment against which he will be measured and evaluated. Each month his performance to date and his expected performance for the year are analyzed in detail, variances are explained, and courses of corrective action considered when there is a likelihood that the profit goal will not be met. Since the profit budget does not provide a complete basis for evaluation and control, effective tight delegation requires some additional control devices. These include:

1. Complete management involvement in the budgeting and reporting system. This usually requires face-to-face discussions every period with divisional managers, an intimate knowledge of the operations being reviewed, and an ability to analyze and interpret financial data.
2. A capable accounting, budgeting, and analytical staff to make the financial information as reliable as possible and to assist management in using the data.

To demonstrate that these devices are necessary to make a budget system effective, let us consider first the problems that might occur if they did not exist. The following unfortunate events are likely to occur:

1. Short-term actions that are not in the long-term interests of the company will be encouraged. If too much pressure is applied to meet current profit goals, the divisional manager will have no alternative but to take short-term action that may well be wrong in the long run. The greater the amount of discretion delegated to the manager, the greater will be the danger of encouraging uneconomic short-term actions (errors of commission) and discouraging useful long-term actions (errors of omission).

2. If the profit budget is used by top management as the sole, or primary, basis for evaluating performances, serious errors could result. Difference between actual and budgeted profits may bear no relationship to the effectiveness of a divisional manager in the current period since many actions he takes in that period affect results in future years.

3. The use of budgeted profit as a firm objective can distort communications between the divisional manager and top management. If a divisional manager is evaluated on the basis of his profit budget, he will be tempted to try to set a profit target that is easily met. This leads to confusion in the planning process prior to the beginning of the year since the budgeted profit may be less than that which could really be achieved. Also, the divisional manager may be reluctant to admit, during the year, that he is likely to miss his profit budget until it is evident that he cannot possibly attain it. This could delay corrective action.

4. If top management relies on the profit budget reports as an early warning of potential trouble, it will be placing its faith in an imperfect instrument. Many important management actions are not reflected in profit performance until long after they have been taken.

In summary, then, if the profit budget is taken as being a firm commitment of a divisional manager against which his actual performance is evaluated, there is a danger that: (1) the manager may be motivated to take uneconomic actions; (2) that this may result in incorrect evaluation; and (3) that this may distort communications and, consequently, affect planning adversely.

The additional devices mentioned above can mitigate these problems:

1. Proposed corrective actions are reviewed in detail with divisional managers. This lessens the likelihood of uneconomic short-term action.
2. Top management evaluates divisional management on the basis of personal observation. The performance of a divisional manager can be judged in part on the basis of the *quality* of his decisions. It is not necessary to wait until the impact of these decisions is reflected in profits.
3. Top management can establish the philosophy that a divisional manager who delays informing top management about incipient problems is committing a serious sin. This attitude, supported by extensive analytical efforts on the part of the finance staff, can improve greatly the quality of the information submitted by the divisions.

The insistence by top management on accurate and immediate communication of problems, together with management's intimate knowledge of individual operations, reduces significantly the likelihood that unexpected adverse situations will develop. In short, management uses the budget system as a means of requiring division management to make a commitment and, subsequently, as a means of getting involved in divisional problems and helping to solve them. Evaluation and control are exercised by top management through personal observation and nonfinancial information, in addition to the accounting reports. The key to successful operation is top management's participation in divisional operations. Note that in such a system *all* divisions are reviewed in detail each period. The profit budget is not used as a basis for "management by exception" because, for reasons previously stated, it is not a satisfactory vehicle for this purpose.

Loose Delegation

Loose delegation is based on a completely different management philosophy from tight delegation. This philosophy is illustrated by the statement: "I hire good people, and I leave them alone to do their jobs."

Under loose delegation, the budget is used essentially as a communication and planning tool. Annually, budgets are prepared, reviewed by top management, adjusted where management deems appropriate, and approved. Monthly, or quarterly, actual results and a forecast for the year are compared to the budget, and differences are analyzed and explained. The budget is not considered a management commitment; instead, it is assumed to be the best estimate of profitability at the time that it was prepared. Subsequently, as conditions and expectations change, these are communicated to top management in the form of revised estimates which are compared to the original budget and differences explained. The fact that the original profit goal has not been met does not necessarily indicate poor performance.

A budget system administered in this way has some advantages over the alternative of using the profit budget as a firm management commitment. First, there is no pressure for immediate short-term actions to increase profits. Secondly, since the emphasis is placed on communication and planning rather than on performance evaluation, there should be less tendency to withhold unpleasant information. Third, top management does not evaluate divisional performance by comparing it with budgeted profits, thereby avoiding the incomplete or misleading conclusions that are possible when the budget is used for this purpose.

Control Devices in Loose Delegation

Although a loose delegation system provides a good basis for planning, it has limited use for control. Management needs two additional devices for this purpose:

1. A means for signaling when a divisional manager is performing unsatisfactorily, that is, an early warning system.
2. A means of evaluating divisional management.

Early Warning System. In loose delegation, the budget system does not assure that top management is informed about all important events. Some type of early warning system that signals when something that requires immediate action is occurring in one of the divisions is necessary. The development of such an early warning system can be much more difficult than the development of an evaluation system. The problem becomes more difficult as the divisional manager's responsibilities become more complex. One conclusion we can safely draw is that the *accounting and budgeting system does not provide a reliable early warning system* for a complex organization. It provides an early warning system only for a limited set of unsatisfactory situations, namely, those that are reflected quickly in profit performance. It does not provide an early warning of unsatisfactory managerial action where the impact of these actions on accounted profit is deferred. The determination that top management action is required depends upon the informed judgment of an individual who is: (a) knowledgeable in the area in which he is evaluating the activities, (b) familiar with the situation, and (c) independent. This means that either top management or someone between top management and the divisional manager must perform this function. In smaller or relatively integrated companies, the president is often able to do this effectively. In a large diversified corporation, only a very unusual top manager is able to rely on his own observations and judgment to monitor divisions constantly to detect unsatisfactory activity.

Evaluating Division Management. Any of several types of organizational arrangements may be used both to evaluate division managers and to serve as an early warning system:

1. Appropriate staff offices may be assigned the responsibility for monitoring divisional activity in their respective fields. For example, the marketing

staff would be responsible for monitoring the marketing activities, the manufacturing staff for production, and the research staff for research and development. When the staff believes that a divisional manager is making questionable decisions in its area, it alerts top management. Once alerted, top management takes whatever action it deems necessary. This arrangement is not without problems, however. If the monitoring is not done tactfully and carefully, the staff groups might be looked upon as spies by operating management, and this, of course, limits their effectiveness.

2. Instead of just one or two persons in the top executive group as is the case in the traditional organization, there may be several, and the group may be designated by a title such as "Office of the President." Each division is assigned to one of these executives. He monitors the divisional activity and takes appropriate action when he feels it is necessary.

3. A committee of top executives, without line authority, may review divisional activity periodically. These persons are chosen for their expertise and are provided with the necessary time to become familiar with divisional activities. The DuPont Executive Committee is an example of this type of organization.

4. The company may be divided into groups of divisions, each headed by a group executive responsible for the operations of the divisions within his group. This arrangement may not be as effective in early warning as the other three because the group executive is *responsible* for the effectiveness of the divisions. He is not, therefore, independent. If a person is held responsible for an activity, he tends to become a filter that blocks unpleasant information concerning this activity from reaching top management.

Whatever the form of organization that is used to provide top management control over divisional operations, management should recognize that the financial control system, or any system, will not provide adequate early warning information or reliable evaluation of divisional activities. If the top manager believes that he cannot monitor divisional activity adequately himself, he should be sure that someone with the necessary time, ability, and objectivity is doing so.

Selection of a Delegation Philosophy

International Telephone and Telegraph Company (ITT) is an example of a company that uses a budget system with tight delegation. To administer this system takes a great deal of top management time. Also, it requires considerable financial insight and ability on the part of top management.[1] Top management people of ITT are said to spend a full week each month in Europe reviewing financial performance with the managers of the European companies. The DuPont control system is an example of loose delega-

---

[1] For a description see Anthony Sampson, *The Sovereign State of ITT* (London: Hodder and Stoughton, 1973).

tion, at least with respect to the *formal control system.* DuPont has a 12-man executive committee, without line responsibility, that reviews the results of the operating departments in detail at least once a quarter.[2]

The control system of most companies falls somewhere in between these two extremes. Paradoxically, the least effective systems are likely to be those that are half way between the extremes. The reason is that each of the extreme systems is based on a management philosophy, and the administration and organization of the control system should be consistent with that philosophy. If it is not, it will tend to be ineffective. We have already described the problems that can exist in a tight delegation system without the necessary management commitment. A loose delegation system without adequate evaluation procedures and an early warning system can be equally dangerous. Some financial control systems are less effective than they could be because they were designed by financial experts who did not take into consideration management's philosophy and style, and who did not recognize the limitations of a profit budget system. For example, a system may be designed to exert tight control by making the divisional manager responsible for his profit goal, even though top management may not be interested in getting into the day-to-day operation of the divisions. In some cases, management may realize that the budget has limited use as an evaluation technique and more or less ignores differences between actual and budget unless they are extreme; therefore, management is administering the budget loosely.

Because of the appearance of adequacy (i.e., analyses of actual performance against budget), however, the fact that there is no systematic formal evaluation system and no early warning system may go undetected. The situation is even worse if top management uses the budgets as firm goals that divisional managers are expected to meet. Then, all of the problems described earlier will result.

In many companies, the function of the budget is not explicitly stated. As a result, there is a great deal of uncertainty on the part of the profit center manager and a great deal of inconsistency on the part of those to whom the profit center managers report. For example, in a single line of command, the budget may be treated at one level as a firm commitment, at another level as a forecast, and at a third level as something in between. Such a lack of explicit decision as to whether or not the profit budget is supposed to represent a firm commitment causes grave problems.

NONBUDGETARY TECHNIQUES

So far in this chapter, we have been concerned exclusively with the appraisal of performance by the use of budgetary techniques. In this part of

---

[2] For a detailed description of the DuPont control system, see *Executive Control— The Catalyst,* by William T. Jerome (New York: John Wiley & Sons, 1961), chap. 13.

the chapter, we discuss nonbudgetary techniques. Specifically, we shall discuss (a) periodic financial evaluation and (b) nonfinancial measures to appraise management performance.

Periodic Financial Evaluation

As described earlier, two of the principal problems with using the profit budget to appraise managerial performance are: (1) the time span that elapses before many important decisions are reflected in financial performance is greater than the time covered by the budget; and (2) the budget uses forecasts of expected conditions that often turn out to be inaccurate. As a result, actual performance against the profit budget may be a poor measure of managerial performance. One technique for overcoming these problems is an after-the-fact analysis of financial results. This analysis is based on two principles: (a) the time period covered should be long enough to make the evaluation valid (e.g., equal to the time span of divisional managers); and (b) the evaluation should be made solely on the basis of what has actually been accomplished.

The benefits from using a period related to the time requirements for evaluation are twofold. First, the impact of important decisions will be reflected in the financial performance data. Second, the motivation to take short-term actions to increase profits is eliminated or, at least, considerably mitigated.

The reason for evaluating performance after the fact is that it is only then that top management knows the conditions under which the divisional manager was working. Since these conditions cannot usually be projected accurately, top management cannot set a reasonable before-the-fact objective. Under these circumstances, it may not be worthwhile to predict conditions and then examine how the assumed conditions differed from the actual. It may be more efficient to eliminate the prediction step and go directly to evaluating what has happened in the light of the actual conditions that existed. Evaluation would take place under three conditions.

First, a time period adequate for fair evaluation should be established for each profit center. Evaluation would then take place at the end of this period. The period would generally be between three and five years, although some profit centers could be evaluated more frequently. For example, a year would be reasonable for a profit center in an integrated company that sells its products exclusively within the company; it is really responsible only for manufacturing costs, and these costs lend themselves to control through an annual budget.

Second, when a manager leaves a division, a terminal evaluation would normally be made. This would not only ensure that the departing manager had been appropriately evaluated, but it would also protect the incoming manager. For example, if the new manager is inheriting problems created by his predecessor, this fact should be evident from the evaluation.

Third, whenever top management becomes concerned about a particular profit center, an evaluation of performance could be requested. This would protect the company should conditions deteriorate sufficiently during the evaluation period to make it obvious that managerial performance was below par.

The evaluation would be conducted by the central finance staff with the assistance of other staff offices. Although the main thrust of the evaluation would be on financial performance, it would also be necessary to evaluate marketing and product positions and organizational and personnel development.

Nonfinancial Measures

After World War I when General Motors and DuPont were developing their now-famous decentralized organizations, the formal measurement of performance was almost exclusively financial. The principle was that if a division earned an adequate return on its investment, the divisional manager would be left alone by top management.

The first major company to deviate formally from the idea of a single measure of performance was the General Electric Company in the 1950s. When General Electric decentralized, it used eight measures of divisional performance.[3] Although there is some disagreement as to which result areas to measure and how to measure them, there appears to be general agreement that profitability, as a single measure of divisional performance, is not adequate for evaluating divisional managers in most instances. It would seem that at a minimum a divisional manager should also be evaluated on his market performance, his product development, his personnel development, and his public responsibility.

The principal differences among companies in measuring divisional management's performance in nonfinancial areas is the degree of formality employed. At one extreme, the measurements are entirely informal and subjective. At the other extreme these measurements are detailed and formal, in which case, we have a system of "management by objectives." The next part of this chapter describes the management by objectives system as it applies to the appraisal of divisional performance.

Management by Objectives[4]

Management by objectives is a system of performance appraisal having the following characteristics:

1. It is a formal system in that each manager is required to take certain prescribed actions and to complete certain written documents.
2. The process involves five steps:

---

[3] For a description of these eight measures see the General Electric (A) case in Chapter 4.

[4] There have been a great many articles and books written about management by objectives (MBO). This literature provides many different definitions of MBO and describes many different techniques for implementation. In this book, we use the term MBO simply to mean the inclusion of nonfinancial goals or targets in the formal annual review and approval of divisional plans.

    a. The manager discusses with the subordinate, the subordinate's description of his own job.

    b. The manager and the subordinate agree to short-term performance targets.

    c. The manager and the subordinate discusses periodically the progress made towards meeting the targets.

    d. The manager and the subordinate agree to a series of checkpoints that will be used to measure progress.

    e. At the end of a defined period (usually one year), the manager discusses with his subordinate his assessment of the results of the subordinate's efforts.

A management by objectives system is much broader than the budgetary control systems. First, the budgetary control system is a *part* of the management by objectives system. Second, the management by objectives system would normally include subordinates with little or no budget responsibility. We are concerned here with management by objectives as it applies to the evaluation of divisional performance.

The divisional managers' job tends to be more clearly defined than, say, for a staff executive, and formal reports on many aspects of his performance (e.g., profits and sales) are usually already available. Consequently, the initiation of a management by objectives system for divisional managers will usually not involve the amount of innovation that would be required for many other types of jobs. The profit budget system would remain the same as before.

Typically, the divisional manager would meet with top management to review his proposed budget. Under a management by objectives system, however, he would add other specific objectives in such areas as sales, product development and personnel development. He might also include personal development objectives for instance. Management by objectives then, as it applies to divisional management extends his profit budget presentation to include specific objectives in other areas and to provide checkpoints for measuring the progress towards meeting these objectives. Performance reviews would now include the divisional manager's progress toward meeting these other objectives.

In performance appraisal, there is one very important difference between management by objectives as it applies to a divisional manager and how it applies to an executive with limited budget responsibility. The *profitability of a division is so important that it tends to overshadow other objectives.* This means that a divisional manager is expected to earn a satisfactory profit *in addition* to meeting his other objectives. If top management perceives that a divisional manager's profit performance is less than satisfactory, the fact that he has met the other objectives may not be given much weight. Conversely, if a divisional manager is perceived to be performing well in the area of profitability, the fact that he has not met some of his objectives may not be held too much against him, unless it is clear that the failure to meet the other objectives will have a serious effect on future profits. It is important that a company using management by objectives for divisional performance evaluation keep this situation in mind. If profits are emphasized to the exclusion of other goals, the management by objectives system exists in name only. Consequently, it is important that top management take a balanced position in evaluating divisional performance. If this is done, the general approach of setting objectives in other areas in addition to profitability improves the ability of top management to control divisional operations.

Case 12–1

Mainline Manufacturing
Company (A)

Background

The Mainline Manufacturing Company, headquartered in a suburb of Cleveland, Ohio, is a broad line manufacturer, distributor, and retailer of electrical hardware and components used in large-scale electrical installations. Although its main works are in Cleveland, the company has branch factories and warehouses in more than a dozen other cities in the United States, Canada, and Europe. Among its subsidiaries engaged in manufacturing, those in Europe are of particular interest to this case. These are:

1. Mainline Ltd., England
2. Mainline, g.m.b.h., Germany
3. Mainline, Italia, S.R.L.

Each of these manufacturing subsidiaries is a self-contained profit center with its own manufacturing, marketing, engineering, and financial organization, under the direction of a chief executive with the title of managing director (or its local equivalent). These managing directors currently report to the company's vice president, European Operations.

Sales and Distribution

Each of the three manufacturing subsidiaries sells in its home country through its own marketing and field sales organization. Since the products of the three subsidiaries do not generally overlap, each subsidiary also has the opportunity to sell its output in each of the other major countries in Europe. Over the years, sales to other than home countries have been handled and controlled in a number of ways.

For many years prior to 1957, these "export" sales were controlled by the domestic Mainline Export Department which also controlled the export sales of the U.S. facilities. These sales were made primarily through agents in the various countries who received a commission (usually 7½ %) on all shipments into their territories regardless of origin. For this commission, the agents were expected to actively solicit orders and to assist in collecting the customers' accounts, which were billed and carried by the Mainline manufacturing companies. In a very few cases, agents carried inventories of selected items, which were billed directly to them and which they in turn billed to their customers on delivery.

About 1961 it was decided to increase the general sales effort in continental Europe with a small force of full-time missionary field salesmen and this force was gradually expanded over the next few years. Because of the proximity of this sales force to the European manufacturing companies, responsibility for its direction, after a trial period, was removed from the jurisdiction of the Mainline Export Department and assigned to the Sales Manager, European Sales Organization, located in London and reporting to the Managing Director of Mainline Ltd., the company which had the largest volume of sales in continental Europe (outside of Germany and Italy).

The success of this missionary effort in expanding sales volume in Europe was so marked that in 1964 the decision was made to further expand the sales effort and, additionally, improve service to customers by setting up sales companies with warehouses at several locations on the continent. The first such sales company was organized in Sweden in 1964 and this was followed by similar companies in Belgium (1964), Spain (1965), and France (1966). In 1965, a central headquarters office was established in Zurich for the administration of the activities of the European Sales Organization which then included the newly established sales companies and those field organizations in countries where no sales company had been established. The Sales Manager, European Sales Organizations, was then moved to this office and a financial controller was assigned to his staff. Accounting for the sales companies and field sales forces was also transferred from Mainline Ltd. in London to the Zurich office. From this point on, all sales company accounts would be maintained by a chief accountant assigned to each company, while the accounts of the field sales force were to be kept in Zurich. Exhibit 1 is a schematic of the current organization.

Accounting

Just as the form of the European Sales Organization has changed and evolved over the years, so also have the concept and methods of accounting, reporting, and control of that organization evolved. When the sales organization consisted only of commission agents, control, such as it was, lay with the Mainline Export Department. The 7½ percent commission paid to the agent, based on f.o.b. factory prices, was charged directly to the factory producing the item sold and a charge was also made to each factory for

Exhibit 1

MAINLINE MANUFACTURING COMPANY (A)

European Organization

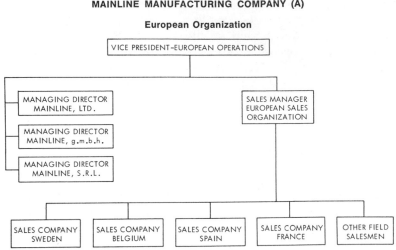

an allocated share of the expenses of the Mainline Export Department. This procedure applied alike to domestic and European production facilities.

The advent of the missionary sales force, which was designed to supplement the activities of the commission agents, created an additional expense which was aggregated by the European Sales Organization and allocated to the manufacturing companies on the basis of sales to a particular territory. At the same time, since responsibility for the field force had been transferred to the European Sales Organization, the allocation of the Mainline Export Department expenses was discontinued. Each factory, at this point, was "paying" the standard 7½ percent commission and a charge for sales force expenses. Although sales expenses as a percent of sales under this arrangement were higher than they had been when control rested with the Export Department, this was considered a legitimate cost of market penetration. Even during this period, however, the extra volume and contribution achieved more than offset the additional expense.

The introduction of the sales companies in 1964–1965 significantly altered this arrangement. With the establishment of company-owned warehouses, sales from the factory to the customer were made and accounted for in one of two ways. On direct factory shipments, called indent sales, the sales company effectively replaced the commission agent and assumed all of the functions performed by that agent. This pattern was little changed from that which had been in effect prior to the introduction of the missionary field sales force. What was different, however, was the fact that the sales company could now purchase goods from the factory for its own inventory and then sell that inventory in the wholesale market. In this case, then, each sales company acted as both agent and wholesaler and, in fact, competed with wholesalers in its assigned territory.

Once the accounts and control were transferred to Zurich, all selling expenses were then charged directly to the European Sales Organization and each of its sales companies. Revenues offsetting these charges came from two possible sources: (1) the 7½ percent "agent" commission, which was still being charged to the factory on the f.o.b. value of all shipments into the territory (both indent shipments direct to a customer and shipments to a sales company warehouse); and (2) the wholesaler markup realized by the sales company on "ex-warehouse" sales.

Control

In the period 1965–1967, each sales company reported as a profit center in the format of Exhibit 2 and the managers of the sales companies were

Exhibit 2

MAINLINE MANUFACTURING COMPANY (A)

Sales Company Profit and Loss Statement

Sales—ex-warehouse		1,520
Cost of sales—ex-warehouse		
Landed cost of goods sold[1]	1,250	
Repair service	20	
Warehouse labor	50	
Other direct	30	1,350
Gross profit		170
Selling and administrative expenses		460
Commissions received on all sales[2]		240
Operating profit (loss)		(50)
Interest on bank loans		30
Net income (loss) before tax		(80)
Income tax (credit)		(40)
Net income (loss)		(40)

[1] f.o.b. = 1,200
Shipping and duty = 50
Landed Cost = 1,250

[2] At 7½ percent f.o.b. value of sales from all factories to this sales territory = $3,200. It is assumed that inventory levels in the Sales Company were unchanged for the period since the Sales Company could be credited with the commissions on goods shipped to the warehouse for inventory. Therefore Indent Sales at f.o.b. = $2,000.

paid a salary plus a bonus which was based entirely on sales volume performance. This arrangement soon proved unsatisfactory as it did not provide adequate incentive to the manager to control his costs. There was, in addition, very little basis for deciding what was a reasonable level of costs for a given level of sales. It became obvious to some, but not all, of Mainline's European Sales Organization that the sales companies were not, in fact, profit centers and that their real mission was to stimulate higher sales at a reasonable cost.

Cost to Sell Concept

This conclusion led to a restatement of the objectives of the European Sales Organization (Exhibit 3) and a revised concept of control reporting (Exhibit 4). The revised control reports, called "Cost to Sell Statements," then became the basis for a new bonus system shown in Exhibit 5.

Exhibit 3

MAINLINE MANUFACTURING COMPANY (A)

European Sales Organization, Statement of Objectives

Purpose

The primary function of the European Sales Organization is to maximize the sale of Mainline products within the assigned territories of operation at an acceptable cost to sell. Thus E.S.O. is considered to be the sales arm of Mainline in Europe.

Long-term

1. The long-term financial objective is to maximize sales of Mainline products in E.S.O. territories at an acceptable net cost to sell.
2. "Net Cost to Sell" is defined as:
   a) Total operating expenses (warehouse, administrative, and selling)
   less
   b) Gross profit realized on ex-warehouse sales
   plus
   c) Cost of Capital, computed at 10 percent on average capital employed
3. For simplicity, "capital employed" will be defined, for the purpose of management control, as follows:
   a) Total accounts receivable (trade and other)
   plus
   b) Total inventories, less a predetermined amount equal to three months budgeted purchases
   c) Cost of Capital will be computed each month on the amounts of receivables and adjusted inventories at the beginning of the month.

Short-term

1. E.S.O. Management—the over-all objectives of the E.S.O. management for the fiscal year 1968–1969 are:
   a) to attain budgeted sales in the territories of the four sales companies at budgeted cost to sell as follows:
   —total budget sales to customers (indent and ex-warehouse) at f.o.b. value = 14,000 dollars U.S.
   —over-all budget cost to sell = 11 percent.

Under the cost to sell concept, a budgeted cost to sell percentage (percentage of budgeted net cost to sell related to the f.o.b. value of all shipments to customers, both indent and ex-warehouse) was to be developed at

Exhibit 4

MAINLINE MANUFACTURING COMPANY (A)

Sales Company Net Cost to Sell Statement

Gross sales at f.o.b. value
    Direct ship 2,000
    Ex-warehouse 1,200
        Total f.o.b. 3,200
Gross warehouse sales at invoice 1,520
Cost of sales 1,350
Gross profit 170
Selling and administrative expense .... (460)
    Net cost to sell before Cost of Capital .... (290)
    Cost of Capital .... (50)
Net cost to sell including Cost of Capital ...... (340)
    Percent total sales at f.o.b. 10.6

(340 ÷ 3,200 = 10.6 percent)

Exhibit 5

MAINLINE MANUFACTURING COMPANY (A)

Incentive Plan for E.S.O. Managers
(Financial Year 1968–69)

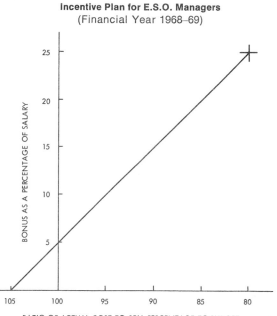

RATIO OF ACTUAL COST TO SELL PERCENTAGE TO BUDGET

the beginning of the year for each of the four sales companies. These percentages were calculated from the sales and expense budgets of each sales company which were initially prepared by the respective sales company managers. These budgets were carefully reviewed first by the Sales Manager and

Financial Controller of the European Sales Organization and then by the Director of Finance, European Operations, before being finally approved by the Vice President—European Operations.

The commission, then charged to each factory for sales into a given territory, was set at a rate equal to the budgeted cost to sell percentage for the corresponding sales company in lieu of the standard 7½ percent rate which had been in effect. For FY 1968–1969, the budgeted cost to sell percentages ranged from 8.4 to 19.6 percent. Commissions at these rates were charged on all shipments by the factories into the sales companies' territories and were credited on the books of the sales companies. These commission credits to the sales companies were omitted from the control reports (Cost to Sell Statements) used as the basis for paying bonuses but were reflected in the official P&L statements used for legal, tax, and consolidation accounting.

The other major difference between the control reports under the cost to sell concept and under the profit reporting center concept was the substitution of a "memorandum interest on capital' charge for the previously recorded actual interest on bank loans. This capital charge, based on the actual investment in receivables and inventories, was more under the control of the sales company manager, while the amount of bank interest paid for each sales company depended on the particular financial arrangements in effect for each company and was outside the scope of the manager's responsibility.

Case 12-2

Mainline Manufacturing
Company (B)

Review

The Cost to Sell concept, described in the Mainline (A) case, was used in FY 1968–1969 as the basis for control and evaluation of the company's four sales companies in Europe. At the close of FY 1968–1969 all sales companies, but one, had achieved a lower Cost to Sell percentage than that which had been budgeted, and the management of the European Sales Organization generally received substantial bonuses. Management was also satisfied with the results achieved over and above the impact on the Cost to Sell percentage. Sales in two of the four companies exceeded budget, and margins on ex-warehouse sales were generally maintained at better-than-budget levels. Expenses in one of these companies were held well in line considering the extra sales volume. One of the two companies which failed to meet the sales budget was also over budget on expenses and no bonus was earned in this case. In the fourth company, although the sales budget was not met, about half the maximum bonus was earned. The short-fall in sales was attributed to start-up problems which also resulted in correspondingly lower costs due principally to delays in staffing the field sales force.

Control—1969–1970

For the Fiscal Year 1969–1970, the vice president of Europe, for a number of reasons, decided that the Cost to Sell concept should be abandoned, and in its place he substituted a profit center reporting format (see Exhibit 1). He also modified the commission paid by the factory to the sales company on each sale. The new commission was to be a straight 10 percent on every sale rather than a different Cost to Sell for each territory.

In an effort to meet his objective of "increasing sales profitably," the vice president of Europe also altered the bonus structure in the following manner.

Exhibit 1

MAINLINE MANUFACTURING COMPANY (B)

Sales Company Operating Performance Statement

F.o.b. value of sales
Indent 2,000
Ex-warehouse 1,200

Total 3,200
Gross warehouse sales 1,545
Sales deductions   25

Net sales 1,520
Cost of sales 1,350

Gross profit 170
Selling and administrative expense 460

Net operating surplus (Cost) .... (290)
Standard commissions at 10 percent of f.o.b. value ..... (320)
Net operating result   30

Profitability = Net operating result/Net sales =   2%

The maximum per cent of salary available as a bonus was maintained at 25 percent but it was divided into two parts. Up to 15 percent would henceforth be based on exceeding a sales quota which would be established by the vice president—Europe. For every whole percentage point that actual sales exceeded quota sales, the sales company manager would receive a 1 percent of salary bonus up to a limit of 15 percent of salary. The second part of the bonus was to be based on the relative profitability of the sales company (see Exhibit 1). The relative profitability measure was to be the ratio between Net Operating Result (positive only) and Net Sales. Each percentage point of relative profitability would be worth 2 percent of salary, up to a limit of 10 percent of salary.

This bonus breakdown is based on the vice president's determination that a 5 percent level of relative profitability was an adequate level to achieve and still maintain a good growth rate. Anything less he felt would be too low and anything greater might tend to restrict sales growth.

Discussion

The vice president—Europe gave several reasons why he desired to change the Cost to Sell concept:

—it overemphasized control of costs at the expense of increased sales.
—it was complicated and confusing to salesmen familiar with sales quota-type bonus systems.
—he preferred a measure which would increase with improved performance rather than decrease.
—the Cost to Sell as a summary measure was one step removed from his objective of "increasing sales profitably."

—the Cost to Sell bonus paid managers on an improvement of a percentage rather than on an absolute amount.

—the fact that different sales companies in different countries had different Cost to Sell percentages might motivate factory managers to favor those countries with a lower Cost to Sell.

—the Cost to Sell percentage was based on a budgeted figure rather than one selected by top management.

He also listed several reasons why he preferred a profit center format:

—it was simple.

—he had control over the goals and targets.

—it permitted evaluation of sales companies on a profit center basis.

—it restored a reasonable balance between costs and sales volume.

—it charged all factories the same commission, thereby motivating a broader market penetration.

—is was a more direct measure of sales and profits.

Case 12–3

Perkins Engines Group

In January 1973, James Felker, Finance Director for the Perkins Engines Group, was speaking about the company's management control system:

In the past two years we have made dramatic improvements in our management control system. The organization of the firm's accounts into cost and profit centers with the associated variance analyses of performance against standards and budgets improved considerably our insight into and control over company operations. A control system like organization structure, however, never stays static and we are now reassessing it to make sure it still fits our new economic challenges.

When it was installed about a year and a half ago, we were in a depressed order period and its emphasis on the control of production costs helped us to hold down our expenses when revenues were at a minimum.

Now, however, we are experiencing a totally different phenomenon. With orders coming in faster than we can fill them, the Supply Division, which is our production unit, is willing to alter their production schedule to fit the changing priorities of the Sales Division, providing that alterations be made to their costs so as not to hurt their performance rating. However, because of outside constraints, union pressure, and supplier capacity limitation, there is considerable doubt that even if the brakes were released on manufacturing cost that output could be increased.

On the other hand, the sales people are worried about not getting the important orders produced and delivered at the promised time. They are concerned both with their profit contribution and with their long-term customer contacts. As a result, they are constantly jockeying with each other and complaining about the inability of supply to produce the needed engines. I know that part of the problem is with our suppliers. We are totally out of castings and can't get our orders for these parts filled. But that's not the only problem. I'm also wondering if we might need to make some alterations in the control system. After all, a control system should motivate the employees to work for the good of the whole company, not just their own department.

Company Background

Perkins Engines Group, with headquarters in Peterborough, England, manufactured and sold diesel engines throughout the world. In the power range covered by its line of engines, Perkins was the largest producer in the world with 1972 sales of more than $280 million (Exhibit 1). Perkins' line consisted of 3-, 4-, 6-, and 8-cylinder engines for the agricultural, vehicle, industrial, and marine markets. In 1973, Perkins had over 40 basic diesel-engine models as well as two gasoline-engine models.

Exhibit 1

SUMMARY INCOME STATEMENT AND BALANCE SHEET*
(Full Year)

	1972 Actual	1973 Forecast as of March 16, 1973
Sales		
Third Party	186	239
Massey-Ferguson	100	113
Total Sales	286	352
Standard variable cost	212	258
Cost allowances	2	8
Direct variable profit	72	86
Decision Costs		
Sales	10	11
Supply	11	11
Engineering	19	20
Services	3	4
Exchng. and consolid. adjustments	—	0
Total Decision Costs	43	46
Net Operating Profit	29	40
Asset Review		
Receivables	37	47
Inventories	38	33
Other current assets	(33)	(47)
Current operating assets	42	33
Net Fixed and Other Assets	56	62
Decision Costs in Inventory	3	3
Total Assets	101	98

* All figures have been disguised and ratios deliberately distorted. Figures are stated in millions of U.S. dollars.

Founded in 1932 to specialize in diesel engines, Perkins had remained an undiversified diesel-engine manufacturer. In 1934, under Frank A. Perkins, the founder, the company sent sales representatives to Russia, India, and South America. Export development was interrupted during the war years of 1939–45 but was resumed after the war.

According to Perkins' management, one characteristic of the diesel engine business was the tendency for large customers to integrate backwards into engine production when their engine purchases became high. Perkins had found its volume thus diminished, particularly by such large vehicle producers as Ford, British Leyland, and Chrysler. In early 1973, management believed that no current customer was in this category.

In 1959, another large customer, Massey-Ferguson Ltd. of Toronto, Canada, had chosen an alternate course of action by making a successful bid to merge with Perkins. In its new relationship, Perkins supplied about 35 percent of its output by value to Massey-Ferguson but remained independent and autonomous in servicing its other customers, many of whom competed directly with Massey-Ferguson. Perkins' management expressed great pride in their own initiative and operational control of the company.

Organization

Perkins' operations included sales, supply (production), and engineering; a group of service departments supported these three main operations. All sales (with the exception of Brazilian sales and those to Massey-Ferguson) were made by five regional sales operations: United Kingdom, North America, North Europe, South Europe, and International (i.e. the rest of the world.) These operations collaborated with the market-development sections to build up Perkins' market share in each area.

In addition to its sales effort, each sales operation was responsible for service and parts for all engines within its territory. Approximately one half of the UK operation's sales went to UK original-equipment manufacturers who then exported their equipment; as a result, the remaining sales operations placed much of their service effort (and expense) on engines for which they had received no sales credit. This service effort was relatively profitable. However, spare-parts inventorying and servicing were complicated by the fact that the sales operation was sometimes not aware that certain engines were in its area because of the mobility of the vehicles they powered.

All Perkins' engines were produced by the Supply Division under Richard Perkins, son of the founder Frank Perkins. Richard Perkins was also Deputy Managing Director and General Manager of the autonomous Brazilian subsidiary with its self-sufficient manufacturing operation.

The vast majority of Perkins' engines were produced in the five factories in Peterborough. The factories produced the full variety of Perkins' 40-plus engine models. The Fletton factory specialized in V8 engine production; headquarters factory No. 2 specialized in a certain 4-cylinder type; the other three factories produced the remaining varieties of engines.

All Perkins' engines were produced on motorized assembly lines; however, the engines differed substantially, even within one product model. Although basic parts might be similar, there was often great variety in accessory equipment. Such variety might involve the simple substitution of one accessory for another; or it might involve boring entirely different holes into an engine block. While acknowledging the difficulty in defining exactly what one engine or engine model was, one manager estimated that the average production was about seven engines in a month. He estimated that maximum production was about 40 engines in a month.

According to Richard Perkins, the company had an adequate labor supply and manufacturing capacity for conceivable future demand. However, many of the company's British suppliers were at full capacity. This tight supply situation compounded by the high frequency of British strikes had made it attractive to increase imports of parts. For example, some of the company's castings were coming from as far away as Argentina.

Perkins' production was scheduled by three separate departments in the Supply Division. The Planning and Procurement Department prepared the company's monthly production program for six months in advance, allocated the engines among customers in times of scarce capacity, and then purchased the parts and materials to fill those production needs. This production program was based on Sales Division forecasts and was coordinated with the Purchase Department. The short-term scheduling of the various production lines was done by the Production Control Department.

At one time, Planning and Procurement had been a separate entity, falling under neither the Sales nor the Supply Division. However, in a company consolidation, Planning and Procurement had been placed in the Supply Division because of the close relationship between purchasing and production planning.

The Management Control System

Perkins' planning system was patterned after the Massey-Ferguson system. The information collected from the books of account was broken down two ways. The first was the legal-entity accounting system which showed the legally reportable results of the individual subsidiaries and the consolidated results of the Perkins Group. The second breakdown formed the management control system. The reports in this system divided the company into profit and cost centers rather than as geographical or legal entities. These reports were used to evaluate managerial performance in each center. Each of the six sales operations was a profit center. The Supply Division, Engineering Division, and support services were cost centers.

The Planning and Reporting Cycle

Senior Massey-Ferguson management began the planning cycle in March. They developed goals for the whole company for the succeeding three years. Massey-Ferguson management then informed Sir Monty Prichard, Perkins' Managing Director and a member of Massey-Ferguson's Board of Directors, of the Massey-Ferguson goals and how Perkins supported them.

Upon receipt of this letter, Sir Monty Prichard, in conjunction with

Felker, sent out a letter to each operating division (Sales, Supply, and Engineering) setting the general Perkins goals for return on sales and return on assets. At the same time, Felker's department instructed each operating division how the company plans would be formed. Neither of these directives set specific revenue or expense targets for the departments; rather, they provided a framework for planning.

By May, the operating divisions had forwarded their plans to the Finance Department for consolidation into Perkins' tentative 2-year plan with key items projected for five years (e.g., sales, capital investment). At the end of May, a presentation involving each operating division was made to the Managing Director; he specified any changes to bring the plan into line with the goals of his March letter. In late June, the plan was presented for approval in Toronto. The final plan was usually approved in November, following a series of discussions.

Perkins' management control involved the comparison of actual results with information generated in the planning process. These results were prepared by the second Friday following the end of each month. Massey-Ferguson headquarters in Toronto received the results by the next Tuesday. A revised forecast for the balance of the year was issued by Perkins on the third Friday after the close of each month. Key sales and expense levels were compared with this revised forecast. Felker felt this constant review and modification of the forecast during the year was a key element in the system's success.

Manufacturing Costs

The heart of Perkins' control system was a manufacturing standard-cost system. Standards for each engine were reviewed annually.

The *direct material costs* of an engine included the vendor's price for the raw materials or finished components incorporated in it, inward freight charges, and import duties, if any. All parts and materials including packing materials and miscellaneous supplies such as paint and oil were given standard costs, which were applied to each engine.

The *direct labor costs* for an engine included only those associated with the machining of parts and the assembly and testing of engines. To determine the direct labor cost, the standard time of each production function was multiplied by that function's standard wage rate. Direct labor costs excluded all costs for material handling, maintenance, inspection, and fringe benefits.

The *direct variable overhead costs* included all indirect supervisory labor, direct-labor overtime and night-shift premiums, wage increases, direct-labor fringe benefits, training time, and normal direct-labor idle-time expenses. It also included processing supplies, cutting tools, and labor and material value lost when material was scrapped. Direct variable overhead was charged to an engine at a rate of 117 percent of direct labor. (The rate was reviewed and redefined every year.)

In addition to the standard costs, the plans provided allowances for increases in costs throughout the fiscal year. These provisions (known as cost allowances) were derived from items like increases in labor contract, price inflation, and labor idle-time.

All costs which were not incorporated in the variable costs for engines were called "decision costs." These were all semivariable or fixed costs not directly related to increases or decreases in engine production (Exhibit 2).

Exhibit 2

U.K. SUPPLY DIVISION: DECISION COST VARIANCE ANALYSIS
(For 1973 as of March 16, 1973)*

By Expense Type (planned decision costs level as of Jan. 1, 1973—10,220)		By Section (planned decision costs level as of Jan.1, 1973—10,220)	
Plant Operations Dept.		*Plant Operations Dept.*	
Overtime and premiums	(119)	Director	2
Salaries and wages	(144)	Plant No. 1	(43)
Fringes	(23)	Plant No. 2	(12)
Administrative expenses	(15)	Fletton	(22)
Indirect materials	(1)	Walton	5
Repairs and		Queen Street	7
maintenance	(2)	Production control	(57)
Income	—	Loss prevention	(4)
Other	(21)	Plant engineering	(144)
Subtotal	(325)	Quality control	(57)
		Subtotal	(325)
Manufacturing Planning Dept.		*Manufacturing Planning Dept.*	
Salaries and wages	51	Director	9
Outside services	13	Facilities	33
Other	(8)	Industrial engineering	18
Subtotal	56	Product cost	(4)
		Subtotal	56
Material Control Dept.		*Material Control Dept.*	
Overtime	(18)	Director	2
Other	(1)	Purchase	(13)
Subtotal	(19)	Planning and	
		procurement	(8)
		Subtotal	(19)
Material Variances		*Material Variances*	12
Rebates	12		
Others	—		
Subtotal	12		
Policy (Holiday Pay)	(34)	*Policy*	(34)
Total Supply Division	(310)		(310)
Forecasted Decision Costs for 1973 as of March 16, 1973	10,530		10,530

* All figures have been disguised and are in thousands of U.S. dollars.

According to Peter Ray, Supply Division Cost Analysis Chief, 80% of these decision costs were personnel related. Throughout the year, any deviations from the planned standard costs and decision costs were recorded as "variances." These variances were analyzed monthly. In addition, a new forecast for the entire year was prepared; this was based on volume, level of inflation, specific supplier increases, and so forth.

For each production department, a labor-efficiency variance was calculated. This was done weekly by comparing the department's total labor inputs (determined from employee time cards) to the standard labor costs for the department's output (calculated by multiplying the number of engines processed through each work center by the department's standard labor cost).

All materials purchased by the company were added to the raw materials inventory at the standard purchase price; the purchase price variance was identified at that time. Materials were not subtracted from that inventory account until the engine was transferred to finished-goods inventory. Under this system, all raw materials and the materials portion of work-in-process inventories were lumped together. A physical inventory was made once a year.

A finished engine was put into finished stock inventory for shipment to a customer either in the United Kingdom or overseas. The ex-works price was recorded as an account receivable, against which was charged the standard cost of the engine. Inventory stocks were officially deleted at that time.

For legal entity reporting purpose, sales to Perkins non-U.K. subsidiaries were made at intercompany prices developed to satisfy tax and customs authorities.

Exhibit 3

SALES OPERATION FORECASTED PROFIT SUMMARY FOR SOUTH EUROPE
(As of March 16, 1973)

	Year-End Forecast	
	Forecast for 1973	Variance from Jan. 1, 1973 Plan
Sales		
Engines	22,828	777
Parts	1,037	37
Total	23,865	814
Standard direct variable profit		
Engines	4,623	389
Parts	336	8
Total	4,959	397
Decision costs	1,464	29
Profit contribution	3,495	368

For management control purposes, however, the effect of intercompany transactions was eliminated. To measure management performance, sales revenues were compared with the direct standard manufacturing variable costs (direct materials, direct labor, and direct variable overhead). From this resulting gross profit figure, the sales-operations decision costs were subtracted (Exhibit 3). This method provided an equivalent basis for evaluation of all sales operations.

All Original Equipment Manufacturer (OEM) customers (including Massey-Ferguson) were subject to the same pricing policy.

Performance Evaluation

Each of the three operating divisions (Sales, Supply, and Engineering) and their subdivisions and each of the support services was evaluated according to its performance versus the 1-year plan. This was accomplished on a month-by-month basis in which year-to-date was compared against plan and the most recent forecast, and the measure of performance varied according to whether the unit was a cost or a profit center.

Each of Perkins' subsidiaries had geographic sales and service responsibilities. With the exception of the independent Brazilian operation, little manufacturing and no engineering was undertaken in these subsidiaries. Each subsidiary reported its results monthly to the Peterborough headquarters where these results were consolidated into Sales Operation Profit Summaries. Each subsidiary and each sales operation was evaluated according to the variation of its profit contribution from the predetermined plan. This was done on both a monthly and a full-year basis (Exhibit 3). A consolidated Sales Division Summary was then calculated from these sales operation reports.

In contrast to the Sales Division, the Supply Division was a cost center. Actual-versus-standard cost comparisons were recorded down to the shop-floor subdepartments. At this level, weekly labor efficiency reports were discussed with the foremen to determine the causes of deviations. Building from this level, the monthly reporting cycle showed the variances in the variable production costs by department and for the whole division (Exhibit 4). It also showed departmental variances in the Supply Division's decision costs; these were broken down by type of expense and by department section (Exhibit 5). In addition to these reports, the Supply Division also generated monthly reports of headcount, productivity, overtime, inventory, engine output, manufacturing arrears, quality, safety, and maintenance downtime.

The Engineering Division and the support services were also cost centers. Since their expenses represented decision costs, each was measured by a decision cost variance analysis. For the Engineering Division, these cost variances were broken down by work category and by type of expense (Exhibit 5). Each of the support services also broke down the decision cost variances by type of expense and by cause.

Exhibit 4

U.K. SUPPLY DIVISION: COST ALLOWANCE FORECAST FOR 1973
(As of March 16, 1973)*

Planned cost allowances as of Jan. 1, 1973 6,052
Variances from Jan. 1, 1973 plan
Material Control Department
    Volume and mix 18
    Purchase price variance 141
    Sourcing variance 157
    Sales of scrap .... (21)
    Freight duty and insurance 3
    Other .... (7)

      Subtotal 291
Manufacturing Planning Department
    Volume and mix 15
    Times revisions .... (17)
    Consumable tools 7

      Subtotal 5
Plant Operations Department
    Volume and mix 75
    Direct labor off standards .... (69)
    Indirect labor and O.T. premiums .... (797)
    Consumable materials .... (26)
    Other 49

      Subtotal .... (768)
Nondepartmental
    Volume and mix .... (17)
    P.P.V. in inventory 5
    Stock loss provision 5
    Duty variance .... (12)
    Other 19

      Subtotal 0

Total Supply Division .... (472)

Forecasted Cost Allowances as of March 16, 1973 6,524

* All figures have been disguised and are stated in thousands of U.S. dollars.

These profit and cost variances were then summarized by operating division in a Sales and Profit Contribution Variance Summary. Also, a Summary Income Statement and Balance Sheet (Exhibit 1) showed the total Perkins performance. The variances in the direct variable profit, decision costs, and assets were then analyzed by cause, and the year-end outcome in each of these areas was projected.

Although Perkins had no formal bonus system, managers were paid and promoted according to their results in comparison with the plan.

Company Opinion

In discussing the Supply Division as a cost center, Felker noted that small percentage variations in many items could cause large changes in profits. While materials constituted 80 percent of the variable standard cost of goods

Exhibit 5

ENGINEERING DIVISION COST FORECAST FOR 1973
(As of March 16, 1973)*

Decision Costs	Forecast for 1973	Variance from Jan. 1, 1973 Plan
Work Category		
Cost saving work	9,243	154
New product	775	—
Supply problems	353	(10)
Product reliability	928	—
Applications	2,933	85
General	1,183	(103)
Total Direct	15,415	126
Administration	3,889	50
Total	19,304	176
Type of Expense		
Salaries	9,008	—
Wages	3,773	—
Materials	1,568	50
Outside assistance	1,170	25
Depreciation	1,045	19
Supply beds	430	188
Consumables	535	29
Other	1,775	(135)
Total	19,304	176

* All figures have been disguised and are stated in thousands of U.S. dollars.

sold, there were nevertheless 9,000 people working in the Peterborough factories. This large labor expense required careful control.

However, C. Joseph Hind, Director of the Engineering Division, felt that cost center concept was not particularly helpful. He believed that the monthly reports of costs and variances did not really indicate whether all the money allocated for each particular development project would be spent by the end of the year. Rather than being elated over any positive monthly or year-end variance in a development expense, Hind was often disappointed, since such a surplus probably meant that the project was lagging. Perhaps more importantly, he sensed that a negative expense pressure might discourage the kind of adventurous development so critical in this industry. Furthermore, he felt cost performance was not a good measure of technical productivity.

A marketing manager mentioned his analogous concern that the Supply Division's cost consciousness could inadvertently cause schedule inflexibilities. These in turn might jeopardize long-term customer relationships. In such a case, the company might be sacrificing long-run profits for short-term savings.

According to Victor A. Rice, Sales Division Director, the company was not concerned with trading off the various ways of using a limited production capacity. He acknowledged that there was a significant problem with suppliers; nonetheless, he believed that the company had no foreseeable problems with internal capacity. In his opinion, while his sales subordinates could benefit from additional leverage for influencing the Supply Division's schedule, they also needed firm direction in making more realistic sales forecasts. In his estimation, the current sales forecasts, by which the future production schedules were set, were highly optimistic and reflected two things: salesmen were overselling in 1972–73, effectively stealing sales from 1973–74; and customers were overordering in anticipation of an allocation cutback because of undercapacity (as had happened in the past).

Rice believed that the system, which evaluated and pointed up problem areas in the performance reports, tended to look only at the actual-versus-forecast results, with perhaps insufficient attention to the pattern with which forecasts changed.

In looking further at the control system which he had helped design two years earlier in his capacity as Finance Director, Rice noted that the responsibility for assets like accounts receivable and inventories was not always assigned on the same basis as the profit contribution responsibility for inventories; the reason was short transit times and direct contact of customers with planning and procurement. Finance had responsibility for all credit and receivables. The North America Sales Operation Manager, however, was responsible for his receivables assets and inventories.

Case 12–4

Binswanger & Steele, Inc.

Alvin Binswanger, President of Binswanger & Steele, Inc., which manufactured office equipment, had introduced a new system for appraising the performance of his top executives in 1969. During 1970, he decided the system, which was called "management-by-objectives," might help solve some problems in the sales area, and in 1971, the system was extended to the national sales manager and the eight regional sales managers. After the 1971 performance appraisals had been submitted and reviewed, several of the company's managers discussed the desirability of extending the system to lower levels of management.

The Management-by-Objectives System

The management-by-objectives system of performance appraisal was based on the concept that evaluation of executives should depend on how the results they achieved compared with their objectives; that is, with reasonable estimates of what was possible.

In October 1968, Binswanger decided to test the system on his key executives. If the system proved successful, he planned to instruct these executives to extend it to the managers who reported to them. The appraisal system then would be introduced to successively lower levels of management each year until it included all employees.

During the first week of October 1968, Binswanger and his key executives met privately to determine their key objectives for their own satisfactory performance for fiscal 1969, beginning November 1, 1968. They agreed that if they exceeded their objectives, they would consider their performance outstanding. If they merely met their objectives, they would consider their performance satisfactory. If they failed to meet their objectives, they would consider their performance unsatisfactory. Bonuses and raises were to be awarded only to the men who exceeded their key result targets.

In December of 1969, at the end of the one-year trial period, each executive met privately with Binswanger to review his individual performance. Each manager's performance exceeded his stated objectives for 1969.

Extension to the Sales Division

In June 1970, Binswanger and Steele's executive committee met to discuss the increasing turnover and evidence of low morale among the company's salesmen. Sales Vice President Ben Weddels attributed these problems to several factors, including management problems generated by the expansion of the sales force from 300 salesmen in 1965 to 500 in 1970 and the increased complexity of the selling jobs caused by a large number of new and more complex products which had been added to the company's line in recent years. Weddels was concerned that he and Ted Forman, the National Sales Manager, might have inadequate control over the sales force. Weddels believed that the management-by-objectives system would be useful in tightening up this control. The executive committee approved Weddel's suggestion that the system be applied to the national sales manager and his eight regional sales managers during fiscal 1971.

In July 1970, Weddels called in Ted Forman to explain the performance appraisal system. Ted Forman, 55 years old, had been with Binswanger & Steele since 1937. During that time he had been a salesman, branch sales manager in four different areas of the country, and regional sales manager in New England for six years before being selected as National Sales Manager in 1970.

Weddels and Forman agreed to appraise Forman's 1971 performance on the basis of satisfactory performance of his regional sales managers. Forman, in turn, was to explain the system to the regional managers and to negotiate objectives for the year with each of them. Weddels gave Forman a memorandum setting forth guidelines for implementing the performance appraisal system (see Exhibit 1).

In September 1970, Forman wrote each of his regional sales managers and asked them to draft their own key result targets (objectives) for the fiscal year ending October 31, 1971. He defined "key result target" as a critical business accomplishment required of a regional sales manager and suggested the following areas as some of those to be defined carefully: net sales, gross profit, gross percentage, operating expenses, branch pretax profit, year-end inventory level, and year-end inventory turnover.

The Midwest Sales Region

One of Binswanger's regional managers was 40-year old Ed Michelson, the Midwest Regional Sales Manager. Ted Forman was aware that Ben Weddels considered Michelson the most effective and promising of the company's regional sales managers. Since Forman was eager to please Weddels, he decided to pay special attention to Ed Michelson's key result targets for fiscal 1971.

Exhibit 1

MEMORANDUM

July 15, 1970

To: Ted Forman
From: Ben Weddels
Subject: Management-by-Objectives Performance Appraisal System

In the fall, the supervisor should invite his immediate subordinates to submit to him what they believe to be their key result targets for the coming year. The supervisor should meet with each subordinate in closed conference and negotiate the subordinate's key result targets. The supervisor should not accept his subordinate's targets without questioning them, and the subordinate should be encouraged not to accept his superior's targets until he understands the complete logic behind them.

During the year, the supervisor should discuss with each subordinate any of his key result targets that do not appear to be on schedule. A plan for attaining off-schedule key result targets should be worked out between superior and subordinate. At the end of the year, the subordinate and supervisor should review the subordinate's key result targets and his actual achievements on a simple worksheet called a Manager Performance Statement.

The supervisor should send the worksheet to the subordinate prior to the appraisal interview and ask him to enter his results next to his agreed-upon targets. The subordinate returns a copy of the worksheet to the supervisor prior to the appraisal interview.

The purpose of the appraisal interview is to give supervisor and subordinate an opportunity to review the subordinate's performance in detail and to help the subordinate understand his strengths and weaknesses so that he can concentrate on improving himself. If a subordinate does not achieve key result targets because of circumstances outside of his control, such as an unanticipated increase in price or a shortage of supply, that fact should be noted in the supervisor's comment column. Such factors should not be counted against a subordinate in his appraisal. Normally, an appraisal interview takes two to four hours.

A supervisor-subordinate meeting is scheduled, during which a plan of action should be drafted for the subordinate to use in the coming year to improve his areas of weakness. This plan of action should be incorporated into the subordinate's key result targets for the coming year. These new targets should be presented about four weeks after the appraisal interview.

Bonuses and raises will be awarded only to those men who exceed their key result targets. One of the most useful indications a supervisor's manager can have of a supervisor's effectiveness is the Manager Performance Statements for the supervisor's subordinates. In other words, Ted, I'll be looking at your regional managers' performance appraisals in order to evaluate your performance for 1971.

Ben Weddels

Ben Weddels

When Michelson received Forman's letter asking for key result targets, Michelson went to the files and reviewed midwestern sales data for the past three years in order to arrive at key result targets for his branches. Meanwhile, Forman reviewed his personal copies of the same data. (Exhibit 2 gives these data.)

Exhibit 2

PERFORMANCE OF MIDWEST REGION AND SELECTED DISTRICTS

District and Year	Net Sales ($000)	Gross Profit ($000)	Percent Gross Profit to Net Sales	Operating Expenses	Pretax Profit
Chicago (June 1970)*					
1968	759	128	16.9	107	21
1969	982	133	13.5	115	18
1970	655	94	14.3	111	(17)
St. Louis (April 1970)					
1968	760	114	15.0	88	26
1969	712	96	13.5	96	0
1970	552	78	14.2	111	(33)
Detroit (September 1969)					
1968	1,940	242	12.5	197	45
1969	1,470	212	14.4	316	(104)
1970	1,990	275	13.8	277	(2)
Dayton (December 1967)					
1968	796	116	14.6	94	22
1969	1,103	152	13.8	112	40
1970	1,226	188	15.3	137	51
Midwest Region Total (9 branches)					
1968	10,637	1,517	14.2	1,219	298
1969	10,576	1,495	14.1	1,455	39
1970	10,038	1,457	14.5	1,415	42

* Date district manager appointed.

The Forman-Michelson Conference

Forman and Michelson met in October 1970 to negotiate Michelson's key result targets for fiscal 1971. During the meeting, there was a cordial atmosphere, but Forman reserved the right ultimately to determine Michelson's objectives. Michelson and Forman agreed that the Midwest region had shown little sales improvement in the past few years. Both men suspected that a business recession may have affected sales, but there was no indication that the recession would affect sales in 1971. Forman got the impression that Michelson's sales estimates were highly conservative and his requests for sales expenses were overly liberal. When the men disagreed, Forman made reference to corporate level marketing data, unavailable to Michelson, that substantiated Forman's claims. Michelson claimed that he did not believe it would be possible to produce the sales volume Forman desired, given the imposition of such low sales expenses. Michelson was not pleased with his conference and said he did not know how he was going to achieve the key result targets budgeted for 1971.

Forman also incorporated into Michelson's 1971 key result targets several items about which Michelson had no previous notice. Forman said that his list of specific targets which would apply to all regional managers had been delayed in preparation. He explained that the specific targets, such as improving sales mix and the market share and sales volume of particular product lines, were intended to help regional sales managers direct their efforts toward areas considered important by top management. Michelson did not argue with Forman's specific targets, but complained that he had had no prior opportunity to determine his region's current status and the feasibility of meeting Forman's targets.

1971 Sales Results—Midwest Region

During 1971, Michelson spent much of his time traveling to the branch offices in his region and working out problems with his branch sales managers. He did not have an opportunity to work out an account analysis with his managers and intended to do this as soon as there was sufficient time. When the fiscal year ended in October, Forman was unable to meet with Michelson for a performance appraisal interview. Instead, Michelson was sent a Manager Performance Statement with the 1971 key result targets and budgeted figures for each target, with instructions to fill in the 1971 actual results. When he completed this task, Michelson returned the worksheet to Forman.

The two men met in early November and, in an hour, reviewed Michelson's Manager Performance Statement. Forman jotted his notes of the meeting in the space provided "for use of executive making appraisal." After the review, he instructed Michelson to prepare 1972 key result targets for the Midwest region, and to study the possibility of introducing the management-by-objectives performance appraisal system to his branch sales managers.

In the meantime, Ben Weddels had seen preliminary 1971 sales figures for the Midwest region which indicated a decline in both net sales and gross profit. He was concerned about this decline, and in mid-November, asked Ted Forman to send Michelson's Manager Performance Statement to his office. Forman was surprised to receive Weddels' request. He had filed Michelson's materials and forgotten about them, but was under the impression that Ed Michelson had done as well as or better than any of the other regional managers in meeting his key result targets. To prove this, Forman prepared an analysis showing which of the regional sales manager's actual results had exceeded their targeted results by 5 percent or more. Of 63 branches, eight had exceeded their gross profit target, and about 12 each had exceeded their net sales, gross profit percentage, branch operating expense, or branch pretax profit target. More branches in the Midwest Region exceeded each of these targets than in any other region except the South Central region. He submitted the details of this comparison analysis with Michelson's performance appraisal (see Exhibit 3) to Ben Weddels.

Exhibit 3

MANAGER PERFORMANCE STATEMENT*

Name: Ed Michelson   *Position:* Regional Manager
Region: Midwest   *For Period:* 1971

Key Results Expected

1. Achieve at branch level 1971 budgeted components in the following categories:
   a. Net sales
   b. Gross profit
   c. Gross profit percentage
   d. Branch operating expenses
   e. Branch pretax profit

Key Results Achieved (include appropriate supporting comment)

	1971 Est. (Michelson)	1971 Budget (Michelson-Forman)	1971 Actual
Chicago Branch			
a. Net sales	$ 690	$ 820	$ 628
b. Gross profit	99	127	68
c. Gross profit percentage ..	14.4%	15.5%	10.9%
d. Branch operating expenses	125	110	91
e. Branch pretax profit	(26)	17	(23)
St. Louis Branch			
a. Net sales	$ 560	$ 720	$ 562
b. Gross profit	84	110	93
c. Gross profit percentage ..	15.0%	15.3%	16.5%
d. Branch operating expenses	125	100	87
e. Branch pretax profit	(41)	10	6
Detroit Branch			
a. Net sales	$2,000	$2,080	$2,151
b. Gross profit	300	300	325
c. Gross profit percentage ..	15.0%	14.4%	15.1%
d. Branch operating expenses	260	250	257
e. Branch pretax profit	40	50	68
Dayton Branch			
a. Net sales	$ 990	$1,190	$1,051
b. Gross profit	150	190	142
c. Gross profit percentage ..	15.1%	16.0%	13.5%
d. Branch operating expenses	140	132	117
e. Branch pretax profit	10	58	25

* Detail on 5 branches omitted.

Exhibit 3—Continued

Regional Total (9 branches)

a. Net sales	$9,890	$10,970	$9,792
b. Gross profit	1,448	1,652	1,456
c. Gross profit percentage ..	14.7%	16.5%	14.9%
d. Branch operating expenses	1,435	1,329	1,224
e. Branch pretax profit	13	323	232

Comment (for use of executive making appraisal)

Net sales off slightly more than 10% for region which was below expectations; however, two branches did exceed budget. Dollar gross profit was severely affected, but again, same two branches were above or near budget. Expense reduction was made, but in my opinion, action was not taken soon enough. Even though Chicago attained expense budget, additional profit should have been realized through closer control of expenses. Profit was disappointing, partially contributed to by chaotic conditions. Greater profit could have been obtained through better planning and expense control.

Key Results Expected

2. Improve sales mix between commercial, institutional, and military. Emphasize new business and re-equipment sales.

Key Results Achieved (include appropriate supporting comment)

		Gross Sales ($000)			
	Chicago	*St. Louis*	*Detroit*	*Dayton*	*Total (9 Branches)*
Commercial					
1970	553	502	924	1,152	7,055
1971	500	403	813	784	5,763
Diff.	(53)	(99)	(111)	(368)	(1,292)
Institutional					
1970	132	74	932	157	2,605
1971	118	125	1,271	223	3,116
Diff.	(14)	51	339	66	511
Military					
1970	9	4	205	0	802
1971	5	12	158	10	778
Diff.	(4)	8	(47)	10	(24)
Government					
1970	1	0	19	14	124
1971	36	53	21	94	627
Diff.	35	53	2	80	503

Comment (for use of executive making appraisal)

Satisfactory on institutional and government. Held steady in military but too great a decline in commercial.

Key Results Expected

3. Increase average gross profit realization to 15.8% or better.

Exhibit 3—Continued

Key Results Achieved (include appropriate supporting comment)

Overall gross profit percentage
 1971 Budget—15.1%
 1971 Actual—13.9%
 (See Target No. 1, *Key Results Expected,* for gross profit percentages of individual branches.)

Comment (for use of executive making appraisal)

15.8% was for all eight regions. Your measurement should be based on your budgeted regional level of 15.1%. Actual percentage attained was 13.9%, which was not satisfactory. However, it is recognized that improvement is difficult under severe competitive conditions, but you must watch this phase closely in the affected areas.

Key Results Expected

4. Institute an inventory of manager development requirements for all branch managers, as well as inaugurate an individual on-the-job development action program for three prospective branch managers.

Key Results Achieved (include appropriate supporting comment)

Inventory of developmental requirements taken for all managers in the midwest region and action program prepared for three.
Action program postponed because of press of business in last quarter of 1971.

Comment (for use of executive making appraisal)

This should be your personal target to continue some training of managers to correct their weaknesses during 1972.

Key Results Expected

5. Improve market share of corporate products. Achieve 5.7% share of market for Exec-Q-Tote portable dictating machine at each branch.

Key Results Achieved (include appropriate supporting comment)

	Exec-Q-Tote 10 *Months' Net Sales ($000)*		
	5.7 Percent Share (estimated)	*1971 Actual (10 months)*	*Difference*
Chicago	22	22	—
St. Louis	84	50	(34)
Detroit	108	92	(16)
Dayton	104	87	(17)
Region Total (9 branches)	605	532	(82)

Comment (for use of executive making appraisal)

Share of market not a satisfactory measurement and you agree that sales of these products need serious attention in 1972.

Exhibit 3—Concluded

Key Results Expected

6. Improve sales volume of noncorporate products. Achieve overall 5% or more increase in sales of typewriter ribbons and supplies.

Key Results Achieved (include appropriate supporting comment)

	Typewriter Ribbons and Supplies (in $000's)		
	1971 Unit Objective	Dollar Sales to 10/31	Percent Achievement
Chicago	292	270	92
St. Louis	124	156	126
Detroit	751	878	117
Dayton	423	396	93
Region Total (9 branches)	3,438	3,639	106

Comment (for use of executive making appraisal)

Generally satisfactory.

Weddels was not happy with the results reported by Forman. According to the performance appraisal system, most of the regional managers, including Ed Michelson, were "below standard." On the other hand, he knew that many of them had faced competitive conditions which could not have been predicted with accuracy.

Alvin Binswanger's Memorandum

Shortly thereafter Ben Weddels received the following memorandum:

November 22, 1971

To: Ben Weddels
FROM: Alvin Binswanger
SUBJECT: Management-by-Objectives Performance
           Appraisal System—1971 Results

Happy Thanksgiving, but no relaxation for managers. We must get together soon to work out our 1972 plan for appraising managers. I am still excited about the management-by-objectives performance appraisal system, and eventually, I would like to extend the system to all levels in the organization and broaden its concept to tie in directly with compensation and development. I would like to hear your views on the system's effectiveness last year. I would appreciate it if you would dig up some answers to the following questions before we meet:

1. Were the key result targets realistic and challenging? Do you think they motivated the men to improve their performance?
2. Did the system help the managers appraise the strengths and deficiencies of their subordinates? Did they use the system to develop plans for improvement? If not, was it the fault of the system or the way the system was applied?

3. What can we do to improve the system?
4. Are we ready at this time to extend the system to the branch sales managers? If so, what steps should we take?

Alvin Binswanger

Alvin Binswanger

PART IV

Special Management
Control Situations

Although the management control process occurs in organizations of all types, in the preceding chapters we have tended to focus on the process as it occurs in industrial companies.

Chapter 13 describes certain control problems that are peculiar to multi-national organizations, particularly the appropriate transfer pricing policy for international transactions and problems relating to fluctuation in monetary exchange rates.

Chapter 14 discusses the special problems of service organizations, that is, organizations that produce and sell services, rather than tangible goods. Two types of such organizations are discussed in some detail: (1) banks and similar financial institutions, and (2) professional organizations.

Chapter 15 discusses nonprofit organizations. The principal difference be-tween these organizations and profit-oriented organizations arises from the absence of a profit measure. Profitability provides both an easily understood criterion for evaluating proposed programs and a good way of motivating and measuring performance. In nonprofit organizations, the task of finding suitable alternatives to the profit measure is difficult.

Chapter 16 discusses project-oriented organizations. The management control of projects differs from the management control that focuses on responsibility centers in several important respects. The chapter discusses these and also the problems of management control in a matrix organization, that is an organization in which persons have responsibilities both to a project and to a functional responsibility center.

Chapter Thirteen

MANAGEMENT CONTROL IN MULTINATIONAL COMPANIES

In this chapter we describe management control problems and practices in multinational organizations. Many of the aspects of controlling foreign operations are similar to those for controlling domestic operations, and these are discussed only briefly. There are, however, several problems that are unique to foreign operations, and most of this chapter is devoted to these problems. Although our discussion is stated in terms of a United States corporation and its foreign subsidiaries, the same general problems exist with respect to the parent company in any country and its foreign subsidiaries.

SIMILARITIES

In general, foreign operations may be organized as cost centers, revenue centers, profit centers, or investment centers, and the considerations that govern the choice of a particular type of responsibility center are in most respects similar to those for domestic operations. One important difference, however, is that even if a foreign operation is a cost center or a revenue center for control purposes, it is often a profit center for accounting purposes. This is because many foreign operations are legal entities, incorporated in the host country, and must therefore maintain a complete set of accounting records for legal and tax reasons.

Most United States companies maintain planning and control systems for foreign operations that are essentially the same as those they maintain for domestic operations. One study showed that 90 percent of large United States multinational corporations responding to a questionnaire used profit budgets in controlling foreign operations and that virtually all of these companies (97 percent) used the same, or essentially the same, system for budgeting and reporting as was used for domestic divisions.[1] One difference in control practices was that return on investment was used as a measure of performance by only 29 percent of the companies, which is much less than the comparable percentage for domestic operations.[2]

In general, the same problems of early warning and evaluation are experienced in controlling foreign operations as were described in Chapter 12 for domestic operations. As might be expected, although the problems are similar, their solution tends to be more difficult because foreign subsidiaries tend to operate in less familiar environments and to be more geographically dispersed than domestic operations. Also, cultural differences make the evaluation of performance more difficult.

TRANSFER PRICING

Of all aspects of management control, transfer pricing represents the greatest difference between controlling domestic and foreign operations. In domestic operations, the criterion for the transfer price system is almost exclusively goal congruence; that is, the principal objective is to develop a transfer price system that insures that actions taken by the divisional manager will be consistent with the best overall interests of the company. Total company profits should change, as the result of any decision, in the same direction and often in the same amount as divisional profits change. Total company profits are rarely affected directly by the transfer price system and, even when they are affected, the reason is that management believes that the action is consistent with the goal congruence objective. For example, divisions may be allowed complete freedom in sourcing, and this may result in some products being produced outside of the company even though inside capacity exists. Freedom in sourcing, however, is nevertheless permitted because top management believes that the short-run loss in profits will be more than off-set by long-run gains resulting from the impact of competitive pressures on the selling division.

In foreign operations, however, considerations other than goal congruence are important in arriving at the transfer price. The most important of these are:

1. Effective income tax rates can differ considerably among foreign countries. A transfer price system that results in assigning profits to low-tax countries can reduce total income taxes.

---

[1] Bursk, Dearden, Hawkins, and Longstreet, *Financial Control of Multi-National Operations,* New York: Financial Executive Research Foundation, 1971, pages 22–24.
[2] *Ibid.,* page 25.

2. Tariffs are often levied on the import value of a product. The lower the price, the lower will be the tariff.
3. For various reasons, a company may wish to accumulate its funds in one country rather than another. Transfer prices are a way of shifting funds into or out of a particular country. Profits can be affected by differing interest rates, changes in exchange rates, different degrees of inflation, and so forth.
4. Government regulations, both United States and foreign, affect the way in which the transfer price can be calculated.

Note that the first and second factors—income taxes and tariffs—tend to work in opposite directions. Although tariffs will be low if the transfer price is low, the profit—and hence the local income tax on the profit—will be correspondingly high. Thus, the net effect of these factors must be calculated in deciding on the appropriate transfer price. The results of this calculation may be modified by the effect of the third and fourth factors.

In addition to the transfer prices for goods sold by one profit center to another, profits and funds can also be affected by:

1. Royalties and service charges made between profit centers; and
2. Funds loaned by one company unit to another.

In this section, we will consider only transfer prices. Essentially the same conditions will apply to royalties, service charges, and the transfer of funds between locations.

Legal Considerations

Almost all countries place some constraints on the flexibility of companies to set transfer prices for transactions with foreign subsidiaries. The reason, of course, is to prevent the multinational company from avoiding the host country's income taxes. Probably the most stringent regulations exist within the United States. They are basically set forth in Section 482 of the Internal Revenue Code.

In general, Section 482 tries to insure that financial transactions between the units of a "controlled taxpayer" (that is, a company that can control transactions between domestic and foreign profit centers) are conducted as if the units were "uncontrolled taxpayers" (that is, independent entities dealing with one another at arm's length). In the words of this regulation:

> The purpose of Sec. 482 is to place a controlled taxpayer on a tax parity with an uncontrolled taxpayer, by determining, according to the standard of an uncontrolled taxpayer, the true taxable income from property and business of a controlled taxpayer. . . . The standard to be applied in every case is that of an uncontrolled taxpayer dealing at arm's length with another uncontrolled taxpayer.

Clearly, the purpose of Section 482 is to prevent the United States multinational corporations from assigning profits to foreign subsidiaries to avoid paying United States' income taxes.

In case of a dispute, Section 482 permits the Internal Revenue Service to calculate what it believes to be the most appropriate transfer price, and the burden of proof is then on the company to show that this price is unreasonable. This is in contrast with most provisions of the Internal Revenue Code, which permit the company to select whatever permissible alternative it wishes, and places the burden of proof on the Internal Revenue Service. The wording is as follows:

In any case of two or more organizations, trades or businesses (whether or not incorporated, whether or not organized in the United States, and whether or not affiliated) owned or controlled directly or indirectly by the same interests, the Secretary or his delegate may distribute, opportion or allocate gross income, deductions, credits, or allowances between or among such organizations, trades or businesses, if he determines that such distribution, apportionment, or allocation is necessary in order to prevent evasion of taxes or clearly to reflect the income of any of such organizations, trades or businesses.

The 482 Regulations provide rules for determining an arm's length price on sales among members of the controlled group. Acceptable intercompany pricing methods, listed in descending order of priority, are as follows:

1. *Comparable uncontrolled price method.* An arm's length price will be ascertained from comparable sales where either or both the buyer and seller are not members of a controlled group. Comparability is based on the similarity of the controlled and uncontrolled sales with respect to the physical properties and factual circumstances underlying the transactions. An uncontrolled sale will be considered comparable if the differences are such that they can be reflected by an adjustment of the selling price, e.g., where the difference is accounted for by a variance in shipping terms. However, a sale will not be considered comparable if it represents an occasional or marginal transaction or is a sale at an unrealistically low price.

Circumstances which may affect the price include the quality of the product, terms of sale, market level and geographical area in which the item is sold; but quantity discounts, promotional allowances and special losses due to currency exchange and credit differentials are omitted.

Lower prices, and even sales at below full cost, are permitted in certain instances such as penetration of a new market or maintaining an existing market in a particular area.

2. *Resale price method.* Where comparable sales are not available, the next preferred method is the resale price method. Under this method, the taxpayer works back from a predetermined price at which property purchased from an affiliate is resold in an uncontrolled sale. This "resale price" is reduced by an appropriate mark-up percentage based on uncontrolled sales by the same affiliate or by other resellers selling similar property in a comparable market. Mark-up percentages of competitors and industry averages are also helpful in this connection.

The Regulations require that this method be used (1) if there are no comparable uncontrolled sales, (2) the resales are made within a reasonable time before or after the intercompany purchase, (3) the reseller has not added significant value to the property by physically altering it, other than packaging, labelling, and so forth, or by the use or application of intangible property.

3. *Cost plus method.* Under this method, the last of the three prescribed methods, the starting point for determining an arm's length price is the cost of producing the product, computed in accordance with sound accounting practices. To this is added an appropriate gross profit expressed as a percentage of cost and based on similar uncontrolled sales made by the seller or other sellers or, finally, an industry rate.

A schematic representation of these three methods appears as follows:

1. *Comparable uncontrolled price method*
   Arm's length price = price paid in comparable uncontrolled sales ± adjustments.
   > *Controlled sale* is where property is sold in a transaction between members of a controlled group.
   > *Uncontrolled sale* is a sale where at least one party to the sale is not a member of the controlled group.
2. *Resale price method*
   Arm's length price = applicable resale price − appropriate mark-up ± adjustments.
   > *Applicable resale price* is price at which property purchased in the controlled sale is resold by the buyer in an uncontrolled sale.
   > *Appropriate mark-up* = applicable resale price × appropriate markup percent.
   > *Appropriate mark-up percent* = percent of gross profit (expressed as a percent of sales) earned by buyer (reseller) or another party in uncontrolled purchase and resale similar to controlled resale.
3. *Cost plus method*
   Arm's length price = cost + appropriate mark-up ± adjustments.
   > *Appropriate mark-up* = cost × appropriate gross profit percent. Appropriate gross mark-up percent = gross profit percent (expressed as a percent of cost) earned by seller or another party on uncontrolled sale similar to controlled sale.

In lieu of one of these three specified methods, the taxpayer is permitted to use another method if he can establish that in view of all the circumstances this other method is "clearly more appropriate."

Puerto Rico. Although not a foreign country, Puerto Rico makes income tax concessions to American companies that manufacture products there, and transfer price problems therefore arise for products shipped out of Puerto Rico that are similar to those involved in international companies. Companies can use either the rules set forth in Section 482, or those in

Revenue Procedure 63–10, which shows alternative ways of arriving at the price for Puerto Rican transfers.

From a management control point of view, there are two important implications of Section 482:

1. Although there are legal restrictions on a company's flexibility in transfer pricing, there is considerable latitude within these restrictions.
2. In some instances, the legal constraints may dictate the type of transfer prices that must be employed. Each of these is discussed below.

Latitude in Transfer Prices

In many multinational companies there is a difference between the transfer prices that management would use purely for control purposes and those legally allowable transfer prices that minimize the sum of the tax and tariff impacts.[3] Since a high degree of subjectivity is involved in applying Section 482 to many goods and services, there can be a considerable range in the permissible transfer price for a particular good or service. Management can minimize the sum of income taxes and tariffs by maintaining transfer prices as far as possible at the appropriate end of the range. For example, if a United States parent company sells a product to a subsidiary in a country with materially lower income taxes than the United States, profits can be shifted to the foreign subsidiary by keeping the transfer price as low as is legally allowable. This practice, however, may cause a problem in control because profits in the foreign subsidiary would be reported as being higher, and profits in the American profit center would be reported as being lower, than would be the case if the transaction took place between independent entities. This problem can be even greater if the transfer is between two foreign subsidiaries because many foreign countries have neither the regulations nor the administrative personnel to monitor effectively the transfer prices of multinational corporations, and transfer prices outside of the United States therefore tend to be more flexible.

There are two extremes of policy in dealing with this problem. Some companies permit profit centers to deal with each other at arm's length and let the impact of taxes fall where it may. With this policy, there is no question about the legality of transfer prices because the subsidiaries are trying to do exactly what the regulations say they should do—deal at arm's length. Under this policy, foreign transfer pricing will be essentially the same as domestic transfer pricing; that is, the objective will be goal congruence. Consequently, the transfer price system supports the management control system. On the other hand, the policy could result in higher total tax costs.

At the other extreme, foreign transfer prices are controlled almost entirely

---

[3] Throughout this chapter, we are assuming that corporations are using transfer prices that comply with Section 482.

centrally with the purpose of attempting to minimize total corporate costs or maximizing dollar cash flow. For example:

In Company 62, an executive explains that the objective is to get as much profit home as possible, so long as foreign subsidiaries' payments are deductible for local tax purposes. He prefers to repatriate funds as royalties rather than as dividends, because royalties are often deductible overseas and because they are classified by the United States as foreign source income—thereby raising the limitation on foreign tax credit. Actually, he feels, there is little basis for charging royalties overseas, because his company's intangibles have little value to the foreign subsidiaries until the subsidiaries themselves develop them.

"The best way to bring money back varies with the situation," he explains. "Some countries allow royalties to be deducted, but are tough on service fees. Others are the other way around. Some have a progressive withholding rate. We call the payments whatever seems best under the circumstances."[4]

Such a policy has the advantages of possibly reducing total costs and in controlling cash flow. It can severely restrict the usefulness of the control system, however, because in some instances the transfer prices may bear little relationship to the prices that would prevail if the buying and selling units were independent. If this policy is followed, the question of what to do about the control system arises.

One possibility is to adjust profits for internal evaluation purposes so as to reflect competitive market prices. For example, the total differences between the prices actually charged and those that would have been in effect had taxation not been a consideration, could be added to the selling subsidiary's revenue and the buying subsidiary's costs when profit budget reports are analyzed. This is a questionable practice, however, and few companies use it. If asked, a company would be required to disclose these adjustments to the Internal Revenue Service, and their existence of course would raise questions concerning the validity of the transfer prices being used for tax purposes.

Most companies that price to minimize taxes and tariffs use the same transfer prices for profit budget preparation and reporting as are used for accounting and tax purposes. The approved budget reflects any inequities arising from the transfer prices. For example, a subsidiary that sells for lower than normal prices might have a budgeted loss. If reports of performance show that the subsidiary loses less than budget, its performance is considered to be satisfactory. In short, the transfer prices are considered both in approving the budget and in analyzing results.

If profit budgets and reports reflect uneconomic transfer prices, care must be taken to be sure that profit center managers are making decisions that are

---

[4] Michael G. Duerr, *Tax Allocation and International Business,* The Conference Board, 1972, page 32.

in the best interests of the company. For example, suppose that Subsidiary A purchases a line of products from Subsidiary B at a price that gives B most of the profit. In these circumstances Subsidiary A can improve its reported profit performance by not selling B's products aggressively and by concentrating its marketing effort on products that add to its reported profits. Such a practice would be contrary to the best interests of the company as a whole. If uneconomic transfer prices are used in budgeting, therefore, it is important to guard against such situations. It may be necessary to use measures of performance other than profitability or, at least, other measures *in addition* to profitability, such as sales volume or market share.

Legal Constraints on Transfer Pricing System

In some instances, legal constraints may require that a particular transfer pricing system be used, or that a preferred transfer system may not be used. For example, the two-step transfer price system described in Chapter 7 might be questioned by the tax authorities simply because it is not mentioned in Section 482 and is not widely known about.

Some constraints are caused by the nature of the product being transferred. For example,

In the oil industry (the biggest single multinational organized industry) the posted price system limits transfer pricing, removes it from the control of the companies and indeed exploits it in favor of the exporting countries. With many other primary products, transfer pricing is either organized by the exporting country through state trading or similar regulation (e.g., Chilean and Peruvian copper exports) or severely limited by specific taxes (e.g., tonnage levies on output or exports).[5]

In other instances, the "full cost" approach implicit in Section 482 may limit a company's ability to transfer some products at less than full costs. For example,

An executive of another large multinational firm suggests that the arm's length concept introduces an air of unreality to management decision making. He explains, "Internal accounting recognizes management objectives and intracompany negotiations, but the IRS accounting does not; and this is what causes much of the trouble with Section 482. For example, management may want to sell a new product without burdening it with parent company overheads. Incremental costing may make perfect sense from the marketing standpoint, but the IRS says the overhead must be allocated."[6]

If legal constraints require the use of transfer prices different from the ones that would be used for control purposes, a company is in the same posi-

---

[5] Crawford, Malcolm. "Transfer Pricing in International Transactions," *Multinational Business,* September 1974, page 1.

[6] Michael G. Duerr. *Tax Allocation and International Business,* The Conference Board, 1972, page 67.

tion as the company that uses one set of transfer prices for taxation and another for control, except that such a company can safely adjust profit center revenues and costs for differences between the legal transfer price and the preferred transfer price in most cases. Since the company presumably would have no objection to using the preferred transfer price for legal purposes, no harm can come from, in effect, keeping two sets of books. A company contemplating such a system should consider the possibility that it might be required to use a different price in two different countries for the same transaction.

Domestic International Sales Corporations

In order to encourage United States companies to develop increased amounts of foreign trade, the Congress has authorized the use of Domestic International Sales Corporations (hereafter referred to as DISC). A DISC receives favorable tax treatment both with respect to the timing of tax payments and the total amount of taxes paid.

A DISC is a separate corporation that buys goods from a United States corporation and sells such goods abroad. The physical handling of the goods can be identical to that used before the DISC was formed. The existence of the DISC simply changes the accounting. Clearly, it is the advantage of a parent company to charge the lowest price possible to the DISC, since the DISC's income tax rates are lower than those of the parent company. Consequently, the transfer price to the DISC is of interest both to management and the Internal Revenue Service.

The rules for transfer pricing between a DISC subsidiary and its parent company are as follows:

Regardless of the actual transfer price charged, the transfer price in intracompany sales to (but not by) a DISC is the transfer price that will let it earn the *largest* amount of taxable income under three rules:

1. Taxable income based on the actual price but subject to Section 482 adjustment.
2. Four percent of qualified export receipts on resale plus ten percent of export promotion expense.
3. Fifty percent of the combined taxable income of the DISC and the related supplier derived from the entire transaction plus ten percent of the export promotion expense.

Under rules 2 and 3, income must *not* be allowed to the DISC to the extent that the allocation causes the supplier to realize a loss on the sale.

Minority Interests

The foregoing discussion has assumed that the intracompany transfers were between wholly owned subsidiaries. The problem becomes more difficult if minority interests are involved, for in these circumstances top management's flexibility in distributing profits between subsidiaries is severely restricted. In this event, it would seem almost mandatory that subsidiaries deal with each other at arm's length, to the extent possible.

There are no easy answers to the transfer price problem. The important point is that management must recognize the problem and give much thought as to what it wishes to do about it. This is a top management policy decision, not one that can be delegated to the controller. Furthermore, such a decision cannot be made in the abstract. A realistic estimate of the costs to the company of ignoring taxes, tariffs, or cash flow will have to be made.

FOREIGN EXCHANGE TRANSLATION

After transfer pricing, the most important problem of control systems for foreign subsidiaries is the translation of amounts expressed in a foreign currency into United States dollars.

Exchange Rates

An exchange rate is the relationship between two currencies. In the situations we will discuss, it is the relationship between the dollar and some other foreign currency. For example, the exchange rates on June 11, 1975 for several types of foreign currency are shown in Exhibit 13–1.

Exhibit 13–1

**EXCHANGE RATES FOR VARIOUS FOREIGN CURRENCIES
ON JUNE 11, 1975**

Country	Monetary Unit	Value of Foreign Monetary Unit in U.S. Dollars	Number of Foreign Monetary Units Equal to One U.S. Dollar
Argentina	Peso	$ .0375	26.7
Australia	Dollar	1.3450	.7
Brazil	Cruzeiro	.1270	7.9
Britain	Pound	2.2850	.4
France	Franc	.2510	4.0
Japan	Yen	.003428	291.7
Switzerland	Franc	.4017	2.5
West Germany	Mark	.4298	2.3

The schedule indicates that on this date a dollar was worth 2.5 Swiss francs, 4.0 French francs, 2.3 West German marks and so forth. This means that banks in foreign countries will accept United States dollars at these rates and, conversely, they will convert dollars into foreign currencies at these rates. Under the system currently in operation, the rate of exchange of the dollar with other currencies can vary significantly over the course of a year. Also, these changes in rates can be different for different currencies.

For example, during a given year, the value of the dollar could increase relative to the pound sterling and decrease relative to the West German mark. At one time the rate of exchange of the currencies of most developed countries was fixed within small limits because the value of each currency was based on a specific amount of gold. Consequently, significant changes in exchange rates were generally confined to third world currencies and an occasional revaluation by one of the developed countries, for example, the British pound in 1967 and the French franc in 1969. At present currencies are not tied to gold. As a result, their values fluctuate with supply and demand. Also, speculative activities can affect exchange rates in somewhat the same way that stock prices fluctuate with buyer and seller expectations. This situation makes the conversion problem now considerably more important to the manager than has been true in the past.

Method of Conversion

It is necessary to convert (or translate) financial statements of foreign subsidiaries into United States dollars before these statements can be consolidated with the parent company's financial statements. Generally accepted accounting principles for this conversion are described in the Statement of Accounting Standards No. 8—Accounting for the Translation of Foreign Currency Transactions and Foreign Currency Financial Statements. In general, balances representing cash and accounts receivable or payable shall be translated at the current rate of exchange. Accounts carried at prices in past exchanges (past prices) shall be translated at historical rates. Accounts carried at prices in current purchase or sale exchanges (current prices) of future exchanges (future prices) shall be translated at the current rate. Revenue and expense items are translated at average rates for the year, except for those related to assets and liabilities that have been converted at historical rates. Such items are translated as historical rates. Any translation gain or loss is written off against income in the period that it was incurred.

Control Problems of Currency Translation. As stated above, the financial statements of foreign subsidiaries must be translated into United States dollars for inclusion in the parent company's consolidated financial statements. The control problem is whether the foreign subsidiaries should be evaluated on the basis of the financial results expressed in local currency or the results expressed in dollars. As with transfer pricing, there are two extreme positions. At one end of the spectrum, profit budgets are approved and reports prepared in the local currency, or actual results are translated into dollars at the same exchange rates that were used in constructing the budget, which amounts to the same thing. At the other end of the spectrum, the profit center manager is responsible for meeting dollar objectives. His budget is approved in United States dollars, using exchange rates in existence at the date the budget was prepared, and actual results are translated into dollars at the current exchange rates. With this practice there will usually be either a profit or a loss that is caused by differences between budgeted and current exchange rates.

In addition to the profit budget variances that are caused by differences betweeɪ. budgeted and current exchange rates, there also will be an exchange gain or loss when the foreign financial statements are translated into dollars, if there has been a change in exchange rates during the period.

As described above, until 1971, exchange rates of most developed countries were relatively stable. Usually, significant currency gains and losses were limited to transactions with developing countries. Such transactions almost always resulted in losses because the monetary unit of most developing countries was deteriorating relative to the dollar. In many instances, the managers of subsidiaries in these countries were expected to minimize exchange losses by acquiring funds from local sources to the extent possible. In such circumstances, it was reasonable to hold the manager of the foreign subsidiary responsible for exchange gains or losses.

In 1971, exchange rates were "floated," and subsequently changes in exchange rates among countries have been frequent. These changes often resulted in significant exchange gains since the value of the dollar often declines. Because of these fluctuations, it has become increasingly common for currency movements in multinational companies to be controlled at headquarters by the treasurer's department. In these circumstances the local manager is no longer able to control exchange gains or losses. Consequently, many companies use the following procedures with respect to currency translation:

1. The budget for the period is translated into United States dollars at the same exchange rates that are used to translate the current operating statements. Thus, no variances are caused by differences between budgeted and actual exchange rates.
2. Gains or losses from translating actual operating results into dollars are eliminated from the budget performance report.
3. If a manager has control over exchange gains or losses, these gains or losses are analyzed separately.

The above procedure has the advantage of separating operating performance from financial performance.

INFLATION

Until 1973, the rate of inflation in many foreign countries was significantly greater than that in the United States. Consequently, the problem of taking account of inflation was important only in certain foreign subsidiaries. Since 1973, inflation has also become a problem in the management control of domestic companies. Thus, much of the discussion in this part of the chapter also applies to domestic profit centers.

The Problems

High inflation causes two problems in management control:

1. When costs are measured in terms of historical acquisition cost, profits may be overstated. Pricing inventory at either Fifo or average cost understates the replacement cost of the inventory, and depreciation based on historical cost understates the amount needed to replace plant and equipment. Furthermore, the purchasing power gains and losses that arise from holding monetary assets and monetary liabilities are not recognized in conventional accounting.

2. Financial statements for different time periods may not be comparable with one another because changes in the value of the monetary unit affect different items in different ways.

Possible Solutions

Few companies adjust their reports to take account of the effect of inflation, either domestically or in foreign subsidiaries. Some possible approaches are outlined below, but it should be emphasized that they are strictly possibilities that have not yet been widely, if at all, used in practice.

One approach to the inflation problem is to attack it on a piecemeal basis. For profit budget preparation and reporting purposes, inventory and plant and equipment could be written up to their replacement values. When this is done, budgeted and actual profits would represent more nearly real profits in terms of constant purchasing power. Variance analysis would segregate that portion of selling price variances and cost variances that were due to changes in the value of money. A disadvantage with this approach is that it would result in performance reports that are inconsistent with the financial accounting records. Managers tend to dislike such reports because they view the operating results as thus calculated as not being "real," but rather figments of the imagination of the accountant or economist. In some countries, property assets are written up to replacement value for accounting purposes, and in these countries this disadvantage would not apply.

Another approach to the inflation problem is to prepare supplemental statements adjusted for general purchasing power changes. This approach is currently (1976) being considered by the Financial Accounting Standards Board for general use in the United States. The proposal being considered by the FASB involves adjusting items by an index of the change in the purchasing power of the monetary unit. In the United States, this is the Gross National Product Implicit Price Deflator. Supplemental statements are fairly difficult to prepare and also are difficult to interpret. Perhaps the most important problem, however, is the likelihood that top management will give only cursory attention to the supplementary report and will use the more familiar historical cost reports for evaluation. If this happens, the supplementary reports will be a waste of time.

A combination of these two approaches could be to adjust the financial statements using price level indexes and other data that apply specifically to the company in question. This would make the figures more realistic, but they would also be more subjective and thus subject to manipulation. These reports would also be subject to problems of interpretation by management, as well as the question of whether management would use them.

A final possibility would be to abandon statements that were based on historical cost and budget and report on the basis of numbers that are adjusted to some form of current value. If this were done, management would have to use these reports since performance reports in conventional terms would not be available. Such a step would be a drastic change from current procedures, and would create a discrepancy between internal reports and those prepared for outsiders; the latter would necessarily be on an historical cost basis.

None of these proposals provides an effective solution to the problem of inflation. If just inventories and property assets are adjusted, only part of the problem is being attacked. If the entire problem is attacked, there is the problem of objectivity and of inconsistencies with conventional reports. Finally, there is the problem of using the information: if the adjusted reports are supplementary to the conventional reports, it is likely that top management will use the conventional reports because these reports are more familiar and because they are consistent with published financial statements.

PPG Industries, Inc.*

In the 1960s PPG Industries, Inc. was faced with the prospect of tax court litigation on the issue of international transfer pricing. The Internal Revenue Service (IRS) contended that PPG had set the price of its products sold to a Swiss subsidiary in 1960 and 1961 in a manner which resulted in an unclear reflection of income and an avoidance of U.S. income tax. The effective tax rate (federal and cantonal) for Swiss companies was considerably less than that for American companies. Management was concerned not only with the size of the alleged deficiency[1] (which totalled over $1,000,000), but also with the precedent that would be set by an adverse decision.

PPG Industries, Inc. (PPG), a manufacturer of glass, fiber glass, chemical, and paint products, was incorporated in 1883. PPG was organized on a product line basis. Each division was responsible for domestic sales of the products it manufactured.

Until 1958 all international activities were managed by a small export department. The export department had been constrained by the fact that selling prices and terms for all products were determined by the divisional personnel responsible for each particular product. The prices charged export customers, particularly for glass products, generally yielded higher margins than domestic sales. Furthermore, export personnel were not free to travel to develop new markets or service existing markets without specific approval from the executive vice president of PPG.

After World War II there was a great shortage of glass manufacturing capacity in the United States. For example, in 1955 and 1956, PPG bought

---

* Material for this case was derived from published sources.

[1] The Service has a procedural rule such that if income which it proposes to reallocate to a U.S. company has already been taxed in another country, the incremental tax burden will only rise to the point where the effective tax rate on the income in question equals the statutory rate in the United States.

more glass from foreign suppliers than it sold to foreign customers. In 1957, capacity caught up with domestic demand, and there were indications that this trend would continue.

In 1958, PPG formed a Swiss subsidiary, known hereafter as PPGI. The stated purposes of this subsidiary were to (1) expand the sale of PPG products outside the United States, (2) develop opportunities outside the United States for the exploitation of PPG technology, and (3) develop opportunities outside the United States where equity investments could be made for the manufacture of products using PPG technology.

In accordance with the above, PPG offered volume discounts to PPGI as follows:

Aggregate Quarterly
Purchases by PPGI
of PPG Products
($000,000) . . . . *Discount Rate*

0–2	None
2–2.2	3% on entire amount
2.2–3	Graduated up to 10%
Over 3	10% on amount over $3

The discounts were subject to the restriction that no product, regardless of the quantity purchased was to be sold to PPGI at a net price that was less than the PPG inventoriable value (which was basically actual direct cost) or replacement cost, whichever is higher, plus 25%. Furthermore, PPG expected a return on sales (after allocation of indirect costs) of at least 10%. If a 10% ROS was not maintained, prices were to be adjusted upward.

PPGI was required to purchase 85% or more of its product needs from PPG. There were other producers in the United States and abroad capable of supplying comparable quality products to PPGI at comparable prices.

In the event a foreign customer dealt directly with PPG rather than with PPGI, PPGI was to receive a 2% commission on such sales. Such business was minimal in 1960 and 1961.

Although PPGI sold the entire range of PPG products, the remainder of this case deals with sales of glass products unless stated otherwise. Sales of glass products represented approximately two thirds of PPGI's sales and substantially all of its profits.

Interest of the Internal Revenue Service

Since the Revenue Act of 1939, the IRS has had the authority to allocate or apportion income between two related company entities if it "determines that such distribution, apportionment or allocation is necessary in order to prevent evasion of taxes or clearly to reflect the income of any such organizations, trades or businesses." In the early 1960s, the Service set up an Office of International Operations, and this office began an accelerated program to scrutinize in detail the transactions among units of multinational companies. By 1968, such operations were resulting in substantial income reallocations. A Treasury Department study indicated that 1,706 possible adjustments of this nature (involving 871 companies) were identified during 1968 and 1969. Of the possible adjustments, 886 were actually made, in amounts totalling $662 million. Of this amount, almost ½ involved adjustments to the transfer price used in international transactions.[2] Significantly, once the issue is raised by the IRS, the burden of proof shifts to the taxpayer. The taxpayer is required to prove that the foreign subsidiary fulfills a valid business purpose, was not set up to evade taxes and that the transfer price calculations proposed by the IRS are unreasonable.

In challenging PPG, the IRS focused on sales into Canada, paying particular attention to sales made through PPGI to CPI and Duplate, two other subsidiaries of PPG.

Activities and Relationships of CPI and Duplate

CPI was a distributor of glass and paint in Canada. Its customers were retailers and industrial users. It also performed some contract work such as glazing buildings. It was 100 percent owned by PPG, and had been fully owned prior to 1960.

Duplate fabricated glass parts for the automotive original equipment market, the largest single Canadian market for glass products. Duplate made automotive sales on a yearly contract basis. As an adjunct to its automotive business, Duplate fabricated double-glazed units, aircraft windshields and a variety of tempered glass for the building trade. The ownership of Duplate had been acquired in stages. By 1960, PPG owned approximately ⅔ of Duplate's stock.

Sales to CPI and Duplate represented approximately ⅔ of the total sales of glass by PPGI, both as of the time PPGI was formed and for the years in question. Each subsidiary was required by PPG to purchase at least 35% of its annual needs from PPGI. The remainder could be purchased from any supplier. Also, should CPI and Duplate request more than 35%, PPGI was obliged to furnish up to 85% of their glass needs.

Activities of PPGI

PPGI's principal function was marketing, which embraced many activities other than strictly selling. Of the total staff of nearly 80 people, approximately 50 concentrated on marketing. The marketing staff spent about half of its time in the field. Its activities included customer contact and service (including after-sale service); contract negotiations; market research; technical assistance to customers; credit arrangements; efforts toward help-

---

[2] The study did not explain why the remaining 820 (1706–886) adjustments were not made. Possible explanations are tax court rulings in favor of the taxpayers or acquiescence by the Service if it was not confident about the case.

ing customers market their products to their customers and market studies to determine potential for old and new products. In 1959 PPGI had 86 customers for glass; in 1965, 568; in 1967, over 700. The growth rate in sales volume was somewhat less dramatic.

Unlike Combination Export Managers (CEMs), which were used by many U.S. manufacturers for foreign sales, PPGI did not process the paperwork for international sales. PPG believed this could be accomplished more easily by its domestic staff. Also unlike a CEM, PPGI accepted the credit risk on sales and negotiated terms to suit its marketing effort. For example, whereas PPGI generally remitted to PPG within 10 days of invoice date, it granted its own customers payment terms ranging from 30 to 180 days.

IRS Arguments

The IRS challenged the transfer price on transactions between PPG and PPGI. The Service contended that PPGI was analogous to a Combination Export Manager of which there were numerous representing U.S. companies in foreign markets. The Service pointed out that for the job of processing the paperwork necessary in the export of various products and performing a selling function by selecting and dealing through foreign distributors to fill a prevailing demand for a particular product, CEMs were generally paid a commission sufficient for them to earn a pretax profit of 2–5 percent on sales. The Service also pointed out that most U.S. manufacturers considered Canada as an extension of the U.S. market; therefore even CEMs were superfluous in dealings in Canada.

The Service changed its position several times with respect to what margin would be appropriate for PPGI. Initially, it argued that PPGI's pretax profit margin should be no higher than those of a sample of businesses which its staff studied and claimed to be comparable to PPGI. These businesses were basically CEMs and had pretax profits of 3.6 percent in 1960 and 2.4 percent in 1961. Later the Service contended that sales into Canada should be treated like commission sales and that PPGI should receive only 2 percent commission (not pretax profit) on such sales and that the remaining sales should be subject to the above mentioned profit ceilings.

PPG Arguments

PPGI insisted that its business was appreciably different from those selected by the Service and, therefore, the use of their profit margins and commission rates was inappropriate. PPGI also pointed out that adherence to these margins and rates would result in PPGI's incurring consistent losses. The earnings of PPG and PPGI for 1960 and 1961 are summarized in Exhibits 1, 2, and 3.

As the discussions with the IRS continued, it became apparent to management that this case might result in litigation. Management consistently believed that the transfer prices used were reasonable and appropriate but nevertheless evidenced some concern in view of a recent case involving Eli Lilly which was settled in the government's favor. (Lilly is summarized in the Appendix)

In addition to legal counsel, management also retained the services of C. Paul Jannis, a cost accounting expert, after the IRS raised some questions as to the propriety of PPG's allocation of indirect costs of production, research, engineering and selling and administration.

When Jannis began his work in 1967, he sought to determine the best method of allocation in terms of accounting theory and feasibility for PPG. As mentioned earlier, PPG was organized on a product line basis. Sales revenue and direct costs were accounted for by individual products, but indirect costs were accounted for by a total product line or division. The glass division had 3 product lines (window, plate and building). The chemical division had 15 product lines.

Jannis realized that the various types of indirect costs had different characteristics themselves, and he considered formulating a different method of allocation for each distinct cost. Ultimately he decided to determine profitability by product, allocating indirect costs to products on the basis of the contribution margin of each product. His calculations are included in Exhibits 1, 2, and 3.

Exhibit 1

PPG INDUSTRIES, INC.
Condensed Income Statements

	Consolidated Sales of PPG (in millions)		Glass Sales to PPGI by PPG (in thousands)	
	1960	1961	1960	1961
Net sales	$628	$603	$7,811*	$7,026*
Direct costs	—‡	—‡	5,162	4,517
Period costs of manufacturing ...	—‡ .	—‡	1,304†	1,358†
Total cost of sales	$438	$434	$6,466	$5,875
Gross margin	$190	$169	$1,345	$1,151
S.G.&A.	90	93	397	416
Other expense, net	8	9	—	—
Pretax profit	$ 92	$ 67	$ 948	$ 735

* Net sales by PPG differ from PPGI cost of sales by the amount of PPGI sales of products acquired elsewhere.

† Period costs are those costs of manufacturing which could not be specically allocated to products. Allocation was made on the basis of contribution, that is, the difference between sales and direct costs.

‡ Breakdown between direct and indirect not available on a consolidated basis.

Exhibit 2

PPGI INCOME STATEMENT, 1960
(Glass Sales Only)

	Sales To (000 omitted)		
	Canadian Affiliates	Others	Total
Net sales*	$7,201	$3,354	$10,555
Cost of goods sold	6,027	2,617	8,644
Less: Volume discount	(318)	(140)	(458)
Net cost of goods sold	$5,709	$2,477	$ 8,186
Gross profit	$1,492	$ 877	$ 2,369
S.G.&A.			
Commissions	$ —	$ 191	$ 191
Freight	112	56	168
Discounts allowed	62	28	90
Employee compensation and			
expenses	282	165	447
Other	27	46	73
Total S.G.&A.	$ 483	$ 486	$ 969
Pretax profit from selling	$1,009	$ 391	$ 1,400
Other expenses, not allocated			330
Pretax profit			$ 1,070

* Includes no revenue from commission sales.

ADDENDUM TO EXHIBITS 2 AND 3

In 1960 and 1961, PPGI also sold paint, chemicals and fiber glass. The subsidiary also incurred expenses in, among other things, attempting to exploit further the technology developed by the parent and licensed to the subsidiary. The effect of such activities on pretax profits in 1960 and 1961 were as follows:

	1960	1961
Sale of paint, etc.	$ 79	$(64)
Other activities	(555)	96
Total	$(476)	$ 32

( ) Indicates net expense.

During the two years, PPGI's assets totalled approximately $15 million and net worth approximately $5 million.

PPG also collected some examples of selling prices on transactions involving outside parties. There were some practical difficulties due to differences in timing, terms of sale, quantities involved and competitive relationships. Nevertheless, PPG found a few instances where the price paid by PPGI for comparable goods in comparable quantities was higher than that charged outsiders:

1. PPGI and another vendor who also purchased from PPG bid on a

Exhibit 3

PPGI INCOME STATEMENT, 1961
(Glass Sales Only)

	Sales To (000 omitted)		
	Canadian Affiliates	Others	Total
Net sales*	$6,631	$2,755	$9,386
Cost of goods sold	5,287	2,173	7,460
Less: Volume discount	(300)	(120)	(420)
Net cost of goods sold	$4,987	$2,053	$7,040
Gross profit	$1,644	$ 702	$2,346
S.G.&A.			
Commissions	$ —	$ 159	$ 159
Freight	296	108	404
Discounts allowed	54	23	77
Employee compensation and			
expenses	297	126	423
Other	6	5	11
Total S.G.&A.	$ 653	$ 421	$1,074
Pretax profit from selling	$ 991	$ 281	$1,272
Other expenses, not allocated			110
Pretax profit			$1,162

* Includes no revenue from commission sales.

European government contract. The other vendor secured the bid by an amount which was less than the difference between the price it paid PPG for raw materials compared with what PPGI paid (the price charged the unrelated vendor being the lower price).

2. In 1960 and 1961 PPG sold substantial amounts of ¼″ plate glass to a domestic manufacturer and distributor of plate glass (not related to PPG) at prices from $0.01 to $0.06 per square foot less than the prices charged to PPGI, depending on the size bracket.[3]

3. In 1961 PPG sold 70,000 tons of liquid caustic soda to Olin Mathieson Company for $25 per ton. In 1961 PPGI paid PPG about $27 per ton for a substantial amount of such caustic soda.

Moreover, for a period of over 60 years ending in the 1950s, PPG sold glass to its west coast distributor (an unrelated corporation) at volume discounts ranging from 5 percent to 15 percent, as compared with the 3 percent to 10 percent volume discounts on sales to PPGI.

Section 482 of the Internal Revenue Code and, the regulations relating to this section are summarized in the text.

*   *   *   *   *

[3] The "size bracket" refers to the area of a sheet of plate glass.

The controversy did go to litigation and the facts and arguments described above are derived from the record of that litigation and from other published sources. For purposes of class discussion, the student may assume that all of these matters were known to management at the time the decision was made as to the action to be taken.

QUESTION

Should management decide to litigate this question, or should it accept the position of the Internal Revenue Service?

Appendix

Eli Lilly & Co. *v.* U.S.*

Eli Lilly had attempted to expand sales abroad through the formation of divisions within the parent company. Unfortunately, company personnel tended to treat international sales like stepchildren. The company decided to form two subsidiaries for international sales, one of which was qualified as a Western Hemisphere Trade Corporation.[1]

In the early 1950s the market for antibiotics was very soft. In order to provide incentive to the managements of the international sales subsidiaries for pushing sales, Lilly elected to modify its method for calculating transfer prices.

The transfer price was to be calculated in such a way as to recover

a) All manufacturing cost (including an allocation of fixed costs);
b) Royalties paid by Lilly to 3rd parties;
c) All operating expenses incurred by Lilly incident to the servicing of the export business.

---

* The material in this appendix was taken from the description of *Eli Lilly & Co.* v. *U.S.*, which appeared in Volume 19 of *American Federal Tax Reports*, pp. 712–37.

[1] Basically, if a corporation qualifies as a WHTC, U.S. taxes on its profits are reduced by approximately 30 percent. See Sections 921 and 922 of the Internal Revenue Code.

Clearly, to the extent accounting profits were to be earned on non-U.S. sales in the western hemisphere, they would be reflected on the books of the WHTC. This served as the basis for a challenge by the IRS under Section 482.

The Service did not dispute the validity of establishing the WHTC for business purposes. The Service challenged the manner in which the transfer prices were established, the lack of comparability with prices charged in uncontrolled transactions and the reasonableness of the ROS and ROI of the WHTC as compared with that of the parent.

In disputing the calculation of research and developments costs and transfer prices, the Service pointed out that there had been no allocation of R&D. If this had been done, the price would have been increased by 30%. The Service argued that normal, recurring sales should be priced in a manner to cover all costs and that R&D was a significant recurring cost for Lilly.

Lilly pointed to sales to the U.S. Government, DOD and GSA, which had been made at prices less than those charged the WHTC, and suggested these sales supported the "arm's length" nature of prices charged the WHTC. The Service claimed that such sales were sporadic and made only to use idle capacity. Furthermore, the products sold were packaged in drums bearing no trademark of Lilly. The Service claimed that these differences destroyed the comparability of the transactions.

Finally, the Service noted that the return on assets for the WHTC was 40% vs. 24% for Lilly during the period under review and that return on investment was 54% and 33% respectively. The Service considered this difference unreasonable, particularly in light of the differing degrees of risk and the functions performed by the two entities.

In support of its position Lilly seemed to place much reliance on the case of *Frank* v. *International Canadian Corp.* In that case a parent sold goods to its Western Hemisphere Trade Corporation at a price which included all the parent's direct costs, a full allocation of manufacturing overhead, delivery charges and a six percent mark-up on those costs and charges. The IRS asserted that a reallocation was necessary under Section 482, but the court found that the price reflected a "reasonable return" and therefore a reallocation of any part thereof was not proper. The provision in the price for a six percent profit distinguishes the Frank case from Lilly. However, Lilly pointed to the following language in the court's opinion as demonstrating that the arm's length standard set forth in the regulations is not the only test for determining true taxable income under Section 482:

> But entirely aside from appellees' position that the Commissioner is precluded from advancing this argument on appeal, we do not agree with the Commissioner's contention that "arm's length bargaining" is the *sole* criterion for applying the statutory language of Section 482 in determining what the "true net income" is of each "controlled taxpayer." Many decisions have been reached under Section 482 without reference to the phrase "arm's length bargaining" and without reference

to Treasury Department Regulations and Rulings which state that the talismanic combination of words—"arm's length"—is the "standard to be applied in every case."

For example, it was not any less proper for the district court to use here the "reasonable return" standard than it was for other courts to use "full fair value," "fair price, including a reasonable profit," "method which seems not unreasonable," "fair consideration which reflects arm's length dealing," "fair and reasonable," or "fair and fairly arrived at," or "judged as to fairness," all used in interpreting Section 482.

Subsequent court rulings have suggested that only a very narrow departure from the arm's length standard was allowed in the particular circumstances of Frank, and that where "the extent of the income in question is largely determined by the terms of business transactions entered into between two controlled corporations it is not unreasonable to construe 'true' taxable income as that which would have resulted if the transactions had taken place upon such terms as would have been appplied had the dealings been at arm's length between unrelated parties." (*Oil Base, Inc.* v. *Commissioner.*) Moreover, even accepting Lilly's interpretation that Frank establishes a criterion of a fair and reasonable price, such a price can best be determined by hypothesizing to an arm's length transaction. The thrust of Section 482 is to put controlled taxpayers on a parity with uncontrolled taxpayers. Consequently, any measure such as "fair and reasonable" or "fair and fairly arrived at" must be defined within the framework of "reasonable" or "fair" as among unrelated taxpayers. Simply because a price might be considered "reasonable" or "fair" as a business incentive in transactions among controlled corporations, does not mean that unrelated taxpayers would so consider it. Thus, even if the arm's length standard is not the sole criterion, it is certainly the most significant yardstick.

The court upheld the Service's claim and ordered a revision in the tax returns of Lilly and the WHTC.

Case 13-2

Macomber Corporation

Macomber Corporation consisted of ten U.S. operating divisions and several foreign subsidiaries. Each division was responsible for both manufacturing and marketing its product lines. There was some transfer of finished goods among divisions, but it was relatively minor. Each division and subsidiary was operated as a profit center. The firm's compensation plan was structured such that the incomes of key line managers were heavily influenced by the pretax incomes of their divisions.

In the early 1960s the Mendell division, with the approval of corporate management, decided to open a plant in Puerto Rico. Within the firm, opinion was mixed as to the success of the venture. While it appeared successful in terms of reported net income and return on investment, there were certain aspects of the Puerto Rican tax laws which some felt obscured the plant's true profitability.

Puerto Rico

The citizens (individual and corporate) of the Commonwealth of Puerto Rico govern themselves and also enjoy the advantages of U.S. citizenship without bearing many of the costs. Puerto Ricans are protected by the U.S. constitution, are serviced by the U.S. postal and judicial systems and use U.S. currency. They are subject to the same tariff regulations (with certain minor exceptions) as are other U.S. citizens. Unlike other U.S. citizens, however, they are exempted from paying federal income taxes.

The Commonwealth itself does levy a tax on profits, ranging from 22 to 48 percent for corporations. However, as an incentive to new industry it exempts from this tax income earned in the first ten years of operations. Such exemptions also apply to new or expanded divisions of firms previously doing business in Puerto Rico.

In 1949 the Commonwealth's gross national product was approximately $750 million. Annual per capital income was $256. There was virtually no industry. Average life expectancy was 46 years. The leaders of the island began a program, which they called Operation Bootstrap, intended to bring an end to economic privation and to improve substantially the quality of life on the island. Due in large part to incentives provided by the government and a spirit of cooperation among government, labor, and industry, the GNP in 1974 was approximately $6.5 billion and per capita income almost $2,000. Average life expectancy in 1974 exceeded 70 years, 90 percent of the population was literate and the median education level of employed persons was 11 years.

The island has a well-developed infrastructure with good roads (over 6,500 miles of expressways and super highways), port facilities, an airport (38 flights daily from the United States), and communication facilities comparable with those on the U.S. mainland.

Puerto Rican firms also received government assistance in the areas of site development, labor training and debt financing. Sites were generally available throughout the island in currently developed industrial parks, port-front locations and elsewhere. A government agency maintained an inventory of factory buildings adaptable to individual requirements for light or moderately heavy industry.

Unemployment on the island was generally around 15 percent. As a result, wage rates were relatively low. In 1974 the average hourly wage for a manufacturing worker was $2.43. In the U.S. mainland the average was $4.42, and in South Carolina, $3.45.

Currently the government was attempting to reduce unemployment, and to this end was subsidizing vocational and technical schools and sharing the cost of various employment training programs. The educational and training programs together with the conditions of the labor market and cultural values on the island combined to provide an environment which many firms considered attractive: relatively high skill levels, high morale, low turnover, low absenteeism and low wages.

The island was served by numerous commercial banks (including large New York banks) and several investment banking houses. New industry financing obtained through these sources was frequently supplemented by financing from the Government Development Bank. Furthermore, if a new firm located a facility in an economically undeveloped area, the government would provide financing for up to 90 percent of the firm's fixed assets and working capital with repayment schedules of up to 25 years.

Truedale Division Proposal

After the normal delays in getting started, the Mendell division plant began operating very efficiently in terms of cost, quality and delivery. As a result, other divisions began to consider moving some operations to the island. In 1970 the Truedale Division did a feasibility study analyzing the possibility of manufacturing part of its Trudy product line, a branded consumer product, in Puerto Rico. Additional manufacturing facilities were required to accommodate the expanding sales volume of this line. Estimated income statements, based on a ten year tax holiday, are shown in Exhibit 1.

Top management of the Macomber Corporation encouraged such moves if they actually were profitable. Questions arose about the effect of such actions on divisional profitability, however.

The first related to the fact that income generated in Puerto Rico became taxable if it were remitted to the United States within ten years. The tax rate was the sum of the 48 percent U.S. rate plus a special 15 percent Puerto Rico rate. As a result of this restriction, Macomber Corporation already had sizeable amounts of cash tied up in Puerto Rico, resulting from the operations of the Mendell division. The corporation could make good use of this cash for expansion of U.S. operations and for acquisitions. In fact, it could not raise equity money (or use stock for acquisitions) because its price/earnings multiple was temporarily low, and it could not

Exhibit 1

ESTIMATED INCOME STATEMENT, EXPANSION OF TRUDY PRODUCT LINE
(000 Omitted)

	If Manufactured in U.S.A.	If Manufactured in Puerto Rico
Revenue	$1,190	$1,190
Cost of sales (all manufacturing and shipping costs)	880	720
Gross margin	$ 310	$ 470
Selling expense (USA)	130	130
Pretax income	$ 180	$ 340
Income tax*	86	86
Net income	$ 94	$ 254

* It was assumed that goods would be transferred from Puerto Rico to the United States at a price that approximated the American total manufacturing cost, and the U.S. Income Tax would be levied on net income as computed on the basis of this cost. Therefore, U.S. income tax would be approximately the same under either alternative.

borrow without issuing a corresponding amount of equity. The financial vice president, therefore, believed that some cost should be assessed to the Trudy division to reflect the impact of this frozen cash on the corporation. One possibility was to discount Puerto Rico earnings at the present value of the cash when it was released ten years hence. At an annual rate of 10 percent, this would mean that each dollar of Puerto Rico cash earnings in the first year would be given a value of 40 cents.

Offsetting this, in part, was the fact that Puerto Rican cash could be used to build and equip Puerto Rican plants. Thus, the Truedale Division argued that if its earnings were discounted, the book value of plant and equipment should be discounted at the same rate, and annual depreciation would be correspondingly lower. Furthermore, Macomber liquid funds in Puerto Rico could be invested in local, well-secured loans at a return of approximately 6 percent. (These were short-term investments because the possibility existed that the political climate in Puerto Rico might change unfavorably, and corporate management regarded long-term investments as unduly risky.)

The Truedale plant would be leased from the government development agency, and the division would install $300,000 worth of new equipment which it would purchase using Macomber Corporation excess funds available in Puerto Rico. The manufacturing cost on Exhibit 1 included $30,000 depreciation on this equipment.

The working capital requirements for the Puerto Rican plant, consisting primarily of inventory, were expected to be approximately $200,000.

If the goods were manufactured in the United States, the plant would be leased, its equipment would cost $300,000, and working capital requirements would be about $200,000. (The lower cost content of inventory in Puerto Rico was offset by the necessity for carrying larger raw material inventory quantities because of delivery uncertainties.)

Finally, the Truedale Division suggested that divisional profitability should henceforth be measured on the basis of after-tax income so that the division would be given credit for the income tax saving it would produce for the corporation.

QUESTIONS

1. Should the additional goods for the Trudy product line be manufactured in the United States or in Puerto Rico?

2. Should the financial value of the Trudy line to Macomber be assessed in terms of pre-tax income, after-tax income, return on investment, or some other measure?

3. On what basis should the calculation of the Trudy Division manager's bonus be made?

Case 13-3

International Publishing
Equipment Corporation

On September 21, 1972, a meeting was held in Lausanne at the International Publishing Equipment Company, SA, of Switzerland (hereafter referred to as the Swiss Company) to discuss several problems concerning intracompany transactions. Attending the meeting were Mr. George Bois, the managing director of the Swiss Company, Mr. Olivier, the controller, and Mr. Barrows, the chief cost accountant. The specific purpose of the meeting was to review a proposal developed by Mr. Barrows for changing the method of transfer pricing. If agreement could be reached, Mr. Bois would recommend to the president of the International Publishing Equipment Corporation that the proposed transfer price systems be adopted throughout the entire corporation.

THE CORPORATION

International Publishing Equipment (IPE) was a large diversified corporation, with headquarters located in Cincinnati, Ohio. It was organized into 16 divisions divided into three groups: Printing Equipment, International, and Electronics. For practical purposes, the divisions were fully owned subsidiaries and each was a profit center.

IPE 1971 sales volume was nearly $500 million. Of these, approximately 30 percent were sales made by the International Group. The sales of the entire corporation increased four-fold in the past 10 years, and sales of the International Group increased eight-fold in this period.

PRODUCTS

IPE manufactured a broad range of products related to the printing and publishing industry, as well as certain other industries. However, since the problem in the case involves the printing and publishing, only these products are described here.

Hot-Metal Typesetting Machines

The hot-metal typesetting machine had been for many years the basic machine for setting type for books, magazines, and newspapers. The operator sits at a keyboard, similar to a typewriter keyboard, and depresses the keys indicated by the letters or numbers in the text. When each key is depressed, a brass mold (called a matrix) with the appropriate letter or number falls into place in a line. Molten lead is poured into the line of matrices and when hardened it becomes a line of type (hence, the name "hot metal"). A number of lines are clamped together to form a page of print. Except for the operator who works at the keyboard, the entire process is automatic. For example, after each line is set the matrices are returned automatically to the magazine.

Although there have been many improvements in hot-metal typesetting machines, the process in 1972 was essentially the same as that used at the turn of the century.

All hot-metal typesetting machines were produced by the Swiss Company in Lausanne. Until 1969, they also had been produced in the Elizabeth, New Jersey plant of the Typesetting Division, a U.S. subsidiary. Competitive products (described below) reduced the overall demand for hot-metal typesetting machines, and it was decided to concentrate all production of these machines in one location.

Retail selling prices in Switzerland ranged from SF 50,000 to SF 150,000, depending on the model. (A Swiss franc was worth approximately $.30 during this period.)

Photographic Typesetting Machines

Photographic typesetting machines use a photographic process for composing instead of lead slugs. The text is punched on perforated paper tape produced either by a computer or directly from a keyboard console. The paper tape is fed into the machine, and the text is composed onto film or paper by means of a spinning-disc phototypesetter. There is also a cathode-ray-tube machine in which type is composed on the tube (similar to a television tube) and photographed. Photographic typesetting machines are relatively expensive but are much more efficient than hot-metal typesetting machines for certain types of application where storage and updating are important. For example, the tapes for telephone books can be stored in a much smaller space than is required with lead type. Also, these tapes can be updated by computers, at much less cost than changing metal type. Where only one use is to be made of the type, as in printing newspapers, hot-metal typesetting is still more economical than photographic typesetting.

Photographic machines were manufactured in two locations in the United States. They sold from SF 230,000 to SF 4,000,000.

Other Products

IPE made several types of printing presses, which were manufactured in the United States, France and Italy. A printing press sold for as much as $1,000,000.

IPE also produced a variety of other equipment to service the publishing industry. These included offset presses, book binders, cutters, collators, gatherers, and trimmers. Each type of equipment was manufactured at a single location or, at most, two locations, in order to maximize manufacturing efficiency.

MANUFACTURING AND SALES

As indicated earlier, the corporation consisted of 16 divisions, divided into three groups. This case is concerned with two of the groups: the Printing Equipment Group and the International Group. Each division in these two groups had two types of activities: manufacturing of one or more of the product lines described earlier and marketing the entire line of printing equipment. Each division, therefore, sold the products it manufactured both to its own customers and to other divisions within the company. Also, it purchased equipment from other divisions and sold this equipment to its customers. International market boundaries were determined geographically; that is, each division had exclusive marketing rights to all International Publishing Equipment in a specific country.

INTERNATIONAL PUBLISHING EQUIPMENT OF SWITZERLAND

The Swiss Company manufactured hot-metal typesetting machines exclusively. It sold these machines to other divisions of International Publishing Equipment as well as to outside customers. Sales to outside customers were made directly by the division's internal sales force in its markets in Europe and by independent distributors in other markets, e.g., Africa. The Swiss Company purchased photographic typesetting machines, printing presses, offset presses, and so forth from other divisions within the company and sold this equipment directly to its customers or through independent distributors. The Company had exclusive marketing rights for all International Publishing Equipment products in Switzerland, Austria, and West Germany as well as certain parts of Africa and Asia. As indicated above, the Swiss Company sold directly in Europe and through independent distributors in other markets. In 1971, the Swiss Company purchased over SF 15,000,000 worth of equipment from eight divisions and sold over SF 10,000,000 worth of hot-metal typesetting machines and service parts to five divisions of the corporation. A little less than one-third of all sales of the Swiss Company were products purchased from other divisions of the company.

INTERDIVISIONAL RELATIONSHIPS

Much of the growth of IPE came from acquisitions. As a result of the historical independence of these divisions, their managers considered themselves to be directors of relatively autonomous units and tended to treat other divisions of the company in the same way that they treated outside suppliers and customers. This attitude was encouraged by the central management in the United States. Divisional managers were expected to operate on an "arm's-length" basis as they had before being merged into International Publishing Equipment. Although not specifically stated, this laissez-faire philosophy was evident from the following situations:

1. There were no transfer-pricing rules or regulations. Each division was free to negotiate whatever discounts it could get. (This tended to be, on occasion, an abrasive and time-consuming task.) However, divisions were not permitted to buy equipment from competitive producers if the particular type of equipment was available in International Publishing Equipment. For example, the Swiss Company could not buy photographic typesetting machines from a competitor. It was not required to sell machines made by another IPE division if it did not choose to do so, however. In general, transfer prices were calculated by subtracting a discount from the domestic retail list prices of the division manufacturing the product. A list of discounts applicable to products which the Swiss Company purchased is as follows:

Product	Price Range	Discount from Local Retail List Price
Offset presses	SF 150,000 to SF 780,000	10%
Printing presses	SF 2,500,000	negotiated
Cutters	SF 46,000	10%
Book binders	SF 25,000 to SF 30,000	20%
Photographic composing machines	SF 230,000 to SF 300,000	25%
Cathode-Ray-Tube composing machines	SF 1,750,000 to SF 2,000,000	5%
Collators	SF 360,000	10%
Gatherers, binders, trimmers	SF 150,000 to SF 2,000,000	negotiated

Hot-metal typesetting machines were sold to other divisions at discounts ranging between 10 percent and 20 percent from the Swiss retail prices.

2. When the production of hot-metal typesetting machines was moved to Switzerland, the manufacturing unit in Elizabeth, New Jersey was closed.

At that time, the Elizabeth Plant turned over to the Swiss Company certain blueprints and patents which it had held. It also provided technical assistance to the Lausanne Plant when it started to produce certain models that had previously been manufactured exclusively at the Elizabeth Plant. In payment for the drawings, patents, and services, the Swiss Company was required to pay a royalty of 5 percent of net sales, including interdivisional shipments, to the Typesetting Division, the U.S. subsidiary which had controlled the Elizabeth Plant.

3. The entire central staff in Cleveland consisted of only 100 people. Each division paid a management fee to the central office equal to 2½ percent of net sales.

4. Outside of the United States, cash was controlled by each division independently. Divisions paid each other as though they were independent companies. The official collection terms were net 30 to net 60 days. Actually, however, the payment time between divisions tended to be longer.

PRODUCT PROFITABILITY

In 1972, the Swiss Company expected to make a net loss on the resale of equipment purchased from other divisions of the company. In preparing the 1972 profit budget, Mr. Bois had been quite concerned about the prospects for the future. He had asked Mr. Olivier, the controller, to find out why the division was losing money on the resale business and what should be done about it. Mr. Olivier, working with Mr. Barrows, the cost accountant, studied the situation and concluded that the problem resulted from the relatively high prices that had to be paid for products that were resold, coupled with a low sales volume in relation to the expenses of the specialized sales force. The laid-down cost in Switzerland, Germany, and Austria, for most products, was so high relative to the potential selling price that there was little room to maneuver to meet competitive prices. Also, there was little incentive to spend money to sell these products aggressively because the amount of potential profit was simply too small to warrant this action.

Since profitability is considered to be a very important element in executive evaluation, Mr. Bois was extremely anxious to submit a reasonably high profit budget for 1973. However, since performance compared with profit budget were also a very important measure of executive accomplishment, Mr. Bois was also anxious to have a profit budget that he had a reasonable expectation of meeting. With one-third of his sales at the break-even point, or less, it did not appear that he would be able to earn a reasonable profit unless he was able to do something about the profit on the International Equipment products that the Swiss company purchased for resale.

At the meeting on September 21 one avenue that Mr. Bois explored with Mr. Olivier and Mr. Barrows was the possibility of negotiating increased discounts from the manufacturing divisions. It was decided that there was little likelihood of a substantial enough reduction to make any real difference. The discount structure had a long history and it appeared unlikely that the manufacturing divisions would voluntarily agree to a significant increase in the discounts from list price.

The next alternative studied was that of reducing substantially the expenses involved in resale operations. This could be done by reducing the size of the sales force and the product specialists, and also by cutting down heavily on advertising. A further possibility was to maintain high prices even though these would be noncompetitive in the market place. However, the consequence of both these actions was likely to reduce sales volume even further, so that any advantage from higher margins and reduced expenses would be lost, and the operation would still remain unprofitable.

The only other alternative seemed to be to stop selling all products not showing a reasonable profit. It was decided that this would not be acceptable to the central office in Cleveland. First, if this action were taken, International Publishing Equipment would be in considerable danger of losing its central European markets for many of its products. Secondly, although Olivier did not know precisely, he estimated that the variable manufacturing and distribution costs probably averaged no more than one-half of the price that the Swiss Company paid for the resale products. Consequently, the corporation would not allow the Swiss company simply to stop selling International Publishing Equipment products. Although, if asked, the central staff would refuse to allow a deliberate cutback on the resale of International Publishing Equipment products, Mr. Bois believed that it would be possible to curtail the sales of some of the less profitable items. The problem was that much of the Swiss company's selling expenses were relatively fixed and would therefore not go down as sales volume was reduced.

Transfer Price Proposal

At this point Mr. Barrows proposed that all resale products be transferred between divisions at the full manufacturing cost. After the product had been sold to an outside customer, the selling division's profit would be apportioned between the two divisions on a previously established percentage basis, taking into account the fixed and variable expenses of each of the divisions.

As Mr. Barrows pointed out, the division selling to the ultimate customer would be motivated to take action in the form of adjusting selling prices or increasing marketing costs to increase sales and maximize profits. Since this type of action would result in increased volume, both the manufacturing division profits and selling division profits would be maximized also. Mr. Barrows believed that, if agreement could be obtained on the principle of profit sharing after the product had been sold, the details could be agreed to subsequently.

Royalty Payments

During the meeting Mr. Bois also expressed concern about the 5 percent royalty payment that was being made to the Typesetting Division. This royalty was equal to nearly half of the net profit on the sales of the hot-metal typesetting machines. Mr. Bois believed that he could with advantage retain this money in the Swiss Company and use it on research and development projects.

He wondered about the justice of giving the Typesetting Division a bonus equal to 5 percent of Swiss Company sales simply because it had developed the hot-metal typesetting machine 60 years or so ago.

QUESTIONS

1. Evaluate Mr. Barrows' proposal. Will it reconcile the difference between divisional interests and corporate interests? If not, why not? If you disagree with this proposal, what would you recommend? What would be an equitable way to divide the profit between the divisions?

2. If some change in transfer pricing is appropriate, should this change also be made in pricing to the independent distributors? Why or why not?

3. What do you think about the royalty payments and management fees paid by the Swiss Company? Could these result in lost profits to the company? If so, how? Could there be any other disadvantages to such fees? What would you recommend in their place?

4. What, if any, changes would you make other than those covered above?

Chapter Fourteen

SERVICE

ORGANIZATIONS

In the preceding chapters our focus, at least implicitly, has been on organizations that produce and sell tangible goods. In this chapter, we discuss management control in organizations that provide intangible services, rather than tangible goods, with particular attention to organizations that provide professional services.

In the Standard Industrial Classification, service organizations include hotels, restaurants, and other lodging and eating establishments; barbershops, beauty parlors and other personal services; repair services; motion picture, television and other amusement and recreation services; legal services; and accounting, engineering, research/development, architecture and other professional service organizations. Because of the similarity of their management control problems, we also include banks, insurance companies and other financial institutions. Government agencies, educational organizations and most other nonprofit organizations are service organizations, but in this chapter we focus on profit-oriented organizations. Nonprofit organizations are discussed in Chapter 15. In the 20th century the fraction of the work force employed in service organizations has been steadily increasing, and in the United States currently more people are employed in these organizations than in organizations that produce goods.

SERVICE ORGANIZATIONS IN GENERAL

• Characteristics of Service Organizations

The production and sale of services, as contrasted with tangible goods, has several important implications for the management control process.

Absence of Inventory. Goods can be held in inventory, and this inventory is a buffer that dampens the impact on production activity of fluctuations in sales volume. Services cannot be stored. If the services available today are not sold today, the revenue from these services is lost forever. By contrast, in order to obtain the advantages of long production runs or for other sound reasons, manufacturers often produce goods for which they have no current orders. Up to a point, they need not be concerned about the fact that these goods are not sold currently; the revenue should be earned in the near future. Thus, because of inventory the manufacturer can earn revenue in the future from production capacity that is not sold today, but the service company has no such option.

To make this problem even worse, the resources available for sale in many service organizations are essentially fixed. In the short run, a hotel cannot increase the number of rooms that it offers for rent, and it does not reduce costs substantially by closing off some of its rooms. An accounting firm, law firm or other professional organization could conceivably lay off some of its professional personnel in times of low volume, but for morale reasons it is most reluctant to do so.

These facts cause great stress to be placed on planning for an amount of available services that is not in excess of what can be sold currently and on marketing efforts to sell these resources each day. For various reasons, full utilization of capacity may not be feasible; for example, a hotel has a fixed stock of guest rooms, but its occupancy rate may vary greatly by days of the week and by seasons of the year. The loss from unsold services is such an important factor that occupancy rates and similar indications of success in selling available services are normally key variables in service organizations of all types.

Labor Intensive. Service organizations tend to be labor intensive, that is, they tend to require relatively little capital per unit of output. It is more difficult to control the work of a labor-intensive organization than that of an operation whose work flow is paced or dominated by machinery. (Some service organizations are becoming capital intensive as computers replace clerks.)

Quantity Measurement. It is easy to keep track of the quantity of tangible goods, both during the production process and when the goods are sold, but it is not so easy to measure the quantity of many services. We can measure the number of patients that a physician treats in a day, for example, and even classify these visits by type of complaint, but this is by no means equivalent to measuring the amount of service that the physician provides to each of these patients. For many services, the amount rendered can be measured only in the crudest terms, if at all.

Quality Measurement. The quality of tangible goods can be inspected, and in most cases the inspection can be performed before goods are released to the customer. If the goods are defective, there is physical evidence of the nature of the defect. The quality of a service cannot be inspected in advance; at best, it can be inspected during the time that the service is being rendered to the client. Judgments as to the adequacy of the quality of most services are subjective; measuring instruments and objective quality standards do not exist. A public accounting firm can measure the number of hours spent on an audit, but not the thoroughness of the work done during those hours. A consulting firm has no objective way of appraising the soundness of its recommendations. A law firm may leave loopholes or ambiguities in documents it drafts that do not come to light until years later.

Historical Development. Cost accounting started in manufacturing companies because of the necessity for valuing work-in-process and finished goods inventories for financial statement purposes. These amounts provided raw data that was easily adapted to use, first for setting selling prices and then for other management problems. Standard cost systems, the separation of fixed and variable costs, and the analysis of variances, built on the foundation of actual cost systems, and the fact that managers in manufacturing companies were accustomed to using cost information facilitated the general adoption of these techniques. Until the last few decades, most books on cost accounting and related subjects dealt only with manufacturing companies.

Because service organizations have no inventories, they did not have the natural impetus to develop cost data that existed in manufacturing companies. It is only in fairly recent years that they have learned, usually by observations of practice in manufacturing companies, of the usefulness of cost information to management. Since World War II, the development of management control systems in service organizations has been rapid.

The literature on control techniques—standard costs, analysis of variances, statistical quality control, production control, inventory control—still tends to emphasize production situations rather than service organizations. For example, in 1972 the Price Commission placed great emphasis on the importance of increasing productivity as the only noninflationary way of justifying higher wage rates. It was able to establish quantitative annual productivity goals for each manufacturing industry, but no one was able even to devise reliable ways of measuring productivity in most service organizations, let alone suggest reasonable goals for improvement.

Although the absence of productivity data means that statistical comparisons are not possible, there is a general impression that service industries are less efficient than manufacturing industries. The following indicates the situation in the Operating Group at First National City Bank, one of the largest banks in the world, as recently as 1970, and the possibilities for improvement that were found to exist:

The Operating Group in 1970 was a discordant tangle of old-fashioned banking functions swamped by frantically accelerating volume; it cried out for austerity.

Costs were rising 15 percent a year; the backlog of uncorrected errors had topped 25,000; work-force turnover was at 50 percent. A decision was made to lower the boom: There would be no cost increases in 1970. "We squeezed out the fat," Mr. White, the new manager, says. "We became kind of serious. Whatever we forecast, we were going to make."

Quality standards were imposed, then time standards. And 111 Wall Street was pulled apart and nailed together again as 23 separate assembly lines, one for each kind of bank transaction. New generations of computers were spawned; overtime was slashed; turnover dropped to 10 percent while total Operating Group employment fell from more than 10,000 to the current 6,500. As efficiency increases, "the processing becomes clearer, more understandable, and hence better," Mr. White says. "Service to customers is improved."[1]

Size. With some notable exceptions, service organizations are relatively small and operate in a single location. Top management in such organizations can personally observe what is going on and personally motivate employees. Thus, there is less need for a sophisticated management control system, with profit centers and heavy reliance on formal reports of performance. (Nevertheless, even a small organization needs a budget, a regular comparison of actual performance against a budget, and the other essential ingredients of a management control system.)

Implications for Management Control

The characteristics listed in the preceding section suggest that there are some differences between management control systems in service organizations and those in manufacturing organizations. These are differences in degree, rather than in kind, however. The essential features are the same in both types of organizations. In both, planning is done in terms of programs and responsibility centers, including profit centers and investment centers for organization units that meet the criteria described in Chapters 6 and 8. The management control process in both organizations involves the steps of programming, budgeting, the measurement of performance, and the appraisal of that performance.

Because of their relatively recent development, systems currently found in service organizations tend to be less advanced than those in manufacturing organizations. Because of the difficulty of measuring both the quantity and the quality of output, judgments about both the efficiency and the effectiveness of performance are more subjective than is the case when output consists of physical goods, which means that there is more room for legitimate differences of opinion about performance. Managers are coming to recognize that performance is not easy to measure; this suggests that a search for better tools for improving its measurement is likely to be eminently worthwhile.

In their details, the management control systems of various types of service organizations vary widely. We shall limit the discussion in this chapter to two types of organizations in which special problems exist, namely, financial institutions and professional organizations.

---

[1] *Wall Street Journal,* June 6, 1975, p. 1.

FINANCIAL INSTITUTIONS

Commercial Banks

In the 1960s commercial banks began to create profit centers for their branches and for their corporate trust, personal trust, investment, and other revenue producing units. In doing so, they had to solve problems not faced by an industrial company.

Perhaps the most serious problem is that of measuring the number that corresponds to gross profit in a manufacturing company, that is, the difference between the cost of obtaining money and the revenue earned on loaning or investing that money. Money is obtained by inducing customers to make deposits. (It is also obtained by borrowing from other financial institutions, but the cost of these funds can be readily measured.) For savings deposits, the bank pays interest, and this interest, plus the cost of servicing accounts, is the cost of money obtained from savings accounts. For checking accounts, however, cost is much more difficult to measure. Commercial banks are prohibited by government regulation from paying interest; therefore, in order to induce customers to make deposits in checking accounts, banks provide a number of free services. The most obvious of these is the processing of checks and deposits, but there are a number of others, ranging from informal advice to handling payroll records and accounts receivable records at no cost or at a price that is less than these services cost.

The problem is further complicated by the fact that some fraction of many corporate checking accounts consists of compensating balances, that is, funds that the corporation is required to leave on deposit as a condition of a loan that the bank has made to it. Conceptually, a compensating balance reduces the net amount of funds made available to the borrower and thus increases his effective interest cost and the rate of return that the bank derives from the loan. As a practical matter, the problem of treating compensating balances separately from other checking account balances is so difficult that banks do not attempt to make the separation in their formal control system, although they may do so in special analyses.

These problems make it difficult to measure the profitability of individual branches and other profit centers.

Some branches typically generate more money in deposits than they loan out; they are "deposit-heavy," while other branches are "loan heavy." Some profit centers make only loans, using funds generated by deposits made in the branches. In order to measure the profitability of these profit centers, the cost of money must be correctly calculated. If it is set too low, too much profit will be reported for the loan-heavy units; whereas if it is set too high, too much profit will be reported for the deposit-heavy units. The problem is further complicated by the fact that government regulations require that a certain proportion of deposits be held in reserves on which low interest rates, in some cases zero, are earned. Arriving at the cost of money is a difficult transfer price problem, and banks have devoted much attention in recent years to the best way of setting this price. Partly in order to arrive at a sound transfer price, and partly for other reasons, banks have also started to analyze carefully the real cost of services that they provide to customers and to measure the profitability of individual customer accounts.

Problems of joint costs and joint revenues are also prevalent in banks. Accounting and check processing are usually done centrally, and the costs of such work must be equitably assessed to the branches. A customer who maintains an account in one branch may use the services of another branch, or may be induced to use services provided by headquarters unit. The branches that "sell" such services should be given appropriate credit, but this is difficult to do in practice.

With these important exceptions, the management control systems in commercial banks are similar to those described in earlier chapters.

Insurance Companies

Insurance companies also deal with money. They collect money in the form of premiums, invest it, and subsequently pay out money in the form of claims, death benefits, or annuities. Many years may elapse between the time a policy is written and the time when benefit payments are completed. The profitability of the policy cannot be known with certainty until the last payment is made, but for management control purposes the company cannot, of course, wait; it needs information currently.

Traditionally, insurance companies measured the performance of their responsibility centers by rough rules of thumb, such as the amount of first-year premiums or the face amount of insurance written. In recent years, they have begun to explore the possibility of measuring the approximate profitability of a policy at the time it is written. For example, the annual premium on an ordinary life policy is arrived at by taking into account life expectancy, estimated investment income, selling costs, and recurring operating costs over the life of the policy, adjusted if necessary to meet rates charged by other companies. Each of these components is set conservatively; for example, the mortality table used in setting premiums understates the actual life expectancy. The ultimate profitability of the policy arises from the difference between these conservative estimates and the actual amounts experienced The true expectations can be estimated, and from them the expected present value of the policy can be determined. Thus, a measure of profitability can be calculated at the time the policy is sold.[2]

With this measure of profitability as a starting point, insurance companies can organize their sales branches as profit centers, and they can also measure

---

[2] For a full description see James S. Hekimian, *Management Control in Life Insurance Branches* (Boston: Division of Research, Harvard Business School, 1965).

the performance of the investment, actuarial, and other parts of the company by comparing actual results with those used in the calculations of the present value of a policy's profitability.

PROFESSIONAL ORGANIZATIONS

Research/development organizations, law firms, accounting firms, medical clinics, engineering firms, consulting firms, investment firms, and advertising agencies are examples of organizations whose product is professional services. These firms differ from manufacturing companies and from other service companies in ways that have a substantial impact on management control problems and practices.

Characteristics

Organizational Goals. In a manufacturing company, and also in some service organizations such as hotels, the name of the game is return on assets employed. The organization is successful if it earns a satisfactory return on assets employed, and capital investment decisions are made according to this return-on-investment criterion. The assets can be measured, and they are reported on the balance sheet. In a professional organization, the amount of tangible assets employed is relatively insignificant. The principal resource of the organization is the skill of its professional staff, and return on investment, as conventionally calculated, provides neither a basis for measuring success nor a criterion for decision making. Thus, the conceptual foundation on which our discussion of measuring the profitability of profit centers and investment centers in manufacturing companies was based, does not apply to these organizations.

As noted above, the output of a professional organization is intangible, is therefore not easy to measure in quantitative terms, and is difficult or impossible to measure in qualitative terms.

Production Standards. The work done by professionals tends to be non-repetitive. No two consulting jobs or research/development projects are quite the same. Thus, it is difficult both to plan the time required for a task and also to set reasonable standards for task performance. This obviously makes it difficult to judge how satisfactory the performance was. Some tasks are essentially repetitive; the drafting of simple wills, deeds, sales contracts, and other documents, the taking of a physical inventory, and certain medical and surgical procedures, are examples. The development of standards for such tasks is worthwhile, although in using these standards, unusual circumstances affecting them must be taken into account. For example, although the drafting of a deed for residential property and the related title search may be a cut-and-dried process in the majority of instances, there are enough situations involving ambiguity in the title or special restrictions in the deed that a "standard time" for deed preparation is at best only a general guide.

With some important exceptions, such as lawyers, professionals are reluctant to keep track of how they spend their time, and this complicates the task of measuring performance. This reluctance seems to have its roots in tradition, and it usually can be overcome if top management is willing to put appropriate emphasis on the necessity of accurate time reporting.

Marketing.   In most professional organizations no clear dividing line exists between marketing efforts and production efforts. In some, such as law, medicine, and accounting, the reason is that the ethical codes of the profession prohibit overt marketing efforts. Since marketing is an essential activity in any organization, if it cannot be conducted openly, it takes the form of personal contacts, speeches, articles, golf games, and similar activities. These activities are carried on by the professionals, who correspond to the production organization in an industrial company. In professions which permit explicit marketing efforts, the professional staff is responsible for developing leads, preparing proposals, and carrying on discussions with prospective clients, all of which are activities that would be conducted by the marketing department in an industrial company. (A few firms do have identifiable market research, proposal writing, and similar groups that are responsible for part of the marketing function, but even in these firms much of the marketing effort is carried on by the professional staff.)

Because marketing is not an identifiable function and because new business is generated by the part-time activities of professional staff members who are primarily engaged in doing production work, it is difficult to assign appropriate credit to the person responsible for the generation of revenue. In a consulting firm, for example, a new engagement may result from a conversation between a member of the firm and an acquaintance in the client company, from the reputation of one of the firm's professionals, as an outgrowth of an existing engagement, from a speech or article, as well as from an explicit written proposal. Moreover, the professional who is responsible for obtaining the engagement may not personally be involved in doing the work. Thus, the practice of assigning responsibility for obtaining a specified share of the market and of measuring performance against this standard, which is common in an industrial company, is difficult, often impossible, to follow in a professional organization. In professions that frown on marketing, firms tend not to give much, if any, thought to the marketing mix, the proper positioning of the product line, and other fundamental marketing concepts.

Professionals.   Professionals often have motivations that are inconsistent with good resource utilization, and their success, as perceived by their professional colleagues, reflects these motivations.

Professionals are motivated by dual standards: (a) those of their organizations, and (b) those of their professional colleagues. The former standards are related to organizational objectives; the latter may be inconsistent with organizational objectives. The rewards for achieving organizational objectives may be less potent than those for achieving professional objectives.

Those professionals who are departmental managers tend to work only part time on management activities. They spend a substantial part of their time doing the same work that their subordinates do. The head of the surgical department in a hospital does surgery. The senior partner in the local office of an accounting firm participates actively in audit engagements. In organizations not dominated by professionals, management tends to be a fulltime job, and managers do not do the same type of work that their subordinates do.

Many professionals, by nature, prefer to work independently. Examples are academicians, researchers, and physicians. Because the essence of management is getting things done through people, professionals with such a temperament are not naturally suited to the role either of managers or of subordinates.

In a professional organization, the *professional quality* of the people is of primary importance, and other considerations are secondary. Therefore, managers in professional organizations spend much of their time recruiting good people and then seeing to it that they are kept happy. The manager has correspondingly less time available for those aspects of the job that relate to efficiency. In a professional organization, the practice of recruiting many and then weeding out unsatisfactory workers is expensive, so management must concentrate on careful preselection.

In some professions, promotion is geared to criteria established by the profession and tends to be a function of time (e.g., four years for assistant professor; eight years for Army major). These criteria may not place much emphasis on efficiency and effectiveness. (There are exceptions; exceptional individuals may shortcut the usual rules if they earn the esteem and recognition of their *professional* superiors.) In some situations, promotions may be influenced by outside qualifications such as degrees, prizes, and published articles; these are not always an accurate reflection of the individual's worth to the organization.

Except for professions such as accounting and management consulting, professional education does not usually include education in management and quite naturally stresses the importance of the profession rather than of management. For this and other reasons, professionals tend to look down on managers. For example, John Kenneth Galbraith, a prominent professor of economics, was quoted as saying: "It (Harvard Business School) is a good school. We should be grateful to it for training people who will shoulder the dull, tedious administrative jobs in organizations."[3] In some hospitals, the administrator's status and pay are below that of all professional people; the chief administrator may not even attend the Board of Trustees meetings in which the professionals and the trustees decide on policies.

Financial incentives tend to be less effective with professional people either because they consider their current compensation to be adequate or because their primary satisfaction comes from their work.

Although the leadership of an organization may require more management

---

[3] *Wall Street Journal*, April 1, 1969, p. 1.

skills than professional skills, tradition often requires that the manager be a professional. Traditionally, the head of a research/development organization was a scientist; the president of a university, a professor; the head of a hospital, a physician. This tradition seems to be diminishing, however.

Professionals tend to give inadequate weight to the financial implication of their decisions. The physician feels that no limit should be placed on the amount spent to save a human life, although in a world of limited resources such an attitude is unrealistic.

Differences Among Organizations.   The characteristics described above are tendencies which are applicable to varying degrees in most professional organizations. There are also differences among professions and among the firms within a given profession that are relevant for management control.

In some organizations, professionals work as a team on an engagement; in others they tend to work as individuals with perhaps some temporary assistance from colleagues. Research/development organizations, accounting firms, engineering firms and consulting firms are examples of the former type, and physicians, some law firms, and investment advisory firms are examples of the latter. The former type requires a matrix organization and the project controls that are discussed in Chapter 16.

Organizations also vary in the proportion of support personnel to professional personnel. In law firms, the proportion is low, that is, each lawyer receives little, if any, staff assistance; in medicine it is low, but growing because of the increasing use of paramedical personnel. In accounting firms and research/development firms, the proportion is relatively high. These firms understand the basic economic principle of division of labor with its favorable impact on profitability. In essence, if a professional sells only his own time, the firm's income is limited by the number of professional man-hours in a working day; but if some revenue producing work is done by lower paid people, the firm's income can be increased by the profit margin on such work.

Organizations also, of course, vary in size and complexity. In small organizations with only one office, the management control system can be relatively simple and informal.

Some implications of these characteristics of professional organizations are discussed in following sections.

Programming and Budgeting

In general, formal programming and budgeting systems are not as well developed in professional organizations as in industrial companies of comparable size. With respect to programming, at least part of the explanation is that in professional organizations the need for a formal programming system is not so great. In industrial companies most program decisions involve commitments to plant and equipment which have a predictable effect for years into the future on both capacity and on costs, and which, once made, are essentially irrevocable. In a professional organization, the principal assets are people, and although short-run fluctuations in personnel levels are avoided wherever possible, changes in the size and composition of the staff are easier to make and are more easily reversed than changes in the capacity of a physical plant. Thus, the program of a professional organization tends to consist only of a long-range staffing plan, rather than a full-blown program for all aspects of the firm's organization.

Professional organizations, particularly research/development organizations, do acquire capital assets, and they therefore need a procedure for making capital acquisition decisions and for following up on asset acquisitions, that is similar to that in industrial companies. The return-on-assets criterion cannot be used for many such decisions, however, so management's intuitive judgment is correspondingly more important.

The fact that budgeting systems are less well developed in professional organizations is difficult to explain, for the need for a formal spending commitment by managers of responsibility centers is at least as great in these organizations as in industrial companies. Probably the explanation is that professional organizations, like service organizations generally, are late in adopting good management control techniques. In preparing budgets, many professional firms do not make full use of such data as do exist, that is, data on past performance in the firm, on costs in other firms that are collected and published by trade associations, and on the behavior of costs as volume changes.

A good budgeting process helps to insure that departments are in balance with one another, and particularly that support departments are at an optimum size to service the professional staff; it determines the size and scope of the firm's operations for the coming year, particularly its capacity to take new business; it identifies the additional staff and other resources that must be acquired; it states permitted levels of spending, and it provides a basis for motivating desired spending performance and for judging actual performance.

Pricing

The criterion of return on assets employed provides both a conceptual basis for analyzing and explaining the behavior of the prices of industrial products in general, and also a practical guide to pricing in individual companies. Since assets, in the conventional accounting sense, are relatively unimportant in professional organizations, the return-on-assets criterion does not provide a rationale for pricing in these organizations.

The problem can be seen most clearly in the case of cost-type government contracts. For contracts that involve the production of physical goods, a price that is equal to cost plus a profit margin based on assets employed is equitable both to the contractor and to the government. If this pricing policy is used for contracts involving professional services, however, the firm would receive only an insignificant amount of profit since it employs relatively small amounts of assets. Clearly, the professional team has a value to the government that is greater than the sum of the compensation paid to individual members of the team. Otherwise, the government would be well advised to hire the persons as individuals, rather than contracting with the professional firm for their services at a higher cost. This higher value of the organization arises for any or all of the following reasons:

1. The firm has assembled a group of competent persons. Considerable time and effort would be required for the government to go through the process of recruiting and screening individuals so as to obtain persons of comparable ability.

2. The firm has identified the skills of these persons, and given them assignments commensurate with these skills. Considerable effort would be required for the government to do this with a group of individuals.

3. The firm has increased the value of these individuals both by skills developed on the job, and by paying for formal training programs.

4. The firm has organized these individuals, taking account not only of professional skills, but also of personality "fits," managerial ability, and other factors.

5. The firm has developed policies and procedures that are useful in assuring that work is done efficiently and effectively.

6. The firm accepts responsibility for the quality, cost, and ontime delivery of its product.

7. The firm assumes risks, both the risk of monetary loss if actual costs exceed prescribed limits and also risks to its reputation if the work is not well done.

8. The firm must absorb the costs of professional personnel when they have no revenue-producing work. The government uses the professional resources only for a limited purpose and for a limited time, and pays only for the time that it uses.

If it is granted that a professional organization is entitled to some profit that is unrelated to the amount of assets employed, the question then arises: how should this profit be calculated? No satisfactory answers to this question have yet emerged.

Many professional firms are organized as partnerships, so that the total of compensation for individual services plus profit winds up eventually as partnership compensation, with the line between these two components being fairly arbitrary. Indeed, for many consulting contracts, the government pays no "profit" as such, although it knows full well that an amount equivalent to profit is built into the daily rates for professionals that are set forth in the contract. For other contracts, the government allows a fee of a few percentage points above costs. The principal determinant for the amount of the fee is tradition. For example, architectural firms have for many years operated on a fee schedule that has never been thoroughly studied as to its rationale.

Lacking any conceptual basis for determining a profit margin, professional firms tend to price strictly according to tradition. In each profession, there is a traditional fee structure, usually related primarily to the time of the professionals, and firms use this structure in their pricing. The fee structure varies widely from one profession to another, and in ways that are unrelated to supply-demand relationships. For example, it is relatively low for scientists and relatively high for accountants.

Control of Operations

Because the resources that a professional organization offers for sale are professional services which cannot be stored in inventory, measures that insure that these services are used the highest feasible percentage of the time are especially important in such organizations. Much attention is, or should be, given to scheduling the time of professionals. The *billed time ratio,* which is the ratio of hours billed to total professional hours available, is watched closely. If, in order to use otherwise idle time for marketing or for public service reasons, some engagements are billed at lower than normal rates, the resulting price variance is another variable that may warrant close attention.

The inability to set standards for task performance, the desirability of carrying out work by teams, the consequent problems of managing a matrix organization, and the behavioral characteristics of professionals, all complicate the planning and control of the day-to-day operations in a professional organization. When the work is done by project teams, control is focused on projects. There is need for a written plan for each project and for timely reports that compare actual performance with planned performance in terms of cost, schedule, and quality, as described in Chapter 16.

The measurement and control of quality is difficult, and procedures used for this purpose are often inadequate. Indeed, the current crisis resulting from the tremendous increase in malpractice payments in the medical profession, and the less dramatic but nevertheless significant increase in suits against the accounting profession are, in part, the result of the failure of these professions to set up adequate quality control procedures. The crisis is leading to increased attention to such procedures.

Because quality usually cannot be measured by physical instruments or by the other inspection procedures found in industrial companies, special control techniques are needed. Perhaps the most important is the creation of an atmosphere such that project leaders are willing to reveal actual or incipient problems to their superiors, rather than hiding them until it is too late to take remedial action. In such an atmosphere, progress reports are important control devices; whereas in an environment in which unpleasant reports invariably lead to destructive criticism, rather than helpful suggestions, the reports resemble works of fiction.

Progress reports are paperwork, which professionals tend to dislike, but they are nevertheless essential. Report requirements that lead to voluminous descriptions of trivial matters should, of course, be avoided. In particular, if the project is truly proceeding without difficulty, extensive documentation of this fact is a waste of time. By contrast, setting up a list of a relatively few (say 10 percent) of the projects that are in trouble and requiring special reports on these projects can be a helpful procedure.

At best, formal reports are unlikely to provide the principal means of finding out about quality problems. Informal conversations, regularly scheduled meetings, and the manager's sensitivity to hints of trouble received from various sources are likely to be much more important.

Especially in professions where public criticism of quality is increasing, internal audit procedures are being introduced as a means of controlling quality. In accounting firms, the report of an audit is reviewed by a partner other than the one who is responsible for it. The proposed design of a building is reviewed by architects who are not actively involved in the project. Under recently enacted legislation, the performance of physicians will be reviewed by peer groups set up for this purpose.

Performance Measurement and Appraisal

At the extremes, the performance of professionals is easy to measure; that is, it is easy to identify and take appropriate action about professionals who do sloppy, incompetent, or inadequate work on the one hand and those who do brilliant work on the other. Appraisal of the large percentage of professionals who are well within either extreme is much more difficult. In some situations, objective measures of performance are available: the recommendations of an investment analyst can be compared with actual market behavior of the securities; the accuracy of a surgeon's diagnosis can be verified by an examination of the tissue that he removed and his skill can be measured by the success ratio of his operations. These measures are of course subject to appropriate qualifications. In most circumstances, however, the assessment of performance is a matter of human judgment. These judgments may be made by superiors, peers, self, subordinates, or clients.

Most common are judgments made by superiors. Professional organizations are increasingly using formal systems to collect such performance appraisals and to use them as a basis for personnel decisions and for discussion with the person involved. Some of these systems require numerical ratings of specified attributes of performance and provide for a weighted average of these ratings. Compensation may be tied, in part, to these numerical ratings. In a matrix organization, performance is judged both by the person's project leader and by the head of the functional unit that is his organizational "home."

Appraisals by a professional's peers, his subordinates or himself are occasionally part of a formal control system. In all cases, information that a superior receives from these sources is an informal input to the judgmental process.

Expressions of satisfaction or dissatisfaction from clients are also an important basis for judging performance, although such expressions may not be forthcoming in many engagements. One firm that sells investment advice to institutional clients keeps a record of letters of commendation or criticism received from these clients, classifies these according to the analysts who made the relevant recommendations, and uses this information as part of its performance evaluation system.

For reasons given earlier, the measurement of the revenue generated by a professional is often not feasible. A few firms have a formal system for doing this. At the time an engagement is contracted for, the persons involved agree among themselves on the percentage of the fee that is equitably attributed to each of them, and revenue associated with each professional is developed by applying these percentages to the actual fee earned on the engagement. Such a procedure can work if there is goodwill and a minimum of wrangling among the persons involved.

The budget can be used as the basis for measuring cost performance, and the actual time required can be compared with the planned time. Budgeting and control of discretionary expenses is as important in a professional firm as in a manufacturing company. A professional's contribution to the firm's profitability is only to a minor extent reflected in such financial measures, however. The major contribution is related to the quality of his work, and its appraisal must be largely subjective. Furthermore, the appraisal must be made currently; it cannot wait until one learns whether a new building or a new control system actually works well or whether a bond indenture has a flaw.

HUMAN RESOURCE ACCOUNTING

The principal asset of a professional organization is its professional staff. The value of this staff does not appear in its balance sheet, however. From 1967 on, accounting literature contains many references to the desirability of accounting for the asset value of human resources in a way that is analogous to the conventional accounting treatment of physical and financial resources.[4]

The only application of this idea in a real situation reported in the literature is in R. G. Barry Corporation, a medium size industrial company. Since 1968 this company has prepared and reported supplementary financial statements in which "management assets" were listed as a balance sheet item. The amounts reported were arrived at by assigning estimated recruiting, hiring, and training costs to persons in each level of management from first-line supervisor on up.

Those involved in installing the system at R. G. Barry stated that it was a basic premise and a testable hypothesis that "decisions will be made differ-

---

[4] See especially Eric G. Flamholtz, *Human Resource Accounting* (Encino, Calif.: Dickerson Publishing Co., Inc.), 1974.

ently and human assets will be managed more effectively with the addition of information provided by a human resources accounting system."[5] Nevertheless, no documented evidence that human resource accounting has had a significant effect on decision making at R. G. Barry has been reported in the literature.

The label "human resource accounting" has been applied to other analytical devices, such as the measurement of the effectiveness of training programs, the cost effectiveness of measures to reduce employee turnover, and the like. There is nothing especially new about these techniques. To reduce ambiguity, it seems desirable to restrict the term "human resource accounting" to accounting, that is, to a formal system for recording the status and flow of economic resources. Viewed in this way, it cannot be said that human resource accounting has had any significant amount of acceptance by business, notwithstanding the contrary impression that is given by the numerous references to it in the literature.

The basic weakness in the present approach is that valuing human resources at their hiring and training costs far understates the real value of these resources to a company. Conceptual alternatives, such as what it would cost to replace the organization's human resources or the discounted net cash flows that human resources are expected to generate, are completely impractical, even more impractical than the concept that the value of a physical asset is the present value of its future earnings.

In assessing damages in negligence suits involving loss of life, and in the analysis of certain social issues, the value of a human being is taken as being the present value of the person's expected future earnings. The effect of this approach is to attribute a high value to young people compared with old people, to males compared with females, to whites compared with members of minority groups, and to business executives compared with clergymen and others in low-paying occupations. More importantly, this approach has the conceptual weakness that it does not take into account the food, shelter and other resources that persons consume at the same time that they generate earnings. In any event, this approach holds no promise as a way of valuing human resources in an organization.

An alternative approach, which does hold promise, starts with the premise that a person's current earnings are an indication of what that person is worth to the company. Just as an office building that generates $50,000 of net rentals is worth twice as much as one that generates $25,000, so a $50,000 professional can be said to be worth twice as much as a $25,000 professional. The value of the office building can be found by capitalizing the net rentals at an appropriate rate, which is the cost of capital. By analogy, the value of

---

[5] R. Lee Brummet, Eric G. Flamholtz, and William C. Pyle, "Human Resource Accounting: A Tool to Increase Managerial Effectiveness." *Management Accounting,* August 1969.

the professionals might be found by capitalizing their current compensation at an appropriate rate, but no one has so far suggested a rational approach to the determination of this rate. Further, the analogy is weakened by the fact that an organization does not own its professionals as it owns its office buildings, although as a practical matter the probability that a professional will stay with the organization can be estimated sufficiently closely to allow for this difference.

The need for a method of valuing human resources was pointed out in connection with the discussion of pricing in the preceding section. Human resource values would also be useful in many other types of management decisions. Thus although there have been practically no worthwhile accomplishments to date, the subject is important, and continued research on it is eminently worthwhile.

Case 14-1

Harley Associates, Inc.

In 1975 Harley Associates, Inc. was one of America's largest advertising agencies. Advertising agencies are retained by many major corporations to assist them in the development and implementation of campaigns to promote sales. Two of the principal groups of advertising work in which agencies engage are the development of strategy and plans for new products, and the maintenance and improvement of the market share of established products. Generally speaking, the most successful partnership between advertisers and agencies are those of long duration. Harley Associates had worked with many of its present clients for more than twenty years, and some other agencies have been associated with clients for as long as a hundred years.

Advertising agencies are remunerated by their clients in one of two ways. First there is the commission basis, whereby the agency receives a rebate of 15 percent of gross billings from the medium in which the advertisement is placed.[1] Out of this amount the agency must meet all of its expenses. The other system, called the fee system, has many variations, but in general the client is billed for specific amounts of work done on his behalf by the agency. This may be on a cost-plus basis or involve a retaining fee plus a reimbursement of expenditures. Harley Associates had worked under various fee arrangements, but its preference was for the 15 percent commission system since it considered that such a system offered greater benefits to both the client and the agency.

Organization

Harley Associates was organized into five divisions of management:
Account Management. The account supervisor and his staff formed the

---

[1] For example, if Harley placed a full-page ad for a client's product in a magazine whose full-page rate was $10,000, Harley would collect $10,000 from the client, but would have to pay the magazine only $8,500.

principal day-to-day contact between the agency and the client organizations. It was their function to work with the client in the development of the marketing plan. In addition, they acted as a liaison among the other areas of management within the agency to coordinate activities on the client's account.

Creative Management. The creative department conceived and developed advertising copy and art work required for prints and advertisements.

Information Management. This group was responsible for planning and conducting copy and market research programs, and for advising on merchandising and product promotion opportunities. It also maintained the agency reference library, and a training group for teaching the sales personnel of clients.

Media Management. Within the framework of the market plan developed by the account manager, this group developed a media strategy that set forth the desired objectives, and then developed a media plan aimed at accomplishing the strategy most effectively. The relations between the agency and the advertising media, including the buying of space and time and the planning of advertisements, was the responsibility of this group.

Administrative Management. This group was concerned with the internal management of the agency, dealing with personnel, financial and office services areas.

As noted above, the direct contact between the agency and the client organization was through the account supervisor. It was the function of account management to coordinate the work with the client and map out the marketing, creative and media strategies to promote the client's product. When an account supervisor was promoted to the position, he would begin with one account, and as he developed he would assume the responsibility for additional accounts. There was also a certain amount of turnover of accounts among the account supervisors so that each supervisor seldom stayed on the same account for more than a few years. The turnover required the supervisors to learn all about a new business each time they were transferred. This was obviously an expensive procedure, but Harley Associates considered it to be an excellent investment. The rationale behind it was that if the person was of high quality, he would be continually on the lookout for new challenges.

The "New Client" Decision

One of the most important decisions faced by the top management of an advertising agency is that of accepting an assignment from a new client. Certain firms have to be excluded from consideration because of the competitive constraint: an agency cannot accept a new assignment involving a good or service (i.e., "product") which is competitive with that of another client.

With the above exception, Harley Associates would consider any new client which satisfied two criteria. If the client had a satisfactory business reputation and was of good standing in the business community generally, and if the product seemed to the agency to be likely to satisfy a consumer need, the agency would be interested in accepting the assignment.

In assessing the profit potential of the assignment, the agency used its experience of past costs. Harley Associates was serving over 150 products for 33 clients in 1975, covering a wide range of product groups. On the basis of the cost data for these, an estimate of the cost of servicing the product under consideration would be made. An estimate would also be made of the amount of advertising required to build up the product to the desired market share, and the amount needed to maintain it thereafter. Since an advertising allowance was usually built into the cost of the product, the agency could determine the amount they were going to be able to spend on the basis of certain volume assumptions. If the advertising allowance seemed to be sufficient to build up and to sustain the product, given the estimates of requirements, there would be a prima facie case for accepting the assignment.

The Introduction of a New Product

When a new product was being considered, the problem of estimating the costs of its introduction was acute. As a first step, the information management group tested the market to determine if there were a consumer need for the product and, if so, to isolate the consumer benefit. This procedure was not the introduction of the product to a limited market (Harley Associates referred to this as test marketing), but rather a gauging of consumer acceptance of the product. To aid in this Harley Associates maintained a research panel of several thousand ordinary citizens around the country.

If it was satisfactorily established that a consumer need for the product existed, a creative strategy was developed, based largely upon the perceived consumer benefit. The product would then be test marketed in order to test the effectiveness of the execution of the strategy. If the first test was unsuccessful, it was assumed that the selling message had not gotten across to the consumer and a change would be attempted in the execution of the strategy. The creative strategy itself was not subjected to question in this process. Such changes were time-consuming, both for the agency and for the client.

After the test marketing was completed, the agency advised the client of its opinion on the probable outcome of launching the product on a full-scale basis. It was only after the decision to proceed had been taken and the advertising expenditures built up that the agency received significant revenue from the assignment. As well as covering current expenses, this revenue had to recompense the agency for the initial costs, so the management judgment early in the assignment concerning the likelihood of success of the product was extremely critical to the profitability of the agency.

Support of an Established Product

The advertising strategy involved in the support of an established product differed from that used in introducing a new one. The uncertainty attached to the market performance of a new product was considerably less acute in the case of an established product, although the constant possibility of product obsolescence remained. In essence, the function of advertising in supporting a product was to maintain constant exposure of the product's advantages to the ultimate user. The agency personnel and the client's marketing department were constantly seeking new ways of presenting the product to consumers with the objective of expanding market share.

Typically a new maintenance campaign would be started after the existing campaign had run for a predetermined period of time. Judgment was involved in deciding how often a new campaign should be initiated. In addition, a drop in the product's market share might be a sign that a new campaign was required. Adjusting to meet competitive advances was an important part of the maintenance of a product.

When a new campaign was being planned the account supervisor would instruct the creative department to prepare plans for a strategy. The account supervisor and his staff would then meet, perhaps several times, with the sales personnel of the client to discuss the plans. Eventually a strategy would be agreed upon and the advertisement, commercial, or other promotional device prepared. The agency's media department would then arrange for the execution of the promotion as specified by the account supervisor.

Profitability of an Assignment

An important part of the agency top management's job was the assessment of the profitability of an account.

The most profitable clients to the agency were those using each advertisement frequently. The major expenses involved in the agency's work were incurred preceding the completion of the commercial or the copy. Thereafter, the work involved in placing the advertisement with the media was small compared with the 15 percent commission obtainable. Obviously, the more a given advertisement was used, the greater was the probability that the contribution (commission less placement costs) would amount to more than the cost of the preparatory work. If, on the other hand, the client's marketing strategy required constant development of new copy, which would be used only once or twice before it was considered obsolete, the agency's profits would be smaller.

The size of the client might also affect the profitability of an account. If numerous people in the client's organization had to clear an advertising plan, which was more likely to be the case with larger clients, this took a great deal of agency personnel's time and effort. The repeated conferences and revisions involved might push up the agency's costs to the extent of rendering the account unprofitable.

Other considerations involved in the top management decision on the retention of an account were frequently of greater significance than cost considerations. For example, even if a particular product was judged to be unprofitable to the agency, the agency might continue to carry this product because of the profitability of other products being carried for the same client. Sometimes a certain product line had to be maintained by the client for competitive purposes even though the client was aware that the line was not showing a profit for him. If this were the case, the amounts spent on advertising such a product would frequently be small as the client would not be anxious to promote the sales of a losing product. The agency would continue, in many cases, to handle such an account. At the same time the agency would attempt to minimize its own expenditures involved in the advertising of such a product.

Cost Collection

In an effort to determine the cost associated with servicing a given account, close attention was paid to the amount of payroll costs associated with that account. Typically, payroll would amount to between 60 percent and 65 percent of the gross revenues of the agency. In many agencies expenses other than payroll ranged from 20–25% of gross revenues leaving the remaining 10–20% as profit before tax.

All employees except those in administrative management filed time sheets on which they recorded the time they had spent on specific accounts during the previous week. Anyone in the administrative department whose work could be allotted to a specific account would also file a time sheet. From the time sheets, 85% of the total payroll cost could be charged directly to the various accounts. Since 85% of the payroll was direct, and 65% of total cost was payroll, it followed that about 55% of cost was direct payroll. This led to a rule-of-thumb method for judging the profitability of an account. If the direct payroll of the account was less than 55% of the gross revenue from the account it was assumed to be profitable.

Of the nonpayroll expenses, about 20% (i.e., 4–5% of revenues) were directly chargeable to the job. Included in direct expenses were travel, entertainment, the cost of rough copies, copy research work, and pretesting of copy. Indirect nonpayroll expenses included rent, which was the largest, telephone expenses, and so on. These indirect expenses were allocated to assignments on the basis of direct labor payroll.

One feature of Harley Associates' cost accounting system which was unusual in the business was that the figures on the profitability of an account were made available only to the chairman, the president, and the treasurer of the company. This was done so that the enthusiasm of the service personnel for their work would not be affected by the profitability of the account. It was thought that an employee might have less enthusiasm for an unprofitable account, and that the quality of his work might suffer as a result. It was considered to be the job of top management to decide which jobs to carry, and that the function of the creative personnel was to execute their tasks as well as they could.

The Electron Industries Situation

Electron Industries was a large manufacturer of an industrial product group. The company comprised many divisions, each of which was autonomous except for those things which affected the image of the company as a whole, including advertising. Some of the company's divisions were clients of agencies other than Harley Associates.

Until recently, each of the divisions of Electron Industries which were clients of Harley Associates had been considered by the agency to be profitable. Early in 1976, however, the profitability to the agency of Electron's International Division had been subjected to question. The client profit and loss statement for the division for the year 1975 is shown in Exhibit 1.

Exhibit 1

CLIENT PROFIT AND LOSS STATEMENT

Client   = Electron Industries, Inc., International Division
Product = Professional Prod.
Period   = Year to 12/31/75

Billing	$348,000
Commissions and Fees	$ 61,800
Direct Payroll	
Account management	18,000
Copy	22,000
Art	10,000
Media	3,000
Administrative	1,500
	54,500
Other Direct Expenses	
Unbillable costs	600
Travel	200
Entertainment	600
	1,400
Indirect Expenses	
Occupancy	8,000
Employee benefits	3,200
Telephone	2,100
Indirect service departments	14,600
Other indirect	6,800
	34,700
Total Expense	90,600
Profit (Loss) before taxes	($ 28,800)

The International Division did not advertise through the mass media. It was equipped to do most of its own art work, so Harley Associates did not have to provide these services to the same extent that they did for other clients. The agency's main function for this division were the development of advertising copy and the placing of advertisements with the media.

The account supervisor had spent considerable time becoming acquainted with International Division's products, and with Electron Industries' objectives in order to convey in the advertising plan a message which would meet with the approval of corporate management. Within the agency he had to ensure that the copywriters were also thoroughly familiar with the subject matter and objectives of the advertising plan, so that the copy would conform to Electron's corporate policy.

Mr. Sykes, a member of the agency's staff at headquarters, had been instructed to prepare a report for a top management meeting at which the profitability to the agency of International Division was to be discussed. The report was to include a statement of all the relevant points at issue, a list of alternative courses of action available to the agency, a brief note on the consequences of each, and Sykes' recommendation.

QUESTIONS

1. Describe a management control system that is appropriate for Harley Associates.

2. What points would you include in the report mentioned in the last paragraph of the case?

Case 14-2

Chemical Bank (A)

Chemical Bank, with deposits averaging well over a billion dollars, was one of the largest banks in the United States. Its banking operations were conducted in a main office and several dozen branch offices located throughout the metropolitan area it served. A partial organization chart is shown in Exhibit 1.

Exhibit 1

CHEMICAL BANK
Partial Organization Chart

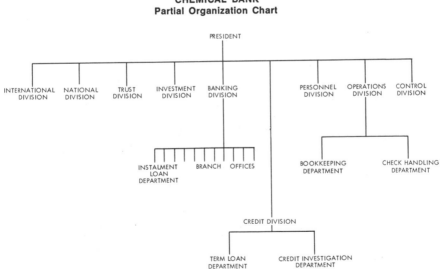

Branch offices operated as if they were independent banks. They served individual, commercial, and industrial customers by accepting demand, savings, and time deposits, by extending various types of loans, and by performing other services normally expected of a bank. The sizes and operating characteristics of the branches varied over a wide range. Average deposits outstanding ranged from $1 million to over $100 million; average loans outstanding, from no loans to over $100 million. Moreover, the ratio of deposits to loans varied considerably from one branch to another; most branches had more deposits than loans, but a few had more loans than deposits. In brief, both the magnitude and composition of assets and liabilities were significantly different among the different branches. Inasmuch as these differences were related to the geographical location of the branches, the difficulty of evaluating and comparing the performances of branches for the purpose of overall planning and control was inherent in the situation. The design and operation of a planning and control system for this purpose was the responsibility of the control division.

Among various reports reaching top management, the quarterly comparative earnings statement (see Exhibits 2 and 3) played a central role in the evaluation of branch performance. The report was designed to show the extent to which branches attained three important goals: (1) branches should operate within their budgets; (2) branches should grow in deposits and loans; and (3) branches should earn satisfactory profits. Accordingly, the statement showed for each branch the budgeted and actual amounts of deposits and loans outstanding, and income, expenses, and earnings for the current quarter, the year to date, and the year to date for the preceding year.

BUDGET

In early November, each branch prepared a budget for the following year for submission to headquarters of the banking division and to top management. The branches were furnished a booklet containing sample forms, 24 pages of detailed instructions, and a brief set of policy guides from top management to facilitate the preparation of their budgets. The policy guide for 1961 is given in its entirety in Exhibit 4. The instructions gave the procedures to be followed in arriving at the budget amounts for specific items. It was, for instance, specified that the starting point for forecasting was to be the prior year's figures on the quarterly basis, that the income item interest on loans was to be derived from the projected volume of loans and loan rates, that painting cost should not be included in the item for building maintenance expense, and so on.

Since Salaries was the biggest single expense item, and the hiring and releasing of employees involved considerable cost, utmost care was required in budgeting this item. Branches were instructed to arrive at staffing requirements for the next year after a thorough examination of anticipated increases in productivity arising from mechanization or otherwise improved operating procedures, of anticipated changes in the volume of activity, and of advantages and disadvantages of using overtime or temporary or part-time help. If the number of the required staff of a branch thus determined exceeded the

Exhibit 2

COMPARATIVE STATEMENT OF EARNINGS, 1960

Branch A

(Dollars)

3rd Quarter			January 1 thru September 30		
1960 Actual	1960 Budget		1960 Actual	1960 Budget	1959 Actual
		Income:			
13,177	12,600	Interest on loans	33,748	35,200	
6,373	4,800	Service chgs.—regular A/C's.	14,572	14,100	
3,816	3,600	Service chgs.—special ck.	11,114	10,700	
1,168	1,300	Safe deposit rentals	4,317	4,500	
2,237	2,154	Installment loans (net)	5,126	5,406	
—	—	Special loans (net)	—	—	
1,010	1,200	Fees, comm., other income	3,321	3,300	
27,781	25,654	Total Direct Income	72,198	73,206	
104,260	102,148	Interest on excess (borr.) funds	324,434	306,166	
132,041	127,802	Gross Income	396,632	379,372	
		Expenses:			
32,363	32,617	Salaries	96,151	97,164	
2,955	2,955	Deferred compensation	8,865	8,865	
5,232	4,689	Employee benefits	14,925	14,067	
11,485	11,489	Rent and occupancy	34,398	33,947	
6,824	7,560	Interest on deposits	20,455	21,780	
9,458	8,090	Other direct	25,688	23,930	
3,128	3,097	Office administration	9,676	9,725	
19,183	17,642	Service departments	57,059	52,399	
6,415	5,061	Indirect and overhead	14,964	14,273	
97,043	93,200	Gross Expenses	282,181	276,150	
34,998	34,602	Net Earnings before Taxes	114,451	103,222	
18,955	18,741	Income tax prov. (credit)	61,987	55,906	
16,043	15,861	Net Earnings after Taxes	52,464	47,316	
12,655,000	12,550,000	Average deposits—Demand	13,134,000	12,650,000	
979,000	1,100,000	Savings	986,000	1,057,000	
55,000	55,000	Time	40,000	43,000	
233,000	190,000	U.S.	213,000	183,000	
13,922,000	13,895,000	Total	14,373,000	13,933,000	
900,000	870,000	Average loans	775,000	827,000	
5.82	5.76	Average loan rate	5.82	5.69	
		Earning rate on:			
4.08	3.95	Excess (borr.) funds	4.05	3.95	
6.50	6.40	Savings deposits	6.46	6.40	
26.5%	27.1%	Net earnings ratio (before taxes)	28.9%	27.2%	
		Memo:			
—	—	Losses—before taxes	—	—	
—	—	Recoveries—before taxes	—	—	

Exhibit 3

COMPARATIVE STATEMENT OF EARNINGS, 1960

Branch B

(Dollars)

3rd Quarter			January 1 thru September 30		
1960 Actual	1960 Budget		1960 Actual	1960 Budget	1959 Actual
		Income:			
951,617	833,300	Interest on loans	2,646,813	2,202,750	
7,015	7,400	Service chgs.—regular A/C's.	24,020	21,900	
8,211	7,600	Service chgs.—special ck.	23,384	22,600	
2,049	2,100	Safe deposit rentals	6,712	7,100	
9,202	9,478	Installment loans (net)	21,402	23,790	
—	212	Special loans (net)	85	556	
8,081	3,100	Fees, comm., other income	22,517	12,800	
986,175	863,190	Total Direct Income	2,744,933	2,291,496	
(191,650)	(121,960)	Interest on excess (borr.) funds....	(430,444)	(121,493)	
794,525	741,230	Gross Income	2,314,489	2,170,003	
		Expenses:			
69,308	62,633	Salaries	197,572	185,634	
5,646	5,646	Deferred compensation	16,938	16,938	
9,180	7,989	Employee benefits	25,833	23,967	
27,674	27,775	Rent and occupancy	82,726	83,375	
15,878	18,230	Interest on deposits	47,589	52,650	
25,637	23,660	Other direct	86,112	71,400	
17,232	17,072	Office administration	53,321	53,606	
89,724	95,719	Service departments	290,082	283,531	
22,406	18,001	Indirect and overhead	53,643	51,166	
282,685	276,725	Gross Expenses	853,816	822,267	
511,840	464,505	Net Earnings before Taxes	1,460,673	1,347,736	
277,212	251,576	Income tax prov. (credit)	791,100	729,934	
234,628	212,929	Net Earnings after Taxes	669,573	617,802	
67,901,000	70,000,000	Average deposits—Demand	69,425,000	72,667,000	
2,354,000	2,700,000	Savings	2,328,000	2,600,000	
74,000	90,000	Time	52,000	66,000	
5,194,000	1,900,000	U.S.	4,086,000	1,733,000	
75,523,000	74,690,000	Total	75,891,000	77,066,000	
72,129,000	65,000,000	Average loans	67,446,000	57,666,000	
5.25	5.10	Average loan rate	5.24	5.10	
		Earning rate on:			
4.08	3.95	Excess (borr.) funds	4.05	3.95	
6.50	6.40	Savings deposits	6.46	6.40	
64.4%	62.7%	Net earnings ratio (before taxes)	63.1%	62.1%	
		Memo:			
—	—	Losses—before taxes	5,559	—	
66	—	Recoveries—before taxes	798	—	

Exhibit 4

COVERING MEMORANDUM FOR 1961 BUDGET INSTRUCTIONS

It is customary for the committee to summarize for your general guidance current thinking regarding deposits, loans, and loan rates. The expectations outlined below are for the overall bank. Therefore, it is important that the head of each earning unit analyze the impact of expected general economic trends on the conditions peculiar to his own area of activity in order to project specific goals which he may reasonably expect to attain.

Deposits

There is every indication that money market conditions will be such that demand deposit levels in our area will expand. In our judgment, we anticipate at least a 5 percent growth in demand deposits for all banks. Our overall goal, however, should be set somewhat higher to reflect an improvement in our relative position. Savings deposits will continue to climb moderately. Current rates for time and savings deposits should be used to project interest costs.

Loans and Loan Rates

In all probability loan demand will slacken seasonally in the early months of 1961; in fact, many economists believe that the decline may continue through the second quarter of the year. We firmly believe that sometime between the March tax date and early in the third quarter, loan demand should strengthen.

For the most part, the recent decline in the prime rate is reflected in the loan rate structure at this time. Accordingly, except where necessary rate adjustments are still anticipated, the existing rate structure should prevail.

Expenses

Before preparing the budget, it is imperative that each supervisor closely evaluate every controllable expense in his area and consider all means of economizing and reducing costs, particularly in such areas as personnel staffing, overtime, entertainment, stationery, etc. The salary administration policies explained on pages 19 and 20 in the Budget Instructions* should be strictly followed.

In order to complete the budget for the entire bank by year-end, your full cooperation is necessary in meeting the deadlines which appear in the attached General Instructions.

BUDGET COMMITTEE

October 7, 1960

---

* The policies referred to are as follows:

Your current appraisal of each employee's performance as E (excellent), AA (above average), A (average), or P (poor) is to be shown immediately following the individual's name on schedule 4A, as a guide for your own budgeting and for the subsequent review by the budget committee.

Exhibit 4—Continued

Salary administration policies, as expressed in Bulletin III of the Personnel Policies Manual, are not expected to change during 1961. Our salary rates are competitive, and as in recent years, any projected increases should be based solely on merit or, where plans are sufficiently advanced, on anticipated bona fide promotions.

In general, the budget committee anticipates that we will be able to maintain our competitive position with total bankwide increases to deserving employees, averaging no more than 5 percent of their salaries. In order to achieve this purpose, all departments must cooperate in observing the following guides:

a) In all cases, *merit* and not length of service is to be the basis for the forecasting of increases.

b) Individual merit increases should be roughly 5 to 5½ percent of the range midpoint, with no increase less than $156 nor more than 10 percent of the range midpoint, ($500 maximum), and in multiples of $1.00 weekly.

c) Individual increases exceeding the guidelines in (*b*) above should be thoroughly documented both in budget submittal and in subsequent actual review for salary purposes.

d) An employee rated average should not receive appreciably more than the midpoint of his salary range. The top half of the range is reserved for those employees who demonstrate above-average performance.

e) In case of promotion, the increase or increases to be scheduled should normally bring the salary within a reasonable period to the minimum for the new job.

number previously authorized by top management, the reason for the difference had to be thoroughly documented and substantiated to banking division headquarters and the budget committee. Top management was extremely critical of subsequent requests by the branches for staff increases which had not been reflected in the budgets.

In general, there were two types of income and expense items—those directly identifiable with a particular branch, and those not directly identifiable with a particular branch. Branches were instructed to budget only those direct expenses under their control. Indirect expenses were allocated to branches by the control division. In addition, the budgeting of certain direct expenses, such as depreciation of fixtures, employee benefits, and deferred compensation, was done by the control division because the branches had only secondary control over these expenses.

DEPOSITS AND LOANS

In the lower part of the comparative statement were shown the budgeted and actual loans and deposits outstanding. Both top management and branch managers exercised a close watch over these primary indicators of the level of the branch's operation. The controller, however, believed that the ultimate test of the office performance should not rest with these items but, rather, with earnings. He maintained that the effect of changes in deposits and loans should and would be reflected in the earnings statement.

EARNINGS STATEMENT

The control division had encountered a number of serious problems in trying to produce an earnings statement that would be most useful for the branches and for the management of the banking division. Some problems were basic to all types of business; some were peculiar to banking. The fundamental cause of the problems, however, lay in the fact that not all income and expense items could be measured precisely or directly identified with particular offices. Specifically, some of the questions asked were these: What should be the basis for determining the credit for a branch that generated deposits in excess of its own requirements for funds? What share of general administrative expenses, including the salaries of top management, should be charged to each branch? How should the expenses of the personnel division, the bookkeeping department, the check clearance department, the credit department, etc., be allocated to branches? The control division resolved some of these problems in the following ways.

Installment Loans

Record-keeping, issuance of coupon books, and part of collection work for installment loans generated by all branches were handled centrally by the installment loan department, and income earned from installment loans was, therefore, credited initially to this department. This income was, in large part, attributable to the branches that generated the loans and was, therefore, redistributed to them. The current procedure was to distribute gross operating income less the cost of "borrowed" funds and operating expenses of the department on the basis of the total direct installment loans generated by the branch during a revolving annual cycle.

An alternative basis that had been considered was to apportion the net income of the installment department according to the number of payments received by branches, since this measure of activity reflected the clerical time spent for coupon handling. This alternative was not adopted, on the grounds that it did not give branches enough motivation to seek more new installment loans, particularly since customers could make their installment payments at any branch they chose. An alternative basis considered was the amount of average loans outstanding. The controller thought this might be more equitable than the currently used basis, but he was of the opinion that the gain to be obtained from the adoption of the new basis was not large enough to offset the additional necessary record-keeping.

Interest on Excess (or Borrowed) Funds

Branches and other operating units with funds available for investment in excess of their own requirements for loans, cash, and other assets shared in the net earnings of the investment division; branches and other operating units whose asset requirements exceeded their available funds were charged for funds "borrowed." There was a wide variation in the ratio of deposits to loans among branches, and some branches were credited with the interest on excess funds in an amount higher than their direct income. An example of the calculation of this important income or charge item is shown in Exhibit 5.

As shown in the top section of Exhibit 5, the first step was to compute the amount of excess (or borrowed) funds for the branch. Funds were divided into two pools: (1) special pool—earnings from special long-term, high-yield, municipal securities, which were considered as an investment of part of the savings and time deposits; and (2) regular pool—earnings from other portfolio securities investments, interest on certain loans, and sundry earnings. As a rule, the special-pool investments yielded a higher rate of return than the regular-pool investments.

Third, branches with savings deposits were credited at the interest rate of the special pool on the basis of their pro rata share of savings deposits. Net savings deposits in excess of the principal of investment in the special pool, together with excess funds other than savings deposits, received pro rata credit from the earnings of the regular investment pool. Branches that borrowed funds were charged at the regular pool rate. In summary, the two rates from the two pools were as follows:

Critical Factor pool rates

Special pool rate: Net earnings of special pool/special pool securities principal (part of total savings deposits)

Regular pool rate: Net earnings from regular pool/excess funds less borrowed funds less special securities principal

For the first three quarters of 1960, the budgeted regular pool rate and special pool rate were 3.95 percent and 7.81 percent; the actual rates, 4.05 percent and 7.88 percent, respectively. Thus, for branch A the interest on excess funds for the first three quarters was calculated as shown in the lower section of Exhibit 5.

Rent and Occupancy Cost

Some branches operated in leased space whereas others operated in bank-owned buildings. The first group was charged with the actual rent paid, but the second was charged with the "fair rental value," which was determined by outside real estate appraisers. The practice was thought to put the two groups on the same footing. The fair rental value charges were internal bookkeeping entries offset by credits to real-estate accounts, which were maintained for each bank-owned building. These accounts, therefore, indicated the profitability of each building. The determination of the fair rental value was not difficult, and there had been no significant controversies involving its calculation.

Exhibit 5

CALCULATION OF INTEREST INCOME ON EXCESS FUNDS, BRANCH A
First Three Quarters of 1960

Calculation of Excess Funds

	(In thousands)	
Total demand deposits	$13,134	
Less: Reciprocal bank balances; float	(727)	
Plus: Treasury tax and loan a/c	221	
Adjusted demand deposits	$12,628	
Less: Reserve at 18%	(2,273)	
Net demand deposits		$10,355
Savings deposits	$ 1,026	
Less: Reserve at 5%	(51)	
Net savings deposits		975
Net deposits available for investment		$11,330
Less: Loans, cash, other assets		(1,229)
Net Excess Funds		$10,101

Calculation of Interest Income on Excess Funds

	Principal		Annual Rate		Three Quarters		Interest
In special investment pool (63%)....$	614,000	×	7.88%	×	¾	=	$ 36,270
In regular investment pool (37%)....	361,000	×	4.05%	×	¾	=	10,962
Savings deposits (100%) ....$	975,000	×	6.46%	×	¾	=	$ 47,232
In regular investment pool—							
demand deposits	9,126,000	×	4.05%	×	¾	=	277,202
Net excess funds $10,101,000							
Interest on excess funds							$324,434

Advertising

General or institutional advertising was charged to other indirect expenses. (See below for the allocation of other indirect expenses.) Advertising related to a specific branch was charged directly to that branch, except that when advertising was placed in mass media, such as radio, television, and newspapers with general circulation, 33 percent of the expense was allocated to other indirect expenses and 67 percent was allocated to the specific branches involved. The theory of the exception was that when mass media were used, the whole bank benefited to a certain extent.

Banking Division Headquarters and General Administration

All expenses of the banking division headquarters, including the salaries of officers in the division headquarters, were allocated to branches on the basis of their prior year's average gross deposits. The figure for average gross deposits was considered as the best single measure of branch activity.

The salaries of general administrative officers of the bank were first allocated among divisions on the basis of the time spent on problems of each division as estimated by each officer. The amount of general administrative salaries thus allocated to the banking division was, in turn, allocated among branches on the basis of gross deposits in the prior year. All other general administration expenses were charged on the same basis.

Bookkeeping Department

Much of the bookkeeping work was centralized for the whole bank. However, since the central department had been established only in 1959, several offices continued to do their own bookkeeping in 1960. The expenses of the central bookkeeping department were, therefore, allocated only to the branches it serviced. There were eight functional cost centers in the bookkeeping department, and each cost center had its own basis of allocation. The bases of four of the cost centers are given below.

1. *Regular Bookkeeping Cost Center.* In the bookkeeping department, a permanent clerical staff was assigned to process the accounts of each branch. Allocations to branches were based on the salaries of this assigned staff, plus fringe benefits and related overhead costs.

2. *Bank Ledgers Cost Center.* Allocation was on the basis of debit and credit activity as determined by an analysis made from time to time. Inasmuch as the main activity of this cost center was the posting of transactions to ledger sheets, the number of debit and credit entries was preferred to any other basis, e.g., number of accounts. A new survey of debit and credit statistics was made by the analysis department whenever it was believed that there had been a material change from the prior survey period and, in any event, at least once a year.

3. *Special Checking Cost Center.* Same as 2.

4. *Special Statement Section.* Allocation was on the basis of number of accounts handled. The activity of the section was to send out special statements on customers' special requests.

Before adoption of the current method based on the cost center concept, weight of statements mailed out had been the basis of allocation for the expenses of the entire department. The current practice was regarded as more accurate, because there were very few temporary movements of staff and machine services from one cost center to another and because there was a significant variation in the activity measures of the cost centers.

According to the controller, the main controversy involving the expenses of the bookkeeping department was not with respect to the basis of allocation but, rather, with respect to the absolute level of expenses of the department. Complaints were heard from those branches serviced by the department to the effect that they were handicapped relative to branches that did their own bookkeeping, because the cost charged by the central bookkeeping department was considerably higher than the cost that would be incurred if the branch did its own bookkeeping. The controller thought branches that had this opinion failed to recognize that the bookkeeping expenses shown in the earnings statements of the branches with their own bookkeeping were only part of the true bookkeeping cost, because an appropriate portion of supervisory salaries, occupancy costs, supplies, etc., was not included in the item. When the bookkeeping was centralized for a branch, the benefit gained from relieving the supervisors of supervising bookkeeping activity usually appeared as increased loans and deposits, and better management generally.

Check Clearance Department

The total cost of this department was divided among 12 functional cost centers, based on the number of employees assigned to each and the volume of its work. The cost of each cost center was, in turn, charged to branches. Examples of the basis of allocation are given below.

1. *IBM proof machine operation—exchanges:* allocated on the basis of number of checks handled.
2. *IBM proof machine operation—deposits:* allocated on the basis of the number of deposit items.
3. *Check desk:* allocated on the basis of number of checks handled.
4. *Transit clerical:* allocated on the basis of number of deposit items.
5. *Supervision:* allocated to the various check clearance department cost centers in ratio to labor costs.

As was the case with the bookkeeping cost centers, the measures of activity (checks handled and number of deposit items) were based on periodic surveys and remained unchanged until significant changes in the relative activity of branches indicated the need for a new survey. Every cost center's activity was reviewed at least once a year for this purpose.

There were two important sources of trouble in allocation of the expenses of the check clearance department. One was that branches cashed checks issued by other branches; the other was that branches received deposits for customers whose accounts were in other branches. In the periodic activity analyses made to determine the basis of allocating cost, the "number of checks cashed" was the number of checks actually cashed in the branch, whether or not the account was located in the branch. Similarly, the "number of deposit items" was the number of deposits made in the branch. Although it had been believed that the effect of these interbranch services largely offset one another, a recent study by the control division indicated that they, in fact, resulted in distortions with respect to certain branches. The control division was currently working on a method of allocation by which the charge would be made to the branch that benefited most; that is, the branch in which the account was located.

Credit Investigation Department

Although most branches had their own credit analysis staffs, they often asked the central credit department to make investigations. The expenses of the central credit investigation department, therefore, were allocated to the branches that requested its service. The basis of allocation was the number of requests for credit investigation weighted by the typical time required for the analysis performed. The weight for the various types of investigation was determined by the analysis department on the basis of an actual time study.

Term Loan Department

Income from term loans was credited to the branches that generated the loans. Officers of the term loan department actively counseled the branches in negotiating terms with customers, in drawing up loan contracts, and in reviewing existing loans. It was therefore necessary that the expenses of the term loan department be allocated to the branches that used its service. The basis of allocation was the number of loans considered, the number of loans outstanding, and the number of amendments to existing loans, weighted by the unit handling time of each of three classes. In order to determine the weight, the analysis department asked the staff of the term loan department to estimate the time spent on each class.

Personnel Division

The expenses of this division were allocated to all operating units in the ratio of the number of employees in each operating unit to the total.

Other Indirect Expenses

Items of a general overhead nature, such as expenses of the accounting division (except the direct cost of examining a branch, which was charged directly), cost of the senior training program, general institutional advertising, contributions, etc., were included under this heading. The basis of allocation of these expenses among branches was the ratio of annual operating expenses (excluding other indirect and interest on deposits) of each branch to the total operating expenses of all branches.

CONTROLLER'S VIEWS ON ALLOCATIONS

The controller believed that some arbitrariness was inevitable in the allocation of the income and expense items described above. With dozens of branches, each with its own operating characteristics, it was impossible to have a "perfect" or "right" system for all of them. What was more important, according to the controller, was agreement on the part of the branch managers that the system was generally equitable. If managers agreed on the fairness of the system, he believed, it was likely to be a success. They therefore, let it be known to branch managers that the system was always open for revision, and he encouraged them to make known any criticisms they had. After the control division had done its best to find a workable system, the initiative for suggesting changes was with the branch managers. The controller said that several changes had been made as a result of branch managers' suggestions.

He warned them, however, against a blind and apathetic acceptance; the acceptance should be positive and constructive. On acceptance of the system, branch managers should be concerned with the reported result and make necessary efforts to improve it. Thus, he said, branch managers were told clearly that the earnings statement was used to evaluate their performance. This, he thought, attached sufficient importance to the matter to prevent any possible indifference.

ATTITUDES OF BRANCH MANAGERS ON ALLOCATIONS

The managers of two offices, A and B, held different opinions about the system. The operating characteristics of these branches were different, as indicated by their comparative statements of earnings for the third quarter of 1960, reproduced in Exhibits 2 and 3. Branch A was relatively small and deposit-heavy, did its own bookkeeping and operated in a leased space, whereas branch B was larger, loan-heavy, used the centralized bookkeeping department, and operated in a bank-owned building. Their annual earnings statements of recent years are shown in Exhibits 6 and 7.

Comment by Manager of Branch A

The statement is useful because I like to see, at least quickly, whether I am within the budget and what caused the deviations from it, if any.

The earnings of our branch are relatively low, because the volume of business is limited by the location. We have more deposits than our loan requirements; consequently, we get credit for the excess funds. In fact, as you see, for the first three quarters of 1960, interest on excess funds was more than four times the total direct income. The 4.05 percent rate on the excess funds seems fair enough, but we try always to increase our own loans in order to increase our earnings. However, the location of our office is a limiting factor.

Since rent and occupancy is the actual rent paid to the owner of the building, we can't have any quarrel about that, but the service department charges are certainly too high. We don't have any control over these costs; yet we are charged for them. I am not complaining that this is unfair; on the contrary, I believe branches should share the burden. My only misgiving is whether those service departments are doing enough to cut down their costs.

About one half of the service department expenses charged to our branch is for check clearing service. Although I don't know the basis of allocation, I don't doubt that it is fair. Besides, even if I should have some questions about the basis, probably it wouldn't reach up there; the communication channel from here to the top is long and tedious.

At present, we do our own bookkeeping, but soon this will be centralized. I have heard some managers complain that the cost charged to them for the centralized bookkeeping is higher than the cost when they did their own bookkeeping. However, such intangible gains as prestige and customer relations may justify

Exhibit 6

CONDENSED ANNUAL EARNINGS STATEMENTS, BRANCH A

(In thousands)

	1960 Budget	1959 Budget	1959 Actual	1958 Budget	1958 Actual	1957 Budget	1957 Actual	1956 Actual	1955 Actual
Total direct income	$ 98	$ 93	$ 90	$ 87	$ 89	$ 99	$ 90	$ 99	$ 82
Interest on excess funds	409	364	381	327	316	299	287	263	355
Gross income	$ 507	$ 457	$ 471	$ 414	$ 405	$ 398	$ 377	$ 362	$ 437
Expenses:									
Salaries	$ 130	$ 129	$ 125	$ 125	$ 125	$ 140	$ 147	$ 132	$ 114
Deferred compensation	12	10	10	8	9				
Employee benefits	19	19	18	17	17				
Rent and occupancy	45	46	45	45	47	47	49	43	43
Interest on deposits	30	30	27	19	19	9	11	6	4
Other direct	32	29	31	30	30	*	*	*	*
Office administration	13	15	13	17	16	*	*	*	*
Service departments	70	58	61	57	57	67	69	62	44
Indirect overhead	18	18	21	19	16	*	*	*	*
Gross expenses	$ 369	$ 354	$ 351	$ 337	$ 336	$ 315	$ 329	$ 296	$ 256
Net earnings before taxes	$ 138	$ 103	$ 120	$ 77	$ 69	$ 83	$ 48	$ 66	$ 181
Average gross deposits	$13,975	$13,550	$13,707	$13,573	$12,948	$14,540	$13,442	$15,057	$21,504
Average loans	$ 820	$ 820	$ 810	$ 746	$ 737	$ 990	$ 927	$ 1,139	$ 1,093

* Changes in accounting procedure make these items noncomparable with later years.

Exhibit 7

CONDENSED ANNUAL EARNINGS STATEMENTS, BRANCH B

(In thousands)

	1960 Budget	1959 Budget	1959 Actual	1958 Budget	1958 Actual	1957 Budget	1957 Actual	1956 Actual	1955 Actual
Total direct income	$ 3,077	$ 2,725	$ 2,532	$ 2,214	$ 2,201	$ 2,338	$ 2,395	$ 1,959	$ 1,172
Interest on excess (borrowed) funds	(177)	157	222	154	263	73	(32)	209	556
Gross income	$ 2,900	$ 2,882	$ 2,754	$ 2,368	$ 2,464	$ 2,411	$ 2,363	$ 2,168	$ 1,728
Expenses:									
Salaries	$ 249	$ 255	$ 256	$ 245	$ 247 ⎤	$ 250	$ 264	$ 236	$ 232
Deferred compensation	22	19	21	17	18 ⎥				
Employee benefits	32	34	33	30	31 ⎦				
Rent and occupancy	111	105	104	104	105	106	108	65	85
Interest on deposits	71	75	66	51	52	19	25	12	10
Other direct	95	93	108	84	86	*	*	*	*
Office administration	71	85	76	86	83	*	*	*	*
Service departments	379	383	360	356	345	361	380	315	224
Indirect and overhead	65	64	72	60	51	*	*	*	*
Gross expenses	$ 1,095	$ 1,113	$ 1,096	$ 1,033	$ 1,018	$ 878	$ 928	$ 829	$ 814
Net earnings before taxes	$ 1,805	$ 1,769	$ 1,658	$ 1,335	$ 1,446	$ 1,533	$ 1,435	$ 1,339	$ 914
Average gross deposits	$77,410	$79,885	$75,853	$72,063	$73,899	$73,415	$69,683	$70,740	$73,433
Average loans	$58,000	$56,000	$49,702	$48,971	$47,095	$50,000	$49,945	$44,460	$28,378

* Changes in accounting procedure make these items noncomparable with later years.

a little higher cost. At any rate, we wouldn't have any choice if top management decides to centralize our bookkeeping. It may be better in the long run.

Although I don't know exactly what items are included in other direct and indirect and overhead expenses, I don't think they are excessive. The control division is trying to be fair.

In summary, I think the statement is useful, but there are many factors you should consider in interpreting it.

Comment by Manager of Branch B

The statement is a fair measure of how branches are doing. It is true that the location of a branch has a lot to do with its operation; in evaluating a particular branch, the location is an important element to be taken into account. To take the extreme case, you don't need a branch in a desert. If a branch can't show earnings after being charged with its fair share of all costs, perhaps the purpose of its existence is lost.

High volume and efficient operation have contributed to our high level of earnings. Our branch has more loans than can be sustained by our own deposits; thus, we are charged with interest on borrowed funds on the theory that we would have to pay the interest if we borrowed from outside. Of course, by increasing deposits we could meet the loan requirements and add to our earnings a good part of the interest on borrowed funds; indeed, we have been trying to lure more deposits to our branch. Quite apart from this special effort, however, we do not neglect to seek more loan opportunities, for loans increase earnings even after the interest charge.

Our office is in a bank-owned building, but instead of controversial depreciation and maintenance charges we are charged with the fair rental value. We are satisfied with this practice.

The bookkeeping of our branch is centralized. I believe we could do it for less money if we did our own bookkeeping; but competing banks have centralized bookkeeping departments, and we have to go along. I suspect there are some intangible benefits being gained, too.

If I really sat down and thoroughly examined all the allocation bases, I might find some things that could be improved. But the fact of life is that we must draw a line somewhere; some arbitrariness will always be there. Furthermore, why should our branch raise questions? We are content with the way things are.

Comments by Banking Division Headquarters

We call this report [Exhibits 2 and 3] our Bible, and like the actual Bible, it must be interpreted carefully. Many factors affect the performance of a branch that do not show up on the report. For example, in an area that is going downhill the manager of a branch has to work terribly hard just to keep his deposits from declining, whereas in a growing area, the manager can read the *New York Times* all day and still show an impressive increase in deposits. The location of the branch in the neighborhood, its outward appearance, its decor, the layout of its facilities—all can affect its volume of business. Changes in the level of interest rates, which are noncontrollable, also have a significant effect on income. At headquarters, we are aware of these factors and take them into account when we

Exhibit 8

BRANCH OFFICE REPORT

1960

Location and Office No. A

#	All Dollar Amounts in Thousands Unless Otherwise Stated	JAN.	FEB.	MAR.	APRIL	MAY	JUNE	JULY	AUG.	SEPT.	OCT.	NOV.	DEC.	YEAR AVERAGE
	DEPOSITS – AVERAGE													
1	Demand – (Ind., Part., Corp.)	14 038	13 473	12 330	12 919	13 108	12 911	12 596	11 907	12 746	12 202			
2	Demand – Banks	50	50	–	–	–	–	–	–	–	–			
3	Special Checking	221	218	220	251	235	216	237	244	236	219			
4	Treas. Tax & Loan Account	118	149	238	124	270	321	235	202	265	196			
5	Savings	987	974	1 001	990	976	1 012	972	978	986	1 013			
6	Christmas Club	15	23	30	35	41	46	51	55	60	63			
7	Time	–	–	–	–	–	–	–	–	–	–			
8	Total	15 429	14 887	13 819	14 319	14 630	14 506	14 088	13 386	14 293	13 693			
	NUMBER OF ACCOUNTS													
9	Demand (Ind., Part., Corp.)	1 515	1 513	1 507	1 503	1 516	1 511	1 514	1 497	1 478	1 473			
10	Demand – Banks	–	–	–	–	–	–	–	–	–	–			
11	Special Checking	868	865	884	892	894	900	905	911	939	948			
12	Savings	585	587	593	589	587	591	595	587	621	645			
13	Christmas Club	540	536	534	538	533	530	526	519	516	511			
14	Time	–	–	–	–	–	–	–	–	–	–			
15	Total	3 509	3 501	3 518	3 522	3 530	3 532	3 536	3 514	3 554	3 577			
	LOANS													YEAR AVERAGE
16	Total Loans – Average	723	755	720	627	672	773	341	889	971	961			
17	Instalment Loan – Volume	20	24	36	31	35	22	25	34	27	39			
18	Spec. Loan Dept. – Month End	–	–	–	–	–	–	–	–	–	–			
	NUMBER OF BORROWERS													
19	Total Loans	48	58	50	49	51	54	55	60	62	63			
20	Instalment Loans – Made	24	37	46	50	32	30	28	45	44	39			
21	Special Loan Dept.	–	–	–	–	–	–	–	–	–	–			
22	Staff – Number of Officers	4	4	4	4	4	4	4	4	3	3			
23	No. of Employees – Auth. Budget	25	25	25	25	25	25	25	25	25	25			
24	Total	29	29	29	29	29	29	29	29	28	28			
25	Overtime & Supper Money Payments (To nearest dollar)	276	135	273	93	496	123	536	370	350	220			YEAR – TOTALS
	SERVICE CHARGES (To nearest dollar)													
26	Regular Checking Accounts	1 543	1 578	1 445	1 225	2 550	858	2 378	1 998	1 997	1 833			
27	Special Checking Accounts	1 017	1 119	1 220	1 397	1 223	1 322	1 313	1 237	1 266	1 340			
28	Total	2 560	2 697	2 665	1 622	3 773	2 180	3 691	3 235	3 263	3 173			

Income and Expense By Quarters And Cumulative

To Nearest Dollar	1st Quarter	2nd Quarter	Jan. thru June	3rd Quarter	Jan. thru Sept.	4th Quarter	Jan. thru Dec.
Gross Income	$ 133 060	131 531	264 591	132 041	396 632		
Gross Expenses	$ 92 050	93 088	185 138	97 043	282 181		
Net Before Taxes	$ 41 010	38 443	79 453	34 998	114 451		
Net After Taxes	$ 18 799	17 622	36 421	16 043	52 464		
Average Loan Rate	5.80	5.83	5.81	5.82	5.82		
Earn. Rate–Excess Funds	4.02	4.06	4.04	4.08	4.05		
Earn. Rate–Savings Deposits	6.52	6.55	6.54	6.59	6.55		

Exhibit 8—Continued

BRANCH OFFICE REPORT—SUPPLEMENT

1960

Location and Office No. A

#	All Dollar Amounts in Thousands	JAN.	FEB.	MAR.	APRIL.	MAY	JUNE	JULY	AUG.	SEPT.	OCT.	NOV.	DEC.	YEAR TOTALS
	Regular Checking Accounts – Number													
1	Opened – New	26	17	7	15	16	17	10	9	14	11			
2	Opened – A/C Trans. within Office	-	1	1	1	4	-	1	-	-	-			
3	Opened – A/C Trans. from other Off.	-	1	1	-	3	-	2	-	1	1			
4	Total Number Opened	26	19	9	16	23	17	13	9	15	11			
5	Closed	24	17	12	17	6	19	9	17	24	14			
6	Closed – A/C Trans. within Office	-	2	1	2	2	-	-	8	6	1			
7	Closed – A/C Trans. to other Offices	4	3	2	1	2	3	1	1	4	1			
8	Total Number Closed	28	22	15	20	10	22	10	26	34	16			
9	Net Opened or Closed	-2	-3	-6	-4	+13	-5	+3	-17	-19	-5			
	Regular Checking Accounts													
	Average Deposits Closed – Monthly													
10	Closed $	16	7	3	15	7	14	4	11	18	7			
11	Closed – Trans. within Office $	-	19	2	4	2	-	-	6	4	1			
12	Closed – Trans. to other Offices $	5	6	2	-	1	3	1	1	2	2			
13	Total Average–Closed Accts. $	21	32	7	19	10	17	5	18	24	10			
	Accounts Since Jan. 1st–Cumulated*													
14	*No. Opened (Line 1)	26	43	50	65	81	98	108	117	131	142			
15	No. Closed (Line 5)	24	41	53	70	76	95	104	121	145	159			
16	*Opened–Current Mo. Avg.(Line 14)$	83	191	162	143	120	102	120	109	114	127			
17	Closed–Total Avg.Bal. (Line 10) $	16	23	26	41	48	62	66	77	95	102			
	Business Development													
18	No. of calls – Customers	3	8	7	4	10	8	6	9	5	5			
19	No. of calls – Prospects	3	4	4	4	1	4	2	6	5	5			
20	Total	6	12	11	8	11	12	8	15	10	10			
21	Spec. Checking Accts – Opened	26	21	31	21	19	22	15	33	37	29			
22	Spec. Checking Accts – Closed	13	24	12	13	17	16	12	25	9	20			
23	Spec. Checking Accts – Net	+13	-3	+19	+8	+2	+6	+3	+8	+28	+9			
24	Savings Accounts – Opened	17	9	22	9	15	24	15	9	52	39			
25	Savings Accounts – Closed	21	7	16	13	17	20	13	15	18	15			
26	Savings Accounts – Net	-4	+2	+6	-4	-2	+4	+2	-6	+34	+24			
27	S.D. Boxes – New Rentals	9	6	3	9	3	6	5	6	4	5			
28	S.D. Boxes – Surrendered	9	4	9	11	12	10	6	7	7	3			
29	S.D. Boxes – Net	-	+2	-6	-2	-9	-4	-1	-1	-3	-3			
30	No. of Personal Money Orders Sold	523	543	583	643	421	467	447	419	452	367			

YEAR TOTALS

Exhibit 9

BRANCH OFFICE REPORT

Location and Office No. B

1960

All Dollar Amounts in Thousands Unless Otherwise Stated		JAN.	FEB.	MAR.	APRI.	MAY	JUNE	JULY	AUG.	SEPT.	OCT.	NOV.	DEC.	YEAR AVERAGE	
DEPOSITS - AVERAGE															
Demand - (Ind., Part., Corp.)	$	76 738	68 526	68 509	68 354	65 716	67 602	66 723	64 335	70 017	70 912				1
Demand - Banks	$	475	475	350	150	275	520	524	350	258	125				2
Special Checking	$	506	506	509	562	534	516	512	508	475	465				3
Treas., Tax & Loan Account	$	1 689	3 065	4 776	1 324	5 078	4 761	4 757	4 786	6 038	6 026				4
Savings	$	2 359	2 301	2 340	2 320	2 359	2 210	2 349	2 328	2 385	2 493				5
Christmas Club	$	19	28	35	45	54	61	67	75	81	89				6
Time	$	-	-	-	-	-	-	-	-	-	-				7
Total	$	81 786	74 901	76 519	73 555	74 016	75 670	74 932	72 382	79 254	80 110				8
NUMBER OF ACCOUNTS															
Demand - (Ind., Part., Corp.)		3 561	3 585	3 631	3 622	3 565	3 556	3 569	3 617	3 619	3 591				9
Demand - Banks		1	1	1	1	1	1	1	1	1	1				10
Special Checking		1 840	1 862	1 853	1 850	1 893	1 891	1 871	1 894	1 885	1 909				11
Savings		1 509	1 510	1 511	1 518	1 507	1 531	1 523	1 526	1 642	1 707				12
Christmas Club		600	602	734	731	728	723	72-	720	715	708				13
Time		-	-	-	-	-	-	-	-	-	-				14
Total		7 511	7 560	7 730	7 722	7 694	7 702	7 685	7 758	7 862	7 916				15
LOANS														YEAR AVERAGE	
Total Loans - Average	$	64 277	67 796	66 835	62 033	61 763	67 926	72 386	71 644	72 356	65 851				16
Instalment Loan - Volume		80	86	134	124	103	110	98	115	90	123				17
Spec. Loan Dept.-Month End	$	3	-	-	-	-	-	-	-	-	-				18
NUMBER OF BORROWERS															
Total Loans		378	381	372	390	398	403	408	430	434	409				19
Instalment Loans - Made		86	83	118	121	97	107	106	120	112	110				20
Special Loan Dept.		1	-	-	-	-	-	-	-	-	-				21
Staff - Number of Officers		8	9	9	9	9	9	9	9	9	9				22
No. of Employees - Auth. Budget		42	42	43	43	43	43	43	43	43	43				23
Total		50	51	52	52	52	52	52	52	52	52				
Overtime and Supper Money															24
Payments (To nearest dollar)	$	756	238	139	127	139	21	195	78	16	80			YEAR - TOTALS	25
SERVICE CHARGES (To nearest dollar)															
Regular Checking Accounts	$	3 081	2 786	2 263	3 048	2 430	3 399	2 520	2 067	2 328	2 876				26
Special Checking Accounts	$	1 963	2 251	2 504	2 834	2 755	2 867	2 365	2 645	2 701	2 674				27
Total	$	5 044	5 037	4 767	5 882	5 185	6 266	5 485	4 712	5 029	5 550				28

Income and Expense By Quarters And Cumulative

To Nearest Dollar		1st Quarter	2nd Quarter	Jan. thru June	3rd Quarter	Jan. thru Sept.	4th Quarter	Jan. thru Dec.
Gross Income	$	766 538	753 426	1 519 964	794 525	2 314 489		
Gross Expenses	$	290 733	280 398	571 131	282 685	853 816		
Net Before Taxes	$	475 805	473 028	948 833	511 840	1 460 673		
Net After Taxes	$	218 109	216 836	434 945	234 628	669 573		
Average Loan Rate		3.18	5.29	5.24	5.25	5.24		
Earn. Rate-Excess Funds		4.02	4.06	4.04	4.08	4.05		
Earn. Rate-Savings Deposits		6.52	6.55	6.54	6.59	6.55		

Exhibit 9—Continued

BRANCH OFFICE REPORT—SUPPLEMENT

Location
and Office No. B

1960

#	All Dollar Amounts in Thousands	JAN.	FEB.	MAR.	APRIL	MAY	JUNE	JULY	AUG.	SEPT.	OCT.	NOV.	DEC.	YEAR TOTALS	#
	Regular Checking Accounts–Number														
1	Opened - New	54	54	38	32	21	32	33	49	43	46				1
2	Opened - A/C Trans. within Office	10	9	50	5	6	10	5	46	8	4				2
3	Opened - A/C Trans. from other Off.	4	4	7	5	1	5	11	9	3	6				3
4	Total Number Opened	68	67	95	42	28	47	49	104	54	56				4
5	Closed	32	17	40	31	47	30	21	39	32	28				5
6	Closed - A/C Trans. within Office	14	19	2	16	35	20	12	7	10	53				6
7	Closed - A/C Trans. to other Offices	5	7	7	4	6	3	3	10	10	3				7
8	Total Number Closed	51	43	49	51	85	56	36	56	52	84				8
9	Net Opened or Closed	+ 17	+ 24	+ 46	- 9	- 57	- 9	+ 13	+ 48	+ 2	- 28				9
	Regular Checking Accounts Average Deposits Closed - Monthly														
10	Closed $	129	37	181	158	160	32	72	42	40	91				10
11	Closed - Trans. within Office $	226	48	31	42	34	694	39	107	346	157				11
12	Closed - Trans. to other Offices $	294	107	15	20	5	247	36	44	70	67				12
13	Total Average - Closed Accts. $	649	192	227	220	199	973	147	193	456	315				13
14	*No. Opened (Line 1)	54	108	146	178	199	231	264	313	356	402				14
15	No. Closed (Line 5)	32	49	89	120	167	197	218	257	289	317				15
16	*Opened-Current Mo. Avg. (Line 14)$	603	907	1 378	1 584	1 544	1 709	2 419	2 634	2 484	3 066				16
17	Closed-Total Avg. Bal. (Line 10) $	129	166	347	505	665	697	769	811	851	942				17
	Business Development													YEAR TOTALS	
18	No. of calls - Customers	129	148	153	115	140	215	117	103	160	136				18
19	No. of calls - Prospects	89	46	39	48	51	44	29	50	33	34				19
20	Total	218	194	192	163	191	259	146	153	193	170				20
21	Spec. Checking Accts - Opened	70	62	28	66	64	55	67	60	91	87				21
22	Spec. Checking Accts - Closed	33	40	37	69	21	57	87	37	100	63				22
23	Spec. Checking Accts - Net	+ 37	+ 22	- 9	- 3	+ 43	- 2	- 20	+ 23	- 9	+ 24				23
24	Savings Accounts - Opened	63	54	54	63	47	65	56	53	173	122				24
25	Savings Accounts - Closed	93	53	53	56	58	41	64	50	57	57				25
26	Savings Accounts - Net	- 30	+ 1	+ 1	+ 7	- 11	+ 24	- 8	+ 3	+116	+ 65				26
27	S.D. Boxes - New Rentals	8	11	7	14	15	10	14	6	15	7				27
28	S.D. Boxes - Surrendered	8	9	8	8	9	13	14	6	14	13				28
29	S.D. Boxes - Net	-	+ 2	- 1	+ 6	+ 6	- 3	-	-	+ 1	- 6				29
30	No. of Personal Money Orders Sold	1 410	1 636	1 578	1 648	1 165	1 140	1 244	1 157	1 134	1 084				30

read the reports. The unfortunate fact is that some managers—for example, those in declining areas—may not believe that we take them into account. Such a manager may worry about his apparently poor performance as shown on the report, and this has a bad psychological effect on him.

One other difficulty with the report is that it may encourage the manager to be interested too much in his own branch at the expense of the bank as a whole. When a customer moves to another part of town, the manager may try to persuade him to leave his account in the same branch, even though the customer can be served better by a branch near his new location. We even hear of two branches competing for the same customer, which certainly doesn't add to the reputation of the bank. Or, to take another kind of problem, a manager may be reluctant to add another teller because of the increased expense, even though he actually needs one to give proper service to his customers.

Of course, the earnings report is just one factor in judging the performance of a branch manager. Among the others are the growth of deposits compared with the potential for the area; the number of calls he makes soliciting new business (we get a monthly report on this); the loans that get into difficulty; complaint letters from customers; the annual audit of his operations made by the control division; and, most important, personnel turnover, or any other indications of how well he is developing his personnel. Some of these factors are indicated in these statistics [see Exhibits 8 and 9], which are prepared at banking division headquarters.

QUESTIONS

The general question is: What are the strong and weak points of the budget-reporting-performance evaluation system of the bank in reference to its branch operations? What improvements would you suggest?

Examples of specific topics you should consider are:

1. What characteristics of banking make its management control system different from that of a manufacturing operation?

2. What is the relationship between the earnings statement and the branch office reports?

3. Would you recommend calculating a return on investment for each branch? If so, how would you determine the investment base?

4. Should noncontrollable costs be omitted from the earnings statement? If so, what items would be affected?

5. In comparing actual with budgeted interest on loans, should a noncontrollable variance be developed which represents the effect of changes in the general level of interest rates?

Case 14–3

Emerson & Hamlin

John Hamlin, the managing partner of Emerson & Hamlin, read with interest a description of the method of appraising and rewarding partners used by Rachlin & Company, as reported in *The Journal of Accountancy,* February 1975. He wondered whether the plan was sufficiently worthwhile to discuss seriously with his colleagues.

Emerson & Hamlin was a single-office public accounting firm which engaged in auditing, management services, and income tax practice. It had 20 partners and 45 other employees, and annual billings of approximately $3 million. Currently, partners were compensated by a relatively small salary plus a share of the partnership income. Each partner's share was determined by the number of "units" assigned to him, as a proportion of the total number of units for all partners. Each partner's units were agreed on between him and Mr. Hamlin. The total number of units increased over time for two reasons: (1) addition of new partners, and (2) rewards for additional responsibilities or performance of existing partners. The total units decreased as partners retired or left the firm, but there was usually a net increase from one year to the next because the firm was expanding.

Mr. Hamlin was 60 and planned to retire in the near future. Privately, he thought that each of the three senior partners (in charge of audit, management services, and tax, respectively) was capable of becoming managing partner. Mr. Hamlin spent approximately 20 percent of his time on billable work, and each of the three senior partners spent about 60 percent.

Rachlin Plan

The plan used by Rachlin & Company, as described in the article, is summarized below.

Each partner has a base draw (or "salary") and any profit remaining above the draws is divided on the basis of points. Points are also used as the basis for determination of a partner's payout in the event of death or retirement. The initial number of points is based on original contributions to the firm (in clientele and/or capital), or points are allowed to be purchased on admittance to partnership.

More points can be acquired from the firm by award in the following manner. At the end of each year the firm considers it has available one point for each $1,000 of annual volume and can award those points not already outstanding. If we assume an annual volume of $750,000 then

> Points available (total authorized) 750
> Total of partners' present points (issued) 525
> Points available for distribution 225

The firm thus has 225 points available to distribute to present or new partners. They can be awarded (issued) or carried over to subsequent years, depending on the recommendation of the Points Committee.

At the partners' December meeting each year, two partners are selected (by secret ballot) to serve as the Points Committee. At the January partners' meeting the Committee presents its recommendations as to awarding points. If there is no veto by 75 percent or more of the partners, then the recommendations of the Points Committee shall be effective for the year beginning January 1.

The first time the Points Committee met, it found it had no criterion for awarding of the points. The initial committee awarded no points, but it did develop an "evaluation analysis." This analysis is based on a partner performance list which Carl S. Chilton, Jr., of Long, Chilton, Payte & Hardin, described in *The Journal of Accountancy,* December 1973, and on material presented by William R. Shaw, of Arthur Young & Company, at the Management of an Accounting Practice Conference sponsored by the Missouri Society of CPA's in October 1973.

The evaluation analysis was a one-page form on which each partner was rated on the 31 criteria, as follows:

A. Workload, production and firm responsibility:
1. Fees produced by partner's client responsibility.
2. Profitability of service for clients (considering hourly rates, markdowns, markups, and so forth).
3. Fees produced by partner individually.
4. Effectiveness in collecting client receivables.
5. Performance and up-to-date knowledge in basic areas of practice (what every partner is expected to know).
6. Performance and up-to-date knowledge in partner's specialized area.
7. Performance in contributing to the management of the firm.
8. Engagement planning and control.
9. Ability to get things done.
10. Ability to delegate and supervise.

B. Client relations:

11. Reputation for "attentive" service.
12. Ability to complete work promptly.
13. Availability to clients when needed.
14. Confidence in the individual and satisfaction with work.
15. Expansion of service to existing clients.

C. *Personal development:*

16. Participation in recruitment.
17. Participation in training programs.
18. Efforts to bring along subordinates.
19. Attitude toward employees.
20. Employee attitude toward person evaluated.

D. *Standing in the community and profession:*

21. Image in the community as a top-level citizen and professional person.
22. Positions of leadership in community organizations.
23. New clients brought in through individual contacts and efforts.
24. Standing within the profession (positions of leadership, and so forth).
25. Participation in professional activities.

E. *General:*

26. Self-motivation (initiative, drive, energy).
27. Leadership (ability to motivate others).
28. Stability and maturity (discerning what is important, reliability in crises).
29. Judgment (when to decide and when to consult).
30. Cooperativeness and team play.
31. Promotion of firm's standing.

On each criterion, a person was rated on the following scale:

1. Disappointing, needs improvement.
2. Erratic, less than expected.
3. Satisfactory, normal expectancy.
4. Excellent, unusually well done.
5. Outstanding, rarely equalled.
0. No basis for judgment.

With a maximum rating of 5 for each criterion, the maximum possible score was 155.

The "evaluation analysis" is prepared three times a year by each partner on himself or herself and each of the other partners. The analyses are submitted to the managing partner, who is authorized to review any deficiencies or "downward trends" with the subject partner. At the end of the year these forms are made available to the Points Committee as a basis for judgment in awarding points.

In addition to specific areas of judgment, the form also provides space for subjective comments on outstanding accomplishments, areas of weakness and efforts to resolve weakness.

The Points Committee reviews the three evaluation forms on each partner for the purpose of awarding the 225 available points. Assuming that all 225 points were awarded, the results could be as shown in Exhibit 1.

Exhibit 1

AWARDING AVAILABLE POINTS

Partner	Present		Awarded	New Totals	
	Points	Percent		Points	Percent
A	250	47.6	50	300	40.0
B	100	19.0	50	150	20.0
C	75	14.3	75	150	20.0
D	75	14.3	25	100	13.3
E	25	4.8	25	50	6.7
Total	525	100.0	225	750	100.0

There are three key ideas which make this system of awarding points effective:

1. It is a method of rewarding the younger partners on a regular (annual) basis, to keep their enthusiasm high, and it allows them to share in increased profits.
2. Points are awarded only out of growth of the firm (if the annual fees did not increase there would be no new points available).
3. Points are never taken away, once awarded, so that no one feels that he or she has surrendered anything.

Chapter Fifteen

NONPROFIT

ORGANIZATIONS*

Most of this book has, at least implicitly, focused on profit-oriented organizations. The management control process in nonprofit organizations is in many respects similar to that in profit-oriented organizations, but in other important respects it is different. The similarities and differences are discussed in this chapter.

CHARACTERISTICS OF NONPROFIT ORGANIZATIONS

The dominant purpose, or at least one of the major purposes, of some organizations is earning profits. Decisions made by their managements are intended to increase (or at least maintain) profits, and success is measured, to a significant degree, by the amount of profits that these organizations earn. (This does not imply that profit is the only objective, or that success can be measured entirely in terms of profitability; that would be, of course, an overly simplistic view of most businesses.)

By contrast, other organizations exist primarily to render a service. Decisions made by their managements are intended to provide the best possible service with the available resources, and the success of these organizations is measured primarily by how much service they render and by how well they render it. More basically (but unfortunately also more vaguely), their success should be measured by how much they contribute to the public welfare. This type of organization is here labelled "nonprofit." Included in this category are government organizations, educational organizations, hospitals and other health care organizations, and religious and charitable organizations,

---

* This chapter is based on Robert N. Anthony and Regina E. Herzlinger, *Management Control in Nonprofit Organizations* (Homewood, Ill.: Richard D. Irwin, Inc., 1975).

clubs and similar membership organizations, foundations, and a variety of other types. They employ approximately 25 percent of the American work force.

Certain characteristics of nonprofit organizations affect the management control process in those organizations:

1. Their tendency to be *service organizations.*
2. The dominance of *professionals.*
3. The absence of the *profit measure.*
4. The lesser role of the *marketplace.*
5. Differences in *ownership and power.*
6. Their tendency to be *political* organizations.
7. A *tradition* of inadequate management controls.

The first two of these characteristics were discussed in Chapter 14. The other five are discussed below.

The Profit Measure

All organizations use inputs to produce outputs. An organization's effectiveness is measured by the extent to which outputs accomplish its objectives, and its efficiency is measured by the relationship between inputs and outputs. In a profit-oriented organization the amount of profit provides an overall measure of both effectiveness and efficiency. In many nonprofit organizations, however, outputs cannot be measured in quantitative terms. Furthermore, even when outputs can be measured, many nonprofit organizations have multiple objectives, and there is no feasible way of combining the several outputs, each of which is intended to accomplish one of these objectives, into a single number that measures the overall effectiveness of the organization.

The absence of a satisfactory, single, overall measure of performance that is comparable to the profit measure is the most serious management control problem in a nonprofit organization. (It is incorrect to say that the absence of the profit *motive* is the central problem; rather, it is the absence of the profit *measure.*)

The profit measure has the following advantages: (1) It provides a single criterion that can be used in evaluating proposed courses of action; (2) it permits a quantitative analysis of those proposals in which benefits can be directly compared with costs; (3) it provides a single, broad measure of performance; and (4) it permits comparisons of performance to be made among responsibility centers that are performing dissimilar functions. The difficulties that arise when the profit measure is not present can be seen by discussing each of these points.

In passing, it should be noted that the measurement problem relates to outputs, not to inputs. With minor exceptions, inputs (i.e., costs) can be measured as readily in a nonprofit organization as in a profit-oriented organization.

1. *No Single Criterion.* Since a nonprofit organization has multiple goals and since these goals usually cannot be expressed in quantitative terms, there often is no clearcut objective function that can be used in analyzing proposed alternative courses of action. The management team of a profit-oriented company may debate vigorously the merits of a proposal, but the debate is carried on within the context of how the proposal will affect profits. The management team of a nonprofit organization often will not agree on the relative importance of various goals; members will view a proposal in terms of the importance that they personally attach to the several goals of the organization. Thus, in a municipality, all members of the management team may agree that the addition of a new pumper will add to the effectiveness of the fire department, but there will be disagreement on how important an expenditure to increase the effectiveness of the fire department is compared to a comparable expenditure on parks, or streets, or welfare. This greatly complicates the problem of decision making.

2. *No Relation between Costs and Benefits.* For most important decisions in a nonprofit organization, there is no plausible way of estimating the relationship between inputs and outputs; that is, there is no way of judging what effect the expenditure of X dollars will have on achieving the goals of the organization. Would the addition of another professor increase the value of the education that a college provides by an amount that exceeds the cost of that professor? How much should be spent on a program to retrain unemployed persons? Issues of this type are difficult to analyze in quantitative terms because there is no good way of estimating the consequences of a given increment of spending.

3. *Difficulty of Measuring Performance.* When both revenues and costs can be measured, one goal of a nonprofit organization should be to break even. But this is never the principal goal, nor is it a very important goal except in times of financial crisis. The principal goal should be to render service, and the amount and quality of service rendered is not measured by the numbers in the financial statements. Performance with respect to the important goals is difficult to measure. The success of an educational institution depends more on the ability and diligence of its faculty than on such measurable characteristics as the number of courses offered, or the student/faculty ratio.

4. *Comparison among Units.* In nonprofit organizations, organizational units can be compared with one another only if they have similar functions. One fire department can be compared with other fire departments, and one general hospital with other general hospitals, but there is no way of comparing the effectiveness of a fire department with the effectiveness of a hospital. Dissimilar profit-oriented companies can be compared with one another in terms of the common measure of profitability.

Market Forces

Most nonprofit organizations are less subject to the forces of the marketplace than are profit-oriented organizations. The market dictates the limits within which the management of a profit-oriented company can operate. A company cannot (or, at least, should not) make a product that the market does not want, and it cannot dispose of its products unless selling prices are in line with what the market is willing to pay. A company cannot survive for long if it cannot equal the performance of its competitors. By contrast, many nonprofit organizations decide what services they should render on the basis of the judgment of their managements, rather than according to what the market wants. And, in many cases, a nonprofit organization need not worry about competition. These differences have important implications for management control.

A profit-oriented company wants more customers. More customers mean more profit. In many nonprofit organizations, however, there is no such relationship between the number of clients and the success of the organization. If the amount of its available resources are fixed by appropriations (as in the case of government agencies) or by income from endowment or annual giving (as is the case with many educational, religious and charitable organizations), additional clients may place a strain on resources. In a profit-oriented organization, therefore, the new client is an *opportunity* to be vigorously sought after; in many nonprofit organizations, the new client is only a burden, to be accepted with misgivings.

Competition provides a powerful incentive to use resources wisely. If a firm in a competitive industry permits its costs to get out of control, its product line to become out of fashion, or its quality to decrease, its profits will decline. A nonprofit organization has no such automatic danger signal.

Because the importance of what the organization does is not measured by demand in the marketplace, managers of nonprofit organizations tend to be influenced by their personal convictions of what is important. As a substitute for the market mechanism for allocating resources, managers compete with one another for available resources. The physics department, the English department, and the library, all try to get as large a slice as possible of the college budget pie.

Ownership and Power

The statement that shareholders "run" a corporation is an oversimplification, but it is unquestionably true that shareholders have the ultimate authority. Although they may exercise this authority only in times of crisis, it is nevertheless there. The movement of stock prices is an immediate and influential indication of what shareholders think of their management. In profit-oriented organizations, policy and management responsibilities are vested in the board of directors, which derives its power from the shareholders. In turn, the board delegates power to the president, who serves at the board's pleasure, acts as the board's agent in the administration of the organization, and who is replaced if there are serious differences of interest or opinion.

In many nonprofit organizations the corresponding line of responsibility is often not clear. In nongovernment organizations, the presumably controlling body does not necessarily represent the source of the organization's power. Instead of being selected formally by those ultimately responsible for the organization, it may be self-perpetuating, selected by outside parties, or selected *de facto* by top management. Its members are seldom paid for their services. They feel little pressure from, or little responsibility to, outside groups.

In government organizations, the diffusion of power is also great. The bureaucracy is often insulated from top management by virtue of job security and rules, and career civil servants may know that they will outlast the term of office of the elected or appointed chief executive. Agencies, or units within agencies, may have their own special-interest clienteles (e.g., Maritime Administration and shipping interests) with political power which is stronger than that of the chief executive of the agency. Top management authority may be divided, particularly in those states where the expenditure authority is vested in committees of independently elected officials, and in local governments administered by commissions whose members each administer a particular segment of the organization (e.g., streets, public safety, welfare, education). In State and Federal governments, there is a division of authority among executive, legislative, and judicial branches. There may also be a vertical division of authority among levels of government (federal, state, and local), each responsible for facets of the same problem. For example, the Federal government finances all major highways and partially finances many minor highways, and state and local governments construct and maintain other highways.

Although the power exercized by the governing board in a nonprofit organization is usually less than that exercized by the board of a profit-oriented organization, the need for an active, involved governing board is actually greater in a nonprofit organization. This is because the vigilance of the governing board is the only effective way of detecting when the organization is in difficulty. In a profit-oriented organization, a decrease in profits provides this danger signal automatically. Boards of trustees and legislative oversight committees therefore should take this responsibility seriously, much more seriously than most of them do.

Politics

Many nonprofit organizations are political; that is, they are responsible to the electorate or to a legislative body that presumably represents the electorate. Elected officials cannot function if they are not re-elected, and in order to be re-elected, they must—at least up to a point—advocate the perceived needs of their constituency, even though satisfying these needs may not be in the best interests of the larger body that they are supposed to govern.

In a democratic society the press and public feel that they have a right to know everything there is to know about a public organization, and media stories tend to exaggerate the sins that they uncover. Consequently, government managers take steps to reduce the amount of sensitive, controversial information that flows through the formal management control system, and this lessens the usefulness of the system.

Government executive organizations must operate within statutes enacted by the legislative branch. These are much more restrictive than the charter and by-laws of corporations; often they prescribe detailed operating practices. It is relatively difficult to change these statutes.

When the Number One person in an organization is elected by the voters, the person is often chosen for reasons other than ability as a manager. Moreover, in some public organizations top management tends to change rapidly because of administration changes, political shifts, military orders, and managers who only dabble in government jobs. Each change requires a "learning lead time" and many of them result in changes in priorities. This rapid turnover tends to result in emphasis on short-run plans and programs which produce quickly visible results, rather than longer-range programs.

Salaries and other compensation of managers in public organizations tend to be relatively low. Consequently, managers of these organizations, especially those near the top of the organization, may be less capable than their counterparts in profit-oriented organizations.

Tradition

In the 19th century, accounting was primarily *fiduciary* accounting; that is, its purpose was to keep track of the funds that were entrusted to an organization so as to ensure that they were spent honestly. In the 20th century, accounting in business organizations has assumed much broader functions. It furnishes useful information about the business both to interested outside parties and to management. Nonprofit organizations have been slow to adopt 20th century accounting and management control concepts and practices.

OUTPUT MEASUREMENT

In a profit-oriented company, the amount of revenue is a good measure of output. For the company as a whole, revenue is measured by the prices charged for goods and services sold in the marketplace. For individual profit centers, revenue is measured both by market prices and by transfer prices. Nonprofit organizations that provide service to individual clients usually can devise similar monetary measures of output. Other organizations must rely on nonmonetary measures.

Pricing

Although prices charged for services rendered are an important consideration in the management control structure, many nonprofit organizations have given inadequate attention to their pricing policies. To the extent that pricing of services is feasible, the following benefits can be achieved:

1. If services are sold at prices that approximate full cost, the revenue figure that is thereby generated is a measure of the quantity of services that the organization supplies. In the absence of such an output measure, it is difficult to measure either efficiency or effectiveness.

2. Charging clients for services rendered makes them more aware of the value of the service and encourages them to consider whether the services are actually worth as much to them as their cost. If revenues generated by full-cost prices are not sufficient to cover total expenses, there is an indication that the service is not valuable enough to society to warrant the cost of providing for it. It may be that the organization's costs are higher than necessary, or that a lower-cost service would satisfy the clients' needs.

3. If services are sold, the responsibility center that sells them can become, in effect, a profit center. The manager of a profit center becomes responsible for operating the unit in such a way that revenue equals expenses. Such a manager is motivated to think of ways of rendering additional service that will increase revenue, to think of ways of cutting costs to the point where the corresponding price is one that clients are willing to pay, to become more vigilant in controlling overhead costs, and in general to behave like a manager in a profit-oriented company.

Notwithstanding these advantages of charging for services rendered, there are many situations in which prices should not be charged.

The most important class of these is *public goods*. Public goods are services which are for the benefit of the public in general, rather than for an individual client. Examples are police protection, as contrasted with a police officer who is hired by the manager of a sporting event; and foreign policy and its implementation, as contrasted with services rendered to an individual firm doing business overseas. In addition to the general class of public goods, prices should not normally be charged for services when it is public policy to provide the services (e.g., welfare investigations; legal aid services), when it is public policy not to ration the services on the basis of ability to pay, when the cost of collecting the revenue exceeds the benefits, or when a charge is politically untenable.

Full-Cost Pricing. As a general rule, prices should be equal to full cost. A nonprofit organization often has a monopoly position. It should not set prices that exceed its cost, for to do so would be taking unjustifiable advantage of its monopoly status. Furthermore, the organization does not need to charge prices that are higher than costs. If it does so, it generates a profit, and by definition no person can benefit from such a profit. Neither should a nonprofit organization price below full cost because that would be providing services to clients at less than the services are presumably worth; this can lead to a misallocation of resources in the economy.

A full-cost pricing policy should normally apply to services that are directly related to the organization's principal objectives, and to services that clients ordinarily take as a necessary concomitant to the organization's principal objectives; but it does not necessarily apply to peripheral activities. Prices for these activities should ordinarily correspond to market prices for similar services. For example, in a hospital, prices for hospital care, surgical procedures, laboratory procedures, X-rays, and meals come within the general rule, but prices in the gift shop in the hospital should be market based.

Although the pricing strategy should normally be to recover full cost for the organization as a whole, it may be desirable to price specific services above or below full cost. The relevant considerations are essentially the same as those that profit-oriented companies consider when they depart from full-cost pricing.

The Pricing Unit. In general, the smaller and more specific the unit of service that is priced, the better the basis for decisions about the allocation of resources and the more accurate the measure of output for management control purposes. An overall price is not a good measure of output because it masks the actual mix of services rendered. For example, a blanket daily charge does not provide as good a measure of output in a hospital as specific charges for room rental, use of the operating room, drugs, and so on. Separate charges for the day of admission (to cover "work up" costs), and for geriatric and infant patients as compared with other patients, are examples of opportunities to make the pricing unit even smaller.

This principle is subject to two qualifications. The first is the obvious one that beyond a certain point, the paperwork and other costs associated with pricing tiny units of service outweigh the benefits. The precise location of this point is of course uncertain. The second qualification is that the pricing policy should be consistent with the organization's overall policy. It is a fact that undergraduate English instruction per student costs less than undergraduate physics instruction, and it would be feasible to reflect these differences in cost by charging different prices for each course that a student takes. Nevertheless, a separate price for each course may well lead students to select courses in a way that the university administration does not consider educationally sound.

Prospective Pricing. As a general rule, management control is facilitated when the price is set prior to the performance of the service, as contrasted with the alternative of reimbursing the service provider for the actual amount of costs incurred. When prices are set in advance, they provide an incentive for the organization to keep costs within the level of anticipated revenue, whereas no such incentive exists when the organization knows that whatever the level of costs may be, they will be recouped. An organization that knows that it is going to recover its costs, whatever they are, is not likely to do much worrying about cost control. When reliable methods of setting prices in advance can be worked out, the incentive is much stronger.

This principle can be applied, of course, only when it is possible to make a reasonable advance estimate of what the services should cost. For many research or development projects, for example, there is no good basis for estimating how much should be spent in order to achieve the desired result, and the reimbursement for such work is necessarily based on actual costs incurred.

Transfer Pricing.   Most nonprofit organizations have not given much attention to developing a sound policy on transfer prices, even though goods and services are transferred from one responsibility center to another to roughly the same degree as is the case in profit-oriented organizations. The basic purposes of a transfer price are the same in both types of organizations; that is, to measure the revenue of the responsibility center that furnishes the product and the cost of the unit that receives the product in a way that aids management decisions and that motivates responsibility center managers to work in the best interests of the organization. The principles for transfer pricing in nonprofit organizations are essentially the same as those in profit-oriented organizations, as discussed in Chapter 7.

Nonmonetary Output Measurement

Prices can be charged only by client-oriented organizations. In other organizations, and also in many circumstances in client-oriented organizations, output must be measured in nonmonetary terms. Output measures can be classified in various ways. They can be subjective or objective; that is, they can be derived from a person's judgment or they may be derived from numerical data. They can be quantitative or nonquantitative. They can be discrete or scalar. They can measure either the quantity of output or the quality of output.

An important way of classifying output measures is according to what it is they purport to measure. Although many different terms are used in practice, they can be grouped into three categories: (1) results measures, (2) process measures, and (3) social indicators.

A *results measure* is a measure of output expressed in terms that are supposedly related to an organization's objectives. In the ideal situation, the objective is stated in measurable terms, and the output measure is stated in these same terms. When this relationship is not feasible, as is often the case, the performance measure represents the closest feasible way of measuring the accomplishment of an objective that cannot itself be expressed quantitatively. Such a measure is called a *surrogate* or a *proxy*. A results measure relates to the impact that the organization has on the outside world.

A *process measure* relates to an activity carried on by the organization. Examples are the number of livestock inspected in a week, the number of lines typed in an hour, the number of requisitions filled in a month, or the number of purchase orders written. The essential difference between a results measure and a process measure is that the former is "ends oriented," while the latter is "means oriented." An ends-oriented indicator is a direct measure of success in achieving an objective. A means-oriented indicator is a measure of what a responsibility center or an individual does. There is an implicit assumption that what the responsibility center does helps achieve the organization's objectives, but this is not always a valid assumption.

Process measures are most useful in the measurement of current, short-run performance. They are the easiest type of output measure to interpret because there presumably is a close causal relationship between inputs and process measures. They measure efficiency, but not effectiveness. Being only remotely related to goals, they are of little use in strategic planning. They are useful in constructing relevant parts of a budget, but only for those activities for which it is feasible to obtain process measures. They are useful in the control of lower-level responsibility centers. Process measures should not be used if results measures are available.

A *social indicator* is a broad measure of output which is significantly the result of the work of the organization, but which is also affected by exogenous forces, and which therefore is at best only a rough indication of the accomplishment of the organization itself. Social indicators are often stated in broad terms (e.g., "the expectation of healthy life free of serious disability and institutionalization"). Such statements are generally not as useful as those expressed in more specific, preferably measurable, terms (e.g., infant mortality rates, life expectancy). Social indicators are useful principally for long-range analyses of strategic problems. They are so nebulous, so difficult to obtain on a current basis, so little affected by current program effort, and so much affected by external influences, that they are of limited usefulness in day-to-day management.

Inputs as a Measure of Outputs

Although generally less desirable than a true output measure, inputs are often a better measure of output than no measure at all. For example, it may not be feasible to construct output measures for research projects. In the absence of such measures, the amount spent on a research project may provide a useful clue as to its output. In the extreme, if no money was spent, it is apparent that nothing was accomplished. (This assumes that the accounting records show what actually was spent, which sometimes is not the case.) When inputs are used as proxy output measures, care must be exercised to avoid undue reliance on them, and the organization should try to develop usable measures of output.

PROGRAMMING

In government organizations particularly, and also in other organizations in which important decisions must be made as to how resources are to be allocated so as to achieve the organization's goals, programming is an important process, more important and more time consuming than in the typical profit-oriented organization. Until fairly recently, the process was carried out informally, but with the development of the Planning-Programming-Budgeting System (PPBS) in the Federal government in the 1960s, it has become increasingly formalized. (Although the name PPBS is no longer used in the Federal government, its essential concepts continue there, and are also being used increasingly in state and municipal governments.)

The programming process described in Chapter 9 is entirely applicable to nonprofit organizations. Only two aspects of it are discussed here: (1) the program structure, and (2) benefit/cost analysis.

Program Structure

Because of the absence of the unifying profit objective, the development of a sound program structure in a nonprofit organization is much more difficult than in a profit-oriented organization. In a business company, the programs are essentially product lines plus research/development and other staff activities, and these are readily identified. In a nonprofit organization it is difficult to decide on the best way of classifying activities into a formal program structure.

Information from the program structure is used for one or more of the following purposes: (1) to facilitate decision making about programs, (2) to provide a basis of comparison of the costs and outputs of similar programs, (3) to set selling prices or provide a basis for reimbursement of costs. The structure should be designed to meet these needs.

The information needed for one of these three purposes may differ from that needed by others. In that case, compromises in designing the structure may be required. In most situations, one of these purposes is clearly dominant, however, and the structure can be designed primarily to provide information needed for that purpose. In public-oriented organizations, the use of information as a basis for making decisions on programs tends to be by far the dominant purpose, whereas in many client-oriented organizations, pricing considerations tend to be dominant.

The program structure consists of three "layers." At the top are a relatively few *program categories* (sometimes called "major programs"). At the bottom are a great many *program elements;* these are the smallest units in which information is collected in program terms. In between are summaries of related program elements, which are here called *program subcategories.*

The primary purpose of the classification of program categories is to facilitate top management judgment on the allocation of resources. Similarly, the primary purpose of the classification into program subcategories is to facilitate middle management judgment on the allocation of resources within programs. The program structure should therefore correspond to the principal objectives of the organization. It should be arranged so as to faciltate making decisions having to do with the relative importance of these objectives. Stated another way, it should focus on the organization's outputs— what it achieves or intends to achieve—rather than on its inputs, that is, the types of resources it uses, or the sources of its funds. A structure that is arranged by types of resources (e.g., personnel, material, services) or by sources of support (e.g., in a university: tuition, legislative appropriations, gifts) is not a useful program structure.

The designation of major programs helps to communicate what the objectives of the organization are. The development of the management control structure may also clarify organizational purpose, and thus suggest improvements in the structure of the organization. Therefore, the program structure should not necessarily correspond to the *existing* categories on which decisions are based; rather, it should correspond to those categories which can reasonably be expected to be useful for decision making in the future.

If is feasible to do so, it is desirable to structure program subcategories and program elements so that each can be associated with a *quantitative* measure of performance, that is of output. At the broad level of program categories, however, no reliable measure of performance can be found in many situations.

Relation to Responsibility.   Although there are advantages in relating program categories and subcategories to organizational responsibility, this criterion is less important than that of facilitating top management judgment. Sometimes the system's designers try to change the organization structure so that it fits the program structure. In general, this should not be done. The system exists to serve the organization, not vice versa. Changes in organizational responsibility should be made if, but only if, such changes help the organization get its job done better. Sometimes the system designer does uncover a situation which would be improved by a reorganization. If the system designer can convince management, fine; otherwise, the system should be designed to fit the organization as it exsts.

Although the program structure need not, and ordinarily will not, match the organization structure, there should be some person who has identifiable responsibility for each program category or subcategory. In some agencies, each program category has its own program manager. This is the *matrix* type of organization, the matrix consisting of program managers in one dimension and functionally organized responsibility centers in the other dimension; it is discussed in more detail in Chapter 16. Program managers may have other responsibilities, and they may have to call on other parts of the organization for most of the work that is to be done on their program. The program managers are advocates of their programs and are held accountable for the performance of their programs.

Benefit/Cost Analysis

The idea that the benefits of a proposed course of action should be compared with its costs is not new. Techniques for analyzing the profitability of proposed business investments involve essentially the same approach. Certain government agencies, such as the Bureau of Reclamation, have made such analyses for decades. Proposals to build new dams were justified on the grounds that their benefits exceeded their costs. Interest in the approach grew rapidly in the 1960s when the Department of Defense applied the concept to problems for which no formal analysis previously had been attempted. It then became fashionable to apply benefit/cost analysis to all sorts of proposed programs in nonprofit organizations. The results of these efforts have been mixed, and there is now considerable controversy about the merits of the approach for certain types of problems.

Although overexuberant advocates and outright charlatans do exist, and their works are properly criticized, there is no doubt that benefit/cost analysis has produced useful results. There are two essential points:

1. Benefit/cost analysis focuses on those consequences of a proposal which can be estimated in quantitative terms. Since there is no important problem in which *all* the relevant factors can be reduced to numbers, benefit/cost analysis will never provide the complete answer to any important problem.

2. However, if *some* of the important factors can be reduced to quantitative terms, it is often better to do so than not to do so. The resulting analysis narrows the area within which management judgment is required, even though it does not eliminate the need for judgment.

Charles Schultze, at the time Director of the Bureau of the Budget, summarized the appropriate role of benefit/cost analysis in a statement which has become a classic:

Systematic analysis is an aid to policy debate. Too often these debates revolve around a simple list of pros and cons. There are no means of making progress in the debate, since participants simply repeat, in different words, their original positions. Systematic analysis is designed to improve this process by:

Uncovering the irrelevant issues.

Identifying the specific assumptions and factual bases upon which alternative recommendations rest, and,

Tracing out the knowable consequences and costs of each alternative.

By this means, systematic analysis is designed to narrow the debate, to focus it on the important issues, and—I underline and stress this—to separate those points about which the judgments of reasonable men can disagree from those which are demonstrably true or false. . . . .

Handled properly, a well constructed numerical estimate can be worth a thousand words. And we seek to encourage quantitative estimates, as part of the systematic analysis of budgetary issues.

But this, most emphatically, does not mean that quantitative estimates are the only elements of systematic analysis. The latter is far broader than the former. Human factors and intangible elements in a decision must not be ignored. And that which cannot reasonably be measured should not be.[1]

Alternative Approaches.   In benefit/cost analysis the general principles

---

[1] From his Statement to the Subcommittee on National Security and International Operations of the Committee on Government Operations, U.S. Senate, 90th Congress, 1st Session, August 23, 1967.

are that (1) a program should not be adopted unless its benefits exceed its costs, and (2) as between two competing proposals the one with the greater excess of benefits over costs, or the one with the lower costs if benefits are equal, is preferable. In order to apply these principles there must be some way of relating benefits and costs.

For many proposals in nonprofit organizations, it is possible to estimate both costs and benefits in monetary terms. These proposals are similar to the capital budgeting proposals for profit-oriented companies, and the method of analysis in nonprofit organizations is essentially the same. A proposal to convert the heating plant of a hospital from oil to coal involves the same type of analysis that would be used for the same problem in an industrial company. Problems of this type are numerous in nonprofit organizations. Unfortunately, they are also relatively unimportant. For most of the important problems a reliable monetary estimate of the benefits cannot be made.

Even if the benefits cannot be quantified, a benefit/cost analysis is useful in situations in which there are two or more ways of achieving a given objective. If there is a reasonable presumption that each of the alternatives will achieve the objective, then the alternative with the lowest cost is preferred. This approach has many applications, simply because it does not require that the objective be stated in monetary terms, or even that it be quantified. All that is necessary is a judgment that any of the proposed alternatives will achieve the objective. We need not measure the *degree* to which a given alternative meets the objective; we need only make the "go/no-go" judgment that the results are adequate. Similarly, if two competing proposals have the same cost, but one produces more benefits than the other, it ordinarily is the preferred alternative. This conclusion can be reached without a measurement of the absolute levels of benefits.

Different Objectives.   A benefit/cost comparison of proposals intended to accomplish different objectives is likely to be worthless. An analysis that attempts to compare funds to be spent for primary school education with funds to be spent for retraining of unemployed adults would not be worthwhile because such an analysis requires that monetary values be assigned to the benefits of these two programs, which is an impossible task. Also, some benefit/cost analyses implicitly assume that there is a causal relationship between the benefits and the costs, that is, that spending $X of cost produces Y amount of benefit. If this causal connection does not exist, such an analysis is fallacious.

BUDGETING

Budgeting is a more important process in a nonprofit organization than in a profit-oriented organization. In a profit-oriented organization, operating managers can safely be allowed to modify plans, provided that the revised plan promises to increase profits. Operating managers of nonprofit organizations, especially those whose annual revenue is essentially fixed, must adhere closely to plans as expressed in the budget. Budgeting is perhaps the most important part of the management control process, and well managed organizations devote much thought and time to it.

The first step in the budgeting process is to estimate the amount of revenue that the organization is likely to receive for operating purposes during the budget year. The next step is to budget expenses that equal this amount of revenue. This matching of expenses to revenue differs from the approach used in profit-oriented organizations because in profit-oriented organizations the amount budgeted for marketing expenses can influence the amount of revenue.

A nonprofit organization should plan to incur expenses that are approximately equal to its revenue. If its budgeted expenses are lower than its revenue, it is not providing the quantity of services that those who provide the revenue have a right to expect. If its budgeted expenses exceed its revenue, the difference must be made up by the generally undesirable actions of drawing down endowment or other capital funds that are intended to provide services to future generations. If the first approximation of budgeted expenses exceeds estimated revenue, the prudent course of action usually is to reduce expenses rather than to anticipate that revenue can be increased.

The budget is structured in terms of responsibility centers. Budget estimates are prepared by responsibility center managers and are consistent with the approved program and with other guidelines prescribed by top management. Budgetees negotiate approval of these estimates with their superiors. Because time does not permit a more thorough analysis, the level of current spending is usually taken as a starting point in these negotiations. The approved budget is a bilateral commitment: the budgetee commits to accomplish the planned objectives within the spending limits specified in the budget, and the superior commits to regarding such an accomplishment as representing satisfactory performance.

Management by Objectives

In addition to estimates of monetary amounts, budgetees should also state, as specifically as possible, the objectives that they expect to attain during the budget year. This part of the budgeting process is relatively new, or at least the organized effort under the label "Management by Objectives" is relatively new, but it is being emphasized increasingly in the Federal government, and is spreading to other types of nonprofit organizations.

If at all possible, the objectives should be quantified so that actual performance can be compared with them. Objectives are output measures. These statements of objectives take the place of the profitability objective which is a key part of the budgeting process in a profit-oriented company. The appropriateness of the revenue and cost estimates in such a company can be judged in terms of whether or not they produce a satisfactory profit.

In a nonprofit organization, such an overall yardstick of judging the estimates in the budget does not exist. In the absence of some substitute, the budgeted costs can be judged in terms of what was spent last year, but this is not a very satisfactory basis for judgment. What the supervisor wants to know is what results will be obtained from the use of the budgeted resources. A statement of objectives that is related directly to the budgeted costs provides this information.

Some organizations use a "management by objectives" procedure that is quite separate from the budgeting process. This separation came about usually because the technique happened to be sponsored by persons who were outside the controller organization. The controller is usually responsible for the budgeting process. Such a separation is undesirable. In discussing plans for next year, both the costs and the results expected from incurring these costs should be considered together.

Fund Accounting

A unique feature of the accounting systems in nonprofit organizations is the use of what are called *fund accounts*. Indeed, a study of accounting in such organizations is often called "fund accounting" as if this were the central feature of the system. Actually, the fund accounts play a relatively minor role in the management control process. A general understanding of their nature and purpose is nevertheless desirable.

In a business accounting system, the available resources for the whole company are, in effect, in one "pot"; that is, the balance sheet lists the assets for the whole organization. In a nonprofit organization, by contrast, the resources may be accounted for in several separate pots, each of which is called a fund. Each fund has its own set of accounts that are self-balancing, and each fund is therefore a separate entity, almost as if it were a separate business. The purpose of this device is to insure that the organization uses the resources made available to each fund only for the purposes designated for that fund.

Omitting several highly specialized funds, the principal funds are:

1. The *general fund* which comprises the resources made available to operate the organization for a specified period of time, usually a year; that is, there is one operating fund for 1975, another for 1976, and so on.
2. A *capital fund* which provides for the construction or acquisition of approved capital assets.
3. The *endowment fund* which holds money entrusted to an organization for endowment purposes. The principal is supposed to be held intact, usually forever, and the earnings on that principal are made available for current use.
4. *Sinking funds,* which are maintained in association with bond issues.
5. *Working capital funds,* also called "revolving funds," which are used to finance inventories and other consumable assets. Their function corresponds

to the function of the inventory accounts in a business, namely, to hold assets in suspense until they are consumed and hence become costs.

To the extent that fund accounting forces a clean separation between operating transactions and capital or endowment transactions, it is a useful device, corresponding essentially to the separation between income statement items and other balance sheet changes in a business. Conversely, to the extent that funds are further segregated as a device for enforcing detailed decisions on spending, they are unnecessary. The same results can be achieved with less effort by other means.

SUGGESTED ADDITIONAL READINGS

ANTHONY, ROBERT N. and REGINA E. HERZLINGER. *Management Control in Nonprofit Organizations.* Homewood, Ill., Richard D. Irwin, Inc., 1975.

GROSS, MALVERN J., Jr. *Financial and Accounting Guide for Nonprofit Organizations.* New York: Ronald Press, 1972.

HAY, LEON B. and R. M. MIKESELL. *Government Accounting.* Homewood, Ill., Richard D. Irwin, Inc., 1974.

KERRIGAN, H. D. *Fund Accounting.* New York: McGraw-Hill Books, Inc., 1969.

Case 15-1

Disease Control Programs

In February, 1967, Mr. Harley Davidson, an analyst in the office of the Injury Control Program, Public Health Service (Department of Health, Education and Welfare) was reviewing DHEW's recently published Program Analysis 1966–1 titled *Disease Control Programs—Motor Vehicle Injury Prevention Program.* Included therein were nine program units, as summarized in Appendix A. Mr. Davidson was a member of a task force established within DHEW to evaluate a series of benefit/cost analyses of various proposed disease control programs. In addition to motor vehicle injury prevention, benefit/cost studies had been made of programs dealing with control of arthritis, cancer, tuberculosis, and syphilis. Mr. Davidson's specific responsibility was to review program Unit No. 8 of the motor vehicle injury prevention program (Increase Use of Improved Safety Devices by Motorcyclists) in order to (a) evaluate the methodology and results of the benefit/cost analysis of Program Unit No. 8, and (b) recommend whether or not the analysis justified the level of funding contemplated in the Program Unit.

THE MOTORCYCLE PROGRAM

The following is the description of Program Unit No. 8 which appeared in Program Analysis 1966–1:

Increase Use of Improved Safety Devices by Motorcyclists

To prevent accidental deaths due to head injuries of motorcycle riders through appropriate health activity at the national, state, and local levels.

Approach. The Public Health Service approach to solving the motorcycle injury problem will involve four phases. Although each of the four phases of activity is identified separately, all will be closely coordinated and carried out simultaneously. The four phases of activity are:

1. A national education program on use of protective head gear aimed primarily at motorcycle users. It will also include efforts to prepare operators of other motor vehicles to share the road with motorcycles.

2. A cooperative program with other national organizations and the motorcycle industry to improve protective and safety devices.

3. Involvement of state and local health departments and medical organizations in programs and activities designed to minimize accidental injury in motorcycle accidents.

4. Conduct surveillance activity on appropriate aspects of the motorcycle accident and injury problem.

The Program Unit was estimated to require the following level of new funding during the 5-year planning period 1968–72:

Estimated Program Level
(millions of dollars)

1968	1.679
1969	1.609
1970	1.575
1971	1.569
1972	1.569

Exhibit 1 gives a summary of the way in which the proposed funds would be spent.

The benefit/cost study estimated that the above program would result in the saving of 4,006 lives over the 5-year period 1968–72 (no reduction in

Exhibit 1

PROPOSED BUDGET FOR PROGRAM TO INCREASE USE OF PROTECTIVE DEVICES BY MOTORCYCLISTS, 1968–1972
(Costs in Thousands)

	1968	*1969*	*1970*	*1971*	*1972*
Total number of persons	42	42	42	42	42
Total costs	$1,679	$1,609	$1,575	$1,569	$1,569
Personnel	504	504	504	504	504
Program	1,175	1,105	1,070	1,065	1,065
Staff:					
Central office	13	13	13	13	13
Regional office	9	9	9	9	9
State assignees	20	20	20	20	20
Personnel	$ 504	$ 504	$ 504	$ 504	$ 504
Evaluation and surveillance	300	300	300	300	300
State projects*	500	500	500	500	500
National TV spots	60	60	60	60	60
Educational TV series	100	100	100	100	100
Safety films	40	40	20	20	20
Publications	100	30	30	30	30
Exhibits	30	30	15	15	15
Community projects	25	25	25	25	25
Campus projects	20	20	20	15	15

* Ten projects at $50,000 per project.

injuries was considered). The cost of the program discounted at 4 percent was $7,419,000; the benefits of the program, based on the lifetime earnings discounted at 3 percent of those whose deaths would be averted, were estimated at $412,754,000. Hence, the benefit/cost ratio equaled 55.6:1. Another measure of program effectiveness was the cost per death averted, $1,860. Exhibit 2 summarizes the benefit/cost ratios and the costs per death

Exhibit 2

**COSTS PER DEATH AVERTED AND BENEFIT-COST RATIOS
FOR ALL PROGRAM UNITS STUDIED**

Program Unit	Program Cost per Death Averted	Benefit/Cost Ratio
Motor Vehicle Injury Prevention Programs:		
Increase seat belt use	87	1,351.4:1
Use of improved restraint devices	100	1,117.1:1
Reduce pedestrian injury	600	144.3:1
Increase use of protective devices		
by motorcyclists	1,860	55.6:1
Improve driving environment	2,330	49.4:1
Reduce driver drinking	5,330	21.5:1
Improve driver licensing	13,800	3.8:1
Improve emergency medical services	45,000	2.4:1
Improve driver training	88,000	1.7:1
Other Disease Control Programs Studied:		
Arthritis	N/A	42.5:1
Syphilis	22,252	16.7:1
Uterine Cervix Cancer	3,470	9.0:1
Lung Cancer	6,400	5.7:1
Breast Cancer	7,663	4.5:1
Tuberculosis	22,807	4.4:1
Head and Neck Cancer	29,100	1.1:1
Colon-Rectum Cancer	42,944	0.5:1

averted for all nine motor vehicle injury prevention program units and for the arthritis, cancer, tuberculosis, and syphilis programs. Exhibit 3 presents, for all programs, the estimated 5-year reduction in numbers of injuries and deaths and the estimated discounted 5-year program dollar costs and benefits.

OVERALL METHODOLOGY

In this effort to apply benefit/cost analysis to the domain of vehicular accidents, three major constraints were laid down:

1. The problem of motor vehicle accidents is examined exclusively in terms of public health concerns. This mandate focused on the role of human factors in vehicular accidents and the amelioration of injury caused by vehicular accidents. In adopting this posture, three major factors in vehicular accident complex—law enforcement, road design, and traffic engineering—were, for

Exhibit 3

**REDUCTION IN INJURIES AND DEATHS AND TOTAL DISCOUNTED PROGRAM
COSTS AND SAVINGS FOR ALL PROGRAM UNITS STUDIED, 1968–72**

Program Unit	Discounted Program Costs ($000)	Discounted Program Savings ($000)	Reduction in Injuries	Reduction in Deaths
Motor Vehicle Injury Prevention Programs:				
Seat belts	2,019	2,728,374	1,904,000	22,930
Restraint devices	610	681,452	471,600	5,811
Pedestrian injury	1,061	153,110	142,700	1,650
Motorcyclists	7,419	412,754	—	4,006
Driving environment	28,545	1,409,891	1,015,500	12,250
Driver drinking	28,545	612,970	440,630	5,340
Driver licensing	6,113	22,938	23,200	442
Emergency medical services	721,478*	1,726,000	†	16,000
Other Disease Control Driver training	750,550	1,287,022	665,300	8,515
Programs Studied:				
Arthritis	35,000	1,489,000	N/A	N/A
Syphilis	179,300‡	2,993,000	N/A	11,590
Uterine Cervix Cancer	118,100‡	1,071,000	N/A	34,200
Lung Cancer	47,000‡	268,000	N/A	7,000
Breast Cancer	22,400	101,000	N/A	2,396
Tuberculosis	130,000	573,000	N/A	5,700
Head & Neck Cancer	7,800	9,000	N/A	268
Colon-Rectum Cancer	7,300	4,000	N/A	170

* Includes $300 million State matching funds.
† This program does not reduce injury; however, it is estimated to reduce hospital bed days by 2,401,000 and work loss days by 8,180,000.
‡ Funding shown used as basis for analysis—includes funds estimated to come from sources other than DHEW.

the most part, excluded. This constraint had the effect of limiting the problem to considerations traditionally within the purview of DHEW, while excluding those elements which are traditionally handled by the Department of Commerce and other Government agencies.

2. The problem of motor vehicle accidents is handled by nine programs which, in the opinion of Committee members, were feasible and realistic. Criteria for determining "feasible and realistic" were not made explicit. However, program proposals which were rejected, such as no person under 21 being allowed to drive, reduction of maximum speeds on all roads by 20 percent, the Federal Government paying for the installation of $100 worth of safety devices on all automobiles, indicate the cultural values and assumed cost factors which were two issues involved in judging "feasible and realistic."

3. The problem of motor vehicle accidents is handled by programs based on what is known today. This constraint ruled out dependence on new findings based on future research. Unlike the other constraints, this ruling, in the minds of the Committee members, constituted a basic condition for

undertaking a benefit/cost analysis of alternative program strategies. Unless the analysis was restricted to "what is known," the "need for more research" would allow one partner in the dialogue to withdraw from the struggle without even having been engaged.

The Report then went on to describe the rationale behind benefit/cost analysis:

The reasoning behind the benefit/cost analysis is quite straightforward. The idea is to allow for a meaningful comparison of the change which results in a given situation as a result of applying alternative programs. In order to bring about this state of affairs, a measurable common denominator is useful for rating program outcome and program costs. This common denominator is dollars. Granting the existence of the common denominator, there must, in addition, be a point on which to take a "fix" in order to support the contention that change has, in fact, taken place. This point for fixing position and shifts in relation to change wrought by program is the baseline.

In this exercise the base line was created by assessing past rates for motor vehicle and pedestrian deaths and injuries. The assumption was made that the current level of program effort in DHEW would remain constant through 1972 with the exception of increases for obligated administrative costs. The observed trend was then projected and applied to the anticipated population distribution for the years 1967–1972. Program costs and savings due to the introduction of the program were limited to the 5-year period 1968–1972, although certain programs were just gathering momentum by the end of this period. . . . The required common denominator was incorporated into the baseline by converting fatalities into lost earnings and by translating lost work days, bed disability days, length of hospitalization, physician visits, and other medical services resulting from injuries into the direct and indirect costs represented by these statistical measures. . . . Throughout this analysis, the total dollar costs and benefit for the 5-year period are discounted to 1968, the base year, to convert the stream of costs and benefits into its worth in the base year . . .

With the baseline and common denominator established, the Committee was able to examine the potential payoff for a variety of program units even though these units differed with respect to such factors as cost of implementation, target group to be reached, method to be employed, and facet of the total program addressed by the proposed program.

With the establishment of the baseline and the development of techniques to convert all elements of the equation to a common denominator, the energies of the Committee were given over to the creation of program units. There are a number of variables which may contribute to the occurrence of a vehicular accident and its resultant injury or death. The skill of the driver, the condition of the road, the speed of the vehicle, the condition of the car, the failure to have or to use safety devices incorporated in the car are just a few of many that are mentioned in the literature. What we know about vehicular accidents is expressed in terms of these variables and as a consequence, program formulations are generally placed in the context of managing these variables, either singly or in combination.

A program unit, as developed by the Committee, usually addressed a single variable.

There are two links needed to effect the benefit/cost analysis in vehicular accidents. The first link is associated with the estimate of reduction that could be realized if a given variable were addressed by a program of some sort. This link is supplied in vehicular accidents by the expertise of the Committee members and recourse to studies on the particular variable in question. The second link is associated with the effectiveness of the program proposed to bring about the estimated reduction. In vehicular accidents this is supplied by the experience with programs of the Committee members and the success in the past of programs, similar in content, devoted to public health problems. . . .

ESTIMATE OF BENEFITS

The benefit/cost studies of the motor vehicle injury prevention programs began with a stipulation of a "base line," or the number of deaths and injuries to be expected if the level of DHEW effort remained constant. Next an estimate was made of the number of deaths and injuries which would be avoided if the proposed program unit were adopted. Finally, the reduction in deaths and injuries was translated into dollar terms. These three steps will now be described as they applied to Program Unit No. 8.

Base Line

The team working on the motorcycle unit had available the information given in Table 1.

Table 1

HISTORICAL DATA ON MOTORCYCLE REGISTRATIONS AND FATALITIES

Year	Total Number of Registered Motor-cycles in the U.S.	Number of Deaths from Motorcycle Accidents	Rate of Deaths per 100,000 Motorcycles
1959	565,352	752	133.0
1960	569,691	730	128.1
1961	595,669	697	117.0
1962	660,400	759	114.9
1963	786,318	882	112.2
1964	984,760	1,118	113.5

The team estimated that (1) the number of registered motorcycles would continue to increase at an increasing rate, and (2) the death rate would decline, in the absence of new safety programs, to a level of 110 deaths per 100,000 registered motorcycles. Accordingly, the number of motorcycle accident deaths to be expected without the safety program was projected as shown in Table 2.

Table 2

PROJECTED BASE LINE CASE

Year	Projected Total Number of Registered Motor-cycles in the U.S.	Projected Number of Deaths from Motorcycle Accidents without Program (based on 110 deaths per 100,000 registered motorcycles)
1968	2,900,000	3,190
1969	3,500,000	3,850
1970	4,200,000	4,620
1971	5,000,000	5,500
1972	6,000,000	6,600

Effectiveness of the Program Unit

Calculation of the anticipated reduction in the number of deaths result-ing from the proposed program unit involved two separate estimates: (1) the effectiveness of the program in persuading motorcyclists to wear helmets and protective eyeshields; and (2) the effectiveness of these devices in reducing deaths (injuries were not considered in the analysis of this program unit). The team's judgment was that the program would result in use of helmets and eyeshields to the degree shown in the following table:

Table 3

ESTIMATED EFFECTIVENESS OF PROGRAM
IN ENCOURAGING PROTECTIVE DEVICES

Year	Estimated Percentage of Motorcyclists Using Helmets and Eyeshields
1968	20
1969	30
1970	40
1971	50
1972	55

Regarding the second factor, the effectiveness of protective devices in reducing deaths, the team relied on a study entitled "Effect of Compulsory Safety Helmets on Motorcycle Accident Fatalities" which appeared in *Aus-tralian Road Research,* Vol. 2, No. 1, September 1964. This study reported that the number of motorcycle fatalities occurring in the Australian state of Victoria in the two years following the effective date of a law requiring the wearing of helmets was only 31 while the number of fatalities projected on the basis of the experience of the two preceding years was 62.5, for a reduction of about 50 percent. Other states, which did not have such a law, had shown a reduction of about 12 percent in the same period, a difference of 38 percent. The Committee concluded that 100 percent usage of helmets and eyeshields by American motorcyclists would reduce the number of deaths by about 40 percent.

Multiplication of the figures for projected usage of protective devices given in Table 3 by 40 percent gave the estimated percentage reduction in deaths, and application of these percentages to the base-line data of Table 2 gave the estimated reduction in number of deaths. The results are summarized in Table 4.

Table 4

ESTIMATED REDUCTION IN DEATHS FROM PROPOSED PROGRAM

Year	Projected Number of Deaths from Motor-cycle Accidents without Program	Estimated Percentage Reduction in Deaths with Program	Estimated Reduction in Number of Deaths with Program
1968	3,190	8	255
1969	3,850	12	462
1970	4,620	16	739
1971	5,500	20	1,100
1972	6,600	22	1,450
5-year total	23,760	—	4,006

Conversion to Economic Benefits

For the purpose of calculating the lifetime earnings lost in the event of a motorcycle fatality, it was necessary to estimate the distribution of fatalities by age and sex. In 1964, approximately 90 percent of the victims of motor-cycle accidents had been male and 10 percent female; similarly, about 90 percent had been in the age group 15–24 and 10 percent in the age group 25–34. The data were not cross-classified, so it was considered necessary to assume that the sex distribution of fatalities in each age group was the same as the overall distribution, i.e., 90:10. Projecting these percentages into the future, it was calculated that, of the 255 fatalities which the proposed program was expected to avoid in 1968, 207 would be males between 15 and 24 inclusive (i.e., $.9 \times .9 \times 255$). Combining this procedure for all categories and years resulted in the estimates of the distribution of death reductions over the 5-year period shown in Table 5.

The final step in calculating the expected benefits of the proposed program was to assign the appropriate dollar benefits to the above estimates of decreases in deaths by age group and sex. This was done by multiplying the decrease in deaths in each sex-age group "cell" in the above table by the applicable discounted lifetime earnings figure for that particular cell.

Table 5

ESTIMATED REDUCTION IN DEATHS BY AGE AND SEX

| Year | Age 15–24 | | Age 25–34 | | Total |
	Males	Females	Males	Females	
1968	207	23	22	3	255
1969	374	42	41	5	462
1970	598	67	67	7	739
1971	891	99	99	11	1,100
1972	1,174	131	130	15	1,450
Total	3,244	362	359	41	4,006

Table 6 shows lifetime earnings by age and sex, discounted at 3 percent used in computing the dollar benefits of reducing motorcycle accident fatalities. (The report contained a detailed description of the methodology used in deriving these amounts.)

Table 6

DISCOUNTED LIFETIME EARNINGS
BY AGE AND SEX

Age	Males	Females
Under 1	$ 84,371	$50,842
1–4	98,986	54,636
5–9	105,836	63,494
10–14	122,933	73,719
15–19	139,729	81,929
20–24	150,536	84,152
25–29	150,512	81,702
30–34	141,356	77,888

The number of deaths saved in each cell of Table 5 was multiplied by the appropriate earnings figure from Table 6, and discounted at 3 percent to the base year, 1968. For example, Table 5 indicates that it was estimated that, in 1968, the lives of 3 females between the ages of 25 and 34 would be saved. The discounted lifetime earnings of females in this age group was found from Table 6 by averaging the discounted lifetime earnings for females 25–29 and 30–34, the average of $81,702 and $77,888 being $79,795. This was multiplied by 3 to give $239,385; using a present value factor of 1 (since 1968 was the base year), the figure derived was $239,385. Similarly, discounted figures were obtained for each year by age group and sex; the results are shown below in Table 7.

Thus, over the 5-year program period, 1968–1972, it was estimated that 4,006 deaths could be averted (Table 5), at a present-value cost of $7,419,000. The present value of the lifetime earnings of the 4,006 persons

Table 7

**DISCOUNTED SAVINGS RESULTING FROM PROGRAM TO PROMOTE USE OF
PROTECTIVE DEVICES BY MOTORCYCLISTS (000's)**

Year	Total	Age 15–24		Age 25–34	
		Males	Females	Males	Females
TOTAL	$512,754	$434,002	$27,164	$48,714	$2,874
1968	36,140	30,347	1,976	3,578	239
1969	61,972	52,423	3,282	5,895	372
1970	97,152	82,363	5,059	9,248	482
1971	139,547	117,928	7,408	13,393	818
1972	177,943	150,941	9,439	16,600	963

whose lives would be saved during this period was shown in Table 7 to be
$412,754,000.

These data were summarized in the form of two measures of program
effectiveness:

(1) *Program Cost per Death Averted* $= \dfrac{\$7,419,000}{4,006} = \underline{\$1,860}$

(2) *Benefit/Cost Ratio* $= \dfrac{\$512,754,000}{\$7,419,000} = \underline{69.1}$

QUESTIONS

1. As Mr. Davidson, prepare a critique of the methodology and findings
of the benefit/cost analysis of Program Unit No. 8.

2. Based on your evaluation of the analysis, would you recommend the
level of funding proposed?

Appendix A

Motor Vehicle Injury Prevention
Program Units

Program Unit 1—Improve Driver Licensing. This program will develop a selective licensing procedure in each State which will screen out the drivers unsafe because of medical conditions.

Program Unit 2—Improve Driver Performance and Behavior by Upgrading Driving Skills, Knowledge and Attitude (Improve Driver Training). An improved program of driver education and training, through classroom work on roads, cars, laws, and personal limitations and behind the wheel supervised driving experience.

Program Unit 3—Improve Driving Performance and Behavior by Decreasing Driving Exposure While under the Influence of Alcohol and Drugs (Reduce Driver Drinking). This program will include a National education program to inform school age children and adults about the effects of alcohol on body functions and driving.

Program Unit 4—Reduce the Exposure of Pedestrians to Injury (Reduce Pedestrian Injury). A national education program will inform elderly persons of personal limitations, e.g., declining vision, and will inform the elderly and young children about traffic control devices, laws, and characteristics of the modern automobile and motor vehicle traffic.

Program Unit 5—Increase Seat Belt Use. A national public education program will use all mass media and organizational approaches to inform individuals about the decrease in risk and other advantages involved in wearing seat belts at all times. Opinion leaders such as clergy and the medical and legal professions will be utilized in transmitting the information.

Program Unit 6—Improve Driving Environment. A national education program will inform the general public about the desirability of changes in vehicle and road design, provide them with an understanding of their relationships to safer driving and create a readiness to accept instruction in their proper use.

Program Unit 7—Develop and Encourage Use of Improved Restraint Systems for Children and Adults (Use of Improved Restraint Systems). Information on the development of restraining devices will be made available to manufacturers and others who can stimulate the production of the devices. A national public education program will use all mass media and organizational approaches, including opinion leaders, to inform individuals about the decrease in risk and other advantages of using the improved restraining systems at all times.

Program Unit 8—Increase Use of Helmets and Protective Eyeshields by Motorcyclists. (Quoted in the text.)

Program Unit 9—Improve Emergency Medical Service. In order to assure adequate and timely care for every injured person, a planned approach would link the community ambulance services and hospitals into an integrated system. An extensive program of remodeling of emergency departments in hospitals is required to redesign, equip, and staff them adequately. Mobile emergency treatment stations (Packaged Emergency Station—PES) dispatched from the hospital to distant points of expected needs is suggested for extending hospital capacity.

Appendix B

Lifetime Earnings Patterns

The calculation of lifetime earnings figures used in DHEW's 1966 series of disease control program analyses was based largely on methodology developed by Mrs. Dorothy P. Rice of the Office of Research and Statistics, Social Security Administration, and reported by her in *Estimating the Cost of Illness.*[1]

The appropriate measure of output loss for individuals was considered to

---

[1] Health Economics Series No. 6, Public Health Service Publication No. 947–6, May 1966.

be year-round, full-time earnings, including wages and salaries before deductions plus wage supplements such as employer contributions for social insurance and private pension and welfare funds. Unpublished mean earnings data for full-time male workers in 1964 by 5-year age intervals were furnished by the Bureau of the Census. Similar data were not available for females, but the Bureau of the Census published *median* incomes for year-round, full-time workers by sex and age. For each age class, it was assumed that the ratio of female to male *mean* income was the same as the ratio of female to male *median* income.

Each mean earnings figure was adjusted upwards to take account of wage supplements by a factor of 1.08268, derived from data published by the Department of Commerce in *Survey of Current Business.*

Although a relatively high proportion of females are housewives and not in the labor market, it was considered desirable to impute a value to their services. For this purpose the 1964 mean earnings of domestic servants, or $2,767, was used. It was recognized that the imputed value was "clearly on the low side," for it made no allowance for the housewife's longer work week and took no account of the size of the household cared for.

The following table presents 1964 mean earnings by age class, adjusted for wage supplements and including an imputed value for housewives' services.

Table A

ADJUSTED MEAN EARNINGS BY
AGE AND SEX, 1964

Age Group	Male	Female
14–19	$2,829	$3,387
20–24	4,634	3,800
25–29	6,373	3,951
30–34	7,532	4,670
35–39	7,953	4,390
40–44	8,305	4,584
45–49	8,229	4,724
50–54	7,435	4,268
55–59	7,174	4,355
60–64	7,113	4,318
65–69	5,981	3,851
70 and over	5,887	3,790

Although Table A presents only cross-sectional data for a single year, 1964, it was assumed that it could also be used to represent the earnings pattern of an average individual over his working lifetime. In other words, an average 20-year-old male in the labor force could expect to earn $4,634 on the average for full-time work over the next five years, $6,373 for the five years after that, and so forth. It was recognized that this assumption might result in a downward bias in the estimate of discounted lifetime earnings because other data indicated that younger workers appeared to benefit more from economic growth than older workers. The evidence for this bias was considered inconclusive, however.

In converting the estimated mean earnings by year into lifetime earnings, several other factors had to be considered.

First, not everyone would have been working or productive had death from the cause under study not interfered. Some victims of fatal accidents would have been too old or too young or unwilling or unable to find a job. For the purpose of the disease control program analyses, it was assumed that if it were not for these illnesses or causes of death, persons stricken would have had the same employment experience as persons in the same age and sex groups. Accordingly, the 1964 labor force participation rates (proportion of all civilians who were employed or looking for a job) were applied and further adjustments were made for the number who would have been employed under conditions of full employment, defined as 4 percent unemployment. The unemployment rates for 1965 were used because 1965 was the most current year of full employment. Without the assumption of full employment, losses due to mortality and disability could not have been isolated from losses due to unemployment. Table B below presents the data used for these adjustments.

Table B

LABOR FORCE PARTICIPATION AND UNEMPLOYMENT RATES BY AGE CLASS

Age Group	1964 Labor Force Participation Rates		1965 Unemployment Rates	
	Male	Female	Male	Female
14	17.7	9.9	6.8	5.2
15–19	44.8	31.9	13.7	14.8
20–24	85.6	49.1	6.3	7.3
25–29	94.7	37.9	3.3	5.7
30–34	96.4	36.2	2.6	5.2
35–39	95.8	41.7	2.6	4.8
40–44	95.4	47.4	2.5	4.4
45–49	95.2	51.4	2.5	3.6
50–54	93.3	50.5	2.6	2.8
55–59	89.6	45.9	3.2	2.9
60–64	77.4	32.7	3.4	2.7
65–69	41.7	17.2	4.2	3.1
70 and over	18.7	5.8	2.7	2.4

The second factor which had to be considered was mortality from causes other than the one under study. Even if a 16-year-old motorcyclist is saved from fatal injury, he may succumb to some other cause before reaching normal retirement. To handle this factor, standard actuarial techniques were used; that is, mortality records were used to determine the proportion of males (females) of age a surviving to age n, and this proportion was then applied to the earnings in year n (adjusted as previously discussed) of any such male whose accidental death was prevented at age a.

Case 15–2

Metropolitan Museum of Art

The "first cut" at the operating budget of the Metropolitan Museum of Art for fiscal year 1973 (i.e., the year ended June 30, 1973) indicated a substantial deficit. Management was considering what, if any, steps should be taken to reduce or eliminate this deficit.

The Metropolitan Museum was organized in New York City in 1870. In 1972 it had over 1,000,000 works of art, the largest collection of its kind in the Western Hemisphere. It had an endowment fund of $150 million.

Governance and Management

The Board.   Fiscal authority for direction of the Metropolitan Museum of Art was vested in the Board of Trustees. The Board was responsible for the broad direction and control of the Museum and for the establishment and approval of basic policies and plan. Meeting quarterly, it also considered important operational matters.

The Director.   The Director was the Museum's Chief Executive Officer. He was responsible for formulating policies and programs for the Board's consideration and for implementing decisions made by the Board. In addition to being responsible for overall planning and administration of the Museum's affairs, he was also involved in fund-raising and negotiating major art acquisitions. He presided at rehearsals of presentations by the Curators and was present at actual presentations made to the Board of Trustees Acquisition Committee. Since 1966, the Director was Thomas P. F. Hoving. Dr. Hoving had achieved national recognition as the Commissioner of Parks of New York City, particularly for his campaign to make New York a "fun city." He earned a Ph.D. in Art History at Princeton in 1959, and was hired as curatorial assistant at the Cloisters, the medieval art department of the Metropolitan. In 1965 he became Curator of the Cloisters.

Curatorial.   The Vice Director, Curator-in-Chief was responsible for 17

709

curatorial departments and the Conservation Laboratory, with a curatorial staff of nearly 200 persons.

The 17 curatorial departments varied considerably in the size of their staffs and collections, and in the range of their activities. While all departments collected art objects, some were more active than others. In general the more active departments were those which collected works of art currently available in the open market.

In addition to collection and display, curatorial departments were responsible for maintaining relations with collectors and art dealers, for developing scholarly and general literature on the collection, and for answering inquiries from the public. Some members of the curatorial staff also taught courses and lectured at the Museum or at other institutions.

Education.   The Vice Director of Education had general responsibility for developing educational programs for students and for the general public. Included in his domain were five departments: the Library, the Junior Museum, Secondary and Higher Education, Community Programs, and the Photograph and Slide Library.

Finance and Treasurer.   The Vice Director for Finance and Treasurer was the chief financial officer of the Museum. Reporting to him were four financial administrators, each with his own staff and task assignment. The Assistant Treasurer was responsible for the physical receipt and payment of funds, accounts receivable, the payroll and general accounting. The Controller prepared the annual budget and was responsible for accounts payable. The Registrar maintained catalogue descriptions of all objects belonging to the Museum, recorded the physical movement of these objects in and out of the Museum, and obtained insurance and custom handling for art shipments. The City Liaison Officer was responsible for developing and maintaining good relations with the New York City administration, in particular those officials with whom the Museum had financial transactions.

Public Affairs.   The Vice Director of Public Affairs, a position that was at the time vacant, had overall responsibility for eight departments, each of which had direct contact with the public. These departments were as follows: public information, information desk, bookshop and reproduction, development and promotion (fund-raising), membership office, publications, exhibition design, and the auditorium.

Operations.   The Operating Administrator had general responsibility for the provision of the Museum's many service functions. These included: guardianship, maintenance, cleaning, purchasing stock room supplies, telephone and office services, and photograph studio, and the several restaurant facilities. This large department employed approximately 400 of the Museum's 800 employees.

Staffing levels for these activities are given in Exhibit 1.

In the late 1960s there was increasing interest among professional staff employees in establishing a union to represent them. Apparently this inter-

Exhibit 1

STAFFING LEVELS: 1967–1971
(Excluding Auxiliary Activities)

	1971	1970	1969	1968	1967
Director and Several Offices	27	23	22	21	20
Vice Director—Curator-in-Chief	199	185	170	172	167
Vice Director for Finance and Treasurer	51	48	46	42	42
Vice Director for Education	63	55	53	52	52
Vice Director for Public Affairs	31	28	28	28	25
Vice Director for Operations	412	407	370	365	361
Subtotal	783	746	689	680	667
100th Anniversary	19	21	—	—	—
Total	802	767	689	680	667

est had been increasing despite efforts by the Museum's administration to be responsive to the needs of the professional staff. The administration had a publicly announced goal of bringing curatorial salaries up to the level received by professors in leading colleges and universities. From 1967 to 1971 there was a 30 percent increase in curatorial salaries. The 1972 budget, prepared in the spring of 1971, called for additional salary increases of between 11.6 percent and 17.9 percent depending on the level of curatorial rank.

The administration had also attempted to increase the extent of participation by professional employees. In 1970 the curators, acting with the backing of the administration, established a Curatorial Forum, which comprised the entire curatorial staff, and had a representative on the Staff Policy Committee, the executive team which made recommendations to the Director and conducted routine business operations.

By April 1972, it appeared to management that the unionization issue was no longer alive and that many of the specific changes that had been introduced had been well received.

Financial Background

The Museum began to suffer operating losses in the late 1960s. Historical financial data are shown in Exhibits 2 and 3.

The emergence of financial problems was not a condition unique to the Metropolitan Museum of Art; many museums were faced with similar situations. The Modern Museum of Art, for example, reported a record deficit of $1.2 million in 1970. Also in 1970, a study conducted by the American Association of Museums found that 44 percent of its members were operating at a loss. Furthermore, at the time of the study the AAM spokesman said that the dismal trend was expected to continue.

Exhibit 2

FINANCIAL RECORD: 1960–1972

Fiscal Year*	Operating Income	Operating Expenses	Surplus (loss)†
1960	$ 4,006,943	$ 3,618,197	$388,746
1961	4,328,603	4,042,561	286,042
1962	5,181,647	4,433,087	748,560
1963	5,066,399	4,605,688	460,711
1964	5,280,503	4,802,832	477,671
1965	5,807,116	5,278,279	528,837
1966	6,128,155	5,698,411	429,714
1967	6,496,767	6,236,532	260,235
1968	7,054,341	7,461,354	(407,013)
1969 ....,..	8,393,332	8,531,833	(138,501)
1970	8,405,569	9,226,513	(820,944)
1971	11,363,519	11,773,117	(409,598)‡
1972 (budget)	12,415,600	13,128,793	(713,193)

* Fiscal year ends June 30.
† For fiscal years prior to 1970 Surplus (loss) is before extraordinary charges.
‡ Plus an accumulated Centennial deficit of $1,121,697.

Two broad explanations were advanced for the growing disparity between revenues and expenses. First, museums, like other entities which relied on a relatively fixed income, suffered from the effects of inflation. Second, in order to adapt to a changing environment museums had incurred new types of expenses.

One cause of the difficulty was the rapid increase in museum attendance. It was noted that the 1971 exhibit entitled the "Drug Scene" at the Museum of the City of New York drew more people in three months of 1971 than the entire museum did in all of 1970. However, the cost of contemporary exhibits was high. The American Museum of Natural History, for example, spent $526,000 for its centennial exhibit "Can Man Survive?"

Another relatively new cost was the emergence of vigorous demands by professional employees for higher pay and more job security. According to Ann R. Leven, Assistant Treasurer of the Metropolitan, this new demand reflected the fact that curators no longer came predominantly from the ranks of the wealthy. Many curators had to live off salaries which were traditionally quite low.

The Metropolitan took action in 1971 to combat the trend of increasing deficits. The actions taken can be grouped into two categories, those which reduced costs, and those which generated additional revenues.

One cost cutting action was a curtailment in the hiring of new personnel. Mr. Daniel Herrick, Vice Director for Finance and Treasurer, instituted the policy of not filling a vacancy unless the position was deemed essential.

A second austerity measure was the decision to close the Museum one day a week (Monday) beginning in July 1971. Prior to this decision the Museum

Exhibit 3
SOURCES OF INCOME 1960–1971

Sources (in 000s)	1960	1961	1962	1963	1964	1965	1966	1967	1968	1969	1970	1971
Unrestricted investment income	2,737	2,890	3,591	3,474	3,621	4,051	4,174	4,380	4,461	4,658	4,670	4,722
Transfer of unrestricted endowment funds*	0	0	0	0	0	0	0	0	0	0	0	844
Appropriation from City of New York	974	1,038	1,191	1,259	1,293	1,385	1,528	1,554	1,678	1,853	1,947	2,323
Grants	0	0	0	0	0	0	0	53	160	577	126	683
Memberships	180	205	234	252	267	289	314	399	415	453	419	1,057
Admission fees	0	65	72	0	0	30	15	0	45	353	390	821
Contributions for general purposes	62	66	20	16	18	17	18	19	181	151	191	204
Other†	64	65	73	66	81	71	81	91	113	137	278	260
Subtotal	4,007	4,329	5,181	5,066	5,281	5,807	6,128	6,497	7,054	8,183	8,021	10,914
Plus: Net income for auxiliary activities	0	0	0	0	0	0	0	0	0	210	385	449
Total	4,007	4,329	5,181	5,066	5,281	5,807	6,128	6,497	7,054	8,393	8,406	11,364

* In 1971 a fixed rate of return (5 percent) was used for the first time to determine endowment income.
† Includes income from slide and photograph sales, guide service, course fees and special seminars.

had remained open to the public seven days a week, 365 days a year. Consequently many maintenance activities had to be performed at odd hours: before the Museum opened and after it closed. These scheduling demands, coupled with ordinary absences, resulted in (1) having to pay guards and maintenance personnel overtime pay, and (2) having to hire temporary personnel on a per diem basis. The budget for 1971–72 estimated that Monday closings would save the Metropolitan nearly $200,000 in annual labor cost. Ten New York City art museums, including the Guggenheim and the Whitney, adopted this policy before the Metropolitan did.

Another cutback was the elimination from the operating budget of various projects which the Museum had planned to carry out. Among the postponed items were the following: (1) the publication of a catalogue of the Museum's programs of research and education; (2) hiring of a specialist for foundation and government fund-raising; (3) installation of a public education gallery dealing with current events in the art world; (4) free acoustiguide equipment; (5) redecoration of the restaurant; (6) development of a computer program for an art catalogue. Perhaps the biggest disappointment to many people was the curtailment of the final Centennial exhibition, "Masterpieces of Fifty Centuries." In the words of Mr. Hoving, "Our budget could no longer afford the expenses involved in the foreign loans that we planned for the last great Centennial show, especially the cost of insurance, which has skyrocketed in the last few years."

At the same time that these cost reduction activities were undertaken the Museum also initiated steps to increase its revenues. One approach was the introduction in 1970 of discretionary admission charges at the main building and at the Cloisters. Mr. Hoving commented that "after investigating different ways of charging admission to the Museum, the pay-as-you-wish plan emerged as the most satisfactory for two reasons. It created no economic barriers for the public and it proved that income was higher than with a set admission fee." (*New York Times,* October 9, 1970.) After a five-month trial period the average contribution per visitor was 64 cents. One reason for the high average was that the Museum "strongly hinted" that one dollar would be a "very nice" contribution for adults, 50 cents for youngsters. The 1971–72 budget estimated that total receipts from the voluntary admission contributions would approximate $1 million. (The Museum found out in 1971 after it purchased electronic counting equipment that the earlier hand-counted records of attendance were about four times too high.)

The introduction of a discretionary admission fee provoked sharp criticism from several sources. Among them Mr. Carter Burden, a New York City Councilman, noted that "of the 15 institutions which receive city funds, with the exception of the Bronx Zoo, the Metropolitan was the only one with a general admission fee." He added, "Our society should be going in the opposite direction."

Another step taken to enhance revenues was the adoption of the fixed rate of return concept for endowment funds. Whereas in past years endowment income was limited to interest and dividends, beginning in 1971 the Museum recorded as income 5 percent of the average market value of unrestricted endowment funds for the three previous years. It was anticipated that over the long run actual capital appreciation combined with dividends and interest would result in an annual yield at least equal to the fixed rate. This approach had the added advantage of making endowment income a constant amount during the course of the fiscal year. (See Exhibit 3.)

Also beginning in 1970 the Museum undertook an energetic campaign to enroll new members. As a result of this campaign 8,667 new memberships were sold by April 1971, bringing in added receipts of $360,000. One spur to get new members was that beginning in April 1971, the prices of individual and family memberships were raised from $15 to $25 and $40 respectively. Because of the price increase the Museum expected only a small increase in memberships for 1972.

The recent history of membership growth, was marred by only one major downturn. This occurred in 1967 when prices were raised. However, there was a short downturn for a few months in the fall of 1968 as a result of the contemporary exhibition, "Harlem on My Mind." One hundred and sixty-five members cancelled their memberships and many others failed to renew. The two major criticisms were an anti-Semitic comment in the catalogue, and the view that this exhibit was not "real" art.

Another approach to enhancing revenues were efforts to make the Museum's auxiliary activities more profitable. Additional merchandising operations were opened and prices on prints, books, and other items were set at levels to bring an optimum return. As a result of these changes the 1971–72 budget anticipated an increase in contribution on these activities from $415,000 to $615,000.

Still another revenue producing activity was the search for nontraditional sources of funds. In 1970 the State of New York broke new ground when it appropriated $18 million for support of the arts. The Metropolitan received a total of $418,500 of the appropriation in 1971, and expected continued support from the state. Another new source of funds was the Federal Government which under the National Endowment for the Arts was expected to make an initial contribution to the Metropolitan of $110,000 in 1972.

Yet by far the largest public contribution came from the City of New York which gave $2.3 million in 1971 to cover the costs of guardianship and maintenance. While the city's contribution to the operating income had declined from 27 percent in 1959–60 to 21 percent in 1970–71, the amount contributed had increased. It was estimated, furthermore, that by 1976 the city would increase its annual commitment by an additional $585,000. (*Wall Street Journal,* July 26, 1971.) Consequently, some administrators at the

Metropolitan felt uneasy when elected city officials began to urge the city to reduce or even eliminate its contributions to the Museum.

Current Financial Situation

During the 1971–1972 fiscal year it became increasingly evident that the financial plans for the year were not going to be met. A deficit of $713,000 was originally budgeted compared to the preceding year's deficit of $1,531,000. The reduction had been planned to be accomplished by keeping 1972 expenditures near the 1971 level ($13.1 million in 1972 versus $12.9 million in the prior year), while revenue was to be increased by $1 million. However, by April 1972 it appeared that the actual deficit for the fiscal year ending June 30 would approximate $1.4 million. The chief reason for this turn of events was that revenue had not increased as planned.

Attendance in the Main Building was down approximately 25 percent from the year before, and admission income was one third below the budgeted figure of $930,000. Mr. Daniel Herrick, the vice director of finance and treasurer, attributed the fall-off to several factors: a post-Centennial slump in public interest, reduced hotel occupancies in New York, and a growing reluctance of New York City residents to go out at night. As a direct result of decreased attendance, the contribution to expenses provided by the restaurant and bookstores was reduced by $130,000.

Two additional factors contributed to lower than planned revenues. In fiscal 1970–71 the Museum undertook a special membership campaign whereby new individual and family members were encouraged to join at the old rates (before new, increased rates went into effect), and existing members were allowed to extend their memberships for an additional year at the old rates. The effect of this campaign was an extraordinary increase in memberships. From 1963 through 1968 membership fluctuated between 20,000 and 23,000 each year. In 1969 it rose to over 24,000, in 1970 to 27,000, and in 1971 to 37,760. However, in early 1972 as memberships began to expire, the renewal rates were lower than anticipated, mostly among the lower membership categories. In the single month of February, for example, 937 individual and family memberships were not renewed. As a result of this higher than anticipated lapse rate, membership income was about $90,000 below the budget. A final financial disappointment was the reduction in grants received by the Museum. New York State reduced its grant to $221,000 from $418,000 the year before, and the National Endowment for the Arts contributed $60,000 less than budgeted. Total grant income was $280,000 short of the budgeted level.

The Budget for 1972–1973

The preliminary budget for the forthcoming year indicated that total revenue would decline slightly to $11.7 million, principally reflecting a further reduction in grants to the Museum. The budget report suggested that there were three principal options to be considered:

Option 1: Deficit $1,000,000. Across-the-board cut in expenditures of 10.3 percent. Staff cut of 36 (excluding auxiliary activities). Requires effecting efficiencies in all departments and certain cutbacks most notably in the Curatorial and Operations area. Reduce advertising. Reduce number of activities for members. Close Monday holidays, 11 A.M. to 1 P.M. Sundays, Friday evenings. Cancel employees' Christmas party.

Option 2: Deficit $500,000. Across-the-board cut in expenditures of 16.4 percent. Staff cut of 60. The effect falls heaviest on those departments with limited program money, cutting deeply into the Curatorial and Operating staffs. Allows for basic maintenance of collections; study rooms would close; conservation and research would stop; exhibitions would be severely limited. Reduce community education activities unless outside funding obtained. Close 83d Street entrance.

Option 3: No deficit. Across-the-board cut in expenditures of 22.5 percent. Staff cut of 91. Merely maintains the Museum as a repository for works of art. Requires a major functional reorganization of the staff. All cataloguing ceases. Closes libraries during the summer, eliminates weekend and summer education programs. Consolidates Development and Membership offices.

When Mr. Herrick was asked whether the administration had considered the possibility of passing the hat among the trustees in order to make up operating deficits, he said:

> The days when a few wealthy contributors would ante up the money to cover a deficit are over. Even the richest person in the world doesn't have an inclination to keep giving money if you have continuing deficits of over $1 million a year. Furthermore, anteing up to fill a deficit is the least attractive type of donation from the viewpoint of most contributors. Philanthropists far prefer to donate money for works of art, buildings, or even endowed chairs before giving to cover operating losses.

Mr. Herrick continued discussing the financial problems of the Museum:

> We are reluctant to cut back expenses especially since the staff takes intense pride in what has been accomplished at the Metropolitan Museum. At a time when other aspects of New York City life are deteriorating, the Museum has been on a planned and vigorous course of greater service to the community in maintaining and communicating the meaning of its collection of works of art to the public.
> We have considered numerous alternative forms of retrenchment but because salaries comprise roughly 70 percent of our total costs (see Exhibits 4 and 5), there is virtually no way to avoid laying off people. Furthermore, this raises the difficult problem of deciding which people to release and how to handle the dismissals. We are even exploring the possibility of converting to a four-day week, perhaps in lieu of salary increases.

Exhibit 4

ADMINISTRATION EXPENSES
(As Budgeted for the Year Ended June 30, 1972)*

	Personal Service	Other Expense	Total
Director and Several Offices	$ 404,095	$ 173,085	$ 577,180
Vice Director, Curator-in-Chief	2,455,227	695,316	3,150,543
Vice Director for Finance and			
Treasurer	555,561	355,910	911,471
Vice Director for Education	783,708	812,586	1,596,294
Vice Director for Public Affairs	467,725	701,815	1,169,540
Vice Director for Operations	3,625,199	1,435,570	5,060,769
Benefits and Allowances	1,764,170	—	1,764,170
Adjustments†	(566,295)	(156,478)	(722,773)
Total Estimated Operating			
Expenses	$9,489,390	$4,017,804	$13,507,194

* As revised 3/31/72.
† Accounting deductions distributed among capital budget, auxiliary activities, the Cloisters.

Exhibit 5

ACTUAL ADMINISTRATION EXPENSES

	1971	1970	1969	1968	1967
Personal service (including benefits and allowances) ..	$ 8,287,400	$ 6,909,700	$6,151,300	$5,422,000	$5,181,400
Other than personal service	3,138,000	2,086,500	1,971,300	1,398,600	1,119,300
Subtotal	$11,425,400	$ 8,996,200	$8,122,600	$6,820,600	$6,300,700
100th Anniversary personal service ..	96,100	210,100			
Other than personal service	1,454,400	1,595,900			
Total	12,975,900	$10,802,200	$8,122,600	$6,820,600	$6,300,700

The fact of the matter is that even if the Museum were to cut its expenditures to create a balanced budget in the forthcoming year, the same problem would recur again next year. As long as the Museum exists in an inflationary economy, where there is an inevitable upward push in terms of wages, fringe benefits, and operating costs, the Museum must seek some means of achieving an adequate and dependable source of funding to maintain the status quo at least.

Possible Repercussions of Cutbacks

The administration was well aware of the possibility that cutbacks might lead to renewed interest in unionization among the professional staff. John Conger, the personnel manager, identified the immediate costs to the

Museum of collective bargaining. First, more time would be spent in negotiating contracts. Second, there was a high probability that the final contract agreement would be more costly to the Museum.

Mr. Hoving stated that the union would have little overall impact on the Museum. "There are very few things they could bargain for. Salaries of curators are at the level of university professors, working conditions are excellent, as is the grievance procedure. A union would actually make management's position stronger. It would absolutely define the areas of bargaining as stipulated by the NLRB. The staff would have much less say on policy matters."

Mr. Herrick noted that "the chances are pretty good that if we decide to have layoffs there may be a professional union. But if there is, that wouldn't be the end of the world."

Case 15-3

Hyatt Hill Health Center

The Hyatt Hill Health Center (HHHC) was established in 1968. It was sponsored by the Follen Hospital, widely considered to be among the leading hospitals in the United States in terms of the quality of its medical care, research, and teaching. The Health Center was established on an experimental basis in order to provide community-centered health care to the residents of the community of Bedford, in which it was located. Bedford is a lower income area which suffers from a heavy incidence of medical, dental, psychiatric and social problems. For example, before the Health Center was established, it was estimated that over 40 percent of Bedford's adults needed dental plates. Also, a significant proportion of its population consisted of confirmed or incipient alcoholics and drug abusers.

Because there were few physicians residing in Bedford, its residents used the emergency room of the Follen Hospital as a substitute for a family physician. As a result, they received sporadic therapeutic medical care and few of them received any preventive care.

The purpose of the Health Center was to provide adequate preventive as well as therapeutic care and to do so by becoming an accepted force in the Bedford community. This wasn't an easy mission, for Bedford was geographically isolated from the rest of the metropolitan area, and its residents, who were largely composed of one closely knit ethnic group, were traditionally suspicious of any "outsiders." Despite the heavy incidence of mental health problems in the area, the residents of Bedford were particularly resistant to receiving the services of social workers and psychiatrists.

Objectives

The experimental nature of the HHHC is readily apparent in the objectives assigned to it by Follen Hospital. These objectives include the following:

1. To be a prevention-oriented, family-centered source of health care, available to all community residents.

2. To deliver less fragmented, more extensive medical services and to utilize clinical information recording methods that will facilitate the delivery of such services.

3. To test the feasibility and success of providing health services that are usually provided by schools and city health departments.

4. To provide for on-the-job training and employment of resident nonprofessionals.

5. To determine the impact that a community health center would have on the utilization of the Follen's facilities by residents of the community in which the center is located.

6. To develop a community health center which can, through the various financing mechanisms available to it, become financially self-sufficient.

The financial objectives of the HHHC—self-sufficiency and reduction of costs for the Follen—were as important to its adminstrators and the Follen Hospital as the medical objectives. This goal, however, was not meant to be attained in the short run, but only after the Center had established itself in the Bedford community.

Organization and Personnel

The Hyatt Hill Health Center was composed of the following departments: Pediatrics, Internal Medicine, Nursing, Mental Health, Social Service, Nutrition, Dental, and Specialists. Most of its practitioners held joint appointments at the Follen Hospital, were considered to be of high professional calibre, and incurred substantial opportunity costs by working at the Health Center.

In addition to its goal of delivering community health care, the HHHC also served as a training ground for members of the Follen Hospital staff who were interested in community medicine. Training activities were conducted in all of HHHC's departments, particularly in the Mental Health, Social Service, and Nutritional departments.

Funding

The Health Center's yearly operating budget of nearly $1,000,000, was funded from a variety of sources, including the Follen Hospital. Follen underwrote the cost of some personnel and equipment. In addition, it completely renovated the building in which the HHHC was located.

In order to gather the data required by Follen Hospital, every practitioner in the Health Center completed the form displayed in Exhibit 1 immediately after every encounter with a patient. The data on the encounter forms were then entered on a computer terminal connected to the Follen Hospital's system. The data were processed at the Follen Hospital to provide the information necessary for compliance with the HEW requirements and sent to the HHHC.

The Control System——Background

Late in 1969, a researcher who was interested in studying the costs of ambulatory medical care facilities visited the Health Center. At the time, Dr. Steven Kyler, the Executive Director, was becoming increasingly concerned over the potential for the achievement of the HHHC's financial self-sufficiency goal. Although the Center had a good financial accounting system for billing and external reporting, it had no management accounting data. Dr. Kyler thus didn't know the total costs of his departments, of different kinds of cases, and of his practitioners. Since the only financial data available to him were the costs of the different line-items on his budget, Dr. Kyler couldn't really assess the feasibility of his Center's accomplishing its financial self-sufficiency goals. He thus agreed to the installation of a management control system which would provide him with the data he wanted.

At that time, there was also an uncomfortable feeling among some of the HHHC's administrative and medical personnel that costs were "above average" for this kind of system and that administrative costs in particular were out of control. They attributed this to the costs involved in setting up the Center; to the additional paperwork required from the HHHC due to its multiple funding sources; to the additional costs of training Bedford personnel; and to general inefficiency in the support departments. However, since the amounts of these costs were not determined, and since there were no standards that could be used to ascertain whether costs were, in fact, too high, there was no way to prove or disprove the feeling that costs were above average.

In addition, some of the HHHC's medical personnel felt that the nursing staff wasn't being efficiently utilized. There was also some concern that the Bedford population of 16,000 was too small to support a Center of the HHHC's size. Some practitioners estimated that a minimum registrant population of 20,000 to 30,000 was necessary for fulfillment of the self-sufficiency goals of the Center. Given the absence of data relating the cost of providing health care to the volume of health care provided, these estimates couldn't be validated.

The New Management Control System

The purpose of the new management control system was to give those individuals having some control over the costs of providing medical services the information which would reveal the impact that their actions had on the level of these costs.

Given this objective, the researcher's first step in the design of the new MCS was to determine to whom this information should be provided. The Health Center was composed of two distinct types of departments: mission units, such as Internal Medicine, which fulfilled the Center's primary mission of providing health care, and support units, such as Accounting, which existed in order to support the mission units in achieving their goals. Theoretically, each mission and each support department could have been designated as a responsibility center, since each represents a subunit of the Health Center whose director had clearly defined authority and responsibility. However, since the objective of the new MCS was to provide information to individuals who directly deliver health services, only the mission departments were designated as responsibility centers. In the Health Center, these departments included the Pediatrics, Internal Medicine, Community Mental Health, Nursing, Dental Health, Social Service, and Nutrition Departments. Since these departments generated revenue by charging fees to their patients, they were further designated as profit centers.

Two types of data were collected. The first type was the fixed cost of running each of the departments. (See Exhibit 2). These costs were fixed in the sense that their level did not depend on the volume or types of health care rendered by the mission departments. Through consultation with the Health Center staff, the fixed cost of the Center for a typical month was established. Next, the fixed cost of the Center was allocated among the mission departments. Some components of the Center's fixed cost, such as salaries, could be directly traced to each department. Other components, such as heat and electricity, were shared costs and were allocated to the mission departments on the basis of their utilization of the component. For example, each department's share of the Center's electric bill was determined by its proportion of the Health Center's square footage. Similarly, the costs of operating the support units were allocated to the mission departments by appropriate utilization measures. For instance, the cost of the accounting department was allocated to the mission departments on the basis of their proportionate share of patients' bills. In some instances, *imputed* costs were employed; thus, if a piece of equipment were donated to the Center, its cost was designated as the price at which that equipment could be purchased from its manufacturer.

The second type of required information was data describing each of the practitioners in a department. This descriptive data included the following items for each practitioner:

1. His salary, on a per minute basis;
2. The total number of minutes he was available to render health services;
3. The number of patients he treated, by type of encounter;
4. The time spent on each type of encounter;
5. The number of walk-in patients he treated;
6. The time spent on walk-in encounters;
7. The number of patients who made appointments he treated;
8. The time spent on encounters for which appointments were made.

These data were obtained from the encounter forms in Exhibit 1. Using these two types of information, a number of calculations were performed.

Exhibit 1

ENCOUNTER FORM, MEDICAL DEPARTMENTS

2 Professional No:

[H][ ][ ]

1 Date

[ ][ ] [ ][ ] [ ][ ]
mo.   day   year

3 Visit:

1 ◯ walk–in

2 ◯ visit kept

3 ◯ visit broken

Date of Birth
_____

Visit location:

1 ◯ HHHC

2 ◯ Home

3 ◯ School

4 ◯ Other

Unit no.: [ ][ ][ ] [ ][ ] [ ][ ]

8 Family no.: [A][ ][ ][ ][ ]

Name: _____

10 Duration of visit:

[ ][ ] minutes

For shared visit, enter time spent by other professional (MD or nurse)

[ ][ ] minutes

12 Assessment status:

1 ◯ not started   3 ◯ complete this visit

2 ◯ in process   4 ◯ complete prior visit

"Treatment Plan" status at this visit:

1 ◯ not needed   3 ◯ short–term, complete

2 ◯ short–term, in process   4 ◯ long–term

13 Check or enter one based on primary reason for visit:

1 ☐ acute prob. or followup   6 ☐ well child visit

2 ☐ chronic problem   7 ☐ prenatal or postnatal

3 ☐ treatment or lab only   8 ☐ health education

4 ☐ checkup or physical   9 ☐ family counseling

5 ☐ school health physical   10 ☐ family planning

Other activity code: [ ][ ]

Comments or chargeable services (injections, treatments, etc.)

14 Code only diagnoses related to primary reason for visit and ENTER CODE below.

A.

B. presumptive / confirmed   C. mild / moderate / severe

1.   1. ☐   2. ☐   1. ☐   2. ☐   3. ☐

2.   ☐   ☐   ☐   ☐   ☐

15 Referrals: Made To:	A in HHHC	B out-side	C Follen	Received From:	D in HHHC	E out-side	F Follen
1. nursing							
2. dental health							
3. nutrition							
4. ENT							
5. eye							
6. speech, hearing							
7. local physician or dentist							
8. medical and specialities							
9. surgical and specialities							
10. mental health							
11. physical therapy							
12. other agencies							

These calculations related the quantities of the various types of medical care rendered to the costs of providing such care. The quality of patient services was controlled by the screening of all professional appointments by the chiefs of the services of the Follen, a continuing peer review by the department chiefs at the Health Center, and the random review of medical records by the utilization review committee at the hospital.

As indicated on the first two columns of Exhibit 2, salary costs were divided into two categories: direct patient care and direct overhead. Direct patient care salary was determined by multiplying the physician's salary for the month by the fraction:

$$\frac{\text{number of minutes spent on direct patient care}}{\text{total minutes available}}.$$

The remainder of the practitioner's salary was designated as direct overhead and represented time spent in activities not reported on the encounter form.

Control of these nonpatient care related activities was achieved through the use of time sheets which measured the time spent in activities such as research, teaching, management, and related activities. They were completed, once every three months, by every Health Center professional. The results were routinely tabulated, translated into full costs, and distributed so that the managers and practitioners could gauge the relative allocation of costs in their nonpatient care related activities.

The average cost for each type of encounter for each physician was determined by multiplying the total number of minutes he spent on that type of encounter by his calculated cost per minute. The cost per minute was calculated as follows:

1. The total cost of the time that a physician spent on patient care in a month calculated as the sum of his monthly salary, plus an allocated share of the total departmental fixed costs. This allocation was determined on the basis of the number of minutes each physician was available, as a proportion of the total number of minutes all physicians were available.

2. This total cost was divided by the number of minutes that the physician spent on patient care to give a cost per minute.

Note that the effect of this calculation was to make all departmental costs including direct overhead cost (i.e., the salary cost of nonpatient care activities) a part of the cost per minute of patient care. For example, the cost per minute of patient care in the Internal Medicine department contained the following approximate elements:

	Percent
Salary of physicians, direct patient care	36
Salary of physicians, other	14 ← absorption rate.
Fixed departmental cost	50
	100

Exhibit 2

COSTS BY DEPARTMENTS

| | Salaries | | Departmental Fixed Cost | | | | | | | | | | | | |
	Direct Patient Care	Direct Overhead	Fringe	Furniture and Equipment	Supplies	Rent	Heat and Power	Evaluation	Med. Rec. and Acctg.	Administration	Service Reps	HHHC Out Patient	General	Total	Percent of Total
Pediatrics	$ 2,400	$ 1,956	$ 610	$ 16	$ 441	$ 162	$ 20	$1,117	$ 817	$ 490	$ 220	$ 40	$ 330	$ 8,619	12.0
Internal Medicine	3,336	1,331	653	23	467	189	33	894	1,170	533	239	43	359	9,270	12.9
Nutrition	537	260	68	4	—	42	7	381	264	189	81	15	127	1,975	2.7
Nursing	4,148	4,371	657	62	320	398	60	394	455	2,313	931	187	1,557	15,853	22.0
Dental	1,140	2,407	493	84	150	162	20	333	0	877	—	71	590	6,327	8.8
Mental Health	737	4,814	554	41	—	382	47	331	187	1,246	—	101	838	9,278	12.9
Social Services	502	4,906	421	30	—	301	40	458	258	1,720	243	139	1,158	10,176	14.1
Specialists	854	447	—	14	—	—	—	269	413	112	51	9	75	2,244	3.1
Eye Clinic	478	172	29	96	—	126	13	165	253	267	—	22	179	1,800	2.5
Laboratory	1,147	645	143	46	275	41	7	—	666	567	243	46	382	4,208	5.8
Radiology	139	392	49	189	272	68	7	—	387	189	80	15	127	1,914	2.7
Therapists	—	—	—	7	—	47	7	39	25	95	40	8	64	332	.5
Total	$15,418	$21,701	$3,677	$612	$1,925	$1,918	$261	$4,381	$4,895	$8,598	$2,128	$696	$5,786	$71,986	100.0

Exhibit 3 contains the results of the calculations described above for the month of September 1970, for each physician in the Medical Department and for that department as a whole.

Exhibit 3

AVERAGE COST PER PROFESSIONAL, INTERNAL MEDICINE

September 1970

Visit Description	Physicians			Total Department
	1	2	3	
Acute problem or followup	$ 9.85	$10.99	$15.47	$10.97
Chronic problem	12.86	15.07	27.51	15.32
Treatment or lab only	2.89	9.97	—	7.11
Check-up or physical exam	24.93	25.93	20.63	24.89
School health physical	8.11	—	—	8.11
Prenatal visit	9.66	—	—	9.66
Walk-in visit	9.45	11.45	19.10	10.73
Appointment visit	16.24	17.63	21.91	17.72
All visits	12.52	13.58	21.21	14.07

Using the data in Exhibit 3, a method for assessing the monthly performance of each physician in the Medical Department (and, similarly, for physicians in other departments) was devised. This method involved comparing actual performance to "average" performance in a normal month. For each practitioner in each department, the number of encounters of each type and amount spent on each encounter type were determined. Using this information and the salary of the practitioner, his average cost for each type of encounter was calculated for the normal month. In Exhibit 4 this quantity is called the "Predicted Standard Cost." If, in a subsequent month, a physician's *actual* average cost for each type of encounter differed from this *predicted* average cost, the difference could have arisen from one or both of two sources. First, the practitioner could have become more or less *efficient* by decreasing or increasing the average amount of time spent on each type of encounter. Second, he could have increased or decreased his capacity utilization by increasing or decreasing the proportion of available time during which direct patient care was provided. The third and fourth columns of Exhibit 4 explain the differences between predicted and actual average costs in terms of changes in the physician's efficiency and capacity utilization:

$$\begin{pmatrix}\text{Average cost} \\ \text{per visit}\end{pmatrix} = \begin{pmatrix}\text{Predicted} \\ \text{standard cost}\end{pmatrix} + \begin{pmatrix}\text{Differential} \\ \text{effect of change} \\ \text{in efficiency}\end{pmatrix} + \begin{pmatrix}\text{Differential effect} \\ \text{of change in capacity} \\ \text{utilization}\end{pmatrix}$$

The Management Control Process

During the development of the control system, the researcher continually consulted with the management and practitioners of the Center. This was

Exhibit 4

SAMPLE MONTHLY PERFORMANCE INDICATORS, INTERNAL MEDICINE

**September 1970
(Physician 2)***

Visit Type	Average Cost per Visit	Predicted Standard Cost†	Differential Effect of Change in Efficiency	Differential Effect of Change in Utilization of Capacity	Total Cost	Total Revenues	Revenue Less Cost
Acute problem	$10.99	$12.22	$−2.53	$+1.30	$1,253	$ 912	$ −341
Chronic problem	15.07	16.66	−2.70	+1.11	1,763	936	−827
Treatment or lab only	9.97	6.66	+2.28	+1.03	60	48	−12
Check-up or physical exam	25.93	24.81	−.07	+1.19	259	80	−179
All visits	13.58	15.91	−3.55	+1.22	3,335	1,976	−1,359

* Numbers do not balance precisely because of rounding errors.
† Standard efficiency and utilization capacity as adjusted for actual total costs in the month of September.

done to insure that the data to be produced by the management control system were understood and reflected the procedures of the HHHC in an equitable manner.

After the MCS was implemented, the data it produced were distributed periodically to the heads of all mission departments and to the administrative officers of the Center. The implications of the data were discussed at executive and departmental meetings. In addition, meetings were held between the Center director and individual practitioners in all departments, during which allocations of time were reviewed using the MCS data as a focal point. The data were, therefore, routinely and actively used in the managerial process.

Results

After implementation of the new system, the average cost per encounter dropped in six of the seven mission departments (see Exhibit 5). The decline

Exhibit 5

AVERAGE COST BY MISSION DEPARTMENT

| Department | Average Cost | | | | Percent Change 3d Quarter 1970 to 2d Quarter, 1971 |
	3d Quarter 1970	4th Quarter 1970	1st Quarter 1971	2d Quarter 1971	
Social service	$43.81	$29.95	$27.31	$23.40	−61%
Mental health	47.25	31.57	27.77	26.21	−57
Dental health	22.69	18.40	15.72	16.22	−33
Nutrition	12.65	11.25	10.45	10.54	−18
Pediatrics	10.59	11.37	12.16	11.19	+ 6
Internal medicine	16.07	14.09	14.72	15.07	− 6
Nursing	35.27	35.16	36.20	32.42	− 9

in costs was most significant in the Social Service, Mental Health, and Dental Health Departments. Smaller drops were recorded for the Nutrition, Internal Medicine, and Nursing Departments. The only department showing an increase in average cost per encounter was the Pediatrics Department, which registered a 6 percent increase.

The sources of these changes in average cost per encounter are indicated in Exhibit 6. The structure of Exhibit 6 is analogous to that of Exhibit 4. The average cost per encounter in each mission department in the first quarter of 1971 was compared with what its average cost in that quarter would have been if its efficiency and capacity utilization had remained as they were in the third quarter of 1970. Thus the difference between the actual cost per encounter and the predicted, or standard cost per encounter, is due to changes in departmental efficiency and capacity utilization.

For example, if the efficiency and capacity utilization of the Mental Health

Exhibit 6

**SOURCE OF THE DIFFERENCE BETWEEN
STANDARD AND ACTUAL COST PER VISIT**
(First Quarter of 1971)

Department	Standard Cost per Visit	Actual Cost per Visit	Difference	Differential Effect of Change in Efficiency	Differential Effect of Change in Utilization of Capacity
Social service	$61.10	$27.31	+ $33.79	+ $ 5.37	+ $28.42
Mental health	53.65	27.77	+ 25.88	+ .23	+ 25.65
Dental health	32.88	15.72	+ 17.16	+ .41	+ 16.75
Nutrition	24.97	10.45	+ 14.52	+ 6.04	+ 8.48
Pediatrics	15.64	12.16	+ 3.48	− .57	− 4.05
Internal medicine	14.72	14.00	+ .72	− .14	+ .86
Nursing	28.34	36.20	− 7.66	− 11.15	+ 3.29

Department in the first quarter of 1971 had remained unchanged from the third quarter of 1970, the average cost per encounter would have been $53.65. The actual cost in the first quarter of 1971 was $27.77. The difference between these two costs ($25.88) was due to an increase in efficiency, which reduced the average cost by $0.23, and an increase in capacity utilization, which decreased the average cost by $25.65.

Managerial Impact

The reactions to the new MCS among the professional staff at the HHHC were mixed. Mr. Hershey, the Assistant Executive Director for Administration, praised the new system:

Before the new system was implemented, a lot of people were worried about how the Center was to become self-supporting and how each department could become self-supporting. The primary impact of the system has been how to get more efficient resource utilization. People in the Social Service and Mental Health never used to consider the costs of the work they did outside the Center in the community. In other departments, people didn't worry about downtime and its cost. The increased cost-consciousness of the staff is shown by the hiring of lower salaried people to perform some tasks that used to be undertaken, unnecessarily, by highly paid professionals.

Dr. Martin, the head of the Evaluation Unit, agreed with Mr. Hershey that the system had led to an increased awareness of costs, but was critical of the way in which the system was implemented:

Before the system, there was relatively little interest in costs, and there was no idea of how to determine what they were. The system made people aware of costs and what they had to do to lower them.

But the system wasn't implemented correctly. What the system never had was the intensive feedback loop it should have had. The staff didn't participate as much as they should have, and the system is too reprimanding and not sufficiently rewarding.

Dr. Strand, the head of the Social Service Unit, said that the system has made him and his staff more aware of time constraints and the need to set priorities, but was worried about the impact of the system:

The system tells us that we should be spending more time on direct patient care and less time out in the communities, doing such things as helping to create a community recreation center. We see these community activities as preventive medicine, but there's no way to measure the long-term effects of these activities. There's a real conflict—these community activities are beneficial, but the more time we spend on them, the less revenue we can generate for the Center.

Dr. Long, head of the Internal Medicine Department, had two complaints about the system:

The only thing that really happened was a greater focusing on cost issues. The system brought about a philosophical change on the part of the Center's administration to increase the volume of direct patient care. I, and many others, think that the system led to a decreased emphasis on the quality of care and on preventive medicine.

Another thing is that administrative costs were never studied. There has not been any perceptible change in administrative costs, nor has any thought been given to altering the physical facilities of the Center.

Chapter Sixteen

MANAGEMENT
CONTROL OF
PROJECTS

A project is a set of activities intended to accomplish a specified end result, of sufficient importance to be of interest to management. In a shipyard, for example, the repair and overhaul work done on a single ship constitutes one project. The accomplishment of a project often involves more than one responsibility center. In a shipyard, each of the production shops (electrical, sheet metal, plumbing, and so forth) is a responsibility center, and several of these shops are usually involved in a single repair and overhaul project. An organization in which employees have responsibilities both to a project and to a responsibility center is called a matrix organization.

In this chapter, we discuss the management control of projects, with special reference to the control problems in matrix organizations.

OVERALL NATURE OF THE PROBLEM

Project management focuses on the accomplishment of a specified end result, that is, the successful completion of the project. Management control of projects therefore differs from that of responsibility centers in two respects:

1. In a project, the focus is on the work involved in producing the end item regardless of which responsibility centers participate in this work, whereas in a responsibility center the focus is on all the work done by that responsibility center.
2. In a project, the time period of interest is the time involved in the total project, whereas in a responsibility center the time period of interest is a calendar period, such as a month.

As will be seen, these two differences lead to a quite different control process for projects than for responsibility centers.

Aspects of Control

Management control of projects has a planning phase and a control phase, as is the case with management control of responsibility centers. In each of these phases, attention must be directed to three aspects of the project: (1) time, (2) cost, and (3) quality.

The time required for each activity involved in the project must be estimated in advance and set forth in a schedule. During the conduct of the project, actual time required is compared with the estimated time and significant variances are brought to light and acted upon.

The cost estimate for a project is prepared in essentially the same way that a responsibility center budget is prepared, except that the focus is on the whole project rather than on a specified time period. In the control phase, actual costs are compared with budgeted costs and appropriate action taken.

The third aspect, quality, refers to the specifications of the project, that is, the desired end product. The term "quality," although customarily used, does not indicate the full scope of this aspect. In the planning phase, the desired end product is stated as specifically as is feasible, and in the control phase, actual quality is compared with these specifications and appropriate action taken.

Each of these three aspects must be considered separately, and they also must be considered jointly, for they interact. A reduction in quality can lead to a corresponding reduction in cost, and time can be shortened by increasing overtime costs, to give two examples. These interactions will be considered in the discussion which follows.

Also, as the project progresses, circumstances may suggest the desirability of revising any or all of the time, cost, or quality estimates. These revisions complicate the control process, as will be discussed.

Work Packages.   Most projects, except the smallest are broken down into pieces, in order to facilitate both planning and control. These pieces are here called *work packages,* or *activities,* although other terms are customary in various industries. A work package is a measurable increment of work which can be related to a physical product, milestone, or other indicator of progress. It should require a relatively short time (usually not more than a month, rarely more than a few months), it should have an identifiable starting point and completion point, and it should be performed in a single responsibility center.

Work packages always encompass the time and quality dimensions; they may or may not include cost information. Often it is not believed to be necessary to collect costs at the level of work packages, and in this case costs are collected in broader categories, which essentially are aggregates of individual work packages.

PROJECT PLANNING

The planning for a project may start with a rough, quite vague idea, which becomes increasingly definite on the basis of discussions, tests, various types of preliminary studies, and negotiations with clients. We start our description at the point where a decision to proceed with the project has been made, and its cost magnitude, the total time required, and the quality aspects have been pretty well agreed to. Such a point cannot be specified concretely, because at any time new information may lead to a change in any of these aspects, as will be discussed below. We shall describe how these general plans are translated into specific schedules and budgets that form the basis for project control. The preparation of these schedules and budgets is done as close to the inception of work on the project as is feasible. If they are prepared at an earlier stage, last-minute changes in the nature of the project are likely to make them obsolete.

Planning the Time Dimension

Several tools are available for constructing the time schedule for the project. They go by such acronyms as PERT (Program Evaluation and Review Technique), CPM (Critical Path Method), LOB (Line of Balance method). Collectively, they are known as techniques for *network analysis.* Essentially, they involve the construction of a network which shows each subgoal, or *event,* that must be completed in order to accomplish the whole project, the time required for the *activity* that is necessary for the attainment of each event, and the chronological sequence in which events must be completed in order to complete the whole project.

Network Analysis.[1] The approach to constructing and analyzing a project network, and the limitations of such an analysis, can be understood from the example in Exhibit 16–1. The example is for a simple situation, but the same principles apply for complex projects involving hundreds or thousands of events.

Section (A) shows a six job network, in which circles represent jobs and arrows indicate job precedence. Four men are available to do this project. The numbers above and below each circle indicate, respectively, the duration and manpower requirement of each job. The "critical path" duration of this network, without considering resources, is eight days.

Section (B) shows the eight-day job sequence for this problem based on standard CPM analysis, and the resulting daily manpower requirements. It can be seen that the available manpower constraint is exceeded on days 3 and 4; thus, this eight-day schedule is resource-infeasible (assuming that the limit of four men cannot be exceeded). In order to complete the project, job

---

[1] This section is adapted from material prepared by Edward W. Davis.

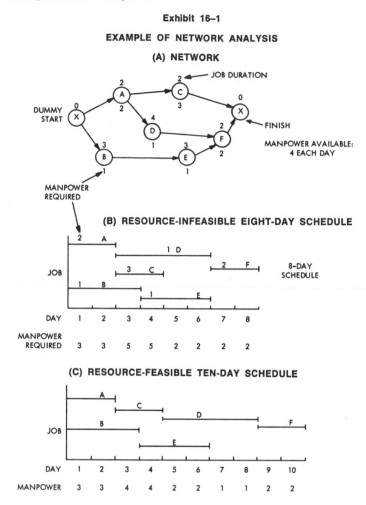

Exhibit 16–1

EXAMPLE OF NETWORK ANALYSIS

(A) NETWORK

(B) RESOURCE-INFEASIBLE EIGHT-DAY SCHEDULE

(C) RESOURCE-FEASIBLE TEN-DAY SCHEDULE

sequencing decisions are required, which will result in the shortest possible project duration, and involving not more than four men each day.

In what order should the jobs of this project be sequenced so as not to exceed the available limit of four men, and yet minimize the increase in project duration? This is the crux of the issue in scheduling project networks under resource constraints.

In spite of this problem's apparent simplicity, there exists today no practical computational scheme for determining optimal solutions to problems of the size and complexity generally encountered in real-life situations. It should be noted that the simple example of Exhibit 16–1 involves only one manpower type for the entire project. If each job required various amounts of several different manpower types (e.g., carpenters, plumbers), and each type were limited in availability, the problem would be much more complicated—and more representative of what actually occurs in practice.

One approach to the simple one-resource problem as described above is to sequence those jobs causing the resource conflicts according to some *heuristic* ("rule-of-thumb") such as the "shortest job first." Using this rule, Job D of the sample problem would be delayed until after Job C, and the resource-feasible schedule of ten days' duration shown in Section (C) is obtained. The drawback of using such a heuristic approach is that we do not know if the resulting schedule is the shortest possible. Thus, there may well be a nine-day solution for this problem which we *might* obtain by using a different sequencing heuristic.

Another approach to the problem would be to formulate it for solution as an integer linear programming problem. This approach will yield the optimal (shortest duration) schedule, but (a) the formulation is extremely cumbersome, requiring dozens of equations for small problems and (b) computation times to solution, even on the largest computers, are quite long, running as high as 12 to 15 minutes for a simple 14 job problem. This approach has generally been discarded as a practical method of solution for network scheduling problems.

A third approach—which would also yield the optimal solution—would be to enumerate all possible job sequences and choose the one producing the shortest project duration. This approach is also impractical, because the number of possible job sequences increases exponentially with an increase in the number of jobs. Stated another way, the decision tree of possible job sequences grows quickly to unmanageable proportions. For example, the decision tree for this very simple problem contains more than 100 nodes, and the tree for a slightly larger example containing 11 jobs contains more than 200,000 nodes! Obviously, then, this approach is also generally infeasible.

A fourth—and more recent—approach involves the techniques of "bounded enumeration." As implied by the name, this approach involves enumerating and searching over only a portion of the decision tree for a given problem. The partial enumeration and search is conducted in such a fashion that the final solution is demonstrably optimal. Bounded enumeration has so far been successfully applied only to small networks of less than 100 jobs and several different resource types. This approach is, however, still in its infancy (first applied in 1967) and holds some promise of ultimately being extendable to moderate sized problems.

Because of its formidable combinatorial proportions, the bulk of effort on the resource-constrained network scheduling problem has been devoted to the development of *heuristic* solution procedures. Dozens, if not hundreds, of elaborate computer-based schemes have been developed in government and industry. Some of these computer programs will quickly produce a *feasible* solution to projects involving hundreds of jobs and many different resource types.

The manager who uses these programs should be aware, however, that irrespective of their complexity—and despite the "best possible solution" claims of their marketers—the "goodness" of the final schedule (relative to the optimum) is generally unknown. Although some heuristic procedures are generally recognized as more effective than others, there is no one heuristic which will perform best, relative to other heuristics, in every given case.

Critical Path and Slack.   Computer programs are available for analyzing project networks. They identify the *critical path,* that is the sequence of events that requires the longest total time. The nature of the critical path is shown in Exhibit 16–2. In order to complete Event B, Event A must first be

Exhibit 16–2

CRITICAL PATH
(Heavy Line Indicates Critical Path)

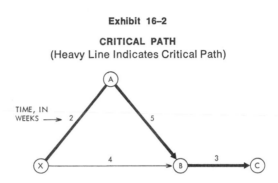

completed; this requires two weeks. A–B requires an additional five weeks. Then B–C, requiring an additional three weeks, is done in order to complete the project. This is the critical path, and it is ten weeks long. Note that in order to complete Event B, activity X–B must also be undertaken, with an estimated time of four weeks. However, Activity B–C cannot be started until *both* A–B and X–B have been completed. Since X–A and A–B require a total of seven weeks, A–B, which requires only four weeks, can be performed any time during this period. Activity X–B is said to have three weeks of *slack*.

There are several management control implications in the concepts of critical path and slack. First, in the control process, special attention must be paid to those activities that are on the critical path, and less attention need to be paid to slack activities (although not so much less that time is allowed to slip by and eat up the amount of slack; the activity then automatically becomes on the critical path). Second, in the planning process, attention should be given to possibilities for reducing the time required for critical path activities; if such possibilities exist, the overall time required for the project can be reduced. Third, it may be desirable to reduce critical path times by increasing costs, such as incurring overtime, but it is not desirable to spend additional money to reduce the time of slack activities.

Probabilistic PERT.   As the PERT system was originally conceived, the estimated times required for each activity in the network were to be arrived at on a probabilistic basis. Three estimates were to be made for each activity:

a most likely time (m), an optimistic time (a), and a pessimistic time (b). The optimistic and pessimistic times were supposed to represent probabilities of approximately .01 and .99 on a normal probability distribution. The most likely estimate was given a weight of 4, and each of the other estimates a weight of 1, and an expected time $(\bar{t})$ for each activity was computed as

$$\bar{t} = \frac{a + 4m + b}{6}$$

Although conceptually elegant, this approach had serious practical difficulties. Engineers and others who were asked to make the three estimates found this to be a most difficult task. It turned out not to be possible, in most cases, to convey what was intended by "optimistic" and "pessimistic" in a way that was interpreted similarly by all the estimators. Furthermore, it was found that estimators tended to make symmetrical estimates, that is, their optimistic and pessimistic estimates were equal distances from the most likely estimate. When this happened, the resulting expected time $(\bar{t})$ was the same as the most likely time, so there was no gain in going through the probabilistic exercise. For example, if the estimates were 3 weeks for a, 5 weeks for m and 7 weeks for b, the expected time was

$$\frac{3 + 4(5) + 7}{6} = \frac{30}{6} = 5$$

Thus, although probabilistic PERT is still referred to in the literature and in formal descriptions of the PERT technique, the probabilistic part is not widely used in practice.

Planning the Cost Dimension

A technique called PERT/Cost attempts to incorporate a cost dimension into the network analysis. Basically, it is an extension of the approach illustrated in Exhibit 16–1, with monetary costs substituted for the man-weeks. The objective is to develop a critical path that is optimum considering both the time aspects and the cost aspects jointly. For planning purposes, PERT/Cost is supposed to identify time/cost tradeoffs, that is, activities in which it would be desirable to increase costs in order to reduce time, and, conversely, activities in which it would be desirable to lengthen the time in order to reduce costs. For control purposes, the PERT/Cost estimates are supposed to provide a basis for analyzing actual times and actual costs jointly.

Experience has shown that PERT/Cost is so complicated as not to be practicable in most situations. In order to control time, the work packages had to be quite small, but great difficulty was experienced in estimating the cost on these small work packages. These difficulties could be overcome by simply assuming that costs were a straight function of time (e.g., $10 per hour) but in this case the cost estimates provided no new information. For this reason PERT/Cost is not widely used as a management control tool (although some defense contractors go through the motions because they are reimbursed by the Department of Defense for the costs of doing so).

For practical reasons, therefore, cost estimates are often made at a level of aggregation that incorporates several work packages. For simple projects, the estimates may be for the whole project as one entity, but if this is done it is not feasible to establish cost checkpoints during the conduct of the project. Lacking such checkpoints, the assumption has to be made that planned spending will proceed at an even rate, for example, that when 25 percent of the project has been completed, 25 percent of the total estimated cost should have been spent. Such an assumption is likely to be, at best, only a rough approximation.

If progress payments are to be made during the course of the project, the cost estimates will usually be in terms of full costs, because these provide a basis for such payments. In other cases, the costs may well include only the direct costs of the project.

In project control, unlike responsibility center control, it usually is unnecessary to separate variable costs from fixed costs since there usually is no need to analyze the behavior of costs in relation to volume.

Planning the Quality Dimension

Presumably, the plan for the project specifies the end product that is desired, and in some cases it may contain considerable detail about the components that make up the end product. To the extent that such information exists, it provides the basis for constructing work packages and specifying their contents. In many cases, however, the nature of the work packages cannot be determined simply from the specifications for the end product, and engineers must develop a concrete plan, perhaps working backward from the end product, first to its components, and then to the activities that are required in order to obtain each component. In a complicated project it is often difficult to describe the work packages concretely enough so that the manager knows exactly when one has been completed, and this complicates the problem of control.

For some projects, there is no written description of the steps that are to be carried out in order to achieve the project's objective, that is, of the work packages. For short, simple projects, or for certain basic research projects where the nature of the work may not be forseeable, this may not be necessary. For other projects, the absence of a written plan greatly complicates the control problem. Furthermore, those who work on projects often find that their time is spent more effectively if they have done as much advance planning as is feasible.

PROJECT CONTROL

As a consequence of the planning process, there exists, for most projects, a schedule and a budget. The schedule shows the time required for each activity, or work package, and the budget shows estimated costs of each principal part of the project, but probably not at the level of individual work packages. In the control process, information on actual cost, time, and quality is compared with these estimates. The comparison may be made each time a designated milestone in the project is reached, or it may be made at specified time intervals, such as weekly or monthly. In the latter case, there is the problem of matching work packages to the work actually done. It is likely that some work packages will be partially complete as of the reporting data, and this makes it necessary to estimate their percentage of completion as a basis for comparing the actual time. A similar procedure must be used for cost comparisons.

Basically, management is concerned with these questions: (1) Is the project going to be finished by the scheduled completion date? (2) Is the completed work going to meet the specifications that were contemplated when the project was approved? and (3) Is the work going to be done within the estimated cost? If at any time during the course of the project, the answer to any of these questions is "no," management needs to know the reasons and what can be done to correct the situation. These three questions cannot be considered separately from one another, for it is sometimes desirable to make tradeoffs among time, quality, and cost. For example, overtime might be authorized in order to assure ontime completion, but this would add to costs; or some of the specifications might be relaxed in order to reduce costs. In any event, a project control system is structured in terms of these three dimensions.

Reports on Cost and Time

Reports on actual cost compared to budget and actual time compared to the schedule are relatively straightforward. In interpreting the time reports, the usual presumption is that if the project manager can complete a work package in less than the estimated time, he is to be congratulated, and if he takes more than the estimated time, questions are raised. The interpretation of the cost reports is somewhat different, for the possibility exists that if actual costs are less than budget, quality may have suffered. For this reason, unless there is some independent way of estimating the costs that should be required, good cost performance is often interpreted as meaning being on budget, neither higher nor lower.

In most companies, cost reports compare actual costs to date with budgeted costs for the work accomplished to date. In some companies, the reports show the current estimate for the entire project compared with the budgeted cost for the entire project. The current estimate is obtained by taking the actual costs to date and adding an estimate of the costs required to complete the project. The latter type of report is a useful way of showing how the project is expected to come out, provided that the estimated costs to complete are properly calculated. In most circumstances, these estimates should be at least equal to the original estimates made for the remaining work; if project managers are permitted to use lower figures, they can hide overruns already incurred by making corresponding reductions in future estimates. Indeed, if overruns to date are caused by factors that are likely to persist into the future, such as unanticipated inflation, the current estimates of future costs may well be higher than the amounts estimated originally.

If only direct costs are matched with work done, reports on indirect costs must be prepared separately. These reports measure costs in a different dimension than do reports on the direct costs of project work. In the case of direct costs, actual costs are compared with budgeted costs for the work actually accomplished. In the case of indirect costs, the actual costs for a period, such as a month, are compared with the budgeted costs for that same period.

Tradeoffs.   The interpretation of time behavior, taken by itself, or cost behavior, taken by itself, is a relatively straightforward type of analysis. For a real understanding of accomplishment, however, one must also consider the interactions between cost and time, and between each of these and quality. Usually such interactions are not set forth in the reports themselves, but they are an important topic in meetings held to discuss progress.

Reports on Output

Reports on time and on cost consist of numbers that come out of a formal system, often from a computer. In part, information on what has been accomplished can also be stated in concrete terms: the completion of a specified component, or of a well defined task of the project, or the achievement of prescribed specifications. Usually, however, the full story of performance cannot be told in such objective terms. The most important information must be conveyed by words, and these reports on what has actually been accomplished usually must be prepared by a project manager personally. Managers usually dislike writing such reports, and even the best reports do not communicate precisely what is going on, because of the limitations inherent in words. There is much difference of opinion as to the appropriate content of such reports.

The question may be raised: If the project is proceeding satisfactorily, why is it necessary to have a report that says so? One possible answer is that even if the project *appears* to be satisfactory, difficulties may surface in the future, and a regular report of progress may help to identify why these difficulties arose and who was responsible for them. In particular, if a controversy arises about the project, a well documented description of "who did what" is a highly desirable starting point in analyzing what went wrong. This reason does not justify lengthy reports on routine happenings, however.

One solution to the performance reporting problem is to classify projects as either high risk or low risk. For low risk projects, the performance reports would be simple, unless a problem was identified. For the high risk projects, the reports would be more detailed and more frequent. Such an approach is taken in research/development laboratories that have many projects underway at any one time and cannot devote an equal amount of management attention to all of them.

Written reports are, by themselves, an inadequate device for controlling progress on any except the most routine projects. An appraisal of performance is very much a matter of management judgment which is arrived at principally by actual observation of the work and by discussions with the persons involved in it. One of the purposes of these discussions is to uncover problems as early as possible, and if this purpose is to be achieved, there must be an atmosphere such that the project leader feels uninhibited about discussing incipient problems.

Revisions

If a project is complex, or if it is lengthy, there is a good chance that the plan will not be adhered to in one or more of its three dimensions: time, cost, or quality. A common occurrence is the discovery that there is likely to be a cost overrun, that is, that actual costs will exceed budgeted costs. When indications of significant deviations of plan come to management's attention, there will naturally be a discussion of what should be done. In the case of a cost overrun, for example, management might decide to accept the overrun and proceed with the project as originally planned; it might decide to cut back on the specifications of the project with the aim of producing an end product that is within the original cost limitations; or it might decide to replace the project leader in the belief that the cost overrun was unwarranted. Whatever the decision, it usually leads to a revision of the original plans for the project, and a revised plan is therefore necessary.

The question then arises: Is it better to track future progress against the revised plan or against the original plan? The revised plan is presumably a better indication of the performance that now is expected, but the danger exists that a persuasive project leader can negotiate unwarranted increases in budgeted costs or that the revised plan will incorporate, and thus hide, inefficiencies that have accumulated to date. In either case, the revised plan is said to be a *rubber baseline,* that is, instead of providing a firm benchmark for measuring progress, it is stretched so as to cover up inefficiencies. This danger can be minimized by taking a hardheaded attitude toward proposed revisions, but even if this is done, there is a tendency to overlook the fact that a revised plan, by definition, does not show what was expected when the project was initiated. On the other hand, if performance continues to be monitored by comparing it with the original plan, the fact that the original plan is obsolete is likely to cause the comparison not to be taken seriously.

A possible solution to this problem is to compare cost performance to *both* the original plan and the revised plan, along the lines indicated in Exhibit 16–3. This summary report starts with the original budget, and in the first section sets forth the revisions that have been authorized to date and the reasons for making them. The lower section shows the current cost estimate

Exhibit 16–3

PROJECT COST SUMMARY
(000 Omitted)

Original budget	$1,000
Authorized revisions to date:	
For inflation	50
For specification changes	200
For time delays	60
For cost savings	(30)
Revised budget	$1,280
Current estimate to complete	1,400
Variance	$ 120

Explanation of Variance:		
Material cost increases	$ 20	
Overtime	60	
Spending variances	40	
	$120	

and the factors that caused the variance between the revised budget and the current estimate of costs.

MATRIX ORGANIZATIONS

In a shipyard that does overhaul work on ships, there are project managers each of whom is responsible for the overhaul work on one ship, and there are managers of the electrical, plumbing, steamfitting, and other shops, each of whom is responsible for the work done by the employees of his shop. Such an organization is called a matrix organization. Because of the overlapping responsibilities, there are difficult management control problems in such an organization.

Not all projects are conducted in matrix organizations. In building a dam, constructing a pipeline, or making a motion picture, employees are hired for the specific project, and equipment is purchased or leased for that project; when the project is completed, the employees are released and the equipment is disposed of. By contrast, in a matrix organization employees are permanently assigned to a functional organization unit, they work temporarily on a project, and when that work is completed they are assigned to another project.

Projects vary widely. In the time dimension, the development of a marketing campaign by an advertising agency may be completed in a few months, while the construction of a nuclear power plant requires at least seven years, and usually longer. In extent of authority, a product brand manager in a consumer goods company may have few people permanently assigned to him, and must count on persuasion with various manufacturing and marketing units to carry out his plans; whereas in a major engineering or consulting project a large force may be assigned full time to the project for a period of months or years, with some supplementary assistance from service units when this is needed. In a research/development laboratory, a typical project will have a nucleus of full-time people, it will have part-time people, and the project leader will draw on the services of test laboratories, computer programmers, model shops, and other specialized activities when the need arises. As to size, a project may involve a single person, or, as in the case of several projects associated with the Apollo space program, it may involve thousands of people full time and the services of many specialized shops and other activities. In view of these variations, not many generalizations can be made about management control that are valid for all types of projects.

The Management Control Problem

The matrix in Exhibit 16–4 suggests the nature of the management control problem in a matrix organization. In a shipyard, one dimension focuses on the projects—the various ship overhaul jobs—and the other dimension focuses on the responsibility centers, the functional shops to which the personnel are permanently assigned. Management control goes on concurrently in both these dimensions. The project manager may be the manager of one

Exhibit 16–4

CONTROL MATRIX IN A SHIPYARD

Jobs	Responsibility Centers				Total by Jobs
	Shop A	Shop B	Shop C	Etc.	
Job 1					
Job 2					
Job 3					
Etc.					
Total by shops					

of the responsibility centers which work on the project, or he may not be associated with any of these responsibility centers. The interests of the project manager often do not coincide with those of the responsibility center managers. The project manager wants full attention given to *his* project, while the responsibility center manager must take into account *all* the projects on which his center works. This conflict of interest is inevitable; it increases the complexity of control. A matrix organization creates tension. As Vancil says, there is "an atmosphere of constructive conflict in which managers in one function know they are working toward the same goal and must compete among themselves to cooperate with other managers."[2]

The larger the project, the more complicated the control problem be-

---

[2] Richard F. Vancil, "What Kind of Management Control Do You Need?" *Harvard Business Review*, March–April 1973, p. 75.

comes. When the TRW Company was working on the Apollo program, for example, the project manager not only had a large office responsible for scheduling the project and dovetailing the operations of the many functional departments involved, but he also had full-time liason people in each of these departments; they were responsible to him for work related to the project, but each was also a member of the functional department, and his overall performance was judged by the head of his department.

The structure of Exhibit 16–4 implies that costs might be collected for each of the cells in the matrix, that is, that there might be a cost element that is unique to a single project in a single responsibility center. This is indeed possible, although in practice it is customary to classify costs differently in one dimension of the matrix than is done in the other dimension. In general, direct labor and material costs are shown in more detail in the project dimension, and overhead costs are shown in more detail in the responsibility center dimension.

For both the planning and the control of direct costs, the project system is more important than the responsibility center system. It is in the project control system that one finds attention devoted to bills of materials, direct labor standards, statistical quality control, and production scheduling. By contrast, individual elements of overhead expense are set forth in detail in the responsibility center control system, whereas overhead costs may be omitted entirely from the data in the project control system, or they may be included as a single lump sum, derived from an overhead rate. This distinction is reflected in the project control cases accompanying this chapter; they focus on labor and material costs rather than on overhead costs.

In attempting to appraise performance, the same dual responsibility exists. The project manager is responsible for accomplishing the project in its time, cost, and quality dimensions, that is, he is responsible for the efficient and effective use of the resources that are made available to him by the functional departments. The responsibility center manager is responsible for seeing to it that the department has the personnel, tools, and other resources that are necessary to do the project work; for training, promotion, salary scales, and other personnel actions; and for seeing to it that available resources are fully used on project work. As one small indication of the distinction, the project manager is responsible for the number of hours that an employee works on the project, but the responsibility manager is responsible for the skills that the employee brings to the project and for the cost per hour.

Case 16–1

Northeast Research
Laboratory (B)

On a Friday morning in late December, 1973, Sam Lacy, Head of the Physical Sciences Division of Northeast Research Laboratory (NRL) thought about two letters which lay on his desk. One, which he had received a few weeks before, was a progress report from Robert Kirk, recently assigned project leader of the Exco Project, who reported that earlier frictions between the NRL team and the client had lessened considerably, that high quality research was under way, and that the prospects for retaining the Exco project on a long-term basis appeared fairly good. The other letter, which had just arrived in the morning's mail, came from Gray Kenney, a Vice President of Exco, and stated that the company wished to terminate the Exco contract effective immediately.

Lacy was puzzled. He remembered how pleased Gray Kenney had been only a few months before when the Exco project produced its second patentable process. On the other hand, he also recalled some of the difficulties the project had encountered within NRL which had ultimately led to the replacement of project leader Alan North in order to avoid losing the contract. Lacy decided to call in the participants in an effort to piece together an understanding of what had happened. Some of what he learned is described below. But the problem remained for him to decide what he should report to top management. What should he recommend to avoid the recurrence of such a situation in the future?

COMPANY BACKGROUND

Northeast Research Laboratory was a multihdisciplinary research and development organization employing approximately 1,000 professionals. It was organized into two main sectors, one for economics and business administra-

747

Exhibit 1

**NORTHEAST RESEARCH LABORATORY
ORGANIZATION CHART**
(Simplified)

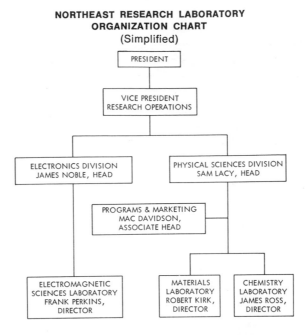

tion and the other for the physical and natural sciences. Within the physical and natural sciences sector, the organization was essentially by branches of science. The main units were called divisions and the subunits were called laboratories. A partial organization chart is shown in Exhibit 1.

Most of the company's work was done on the basis of contracts with clients. Each contract was a project. Responsibility for the project was vested in a project leader, and through him up the organizational structure in which his laboratory was located. Typically, some members of the project team were drawn from laboratories other than that in which the project leader worked; it was the ability to put together a team with a variety of technical talents that was one of the principal strengths of a multidisciplinary laboratory. Team members worked under the direction of the project leader during the period in which they were assigned to the project. An individual might be working on more than one project concurrently. The project leader could also draw on the resources of central service organizations, such as model shops, computer services, editorial, and drafting. The project was billed for the services of these units at rates which were intended to cover their full costs.

INCEPTION OF THE EXCO PROJECT

In October, 1972, Gray Kenney, Vice President of Exco, had telephoned Mac Davidson of NRL to outline a research project which would examine the effect of microwaves on various ores and minerals. Davidson was Associate Head of the Physical Sciences Division and had known Kenney for several years. During the conversation Kenney asserted that NRL ought to to be particularly intrigued by the research aspects of the project, and Davidson readily agreed. Davidson was also pleased because the Physical Sciences Division was under pressure to generate more revenue, and this potentially long-term project from Exco would make good use of available manpower. In addition, top management of NRL had recently circulated several memos indicating that more emphasis should be put on commercial rather than government work. Davidson was, however, a little concerned that the project did not fall neatly into one laboratory or even one division, but in fact required assistance from the Electronics Division to complement work that would be done in two different Physical Sciences Laboratories (the Chemistry Laboratory and the Materials Laboratory).

A few days later Davidson organized a joint client-NRL conference to determine what Exco wanted and to plan the proposal. Kenney sent his assistant, Tod Denby, who was to serve as the Exco liaison officer for the project. Representing NRL were Davidson; Sam Lacy; Dr. Robert Kirk, director of the Materials Laboratory (one of the two Physical Sciences laboratories involved in the project); Dr. Alan North, manager of Chemical Development and Engineering (and associate director of the Chemistry Laboratory); Dr. James Noble, Executive Director of the Electronics Division; and a few researchers chosen by Kirk and North. Davidson also would like to have invited Dr. James Ross, director of the Chemistry Laboratory, but Ross was out of town and couldn't attend the pre-proposal meeting.

Denby described the project as a study of the use of microwaves for the conversion of basic ores and minerals to more valuable commercial products. The study was to consist of two parts:

Task A—An experimental program to examine the effect of microwaves on 50 ores and minerals, and to select those processes appearing to have the most promise.

Task B—A basic study to obtain an understanding of how and why microwaves interact with certain minerals.

It was agreed that the project would be a joint effort of three laboratories: (1) Materials, (2) Chemistry, and (3) Electromagnetic. The first two laboratories were in the Physical Sciences Division, and the last was in the Electronics Division.

Denby proposed that the contract be open-ended, with a level of effort of around $10,000–$12,000 per month. Agreement was quickly reached on the content of the proposal. Denby emphasized to the group that an early start was essential if Exco were to remain ahead of its competition.

After the meeting Lacy, who was to have overall responsibility for the project, discussed the choice of project leader with Davidson. Davidson proposed Alan North, a 37-year-old chemist who had had experience as a project leader on several projects. North had impressed Davidson at the pre-proposal meeting and seemed well suited to head the interdisciplinary team. Lacy agreed. Lacy regretted that Dr. Ross (head of the Laboratory in which North worked) was unable to participate in the decision of who should head the joint project. In fact, because he was out of town, Ross was neither aware of the Exco project nor of his laboratory's involvement in it.

The following day, Alan North was told of his appointment as project leader. During the next few days, he conferred with Robert Kirk, head of the other Physical Sciences laboratory involved in the project. Toward the end of October Denby began to exert pressure on North to finalize the proposal, stating that the substance had been agreed upon at the pre-proposal conference. North thereupon drafted a five-page letter as a substitute for a formal proposal, describing the nature of the project and outlining the procedures and equipment necessary. At Denby's request, North included a paragraph which authorized members of the client's staff to visit NRL frequently and observe portions of the research program. The proposal's cover sheet contained approval signatures from the laboratories and divisions involved. North signed for his own area and for laboratory director Ross. He telephoned Dr. Noble of the Electronics Division, relayed the client's sense of urgency, and Noble authorized North to sign for him. Davidson signed for the Physical Sciences Division as a whole.

At this stage, North relied principally on the advice of colleagues within his own division. As he did not know personally the individuals in the Electronics Division, they were not called upon at this point. Since North understood informally that the director of the Electromagnetic Sciences Laboratory, Dr. Perkins, was quite busy and often out of town, North did not attempt to discuss the project with Perkins.

After the proposal had been signed and mailed, Dr. Perkins was sent a copy. It listed the engineering equipment which the client wanted purchased for the project and prescribed how it was to be used. Perkins worried that performance characteristics of the power supply (necessary for quantitative measurement) specified in the proposal were inadequate for the task. He asked North about it and North said that the client had made up his mind as to the microwave equipment he wanted and how it was to be used. Denby had said he was paying for that equipment and intended to move it to Exco's laboratories after the completion of the NRL contract.

All these events had transpired rather quickly. By the time Dr. Ross, director of the Chemistry Laboratory, returned, the proposal for the Exco project had been signed and accepted. Ross went to see Lacy and said that he had dealt with Denby on a previous project and had serious misgivings about working with him. Lacy assuaged some of Ross's fears by observing that if anyone could succeed in working with Denby it would be North—a flexible man, professionally competent, who could move with the tide and get along with clients of all types.

CONDUCT OF THE PROJECT

Thus the project began. Periodically, when decisions arose, North would seek opinions from division management. However, he was somewhat unclear about whom he should talk to. Davidson had been the person who had actually appointed him project leader. Normally, however, North worked for Ross. Although Kirk's laboratory was heavily involved in the project, Kirk was very busy with other Materials Laboratory work. Adding to his uncertainty, North periodically received telephone calls from Perkins of the Electronics Division, whom he didn't know well. Perkins expected to be heavily involved in the project.

Difficulties and delays began to plague the project. The microwave equipment specified by the client was not delivered by the manufacturer on schedule, and there were problems in filtering the power supply of the radio-frequency source. Over the objection of NRL Electromagnetic Sciences engineers, but at the insistence of the client, one of the chemical engineers tried to improve the power supply filter. Eventually the equipment had to be sent back to the manufacturer for modification. This required several months.

In the spring of 1973, Denby, who had made his presence felt from the outset, began to apply strong pressure. "Listen," he said to North, "top management of Exco is starting to get on my back and we need results. Besides, I'm up for review in four months and I can't afford to let this project affect my promotion." Denby was constantly at NRL during the next few months. He was often in the labs conferring individually with members of the NRL teams. Denby also visited North's office frequently.

A number of related problems began to surface. North had agreed to do both experimental and theoretical work for this project, but Denby's constant pushing for experimental results began to tilt the emphasis. Theoretical studies began to lapse, and experimental work became the focus of the Exco project. From time to time North argued that the theoretical work should precede or at least accompany the experimental program, but Denby's insistence on concrete results led North to temporarily deemphasize the theoretical work. Symptoms of this shifting emphasis were evident. One day a senior researcher from Kirk's laboratory came to North to complain that people were being "stolen" from his team. "How can we do a balanced project if the theoretical studies are not given enough manpower?" he asked. North explained the client's position and asked the researcher to bear with this temporary realignment of the project's resources.

As the six-month milestone approached, Denby expressed increasing dissatisfaction with the project's progress. In order to have concrete results to report to Exco management, he directed North a number of times to change the direction of the research. On several occasions various members of the project team had vigorous discussions with Denby about the risks of chasing results without laying a careful foundation. North himself spent a good deal of time talking with Denby on this subject, but Denby seemed to discount its importance. Denby began to avoid North and to spend most of his time with the other team members. Eventually the experimental program, initially dedicated to a careful screening of some 50 materials, deteriorated to a somewhat frantic and erratic pursuit of what appeared to be "promising leads." Lacy and Noble played little or no role in this shift of emphasis.

On June 21, 1973, Denby visited North in his office and severely criticized him for proposing a process (hydrochloric acid pickling) that was economically infeasible. In defense, North asked an NRL economist to check his figures. The economist reported back that North's numbers were sound and that, in fact, a source at U.S. Steel indicated that hydrochloric acid pickling was "generally more economic than the traditional process and was increasingly being adopted." Through this and subsequent encounters, the relationship between Denby and North became increasingly strained.

Denby continued to express concern about the Exco project's pay off. In an effort to save time, he discouraged the NRL team from repeating experiments, a practice that was designed to insure accuracy. Data received from initial experiments were frequently taken as sufficiently accurate, and after hasty analysis were adopted for the purposes of the moment. Not surprisingly Denby periodically discovered errors in these data. He informed NRL of them.

Denby's visits to NRL became more frequent as the summer progressed. Some days he would visit all three laboratories, talking to the researchers involved and asking them about encouraging leads. North occasionally cautioned Denby against too much optimism. Nonetheless, North continued to oblige the client by restructuring the Exco project to allow for more "production line" scheduling of experiments and for less systematic research.

In August, North discovered that vertile could be obtained from iron ore. This discovery was a significant one, and the client applied for a patent. If the reaction could be proved commercially, its potential would be measured in millions of dollars. Soon thereafter, the NRL team discovered that the operation could, in fact, be handled commercially in a rotary kiln. The client was notified and soon began planning a pilot plant that would use the rotary kiln process.

Exco's engineering department, after reviewing the plans for the pilot plant, rejected them. It was argued that the rotary process was infeasible and that a fluid bed process would have to be used instead. Denby returned to NRL and insisted on an experiment to test the fluid bed process. North warned Denby that agglomeration (a sticking together of the material) would probably take place. It did. Denby was highly upset, reported to Gray Kenney that he had not received "timely" warning of the probability of agglomeration taking place, and indicated that he had been misled as to the feasibility of the rotary kiln process.[1]

---

[1] Ten months later the client was experimenting with the rotary kiln process for producing vertile from iron ore in his own laboratory.

Work continued, and two other "disclosures of invention" were turned over to the client by the end of September.

PERSONNEL CHANGES

On September 30, Denby came to North's office to request that Charles Fenton be removed from the Exco project. Denby reported he had been watching Fenton in the Electromagnetic Laboratory, which he visited often, and had observed that Fenton spent relatively little time on the Exco project. North, who did not know Fenton well, agreed to look into it. But Denby insisted that Fenton be removed immediately and threatened to terminate the contract if he were allowed to remain.

North was unable to talk to Fenton before taking action because Fenton was on vacation. He did talk to Fenton as soon as he returned, and the researcher admitted that due to the pressure of other work he had not devoted as much time or effort to the Exco work as perhaps he should have.

Three weeks later, Denby called a meeting with Mac Davidson and Sam Lacy. It was their first meeting since the pre-proposal conference for the Exco project. Denby was brief and to the point:

Denby: I'm here because we have to replace North. He's become increasingly difficult to work with and is obstructing the progress of the project.

Lacy: But North is an awfully good man . . .

Davidson: Look, he's come up with some good solid work thus far. What about the process of extracting vertile from iron ore he came up with. And . . .

Denby: I'm sorry, but we have to have a new project leader. I don't mean to be abrupt, but it's either replace North or forget the contract.

Davidson reluctantly appointed Robert Kirk project leader and informed North of the decision. North went to see Davidson a few days later. Davidson told him that although management did not agree with the client, North had been replaced in order to save the contract. Later Dr. Lacy told North the same thing. Neither Lacy nor Davidson made an effort to contact Exco senior management on the matter.

Following the change of project leadership, the record became more difficult to reconstruct. It appeared that Kirk made many efforts to get the team together, but morale remained low. Denby continued to make periodic visits to NRL but found that the NRL researchers were not talking as freely with him as they had in the past. Denby became sceptical about the project's value. Weeks slipped by. No further breakthroughs emerged.

LACY'S PROBLEM

Doctor Lacy had received weekly status reports on the project, the latest of which is shown in Exhibit 2. He had had a few informal conversations about the project, principally with North and Kirk. He had not read the

Exhibit 2

WEEKLY PROJECT STATUS REPORT

PROJECT/ACCOUNT STATUS REPORT	ORG 325	PROJ/ACCT 3273	SUB 000	W/O 000	WEEK ENDING DATE 12-22-73	TYPE PROJ	REV TYPE INDUS	PRICE SCA	CLIENT YD	INT/DOM DOMESTIC	NOTICES	PAGE 1

DIVISION PHYSICAL SCI	DEPARTMENT CHEMISTRY LAB	SUPERVISOR ROBERT KIRK	LEADER ROBERT KIRK	PROJECT TITLE MICROWAVES IN CONVERSION OF BASIC ORES AND MINERALS

INST EXCO	READY DATE 11-06-72	STOP WORK DATE --	TERM DATE 11-06-74	BURDEN % 28.00	OVERHEAD % 105.00	FEE % 15.00

TRANSACTIONS RECORDED 12-15-73 - 12-22-73

COST CATEGORIES	OBJECT CODE	DOLLARS PTD13WK1	DOLLARS TO DATE	LABOR HOURS ESTIMATE	LABOR HOURS TO DATE	LABOR HOURS BALANCE
SUPERVISOR	(11, 12)		560			36
SENIOR	(13)	192	17986			1348
PROFESSIONAL	(14)	150	16787			1678
TECHNICAL	(15)	529	5299			1037
CLER/SUPP	(16, 17, 18)		301			84
OTHER	(10) (19)	72	72			12
LABOR (S. T.)		943	41005			1644
BURDEN		248	11481			
OVERHEAD		1227	55110			
OVERTIME PREM	(21)	160	1540			
OVS./OTH. PREM	(22-29)	242	476			
TOTAL PERSONNEL COSTS		2820	109612			
TRAVEL	(56-59)		776			
SUBCONTRACT	(36)					
MATERIAL	(41, 42)		3726			
EQUIPMENT	(43)					
COMPUTER	(37, 45)					
COMMUN	(62, 63, 70, 71)	2	507			
CONSULTANT	(74, 75)					
REPORT COST	(44, 47)					
OTHER M&S		54	99			
TOTAL M&S COST		56	5098			
COMMITMENTS			26847			
TOTAL LESS FEE		2876	141557			
FEE (15.00)		158	24376			
TOTAL		3031	165933			

LAST BILLING:
DATE 11-30-73
AMOUNT 11350
ACCOUNT STATUS TO DATE:
BILLED 154583
PAID 154583

	ESTIMATED	BALANCE
COMMITMENTS	250435	108878
	37565	13189
	288000	122067

TIME BALANCE % 39.4
COST BALANCE % 43.5
TIME BALANCE WKS. 41

COMMITMENT STATUS TO DATE

PO NO		OBJ	VENDOR/DESCRIPTION	TOTAL	CHARGES	BALANCE
A61289	11-21-73	41	MINNESOTA MINING	111	61	50
A61313	11-23-73	41	ALDRICH CHEMICAL	348		348
A95209	11-28-73	43	TENNECO CHEMICAL CO	5		5
A95093	11-15-73	41	UNION CARBIDE CORP	23194		23194
B95104	11-19-73	37	SCIENTIFIC PRODUCTS	600		600
B95232	11-25-73	41	VAN WATERS & ROGERS	2500		2500
018046	12-15-73	57	ROGER MD	300	150	150
					T	26847

LABOR

ORG	ID	W/E DATE	T/S NO	OBJ	NAME	HOURS WEEK	TO DATE
322	02345	12-22-73	363073	13	KIRK	6.0	150
322	02345	12-22-73	363073	22	KIRK	6.0	
322	03212	12-22-73	363082	13	DENSMORE	8.0	25
322	03260	12-22-73	236544	14	COOK	15.0	30
325	12110	12-08-73	C30093	15	HOWARD	15.0	82
325	12110	12-15-73	236548	15	HOWARD	36.0	
325	12110	12-22-73	376147	15	HOWARD	8.0	
325	12357	12-22-73	376149	15	SPELTZ	15.0	68
325	12369	12-22-73	376150	15	GYUIRE	15.0	17
325	12384	12-22-73	R08416	15	DILLON	40.0-	44
325	12397	12-22-73	336527	15	NAGY	31.0	31
325	12397	12-22-73	336527	21	NAGY	15.0	
652	12475	12-22-73	236548	15	KAIN	8.0	20
652	12475	12-22-73	236548	21	KAIN		

	HOURS	DOLLARS
LABOR (STRAIGHT TIME)	117.0	943
PAYROLL BURDEN		248
OVERHEAD RECOVERY		1227
OVERTIME PREMIUM LABOR	30.0	160
OTHER PREMIUM LABOR	6.0	242
TOTAL PERSONNEL COSTS		2820 S

MATERIALS & SERVICES

PO NO	REF NO	OBJ	DESCRIPTION	REQUESTOR	
61289	54065	48	REA EXPRESS	KIRK	42
17234	87413	48	GED SUPPLY CO	COOK	10
	04461	71	448 P.T.&T. 326-6200	NAGY	2
			TOTAL M&S COSTS		56 S
			FEE		158
			TRANSACTION TOTAL		3034 T

reports submitted to Exco. If the project had been placed on NRL's "problem list," which comprised about 10 percent of the projects which seemed to be experiencing the most difficulty, Lacy would have received a written report on its status weekly, but the Exco project was not on that list.

With the background given above, Lacy reread Kenney's letter terminating the Exco contract. It seemed likely that Kenney, too, had not had full knowledge of what went on during the project's existence. In his letter, Kenney mentioned the "glowing reports" which reached his ears in the early stages of the work. These reports, which came to him only from Denby, were later significantly modified, and Denby apparently implied that NRL had been "leading him on." Kenney pointed to the complete lack of economic evaluation of alternative processes in the experimentation. He seemed unaware of the fact that at Denby's insistence all economic analysis was supposed to be done by the client. Kenney was most dissatisfied that NRL had not complied with all the provisions of the proposal, particularly those that required full screening of all materials and the completion of the theoretical work.

Lacy wondered why Denby's changes of the proposal had not been documented by the NRL team. Why hadn't he heard more of the problems of the Exco project before? Lacy requested a technical evaluation of the project from the economics process director and asked Davidson for *his* evaluation of the project. These reports are given in Exhibits 3 and 4. When he reviewed these reports, Lacy wondered what, if any, additional information he should submit to NRL top management.

Exhibit 3

TECHNICAL EVALUATION

by Ronald M. Benton
Director, Process Economics Program

Principal Conclusions

1. The original approach to the investigation as presented in the proposal is technically sound. The accomplishments could have been greater had this been followed throughout the course of the project, but the altered character of the investigation did not prevent accomplishment of fruitful research.
2. The technical conduct of this project on NRL's part was good despite the handicaps under which the work was carried out. Fundamental and theoretical considerations were employed in suggesting the course of research and in interpreting the data. There is no evidence to indicate that the experimental work itself was badly executed.
3. Significant accomplishments of this project were as follows:
   a. *Extraction of vertile from iron ore by several alternative processes.* Conception of these processes was based on fundamental considerations and demonstrated considerable imagination. As far as the work was carried out at NRL, one or more of these processes offers promise of commercial feasibility.
   b. *Nitrogen fixation.* This development resulted from a laboratory observation. The work was not carried far enough to ascertain whether or not the process offers any commercial significance. It was, however, shown that the yield of nitrogen oxides was substantially greater than has previously been achieved by either thermal or plasma processes.
   c. *Reduction of nickel oxide and probably also garnerite to nickel.* These findings were never carried beyond very preliminary stages and the ultimate commercial significance cannot be assessed at this time.
   d. *Discovery that microwave plasmas can be generated at atmospheric pressure.* Again the commercial significance of this finding cannot be appraised at present. However, it opens the possibility that many processes can be conducted economically that would be too costly at the reduced pressures previously thought to be necessary.
4. The proposal specifically stated that the selection of processes for scale-up and economic studies would be the responsibility of the client. I interpret this to mean that NRL was not excluded from making recommendations based on economic considerations. Throughout the course of the investigation, NRL did take economic factors into account in its recommendations.
5. Actual and effective decisions of significance were not documented by NRL and only to a limited extent by the client. There was no attempt on NRL's part

Exhibit 3—Continued

to convey the nature or consequences of such decisions to the client's management.

6. The NRL reports were not well prepared even considering the circumstances under which they were written.

7. It is possible that maximum advantage was not taken of the technical capabilities of personnel in the Electromagnetic Sciences Laboratory. Furthermore, they appeared to have been incompletely informed as to the overall approach to the investigation.

8. There was excessive involvement of the client in the details of experimental work. Moreover, there were frequent changes of direction dictated by the client. Undoubtedly these conditions hampered progress and adequate consideration of major objectives and accomplishments.

9. In the later stages of the project, the client rejected a number of processes and equipment types proposed by NRL for investigation of their commercial feasibility. From the information available to me, I believe that these judgments were based on arbitrary opinions as to technical feasibility and superficial extrapolations from other experience as to economic feasibility that are probably not valid.

Evaluation of Client's Complaints

Following are the comments responding to the points raised by the client management during your conversation:

1. *Client anticipated a "full research capability." He had hoped for participation by engineers, chemists, economists and particularly counted on the provision of an "analytical capability." It was this combination of talents that brought him to NRL rather than [a competitor]. He feels that the project was dominated almost exclusively by chemists.*

    This complaint is completely unfounded. All the disciplines appropriate to the investigation (as called for in the proposal) were engaged on the project to some degree. In addition, men of exceptional capabilities devoted an unusually large amount of time to the project. The client never officially altered the conditions of the proposal stating that no economic studies should be performed by NRL and there was no explicit expression of this desire on the part of the client until near the project termination.

2. *The analytical services were poor. They were sometimes erroneous and there were frequent "deviations." Data was given to the client too hastily, without further experiment and careful analysis, and as a result a significant amount of the data was not reproducible. NRL was inclined to be overly optimistic. "Glowing reports" would be made only to be cancelled or seriously modified later.*

    There is no way of determining whether the analytical services were good or bad, but one can never expect all analytical work to be correct or accurate. Because the client insisted on obtaining raw data they would certainly receive some analyses that were erroneous. With respect to the allegation that NRL was overly optimistic, there were no recommenda-

Exhibit 3—Continued

tions or opinions expressed in the NRL reports or included in the client's notes that can be placed in this category. Whether or not there were verbal statements of this kind cannot of course be ascertained.

3. *There were "errors in the equations and the client was not informed of the changes." This refers to the case of a computer program that had not been "de-bugged." It was the client who discovered the errors and informed NRL of the discrepancies. (The program was eventually straightened out by the Math Sciences Department.)*

    The client's complaint that they were given a computer program which had not been "de-bugged" is valid, but it is not certain that the project leadership gave them the program without exercising normal precautions for its accuracy. The program was developed by a person not presently with NRL and for another project. He transmitted it without any warning that "de-bugging" had not been conducted. It is even possible that the existence and source of error could not have been determined in his usage and would only appear in a different application.

4. *NRL told the client that the "vertile from iron ore" process could be handled commercially in a rotary kiln. Client prepared elaborate plans for this rotary kiln process and then was informed by his Engineering Division that this was completely infeasible. Plans were then shifted to a fluid bed process and much time and money had been wasted. Client claims that he was not warned that in the fluid bed agglomeration would probably take place. Agglomeration did take place the first time this process was tried ("open boats") and the client was greatly upset.*

    It is unclear whether the original suggestion that a rotary kiln be used in the vertile process came from the client or NRL. In any event, it is a logical choice of equipment and is used for the production of such low cost items as cement. Without the benefit of at least pilot plant experience that revealed highly abnormal and unfavorable conditions leading to excessive costs, no one would be in a position to state that such equipment would be uneconomic. It is true that a completely standard rotary kiln probably could not be employed, if for no other reason than to prevent the escape of toxic hydrogen sulfide gas from the equipment. At least special design would be needed and probably some mechanical development. However, it is rare that any new process can be installed without special design and development and it is naive to expect otherwise.

    I do not know, of course, how much time was actually spent on the "elaborate plans" for the vertile process using a rotary kiln. I can, however, compare it with generally similar types of studies that we carry out in the Process Economics Program. For this kind of process we would expend about 45 engineering man-hours, and the design calculations would be more detailed than the client's engineer made (his cost estimates incidentally reflected inexperience in this field). I doubt, therefore, that this effort represented a serious expenditure of money and would not have been a complete waste even if the process had been based on a partially false premise.

Exhibit 3—Continued

The contention that the client was not informed of the agglomerating properties of the vertile while the reaction was taking place seems unlikely. The client's representatives were so intimately concerned with the experimental work that it would be unusual if the subject had not been raised. Moreover, it is doubtful that the client would have been deterred by NRL's warning, in view of their subsequent insistence that considerable effort be devoted to finding means by which a fluid bed could be operated.

5. *The meetings were poorly planned by NRL.*

There is no way of evaluating this complaint, but certainly the extreme frequency of the meetings would not be conducive to a well organized meeting.

6. *Experimental procedures were not well planned.*

Apparently this refers to the client's desire that experiments be planned in detail as much as three months in advance. Such an approach might conceivably be useful merely for purposes of gathering routine data. It is naive to think that research can or should be planned to this degree and certainly if NRL had acceded to the request it would have been a fruitless time-consuming exercise.

7. *Economic support was not given by NRL.*

As mentioned above, the proposal specifically excluded NRL from economic evaluations, but NRL did make use of economic considerations in its suggestions and recommendations.

8. *NRL promised to obtain some manganese nodules but never produced them.*

Manganese nodules were obtained by NRL but no experiments were ever run with them. Many other screening experiments originally planned were never carried out because of the changed direction of the project. It seems likely, therefore, that the failure to conduct an experiment with manganese nodules was not NRL's responsibility.

9. *The client claims that he does not criticize NRL for failing "to produce a process." He says that he never expected one, that he wanted a good screening of ores and reactions as called for in the proposal, and that he had hoped for results from the theoretical studies—Task B. This he feels he did not get. We did not do what the proposal called for.*

The statement that a process was not expected seems entirely contrary to the course of the project. There was universal agreement among NRL personnel involved that almost immediately after the project was initiated it was converted into a crash program to find a commercial process. In fact, the whole tenor of the project suggests a degree of urgency incompatible with a systematic research program. It is quite true that the theoretical studies as a part of Task B were never carried out. According to the project leader this part of the proposal was never formally abandoned, it was merely postponed. Unfortunately, this situation was never documented by NRL, as was the case with other significant effective decisions.

Exhibit 3—Concluded

Additional Comments

1. It appears that the first indication that the client expected economic studies or evaluations of commercial feasibility occurred during the summer of 1973. At this time the project leader was severely criticized by the client's representatives for having proposed a process (hydrochloric acid pickling) that was economically infeasible. The basis for this criticism was that hydrochloric acid pickling of steel had not proved to be economically feasible. It is totally unreasonable to expect that NRL would have access to information of this kind, and such a reaction would certainly have the effect of discouraging any further contributions of an economic or commercial nature by NRL rather than encouraging them.

   Actually it is patently ridiculous to directly translate economic experience of the steel industry with steel pickling to leaching a sulfided titanium ore. Nevertheless, I directed an inquiry to a responsible person in U.S. Steel as to the status of hydrochloric acid pickling. His response (based on the consensus of their experts) was diametrically opposite to the client's information. While there are situations that are more favorable to sulfuric acid pickling, hydrochloric acid pickling is generally more economic and is becoming increasingly adopted.

2. The reports written by NRL were requested by the client, but on an urgent and "not fancy" basis. If such were the case, it is understandable that the project leader would be reluctant to expend enough time and money on the report to make it representative of NRL's normal reports. However, the nature of the reports seems to indicate that they are directed toward the same individuals with whom NRL was in frequent contact, or persons with a strong interest in the purely scientific aspects. The actual accomplishments of the project were not brought out in a manner that would have been readily understandable to client's management.

Recommendations

It is recommended that consideration be given to the establishment of a simple formal procedure by which high risk projects could be identified at the proposal stage and brought to the attention of the Division Vice President. There should also be a formal procedure, operative after project acceptance, in which specific responsibilities are assigned for averting or correcting subsequent developments that would be adverse to NRL's and the client's interests.

Some of the factors that would contribute to a high risk condition are insufficient funding, insufficient time, low chance of successfully attaining the objectives, an unsophisticated client, public or private political conditions, and so forth. The characteristics that made this a high risk project were certainly apparent at the time the proposal was prepared.

Exhibit 4

NORTHEAST RESEARCH LABORATORY

MEMORANDUM

January 8, 1974

To: Sam Lacy
From: Mac Davidson
Re: The Exco Project—Conclusions

The decision to undertake this project was made without sufficient consideration of the fact that this was a "high risk" project.

The proposal was technically sound and within the capabilities of the groups
assigned to work on the project.

There was virtually no coordination between the working elements of Physical
Sciences and Electronics in the preparation of the proposal.

The technical conduct of this project, with few exceptions, was, considering the
handicaps under which the work was carried out, good and at times outstanding. The exceptions were primarily due to lack of attention to detail.

The NRL reports were not well prepared, even considering the circumstances
under which they were written.

The client, acting under pressure from his own management, involved himself
excessively in the details of experimental work and dictated frequent
changes of direction and emphasis. The proposal opened the door to this
kind of interference.

There was no documentation by NRL of the decisions made by the client which
altered the character, direction and emphasis of the work.

There was no serious attempt on the part of NRL to convey the nature or
consequence of the above actions to the client.

Less than half of the major complaints made by the client concerning NRL's
performance are valid.

The project team acquiesced too readily in the client's interference and management too easily to the client's demands.

Management exercised insufficient supervision and gave inadequate support
to the project leader in his relations with the client.

There were no "overruns" either in time or funds.

Case 16–2

Construction Associates, Incorporated

Construction Associates of Syracuse, New York, did general construction work. In April of 1965, the company had three jobs in progress—a six-family apartment house, a gas station, and a four-store addition to a shopping center.

The owner of the shopping center, Mr. Mahara, had recently returned from Akron, Ohio, where he had discussed with the executives of a large tire company the possibility of opening a tire sales and service shop in his shopping center. Mr. Mahara decided that a tire shop would be a profitable addition to his shopping center and on the morning of April 2, 1965, he decided to proceed at once to arrange for the construction of a suitable building to house the tire shop in one corner of the shopping center parking lot. He then called Mr. Heitman, the president of Construction Associates, to arrange a meeting to discuss plans for the building. During their meeting Mr. Mahara and Mr. Heitman agreed that a suitable building for the new tire shop would be a one-story frame structure somewhat similar in exterior design to the gas station that Construction Associates had under construction at that time.

Although the time was short, Mr. Mahara was anxious to have the tire shop building completed by the time the addition to the shopping center was completed. He felt that the grand opening of the tire shop should be tied in with the opening of the four stores in the new addition. The construction schedule for the addition, which was easily being met, indicated that the shopping center addition would be completed in 51 working days after April 2.

Following his meeting with the shopping center owner, Mr. Heitman spoke with Mr. Bevis, Construction Associates' planning specialist. Realizing time was short, Mr. Heitman asked Mr. Bevis to plan immediately the construction schedule for the tire shop building. Mr. Bevis was instructed to use the plans and costs of the gas station under construction as guidelines for his preliminary planning of the tire shop.

In his initial analysis of the problem Mr. Bevis noted the following construction relationships generally observed in construction of this type:

1. A preliminary set of specifications would have to be completed before work could begin on the set of blueprints and before the foundation excavation could begin. After the excavation was completely finished, the foundation could be poured.

2. The preparation of a bill of materials would have to be deferred until the final set of blueprints was prepared. When the bill of materials was completed, it would be used to prepare order invoices for lumber and other items. Construction of the frame could not begin until the lumber had arrived at the construction site and the foundation had been poured.

3. After the frame was completed, electric work, erection of laths, plumbing, installation of millwork, and installation of siding could begin.

4. Painting of the interior walls could not start until the electric work, plastering of the walls, and plumbing were completed. Plastering of the walls could not begin until the laths were erected.

5. The final interior decorating working could not begin until the interior walls were painted and the trim installed. Installation of trim could not begin until the millwork was completely installed.

6. Painting of the building's exterior could not proceed until the windows and exterior doors were installed. Installation of the windows and doors, in turn, could not start until the siding was in place.

After studying the plans and construction schedule of the gas station under construction, Mr. Bevis developed an estimate of the time required to complete each step of the building of the tire shop. The estimates (Exhibit 1) were in most cases developed from the figures given Mr. Bevis by the foremen on the gas station job. Mr. Bevis had found in the past that figures of this type were usually quite accurate. One exception to this were the figures obtained from the carpenter foreman, who was sometimes a little too pessimistic about his estimates.

As he studied the time estimates he had put together for the tire shop job, Mr. Bevis realized that some of the steps would have to be rushed in order to complete the job in 51 days. To provide more usable information on the effects of rushing some of the construction steps, Mr. Bevis estimated the extra cost of reducing the normal time required for each step by one or more days (Exhibit 1). These costs would increase the cost of the tire shop over what might be called the cost under "optimal conditions," (i.e., the cost incurred if each step could be performed at normal pace without undue rushing, overtime, etc.). Realizing that any extra costs should be kept to an absolute minimum, Mr. Bevis tried to develop a construction schedule which rushed only those activities where the extra cost was not too high. After several hours of work, Mr. Bevis devised the following tentative construction plan:

Step	Planned Duration (days)	Step	Planned Duration (days)
A	8	J	5
B	5	K	15
C	5	L	6
D	3	M	7
E	1	N	6
F	4	O	3
G	3	P	2
H	4	Q	6
I	7	R	6

Deciding the plan needed further work, Mr. Bevis put all his notes on the tire shop job into his briefcase to do further work at home that evening.

Exhibit 1

CONSTRUCTION ASSOCIATES, INCORPORATED

Step	Estimated Time Required to Execute Step (days under optimal cost conditions)	Days Reduction	Cost
A. Prepare preliminary specifications	10	2	$ 10
		3	120
B. Excavate foundation	5	1	200
C. Pour foundation	6	1	180
D. Electric work	5	2	200
E. Lath work	2	1	20
F. Plumbing	6	2	80
G. Plaster walls	4	1	40
		2	100
H. Paint interior walls	5	1	70
		2	150
I. Millwork installation	10	2	200
		3	350
J. Trim installation	8	2	90
		3	150
K. Erect frame & roof	15	2	1,000
		4	2,500
L. Final interior decoration	8	2	100
		4	800
M. Installation of siding	7	1	100
		3	600
N. Paint exterior	7	1	50
		2	150
O. Blueprints finalized	5	2	70
		3	120

Exhibit 1—Concluded

Step	Estimated Time Required to Execute Step (days under optimal cost conditions)	Days Reduction	Cost
P. Prepare bill of materials and order invoices 3		1	50
		2	170
Q. Time required to receive lumber after order is sent 8		2	100
		4	290
R. Window and exterior door installation 6		1	100

QUESTION

What schedule would you recommend?

INDEX

INDEX

*This book has been set in 10 point and 9 point
Times Roman, leaded 2 points. Part numbers
are 14 point Trade Gothic Extended and part
titles are 14 point Trade Gothic Extended Bold.
Chapter numbers are 12 point Trade Gothic Extended and chapter titles are 14 point Trade
Gothic Extended Bold. The size of the type page
is 27 by 46 picas.*

Management control covers the whole of an organization. Each operational control procedure is restricted to a subunit, often a narrowly circumscribed activity. Just as management control occurs within a set of policies derived from strategic planning, so operational control occurs within a set of well-defined procedures and rules derived from management control.

Control is more difficult in management control than in operational control because of the absence of a valid, objective standard with which actual performance can be compared. A good operational control system can provide a much higher degree of assurance that actions are proceeding as desired than can a good management control system.

An operational control system is a *rational* system; that is, the action to be taken is decided by a set of logical rules. These rules may or may not cover all aspects of a given problem. Situations not covered by the rules are designated as exceptions and are resolved by human judgment. Other than these exceptions, application of the rule is automatic. The rules in principle can be programmed into a computer, and the choice between using a computer and using a human being depends primarily on the relative cost of each resource.

In management control, psychological considerations are dominant. The management control system at most assists those who take action; it does not directly or by itself result in action without human intervention. By contrast, the end product of an inventory control system can be an order, such as a decision to replenish a certain inventory item, and this order may be based entirely on calculations from formulas incorporated in the system. (The formulas were devised by human beings, but this is a management control process, not an operational control process.)

In a consideration of operational control, analogies with mechanical, electrical, and hydraulic systems are reasonable and useful, and such terms as feedback, network balancing, optimization, and so on are relevant. It is perfectly appropriate, for example, to view an operational control system as analogous to a thermostat which turns the furnace on and off according to its perception of changes in temperature. These analogies do not work well as models for management control systems, however, because the success of these systems is highly dependent on their impact on people, and people are not like thermostats or furnaces; one can't light a fire under a human being simply by turning up a thermostat.

The management control system is ordinarily built around a financial structure, whereas operational control data are often nonmonetary. They may be expressed in terms of man-hours, number of items, pounds of waste, and so on. Since each operational control procedure is designed for a limited area of application, it is feasible to use the basis of measurement that is most appropriate for that area.

Data in an operational control system are often in real time (ie., they are reported as the event is occurring) and relate to individual events,